TWO KINGDOMS

TWO KINGDOMS

THE CHURCH AND CULTURE THROUGH THE AGES

ROBERT G. CLOUSE
RICHARD V. PIERARD
EDWIN M. YAMAUCHI

MOODY PRESS
CHICAGO

The use of selected references from various versions of the Bible in this publication does not necessarily imply publisher endorsement of the versions in their entirety.

Library of Congress Cataloging in Publication Data

Clouse, Robert G., 1931-
Two kingdoms : the Church and culture through the ages / by Robert G. Clouse, Richard V. Pierard, Edwin M. Yamauchi.
p. cm.
Includes bibliographical references and indexes.
ISBN 0-8024-8590-1
1. Church history. 2. Christianity and culture. I. Pierard, Richard V., 1934- . II. Yamauchi, Edwin M. III. Title.
BR145.2.C56 1993
261'.09--dc20 93-13410
CIP

1 3 5 7 9 10 8 6 4 2

Printed in the United States of America

To our wives—
Bonnidell, Charlene, and Kimie

About the Authors

ROBERT G. CLOUSE (B.D., Grace Theological Seminary; M.A., Ph.D., University of Iowa) is professor of history at Indiana State University. He has served as president of the Central Renaissance Conference and director of the Conference on Faith and History. His numerous articles have been published in *The Bulletin of the Evangelical Theological Society, Harvard Theological Review, Grace Journal, Fides et Historia,* and others. He is coeditor of *Protest and Politics: Christianity & Contemporary Affairs* and *The Cross and the Flag.* He has contributed to the *New International Dictionary of the Christian Church,* the *Evangelical Dictionary of Theology, Great Leaders of the Christian Church,* and the *Dictionary of Christianity in America.* He also served as editor of *The Meaning of the Millennium*; *War: Four Christian Views*; and *Wealth & Poverty: Four Christian Views*.

RICHARD V. PIERARD (B.A., M.A., California State University; Ph.D., University of Iowa) is professor of history at Indiana State University. He is the author (or coauthor) of *Twilight of the Saints, Streams of Civilization II, Bibliography on the Religious Right,* and *Civil Religion and the Presidency.* He has contributed to the *New International Dictionary of the Christian Church,* the *Lion Handbook of the History of Christianity,* the *Evangelical Dictionary of Theology, Great Leaders of the Christian Church,* and the *Dictionary of Christianity in America.* He has served as secretary-treasurer of the Conference on Faith and History and as president of the Evangelical Theological Society.

EDWIN M. YAMAUCHI (M.A., Ph.D., Brandeis University) is professor of history at Miami University (Ohio) and a senior editor for *Christianity Today*. He has served as president of the Conference on Faith and History from 1974 to 1976. In addition to countless articles and reviews in a wide variety of periodicals, he has written more than a dozen scholarly texts over a twenty-five-year period, including *The Stones and the Scriptures; Pre-Christian Gnosticism*; *The Scriptures and Archaeology*; *Harper's World of the New Testament*; *Foes From the Northern Frontier*; and *Persia and the Bible.* He has also contributed to more than three dozen books and reference works, including the *New Dictionary of Christian Theology, The Illustrated Bible Dictionary,* and *Great Leaders of the Christian Church*.

CONTENTS

List of Illustrations

Credits

Photos

Alaska Division of Tourism: p. 307

Billy Graham Center Museum, Wheaton College: pp. 289, 409, 447, 509, 529

Christian History magazine: pp. 177, 403, 473, 485, 535, 577, 583

Robert G. Clouse: pp. 49, 99, 111, 123, 135, 183, 209, 231, 237, 251, 263, 325, 337

Loizeaux Brothers: p. 453

Edwin Yamauchi: p. 61

Other

Art by Ron Mazellan: pp. 73, 85, 129, 385, 429, 523, 547

Time lines, charts, and maps by Mary Ragont

PREFACE

The story of the church is an exciting one, and it never ceases to encourage and animate Christians wherever they may be. This is because the good news of the crucified and risen Savior is not restricted to any particular nation or period of time. As Jesus was about to depart from His tiny band of followers and return to His Father in heaven, He told them that they were to go and make disciples of all nations. They would be empowered by the Holy Spirit to proclaim the gospel message, not just to the people in their immediate vicinity but also to the ends of the earth (Matt. 28:19; Acts 1:8). This meant that from the very beginning Christianity would be global in its dimensions. In the following pages we will see how a movement of faith that originated in an obscure part of the mighty Roman Empire mushroomed in size and spread until its spiritual power was felt throughout the world.

To be sure, the history of Christianity is marked by failures as well as successes. This should come as no surprise since the church, although instituted by God (Matt. 16:18), was still a human institution, and its leaders and ordinary members lived in a fallen world where the power of sin held sway. The narrative will not sidestep the faults and misdeeds of Christians, particularly when they became captive to the culture in which they lived, because that is part of the whole story. Yet, in spite of these shortcomings, the gospel has gone forth. When God's witnesses failed and all seemed to be lost, others were raised up who carried on the work. Consequently, as the twentieth century draws to a close, there are more followers of Christ in the world than at any other time in history. In fact, in those areas where the faith has not had as great an impact on culture the church seems to be growing most quickly.

To cover two millennia of the history of Christianity is a daunting task, but we believe a retelling of it will be of great value to the generation of believers who are entering the third millennium. Each of us has spent three decades teaching history from a global perspective and is convinced that the church must be understood in this fashion. We have also come to the material with our own commitments as Christians, and we have wrestled with the issues of faith and our studies through our involvement in the Conference on Faith and History.

As it is physically impossible in one volume to mention every person, idea, and movement that was significant in the epic of the church, necessity has required us to be selective. We have tried to be balanced in our treatment of the various manifestations of Christianity, but we did opt to focus on some neglected aspects of it. Thus, we devoted more space to the modern era than is customary in such books, and we have underscored the involvement of Protestant evangelicals. We have given less attention to doctrinal and ecclesiastical controversies and the institutional development of specific denominations, and in the modern period we concentrate considerably on the church outside the Anglo-American areas.

It will be up to the reader to decide whether we have been fair in our approach. However, whether or not one agrees with our choices and emphases, he or she will surely recognize that the survival and growth of the church is a remarkable tribute to the power of God in the world. After all, that is the underlying message of the book.

We wish to acknowledge with gratitude the assistance of Charlene Pierard in the preparation of the manuscript, the continuing support of our editors at Moody Press—Garry Knussman, Joseph O'Day, Robert Ramey—and our publisher Greg Thornton. Without their encouragement and patience this book would never have become a reality.

PART 1

THE EARLY AND MEDIEVAL CHURCH

(A.D. 1 – 1450)

1

THE FOUNDING OF THE CHURCH

The world had never seen a political system so dynamic and extensive as the empire centered in Rome. The Romans used a dating system based on the beginning of their community, A.U.C. (*ab urbe condita*—"from the founding of the city [of Rome]"). However, an obscure monk, Dionysius Exiguus, replaced the Roman reckoning with a new method that centered on the pivotal role played by Jesus Christ as the "hinge of history." Thereafter, Christians dated events B.C. (before Christ) and A.D. (*anno Domini*—"in the year of our Lord"). Thus, the birth of Jesus was seen as occurring in the year one and the founding of Rome in 753 B.C. This dating system, introduced in A.D. 525, became accepted in the West and eventually throughout the world, although in deference to the sensitivities of adherents to other religions some people today have replaced B.C. and A.D. with B.C.E. ("before the common era") and C.E. ("common era").

From our viewpoint more than nineteen centuries later, it is wholly remarkable that a Jew, who lived in an obscure corner of the Roman Empire and suffered a disgraceful death on a cross, should have inspired a movement that spread throughout the world and transformed countless lives. To this day, Christians believe that Jesus of Nazareth was not only the promised Messiah of the Old Testament (the "Christ" or "Anointed One" who would bring salvation and deliverance to His people) but also the risen Son of God.

The Political Background (Rome)

The Christian faith was born in a period of political transition. A small city-state in Italy that some centuries earlier had been transformed into a republic gradually spread its power throughout the Mediterranean world by crushing its rival in North Africa (Carthage) and winning over the Hellenistic successor states of Alexander the Great's empire in the East. In the first century B.C. Julius Caesar arose as an ambitious politician and ruthless military leader. In 60 B.C. he formed a secret alliance (triumvirate) with Crassus, the wealthiest man in Rome, and Pompey, a young but brilliant general. Together, Crassus and Pompey had crushed the slave revolt of Spartacus in 71 B.C., and the latter had been commissioned to deal with Rome's formidable rival, Mithridates, in the eastern Mediterranean. While in the East, Pompey intervened in a quarrel between two brothers over the office of the high priest, entered Jerusalem (63 B.C.), and established Roman rule in Palestine. Judaea was converted into a client kingdom and placed under Roman supervision. In order to gain military glory, Crassus undertook an ill-advised campaign against the Parthians that resulted in his death at the battle of Carrhae in northern Mesopotamia in 53 B.C.

In a brilliant series of campaigns as proconsul of Gaul (58–51 B.C.) Caesar won public acclaim and alarmed Pompey and most of the Roman Senate by his growing power. Defying the order of the Senate to lay down his arms, he crossed the Rubicon River in northern Italy and marched south in 49 B.C., touching off a civil war that was settled by his victory at Pharsalus in Greece the following year. Caesar pursued Pompey to Egypt where he was killed on the order of King Ptolemy XII. While in Egypt, Caesar became enamored with the legendary Queen Cleopatra, the sister and wife of Ptolemy. Grateful for Jewish aid received while he was besieged at Alexandria (Egypt), Caesar granted the Jews special privileges, including permission to observe the Sabbath, exemption from the military draft, and the right to send offerings to the Temple in Jerusalem.

Just as he was on the verge of achieving the status of an absolute dictator, Caesar was assassinated (44 B.C.) and the Roman world

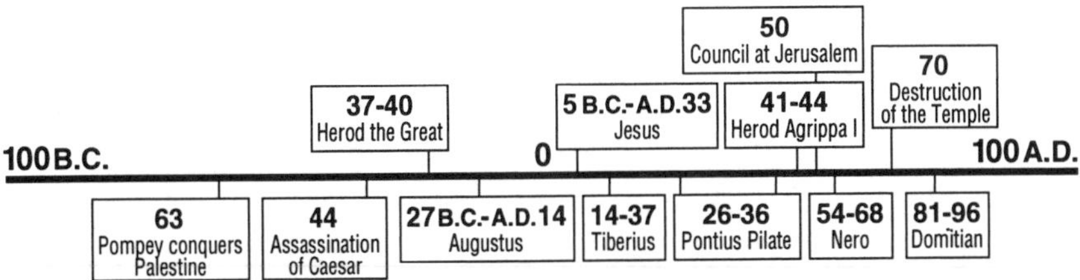

was plunged once again into civil war. Within a year a second triumvirate had been formed that included Caesar's heir, Octavian; his right-hand man, Mark Antony; and Lepidus, the governor of northern Italy. They defeated the forces of Caesar's assassins and divided control of the Roman world among themselves. Antony, who was married to Octavian's sister and had received the East, became hopelessly infatuated with the beautiful Cleopatra. He divorced his wife, married the Egyptian queen, and declared her son rather than Octavian as Caesar's heir. In the war that followed, Octavian defeated Antony at the famous naval battle of Actium in 31 B.C., and Antony and Cleopatra committed suicide the following year.

This left Octavian unopposed, and when he established the imperial regime in 27 B.C. the Senate hailed him as Augustus ("revered"). He became the first and arguably the best of the Roman emperors. He cleverly consolidated all the major powers of state into his hands without alienating the senators, unlike the arrogant Caesar. He was responsible for many wise and far-sighted measures that governed both Rome and the provinces. He boasted in his autobiography that he had transformed Rome from a city of brick into a city of marble.

Augustus's piety, depicted in the Altar of Peace that still stands today, resulted in the restoration of eighty temples. He also attempted to regulate morals and encourage marriages and births, and according to his censuses the population of Italy grew 15 percent in a twenty-two-year period. At this time, Jesus was born in Bethlehem in Judaea where his parents had journeyed for a census. Although sporadic warfare continued on the frontiers, Augustus had initiated the era of the "Roman peace" (*Pax Romana*).

Although the various offices and powers that he had amassed technically could not be passed on to an heir, Augustus was able to circumvent the various legal restrictions and named his stepson Tiberius as his successor. This marked the founding of the Julio-Claudian line of emperors. An able soldier who had secured the frontier on the middle Danube, Tiberius (A.D. 14–37) tried conscientiously to govern the empire and carry out the policies of Augustus. His reign was, however, marred by a proliferation of treason trials. The aging emperor fell under the influence of the sinister chief of the praetorian guard, Sejanus, who in 26 persuaded him to retire to his luxurious villa on the island of Capri. Meanwhile, Sejanus plotted against various members of Tiberius's family, but he was exposed and summarily executed in 31.

His protégé, Pontius Pilate, served as procurator (governor) of Judaea (A.D. 26–36). Insecure at the loss of his patron and fearful that criticism of his administration would result in his dismissal or worse by Tiberius, he had Jesus of Nazareth crucified, most likely in 33.

The next emperor, Gaius Caligula (A.D. 37–41), was mentally unbalanced and noted for his extreme cruelty and sexual excesses. He claimed to be divine and demanded worship, but his attempt to have a statue of himself erected in the Jewish Temple in Jerusalem failed.

Assassinated after four years of misrule, he was followed by his uncle Claudius (A.D. 41–54). A victim of polio, who was not seriously regarded at Rome, he proved to be a conscientious emperor who expanded the empire's borders and developed an effective bureaucracy. He appointed freedman (ex-slaves) to several administrative posts, including Pallas as treasury secretary. Paul conducted most of his missionary activities during the reign of Claudius. He was imprisoned at Caesarea under Felix, the brother of Pallas, who was the governor of Judaea. Unfortunate in his choice of wives, Claudius's last spouse, the ambitious Agrippina, even fed him poisoned mushrooms so her son by a previous marriage, Nero, could succeed to the throne.

Nero (A.D. 54–68) began his rule well under the guidance of the philosopher Seneca and the head of the praetorian guard, Burrus, and soon eliminated his domineering mother. In 64 the capital city was devastated by a fire. Although it is probable that he was not responsible for it, despite the accusation of ancient sources, he diverted blame from himself by making the rapidly growing sect known as "Christians" scapegoats and having them executed in his gardens. In the ensuing persecutions Paul and Peter were martyred at Rome.

A megalomaniac who built the magnificent Golden House to display the crowns he won in the Panhellenic games in Greece and erected a one-hundred-foot high bronze statue of himself as Apollo, Nero became increasingly paranoid as plots swirled around him. He ordered Seneca and his brother Gallio (the governor at Corinth before whom Paul appeared) to commit suicide, but the praetorian guard and Senate turned against him and he killed himself, lamenting his fate with these words: "What a great artist perishes."

After three generals rapidly succeeded each other in a tumultuous year-long struggle for the succession, Vespasian (A.D. 69–79) emerged victorious and established the Flavian line of emperors. He had served ably in Britain under Claudius and had been directed by Nero to suppress the Jewish revolt that had begun in 66. When he was acclaimed emperor by his troops, he left his son Titus behind to complete the conquest of Jerusalem. He restored the public finances, further extended the boundaries of the empire, and began construction on the vast public amphitheater, the Colosseum.

The brief reign of Titus (A.D. 79–81) was marked by another fire in Rome, the completion of the Colosseum, and the unexpected eruption of Mount Vesuvius, which buried the cities of Pompeii and Herculaneum. He was popular except for his involvement with the Herodian princess Bernice (Acts 25:23).

Domitian (A.D. 81–96), the younger brother of Titus, ruled as a despot. He demanded to be addressed as "Lord and God" (*Dominus et Deus*) and persecuted Christians and Jews alike. Domitian's reign of terror, during which John wrote the Apocalypse (the book of Revelation), was cut short by his assassination in a palace coup.

THE RELIGIOUS BACKGROUND (JUDAISM)

For centuries after the destruction of the kingdoms of Israel and Judah at the hands of the Assyrians and Babylonians, various foreign peoples ruled over the region south of Syria known originally as "Canaan" or "Israel" but called by the Romans "Palestine." Under the Assyrians the province of Samaria was settled by foreigners who brought in their pagan religion. The exiles who returned to Judah, now renamed the province of Judaea, and rebuilt the Temple had great doubts about the racial purity of their neighbors, and the two coexisted in a state of permanent hostility. The inhabitants of Judaea were called Jews and were noted for their strict observance of the historic faith. Also, many Jews (in the *Diaspora*, or dispersion) were scattered throughout the Hellenistic world of the eastern Mediterranean and western Asia.

Four decades after the Maccabean revolt against the Syrian rulers of Judaea in the second century B.C., an independent Jewish kingdom was established in 128 B.C. by the high priestly Hasmonaean family under John Hyrcanus. In order to secure their position, the Hasmonaeans even made a treaty of alliance with the Romans. The next years were marked by constant struggle until finally Pompey intervened in 63 B.C. to end the civil strife. Judaea was now a Roman protectorate.

In the southern part of Judaea were a people called the Idumaeans. They settled there after being forced out of their old homeland of Edom by the Nabataean Arabs. In 126 B.C. the Hasmonaean rulers compelled them to convert to Judaism. The governor of Idumaea, Antipater, was strongly pro-Roman, and he persuaded the Jews to come to the aid of Julius Caesar in Egypt, who in turn named him procurator of Syria in 47 B.C. His son Herod was a friend of both Caesar and Antony, and he sided with the Romans against the Parthians. The Senate named him "King of the Jews" in 40 B.C. and authorized him to rule the Judean kingdom in the interests of the Romans as their friend and ally. In 37 B.C. Herod then ousted the Hasmonaean king and married a royal princess in an effort to legitimize his rule in the eyes of the Jews, many of whom regarded him as a foreign usurper. When Octavian defeated Antony, Herod quickly switched his loyalty to the victor.

Commonly known as Herod the Great, he was the most prodigious builder in Jewish history. He completely refurbished the Temple, making it into a dazzling architectural monument that was still under construction in Jesus' lifetime (John 2:20). He also built a splendid palace for himself and a fortress overlooking the Temple that he called the Antonia after his patron, a deep-water seaport on the Mediterranean named Caesarea, and a settlement for his veterans in Samaria that was renamed *Sebaste*, the Greek word for Augustus.

An extraordinarily suspicious and brutal ruler, he murdered most of the leading Hasmonaeans, including his own wife, and several of his sons. An example of Herod's paranoia was his alarm over the news that a possible rival had been born in Bethlehem (Jesus) and his order to slaughter the young children in the area.

After his death in 4 B.C., Herod's holdings were divided among three of his sons. Archelaus (mentioned in Matt. 2:22) succeeded him in Judaea and Samaria, but his misrule was so bad that Augustus responded to a formal request of the Jewish aristocracy to remove him and convert the territory into a Roman province. It was administered by an imperial procurator who was under the governor of Syria. Philip ruled the Gentile region of the northeast (Luke 3:1), while Antipas inherited Galilee and Perea (the Transjordan). The latter had John the Baptist executed at the behest of his wife Herodias. He also had a brief encounter with Jesus, whom Pilate sent to him for judgment.

Procuratorial rule was suspended between A.D. 41 and 44 when Herod Agrippa I, the grandson of Herod the Great, who was reared in Rome and was a personal friend of both Caligula and Claudius, was granted power to rule over a territory in Palestine roughly equivalent to that of his grandfather. After his sudden death, recorded in Acts 12:23, the procuratorship was restored because his son, Agrippa II, was regarded as too young to rule. Paul testified before the younger Agrippa (Acts 25:23–26:32), who sought to prevent the outbreak of the Jewish revolt in 66 and remained loyal to Rome during this trying time.

In the first century A.D. there were several important Jewish sects. The ethnically mixed Samaritans from the area north of Judaea were the most despised. They held to their own version of the Torah (the first five books of the Old Testament) and insisted on worshiping at their holy place at Mount Gerizim (John 4:20). Jesus traveled through Samaria where He confronted the woman at the well and shocked Jewish sensitivities with His tale of the "good Samaritan." The early Christians found a receptive audience there (Acts 8:4–25). About five hundred Samaritans still survive in Israel today.

The Sadducees claimed descent from Zadok, the high priest at the time of David and Solomon. Most belonged to the aristocratic families who controlled the office of high priest. They accepted only the Torah as authoritative and refused to believe in angels or the bodily resurrection. The chief priest who condemned Jesus and tried to keep Peter from preaching about His resurrection was a Sadducee. As their only reason for existence was the Temple, they did not survive the destruction of Jerusalem in A.D. 70.

Sadducees predominated in the Sanhedrin, the Jewish council or high court, composed of seventy men. Presided over by the high priest, it had considerable authority to try religious cases, but the issuance of death sentences required action by the Roman governor.

The Pharisees, a much stricter group that was a minority in the Sanhedrin, arose under the Hasmonaean priest-kings. The name means "separated ones." Many of them were scribes, teachers of the law who interpreted the Scriptures according to oral traditions that they traced back to Moses. They sought to "make a hedge about the Law," that is, they took the most extreme precautions to avoid even the least violation of the law. Jesus condemned this excessive zeal as hypocrisy. Among the most devoted teachers of the law who belonged to the Pharisaic party were Rabbi Hillel, who uttered the "silver rule"—"Do not do to others that which is hateful to you"—and Gamaliel, who was the teacher of Saul of Tarsus. Before his conversion Saul was a devoted Pharisee.

They were willing to accommodate to the Roman rulers and opposed the Jewish freedom fighters. After the great revolt was crushed, Emperor Vespasian permitted them to open a rabbinical school at Jamnia, and their oral discussions, the Mishnah, were written down around A.D. 200. This and the later commentaries known as the Gemara composed the Talmud, the great repository of legal traditions that Orthodox Jews to this day regard as authoritative for faith and life.

The Essenes, an extreme separatist group, are not mentioned in the New Testament, but other contemporary sources describe their life and beliefs. Their community at Qumran produced the famous Dead Sea Scrolls, first discovered in 1947. Although some Essenes were married and lived in villages, they attained their highest ideal at Qumran, located near the Dead Sea. The members of this community were celibate, held property in common, practiced repeated immersions in water, and ate together. Their unnamed leader, called the "Teacher of Righteousness," was persecuted by the high priest. They looked for two Messiahs—a priestly one from the tribe of Levi and a kingly one from Judah. They saw themselves as living in the last days before the final war between the sons of light and the sons of darkness. No more was heard of the Essenes after the Roman destruction of Qumran in A.D. 68.

In A.D. 6 an assessment (census) for the collection of Roman taxes provoked an unsuccessful uprising led by Judas of Galilee. He regarded the payment of tribute by Israel to a pagan ruler as treason to God. His followers were known as the Zealots because they manifested zeal for the law of God. Although at first their group was a religious party, it rapidly became a national resistance movement as well. Two of Judas's sons were crucified by the procurator Tiberius Alexander in A.D. 46 and a third son was a leader in the war against Rome. One of Jesus' twelve disciples was called a "zealot" (Luke 6:15). The enemies of Jesus who sought Pilate's approval for His execution alleged that Jesus had claimed to be a king. Paul was mistaken for

Roman Territories (B.C. 50-100 A.D.)

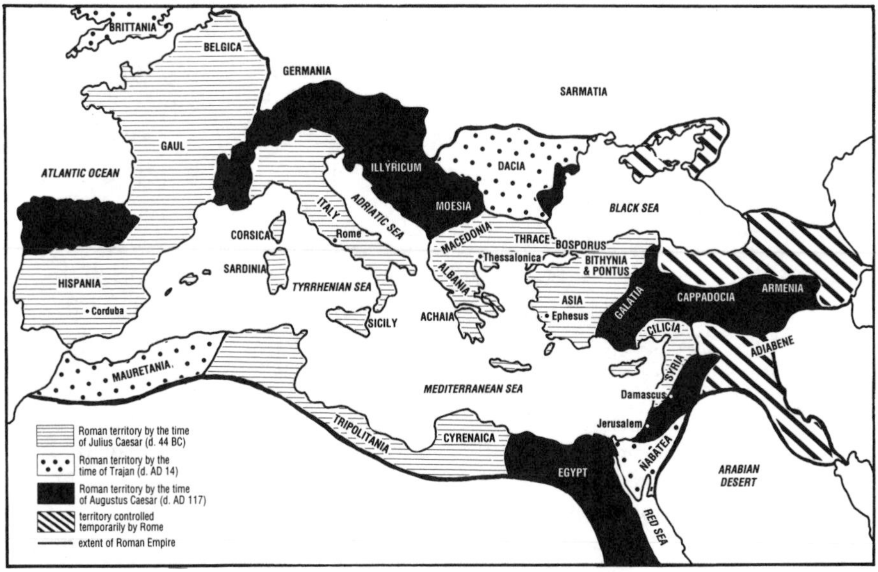

an Egyptian messianic figure who had rallied anti-Roman sentiment in Jerusalem (Acts 21:38). Radical Zealots in the late 50s began assassinating Jews who collaborated with the Romans, and attempts of the governors to suppress what was becoming a guerrilla movement led to the Jewish-Roman War of 66–74.

A later messianic figure, Simon Bar-Kochba, led the second Jewish revolt in 132–35, which the Emperor Hadrian crushed. Jerusalem was then transformed into the Roman city of Aelia Capitolina, from which Jews were banned. After this disaster, Jewish leaders abandoned hope in the imminent coming of a messiah who would deliver the people from foreign oppression and establish a kingdom of righteousness. Since they had not anticipated a virgin-born, crucified and resurrected, divine person as the Messiah, it is understandable that most Jews did not acknowledge Jesus as the one for whom they were looking.

With the destruction of the Temple, the primary institution of Judaism became the synagogue, the local assembly for prayer and worship. Synagogues originated in the post-Exilic period, and "places of prayer" existed in Egypt by 250 B.C. The gospels report that Jesus taught and performed miracles at synagogues in Nazareth and Capernaum. To form one required a quorum of ten men. It was led by a "head of the synagogue" such as Jairus (Luke 8:41), who acted with a group of elders. There was also an "attendant" (*hazzan*) who cared for the Scripture scrolls (Luke 4:20).

Synagogue services included such features as the recitation of the *Shema* prayer (Deut. 6:4–9), the prayer stance facing Jerusalem, the "Amen" response from the congregation, the reading of selections from the Torah scrolls (Acts 15:21), translation of the Hebrew Scriptures into Aramaic paraphrases, a sermon, and a benediction. While standing, one recited the "Eighteen Benedictions," to which at the end of the first century A.D. a nineteenth was added, a curse against the *minim* or heretics, an obvious allusion to the Christians.

Any male could be called upon to pray or to read portions from Scriptures. On one occasion Jesus read from the prophet Isaiah in the Nazareth synagogue. A competent individual could also be invited to give the sermon (see Acts 13:15, 42; 14:1; 17:2). There is no evidence that the early synagogues had segregated gallery seating for women, such as was the case in the Middle Ages.

As the major community building, the synagogue was used for religious services, teaching of the children, and as places of judgment and punishment for offenders (Mark 13:9; 2 Cor. 11:24). Apostates could be excommunicated (John 9:22; 12:42). The archeological remains of more than one hundred synagogues exist in Palestine, three of which date back as far as the first century A.D.

THE FOUNDATIONAL MINISTRY OF JESUS

There are some important extrabiblical references to Jesus. The Roman biographer Suetonius (early second century) relates that Claudius expelled the Jews from Rome "on account of the riots in which they were constantly indulging, at the instigation of *Chrestus.*" This was probably a reference to Christ. Acts 18:2 refers to the arrival of Aquila and Priscilla at Corinth "because Claudius had commanded all the Jews to leave Rome."

The historian Tacitus, writing in A.D. 115, describes how Nero blamed the Christians for the devastating fire of 64. He reports that "they got their name from Christ, who was executed by sentence of the procurator Pontius Pilate in the reign of Tiberius." Pliny the Younger, governor of Bithynia in northwestern Asia Minor, wrote the Emperor Trajan to ask what he should do with the Christians. His interrogations had revealed that they were "meeting on a certain fixed day before sunrise and reciting an antiphonal hymn to Christ as God."

Flavius Josephus, the Jewish writer who wrote a comprehensive history of his people in A.D. 93, the *Antiquities of the Jews*, notes that the high priest Annas, "convened a judicial session of the Sanhedrin and brought before it the brother of Jesus the so-called Christ—James by name—and some others, whom he charged with breaking the law and handed over to be stoned to death." In another longer and more controversial passage where scholars have found that a later Christian editor tampered with the text, Josephus dealt with Jesus. The probable interpolations are in italics.

> At this time there appeared Jesus, a wise man, *if indeed one should call him a man.* For he was a doer of startling deeds, a teacher of people who receive the truth with pleasure. And he gained a following both among many Jews and among many of Greek origin. *He was the Messiah.* And when Pilate, because of an accusation made by the leading men among us, condemned him to the cross, those who had loved him previously did not cease to do so. *For he appeared to them on the third day, living again, just as the divine prophets had spoken of these and countless other wondrous things about him.* And up until this very day the tribe of Christians, named after him, has not died out. (*Antiquities* 18.3.3)

Although He undoubtedly knew Hebrew and Greek as well, Jesus customarily spoke in Aramaic, a Semitic dialect that originated in Syria but had become an international language as early as the eighth century B.C. He gently raised Jairus's daughter by saying to her "'*Talitha koum!*' (which means, 'Little girl, I say to you, get up!')" (Mark 5:41), and effected the healing of the deaf and mute man by commanding "'*Ephphatha!*' (which means, 'Be opened!')" (Mark 7:34). On the cross He cried out with the poignant lament, "'*Eloi, Eloi, lama sabachthani?*'—which means, 'My God, my God, why have you forsaken me?'" (Mark 15:34).

Although Jesus was literate (John 8:6), He left no writings. The disciples may have jotted down some of His sayings, but most of them were passed on orally. Outside of the four gospels, relatively few quotations of Jesus have been preserved. The best known is the Lord's Supper passage, 1 Corinthians 11:23–25. Also, various apocryphal works, like *The Gospel of Thomas*, contain statements attributed to Jesus, but the church has never accepted these as authoritative. Matthew, Mark, Luke, and John preserve a great many sayings, but each gospel writer selected these for a particular audience. For example, Matthew, who quotes frequently from the Old Testament, addressed a Jewish-Christian constituency.

Most scholars feel that the gospel by John Mark, who was a companion of Paul and Peter (Col. 4:10; 1 Peter 5:13), was written about a generation after the death of Jesus. The other synoptic gospels, Matthew and Luke, drew heavily from Mark and a common source of sayings called *Quelle* ("source"). Matthew was one of the original twelve disciples, while Luke accompanied Paul on his travels and wrote a second volume, the Acts of the Apostles. Since the latter ends with Paul under house arrest in Rome before the great fire, it probably was penned about A.D. 62. Luke must have composed his gospel before this date.

The gospel of John was written much later, near the end of the first century, either by the apostle John or a close follower of his. There are numerous differences between this and the synoptics. John concentrates on Jesus' ministry in Jerusalem and says little about the work in Galilee. In the synoptics Jesus teaches in short, pithy sayings and parables; in John He delivers long discourses. He is portrayed as "the Son of Man" in the synoptics whereas John highlights affirmations of His deity and oneness with the Father. John also specifies an evangelistic goal—to convince readers that Jesus is the Christ and that they might find life in His name (John 20:31).

Although there have been perennial "Quests for the Historical Jesus," many basic facts about Him are beyond dispute. He was born in Bethlehem to Mary and her spouse Joseph, both of Davidic lineage, during the reigns of Herod the Great and Augustus. In contrast to the apocryphal infancy gospels that appeared in the second century (and later) and that abound in stories of miracles by the youthful Jesus, only one incident in His childhood is reported in the New Testament (by Luke), when the precocious twelve-year-old boy became separated from His parents and engaged in discussion with the teachers in the Temple in Jerusalem.

The gospels speak of the brothers and sisters of Jesus, but only the former are named (Mark 3:31; 6:3; Matt. 12:46; 13:55–56). During His lifetime they were skeptical about His claims (John 7:5), but later two of them became followers and contributed the letters of James and Jude. In fact, James became the leader of the church in Jerusalem (Acts 15) and according to Josephus was martyred in 62. Jesus grew up in Nazareth in Galilee, a village so obscure that it is not mentioned either in the Old Testament, Josephus, or the Talmud. His father was a carpenter and apparently died while Jesus was young.

He began His public ministry in the fifteenth year of Emperor Tiberius's reign, after first being immersed in the Jordan River by His cousin John (the Baptist). He assembled a band of twelve disciples, some of whom were simple fishermen, such as John, James, Peter, and Andrew. Also in His entourage were a hated tax collector (Matthew) and a former Zealot (Simon), certainly a study in contrasts. For at least three years Jesus carried out an itinerant ministry of teaching and miracles from His base at Capernaum on the western shore of the Sea of Galilee, but on three occasions recorded in John He journeyed to Jerusalem for the Passover festival.

Jesus taught that Yahweh was establishing the Kingdom of God and that people had to accept Him as God's Son if they were to enter into this realm. Jesus' consciousness of His close relation to God was characterized by His extraordinary use of the Aramaic familiar term for "father," *Abba*, in addressing God (Mark 14:36). Functioning as the envoy of God, He exercised the power to reinterpret Moses' law, heal the sick, and forgive sins. He maintained that the law was to be fulfilled not by mere external acts but by internal purity. He taught people to love not only their friends and fellow Jews but also their enemies and even the Gentile "dogs."

He performed numerous miracles—referred to in the gospels as "acts of power" or "signs." They included fifteen healings, five exorcisms of demons, five miracles over nature, and two reanimations of dead people. These convinced the disciples of His divine mandate and won many to the cause, but skeptics said His powers were from Beelzebul. In fact, by His teachings and activities Jesus succeeded in offending people from all the Jewish groupings except the Samaritans. By overturning the tables of the money changers and chasing the pigeon sellers out of the Temple precincts, He challenged the authority of the Sadducean high priest. By deliberately healing on the Sabbath, criticizing the punctilious observation of the ritual law by the hard-line Pharisees, and denouncing them as hypocrites, He alienated members of that sect. By acknowledging the legitimacy of taxation ("Render to Caesar the things that are Caesar's"—Matt. 22:21 NASB) He outraged Zealot sympathizers. Also, He may have alluded to the Essenes in the Sermon on the Mount when He referred to people who taught that one should love his neighbor but hate his enemies (Matt. 5:43).

He discouraged those who saw Him as the Messiah according to popular expectations, that is, one who would establish a political kingdom (John 6:15). In fact, He revealed His messianic identity to only a select few, such as the woman of Samaria (John 4:26) and the twelve, but on the latter occasion even Peter could not believe that

Jesus was destined for rejection by the religious leaders and a cruel death (Matt. 16:16–23).

Though hailed by the Passover crowd in Jerusalem on what the church later called Palm Sunday, growing opposition and hostility culminated in Jesus' arrest, an act that was aided by His betrayal by a member of His inner circle, Judas Iscariot. He was examined before the Sanhedrin, which had illegally convened before dawn on Friday, first by Annas and then Caiaphas, the former and current high priest. When asked point blank whether He was the Christ (Messiah), Jesus answered straightforwardly: "I am. And you will see the Son of Man sitting at the right hand of the Mighty One and coming on the clouds of heaven" (Mark 14:62; cf. Dan. 7:13). This convinced the religious leaders that He was a blasphemer, but when they turned Him over to the Roman governor for capital punishment, they charged that He claimed to be the King of Jews.

The procurator Pontius Pilate had had numerous problems with his Jewish subjects, and his relations with them were not always the best. He realized Jesus was innocent and wanted to let Him go, but the chief priests pressed for His death and a mob outside the palace shouted for the release of Barrabas who had been involved in armed insurrection. As Pilate was by this time extremely uneasy about his own position in Rome, he reluctantly ordered Jesus' execution.

He was led outside the city to a hill called in Aramaic *Golgotha* (Latin *Calvary*) or "place of the skull." Some claim that the Church of the Holy Sepulchre was later built on this site. There He suffered crucifixion, an agonizing form of death through exposure, flanked on both sides by two robbers. However, because death came so swiftly, His leg bones were not smashed as were those of the two men beside Him.

Since Sabbath burials were not allowed, Jesus was hastily interred before sundown in a tomb donated by His admirer Joseph of Arimathea. Then, early on Sunday morning the women who came to finish anointing the corpse discovered that the circular stone closing the entrance was dislodged and the tomb was empty. Some explained this puzzling event by maintaining that His disciples had stolen the body, but over the next forty days Jesus showed Himself alive—audibly, visibly, even tangibly—to His followers on at least ten occasions. Since women in the Jewish society of that day were not accepted as legal witnesses, it is noteworthy that His first manifestations were to them rather than to such apostles as Peter and John.

According to the testimony of Paul (1 Cor. 15:3–7), the risen Savior

Early Churches

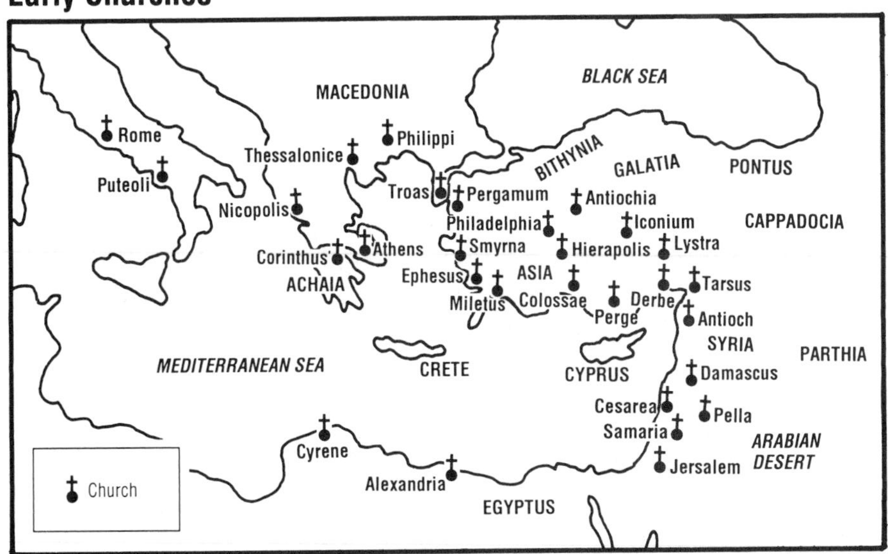

also appeared to the despairing Peter, who had denied Him three times and had returned to his work as a fisherman, his skeptical brother James, and five hundred "brethren," the majority of whom were still alive at least twenty years after the event. Instead of disappearing from the scene like the Essenes of Qumran, the disciples of Jesus, unshakably convinced of His resurrection, grew in strength and numbers as they preached the good news that Jesus was indeed the Christ who had died for the sins of all people and had risen to ensure their salvation.

THE PROMINENT LEADERSHIP OF PETER

Peter is the disciple most prominently featured in the gospels and early chapters of Acts. A fisherman from northern Galilee (Mark 1:16–18), he and his brother Andrew were originally followers of John the Baptist. He was married (1 Cor. 9:5), and Jesus once healed his mother-in-law at the family home in Capernaum (Mark 1:29–31). His original name was Simon Bar-Jona, but Jesus bestowed on him the nickname "Rock," *Cepha* in Aramaic and *Petros* in Greek (Matt. 16:18). Together with James and John, the sons of Zebedee, Peter belonged to the inner circle who witnessed the raising of Jairus's daughter and the transfiguration (Mark 5:37; 9:2).

After his disgraceful denial at the time of Jesus' arrest, Peter was transformed by the appearance of the risen Christ. When the empowering of the Holy Spirit came on the disciples on the Day of Pentecost (the Jewish festival of *Shabuoth*, or "Weeks"), he boldly preached a sermon that led to the conversion of three thousand people. Peter and John then healed a crippled beggar by the Temple entrance, and in spite of the Sanhedrin's orders to cease, the apostles continued to proclaim Jesus' resurrection.

When Ananias and Sapphira lied about how much they had given to the church, Peter exposed their duplicity and the couple fell dead under divine judgment. He also offered his blessings to the Samaritans who had accepted the gospel but condemned the magician Simon Magus who wanted to buy the power of the Holy Spirit. (This was the source of the medieval term "simony" for the purchase of a church office.)

Most significantly, despite an initial reluctance to allow Gentiles in the Christian fellowship, Peter obeyed the vision to welcome Cornelius, a Roman centurion (military commander). However, later he backslid briefly and refused to eat with Gentiles, and for this he was rebuked by Paul (Gal. 2:11–14). Though his mission was primarily to the Jews (Gal. 2:7), Peter did support Paul's position at the Council of Jerusalem that Gentiles should be accepted without having to become Jews first.

As Peter's later movements are not recorded in Acts, they are difficult to reconstruct. Some Christians at Corinth claimed him as their head (1 Cor. 3:22). Also, he is credited with the letters 1 and 2 Peter, probably sent from Rome. Two later writers, Ignatius and Eusebius, refer to his martyrdom in Rome in the persecutions after the great fire, and admirers in the second century erected a shrine to his memory in the Vatican area. There is, however, no evidence that he was the founder of the church in Rome or its first bishop.

The Gentile Mission of Paul

Undoubtedly the greatest missionary and theologian of the New Testament church was Paul, whose activities are chronicled in Acts. Originally named Saul, he was from the tribe of Benjamin (Phil. 3:5) and was born in Tarsus, the major city of Cilicia in southeastern Anatolia. His Jewish father had obtained Roman citizenship that automatically passed to the son. Though Tarsus was a center for the study of Greek philosophy, Saul most likely left home at an early age to be educated under the famous rabbi Gamaliel in Jerusalem.

There he became a Pharisee and surpassed his fellows in his zeal for the law (Gal. 1:14). Saul's first recorded contact with the young church was at the stoning of Stephen, the first Christian martyr, where he was an approving bystander. Alarmed at the growth of the new movement, he became an ardent persecutor and was responsible for imprisoning men and women, forcing them to deny their Savior publicly, and even approving their deaths. Later he bitterly regretted his role in persecuting the church (1 Cor. 15:9; Gal. 1:23; 1 Tim. 1:13).

Not content with rooting out this "heresy" in Palestine, Saul obtained authorization from the high priests to attack the Christian community in Damascus. So intent was he in carrying out this mission that contrary to custom he traveled during the heat of the day. While on the way Saul was struck down by a blazing vision of the risen Christ who rebuked him for his attitude. Because he was temporarily blinded by this, Saul's companions had to lead him into the city. Though most Christians feared him, Ananias responded to the Lord's command in a vision to receive him as a brother. Then Saul recovered his sight and became as devoted a follower of Jesus as he once had been a fanatical opponent.

After his dramatic conversion Saul spent three years in "Arabia" (probably the southern part of modern-day Jordan) and in Damascus (Gal. 1:17). He then made a short visit to Jerusalem and returned to Tarsus. After ten years, Saul was called to assist in the ministry in Antioch, the major city in northern Syria and the place where the believers were first called "Christians" (Acts 11:26). Accompanied by Barnabas, he went to Jerusalem to assist during the famine of A.D. 46–47.

The Antioch church named the two as missionaries, and, accompanied by Barnabas's cousin, the young John Mark (Col. 4:10), they set out for Cyprus and southern Anatolia. They preached at Salamis and Paphos on the opposite ends of the island. Saul exposed the false teachings of a sorcerer at the court of Sergius Paulus, the proconsul (governor) of Cyprus, and won the latter to Christ. At this point in his narrative Luke introduces Saul's Roman name, *Paul* (Acts 13:9), a Latin name that means "small."

When they arrived at Perga on the mainland, John Mark abandoned the party. (Because of this lapse, Paul refused to take Mark on his second missionary journey.) Barnabas and Paul went into the interior of southern Galatia and visited Antioch in Pisidia, Iconium, Lystra, and Derbe. Speaking in synagogues first, they were most successful in winning the "God-fearers," Gentiles who attended the houses of worship but had not yet fully converted to Judaism by being circumcised.

After returning to Antioch, Paul apparently reprimanded Peter for disassociating himself from Gentile believers and wrote the letter to the Galatians to warn them against the false teachers of legalism who were undermining the principle of salvation through faith in Christ, apart from Mosaic law. Because so many Gentiles had turned to Christianity, a great debate ensued as to whether their initiation into Judaism through the rite of circumcision should be required as well. To settle the question, a church council was convened at Jerusalem around A.D. 50. Paul was supported in his position by Peter and James, the leader of the church there. The council decided to accept Gentiles as such, but they were directed to abstain from food offered to idols, eating meat containing blood, and unchastity.

After a sharp disagreement, Barnabas and Mark left on a mission to Cyprus while Paul took Silas (also called Silvanus), a Roman citizen from Jerusalem, on a second journey to Asia Minor. While revisiting the churches in Galatia, they were joined by the young man Timothy, who was part Jewish. At some point after the trio reached the west coast of Anatolia, the physician Luke became a member of the party. In the city of Troas (near ancient Troy) Paul received the famous "Macedonian call," a vision of a man in northern Greece who urged them to "come over and help us."

At once they crossed the Aegean Sea and went to Philippi, the largest city in the region. They contacted some Jewish women at a place of prayer and a number of them were converted. One, a wealthy seller of purple cloth named Lydia, welcomed them into her home. When Paul exorcised a slave girl who was being used for divination, her owners incited a mob against them, and Paul and Silas were thrown into prison. At midnight an earthquake released all the prisoners, and the terrified jailer turned to Christ in faith at Paul's urging. When the authorities learned that they were Roman citizens, they were immediately released and allowed to resume their travels.

After evangelizing in Thessalonica and Berea, Paul reached Athens. Stirred by the religiosity of the great city, he preached his famous sermon to the Areopagus Council at the Royal Stoa in the Agora (not on Mars Hill as is commonly believed). The Athenian philosophers listened intently as Paul declared to them the identity of the "Unknown God" they worshiped, but they were offended by his reference to the resurrection of Jesus, a concept the Greeks regarded as both impossible and undesirable. He did not win many converts in this intellectual metropolis.

He had much more success in the great maritime center of Corinth. There he worked as a tentmaker alongside Priscilla and Aquila, who recently had come from Italy. He began teaching in the synagogue and made some important converts. This upset many in the Jewish community, and they brought him before the court of the governor, Gallio, Seneca's brother. As Gallio was indifferent to matters of Jewish religious practice, he dismissed the charges against Paul. After a year and a half he returned to Jerusalem.

The "Third Missionary Journey" was spent primarily in Ephesus, the metropolitan city of the province of Asia in western Anatolia. With a population of around 250,000, it was the fourth largest city in the Roman world. It boasted one of the Seven Wonders of the World—the temple of Artemis, whom the Romans called Diana. The 361-by-240-foot temple was the largest structure in the Greek-speaking world and the first of such size to be built entirely of marble. Statues of Diana show her breasts covered with objects, indicating that she was a fertility goddess.

Paul's three-year ministry at Ephesus had been preceded by that of Apollos of Alexandria, an intelligent and fervent speaker. Apollos had lacked understanding of basic Christian doctrine, but Priscilla and Aquila, by now residents of the city, gave him instruction. For three months Paul taught in the synagogue and then for the next two years daily in the hall of Tyrannus. Some scholars believe that he spent the early hours of the day at his tent-making and then during the midday proclaimed the gospel. He spoke with such enthusiasm that people would forego their customary rest time to hear him, and through these public lectures he may have won the friendship of the prominent officials who later warned him of danger (Acts 19:31).

Not only did he overcome the Jewish exorcists who threw their occult formulations into a bonfire (the Ephesian *grammata*, magical combinations of meaningless letters like our "abracadabra," which were famed in antiquity), but also he won so many pagans to Christ that it affected the lucrative business of the silversmiths who made statues of Artemis. Their leader incited a mob to protest Paul's missionary work, and only with great difficulty was the local magistrate able to disperse the crowd.

During his stay at Ephesus in A.D. 56 he wrote 1 Corinthians and, while traveling in Greece later that year, 2 Corinthians. In Corinth he penned his great letter to the Romans, which was delivered by Phoebe, a deaconess. In it he developed his theology of salvation by grace through faith in Christ for Jew and Gentile alike. Then he returned to Palestine with a collection that he had gathered from the Greek churches to assist impoverished Christians in Judaea.

Although the prophet Agabus warned Paul of the dangers awaiting him in Jerusalem, he went anyway. To demonstrate that he really was not an apostate from Judaism, Paul agreed to accompany some Nazirites to the Temple and pay for their sacrifices. However, a rumor spread that he was bringing a Gentile into the area reserved only for Jews and a riot ensued. The inner precinct of the Temple was separated from the area open to non-Jews by a four-foot stone railing that contained the ominous warning that any Gentile who entered this enclosure placed his life in jeopardy.

The timely intervention of Roman troops from the Antonia fortress rescued Paul from a lynch mob. He then asked for a chance to explain the situation in Aramaic, the dialect of the people, but his speech so enraged the crowd that the captain took him into protective custody. He was about to scourge the prisoner (flogging was used for interrogation) but stopped when Paul revealed his Roman citizenship. A tumultuous hearing before the Sanhedrin followed, where Paul claimed that as a Pharisee he was being called into question for his belief in the resurrection.

When the Roman commander learned of a conspiracy to murder Paul, he had him taken under armed guard to Caesarea on the coast. There a lawyer for the Jewish leaders accused him before the procurator. A few days later, Paul presented the gospel so eloquently to Felix and his Jewish wife Drusilla, the sister of Herod Agrippa II, that the governor "trembled." Felix, however, was more interested in the prospect of receiving a bribe than in the message of righteousness and allowed Paul to languish in prison for two years (A.D. 57–59).

When the new governor Festus met with the Jewish authorities, he was immediately confronted with the case. He welcomed the desire of Herod Agrippa II and his sister Bernice to hear Paul's defense. The king acknowledged that the charges against him were groundless but rejected the gospel message: "Do you think that in such a short time you can persuade me to be a Christian?" (Acts 26:28). However, since Paul realized that a dismissal of the case was hopeless, he took advantage of his legal right as a citizen to appeal directly to Nero's court, and Festus sent him to Rome.

Paul's Missionary Journeys

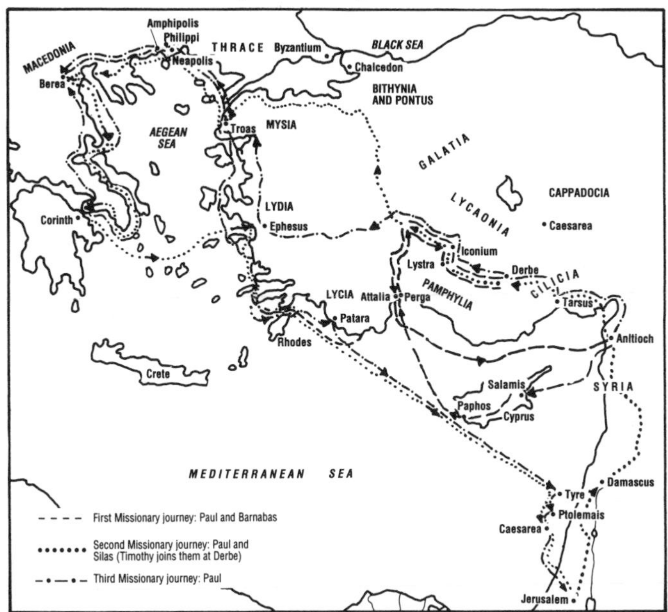

As winter was approaching, the ship on which Paul and two companions were traveling was caught up in a massive storm and broke up on the beach of Malta, south of Sicily. Paul, who had survived three other shipwrecks (2 Cor. 11:25), persuaded the soldiers not to kill the prisoners on the vessel, assuring them that none would escape. In the spring Paul and his escort resumed their journey to Rome, where he was placed under house arrest. Although chained to members of the praetorian guard, he was free to receive guests, including a delegation from the synagogues. The book of Acts ends with the apostle imprisoned in Rome, a period that could have lasted as long as two years, A.D. 60–62.

During this time Paul composed the prison epistles—Philippians, Philemon, Colossians, and Ephesians. It is assumed that he was released, either because his accusers from Jerusalem did not arrive or they failed to present a convincing case. Although there is no direct evidence, he apparently revisited churches in Macedonia and Asia Minor, and he may have even journeyed to Spain (Rom. 15:24). In this period Paul wrote his pastoral epistles—1 and 2 Timothy and Titus. Later Christian sources suggest that he suffered martyrdom toward the end of Nero's reign, more mercifully by the sword as a Roman citizen instead of by crucifixion.

Other Jewish Christians

The last of the twelve apostles to die was John, to whom Irenaeus ascribed the gospel, the three letters, and the book of Revelation. He is believed to have been bishop of Ephesus, and his exile to the island of Patmos (Rev. 1:9) apparently occurred during the persecution in Domitian's reign. Thus, the Apocalypse reflected the tensions of that time.

Not all Jewish Christians were happy with Paul's solution to the problem of Gentile believers. Opposing him in Galatia were the "Judaizers" who insisted on the importance of circumcision. Individuals from this group later composed such apocryphal works as *The Gospel of the Nazareans*, *The Gospel According to the Hebrews*, and *The Gospel of the Ebionites*, which are quoted in the church Fathers.

The Ebionites (literally "The Poor") are mentioned by Irenaeus and Origen. They were Jews who accepted Jesus as the Messiah while continuing to maintain their identity as Jews. They regarded Paul as an apostate from the law, denied the virgin birth, practiced circumcision, and observed the Sabbath, Passover, and other Jewish festivals. Various other minor Jewish Christian groups, such as the Elchasaites, survived east of the Jordan until the fifth century.

How the Early Church Functioned

Christians in Palestine, who were almost all Jews, still went to the Temple up to its destruction in A.D. 70. They also attended the synagogues, although toward the end of the first century they were expelled from most congregations and, as mentioned above, a curse upon "heretics" was introduced into the daily prayers. Since Christians met regularly on the first day of the week, this differentiated them from the Jews who assembled on the Sabbath. Unlike the repeated cleansings, which Jews practiced in their *miqvaoth* (ritual baths), Christian baptism became an initiation rite.

Also, Christians had no sacerdotal caste of priests (*kohanim*), but like the Jews they chose "elders" (*presbyteroi*), or "overseers" (*episcopoi*), who presided over their congregations. The complaints of the Greek-speaking Jews in the Jerusalem church that their widows suffered discrimination in the food distribution led to the selection of seven men as deacons (*diakonoi* or "servants") to care for the physical needs of the believers (Acts 6). Two of them, the martyr

Stephen and Philip, who evangelized Samaria and won the treasurer of the distant kingdom of Meroe in Nubia, were eloquent preachers. Some women, such as Phoebe, served as deaconesses, and older widows whom the church supported engaged in a variety of social ministries (1 Tim. 5:9–10).

Although most Christians were of humble background, there were a few noteworthy exceptions. A key role in the Corinthian community was played by Erastus, the director of public works (Rom. 16:23; 2 Tim. 4:20). In Corinth archeologists have also uncovered large houses (obviously belonging to well-to-do people), which may be like those used for church meetings, although they could probably hold only forty to fifty worshipers.

In fact, for the better part of three centuries the Christians assembled in homes, not in public structures. The earliest archeological evidence of such is "St. Peter's House" located near the synagogue in Capernaum. A later Byzantine octagonal structure marked the site of the early church, which was made of basalt stones and paved with cobblestones. Researchers have found in it pottery, coins, and fishhooks. The kind of cobbled floor illustrates how a coin could be lost in the cracks (Luke 15:8). The walls were such that they could not support a masonry roof but only one made of branches, straw, and earth (cf. Mark 2:1–12; Luke 5:18–26). Toward the end of the first century the walls and floor of the main room were plastered, reflecting the transformation of the structure from a home to a church.

During His brief lifetime Jesus managed to bewilder and offend a variety of Jewish groups. When He was put to death, His followers despaired, and it was only their intense conviction that He was resurrected that inspired them to defy persecution and to spread the gospel to Jews and Gentiles alike. Foremost among the missionary apostles was Paul, who had once been the most fanatical of persecutors. Through tireless effort he spread the Christian message throughout Asia Minor and Greece. His profound letters established the basis of a distinctive Christian theology. Those letters together with the four gospels portraying the life and teachings of Jesus form the core of the New Testament. The Jewish-Christians' belief that the Messiah had come and triumphed over death enabled them not only to survive the turmoil of the Jewish revolt and the destruction of the Jerusalem Temple, but also to disseminate the gospel throughout the Mediterranean world. Their critical decision that Gentiles would be admitted into the fellowship without requiring them to become Jews first, ensured that Christianity would not be just another Jewish sect but a universal faith applicable to all people. Already by the end of the first century the majority of Christians were Gentiles.

2

THE CHURCH IN THE ROMAN STATE

As Christians spread the good news of salvation, they faced formidable obstacles, including a hostile pagan society, rival religious groups, and sporadic persecutions by the civil authorities. In spite of these barriers, their faith countered the challenge of divisive heresies and spread rapidly through the Roman Empire in the second and third centuries. With Emperor Constantine's embrace of Christianity in A.D. 312, the nature of church-state relations changed dramatically from what they had been.

Mystery Religions and the Imperial Cult

Since the traditional Greco-Roman religion failed to satisfy the spiritual hunger of the masses, a variety of so-called mystery religions from the East found acceptance in the Roman world. These functioned as close-knit secret societies, whose members were carefully chosen and initiated. Each appealed to a different segment of society.

One of the first mysteries to be admitted into Rome was the cult of the *Magna Mater*, or "Great Mother," Cybele of Asia Minor, whose roots go back to the Stone Age. In 204 B.C. during Hannibal's invasion of Italy, the Romans in desperation imported the cult object of Cybele, who was honored with a temple on the Palatine Hill. However, Roman citizens themselves were not permitted into the cult until a century later. Cybele had a lover named Attis who was unfaithful to her. Thirsting for revenge, she drove him mad so that he castrated himself. As a result, the priests of Cybele were required to be eunuchs. (Paul's harsh remarks about the Judaizers in Phil. 3:2 may refer to this act of castration.)

A gory ritual in the Cybele cult was the *taurobolium*. Here an initiate would stand in a pit while a bull was slaughtered over him, drenching him in a shower of warm blood. Her festivities included a procession of priests flagellating themselves to the accompaniment of drums and cymbals as they mourned the death of Attis. During the second century the notion of resurrection was introduced into this cult, perhaps as a reflection of the impact of Christianity.

Another mystery religion was an updated version of the ancient Isis-Osiris cult. To unite his subjects, Ptolemy I of Egypt (323–285 B.C.) replaced Osiris with a hybrid Egyptian-Greek god, Serapis, who served as a new consort for the female deity Isis. She quickly became popular in the Greco-Roman world, and by 150 B.C. the cult was one of the more widely practiced in Athens. Within another fifty years it had entered Italy. For a century the Roman authorities tried to suppress the cult, but Caligula favored it and even built a large temple to Isis and Serapis on the Campus Martius. Domitian and Commodus were other emperors who honored the goddess. The colorful rituals of Egyptian origin included processions with shaven priests garbed in white linen and priestesses rattling sistrums. The Isis cult was especially appealing to women.

The leading Syrian mystery religion was the cult of the goddess Atargatis of the city of Hierapolis (Bambyce) on the Euphrates River. Like the priests of Attis her ministrants were eunuchs. These were notorious as beggars who beat themselves to attract attention and alms. Nero had some regard for the rites of this Syrian goddess, and Alexander Severus built a temple for her in Rome.

One noteworthy mystery religion was promoted by Julia Domna, the wife of Septimius Severus. She was the daughter of the high priest of the sun-god worshiped at Emesa (Homs) in Syria. When her grandnephew Elagabalus became emperor, he elevated his hometown sun-god to be supreme in the empire. However, he was so despised that his god did not enjoy much popularity, but Aurelian a half-century

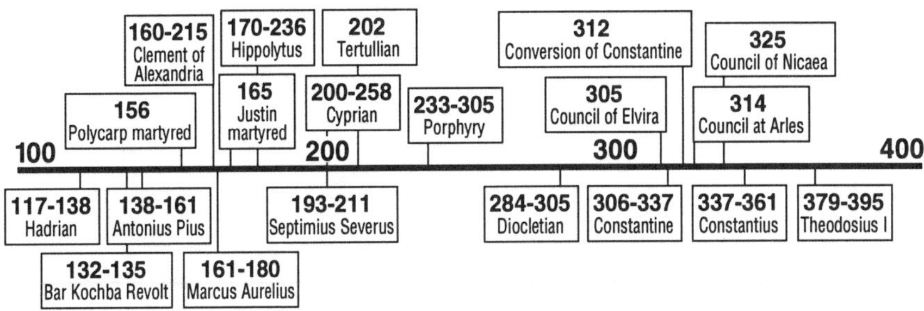

later reintroduced the Emesan god as the *sol invictus*, the "Unconquerable Sun." He built a magnificent temple in Rome and the birthday of the god was celebrated on December 25, just after the winter solstice.

Mithraism, which revolved around the Persian god Mithras, was the most potent rival to Christianity. The earliest contact between the Romans and worshipers of Mithras resulted from Pompey's conquest of the Cilician pirates in 67–65 B.C., but Mithraism did not develop as a mystery religion until 150 years later. The sanctuaries of Mithraism were *mithraea*, small cavelike structures. There may have been hundreds of these in the capital. In some places, such as at San Clemente and Santa Prisca in Rome, mithraea and churches stood side by side.

In every mithraeum was a *tauroctony*, a carved relief of Mithras stabbing the bull. Since only few Mithraic texts have survived, scholars are uncertain as to the exact significance of this deed. Mithras is usually accompanied by two figures, Cautes and Cautopates, who represent the rising and the setting sun. Because some of these reliefs are accompanied by signs of the Zodiac, the tauroctony may also have had astrological significance. The initiates, who were all males, progressed through seven grades that corresponded with the five known planets, sun, and moon. By the early second century Mithraism had spread among Roman merchants and soldiers, particularly in the more distant areas of the empire like Britain, Germany, and the Danube.

The one religious development that most directly threatened the survival of Christianity was the imperial cult, or "emperor worship." Its beginnings lay with the declaration by Augustus and the Senate that Julius Caesar after his assassination in 44 B.C. was "divine." As emperor, however, Augustus discouraged divine honors for himself in Rome but accepted them from the East, where Herod the Great built temples to him at Caesarea and Sebaste. When Agrippa created the Pantheon in Rome, Augustus declined to have it dedicated as a temple to himself. Only after his death did the Senate formally deify him.

Tiberius forbade the deification of his mother, the Empress Livia, and the Senate, which regarded him as an evil emperor, denied such an honor to him as well. The cruel Caligula, however, not only demanded divine honors for himself but even had his sister Drusilla deified after her death. Claudius was unenthusiastic about divine honors, but he did agree to accept a temple in his honor in the recently conquered province of Britain as a sign of political loyalty.

The vain Nero had ordered a gigantic statue of Apollos Helios with his own visage erected, but he declined to have a temple of *Divus Nero* ("divine Nero") built. He commented: "The princeps does not receive the honor of a god until he has ceased to be among men," but at his death the Senate denied him this honor. Vespasian, who was regarded as a good emperor, joked as he was dying, "Dear me! I must be turning into a god." His popular son Titus, whose brief reign was cut short by illness, was elevated to divinity after his death by his brother Domitian. Some scholars feel that Domitian, who required people to address him as "Lord and God," may have persecuted Jews and Christians because they refused to acknowledge his divinity. Some also maintain that the background idea of Revelation 13 was the establishment of the cult of Domitian at Ephesus, which included his huge statue.

The imperial cult had both political and religious significance. In all provinces it was organized by civil magistrates as an institution that reflected loyalty to Rome. The wealthy citizens of Asia Minor who tended the imperial cult centers were called *Asiarchs* (Acts 19:31). Some seventy temples and shrines were erected throughout this province in honor of the emperor. Though in many respects the emperors were treated like gods, there is no evidence that any prayers were offered to them for healing from diseases.

Christians, who were quite willing to pray for the emperor (1 Tim. 2:2) and to obey the Roman authorities (Rom. 13:1–2; 1 Peter 2:17), were, however, not about to offer sacrifices to the emperor. Jews had also taken this stance but their faith was tolerated as a national *religio licita* ("recognized religion.") The new sect of Christians, which soon encompassed many ethnic groups, was suspected of being an immoral, secret society. Those who refused to sacrifice to the emperor were considered guilty of treason and persecuted accordingly.

Roman Persecution and Christian Martyrs

The earliest persecutions of Christians were by Jewish authorities in Palestine. The first martyr recorded in Scripture was the deacon Stephen (Acts 6–7), who was stoned by a mob, perhaps in the year A.D. 36. The next was James the son of Zebedee, one of the original twelve apostles, who was killed by Herod Agrippa I in 44 (Acts 12). According to Josephus and Eusebius, James the brother of Jesus and also head of the Jerusalem church, was stoned at the instigation of the high priest in 62, shortly after the death of the governor Festus.

Claudius's expulsion of the Jews from Rome, recorded by Suetonius, may have resulted from unrest occasioned by Jewish Christians who were preaching Christ in the synagogues. Nero wanted to make Christians the scapegoats for the fire in the capital in A.D. 64. Suetonius said laconically, "Punishment was inflicted on the Christians, a class of men given to a new mischievous superstition." Tacitus's vivid description of Nero's brutality has stirred imaginations for centuries:

> Consequently, to get rid of the report, Nero fastened the guilt and inflicted the most exquisite tortures on a class hated for their abominations, called Christians by the populace. Christus, from whom the name had its origin, suffered the extreme penalty during the reign of Pontius Pilate. . . . Mockery of every sort was added to their deaths. Covered with the skins of beasts, they were torn by dogs and perished, or were nailed to crosses, or were doomed by the flames and burnt, to serve as nightly illumination when daylight had expired. Nero offered his gardens for the spectacle.[1]

A late Christian source (Sulpicius Severus) reports: "At that time Paul and Peter were condemned to death, the former being beheaded with a sword, while Peter suffered crucifixion." Some popular traditions, however, have no historical foundation. One is that as Peter was fleeing Rome to avoid the Neronian persecution, he encountered Jesus on the Appian Way. He said, "Where are you going, Lord?" (*Quo vadis domine?*) Jesus replied, "I am going to Rome to be crucified again." Thereupon the apostle returned to the capital to meet his fate. Another legend maintains that Peter asked to be crucified upside down.

Eusebius indicates that around the year 95 Domitian banished many Christians from Rome, including his niece Flavia Domitilla. Her husband Clemens, who was the emperor's cousin, was executed for "atheism," which at that time meant a conversion to Judaism. Only some centuries later did the idea surface that Clemens was a Christian. Other indirect evidence of persecution under this emperor was John's banishment to Patmos (Rev. 1:9) and some comments in *I Clement*.

An explicit reference to persecution is contained in the letter of the Roman governor Pliny to Trajan (c. A.D. 112). He asked the emperor for advice on whether he should take action against those who had been accused as Christians, since he was uncertain whether "the mere name of Christian" was a punishable offense. He believed in any case that their "stubbornness and unshakable obstinacy" should be punished. He also reported that he had used torture to interrogate "two slave-women, whom they call deaconesses" to learn about Christian practices.

For some unknown reason Ignatius, bishop of Antioch, went to Rome during the reign of Trajan and suffered martyrdom there. His close friend Polycarp was later martyred in Smyrna after he had refused to deny Christ with these memorable words: "Eighty and six years have I served Him and He has done me no wrong. How then can I blaspheme my King who has saved me?"

The legal basis for the persecution of Christians is still a matter of scholarly debate. On various occasions they were accused of "treason," "crimes," "shameful deeds," and "obstinacy." Prejudice and misunderstanding fed a variety of popular rumors. Christians who refused to take part in pagan ceremonies and activities were suspected of being disloyal and antisocial. Because they addressed each other as "brothers" and "sisters" and met secretly, they were charged with immorality. References in the Lord's Supper to eating the flesh and drinking the blood of Christ gave rise to the suspicion of cannibalism.

Justin Martyr was killed in the reign of the Stoic emperor Marcus Aurelius, while the heroism of the martyrs at Vienne and Lyons in southeastern Gaul (France) in A.D. 177 is one of the great stories of Christian history. Eusebius describes how forty-eight Christians were slain in the amphitheaters before bloodthirsty crowds of pagans, including the slave woman Blandina who was gored by a bull. Marcus Aurelius contemptuously dismissed these martyrs as obstinate fools.

His son Commodus was a playboy emperor who amused himself with gladiatorial games and left the Christians alone. However, a dozen were executed by the governor of Scilli in North Africa in A.D. 180, and a number of Christians were killed in the province of Asia. The latter may have been Montanists, as this group was particularly zealous in courting martyrdom. In 202 five were slain at Carthage, the best known of whom were Perpetua, a nursing mother, and her slave Felicitas. The diary of Perpetua, which recorded the visions that God sent to encourage her, was especially popular among the Montanists, since they emphasized the importance of direct revelations by the Holy Spirit.

Leonides, the father of the famed scholar Origen, was killed at Alexandria in 202. The son wanted very much to join his father, but his mother frustrated the attempt by hiding his clothes. Later in 206 eight of Origen's students were slain. In 211 a Christian soldier was executed for refusing to wear a laurel wreath because of its pagan associations. Tertullian, who praised the example of this military martyr, discouraged Christians from serving in the army since this would involve compromise with pagan practices.

The first systematic attempt to wipe out Christianity throughout the empire occurred in 250 under Decius, one of the ephemeral "Barracks Emperors." He required everyone to make offerings in honor of himself and to swear oaths by his fortune as evidence of their loyalty. People had to obtain a *libellus*, a document that certified that they had sacrificed. Those who refused to participate in this civil-religious rite faced harsh consequences. Several bishops were executed, including Fabian of Rome, Alexander of Jerusalem, and Babylas of Antioch. Others were imprisoned, such as Dionysius of Alexandria; Origen died after undergoing torture in 251. Literally hundreds were martyred for their faith at this time.

Cyprian, bishop of Carthage, describes in his writings the problems raised by the persecutions. Much to his dismay, the great majority of Christians out of fear lapsed from the faith and offered sacrifices to protect themselves. Cyprian himself went into hiding and justified this by referring to Jesus' advice to flee (Matt. 10:23). Some compromised by purchasing *libelli* without actually sacrificing.

After Decius's passing, the church leaders took differing positions toward those who had faltered. Novatian, a counter-bishop in Rome, adopted the most rigorist stance and excluded all who had lapsed. However, Cyprian and Cornelius, the regular bishop of Rome, agreed to allow those who had bought *libelli* back into the fellowship after a suitable show of repentance, while those who had actually sacrificed would only be readmitted on their deathbeds.

A few years later Valerian drafted a series of edicts aimed at the leaders of the church. These edicts exiled bishops, forbade all Christian assemblies, and provided for the dismissal of Christian servants from the imperial household and their banishment to work on the imperial estates. One result was the execution of the bishops Cyprian and Sixtus II of Rome.

The final persecution took place under Diocletian, the last great pagan emperor before Constantine. Diocletian and his assistant Galerius were offended by Christians who made the sign of the cross just as pagan priests attempted to foretell the future by looking at the entrails of sacrificial animals. He therefore issued four increasingly severe edicts. According to Eusebius, "an imperial letter was everywhere promulgated, ordering the razing of the churches to the ground and the destruction by fire of the Scriptures."[2] Those who handed over Scriptures and other sacred objects were known as *traditores* (traitors). Church leaders were jailed and pressured to sacrifice to the emperor. In the city of Nicomedia alone 268 Christians were executed. A second edict provided for the imprisonment of all the higher clergy, while a third offered them amnesty if they would sacrifice. The fourth ordered all Christians to sacrifice or face the penalty of death or forced labor.

The persecutions abated when Diocletian retired in 305. Galerius conceded that the policy had failed and issued an edict of toleration in 311, even as he was wracked by terrible suffering from a malady that contemporary church figures interpreted as divine punishment. Two years later Constantine ended the era of persecution with a decree: "Our purpose is to grant both to the Christians and to all others full authority to follow whatever worship each man has desired."

Church Expansion and Growing Influence

After the Romans destroyed the Temple and much of Jerusalem in A.D. 70 and then transformed it into a pagan city following the second Jewish revolt in 135, they declared it out of bounds for Jews and thus for Jewish Christians as well. As this severely undermined the position of Jerusalem, Christians developed new centers elsewhere. One of the first to emerge was Antioch in western Syria, where the disciples had first been given the name "Christian" (Acts 11:26).

Some 150 miles northeast of Antioch lay the important trade city of Edessa (modern Urfa). It was captured by the Romans in A.D. 116 and fully incorporated into the empire in 216. When Christianity actually

The Colosseum in Rome

arrived in eastern Syria is highly disputed, because the sources of information are quite late and of dubious reliability. One legend claims that a disciple of Jesus carried out the evangelization of Edessa, but the first actual Christian king was Abgar IX, who ruled at the end of the second century. The sixth-century *Chronicle of Edessa* records that in 201 a church there was destroyed by a flood. It is generally agreed that Edessa was the first autonomous city-state as such to adopt Christianity.

The apocryphal *Gospel of Thomas* and the *Acts of Thomas* may have been composed in Edessa in the second or third centuries. The former is significant for its extremely ascetic character and the latter for its docetic portrayal of Jesus. Syrian Christianity was noted for its negative attitude toward marriage and procreation. The disciple Thomas himself has an interesting legendary career. Although one writer states he was buried in Edessa, others maintain that he carried the gospel to Parthia (Persia) or that he reached India and was martyred there. It is definitely known that Christianity in Persia used the Syriac language. Also, because of the ongoing struggle with Rome, the Persians persecuted the Christians whom they regarded as aligned with their enemies in the West.

Christianity came to Armenia, the mountainous region east of the Black Sea, in the third century when Gregory the Illuminator (c. 240–

332) won King Tiridates to Christ in 301. Armenia therefore was the first nation as such to embrace Christianity. Important biblical manuscripts and Christian compositions in the distinctive Armenian script have survived.

Scholars are in the dark as to precisely how Christianity came to Egypt, although it was probably brought by Jewish converts. The tradition that Mark founded Christianity there is so late (Eusebius in the fourth century) that many doubt its validity. The once popular notion that the majority form of early Christianity in Egypt was heterodox has been refuted by the papyrus documents uncovered there in recent years. Of the fourteen Christian papyri that can be dated before 200, only one, a Greek fragment of the *Gospel of Thomas* from Oxyrynchus, could be considered nonorthodox.

The first convert from the Sudan (Nubia or the Upper Nile region) was the famed "Ethiopian eunuch" won by Philip (Acts 8:26–40), treasurer of Queen Candace of the Kingdom of Meroe. As used by the Greeks and Romans the term *Ethiopian* simply meant "black" (literally "sunburned"). Unfortunately, there is no textual or archeological trace of Christianity south of Egypt until the fourth century. At that time it was brought to the court of Axum, a kingdom in the eastern part of modern Ethiopia, by Frumentius of Tyre. King Ezana (320–60), who converted to Christianity, then introduced it into the Nile Valley.

Cyrene in Libya had a strong Jewish community, and some of the Cyrenians had a synagogue in Jerusalem as well (Acts 6:9). Among the early Cyrenian converts were Simon, who carried the cross (Mark 15:21), and his sons Alexander and Rufus (Rom. 16:13), who not only helped to evangelize Antioch (Acts 11:20) but perhaps also their homeland. It was probably from Cyrene that the gospel spread to Tripolitania in western Libya and then to Carthage in Tunisia.

Carthage, originally a Phoenician colony and then the capital of Proconsular Africa, was an important outpost of Roman civilization. It is not certain when Christianity reached this metropolis, but the nearby town of Scilla was the scene of several early martyrdoms. Tertullian, the first important Latin spokesman for Christianity, was active in the city around 200. The earliest known bishop of Carthage, Agrippinus, called a council there in 220 to consider the rebaptism of reformed heretics. The city's best-known bishop, Cyprian, shepherded his flock in the midst of the Decian persecution and took a leading part in the controversies over the readmission of the lapsed. A council in 256 was attended by eighty-seven bishops from across western North Africa.

The faith had spread into Germany by the late second century, as there were reports of Christians at Mainz around 200. By the mid–third century there were bishops at Trier (the Roman provincial capital) and Cologne. Maternus, a bishop at the latter, attended councils in Rome (313) and Arles (314). Also, there were probably bishops at this time in Mainz and Augsburg.

Christianity was brought into the region of southeastern Gaul (France) from Asia Minor, where the churches at Vienne and Lyons in the Rhone river valley were especially active. Eusebius records that the news of the martyrdom of around fifty believers in A.D. 177 was conveyed in a letter to "brethren in the provinces of Asia and Phrygia." Irenaeus, one of those who had come from the East, succeeded the martyred Pothinus as bishop at Lyons. By the mid–third century bishops were established in Arles, Vienne, Toulouse, Rheims, and Paris. Sixteen Gallic bishops were present at the Council of Arles.

Although both the New Testament (Rom. 15:24, 28) and Clement of Rome suggest that Paul may have gone to Spain, Spanish Christians have long held that their country was evangelized by the apostle James. Although his relics are venerated at the famous shrine of Santiago de Compostela (Santiago and San Diego are Spanish forms of St. James), this legend did not become current until the eighth century. The first major Christian assembly in Spain was the Council of Elvira (c. 305), which laid down rigorous rules of penance for various infractions and demanded clerical celibacy. Moreover, Hosius, bishop of Cordoba, was an influential adviser to the Emperor Constantine.

A popular legend in Britain holds that Joseph of Arimathea took the Holy Grail (the cup used at the Last Supper) to the island. A thorn tree in the Glastonbury monastery is said to have sprouted from the thorns of Jesus' crown, which Joseph also brought. More realistic are the statements by Tertullian and Origen that Christianity had reached Britain by their day (early 200s). There were three British martyrs in the Decian persecution and five Britons attended the Council of Arles. Ample archeological evidence of the Christian presence in Britain dates from the fourth century.

At the time of Constantine's accession to power somewhere between 5 and 15 percent of the population in the empire had become Christian. By 325 (when the landmark Council of Nicaea met) Christians were a majority in Asia Minor, Thrace, Cyprus, Edessa, and Armenia. They were an important segment of the population in Syria,

Greece, Italy, Egypt, Proconsular Africa, Numidia (Algeria), and southern Gaul, but were still thinly represented in Arabia, Mauretania (Morocco), Tripolitania, the Black Sea coast, northern Gaul, Britain, Germany, and the Danubian region.

The Organization of the Church

Since the early disciples were Jewish, they visited the Temple in Jerusalem and attended synagogues until they were expelled. The apostles and other teachers, gifted by the Holy Spirit with a diversity of talents, provided leadership. Deacons and deaconesses were chosen to assist in more mundane matters such as the distribution of food. There was no formal priesthood because all believers constituted a "holy priesthood" (1 Peter 2:9), whose high priest was the exalted Jesus. Their sacrifices were a spiritual liturgy (Rom. 12:1) that involved offerings of praise and good works (Heb. 13:15–16).

Gradually, distinctions began to be made between the laity (Greek *laos*, "people") and the ordained clergy, and stratification developed within the church. Clement of Rome at the end of the first century introduced the term "layman," and Clement of Alexandria was the first to use the word "clergy" (taken from the Greek word *kleros* or "lot") to refer to individuals who exercised a permanent ministry in the church.

During the early centuries the biblical ideal of the priesthood of believers persisted. Tertullian wrote, "Are we lay people not priests also?" Origen declared, "Or are you ignorant that to you also, that is, to all the Church of God and to the people of believers, the priesthood was given?"[3] But the reality was far different. Origen complained that the bishops in large cities refused to allow "even the noblest of Jesus' disciples" to speak. Origen himself created quite a controversy when he was asked by bishops in Palestine to speak in churches when he was not yet ordained. As time passed, the gap between the two groups widened, and eventually the Ecumenical Council at Carthage (398) formally prohibited laymen from teaching in the presence of clergymen without the latter's consent.

Deacons provided a variety of services in the early centuries. They distributed the eucharist, assisted at baptisms, acted as ushers, served as messengers, administered funds for widows and orphans, and supervised church property. Deacons also were responsible for burials and had charge of cemeteries, and served as assistants to bishops. Deaconesses (female deacons) such as Phoebe (Rom. 16:1;

1 Tim. 3:11) played a vital role in the early church. They assisted at the baptism of women and ministered to women who were sick. The *Apostolic Constitutions* (fourth century) required deaconesses to be either virgins or once-married widows, who were to be ordained by a bishop. In general, widows occupied a position similar to deaconesses. Paul had counseled the younger ones to remarry (1 Tim. 5:14), while the older (usually those over sixty) were to receive assistance from the church, provided they were of good character and had a record of doing good deeds. Origen stated that in his day the "order of widows" was considered an ecclesiastical rank. They nursed the sick and evangelized pagan women.

The lector (reader of the Scriptures in the liturgy) was first mentioned by Tertullian. By the mid–third century they were regarded as a definite order, usually the first stage in the clerical hierarchy. According to the *Apostolic Church Order* (c. 300), "For Reader, one should be appointed, after he has been carefully proved . . . capable of clearly interpreting, mindful that he assumes the position of an evangelist." By the fourth century the lector read from other Scriptures, but the deacons or higher clergy read the gospel. Besides the lectors, other orders of the lower clergy included acolytes, exorcists, and subdeacons. In the mid–third century, according to a letter cited by Eusebius, the following clergy were serving at Rome: one bishop, forty-six presbyters, seven deacons, seven subdeacons, forty-two acolytes, and fifty-two exorcists, readers and doorkeepers.

The Greek word translated "elder," *presbyteros*, meant an older man. (The English word "priest" was derived from an Old Saxon contraction of presbyter to *prester* or *priester.*) In the New Testament church the elders (presbyters) constituted the collective leadership of a local congregation (Acts 11:30; 15:6; 1 Tim. 5:17). Peter considered himself an elder (1 Peter 5:1). Early Christian texts such as Polycarp's *Epistle* indicate that a plurality of elders was in charge of a congregation. Twelve presbyters led the important church at Alexandria.

In the New Testament the word *episcopos*, translated "bishop" or "overseer," was simply another term for presbyter (Acts 20:17, 28; Phil. 1:1). Clement testified that this was also the case at Rome at the end of the first century. However, at Antioch a few decades later Ignatius introduced a "monepiscopacy" that distinguished between the presbyters and a single "bishop" who presided over them. This pattern of a threefold ministry (deacons and presbyters, under a single bishop in a city) prevailed in most urban churches by the middle of the second century. The presbyters served as a council of advisors to the bishop. In time, subcongregations (parishes) formed in addition to the bishop's own church. The bishop's church location eventually came to be known as the "cathedral" because his chair (Latin *cathedra*) was there. At the various local churches presbyters, now beginning to be called "priests," were assigned to "celebrate," i.e., conduct the Eucharist (Lord's Supper).

Gradually the bishop assumed most of the preaching and teaching functions in the church. Hippolytus (third century) reports that only the bishop possessed the power to ordain priests/elders, although the congregations did have to ratify his choices. At Alexandria the twelve leading presbyters elected the new bishop from within their own ranks. Congregational approval was needed for the selection of a new bishop, but the presence of three bishops was required if one were to be ordained. The leading bishop of a province was known as a "metropolitan bishop." The most influential ones were those of Caesarea in Palestine, Antioch, Alexandria, Rome, and (after 330) Constantinople.

Later Roman Catholic tradition holds that Peter was the founder and first bishop of the church at Rome. Drawing upon the scriptural authority ascribed to him in Matthew 16:18, the early medieval church regarded Peter and his successors in Rome as "popes" (from the Latin word *papa*, "father") "or "pontiffs" (from the Latin *Pontifex Maximus*, the highest "bridge maker" or priest). The earliest list of the bishops of Rome, compiled by Irenaeus, contains the name of Peter and his two shadowy successors, Linus and Anacletus, as well as the first clearly attested bishop, Clement (A.D. 91–101), who is known from his epistle to Corinth.

An important controversy over authority occurred near the end of the second century when Victor I (A.D. 189–98), an African who was the first clearly Latin bishop of Rome, threatened to cut off fellowship with the Christians of Asia Minor over the Quartodeciman controversy. The Asians followed Jewish practice and linked the date of Easter with the Passover, which fell on the fourteenth (Latin, *quartodeciman*) day of Nisan. Since this date came from the lunar calendar, Easter often was not observed on a Sunday. The Roman church insisted that since Jesus rose on the first day of the week, Easter should always fall on Sunday. Irenaeus of Lyons, though he agreed with the Roman practice, intervened to achieve peace between the two communities by persuading the Roman pontiff to allow the Asians to continue their divergent practice.

Early Church Expansion

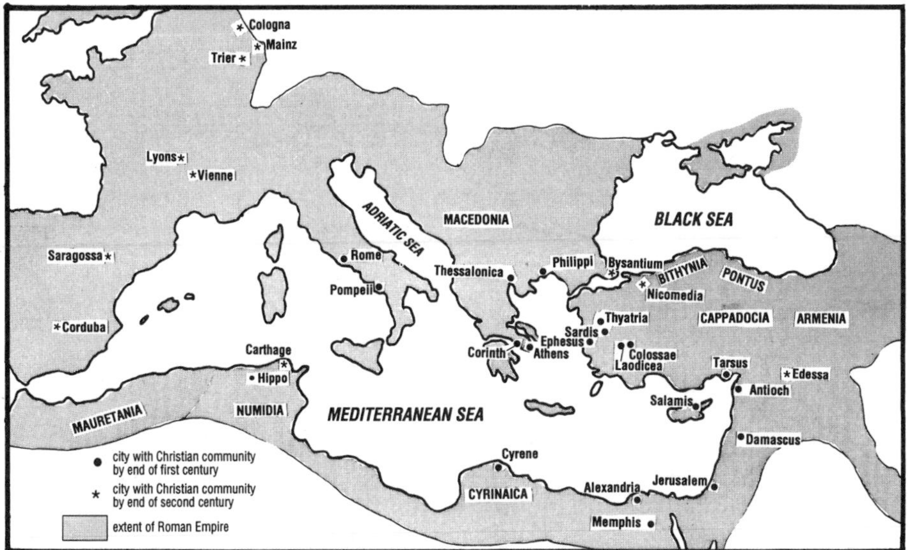

As the early "popes" were not always paragons of virtue, various people challenged their authority. For example, Hippolytus sharply criticized Bishop Zephyrinus (A.D. 198–217) as an uneducated, avaricious man and accused Callistus (217–22) of theological error and lax discipline:

> He laid it down that, if a bishop was guilty of any sin, even a sin unto death, he ought not to be deposed. In his time men who had been twice married, and thrice married, began to be ordained to clerical office as bishops, priests, and deacons. If also, however, any one in holy orders should get married, Callistus permitted such a one to continue in holy orders as if he had not sinned.[4]

Hippolytus also attacked Urban I (222–30) and Pontian (230–35), but then Emperor Maximinus Thrax exiled both him and Pontian to the Sardinian mines. Under these dismal conditions the two were reconciled and Hippolytus urged his supporters to accept the recognized leadership of the Roman church. Another struggle occurred during the bishopric of Cornelius (251–53). He favored the readmission of those who had lapsed during the Decian persecution, but Novatian and his hard-line followers from Spain to Mesopotamia vigorously opposed their restoration.

In the mid–third century, Cyprian of Carthage appealed to the bishop of Rome to confirm some of his decisions. His treatise, *On the Unity of the Universal Church* (251), speaks of "the chair of Peter" and stresses the role of the Roman bishopric as the focal point of unity in the church. His most memorable phrase is, "One cannot have God as a father who does not have the church as mother." Yet Cyprian disagreed sharply with Bishop Stephen (254–57) over the issue of baptism. The latter recognized the baptisms performed by Novatianists and even Marcionites, whereas for Cyprian such rites were totally invalid.

Pagan Attacks and Christian Apologists

Romans such as Suetonius and Tacitus viewed Christianity as a "mischievous superstition." Christians were suspected of atheism, disloyalty, immorality, and cannibalism. In a third-century work called *The Octavius*, in a conversation between a Christian and a pagan, the North African writer Minucius Felix places some of these accusations in the mouth of the pagan spokesman, Caecilius:

> Having gathered together from the lowest dregs of the people a number of ignorant men and credulous women always ready to believe anything, they have formed a rabble of impious conspirators; at their nocturnal gatherings, solemn fasts, and barbarous meals the bond of union is not any sacred rite but crime. It is a people that lurks in darkness and shuns the light, silent in public, talkative in corners; they despise our temples as tombs, insult our gods, ridicule our ceremonies, and in need of pity themselves profess (if allowed) to pity our priests; half naked themselves, they contemptuously refuse offices and dignities.[5]

He also added, "Again, to say that a man who had suffered capital punishment for a crime and the death-dealing wood of the cross are objects of their veneration, is to assign fitting altars to abandoned wretches, and to assert that they worship what they deserve to worship."[6] Even an educated man like Fronto, the tutor of Marcus Aurelius, asserted that Christians were guilty of immorality during their banquets. The satirist Lucian made fun of gullible Christians who showed generosity even to charlatans.

More serious were the thoughtful attacks of Celsus and Porphyry. Celsus, who has been called the "Voltaire of the Second Century," wrote *The True Doctrine* in A.D. 178. Although the original has not survived, most of its content was recorded in Origen's *Contra Celsum*, written about seventy years later. Celsus ridiculed the God of the Old Testament as blasphemously anthropomorphic, while his own concept of the deity was a passionless, unchanging being that existed beyond the realm of human thought. For Celsus the teaching of the incarnation was a particular affront. Not only did he deny that Old Testament prophecies were fulfilled in Jesus but he also repeated the slander (also found in the Talmud) that Jesus was the illegitimate son of a Roman soldier. Celsus insisted that Jesus was in reality a wicked sorcerer who learned his lore in Egypt and performed miracles through magic. As for the resurrection, the witnesses to it were unreliable, and in any event bodies once decayed could never return to life. Celsus also described Christians as ignorant people who shirked their public responsibilities.

Porphyry, who was born in Tyre in 233, was a more erudite critic. Some feel he may have been a Christian in his early days. He was a student colleague of Origen in Alexandria and then went to Rome where he became the principal follower of Plotinus, the renowned Neo-Platonist. Porphyry's *Against the Christians*, which Constantine himself ordered burned, was refuted by Eusebius, Jerome, and Augustine. He accused Origen of using allegory to gloss over difficulties in the Old Testament, and like modern liberal biblical critics he held that Daniel was a prophecy written after the events and pointed out apparent discrepancies within the four gospels. He suggested that either Jesus was drunk when he rebuked Peter as Satan or he must have been dreaming when he bestowed the keys of the kingdom on such a person. Although Jesus may have been a wise man, he should not have been apprehensive in the Garden of Gethsemane nor silent before his accusers. If he really had risen from the dead, he should have shown himself to Pilate and the high priest rather than to humble women. Porphyry also asked, "What became of the innumerable souls, who can in no way be faulted, if he in whom they were supposed to believe had not yet appeared among humankind?"

Fortunately, the early Christian community possessed a group of learned and articulate spokesmen for the faith known as the "Apologists" (from the Greek *apologia*, "defense"). They refuted both the popular misconceptions and scholarly objections to Christianity.

According to Eusebius, Quadratus and Aristides in A.D. 125 presented some books defending Christianity to the Emperor Hadrian. In his work Aristides divided humankind into four nations—Barbarians, Greeks, Jews, and Christians. Then he showed the folly of the gods worshiped by the Barbarians (Chaldeans and Egyptians) and the Greeks, praised the Jews for their monotheism and morality, and argued for the superiority of Christianity. It is not known whether Hadrian read these apologies, but he did send a rescript to his governor Fundanus instructing him to receive accusations against Christians only if they had broken some specific laws.

By far the most important Apologist was Justin Martyr. Born of Gentile parents in Samaria, Justin pursued truth through a variety of philosophies before finding it in Christ. He is remembered as the first Christian thinker who sought to reconcile the claims of faith and reason, and this is seen in his two apologies and his dialogue with Trypho, a Jew.

Justin's lengthy *First Apology* (c. A.D. 155), dedicated to the Emperor Antoninus Pius and his two adopted sons, defended the faith against various pagan attacks. He argued that Christianity was not a novelty but the fulfillment of Old Testament prophecies, which were older than the Greek philosophies. Numerous quotations from the latter revealed his thorough acquaintance with Euripides, Xenophon, and especially Plato. Here Justin set forth a doctrine of the Logos (the Word) that enabled him to acknowledge the existence of partial revelations of truth in thinkers like Socrates who had lived before the coming of Christ, the entire Logos. All people shared in the "generative" Word, but Christianity was the only truly rational belief system. Pagan myths and mystery religions that resembled Christianity were demonic falsifications.

Trypho was a Jewish survivor of the Bar Kochba War. Some time after A.D. 135 he encountered Justin in Ephesus and questioned him about the Christian faith. Justin endeavored to win Trypho by expounding Old Testament prophecies and citing foreshadowings of the cross in natural objects. Trypho listened with interest but objected that he could not accept as Messiah an allegedly divine man who had been crucified like a criminal. Later, after he had moved to Rome, Justin wrote the shorter *Second Apology* to protest a particular case of injustice against Christians there. Around 165 he and six others were condemned for refusing to sacrifice to the emperor, thereby earning the name of Justin "Martyr."

One of his students was the Syrian Tatian, who is best known for his *Diatessaron*, a harmony of the four gospels. In *Oration to the Greeks* he "said goodbye to the arrogance of the Romans and the nonsense of the Athenians" by repeating scandalous stories about the Greek philosophers and denigrating the erotic statues and literary works of the Greeks. He then contrasted all this with the divine purity of Christianity.

Athenagoras's *Plea On Behalf of the Christians* was addressed to Marcus Aurelius and Commodus in the late A.D. 170s. He refuted the accusation of atheism by showing that certain Greek philosophers had also rejected polytheism in favor of monotheism. His explicit mention of the Trinity is the oldest known reference to this doctrine.

Around the same time Theophilus of Antioch wrote an address *To Autolycus*, which attacked paganism and emperor worship, and argued for the priority of Moses and the prophets over the Greek thinkers. He even worked out a detailed chronology of the world that dated the Creation to 5,695 years before his day. The philosophic approach of these Apologists could be seen in their emphasis on God and his Logos coupled with a deliberate silence about Jesus.

The aforementioned Minucius Felix presented a spirited defense of Christianity in Octavius. His approach was the use of rational arguments rather than quoting Scripture. An example of his method was the response of the Christian to his dialogue partner:

> The fact that our number is increasing daily is no proof of error, but evidence of merit; for when men live an honorable life, their own friends remain constant and are joined by others. Lastly, we easily recognize each other, not by external marks, as you imagine, but by the stamp of innocence and modesty; we love one another (which annoys you), since we do not know how to hate; we call ourselves brethren (which excites your ill-will), as being children of one and the same Father.[7]

In some ways this work resembles the *Apology* of the great Tertullian, whose stirring defense of Christianity reverberates even today with memorable phrases. Although trained in Latin rhetoric, Tertullian was adamant against accommodating Christianity with Greek philosophy: "What indeed has Athens to do with Jerusalem? What has the Academy to do with the Church? What have heretics to do with Christians? Away with all attempts to produce a Stoic, Platonic, and dialectic Christianity!" It was Tertullian who said "the blood of the martyrs was the seed of the church." He declared defiantly, "We are but of yesterday, and we have filled everything you have—cities, tenements, forts, towns, exchanges, yes, and camps, tribes, palace, senate, forum. All we have left to you are the temples!"[8]

THE CHALLENGE OF GNOSTICISM

The term "gnosticism" designates a variety of religious movements in the early Christian centuries that held that salvation came through a secret "knowledge" (Greek *gnosis*) of one's origins. It was characterized by a cosmological dualism that opposed the spiritual to the material world and distinguished between the transcendent God and the foolish creator of the material world. The material creation was seen as evil, but "sparks" of divinity were encapsulated in the bodies of certain "spiritual" individuals who were destined for salvation. These individuals were ignorant of their heavenly knowledge, but God sent down to them a "redeemer" who brought them salvation in the form of secret knowledge about their origin and their destiny. Thus awakened, the "spirituals" escaped from the prison of their bodies at death and passed through the planetary regions controlled by hostile demons to be reunited with God.

In the second and third centuries orthodox Christian writers zeroed in on Gnosticism, accused its adherents of immorality, and portrayed the various groups as heretical perversions. Although a few scholars claim there was a pre-Christian gnosticism, in fact only a rudimentary form existed at the end of the first century, possibly evidenced in the traces of a docetic Christianity (see 1 John). Ignatius of Antioch firmly protested against the docetists who denied the incarnation of Christ and said His humanity and sufferings were only in appearance.

Though the church Fathers unanimously regarded Simon of Samaria as the first Gnostic, the earliest authority, Acts 8, describes him only as a magician. According to later writers, Simon also claimed to be divine and taught that his companion, a former prostitute, was the reincarnated Helen of Troy. His successor, another Samaritan named Menander, taught at Antioch a few decades later and said that those who believed in him would not die, but his own death invalidated the claim.

A disciple of Menander was Saturninus of Antioch. He taught that the "unknown Father" created angels, who in turn made the world and mankind. Man was a powerless being, like a worm, until a "divine spark" set him on his feet. Christ the Savior appeared as a man "in semblance," and He came to destroy the God of the Jews, who was one of the creator angels and to redeem those endowed with the divine sparks. Cerinthus, a contemporary, maintained that

The Carrawburgh Mithraeum at Hadrian's Wall

the world was not made by the supreme God but by a lesser power, the "demiurge," who was ignorant of the God above all. He also asserted that "the Christ" (a higher divine power) descended upon the human Jesus in the form of the dove and then departed from him before the crucifixion, as Christ could not suffer.

A major Gnostic was Marcion, a native of Pontus in Asia Minor who came to Rome around A.D. 140. He was so successful in attracting followers that he organized a separate Christian community. His rival sect gained converts all over the empire and constituted one of the chief dangers to the orthodox church in the later second century. In some respects Marcion's teachings differed from the typical Gnostic systems. Because he was unable to reconcile the anthropomorphism of the Old Testament with the philosophical concept of God, he concluded that there were two deities—the inferior God of the Old Testament and supreme God of the New Testament. The former as the creator, though not evil, was incompetent and ignorant. The Old Testament was a valid revelation for the Jews but not for Christians. Rather than being born of a woman, Christ was sent from the Father and suddenly appeared at Capernaum. He did not experience birth, but he did suffer and die.

Basilides, who flourished in Alexandria during Hadrian's reign, was inspired by Menander. According to Irenaeus, he taught that from the supreme or transcendent God "emanated" such things as Mind, Logos, Understanding, Wisdom, and Power. These emanations in turn created 365 heavens, the chief and last of which was the God of the Jews. Although a lower spiritual being, he tried to put mankind in bondage to him. In order to free humanity the transcendent God sent his "Mind" (Greek *Nous*) into the world, and it dwelt in Christ, a man who worked miracles. But since he could not suffer, he escaped death by a ruse. Simon of Cyrene not only carried his cross but was also mistakenly crucified, while the invisible Jesus stood by laughing.

There are striking parallels to this account in two of the Coptic tractates found at Nag Hammadi in Upper Egypt in 1945. One of the most important manuscript discoveries relating to early church history ever made, they greatly expanded our fund of knowledge about gnosticism.

The most famous Gnostic, Valentinus, was educated in Alexandria and came to Rome around A.D. 140. After two decades of conflict with the church there he moved to Cyprus. Several of his disciples founded their own Gnostic schools. Valentinus argued that the divine world of the *pleroma* ("fullness") consisted of four dualities together with eleven pairs of male-female *aeons* (emanations). The last of these aeons was Sophia (wisdom), who became filled with curiosity and the desire to know the Unknowable. Her revolt resulted in the emergence of the demiurge (identified with the Old Testament God), who created the world and humankind. The latter was divided into three classes: (1) the *hylic*, the material or flesh (created of the dust of the earth); (2) an intermediate group, the *psychic* or "soulish"; and (3) the *pneumatic*, in whom was implanted the element of spirit. The hylics were unbelievers immersed in nature and the physical universe. The psychics were the ordinary Christians who lived by faith. The pneumatics were the true Gnostics, who were saved by the awareness or "knowledge" of the divine nature of their spirits.

Scholars have identified no less than five of the Nag Hammadi tractates as Valentinian, although none of these explicitly claim his authorship. He may have even been the author of the famous *Gospel of Truth.* The Valentinians were certainly the most successful of the Christian Gnostics. They pioneered in scriptural commentaries, particularly on John's gospel, which was their favorite. The commentary by Heracleon is the first known work of this type on any New Testament book. Some of their ideas even influenced major thinkers like Clement of Alexandria, but they evoked strong refutations from Irenaeus, Tertullian, and Origen.

Emperor Constantine and Legalized Christianity

To manage the vast empire, Diocletian instituted a complex structure called the Tetrarchy, or "rule of four." He reigned as the "Augustus" in the East, assisted by his "Caesar," Galerius, while Maximian ruled in the West with his "Caesar," Constantius. After Diocletian retired in 305, a struggle for sole power ensued, involving up to seven rivals.

Constantine was the son of Constantius and Helena, a former barmaid. When his father, who had become the Augustus of the West, died in 306, the troops hailed the son as their leader. Although Constantine sought divine aid against his enemy Maxentius by turning to Christianity, it is unlikely that he did this to win the favor of Christians, as they were a small minority. Some see his conversion as syncretistic, since the *sol invictus* was recognized on his triumphal arch in Rome. He had come from Illyria where the sun cult held sway, and this may have predisposed him to monotheism. Most scholars, however, are convinced of Constantine's sincerity, even though he was not baptized until just before his death.

The decisive vision in A.D. 312 was described by Lactantius, a Christian teacher of rhetoric and later tutor of the emperor's son:

> Constantine was directed in a dream to mark the heavenly sign of God on the shields of his soldiers and thus to join battle. He did as he was ordered and with the cross-shaped letter X, with its top bent over, he marked Christ on the shields. [This was the *labarum* or Constantinian monogram, the combination of the first two letters of Christos—the Chi and the Rho.][9]

A variant version is found in Eusebius's *Life of Constantine*: "He saw with his own eyes the trophy of a cross of light in the heavens, above the sun, and an inscription, 'Conquer by this,' attached to it." Be that as it may, while following the heavenly sign, he defeated the forces of Maxentius at the Battle of the Milvian Bridge near Rome.

In 313 Constantine and his eastern colleague Licinius agreed to grant toleration to Christians and restore property that had been confiscated from them. This is commonly known as the "Edict of Milan," although there is considerable scholarly debate over just what actually transpired in Milan. Constantine gave the Lateran Palace to the Bishop of Rome, legalized bequests to churches, began the construction of basilicas—the first public structures to be used as church buildings—and supported clergy, virgins, and widows from public funds. His mother Helena went on a pilgrimage to Palestine in 326, "discovered" the birth and burial places of Jesus and had churches built there, and brought back many noteworthy relics.

Before long the cooperation with Licinius unraveled, and the latter purged Christians from his court and army. In the war that followed, Constantine triumphed at Adrianople in 324 and became sole emperor. In 330 he moved the imperial capital eastward to the Greek colony of Byzantium on the Bosporus and renamed the city Constantinople. The new buildings were patterned after those in Rome and included a palace, forum, and hippodrome. At his death in 337 he was buried in the Church of the Twelve Apostles there. The Eastern Orthodox churches regard him so highly that they still refer to him as the "Thirteenth Apostle."

To a world torn by ethnic and class differences and rife with economic and political problems, Christianity offered the vision of a fellowship of love and peace in this life and the hope of life eternal after death. Though far from blameless, Christians at their best demonstrated lives of compassion and a death-defying faith through their martyrdoms. Despite the rivalry of mystery religions, the disdain of philosophers, the prejudices of the masses, and persecution by the state, Christians won more and more converts, including men of intellect who could defend the faith against slanders and warn the church against the beguiling elitism of heresies like Gnosticism. Christianity ultimately triumphed in the conversion of the Emperor Constantine, a momentous development that brought immediate benefits but also long-term problems as the affairs of state and church became increasingly intertwined.

3

DOCTRINAL DEVELOPMENT IN THE CHURCH

While defending itself against external attacks and insidious heresies, the Christian church also engaged in defining its beliefs regarding the Scriptures, the nature of Christ, and the Godhead. Christians had to clarify their relationship to Judaism and its sacred writings. They enlisted Greek philosophy and Latin rhetoric in the theological task. To resolve doctrinal issues and draw the line separating orthodoxy from heterodoxy, a number of church synods and councils were convened, where political considerations, personality differences, and varying traditions led to acrimonious discussions.

The Development of the Biblical Canon

The term *canon* (Greek: "ruler" or "measuring rod") came to be used for the list of books recognized by Christians as the divinely inspired writings. At first, all they had were the Hebrew Scriptures. These were divided into three sections: the Law (*Torah*) or Pentateuch—the five books of Moses, the Prophets (*Nevi'im*), and the Writings (*Ketuvim*). Though some contend that the Jews did not formally recognize the last category of books as canonical until A.D. 90, more recent research has tended to push the date of their official acceptance back to the second century B.C.

The Hebrew Scriptures were arranged in twenty-two or twenty-four books that correspond to the present thirty-nine books of the "Old Testament," the term Christians use. They were written on leather scrolls, one of the oldest examples of which is the Isaiah Scroll, found among the famous Dead Sea Scrolls of the Qumran community. Other Jewish writings include several books and fragments known as the Old Testament Apocrypha (accepted by the Roman Catholic church as canonical) and the Pseudepigrapha, works that were falsely ascribed to famous personages such as the book of Enoch, which is cited in Jude 14. Actually, there was much debate among the church Fathers about the extent of the Old Testament canon. Some were willing to include part of the Apocryphal books, while others excluded Esther because it does not mention God.

With the exception of Jerome and Origen, the Fathers were not conversant in Hebrew. Consequently, for the postapostolic period the Christian Old Testament was the Septuagint, the Greek translation that had been prepared in Ptolemaic Alexandria in the third and second centuries B.C. In fact, the overwhelming majority of citations in the New Testament come from the Septuagint rather than the Hebrew text.

The Christian Scriptures emerged gradually over a long period of time. The apostolic Fathers (late first–early second centuries) were familiar with the gospels, Acts, and some epistles. For instance, Clement of Rome cites Hebrews and several Pauline epistles, while Ignatius's references to seven of Paul's letters implies that a collection of them existed. Polycarp's letter to the Philippians (c. 110) has allusions to fifteen books. To be sure, the apostolic Fathers did not treat these works as Scripture in the same way that they did the Old Testament, but they still recognized that the books were imbued with apostolic authority. According to Justin (c. 155), many churches were using the gospels along with the Old Testament in their services.

Another influence on the development of the canon was the Montanist movement. This arose in the second century in western Asia Minor, where Montanus and two women, Prisca and Maximilia, claimed the direct inspiration of the Holy Spirit and uttered prophecies while in a state of ecstatic frenzy. The Montanists maintained that they were totally possessed by the Spirit, who was inaugurating a

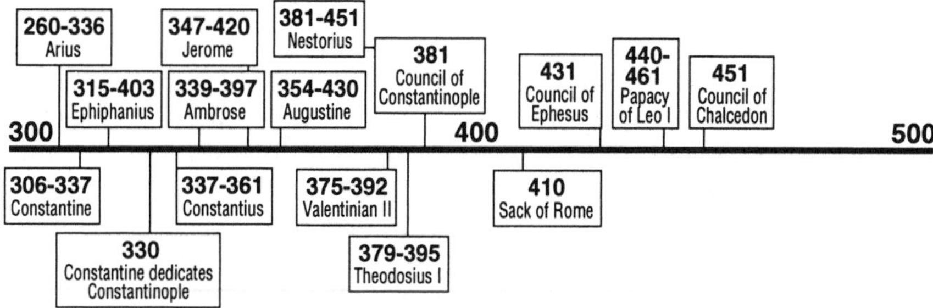

new age of revelation. They believed that the New Jerusalem described in Revelation 21 would soon descend on the town of Pepuza in Phrygia. They also observed strict fasts, forbade remarriage for widowers, welcomed martyrdom, and appealed to the gospel of John, Hebrews, and Revelation as justification for their rigid practices. In reaction, critics of Montanism questioned the inspiration of these books.

When a heretic, Marcion, who rejected the Old Testament but made the first formal listing of Christian books (this included an edited gospel of Luke and ten Pauline letters), the church Fathers responded by defining their own position regarding the Hebrew Scriptures and early Christian writings. Irenaeus (c. 180) and others affirmed the Old Testament, which they especially valued for its prophecies fulfilled in Jesus. He also explicitly acknowledged apostolic writings as Scripture and was the first to use the terms Old and New Testament. He recognized only the four gospels (Matthew, Mark, Luke, and John) as inspired and urged that the apocryphal gospels, which had proliferated by his time, be rejected.

Clement of Alexandria (c. 200) used all of the New Testament books except James, 2 Peter, and 3 John. Like earlier writers, he also cited a variety of other books, but subsequent Fathers referred less and less to these. Some Greek manuscripts of the New Testament from the fourth century still contained such works as the *Epistle of Barnabas*, the *Shepherd of Hermas*, *1* and *2 Clement*, and the *Didache.* In the third century Clement, Origen, and Hippolytus of Rome agreed on the canonical status of twenty-two books. The Muratorian Canon, a Latin text that may have originated around 200, lists twenty-four books, omitting Hebrews and 1 and 2 Peter. The Syriac New Testament, the Peshitta (c. 400), left out 2 Peter, 2 and 3 John, Jude, and Revelation.

Another early writer, Eusebius (c. 325) mentioned three categories of Christian writings: (1) those that were universally accepted as Scripture, (2) the books that were still questioned by some churches, and (3) the spurious or false books. In the first group were twenty of the twenty-seven New Testament books. In the second were Hebrews, James, 2 Peter, 2 and 3 John, Jude, and Revelation, which were still in dispute. The other popular books of the time were relegated to the third category. Athanasius of Alexandria listed all twenty-seven books as well as the thirty-nine books of the Old Testament in his Festal Letter of 367, thus indicating that most Christians had reached a consensus on the New Testament.

The Earliest Christology

One of the thorniest problems facing the early church was the development of the doctrine of Christ, or "Christology" as theologians call it. In the gospels Jesus referred to Himself some eighty times as "the Son of Man." This phrase, borrowed from Daniel, expressed His unity with humankind. Elsewhere in the New Testament it is only used four times. Throughout the New Testament Jesus is also called the "Son of God," a title that has messianic and apocalyptic implications, as its use in a Dead Sea scroll suggests. It conveyed the unique relationship He had to God the Father. During His ministry as a matter of respect Jesus was addressed as "Lord." He welcomed the title because it indicated that He was the Lord God (Ps. 110, as cited in Mark 12:35–37). His resurrection demonstrated that He was the "Lord" in an exalted sense (Acts 2:36; Phil. 2:9–11), and this was recognized by the use in the early church of the Aramaic term *Maranatha*, "Our Lord, come!" (1 Cor. 16:22).

The postresurrection appearances of Christ not only persuaded the early Christians that He had risen from the dead, but also that He was now at the right hand of God. The apostle Paul preached that Jesus was the crucified, resurrected, and exalted Lord. His epistles used the title *Kyrios* (Lord) more than 200 times, and since this Greek word was used in the Septuagint for *Yahweh*, its application to Jesus conveyed divine qualities (Rom. 10:13; 1 Cor. 2:16).

The gospels depicted Jesus as exercising divine powers—healing the sick, forgiving sins, and calming storms. When He declared His preexistence and equality with the Father, the Jews almost stoned Him for blasphemy (John 5:17–18; 8:58; 10:33–36). Among the passages that explicitly declare His deity are John 1:1; 1:18 (with the reading "only-begotten God"); 20:28; Romans 9:5; Philippians 2:6; Colossians 1:19; Titus 2:13; Hebrews 1:8–9; 2 Peter 1:1; and 1 John 5:20. The early Christians composed hymns in honor of Christ, possible examples of which are John 1:1–18; Philippians 2:5–11; Colossians 1:15–20; and Revelation 5:9–14.

These statements about Jesus Christ in the New Testament left to theologians the difficult task of reconciling His humanity and deity. They had to affirm the oneness of God without denying the lordship of Jesus and the lordship of Jesus without detracting from the oneness of God. One of the earliest solutions was suggested by the Ebionites, a late first-century Jewish-Christian group. They essentially saw Jesus as an ordinary man of unusual virtue and taught that at His baptism the Holy Spirit came and gave Him special divine authority.

More complex solutions, however, were proposed by the prominent Greek and Latin churchmen who are customarily referred to as the church Fathers. Traditionally, they are classified as the "Ante-Nicene" (before 325) and "Post-Nicene" (after 325) Fathers.

The Ante-Nicene Fathers

The four leading Ante-Nicene Fathers were Irenaeus, Clement, Origen, and Tertullian.

Irenaeus

Irenaeus (c. A.D. 115–c. 202) was a theologian who was born in Smyrna (Asia Minor) and who then moved to Gaul where he became bishop of Lyons after the martyrdoms of 177. Truly a living link with the apostolic age, he had learned from Polycarp who in turn had known the apostle John.

In the *Demonstration* he drew upon Old Testament teachings to support Christian doctrines, but far more important was his *Against Heresies*, a refutation of Gnostic views. In opposition to the Gnostics he affirmed the existence of one God who is also the Creator, the goodness of the creation, and the literal resurrection of the body. He also insisted that salvation is obtained by faith, not through secret knowledge. In contrast to the bewildering variety of revelations claimed by the Gnostics, Irenaeus recognized only the four gospels and the unity of doctrine found in the "Rule of Faith" (*regula fidei*). This was a body of teachings that had been handed down through the succession of bishops from the apostles and as a summary of beliefs often was presented to new converts in preparation for baptism. Drawing upon Pauline doctrine, he presented Christ as the new Adam who renews creation and Mary as the new Eve. Through salvation in Christ men are made like God and fulfill their original destiny as bearers of the image of God.

Clement of Alexandria

Clement of Alexandria (160–215) was a teacher who expressed Christian doctrine in terms of Greek philosophy. Born in Athens of pagan parents, after his conversion he directed the catechetical school in Alexandria, which trained believers who had not yet received baptism. During the persecutions of Severus (202), he was forced into exile in Cappadocia, where he later died.

In addition to some minor essays, Clement produced the important trilogy, *Exhortation to the Greeks*, *Instructor*, and *Miscellanies.* In the second of these he laid down rules for proper behavior and insisted that Christians should not adorn themselves with jewelry but rather give their wealth for the poor. He also maintained that men should not shave because God had given them beards just as he had given women their locks of hair.

The third book consists of unsystematic, random thoughts based on classical texts designed to lead the mature Christian through true *gnosis* to perfection. Instead of viewing philosophy as an enemy, Clement enlisted it as an ally and pointed out that some Christians "fear Greek philosophy as children fear ogres—they are frightened of being carried off by them. If our faith is such that it is destroyed by force of argument, then let it be destroyed."[1]

Origen

Origen (c. A.D. 185–c. 251) was the leading scholar of the early church. Born into a devout Christian family in Alexandria, as a teenager he had to start supporting his family because his father had been martyred. According to Eusebius, in his youthful zeal Origen took Matthew 19:12 in too literal a sense and made himself a eunuch for "the sake of the kingdom of heaven." Renowned as a practitioner of the "simple lifesyle," he went without shoes, possessed only one cloak, fasted regularly, and slept on the floor.

As Alexandria was the major center of scholarship in the ancient world, Origen studied under the noted Neo-Platonist Ammonius Saccas and at the age of eighteen succeeded Clement as head of the catechetical school. Because of his brilliant reputation, Origen traveled widely, lectured in many cities, and even had an audience with the mother of Emperor Alexander Severus. While visiting Caesarea in Palestine, he was ordained by its bishop, much to the displeasure of the bishop of Alexandria who refused to allow him to return to the catechetical school. Therefore from 231 he resided at Caesarea.

Origen, who authored more than 2,000 works, was one of the most prolific writers of antiquity. He was supported by a wealthy Christian named Ambrose, who provided him with a team of seven stenographers. The first great textual critic of the Bible, he labored for forty years on the *Hexapla*, six side-by-side columns of Hebrew and Greek versions of the Old Testament. He also produced commentaries on nearly every book of the Bible, the best known of which were on the Psalms and the gospel of John.

Influenced by the first-century Jewish scholar Philo and Clement of Alexandria, Origen advocated an allegorical interpretation of the Bible. This methodology looked beyond the literal text for moral and spiritual meanings. He interpreted Scriptures with symbolical equations: "silver" equals "word"; "clouds," "holy ones"; "linen," "chastity"; "bottle," "body"; and so on. The allegorical approach to Scripture was the interpretive method preferred by the medieval church.

Only a fraction of Origen's literary output has survived. His most important theological work is *On First Principles*, where he used Platonic concepts to explain the "eternal generation" of the Son from the Father as a process of emanation, just as a thought arises from a mind and brightness from light. Origen saw the Son as "a second God," who was less than God himself but superior to all created beings. One should therefore pray only to the Father and not to the Son. This view of the relationship of the Son to the Father, Subordinationism, was widely held in the second and third centuries.

Origen was the first to interpret Christ's atoning death as designed to ransom humankind from the clutches of the devil. He did not regard the Son's participation in human nature as eternal but only temporary. At the crucifixion it was Christ's human soul that suffered, not the divine *Logos*, or Word, who was incapable of suffering. He also emphasized man's free will and the goodness of creation, and accepted the Platonic idea of the preexistence of souls. He denied the permanence of the resurrection body, viewing it as a stage on the way to the believer's transformation into pure spirit. He also suggested the possibility that the love of God would eventually bring about the salvation of everyone, including Satan and his demons.

Origen himself died during the Decian persecutions, but his leading student, Gregory Thaumaturgus ("Wonder Worker"), played a major role in establishing Christianity in Cappadocia, later a center of Christian thought. Although controversial, Origen's ideas were a dominating influence for centuries. However, thanks to the aggressive heresy-hunter, Epiphanius, bishop of Salamis in Cyprus (c. 315–403), a reaction set in against many of his views. Even Jerome, who at first was an admirer, eventually became one of his most outspoken critics. Origen's teachings were condemned as heretical by the Fifth Ecumenical Council at Constantinople (553), although many modern scholars question whether these were actually his views or those of his overly enthusiastic followers, the Origenists.

Since the early centers of Christianity were in the eastern half of the empire—Alexandria, Antioch, Ephesus, and Constantinople—almost all of the early church Fathers wrote in Greek. Even in the capital the majority of Jewish-Christians regarded Greek rather than Latin as their language, and only in A.D. 189 was the first Latin-speaking bishop of Rome chosen, Victor I. The linguistic line also carried through into North Africa. Egypt and Cyrenaica were Greek-speaking, while Tripolitania and the regions farther west were Latin speaking.

Tertullian

Thus, the first significant "Latin" church Father was a native of Carthage, Tertullian (c. A.D. 155–c. 215). The son of a centurion, he studied law and may have practiced in Rome. He was converted in middle age and at once became a passionate defender of Christianity. He wrote in Greek as well as his native Latin and was competent in philosophy, literature, history, logic, and psychology. Of his enormous literary output thirty-one works have survived. They are customarily divided into three categories—apologetic, controversial, and moral-ascetical.

The *Apology*, an erudite defense of the faith in the face of murderous persecution, is one of the most brilliant works of this type. In *The Spectacles* Tertullian denounced the popular gladiatorial games and rejoiced in the prospect that one day the Roman officials who condemned Christians to these games would themselves be enveloped

Origen of Alexandria

in the fires of hell. He urged Christians to avoid any occupation that would involve compromise with paganism, including service as teachers, soldiers, or public officials.

Although personally familiar with Jews, Tertullian was harshly critical of Judaism. In *Against the Jews* he declared that God had passed them by and that the Gentiles' reception of Jesus meant the end of Judaism as a faith. He was hostile to most attempts to accommodate Christianity to Greek philosophy, yet his works reveal the influence of Stoicism. From this pre-Christian system he obtained the idea that just as the body is derived from the bodies of one's parents, so also the soul is derived from their material souls, a teaching known as Traducianism. He was the first theologian to articulate a doctrine of original sin that clarified how Adam's sinful nature was transmitted.

Among his controversial works is *Against Praxeas*, one of the clearest treatises on the doctrine of the Trinity. He apparently was the first writer to use the term itself and to express the ideas of three persons in one substance. By affirming the physical reality of the incarnation in *Against Marcion* and *On the Flesh of Christ*, Tertullian refuted those heretics who saw Christ's humanity as only an appearance. His love for paradox was reflected in a famous statement about the gospel of Jesus Christ: "It is immediately credible because it is foolish. He was buried and rose again. It is certain, because it is impossible."[2]

In his later years Tertullian devoted more attention to moral concerns. He was attracted to Montanism and because of this criticized the church for being spiritually lax. Although earlier in his career he had counseled people to flee persecution, now he rejected such an action. In *To His Wife* he depicted the wonderful blessings of a Christian marriage and contrasted this with the problems of a mixed marriage, where a pagan husband created difficulties for a Christian wife. In *On Monogamy* Tertullian followed the Montanist line in opposing remarriage after the death of one's spouse. In *The Feminine Cult* he joined other puritans in the history of the church in condemning feminine fashions as immodest. He urged Christian women to hide their beauty rather than enhance it with jewelry, cosmetics, and dyes, and recommended that both the married and unmarried wear veils.

THE POST-NICENE GREEK FATHERS

The Post-Nicene Fathers are traditionally categorized by whether they wrote in Greek or Latin. Among the noteworthy Greeks were Eusebius, Athanasius, the Cappadocians, and John Chrysostom.

Eusebius

Eusebius (c. 260–c. 339), bishop of Caesarea in Palestine, and a prolific writer, was the "Father of Church History." Although an active participant in the controversies of his time, he was also a biblical scholar, apologist against paganism, and interpreter of the emperor's duties. Although he published significant works in all of these areas, his reputation really rests on the *Ecclesiastical History*, which traces the story of the church from the apostolic age to his own time. With its extensive quotations from earlier writings it is a rich mine of information. He was also a major figure in the Christological debates.

Athanasius

Athanasius (c. 300–373) was ordained a deacon by the bishop of Alexandria, accompanied him as secretary to the Council of Nicaea, and succeeded him in 328. Athanasius was often in conflict with the Roman emperor, the Arians, and other factions in Egypt, which led to his banishment on five occasions and his spending more than sixteen years in exile between 335 and 366. His works fall into three categories—theological, polemical, and ascetic. Among the more significant are *On the Incarnation*, *Apology Against the Arians*, and a biography of Antony, the founder of monasticism. The Athanasian Creed, still used in some church liturgies, was believed to have been written by the great Alexandrian bishop, but scholars discovered that it had originated in the fifth century and was a compilation from various orthodox sources.

The Cappadocian Fathers

The Cappadocian Fathers were the most vigorous champions of Nicene orthodoxy against the Arians in the later fourth century. This trio of theologians—Basil of Caesarea, his brother Gregory of Nyssa, and their friend Gregory of Nazianzus—all came from Cappadocia in modern-day eastern Turkey. Basil of Caesarea (330–79), often referred to as Basil the Great, was educated in the leading schools of his day. After a brief career in the world, he became a monk and through his writings on monastic organization greatly influenced its development in both the Eastern and Western churches. After a while he returned to the public ministry and in 370 accepted the post of bishop in his hometown, the principal city of Cappadocia. There he defended Nicene orthodoxy against Arians and those who questioned the Holy Spirit's divinity.

His younger brother, Gregory of Nyssa (c. 335–95), was a teacher of rhetoric who was appointed in 372 as bishop in the town of Nyssa. From this point on he was continually embroiled in ecclesiastical politics and struggles with the Arians. At the Second Ecumenical Council at Constantinople in 381 he was one of the most vocal defenders of the Nicene position. In the work *Against Eunomius*, Gregory affirmed both the full divinity and the full humanity of Christ, but he spoke of Christ's passive body mixing with his active divinity like a drop of vinegar in the ocean.

Gregory of Nazianzus (c. 329–90), one of the major theologians of the Eastern church, was the son of the bishop of Nazianzus in Cappadocia and was educated at major academic centers in the eastern Roman empire. As a student in Athens he became a friend of Basil, and this connection led to the latter securing for him the position of bishop in the village of Sasima. In 379 Gregory became bishop of Constantinople and vigorously contended for Nicene orthodoxy at the ecumenical council there. However, critics charged that he had held the earlier post without ever having visited his diocese and thus his appointment as bishop in the imperial capital violated canon law. Being one who disliked personal controversy, Gregory resigned in 381 and retired to his home at Nazianzus.

He was a brilliant writer who composed thousands of poems and compiled a collection of his own letters. His *Theological Orations* (380), which includes an eloquent funeral sermon for Basil, are among the finest examples of Greek rhetoric. He was influential in refuting Apollinarianism (denial of the full humanity of Christ), defending the doctrine of the Trinity, and expounding the deity of the Holy Spirit.

John Chrysostom

John Chrysostom, the "Golden-Mouthed" (c. 347–407), was the most eloquent preacher of the early church. He was born into a wealthy home at Antioch in Syria and studied law under the great rhetorician Libanius. Then John turned from pursuing a career in law and became a monk, but soon he returned to Antioch and entered the service of the church. During the following decade he gained the reputation as an outstanding preacher with some of his finest sermons directed at the moral reformation of the church and city. They were so powerful that the congregation at times interrupted them with applause. Once when he rebuked an audience for clapping, the people applauded his rebuke.

Of all the Fathers only Augustine matches John Chrysostom in the sheer quantity of works that have survived. Some six hundred sermons exist, each of which must have required an hour to preach. The ones on various books of the Bible gave him the reputation as perhaps the greatest of all expository preachers. His sermons were marked by deep spiritual understanding, literal interpretation of the texts, and immediate practical applications. Unfortunately, his harsh criticisms of Jewish practices were utilized by anti-Semites in the Middle Ages and have had a negative impact on Jewish-Christian relations ever since.

Because of his fame, the emperor pressured John Chrysostom into becoming the bishop of Constantinople in 398. However, unlike many popular preachers of later times, he fearlessly denounced the immorality rampant in public life as well as in the church and set a good example by living modestly. Instead of holding lavish banquets he ate alone. He halted construction on an elegant bishop's residence and sold the expensive marble pillars to help support hospitals. His uncompromising standards and forthright criticism of Empress Eudoxia, whom he referred to as a "Jezebel," brought upon him persecution, assassination attempts, and repeated banishment from the city. He died in exile in 407, but his remains were brought back with honors to Constantinople in 438. The son of Eudoxia (Emperor Theodosius II) publicly repented for his parents' wrongdoing.

THE POST-NICENE LATIN FATHERS

The three most distinguished Latin Fathers were Jerome, Ambrose, and Augustine, and together with Pope Gregory the Great they are known as the "Four Doctors of the Western Church."

Jerome

Jerome (c. 347–420) was a monastic leader, controversialist, and above all translator of the Vulgate, the accepted Latin version of the Bible. Born of wealthy parents in Dalmatia, he was educated at Rome, Trier, and Aquileia near Trieste. Inspired by the monastic ideal, Jerome became a hermit and settled in Syria where he learned Hebrew with the help of a Jewish Christian. His dedication to scholarship was such that he took his library along into the desert, but then he had a disturbing dream in which Jesus challenged his claim to be a Christian, saying, "You lie, you are a Ciceronian, not a Christian, for where your treasure is, there is your heart." For fifteen years after this Jerome refused to study classical literature.

Nevertheless, his reputation for learning led to his appointment as secretary to Bishop Damasus of Rome. While there Jerome scandalized his peers by leading Bible studies for wealthy women, teaching them Greek and Hebrew, and urging them to adopt an ascetic lifestyle. After Damasus's death in 384 he left Rome in the company of his friends Paula and her daughter Eustochium. After visiting monasteries in Egypt, they settled in Bethlehem where Jerome established a monastery and Paula a companion convent. He got the idea from his friends Rufinus and Melania the Elder who had set up a similar double monastic foundation on the Mount of Olives in Jerusalem.

Jerome was an exceptionally effective writer. He translated into Latin important works of Eusebius, Origen, and Pachomius, the founder of cenobitic (communal) monasticism. He also compiled *On the Lives of Illustrious Men*, which contained biographies of pagan and Christian writers (including himself), and produced learned commentaries on both the Old and New Testaments.

In 382 Damasus asked Jerome to revise the Old Latin version of the Bible, and the result was a more accurate translation based upon the original languages of the Bible. Many criticized this new "Vulgate" (language of the people) version, including Augustine who believed in the inspiration of the Greek language translation of the Old Testament, the Septuagint. Jerome labeled his detractors as "asses with two legs" who preferred to drink from "muddy rivulets rather than drink the clear fountain of the original Greek."

Although the Vulgate was not immediately accepted, it later became the preferred version of the medieval church, and some of Jerome's renderings affected the course of Catholic theology. For example, his translation of the Greek passive participle *kecharitomene* in Luke 1:28 by the phrase *gratia plena* ("full of grace") implied that Mary was not simply favored with grace but also that she had an abundance of grace to bestow on others. At the time of the Reformation Luther discovered that Jerome had mistranslated the word for "repentance" (*metanoia*) as "penance." The Council of Trent in 1546 decreed the Vulgate as the official Bible of the Roman Catholic church.

Jerome dealt harshly with those who disagreed with him. On one occasion he denounced Helvidius who suggested that Mary had borne other children because the gospels speak of Jesus' "brothers and sisters." Jerome argued instead for the "perpetual virginity" of Mary and said these were "cousins." He also attacked Jovinian, an ex-monk who maintained that virginity was not superior to marriage, by saying that virginity was the highest value and that he hoped marriage would produce children who might embrace virginity. In other polemical works he contended for the veneration of martyrs, monasticism, and clerical celibacy and wrote against Pelagianism.

Ambrose

Ambrose (c. 339–97), born in Trier, was the son of an imperial official. After practicing law for a time, he became the provincial governor of northern Italy. In 374 after restoring order during an acrimonious struggle over the bishopric of Milan, he suddenly found himself to be the popular choice for the position. Within eight days

LOCATIONS OF EARLY CHURCH FATHERS

NAME	LOCATION
Ambrose	Milan
Athanasius	Alexandria
Augustine	Carthage
Basil	Cappadocia
Clement	Alexandria
Cyprian	Carthage
Ireneaus	Lyons
Jerome	Bethlehem
Justin	Ephesus, Rome
Origen	Alexandria
Tertullian	Carthage

he was baptized, ordained, and installed as the new bishop of Milan. Ambrose proceeded to uphold high standards for his priests, exalted the Virgin Mary, and persuaded many women to take the vow of virginity. He also wrote hymns that influenced the liturgy of the medieval church.

Ambrose was an impressive scholar in both Latin and Greek, an effective speaker, and an able administrator. Not only did he fight against the restoration of paganism, but he also was a vigorous champion of Nicene orthodoxy. In a dramatic episode in 386, Ambrose resisted Valentinian's order to surrender his cathedral to the Arians, declaring, "The emperor indeed is within the church, not above the church." Assuming the supremacy of the church over the state, he added emphatically, "Bishops ought to judge laymen and not laymen bishops." In 390 when Emperor Theodosius brutally quelled a riot in Thessalonica by slaughtering 7,000 people, Ambrose excommunicated him and forced him to repent publicly. In fact, his defense of the church's rights laid the foundation for church-state relations in medieval western Europe.

The Greatest Latin Father

The greatest of the Latin Fathers was the North African, Augustine (354–430). Born in Thagaste, Numidia, he studied at Madaura and Carthage. Although his father did not become a Christian until much later, his devout mother Monica prayed constantly for her wayward son. Augustine recounts in his autobiographical *Confessions* his rebellious youth and efforts to escape from her influence. Inspired by Cicero's writings, he studied philosophy and then joined the Manichaeans. For nine years he was a "hearer" of the sect but dropped out in 382 after one of its leaders could not answer his questions. He also lived with a mistress for thirteen years, who bore him a son, but at his mother's urging he left her in order to marry a more respectable woman. When the marriage was delayed, he found that he could not contain himself and took up with another concubine. It was this compulsive sexual appetite that caused Augustine to utter the infamous prayer, "Lord, give me continence and chastity, but not now."

In 382 Augustine left home to work in Rome and three years later became a teacher at the imperial court at Milan. Here he was influenced by Ambrose, whose ability to draw upon Greek philosophical ideas for his preaching and writing as well as for his eloquent sermons appealed to the young scholar and led him to reconsider the faith he had spurned. In the *Confessions* he describes how he was converted. One summer day in 386 he thought he heard a child's voice saying, "Take and read, take and read." He then turned and saw a Bible lying open to Romans 13:13–14: "Not in reveling and drunkenness, not in debauchery and licentiousness, not in quarreling and jealousy. But put on the Lord Jesus Christ, and make no provision for the flesh, to gratify its desires" (RSV). Immediately he received Christ as his Savior and Lord, and the godly Monica, who died soon afterward, saw her prayers answered.

After this dramatic event, Augustine resigned his teaching position and went into seclusion to prepare for baptism. In 387 Ambrose baptized him, and he returned to Thagaste to establish a monastic community. During a visit to the town of Hippo in 391, the populace persuaded him to accept ordination by the local bishop, a Greek who had difficulty preaching in Latin. The elderly man assigned him preaching duties, and at his death four years later Augustine was named bishop of Hippo. He served there the remainder of his life and distinguished himself as a pastor, preacher, writer, administrator, and leader in the African church.

When the Germanic Goths captured Rome in 410, it sent shock waves across the entire empire, with pagans blaming Christians for the disaster. To refute these charges Augustine penned his masterpiece, *The City of God.* In it he argued that there are two "cities" or communities—the City of Man and the City of God. The former is temporal and transitory; the latter is spiritual and eternal. He also rejected the premillennialism (also known as chiliasm, from the Greek word for "one thousand") of the early church and equated the reign of Christ and his saints with the entire history of the church, thus denying the idea of a literal, future kingdom of God on earth. He was the first orthodox theologian to teach amillennialism.

Augustine's theology was worked out in his struggle with three important heresies: Manichaeism (388–405), Donatism (394–411), and Pelagianism (412–30). Manichaeism was a missionary-minded, syncretistic religion founded by Mani (216–77). He grew up among the Elchasites, an obscure Jewish-Christian community in Mesopotamia. At twenty-four he received a revelation that led him to reject his heritage and accept a form of Gnosticism. Drawing on elements from Babylonian, Buddhist, Jewish, and Christian sources, Mani taught that he was the successor of Plato, Buddha, Zoroaster, Jesus, and Paul. The fundamental concept of his dualist system was that there are two uncreated principles: Light (Goodness) and Darkness (Evil). The created world is the battleground between these opposites. Knowledge, spirit, and soul are manifestations of Light, but ignorance, matter, and the body reveal Darkness. The faithful are redeemed through awareness of this struggle and by following a lifestyle of abstinence from meat, wine, sex, and labor. Mani himself went to India and Persia where at first he was accepted, but eventually his enemies at the Persian court secured his execution.

In *Against the Manichaeans*, Augustine maintained that evil actually originated in the human will (that is, original sin) and was not an eternal principle. God is the sole Creator and sustainer of all things, and evil is the deprivation of some good that one ought to possess. Physical evil comes from human imperfection and moral evil from the exercise of free will. Christ gives victory over both forms of evil.

Donatism, named for the group's leader Donatus, was a divisive movement in North Africa that insisted on the "pure church." In 331 the Donatists denounced Caecilian, bishop of Carthage, because he had been consecrated by those who had surrendered Scriptures during the persecution of Diocletian. They maintained that the sacraments administered by such an "impure" cleric were invalid, and consequently they left the main body of the church and started their own separatist group. Earlier, in 314, the Council of Arles condemned the Donatists because of their practice of "rebaptism," and labeled them schismatics. Constantine sided with the mainline, or "Catholic," church. The Donatists refused to submit, however, asking, "What has the Emperor to do with the church?" In the ensuing struggle with the imperial forces, many Donatists were killed, and some of their more extreme members, the Circumcellions, terrorized the Catholic churches of North Africa.

Although Augustine at first advocated leniency toward the Donatists, the violence of the struggle led him to take the offensive. He affirmed the church's claim to universality and sarcastically remarked, "These frogs sit in their marsh and croak 'We are the only Christians!'" The church in this world is bound to be a "mixed body," and Christ, who is its head rather than human ministers, guarantees the validity of the sacraments. Thus, the Donatists' insistence on rebaptism is heretical and they deserve to be punished. The imperial commissioner adopted Augustine's position and outlawed the movement, confiscating its property and fining those who refused to rejoin the Catholic church. Augustine's arguments, based on Luke 14:23 (forcing people to come to the master's feast), had a tragic effect when the medieval church used them to justify the persecution of heretics.

Augustine's later years were taken up with the Pelagian issue. Pelagius was a British lay monk who taught in Rome in the late fourth century. He and his chief disciple, the highly combative Celestius, fled to North Africa in 410 ahead of the Goths and engaged in a long dispute with Augustine. Pelagius then went to Palestine and disappeared from history, but the literary debate with other Pelagians continued. They taught that men through their own efforts can take the first steps toward salvation. Although Adam's sin was a bad example, it was personal and not passed on through the race. The God-given human nature enables them to choose good, and both keeping the law and receiving the freely given grace of God help people enter heaven. "God assists us when we choose the good," so the Pelagians affirmed.

In response Augustine developed his theology of predestination, original sin, and grace. He stressed God's predestination but not in a sense that it excused people from responsibility for their sins. Romans 5:12 reveals that all humankind sinned through Adam, and this sin has been transmitted through an inherited legal liability. Individuals could be rescued from this hopeless situation only by God's grace. Faith in Christ brings the infusion of God's love in the human soul, and baptism removes the guilt of original sin.

The Council of Carthage in 416 condemned Pelagius's doctrine, but the war of words between Augustine and Julian of Eclanum, the leading Pelagian, did not cease. Pelagianism was again condemned at the Council of Ephesus in 431, but it persisted in France throughout the century.

Augustine made other contributions to Christian thought as well. In *On Christian Doctrine* he set forth the subjects one should know in order to understand the Bible. A century later Cassiodorus used these ideas to formulate the "seven liberal arts," which were the foundation of education during the Middle Ages—grammar, rhetoric, logic, arithmetic, geometry, music, and astronomy. Moreover, the one-time libertine came to believe that the only legitimate purpose of sex was procreation. This principle was to be the justification for the Roman Catholic church's opposition to the use of contraception, as it supposedly frustrated the natural purpose of sexual relations.

Although most Christian leaders prior to Augustine had been pacifists, he taught that a person could serve in the army and yet follow the Lord. His "just war" theory, which even today is still widely held, consisted of giving a Christian twist to the rules of warfare developed by classical thinkers like Plato and Cicero. War must be fought to restore peace and to obtain justice. It must always be under the direction of the legitimate ruler and be motivated by Christian love. It must be a last resort, after all else has been tried and failed. War must pursue limited objectives rather than the total destruction of the enemy. It must be conducted in an honorable and proportionate manner, without unnecessary violence, massacres, and looting. The immunity of noncombatants must be observed.

In 429 the Germanic tribe known as the Vandals crossed into Africa and besieged Hippo the following year. Augustine died then, despairing that his life work had been in vain, but he could not have been further from the truth. Few individuals have affected the church and Western civilization as much as this bishop of an obscure North African town.

EARLY THEOLOGICAL CONTROVERSIES

Monarchianism

The Monarchian controversy, which developed around A.D. 200, was the opening round in two centuries of debate over the nature of the Godhead. It emphasized the unity, or oneness, of God at the expense of the separate identities of Father, Son, and Holy Spirit. Dynamic Monarchianism was a form of Adoptionism, the view that the Father adopted the man Jesus and endowed him with divine power. A leading proponent of this idea was Paul of Samosata, bishop of Antioch (260–68). He objected to worshiping Christ and taught that Jesus was not the Son of God who came down from heaven but rather an inspired man, "just like us, though better in every way since he was of the Holy Spirit." Paul was an official under Zenobia, queen of Palmyra, who controlled Antioch. He was condemned at synods in Antioch in 264 and 268.

Whereas the appeal of Dynamic Monarchianism was limited to intellectuals, this was not so with the other branch of the movement, Modalist Monarchianism. It held that God revealed Himself as Father, Son, and Holy Spirit only as a temporary succession of modes or operations, and not as eternal characters in the Godhead. Another name for the view was Sabellianism. Sabellius, a Libyan, was condemned in Rome (c. 220) for teaching that God was a monad with three energies that appeared in history as Father, Son, and Holy Spirit for the purpose of creation and salvation. Since modalists preserved the full divinity of Christ, the doctrine was widely accepted, even by the Roman bishops Zephyrinus and Callistus. It had a special appeal as an answer to the plain man's fear of polytheism.

Arianism

Arianism, the Christological controversy of which the debate over Monarchianism was the immediate predecessor, was initiated by a priest in Alexandria named Arius (c. 260–336), who declared that the Son was not eternal, not equal to the Father, "did not exist before he was born," and "has nothing proper to God in proper substance. For he is not equal, no, nor one in essence with him." Christ was a creature who was given divine favor. Arius's ideas won several supporters, above all Eusebius, bishop of Nicomedia, an important city near Byzantium. Arius was a very clever propagandist

Augustine of Hippo

who expressed his views in verse for the populace. He even won over 700 "holy virgins" to his side.

In 325 a local council of bishops at Antioch condemned Arianism. Later that year Constantine called the first "ecumenical council" at Nicaea, which 250 bishops attended. It rejected the stance of Arius and affirmed that Christ was "true God from true God, begotten not made, of one substance (*homoousios*) with the Father." The key word, *homoousios,* was suggested by Constantine, who was influenced by his advisor, Hosius of Cordoba. By 328, however, Eusebius of Nicomedia and Theognis of Nicaea, who had been exiled because they refused to condemn Arius, were restored to their bishoprics, and Arius himself was rehabilitated at the Synod of Tyre in 335.

At his death in 337 Constantine was succeeded by his three sons—Constantine II (d. 340), Constans (d. 350), and Constantius (d. 361). Constantine II controlled the West; Constans, Illyricum and Africa; and Constantius, the East. Although his brothers adhered to Nicene orthodoxy, Constantius was a convinced Arian. Constantine II ordered the restoration of Athanasius who had been exiled from Alexandria, an action that Bishop Julius of Rome strongly supported.

However, ninety-seven bishops meeting in Antioch rejected Athanasius's claim, and they promulgated the Creed of Antioch, which defined the Trinity as three individualities (*hypostases*) united by mutual harmony in a single will. To resolve the differences between the West and the East a conference was held in 342 at Sardica (modern Sofia in Bulgaria), but the Eastern bishops walked out, vehemently denouncing Athanasius. Julius and the Western bishops responded just as emotionally.

In 350 Constans was killed in an uprising and three years later, after he had become the sole emperor, Constantius allowed the restoration of Arianism. Thus, three decades after the Council of Nicaea the world "awoke with a groan to find itself Arian," as Jerome put it. Athanasius denounced the emperor as "worse than Ahab" and the "forerunner of Anti-Christ."

In a further attempt to settle the dispute, a council at Sirmium in 356 drafted a credal formulation that it hoped would be acceptable to both sides. This statement, later known as "the Blasphemy of Sirmium," asserted that the Son was subordinate to the Father and omitted the use of the word *homoousios*. After the death of Constantius and the brief reigns of Julian the Apostate (361–63) and Valens in the East (364–78), Nicene orthodoxy once more held sway in Constantinople, and Athanasius's stubborn advocacy of Christ's equality with the Father was vindicated.

Apollinarianism

A significant effort to counter Arianism was Apollinarianism, but it ended up being just as serious a deviation from orthodoxy. Apollinaris, bishop of Laodicea (c. 315–92) and a follower of Athanasius, was the son of a noted Alexandrian rhetorician. When Julian forbade Christians from teaching the classics, Apollinaris and his father defied the emperor by rewriting biblical texts in classical literary forms.

In opposition to the Arians, Apollinaris argued that, if the fusion of the divine and human in Christ had really occurred, He must have had a body devoid of human personality. As he put it, humans are made up of body, soul, and spirit (mind), and this last element is what constitutes the intellectual core of the personality. In the case of Christ the spirit was replaced by the Logos (the divine intellect), because it was impossible for two personalities to merge into one. Thus, while He possessed perfect Godhood, He lacked complete manhood.

The Apollinarians argued that only a Son who is not of the same nature as the sons of Adam can redeem them. Through faith in

Christ, the human intellect is brought under the control of divine intellect (or mind) and receives new life. After this, the human flesh is sanctified by its union with Christ's body, and the new intellect within the Christian joins itself with Christ and shares in the destruction of the bent toward sinning. In short, Apollinarianism denied Christ's full humanity.

This teaching was vigorously challenged by the Cappadocian Fathers and the church at Antioch. For example, Gregory of Nazianzus objected: "What has not been assumed cannot be restored; it is what is united with God that is saved." Apollinarianism was rejected at synods in Rome and Antioch before finally being condemned at the Second Ecumenical Council of Constantinople in 381. Influenced by the Cappadocians, who opposed all efforts to deny the full deity of the Son or the Holy Spirit, the council also affirmed that in God there are three *hypostases* (individual substances) and only one *ousia* (essence).

This solution had already been accepted by the Western church, which defined the Godhead as a Trinity of three persons in one substance. In addition, the council reaffirmed the "Nicene Creed" of 325, while adding a clause on the deity of the Holy Spirit, and it is this version of the confession that is recited in churches today.

Theologians at Antioch, however, resisted Apollinarianism by contending that the divine and human were joined in Christ through a harmony or purpose but that there was no essential unity as such. Christ's humanity was complete, and Mary was the mother of this human nature alone. This led to another Christological conflict between Antioch and Alexandria that revolved around the views of Nestorius, bishop of Constantinople from 428 to 431.

Nestorianism

Nestorius, who had been educated at Antioch, openly criticized the use of the term, *Theotokos* (Bearer of God) for Mary and suggested instead *Christotokos* (Bearer of Christ). He also emphasized the complete humanity, as well as divinity, of Christ. He declared, "I hold the natures apart, but unite the worship." This led to a sharp controversy in which he was accused of denying the unity of the two aspects of Christ. In the process of explaining his doctrine, Nestorius attacked the exponents of Alexandrine Christology, and Cyril, bishop of Alexandria (375–444), responded by heaping abuse on him.

The acrimonious dispute between the two religious centers was the result of theological rivalries, personal ambitions, and regional differences. The teachers at Antioch followed a literal-historical approach to exegesis, in contrast to the allegorical method of the Alexandrians. The Antiochene theologians taught that the eternal Logos had entered into the man Jesus, whereas the Alexandrian school held that the Logos had become the person of Jesus. The Antiochenes cited Matthew 3:16, whereas the Alexandrians appealed to John 1:14.

Cyril and Nestorius became bitter enemies. However, the astute and unscrupulous Cyril was the better politician. He persuaded Bishop Celestine to call a synod in Rome to condemn Nestorius and had the action repeated at a synod in Alexandria. But the controversy spread, and in 431 Emperor Theodosius II convened the Third Ecumenical Council at Ephesus to consider the charges raised by Cyril. Fearful that he would not get a fair hearing at the council, Nestorius refused to attend. The session opened before the representatives from Antioch arrived, and Cyril convinced the 198 bishops to condemn Nestorius as a heretic. When the forty-three Antiochene bishops arrived, they held a rump session and repudiated the Christology of Cyril. In the face of the deadlock the emperor deposed both bishops, but Cyril cleverly obtained reinstatement while Nestorius was exiled to a monastery and then to an oasis in the Egyptian desert.

Scholars now acknowledge that Nestorius had not taught the doctrine later called Nestorianism, which held that the human Jesus and the divine Christ were two distinct persons. However, his followers did adopt this view. The church they founded spread eastward to Mesopotamia, Persia, central Asia, and even China.

Monophysitism

A further Christological controversy revolved around the teaching of Eutyches (378–454), head of a large monastery at Constantinople. He maintained that Jesus had a single nature, a deified human nature, so that all Christ's human attributes belonged to the one being, the humanized Logos. After the union of the divine and human natures at the incarnation, Christ had only one nature. Known as Monophysitism, this teaching holds that the Lord's humanity was totally absorbed by his divinity in *monophysis* (one nature).

Accused of heresy and condemned by a synod in Constantinople,

Eutyches, who was the superior of hundreds of monks and a person of great influence in the city, persuaded Theodosius to convene the so-called "Robber" Council of Ephesus (449) where his orthodoxy was recognized. But when the emperor died in 450, Eutyches's fortunes suddenly reversed. The new empress, Pulcheria, and her husband, Marcian, supported the position of Bishop Leo of Rome, who affirmed in his "Dogmatic Epistle," or *Tome* (449), that even after the incarnational union the two natures in Christ each preserved their characters. This happened in such a way that their qualities could be communicated to each other, so that what was true of the human nature could be attributed to the divine nature and vice versa.

To deal with the matter, Marcian convened the Fourth Ecumenical Council at Chalcedon, a city near Constantinople in 451. It was attended by a record number of 520 bishops representing both the Western and Eastern churches, and it reversed the decision of the Robber Council. It also condemned the Nestorian view of the separation of Christ's two natures and Eutyches's merger of the two into one. Drawing upon the Tome of Leo, the council concluded that in Christ were two natures—a perfect human and a perfect divine one. The famous Chalcedonian definition made clear that in Christ are "two natures, unconfusedly, unchangeably, indivisibly, inseparably." It added:

> Wherefore, following the holy Fathers, we all with one voice confess our Lord Jesus one and the same Son, the same perfect in Godhead, the same perfect in manhood, truly God and truly man, the same consisting of a reasonable soul and a body, of one substance with the Father as touching the Godhead, the same of one substance with us as touching the manhood, like us in all things apart from sin; begotten of the Father before the ages as touching the Godhead, the same in the last days, for us and for our salvation.

Other important decisions of the council included the affirmation of the title *Theotokos,* a declaration that the archbishops of Rome, Constantinople, Alexandria, and Antioch would be known as patriarchs, and the elevation of Constantinople in the church to a place second only to Rome. The church of Rome, however, rejected the last point.

The theological definitions of the four ecumenical councils (Nicaea, Constantinople, Ephesus, and Chalcedon) have been accepted by the major Christian communities, but not all agreed to the Chalcedonian Christological formulation. Bishops from Egypt objected to the teaching on two natures: "We would prefer to die at the hands of the emperor and the council than at home." In fact, a pro-Chalcedonian patriarch, Proterius, was lynched by a mob of Christians in Alexandria.

Numbered among the Monophysite bodies were the Coptic churches in Egypt and Ethiopia, the Armenian Orthodox church (which rejected the council's "two natures" decision in the following century), the Jacobites in eastern Syria, and the Church of St. Thomas in South India. This explains why most Christians in the Middle East today are Monophysites.

Although the final canon of the New Testament was not established until the fourth century, by the later second century common agreement existed on about 80 percent of the New Testament. Its vivid presentation of a risen Savior, who was both human and divine, forced theologians to use Greek philosophical concepts and Latin legal terminology in their efforts to express the nature of Jesus Christ and the Trinity. During the fourth century, doctrinal controversies revolved around the relationship of the Son to the Father; in the fifth, they focused on the nature of the Son. In spite of the shameful bickering of bishops and the misunderstandings and misrepresentations of the views of those who differed, four ecumenical councils succeeded in expressing the divine mysteries in credal terms that have satisfied the vast majority of Christians—Catholic, Orthodox, and Protestant. More mundane ecclesiastical, liturgical, and political matters, however, continued to plague and divide Christians.

4

THE CHURCH AFTER CONSTANTINE

The conversion of Constantine enabled Christianity to "triumph," that is, it became the dominant religion in the Roman Empire by the end of the fourth century. But this development entailed complications, since church and state became increasingly intertwined. The efforts of the ecclesiastical hierarchy of deacons, priests, bishops, and popes to maintain both doctrinal and moral discipline led to personality clashes and political struggles within the church. However, official recognition and imperial financial support made possible the building of elaborately decorated churches and cathedrals.

CHURCH AND STATE

As mentioned earlier, in A.D. 337 the empire was divided among Constantine's three sons. The succession was not smooth, and only after a long period of civil war did Constantius, a supporter of the Arian position, emerge as sole emperor in 350. Claiming to control the church as "bishop of bishops" (*episcopus episcoporum*), he exiled such leaders as Athanasius, Hilary of Poitiers, and Liberius, bishop of Rome.

Julian, whom Christians dubbed "the Apostate," the son of a half-brother of Constantius, followed him to the throne in 361, and under his sponsorship occurred the final but futile resurgence of paganism. Although an ordained lector, Julian turned against Christianity because of the disgraceful conduct of Constantius, who had executed his father and other relatives, and became an adherent of Neo-Platonism. Perhaps to undercut Christianity's claim as the successor of Judaism, Julian ordered the rebuilding of the Temple in Jerusalem. (Christians were now interpreting the destruction of the Temple in A.D. 70 as a fulfillment of the prophecy in Daniel 9:27 and as a judgment on the Jews for rejecting Jesus as their Messiah.) But the project was frustrated by mysterious fires breaking out on the site, which later Christian writers portrayed as a direct intervention of God.

Julian challenged the Christians in other ways as well. He decreed that only those who believed in the classical texts could teach them, thus depriving many Christians of their posts as educators. He wrote a polemic entitled *Against the Galileans*, which condemned Christians for abandoning Jewish traditions and denied the New Testament claims of the fulfillment of Old Testament prophecies. He cynically asked why there was so much unbelief if Christ really had performed all the miracles recorded in the gospels. Disgusted by the rapid proliferation of the relics of martyrs, he protested: "You have filled the whole world with tombs and sepulchers." However, Julian did express admiration for the social concern of Christians: "These godless Galileans feed not only their own poor but ours; our poor lack our care." He credited the spread of Christianity to their charitable practices.

In 363 the thirty-two-year-old emperor launched a military campaign against the Persian Sassanians, and during one battle was killed by a spear thrust into his abdomen. Christian critics labeled this as a fitting judgment, since he had sought guidance from the pagan gods through the reading of animal entrails. Accordingly, later generations interpreted Julian as an important symbol of the struggle against paganism and the ultimate victory of Christianity, and numerous legends grew up around him. The best known was his alleged death utterance, "You have conquered, O Galilean." Another popular story was that of a Christian who was martyred under Julian. As he was dying, his tormentors asked, "Where is your carpenter now?" He replied, "He is making a coffin for your emperor."[1]

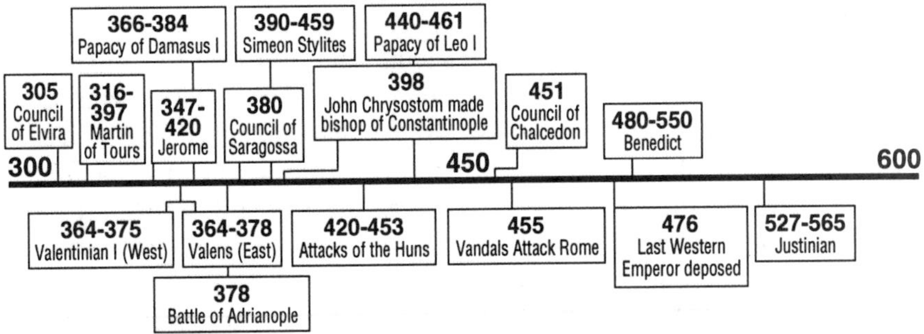

A year after his death the realm was again divided. Valentinian I (364–75) ruled a Western empire with its centers at Trier, Milan, and Sirmium, and in the East his younger brother Valens reigned at Constantinople. Valens was the first emperor to have to deal with the Germanic tribes who were pressing in on the empire. The next emperor, Theodosius I (379–95), a Spaniard and the last person to rule an undivided empire, is often referred to as "the Great." He quickly regained control over both the East and West, and in 381 he denied Arians the right to assemble and ordered them to surrender their churches to the orthodox, thus dealing a deathblow to the movement in the empire. He also summoned the Eastern bishops to a council at Constantinople, which, as explained in chapter 3, reaffirmed the actions of the Council of Nicaea, condemned Apollinarianism, reformulated the Nicene Creed, and accorded the "New Rome" (Constantinople) equal status with the Rome in Italy.

Theodosius moved to stamp out pagan practices, authorized the destruction of their shrines, and appropriated their wealth for the endowment of churches. Encouraged by the imperial attitude, rampaging Christian mobs destroyed pagan worship centers such as the famous Serapeum in Egypt. When, however, Theodosius brutally massacred 7,000 citizens of Thessalonica in reprisal for a minor insurrection, Bishop Ambrose of Milan compelled him to do public penance.

In 395 he was succeeded by his two young sons, Honorius in the West and Arcadius in the East. Much of the power in the West rested in the hands of Stilicho, a German Vandal who was the commander of Honorius's troops. Honorius was threatened by the Germanic Visigoths and sought refuge in the city of Ravenna in northeastern Italy. His stepsister, Galla Placida (392–45), then played a remarkable role in state and church affairs. First, she was taken hostage by the Visigoth leader Alaric and married to his brother. After her husband's death, she went briefly to Honorius's court to escape the on-going political struggles in Italy and then moved to Constantinople. When Honorius died in 323, she returned to Ravenna with her young son Valentinian III and essentially ruled on his behalf. An ardent champion of orthodoxy, she opposed the supporters of Pelagianism and Manichaeism and was an important figure in the religious conflicts of the time. To this day, her tomb at Ravenna is renowned for its stunning mosaics.

During the fifth century the West suffered further attacks from the "barbarian" tribes—both the Asiatic Huns and various Germanic groups. The city of Rome itself was sacked twice during the course of the century. The Western Empire had now so declined in political significance that a German chieftain named Odovacer deposed the emperor at Ravenna in 476, a date that later was regarded as the "fall of Rome," but, in fact, the event went relatively unnoticed at the time.

In the East the most noteworthy development after Theodosius's death was the controversy engendered by the uncompromising preaching of John Chrysostum during his brief tenure as bishop of Constantinople (398–403). He not only criticized other bishops but even the empress herself. Under Emperor Theodosius II (408–50), the famous Theodosian walls of Constantinople were built and a major law code was compiled. He also became involved in the struggle over the definition of Christology that so divided the church leaders.

By far the greatest of the Eastern emperors was Justinian (527–65). A military commander from Illyria who succeeded his uncle as emperor, he was the last Eastern ruler whose native tongue was Latin. His greatest achievements were the codification of Roman law (the Justinian Code) and the construction of the renowned church of Hagia Sophia. With its spectacular 184-foot dome this was one of the greatest architectural achievements in Christian history.

The Eastern realm came to be known as the Byzantine Empire, taking its name from Byzantium, the previous city on the site of Constantinople. One of its distinctive features was Caesaropapism, the principle that the political ruler was also the head of the church. Thus, Justinian, who was an ardent champion of orthodox Christianity, forced 70,000 pagans in Asia Minor to convert. He also closed the great philosophical schools in Athens—the Academy founded by Plato and the Lyceum founded by Aristotle.

Justinian's forces regained control of much of the Mediterranean territories that had been overrun by the Germanic invaders, but these campaigns left Italy in ruins. The Empress Theodora, a former entertainer and a woman who possessed great political acumen, functioned as coruler with Justinian. She promoted moral reform, the establishment of hospitals, and the arts. Although she was sympathetic to the Monophysites, her husband persecuted them. This alienated many Christians in Egypt and Syria from the Byzantine Empire and paved the way for the triumph of Islam in the next century.

THE CLERICAL HIERARCHY

In the fourth century, the relatively simple structure of the pre-Constantinian church described in chapter 2 became much more complex. Deacons continued to perform the eucharistic and service functions and even led some rural congregations. However, a ruling of the Council of Nicaea deprived them of any authority to preside over the Eucharist. Still, since deacons had become the special assistants of the bishops, they often were more highly esteemed than priests, especially the Collegium of Seven Deacons in Rome, which for all practical purposes served as the bishop's cabinet. When the burden of responsibilities became more than the seven could handle, the office of subdeacon was created in Rome. By the end of the third century the subdiaconate had become a relatively widespread institution.

The head of the diaconate was the archdeacon, and he exercised enormous influence. In fact, bishops were frequently chosen from the ranks of the deacons, and some were even named to the Roman See, for example, Leo I (440) and Gregory I (590) who were major figures in the development of the papacy. Among the other important bishops elevated from the archdiaconate were Caecilian of Carthage (311) and Athanasius of Alexandria (328).

Another order, referred to in chapter 2, was the "widows," who were appointed but not ordained. Their functions, which included a ministry of prayer and service to the women in the congregations, were taken over by the order of deaconesses in the third century. A document of that period, the *Didascalia,* spelled out their duties as teaching, caring for the sick, seating women in church services, and assisting at baptisms. The last-mentioned function was particularly noteworthy, since the candidates usually were baptized (immersed) while nude and were also anointed. Thus, the service of deaconesses were required in order to counter charges of impropriety.

The requirement for ordination as a deaconess was that a woman be unmarried or a once-married widow. Although the Theodosian Code (438) set sixty as the minimum age for a deaconess, the Council of Chalcedon (451) reduced this to forty and forbade the woman to marry after ordination. But then the development of the practice of infant baptism eliminated the need for the assistance of deaconesses at baptismal ceremonies. In the sixth century two church councils in the West abolished the office, but it continued in some places, especially in the East.

The gulf between clergy and laity (see chapter 2), which already in the third century was quite substantial, grew steadily wider. The word "priest" (Greek *hieros,* Latin *sacerdos*) came increasingly to be used for the congregational leader instead of the early church term "presbyter" (elder). As the practice of monepiscopacy (single bishop) became the norm, bishops assumed the administrative and teaching functions while the liturgical duties were left to the priests. The Council of Nicaea confirmed the priest's right to preside over the Eucharist without the bishop being present, since by then this was the universal practice.

As the desire grew that the ones who administered the sacraments should be ceremonially pure, it logically followed that some would demand of the clergy sexual continence. Origen spoke of "perfect priests who keep themselves in act and in thought in the state of virgin purity." Ambrose argued that the clergy must be free from defilement by sex as they offered the church's sacrifice. The Council of Elvira ruled, "Bishops, presbyters, and deacons—indeed, all clerics who have a place in the ministry—shall abstain from their wives and shall not beget children. This is a total prohibition: whoever does so, let him forfeit his rank among the clergy."

The issue of clerical celibacy was hotly debated during the next two centuries. Justinian demanded that bishops be celibate and ordered those who were married to send their wives to a distant convent. In the Western church celibacy was finally made a universal rule in the thirteenth century, in large measure because of the problems involved in the inheritance of church property by the offspring of clergy. However, even today in the Eastern church lower orders of clergy are allowed to marry, although bishops must be chosen from those who are celibate, in other words, monks.

Priests also were expected to be mature individuals, and candidates for the priesthood usually were thirty to thirty-five years old. Bishops generally served in lower offices before advancing to a diocese, and the first recorded list of a progression of offices a person would hold before becoming a bishop was provided by Damasus of Rome (366–84). This ideal now and then was disregarded, as for example, Ambrose, who was baptized at the age of thirty-four and then made bishop of Milan eight days later. Most likely, however, newly appointed bishops would be forty-five to fifty years of age. They often designated their successors, and the third-century custom of three bishops being present at the ordination of a new one became the rule. Also, the ordination of priests was now the sole prerogative of the bishops.

The filling of prominent sees sometimes became tumultuous affairs, as exemplified by the election of Damasus I. The supporters of the two rival candidates savagely attacked each other, and on one occasion a mob of Damasus's partisans killed 137 people when they assaulted the basilica of the other candidate.

Damasus is historically significant in the development of the institution of the papacy, because he was the first to affirm Rome as the Apostolic See and to claim the authority allegedly given to Peter by Christ in Matthew 16:18. He also worked diligently to strengthen the position of the Roman bishopric in relation to the others, especially those in the East, by promoting the veneration of martyrs and pilgrimages to their burial places in Rome (the famous catacombs), and by making Latin the liturgical language of the Roman church. He also encouraged Jerome to undertake a new Latin translation of the Bible, the Vulgate, which as noted above eventually became the standard of the Western church.

As the political significance of the city of Rome itself declined, the fifth-century bishops took advantage of the opportunity to expand on the authority claimed by Damasus. Innocent I (401–17) interfered in eastern affairs by supporting John Chrysostom against the patriarch of Constantinople, and in the West he backed Augustine in the Pelagian controversy. In so doing he claimed, as no other Roman bishop had before, the right to serve as the supreme arbiter in doctrinal matters.

Leo I (440–61), also known as "the Great," insisted that Peter had the primacy among the apostles. As his successors, the Roman bishops inherited his role as leader and teacher, and Peter spoke through them. Leo exercised this authority both by his severe criticism of the Manichaeans and Pelagians and by becoming involved in the Council of Chalcedon, which adopted his explanation of Christ as one person in two natures.

Gelasius I (492–96) was the first to be called the "Vicar of Christ." He also proclaimed the influential political doctrine of the "two swords." This held that there were two powers that govern the world, the sacred and the secular, and that the ecclesiastical, under the authority of the Roman See, was superior to the temporal power, such as that of the emperor.

Sins and Church Discipline

Clergy were expected to live up to higher standards than the laity. A fourth-century church council decreed that the clergy must not witness the plays at weddings or banquets but must leave before the players enter. Moreover, priests and deacons were not to enter taverns.

These councils customarily made rulings on matters of doctrine and behavior that were called "canons." The earliest known examples are the eighty-one canons of the Council of Elvira (305), which were remarkably severe. For instance, consecrated women who were unfaithful to their vows of virginity, men who practiced homosexuality, and women who had abortions were denied communion for life. The Council of Ancyra (314) prescribed ten years' excommunication for the sin of abortion.

From the early third century the Greek word for "repentance" (*metanoia*) was translated by the Latin *paenitentia.* The latter term signified not only remorse but also works of "penance" or "satisfaction," such as charity, weeping, prayer, fasting, or abstaining from marital relations for periods ranging from five years to life. Distinctions were made between lesser or "venial" (pardonable) sins and far more serious "mortal" (deadly) sins. According to Tertullian the latter included idolatry, murder, and adultery. Augustine went even further and affirmed that any violation of the Ten Commandments required public penance.

Those accused of committing some specific sin but who were sorry about their offenses were formally enrolled in a class of penitents. In some regions they had to wear a special garb made from goatskin and cut their hair short. They were permanently excluded from the clergy, from holding public office, and from marital intercourse. Such "mourners" or "kneelers" were not permitted inside the church building but had to stand in the forecourt. After the prescribed penance had been carried out, a public reconciliation took place with

The Hagia Sophia Church in Constantinople

the laying on of the hands of the bishops. The increasingly severe demands of penance led some to postpone it until the time of death.

In the fifth century the public confessions of sins gradually began to be replaced by private or "auricular" (to the ear) confessions, that is, to priests. This practice owed much to the stimulus of Celtic monastic piety. The earliest evidence for this form of private penance is found in the proceedings of the Third Synod of Toledo (589). It decreed that believers should confess their sins during Lent and then be publicly reconciled on Maundy Thursday prior to receiving communion on Easter.

The Sacraments and Liturgical Worship

The Latin word *sacramentum* originally meant "oath," such as that taken by soldiers; the recital of the creed at baptism was considered an oath to serve Christ. It was used to translate the Greek word "mystery," and in the early church it came to have the technical meaning of a ceremony instituted by God to channel divine grace to the individual believer. The two most significant sacraments at this time were baptism and communion, although the medieval church would later expand the number greatly.

The earliest reference to infant baptism is found in the writings of Tertullian, who opposed the practice. Cyprian, however, accepted it and urged believers not to wait the customary eight days (the procedure in circumcision) before baptizing their babies. Origen even claimed that infant baptism was an apostolic practice, but several prominent fourth-century figures, including the Cappadocian Fathers, John Chrysostom, Jerome, and Augustine, were not baptized until they were adults. By the fifth century it was the normal procedure in the Western church, and eventually it would be justified by the belief that original sin was "washed away" in the rite of baptism.

When adults wished to become Christians, they first became "catechumens," that is they were instructed in the creed and the Lord's Prayer and then examined as to their knowledge and personal conduct. The process could take as long as three years, but eventually it was shortened to the period of Lent. Baptisms usually took place on Easter morning after fasting and a vigil. The early third-century writer Hippolytus describes the procedure:

> On the Saturday those who are to receive baptism shall be gathered in one place at the bishop's decision. They shall all be told to pray and kneel. And he shall lay his hands on them and exorcise all alien spirits, that they may flee out of them and never return into them. And when he has finished exorcising them, he shall breathe on their faces; and when he has signed their foreheads, ears, and noses, he shall raise them up. And they shall spend the whole night in vigil; they shall be read to and instructed. . . . At the time when the cock crows, first let prayer be made over the water.[2]

Before entering the water the candidates would face west (a region associated with Hades), stretch out their hands, and renounce Satan and all of his works. In some cases they even ceremonially spat on Satan. They were then anointed on the breast and shoulder with an oil from which evil spirits had been exorcised. Following the baptism was a further anointing with "chrism," a special oil scented with balsam.

The account of Hippolytus continues: "And they shall put off their clothes. And they shall baptize the little children first. . . . And next they shall baptize the grown men; and last the women, who shall have loosed their hair and laid aside the gold ornaments." The officiating priest and assisting deacon stood in the water and asked every candidate three questions: "Do you believe in God the Father Almighty? Do you believe in Christ Jesus, the Son of God? Do you believe in the Holy Spirit in the Holy Church?" After each response, the priest immersed the candidate.

Until the fourth century, bishops presided over the baptismal rituals. But as the practice of infant baptism grew more common, a procedure that the priest carried out soon after the birth of a child, it was not always possible for the bishop to be present. This led to a separate rite of confirmation, whereby the bishop laid his hands on and anointed the heads of those already baptized by a priest. Councils in Spain and France in the fourth and fifth centuries directed bishops to "confirm" the baptisms carried out by priests.

Tertullian identified the postbaptismal laying on of hands as the gift of the Holy Spirit, which led to a controversy over whether the Spirit was given at baptism or confirmation. Innocent I claimed, "It belongs solely to the episcopal office that bishops consign and give the Paraclete Spirit." In his opinion, the Holy Spirit was bestowed when the bishop made the sign of the cross and anointed the baptized on the forehead with chrism.

One of the earliest descriptions of the other major sacrament, communion, or the Eucharist ("thanksgiving"), is found in the second-century writings of Justin Martyr. He explained that the rite included the presentation of bread and wine mixed with water, a prayer of thanksgiving, the congregational "Amen," and the distribution of the elements by deacons. By the following century the ceremony had become more elaborate. Hippolytus reported that it included the presentation of the elements by deacons to the bishop, his exhortation "lift up your hearts" (*sursum corda*) and prayer, a recounting of the salvation story and Jesus' words of institution, the formal offering ("oblation") of the bread and cup, the invocation of the Holy Spirit, and finally the distribution of the bread and wine by the priests and deacons. Elements added in the fourth and fifth centuries included readings from the Old and New Testaments, the singing of psalms and alleluias, sermons, prayer, the *Kyrie eleison* ("Lord have mercy") response, the *trisagion* ("Holy, Holy, Holy"), and other prayers such as the *Pater noster* ("Our Father"—the Lord's Prayer).

Cyprian spoke of the Eucharist as "the sacrifice of the Lord's passion" that was offered by the bishop functioning as a priest before the altar. The Eastern Father Cyril described it as a "propitiatory sacrifice." For Ambrose it was perfected by the priest's consecration and not by the reception of the elements, an emphasis that laid the groundwork for the later medieval doctrine of transubstantiation.

Before the communion service began, penitents and those who were not baptized were dismissed, that is, asked to leave. (The word *Mass,* which was given to the Eucharistic ceremony after the fifth century, comes from the Latin *missa*—"dismissal"—usually referring to the sending forth of the congregation at the close of the service.) Before the penitents departed, the deacon gave a lengthy admonition while they knelt, the congregation prayed the *Kyrie* for them, and the bishops concluded with a prayer of dismissal. The service then continued to the communion proper.

In Cyprian's time the Eucharist was celebrated daily. However, as the years passed, it took on the character of a fearful mystery and fewer and fewer people observed the rite. John Chrysostom's lament reflects the change: "In vain is the daily sacrifice, in vain do we stand before the altar; no one partakes."

There were a variety of other services in the churches. In addition to the regular Sunday worship and daily Eucharist were the morning Laudes (or Matins), evening Vespers, and special afternoon services ending the fasts on Wednesday and Friday. Two or three chapters of the Old Testament were read at the weekday services, so that all the books were covered in a cycle of three years. The four gospels would be read at the Eucharist observance in a cycle of three years. By the fifth century each feast was assigned specific texts, and lectionaries (books providing scriptural readings) came into use.

Before long only the ordained clergy engaged in preaching. Among the best surviving sermons from the early church are the two hundred homilies of Origen. Most were on Old Testament topics but thirty-nine were based on Luke. These were delivered extemporaneously after the reading of the day's text. Like many a modern day preacher, Origen expressed annoyance at the lack of attention of some in the congregation "who do not at all understand what is said, but their mind and heart are on business dealings or on acts of the world or on counting their profit."

Sermons remain from other giants of the pulpit in the Eastern church, such as Basil of Caesarea and Gregory of Nazianzus, and John Chrysostom, the greatest preacher of the East, has left 600 sermons. The latter instructed his parishioners about daily concerns and essentially engaged in dialogue with them, but at times his tongue could be sharp. As he told the greedy rich in Antioch, "The world is meant to be like a household, wherein all the servants receive equal allowances, for all men are equal, since they are brothers." Chrysostom was a spell-binding orator who often went on for two hours, but on the other hand, a more run-of-the-mill preacher, Caesarius of Arles (sixth century), had to limit his sermons to fifteen minutes and order the doors of the church shut to keep his hearers from leaving.

In the West Augustine, who sat at the feet of Ambrose, himself a master of pulpit oratory, was by far the greatest preacher. More than five hundred of his sermons survive, and his work *On Christian Doctrine* is regarded as the first significant treatise on homiletics. In fact, his sermons were bound as "homiliaries"—collections of sermons that other preachers could use with their congregations.

Since musical instruments were associated with pagan festivals, unaccompanied vocal music was the Christian practice, hence the expression *a cappella* ("as in the chapel"). There is only little evidence that Christians might have used the lyre and cithara. In fact, a canon of Basil from 375 imposed a penance of seven weeks for a lector who learned to play the guitar; if he continued the practice he was to be excommunicated. The organ, which was an instrument used at the imperial court, was only introduced into the church after the seventh century. Various writers waved aside the objection that musical instruments were used in the Old Testament by maintaining this was a concession to the Jews.

One of the earliest collections of hymns was the second-century Odes of Solomon, which were composed in Syriac. Somewhat later Ephraem the Syrian (306–73) established choirs at Edessa and composed numerous hymns in his tongue. He greatly influenced Romanos Melodos (485–560), the leading early Byzantine hymn writer who produced *kontakia,* verse sermons that were chanted. One entitled "Standing Up," which was dedicated to Mary, is still used in the Greek Orthodox liturgy.

Though Hilary of Poitiers (315–67) first introduced liturgical hymns into the West, Ambrose is commonly regarded as the "father of liturgical hymnody." Best known is his use of antiphonal singing, that is, the singing of verses from the Psalms alternately by two choirs. Augustine was greatly moved by the liturgical music he heard at the cathedral of Milan and records in his *Confessions*:

> But when I recall the tears that I shed upon hearing the singing of the Church in the first days of my recovered faith, and that now I am moved not by the singing but by what is sung when it is sung with a clear voice and the proper modulation, I again acknowledge the great utility of this institution.

Liturgical music was monophonic singing on a diatonic scale. Church leaders like Athanasius were opposed to melodic elaborations, dancing, clapping hands, and the shaking of sistra. The last was seen as a practice borrowed from the cult of Isis.

Although no explicit references exist to women singing in the church during the first two centuries, they undoubtedly participated in congregational singing. In the third century Paul of Samosata, Ephraem of Edessa, and others organized female choirs. On the other hand, some insisted that the Pauline injunction for women to be silent in the church also extended to their singing. Cyril of Jerusalem declared that "virgins should sing or read the psalms very quietly during the liturgy. They should only move their lips, so that nothing is heard, for I do not permit women to speak in church."

The practice of using boys in liturgical music began in the sixth century. Germanus of Paris (d. 576) reports that at the beginning of Mass, three youths sang the threefold *Kyrie eleison* in unison. Since readings in the church now were being chanted, a regulation of Justinian allowed a boy to become a lector in his eighth year.

Holy Days and the Christian Calendar

From the earliest times, Christians met for worship on the first day of the week, presumably because it was when Christ's resurrection occurred, though this justification was rarely mentioned by the early church Fathers. The second-century *Gospel of Peter* identified Sunday as the "Lord's Day" (see Revelation 1:10). Apparently to distinguish themselves from the Judaizing practices of many early believers, Gentile Christians abandoned the Sabbath observance and worshiped on Sunday. Other early writers honored Sunday as the first day of creation. Finally, in 321 Emperor Constantine made Sunday a legal holiday.

The exact day of Jesus' birth is unknown. The Gnostic Basilidians in Egypt (late second century) commemorated Jesus' baptism on January 6, and by the early fourth century many Christians in the East were celebrating both his nativity and baptism then. The following day was devoted to the Epiphany ("manifestation") to the Magi (wise men), when people sang Ephraem's hymn: "The whole creation proclaims, the Magi proclaim, the Star proclaims: Behold the king's son is here."

In 274 Emperor Aurelian decreed December 25 as the celebration of the "Unconquerable Sun," the first day in which there was a noticeable increase in light after the winter solstice. The earliest mention of a Feast of the Nativity on that date is found in a document

The Spread of Monasticism

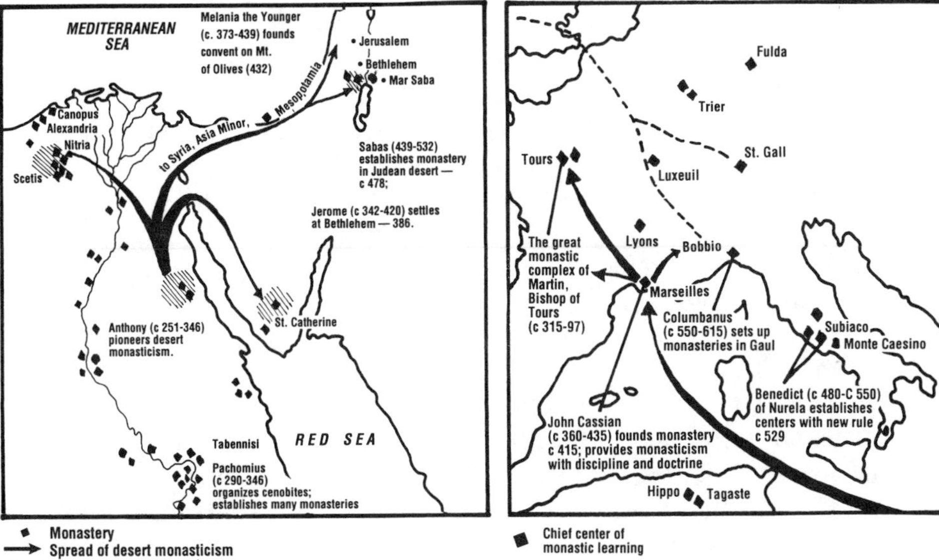

composed in 336. Some feel Constantine (who died in 337) may have selected this day for Christmas because of a deep-seated respect for the popular pagan solstice festival. Others argue that the date was chosen as a replacement for it, that is, to honor the "Sun of Righteousness." Firmly established in the West within a few decades, another century passed before the Eastern church adopted December 25. The many controversies about the person and nature of Christ contributed to the shift in emphasis from His baptism to His birth. The only hold-out was the Armenian church, which still observes the nativity on January 6.

By the fourth century Epiphany was regarded in the East as a holy day equal with Easter and Pentecost, since it celebrated Jesus' birth, baptism, adoration by the wise men, and also the changing of the water into wine at Cana. In the West the emphasis on His baptism was dropped, and Augustine ranked it as equal in importance with Christmas because, he said, it was the day on which the Lord manifested Himself to pagans.

Christians in Spain first observed Advent, a season preceding Christmas, and the Council of Saragossa (380) established a period of three weeks. During the sixth century this had risen to five Sundays, but Gregory the Great reduced it to four. Some time prior to the sixth century the Eastern church added the four feast days of the Virgin Mary to the calendar—her nativity, the manifestation to Simeon in the Temple, the conception of Christ, and her assumption into heaven. Later these feasts were brought to the West.

An elaborate celebration of Christ's death and resurrection developed from the simple second-century pattern of Wednesday and Friday fasts. In the fourth century, Christians were observing weekly fasts on Friday and a forty-day period of self-denial in preparation for Easter, when they abstained from meat, fish, eggs, dairy products, and wine. This period, known as Lent, was the time when catechumens would be prepared for baptism and public penance made. Ashes were commonly sprinkled on the penitents, which was the forerunner of the medieval church practice of doing so to all worshipers at Lent.

The high point of the Christian year was Holy Week, culminating in the "Pasch," or Easter Sunday. Pasch was the Aramaic term for the Jewish Passover, which was the background of the Last Supper and the Christian view of Jesus as the Passover lamb (Mark 14:12–16; John 1:29; 1 Corinthians 5:6–8). In the second century the Pasch was celebrated with a vigil, fasting, Scripture reading, chanting, and the Eucharist.

At first it took place at the same time as the Jewish feast (Nisan 14), the date of which shifted from year to year on the basis of the lunar calendar. The church at Rome, however, insisted that Easter be celebrated on a Sunday because Christ rose from the dead that day. As discussed earlier, many Christians in Asia Minor who followed the Jewish calendar resisted this innovation, but eventually they yielded on the question. Because there were differences between the East and West as to the actual date of the paschal event, the Council of Nicaea determined that Easter would be celebrated on the first Sunday following the full moon that occurred on or after the spring equinox. Thus Easter could be as early as March 22 and as late as April 25.

Fifty days after Easter was Pentecost, the feast of the descent of the Holy Spirit upon the apostles (see chapter 1). It was already being observed in the second century and was next in importance to Easter. Pentecost was also a popular occasion for baptisms, and in the English-speaking church it came to be known as "Whitsunday" because of the white clothing worn by those who received baptism.

The Cult of Martyrs and Relics

Although Stephen, most of the apostles, and many other earlier Christians were the first martyrs of the church, the earliest record of the cult of the martyrs is the story of Polycarp of Smyrna, who was killed in 156. His remains were gathered and buried by Christians who remarked, "There the Lord will permit us to meet together in gladness and joy and to celebrate the birthday of his martyrdom." Annual celebrations of the martyrs Hippolytus, Callistus, Pontianus, and Fabian occurred in the third century. At that time the feast of Peter and Paul began to be observed on June 29.

When the persecutions ended, veneration of the martyrs themselves was transferred to their relics, and their burial sites were thought to possess special healing powers. As Gregory of Nyssa noted, Christians could have a religious experience at these final resting places: "Those who behold them embrace, as it were the living body in full flower, they bring eye, mouth, ear, all the sense into play, and then, shedding tears of reverence and passion, they address to the martyr their prayers of intercession as though he were present." Small chapels (*martyria*) were built over these crypts at first, which were later replaced by martyr basilicas. By the end of the sixth century such places were centers of ecclesiastical life.

The feast of a martyr included a vigil and Mass at the site, with readings from the Scriptures and a recounting of the martyrdom. The commemorative banquet that was held at the scene often became a raucous occasion. The Council of Elvira forbade women from participating in the vigils at a martyr's grave because of the drinking and carousing that might occur. However, only isolated voices, such as that of Vigilantius of Aquitaine, were raised against the excesses of the martyrs' cult. Augustine also noted the abuses connected with the cult when he complained that the relics of individual martyrs were divided up and scattered and some were even manufactured.

To counter the problem, Emperor Theodosius made a law forbidding the transfer, dismemberment, or sale of the bones of martyrs, but this was soon disregarded. For instance, when the tombs of martyrs in the catacombs were threatened by plundering invaders, the Roman bishops had their remains taken to churches inside the city. Relics were simply stolen as well. For example, those of St. Mark were taken from Alexandria by the Venetians and St. Nicholas from Myra by sailors from Bari. Eventually the supply became so great that the medieval church could require the altars in every church to contain the relics of a saint. They were housed inside the altar itself or in ornately decorated caskets known as reliquaries.

Christian Architecture and Art

The earliest Christians met in homes, which were gradually transformed into house churches, but after Constantine's conversion large structures called basilicas were constructed. These were rectangular buildings with two rows of columns in the interior and an apse at the end, which were utilized by the secular authorities as law courts. When his mother Helena made her famous visit to the Holy Land, she had basilicas built over a cave identified as the birthplace of Jesus (Church of the Holy Nativity) and at the traditional location of Calvary and His tomb (Church of the Holy Sepulchre). Other basilicas were erected at Constantinople and Rome, including St. Peter's on the Vatican Hill and the massive Lateran Basilica that was 312 feet long and could hold 3,000 worshipers.

In the Western churches chancel screens were built separating the congregation from the priests, while in the East a solid wall with doors, the *iconostasis,* completely blocked the view of the worshipers. From the sixth century an elevated platform called the *ambo* was added, which was used for the Scripture readings and the delivery of sermons.

Every church had a baptistry that was at times housed in a separate building. Over 300 baptistries constructed between the third and seventh centuries have been discovered. Because the baptismal pools were shallow, persons were immersed kneeling and bending over. The majority of the baptistries were either round or octagonal, since eight was considered the symbol of immortality.

Examples of the earliest Christian art, dating back to about 200, can be found in the Roman catacombs. One of the best-known works is the *Adoration of the Magi* found in the catacomb of St. Priscilla. The three Magi, dressed in Persian garb, are depicted presenting gifts to the infant who rests on the lap of his mother. Another popular subject in the catacombs is the miracles of Jesus, such as His turning water into wine, multiplying the loaves and fishes, and raising Lazarus from the dead. Some depictions are based on pagan models, such as a youthful shepherd carrying a lamb to represent Christ as the Good Shepherd. He is also portrayed as a teacher and lawgiver.

At first his passion was not depicted. It is not until 432 that the crucifixion was the subject of a door panel on a church in Rome (St. Sabine). In the fourth century, imperial iconography, which represented the emperor as semi-divine, began to be used to portray Christ as the all-powerful ruler of the universe. Another important art form was the relief sculptures contained on sarcophagi.

A major influence in the development of Christian art was Constantine himself. He was the leading patron of the arts in the fourth century, and, thanks to his generous support, skilled craftsmen began making such objects as chalices from the finest materials—ivory, glass, gold, silver, and precious stones. He also had the interiors of churches decorated with brilliant mosaics made of small squares of brightly colored stone and glass. Other types of art found in the churches were wall frescoes and sculptures of prominent personages.

The antipathy toward serious art expressed by such individuals as Tertullian, who urged artists who became believers to give up their craft, rapidly died out. No longer did one hear such negative views expressed like that of Eusebius, who rebuked Constantina, the sister of Constantine, for requesting a portrait of Christ. In fact, Christians in the East began making two-dimensional figures of the Holy Family and of saints that they called *icons,* sacred images that were venerated.

Since Theodosius I destroyed pagan temples and gave their riches to the new churches founded on their sites, the fifth century was a period of extraordinary creativity. It was marked by the construction of elaborate churches, baptistries, mausoleums, martyria, and monasteries in such centers as Rome, Milan, Ravenna, Naples, Constantinople, Thessalonica, and Ephesus. Even in the distant Jordanian city of Jerash seven basilicas were erected.

MONASTICISM

Beginning in the late third century, the monastic movement brought a new dimension to Christian life. This was a reaction to the growing worldliness and institutionalization of the church. Already at the time of Constantine approximately 10 percent of the empire's population was Christian, and a century later the number professing the faith approached 90 percent. Since the extraordinary growth led to a decline in zeal, many sincere believers decided to drop out of society and dedicate themselves to spiritual exercises and preparation for the next world. These monks and nuns, who denied themselves all physical comforts, rejected sex and marriage, and ate and slept little, replaced martyrs as the new heroes of the faithful.

The most important early leader was Anthony of Egypt (c. 251–356). He was the founder of *anchoritic* monasticsm, that is, monks living in solitude as hermits. From a wealthy Coptic family, as a youth of twenty Anthony became deeply convicted by Jesus' command to the rich young man to sell all his possessions, give to the poor, and follow Him (Matthew 19:21). Thus, he sold his property and took up the life of a hermit under the direction of an older ascetic. As he progressed in the solitary life, he moved farther into the desert, finally spending twenty years in a ruined fort by the Red Sea. During all this time he struggled against demonic powers who challenged his devotion to Christ. He overcame them by fasting, vigils, prayer, and Bible study.

When Anthony returned to civilization, he was more than a hero. Like the martyrs themselves, he was a paragon of holiness. He healed the sick, mediated controversies, and taught the wisdom he had learned. As disciples were attracted to him, loose communities of hermits formed who imitated the conduct of this spiritual role model. Athanasius's *Life of Anthony* spread his fame throughout the church, and by the time of his death thousands of Christian ascetics lived in the Egyptian desert.

Another early monastic leader, the Egyptian Pachomius (c. 292–346), was the originator of *cenobitic*, or communal, monasticism. After becoming a Christian he first spent six years as a hermit. Then in 323 he received a vision to establish a monastery at the remote village of Tabennesi in southern Egypt. By the end of his life he had founded in the same area eight more monasteries and two convents whose members totaled 7,000. Residents in his communities dedicated themselves to chastity, poverty, and obedience. They prayed as often as twelve times a day, but the austerities practiced there were not as severe as among the anchorites. Because of the work of men like Anthony and Pachomius, Egyptian monasticism flourished in the fifth and sixth centuries, and as many as 50,000 monks were living as hermits or in communities.

From Egypt the movement spread to Palestine where Hilarion (293–371) settled in Gaza and introduced anchoritic monasticism. The hermits, who lived in the Judaean desert in separate cells or caves known as *lauras,* were under a single abbot and came together on Saturday nights to observe a vigil and communion. Jerome also spent several years as a hermit in Syria, and when he returned to the

The Empress Theodora, Wife of Justinian

West to work for Damasus, he sought to generate interest in the ascetic ideal. His promotion of monasticism disturbed many in Rome because people there found the shabby clothing, unkempt hair, and foul odor of ascetics to be disgusting. However, as mentioned in chapter 3, he left in 385 to establish a monastery in the East, and two women accompanied him. Another preceded him and one came later, all of whom directed convents.

These four women—Melania the Elder, Paula, Eustochium, and Melania the Younger—came from aristocratic backgrounds, but paradoxically gained great freedom and prestige by their lives of renunciation. Not only did they use their great wealth to fund monastic enterprises, but they also studied religious literature, copied the Scriptures, and served as advisors on theological issues.

Some forms of Eastern monasticism were unusually ascetic, such as in Syria where a novel form of world-rejection was practiced by the "stylites" (Greek for "pillar"). These were hermits who escaped not horizontally into caves but vertically to the tops of isolated pillars. The best known was St. Simeon Stylites (c. 390–460). He began as an ordinary hermit on the Egyptian model, spending ten years in a lonely cell near Antioch. Then in 423 he mounted a pillar and gradually extended it upward until by 430 it was sixty feet high. For thirty years he sat on a column only three feet in diameter with a manacle around his neck and engaged in meditation and conflict with demons. His piety attracted many pilgrims who sought his prayers and advice, and his counsel was even solicited by several emperors and the Councils of Ephesus (431) and Chalcedon (451). This conspicuous display of asceticism was taken to the extreme by Daniel the Stylite (d. c. 490) who inherited Simeon's pillar and lived on it for three decades. It was said that his legs were completely putrified by the time of his death. As the divisions between the orthodox and the Monophysites grew in intensity and the number of stylites increased, it became common to encounter pillar saints perched on adjacent columns shouting theological abuse at each other across the Syrian landscape.

Monasticism arrived in Cappadocia during the fourth century, and the theologians Basil of Caesarea (the Great) and Gregory of Nazianzus were notable figures in the movement. Basil is particularly important because he had his monks minister to the physical needs of the poor and sick, and his *Rule,* which directed them to live in communities rather than as hermits, profoundly influenced the development of monasticism in the Eastern church. A disciple of both men was Evagrius Ponticus (345–99), who left Constantinople for Jerusalem and came under the influence of Melania the Elder. She encouraged him to adopt the ascetic life and then to go to Egypt where he lived in the desert. The first monk to write extensively, Evagrius set forth the view that through asceticism and contemplation one could rise above temptation and live without sin.

The monastic ideal quickly spread to the Western church. The work of Martin of Tours (316–97) was especially significant. Originally a soldier from Pannonia (Hungary), he left the army, became a monk, and established the first monastery in Gaul at Ligugé near Poitiers around 360. After his election as bishop of Tours in 372, he continued to live as a monk at a foundation he established in Marmoutier. An admiring biographer, Sulpicius Severus, wrote of Martin shortly after his death: "For although the character of our times has been such as not to afford him the opportunity of martyrdom, he nonetheless will share the martyr's glory." Martin was the first nonmartyr to be elevated to sainthood ("canonized") by the church.

Another important Western figure was John Cassian (c. 360–433). After spending seventeen years in monasteries in Palestine and Egypt, he went to Marseilles around 415 and established monasteries for both men and women. His *Conferences,* an account of his discussions with the leaders of Eastern monasticism, and *Institutes,* a set of rules for the monastic life, popularized the Eastern experience in the West. They were used by later monastic writers and continue to this day to be classics of Christian devotion and mysticism.

From Gaul the monastic movement spread to Ireland, where, as will be shown in chapter 5, the Celtic form of Christianity was that of monasticism. In fact, all the clergy in fifth- and sixth-century Ireland were monks. The institution was also introduced into northern Britain by Ninian (c. 360–432), an admirer of Martin of Tours and his monastic lifestyle, who evangelized the people known as the Picts.

The greatest creative personality in Western monasticism was Benedict of Nursia (c. 480–550). He came from a well-to-do family that sent him to Rome to be educated. He, however, grew disgusted with the corruption of the city and withdrew to a remote area where he lived as a hermit in a cave. Benedict's retreat soon was discovered by shepherds, and many people came to him for comfort and advice. Other hermits gathered around him and under his leadership twelve communities were formed. After conflict broke out among the groups, he left with a small band of followers and founded a cenobitic monastery at Monte Cassino, an isolated mountaintop between Rome and Naples.

For this he wrote a *Rule* that became the standard for Western monks. Drawing upon ideas from Basil, John Cassian, and an anonymous rule, it portrayed the monastery as a stable, self-supporting community devoted to Christ. Its members renounced all personal possessions, were celibate, and remained there for life. The head of the community was the abbot, who was to be obeyed without question, but in turn he was required to consult the members in matters of common concern. The tasks of the monks were threefold: they worshiped God, labored in the fields, and studied the Bible. Benedict looked unfavorably upon extreme asceticism, and his Rule was not as severe as the Eastern monastic tradition.

The Benedictines made a real effort to practice genuine Christianity in an age of increasing indifference. This could be seen in their worship cycle as well as their daily activities. Their worship involved seven fixed hours of prayer: Vigils at 2:00 A.M., Lauds at first light, Prime at 6:00 A.M., Terce at 9:00 A.M., Sext at noon, Vespers at 4:30 P.M., and Compline at 6:00 P.M. But the monks were also required to work in the fields and perform chores around the monastery. This emphasis upon work contributed enormously to elevating the value of labor in Western society. Further, the monastery was central to the advancement of learning. In their schools the monks learned to read and write, and they created libraries consisting of the Bible, the Fathers, and secular classical literature, books that they meticulously copied by hand. Without these libraries most of the learning of classical antiquity would have been lost.

Still, there was often tension between the monastic leaders and the ecclesiastical hierarchy. With the exception of the Celts, most of the monks were laymen. For example, Benedict refused ordination, Jerome and Martin were ordained against their will, and the Egyptian hermit Ammon (c. 350) cut off his right ear so he could disqualify himself for ordination. One writer, John of Lycopolis, expressed a typical monastic antipathy to the priesthood by advising, "If you desire to escape trouble, don't leave the desert, for in the desert no one can ordain you a bishop."

In the three centuries after Constantine's conversion the church consolidated its power and prestige. In western Europe the Christian leadership provided stability during the Germanic invasions and the collapse of the Roman political order. Elaborate liturgies were formulated to celebrate baptism and communion, and numerous holy days were added to the Christian calendar. In contrast to the establishment of Christianity and the consequent decline of personal piety, the monastic movement provided a genuine spiritual alternative. Thus monks made up the missionary force that would lead in the expansion of Christianity into other lands in the following centuries.

5

EUROPEAN EXPANSION OF THE CHURCH

Internal struggles and barbarian migrations drastically transformed the political situation in the western Roman Empire in the fourth and fifth centuries, and it broke up into a number of German successor kingdoms. From the fifth to the tenth centuries Christianity spread beyond the confines of the old Roman Empire to the Celts in Ireland, the Germans east of the Rhine, and the Slavs in central Europe. At the same time it endured challenges by attackers who beset Europe from three directions—the Vikings from the north, the Magyars from the east, and the Muslims from the south. Eventually the first two groups were won to the Christian faith, but the latter occupied the traditional centers of Christianity in the Middle East and North Africa and invaded Spain.

THE GERMANIC MIGRATIONS

Although their origins are shrouded in mystery, the Germanic tribes seemed to have concentrated in the Baltic and North Sea coastal regions during the first millennium B.C. They gradually displaced the Celtic peoples who had occupied the area known today as Germany, and by the first century B.C. were in contact with the expanding Romans. In the following century they checked the Roman advance east of the Rhine and a border (called the *limes*) was drawn between them. An uneasy peace followed, and Germans as individuals and in small groups infiltrated the empire. Many of them served in the armies or simply settled there. But as population growth took place in the areas beyond the imperial frontiers, the isolated tribes began coalescing into larger confederations. Along the North Sea coast and Danish peninsula were the Angles, Saxons, and Jutes. In the Rhine valley were the Franks and Alemans, while the Vandals, Burgundians, and Lombards were located in the Oder and Vistula river areas. The Ostrogoths and Visigoths settled west and northwest of the Black Sea.

Another outside group was the Huns, a nomadic people from the central Asian steppes, legendary for their bravery and ruthlessness. They were expert horsemen who fought as lightly armed, mounted archers, who after having failed in efforts to penetrate China, moved westward. Historians disagree as to how centralized the Hunnic organization was, but their cavalry units clearly were highly effective. When they reached eastern Europe, they terrorized the Goths living along the imperial frontiers. Their presence triggered a whole new wave of migrations traditionally called the "barbarian invasions."

The most immediately threatened people was the Visigoths, and they sought permission to cross the Danube and settle within the empire. Christianity had already taken root among them, thanks to the work of Ulfilas (c. 311–c. 381). Of Cappadocian ancestry, he lived among the Goths as a captive and then was taken to Constantinople. There he became a Christian and acquired a mastery of Greek and Latin. In 341 he was ordained by the Arian bishop, Eusebius of Nicomedia, and went back to the Goths as a missionary. A man of great linguistic skill, he created an alphabet using Greek letters to represent Gothic sounds, reduced the language to writing, and translated the Bible into it. However, as the contemporary historian Philostorgius observed, he omitted the books of Kings "because they are only stories of battle, and the Gothic tribes were especially fond of war and more in need of restraint than encouragement in this regard." The conversion of the Visigoths to Arianism would have a profound impact on their relations with other Christian peoples as they moved through the empire.

In 376 Emperor Valens reluctantly allowed the Goths to enter his domains and gave them land in return for military service. However,

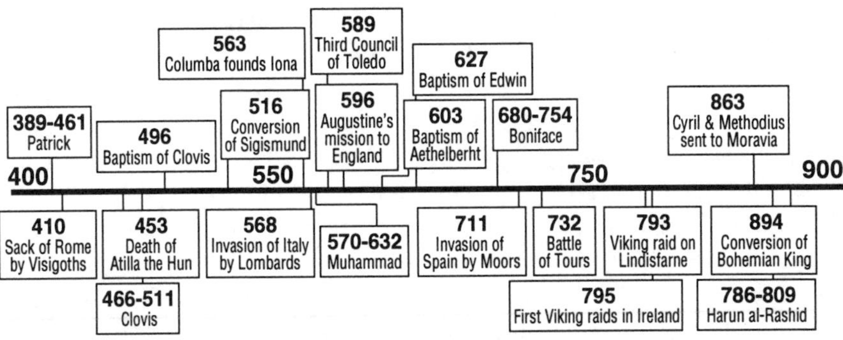

the greedy, corrupt Roman officials responsible for settling the Visigoths in Thrace made them pay for supplies that the emperor had promised to give them. During negotiations to resolve these problems, hostilities broke out, and in 378 Valens personally led an army to deal with the restive Goths. In the ensuing battle of Adrianople the imperial forces were defeated and the emperor killed. Although traditionally regarded as a major turning point in Roman imperial history, recent scholarship has downplayed the importance of Adrianople. The reason is that the battle occurred in that part of the empire that survived for another thousand years. The new emperor, Theodosius I, recognized the Goths as *foederati*, allies sworn to serve with the Roman armies, and settled them on imperial lands in Bulgaria. Later he used them in his effort to reestablish authority over the Western Empire.

Still, the Visigoths were dissatisfied with this status. Under the leadership of Alaric they rebelled in 396 and ravaged Greece, and in 402 invaded Italy. A few years later they turned on the "Eternal City" (Rome) itself. At first Alaric was bought off by a bribe, but then in 410 his Visigoths sacked the city, something that had not occurred for eight centuries. Jerome in faraway Bethlehem wrote when he heard of this disaster: "Who would believe that Rome fights no longer for glory but for her very existence, and no longer even fights but purchases her life with gold?"

While Alaric was invading Italy, the Roman troops on the German frontier were recalled. This enabled various Germanic tribes to move freely into imperial territory, the most important of which were the Vandals. They advanced southward into Spain in 409, but the Romans with the help of the Visigoths pressured them into moving on to North Africa. As a reward for this assistance, the Visigoths were allowed to settle in southwestern France and then in most of Spain.

By the late sixth century approximately 200,000 Visigoths ruled over a population of eight million Hispano-Romans. The latter were overwhelmingly Catholic (Trinitarian), whereas the Visigothic warrior aristocracy was Arian. Since this was the source of serious tension between the two groups, King Reccared (586–601) decided to adopt the Catholic views of his Roman subjects, and at the Third Council of Toledo in 589 he persuaded the Arian bishops to do likewise. This enabled the assimilation of the two peoples and inaugurated a period of close cooperation between church and state that lasted until the Muslim conquest of Spain in the eighth century.

As a device to counter ongoing Arianism, the Council formally inserted the *filioque* ("and from the Son") clause into the Nicene Creed to define the procession of the Holy Spirit. The Eastern church would later object to the emendation as an innovation. (Actually the Eastern churchmen felt slighted at not having been consulted about this.) This action was the work of Isidore, bishop of Seville, who served as advisor to several Visigothic kings. The most outstanding of a succcession of bishops distinguished for their learning, political acumen, and firmness of purpose, Isidore was especially critical of the anti-Jewish attitudes of his fellow Spaniards (there was already a large Jewish population there). He was suspicious of Byzantine (Eastern) Christianity as well. In addition to his other activities, he produced many influential works, including the earliest medieval encyclopedia, the *Etymologies*. Isidore's writings were especially used by Irish and English churchmen.

The Vandals under their leader Gaiseric crossed the Strait of Gibraltar in 429 and subdued western North Africa. Then they built a powerful fleet and raided the Mediterranean islands and southern Italy. In 455 they captured and looted the city of Rome even more thoroughly than the Visigoths had in 410. The Vandals were extremely committed Arians who persecuted Catholics and exiled 5,000 clergy to the southern desert. In 484 a council at Carthage that the Vandals controlled even declared Catholicism a heresy. After Gaiseric's death the kingdom declined rapidly, and the area was reconquered by Justinian in 534.

Meanwhile, the Huns, who had temporarily situated themselves north of the Danube and harassed German and Slavic tribes alike, served as mercenary soldiers and received tribute money from the Roman emperors. However, in 450 the emperor refused to continue making the agreed payments, and Attila, who had become sole ruler of the Huns after 445, then led an army into the empire itself. In 451 a confederacy of Gallo-Romans, Visigoths, and other Germans defeated his forces at a battle near Chalons in France and forced his withdrawal to the Danube. The next year he attacked Italy and encountered little resistance, but Leo I came north from Rome and persuaded the leader of the Huns to leave. An epidemic that devastated Attila's army may have been the real reason for his withdrawal from the apparently defenseless Italian territories. In 453 Attila died and the Hunnic threat to the empire was ended, but in later Christian legend he came to be seen as "the scourge of God," the fearsome instrument of divine retribution.

Two other invasions of the Western Empire during the fifth century led to the formation of significant successor states. In Italy an Ostrogothic kingdom was set up in 493 by Theodoric (c. 455–526). He was the son of the Ostrogothic ruler in the Roman province of Pannonia (Hungary) and was educated at the imperial court in Constantinople. An Arian Christian, he succeeded to the tribal leadership in 475. The emperor was relieved when he and his Goths moved into northern Italy, deposed the imperial claimant there, established a new capital at Ravenna, and restored stability. Although a warrior-leader, Theodoric was also an effective administrator who had a good grasp of the Roman imperial system, and he relied on Roman officials rather than entrusting the Goths with the civil administration. In essence he established a dual society, the Roman and the Gothic, each with its own laws, rulers, and religious practices. The military side was under the Goths and the culture was controlled by the Romans.

Even though he and his Goths were Arians, Theodoric displayed a remarkable tolerance toward the Catholic faith of the native Italians. "We cannot command the religion of our subjects, since no one can be forced to believe against his will." However, shortly before his death Theodoric had serious misunderstandings with the Roman population who did not particularly like their Arian ruler. He accused several prominent figures of treason, including Boethius (c. 480–c. 525), the greatest Christian philosopher of the day, whom he had executed. While in prison, Boethius wrote his famous *Consolation of Philosophy*.

The best example of the Arian Ostrogothic ruler's use of Catholics in his administration is that of Cassiodorus (c. 477–c. 570). He set out to put literary studies in the service of the Christian religion by collecting and preserving both classical and Christian writings. His works on theology and liberal arts were widely used in the Middle Ages. After Theodoric's death the Ostrogothic kingdom rapidly crumbled and was reincorporated into the Byzantine Empire of Justinian in 552. The city of Rome by then had become a cultural and economic backwater.

The Burgundians were a Germanic tribe displaced by the Huns who moved westward into southeastern France in the later fifth century. Although Arians, they did have good relations with the Latin Catholics in the old Christian centers they occupied, and in 516 their king Sigismund decided to convert to Catholic Christianity. A far more important development was the invasion of the Franks, a coalition of Germanic peoples, who settled in northern France. They were the only German tribe to enter the empire as pagans and not as Arian Christians.

The first great Frankish king, Clovis (466–511), brought all the various tribes under his rule, and inflicted defeats on the Visigoths, Burgundians, and Alemans. Although a pagan, Clovis was married to a Catholic princess, Clotilda. According to Frankish legend, Clovis was battling the pagan Alemans and turned to his wife's God for help. He promised to accept Christ if he were victorious, and when the war concluded favorably, he and 3,000 of his warriors were baptized on Christmas Day, 496, by the bishop of Reims. Clovis was the first German ruler to become a Catholic, and his conversion was the most significant religio-political event of this type since that of Constantine because it laid the foundation for the later alliance between the Franks and the papacy.

However, the action did not lead to holy living. Gregory of Tours vividly recounts in his contemporary *History of the Franks* (573–91) the dissolute living, quarreling, intrigues, and assassinations that characterized the rule of Clovis's successors, the Merovingians. Gregory, the leading churchman of the Merovingian period, looked back fondly at the life of St. Martin of Tours, who had done so much to win the pagan peasantry and advance monasticism in Gaul, and compared it to the sad situation of his day. For example, the Merovingian rulers had no qualms about seizing church property and installing their favorites as bishops. An extraordinarily violent bunch, they constantly struggled with each other and even brought thank offerings to St. Martin's shrine after cutting the throats of their rivals. Clerical discipline itself became so bad that two bishops had to be deposed for violence and adultery.

Despite the nominal character of Frankish Christianity, the rulers did have their children baptized, and by the seventh century almost the entire population had received baptism. But few people worked at their faith, communion was seldom taken, and little attention was paid to the clergy's sermons. It is recorded that Hilary of Arles shouted at those leaving his service before the sermon that they would not get out of hell so easily, and Caesarius of Arles locked the doors of the church to keep his parishioners from walking out before he preached.

The last major Germanic people to enter the empire were the Lombards. Justinian had allowed them into Pannonia as allies against the Ostrogoths, and their soldiers participated in his war in Italy. But by destroying the only power that could keep them out, the Arian Lombards were able to return to Italy in 568 as conquerors. They took over most of northern and central Italy, imposed their institutions on the area, and engaged in rivalry with the papacy for control of Italy. In the following century they switched to Catholic orthodoxy.

By the end of the sixth century a variety of Germanic successor states had now come to occupy the territory of the Western Roman Empire. But it would be inaccurate to speak of "the fall of Rome," as so often is done in popular literature. The fact is that the fifth-century emperors simply gave away or lost control of the empire's territory to Germanic rulers. Theoretically, they were subordinate to the authority of the emperor, but in reality he received no material benefits from and could not exercise any authority over his Germanic subjects. Thus, the Western Empire simply delegated itself out of existence. However, Roman culture maintained continuity, as the tribes were more or less assimilated and were at least nominally Christian.

CHRISTIANITY IN THE BRITISH ISLES

Christianity had established a foothold in Roman Britain among the common people, and as many as thirty bishops may have been serving there by the late fourth century. Thus, the Anglo-Saxon invasions may have weakened but did not wipe out the Celtic church. Even as the Roman army units were withdrawn around 400 to deal with continental problems, Britain was subjected to raids by the Picts and Irish. The Saxons were recruited as mercenaries to provide defense against these invaders. Thus, they entered Britain in the same way that the Franks and Visigoths came into the empire, and they assumed the role in society once held by the Roman army. Growing numbers of Saxons, along with Angles and Jutes, established themselves in eastern and northern Britain because of these agreements, but few were Christians.

Works referring to the early history of post-Roman Christianity are those of Nennius (c. 800), who mentions the ministry of Patrick in Ireland and the legendary King Arthur who fought the Anglo-Saxons, and the *Ecclesiastical History of the English People*, a comprehensive account by the Venerable Bede (673–735), a monk at Wearmouth and Jarrow in northern England. Although little hard information is available, it is known that Ninian took the gospel to the Picts in southwestern Scotland at the end of the fourth century. He established a famous monastery church at Whithorn and ministered among the people in this remote area. The Welsh were evangelized in the sixth century by a shadowy ascetic named Dewi, or St. David, who founded a dozen monasteries. When in the eleventh century the Welsh asserted their independence from the English church, they made the bold but unlikely claim that David had been made "archbishop of the whole British race" by the patriarch of Jerusalem.

It is uncertain when Christianity first reached the Emerald Isle, but an early chronicle reports that an individual named Palladius was sent from Rome in 431 to be the bishop of "the Irish believing in Christ." However, the real credit for the evangelization of Ireland is given to Patrick (c. 389–c. 461). All that is definitely known of him comes from his two surviving writings: *The Confessions* and *A Letter to the Soldiers of Coroticus*. The later biographies of Patrick were embellished with many fanciful legends and miracle stories.

From a Christian family in Britain, Patrick was captured at sixteen by raiders and taken to Ireland as a slave. After spending six years as a shepherd, he escaped and returned to his family. Soon after he received a vision in which he heard the voice of the Irish crying out to him: "We ask thee, boy, come and walk among us once more." In response he studied at a monastery in Gaul and then went to Ireland. He arrived around 432, already consecrated as a bishop, and spent the next thirty years there. He preached, founded numerous churches and monasteries, and even won some members of the family of the High King at Tara. In 444 he established his cathedral at Armagh, which became the educational and administrative center of the Irish church.

The unique feature about the church founded by Patrick was that it was based upon monasticism rather than diocesan organization and cathedral clergy. This structure resulted from the peculiar situation of Irish society, as the land was divided between 80 and 100 unstable clans (kingdoms) and possessed virtually no towns. In such a fluid situation it was impossible to establish regular dioceses. The

Celtic Cross in Front of an Irish Round Tower

monasteries, endowed with lands and herds, were usually controlled by abbots appointed by local chieftains (kings). Another reason for the monastic emphasis was the ability of monks to fill the place in Irish society formerly occupied by the magicians (druids) and poets, who had performed the function of priests and scholars. In the preliterate pagan society these individuals had memorized the laws, genealogies, and legends that enabled the preservation of the records of these kingdoms and the "historical" basis for their separate existence.

Thus, the monks assumed the role of the existing elites and were able to win the population to Christ. They were also noted for their asceticism and dedication to the simple lifestyle. At the same time, however, they had a great enthusiasm for scholarship, which may had been encouraged by continental scholars who had fled before the Germanic invasions. The best Latin in Europe was taught in the monastic schools during this period, and the Irish were especially skilled at teaching Latin as a foreign language because they had never been part of the Roman Empire and partaken of its culture. This was to give them a advantage when they engaged in evangelism among the Germanic peoples. Since the tradition of itinerancy remained strong among the Irish monks, they were able to carry out effective missionary work. Ireland essentially was the center of literary and artistic culture in the West, surviving evidences of which include the ornately illustrated *Book of Kells* and *Lindisfarne Gospels* (early eighth century) and the exquisitely sculptured Celtic crosses found on the island.

Augustine of Canterbury

The greatest pope of the early Middle Ages, Gregory I, was strongly committed to renewal of the church in the West. He was particularly interested in the extension of Christianity to Anglo-Saxon England. The legend is that, while he was still a monk, he saw some English boys offered for sale on the Roman slave market. He asked, "Who are they?" and the response was, "Angles." Gregory then said, "They are not Angles but angels." Whatever the case may be, he had in fact carefully planned the mission to Britain.

In 596 he dispatched a team of forty monks under the leadership of Augustine, the prior of an important monastery in Rome. They arrived the following year at the court of King Aethelberht (Ethelbert) of Kent, a leading figure among the twelve Anglo-Saxon rulers of Britain. Since his queen Bertha (daughter of the Frankish king) was already a Christian, Augustine was able to persuade him to receive Christ, and he was baptized in 603. As King Aethelberht's capital was at Canterbury, he offered Augustine, who now had been made archbishop by Gregory, a palace to use as his episcopal seat. This is why the center of English Christianity came to be located here rather than in the larger city of London. Gregory also advised Augustine to adapt pagan practices to the Christian context rather than condemn them outright, and through this means he won the Anglo-Saxons to Christ.

A long and confusing period of struggle among the various Anglo-Saxon kings followed. The problem was that although the new rulers who had come from Germany were pagans, a kind of grassroots Christianity persisted among the Celtic Britons, and this was reinforced by Irish missionaries who were starting to come to Britain. At the same time, the two-century separation between the Celts and Rome had led to the development of differences in discipline and practice between their expressions of the Christian faith. Augustine tried vainly to reconcile the two, and this remained a decisive issue in English religion during the seventh century. Some of the kings even contemptuously saw Christianity as the faith of their serfs and their enemies, the Celts.

The Catholic mission to Kent extended its influence northward in 625 when a daughter of Aethelberht married Edwin, king of Northumbria, the foremost Anglo-Saxon ruler. One of the Roman missionaries, Paulinus, accompanied the queen to York and began preaching to the king's followers. Edwin then summoned a council in 627 where Paulinus was allowed to discuss the merits of Christianity. He asked his advisers what they thought of the new faith, and one of them replied:

> O King, the life of man is like the flight of a swallow through our banquet hall, out of the dark and the cold for a moment through the light and warmth and into the cold and dark again. A religion which can tell us more about that dark beyond certainly ought to be followed.[1]

Acting on this counsel, Edwin decided to become a Christian and was baptized at York on Easter Sunday of that year. As he was already a bishop, Paulinus established a cathedral at York, which soon became the other major center of English Christianity.

Edwin and Paulinus did much to convert the neighboring regions of Lincolnshire and East Anglia to Roman Christianity. After Edwin's death in 633, however, leadership passed to another branch of the Northumbrian royal house, the one headed by Oswald. The latter had been baptized in the Celtic church, and upon assuming power he turned to the Irish monks who replaced Paulinus and his co-workers. One result of the changes was that Oswald gave the Irish monk Aidan the island of Lindisfarne for a new monastery, and this functioned as the center of Celtic Christianity in Northumbria.

The differences that had arisen between the Celts and Romans (Catholics) were difficult to reconcile and prevented the establishment of a common front for converting the pagans in Britain. For example, the Celts often had a single bishop ordain a new one, whereas the Romans required the presence of at least three bishops at an episcopal consecration.

Another difference was over the "tonsure" of the priests, that is, how their hair was to be cut and head shaved. The Celts removed all the hair from the ears upward and left a small tuft on top like a halo, while the Romans shaved the top and left a little rim around the ears like a crown of thorns.

A third dispute was over the date of Easter. The Irish followed an old and faulty calendar, whereas the Romans had worked out the date more precisely. Thus, in 664 the Celts celebrated Easter on April 14 and the Romans on April 21. The Synod of Whitby (664) settled the issue of the Easter date, and its decision was gradually accepted by the various Celtic churches. This paved the way for the uniting of the two factions and resolved the most serious problem in the early history of the British church.

Celtic Missions

A remarkable feature of Celtic Christianity was its fervent missionary zeal, which resulted in the founding of monasteries in the sixth and seventh centuries in Scotland, England, Belgium, northern Germany, France, and even Italy.

Among the foremost figures in the movement was Columba (521–97). Although a devout monk, he was a pugnacious individual who seemed to be constantly involved in conflicts. His fellow monks finally exiled him from Ireland and ordered him to atone for his deeds by winning an equal number of souls for Christ as those whose deaths he had caused. At the age of forty-two he sailed with twelve companions for the lonely island of Iona off the west coast of Scotland, where he lived austerely in a tiny hut within his monastery and showed great compassion for the poor and needy. He spent the next thirty-four years evangelizing the neighboring islands and the Scottish mainland. One convert was Brude, the king of the Picts.

Columbanus (c. 540–615) was an Irish cleric with a great passion for learning, who in 590 left to pursue missionary work on the European continent. He established monasteries in various parts of France, most notably Luxeuil, which for a time was the premier foundation in the land. When the monks got into difficulties with the Burgundian ruler in 612, they moved into northern Italy, where in the midst of the Arian Lombards Columbanus founded his most famous monastery, Bobbio. One of his co-workers, Gall (c. 550–645), labored in Switzerland and opened a small abbey. It later became the Benedictine monastery of St. Gallen, which is known to this day for its magnificent library.

Columbanus's variety of monasticism was extremely intense, with food, clothing, sleep, and personal comfort severely restricted. The monks conducted eight services every day, and they sang through the Psalms almost continuously. A monk who failed to respond with an "Amen" was corrected with six blows, and one who told idle tales could receive fifty blows. The rigor of the Rule of Columbanus eventually gave way to the more moderate Benedictine pattern.

The prestige of Irish asceticism, the monks' reputation for holiness (it was said they were "drunk with God as with wine"), and the emphasis on biblical studies attracted many visitors to these foundations. Ireland now provided the spiritual facilities once offered by the desert monasteries and ascetic teachers of Egypt and Palestine, access to which now had been cut off by the Arab conquest. More than two hundred Franco-Irish monasteries were known to have been founded in the seventh century, and from them flowed numerous missionary ventures.

One was that of Amandus of Aquitaine (c. 584–675) who ministered first among the Basques and Danubian Slavs and then became bishop of Maastricht. He is remembered as the "Apostle of Belgium" for his forty years of work among the Flemish peoples.

The Anglo-Saxon Continental Missions

By the early eighth century Christian culture had become so firmly rooted in Britain that the English began to replace the Irish as missionaries to Europe. One leader in this work was Willibrord (658–739) from Northumbria. In 690 he and a group of companions journeyed to Frisia and began a work in the ruined Roman fort of Utrecht. They were supported in this venture by the Frankish rulers who wished to extend their authority over the area.

Willibrord's heir in the Frisian mission was another Anglo-Saxon monk, Wynfrith (680–754), known to posterity as Boniface. The future "Apostle of Germany" was born in Devon and educated at a Benedictine monastery in England. After working for three years with Willibrord in Frisia, Boniface moved south and organized churches in Hesse, Thuringia, Franconia, and Bavaria. On a visit to Rome in 722 he was consecrated bishop-at-large for Germany by Pope Gregory II. Then he returned to his field of labor and performed what was one of the more touching legendary exploits of the early Middle Ages. At Geismar (near Fritzlar) was a huge oak tree that the Hessians held as sacred to their god Thor. Boniface told them that he would chop it down to prove that Thor was no god and demonstrate the superiority of the Christian God. As a storm gathered, the trembling onlookers expected to see Boniface struck dead with lightning. But just as the axe hit the tree, a sudden gust of wind tore it into four parts, which he then split into boards and used to build a chapel dedicated to St. Peter.

In the following years Boniface divided the German territories into dioceses and founded Benedictine-style monasteries, the most important of which was at Fulda. He also set up schools that trained both priests and laypeople, which served as missionary centers and places of learning. He inspired many in England to join him in missionary and monastic endeavors, one of whom was a woman, Lioba. She became abbess of the Tauberbischofsheim convent and was celebrated for her knowledge not only of the Scriptures but also of canon law and church history.

Unlike the Celtic missionaries, Boniface was not a rugged individualist but rather a statesman, organizer, and above all a servant of the papacy. More than anyone else, he was responsible for building the medieval German church. With the help of Anglo-Saxon monks and nuns he destroyed the last strongholds of German paganism and founded abbeys and bishoprics in their place. Since Germany east of the Rhine was still a land without towns, the bishops' seats became the new centers of urban life.

In addition to his work among the pagan Germans, Boniface was the reformer of the Frankish church. The decadent Merovingian dynasty had yielded the substance of its power to the Mayors of the Palace, who in spite of their military ability did nothing to advance culture or clean up the church. One of them, Charles Martel, confiscated church property and used the abbeys and bishoprics to reward his friends. Boniface condemned this corruption in a letter to the pope:

> All their crimes do not prevent their attaining the priesthood; at last rising in rank as they increase in sin they become bishops, and those of them who can boast that they are not adulterers or fornicators, are drunkards, given up to the chase, and soldiers, who do not shrink from shedding Christian blood.

However, in a series of councils where he acted on behalf of the pope, he succeeded in bringing about the reorganization of the Frankish church under metropolitan bishops responsible to Rome.

Now weary of ecclesiastical politics, Boniface returned to the mission field seeking martyrdom. Soon he found the death for which he longed, as he and a band of followers were massacred by pagan Frisians at Dokkum (Holland). In accordance with his wishes he was laid to rest under the altar at Fulda, where his relics remain to this day.

The Irish and English monks had made western Europe a Christian land by converting the humble peasant folk to their faith. The

Boniface, "Apostle to the Germans"

work of Boniface in particular affected the development of the Catholic church, because his missionary labors brought a great part of the Germanic peoples into the framework of a Christian Europe, while his activities in Gaul created closer ties than had ever existed before between the Frankish church and the papacy.

THE VIKING INVASIONS

The Vikings (also known as Norsemen or Northmen) were a seafaring folk from Scandinavia who were ethnically and linguistically related to the Germans. Between the late eighth and the early eleventh centuries they traded with and attacked Europeans from Spain to Russia, with their most destructive activities occurring in the British Isles and France. They also engaged in peaceful settlement in the North Atlantic islands, Iceland, Greenland, and briefly North America.

There is much historical debate as to why the Vikings carried out their raids and how the small, poor, and remote Scandinavian countries could send forth so many warrior-seamen. Explanations include a population explosion, pressures of Slavic expansion from the southeast, climatic changes, and advances in shipbuilding and navigational technology. This era of migration also coincided with the time when orderly government was being established in Scandinavia, and many hitherto independent groups were gradually being unified under the kings of Denmark, Norway, and Sweden. Perhaps as internal stability was achieved, the more aggressive and violent individuals went to other places. Although all three peoples participated in the journeys, only those from Norway and Denmark operated in Western Europe. The Swedes, who ruled the Baltic Sea, penetrated the Slavic lands of eastern Europe.

The Vikings may have first been greeted as traders, but the populations of the British Isles and France soon discovered that they preferred piracy to peace. Their raids terrified the residents of coastal and riverbank communities, and if we may judge from their names and deeds, their ferocity was unbounded. Such men as Erik Bloodaxe, Harald Bluetooth, and Thorkill the Skullsplitter made a business of war, worked themselves into frenzies, howled like wolves, and gnashed their teeth on their iron swords. Many prayed with the people of France, "From the fury of the Northmen, O Lord deliver us."

In 795 the Vikings began almost incessant hit-and-run attacks in Ireland, but in the 830s they started settling along the coast. Their ports later developed into towns like Dublin, Limerick, Cork, and Waterford. Further invasions followed, and the resulting hardships were such that a contemporary Irish chronicle lamented:

> If a hundred heads of hardened iron could grow on one neck, and if each head possessed a hundred sharp indestructible tongues of tempered metal, and if each tongue cried out incessantly with a hundred ineradicable loud voices, they would never be able to enumerate the griefs which the people of Ireland—men and women, laymen and priests, young and old—have suffered at the hands of these warlike, ruthless, pagans.[2]

The famous Irish round towers, defensive fortifications to which the local folk retreated when Viking attackers appeared, date to this period. However, by 1000 the threat had subsided as the Vikings now had intermarried with the native Irish and accepted Christianity.

In England the first Viking raids occurred in the late eighth century. The "Holy Island" of Lindisfarne was assaulted in 793, and one report declared that the monastery's church sanctuary was "spattered with the blood of the priests of God, and despoiled of all its ornaments." Bede's monastery at Jarrow was burned and the structures on the island of Iona repeatedly ransacked. From the Vikings' standpoint, plundering churches and monasteries made good sense. They were easily accessible and wealthy establishments that contained rich treasures like gold reliquaries, jewel-encrusted book covers, and liturgical ornaments.

In 865 a Danish force led by the sons of Ragnor Lodbrok conquered Mercia and Northumbria. However, they were unable to subdue Wessex, which was ruled by the forceful King Alfred the Great, a distinguished scholar as well as competent warrior. They concluded a peace treaty with him in 878, and the Danish leader, Guthrum, consented to be baptized and leave the area. In effect, the land was divided between the Saxons and Danes, and the Viking territory was henceforth called the Danelaw. Considerable Danish immigration into the area followed, and the newcomers gradually became Christians. A second Viking wave occurred between 980 and 1035, and from 1016 to 1035 a Danish king, Cnut (Knute), occupied the English throne. The leader of a mighty Scandinavian empire, King of Denmark (1019) and Norway (1028), Cnut also was a fervent Christian who even invited missionaries to evangelize his native land.

In the ninth century both Norwegian and Danish Vikings raided French cities along the Seine and Loire rivers, like Rouen, Nantes, and Paris, and later Bordeaux and Toulouse as well. Instead of returning home for the winter as they customarily did, the Vikings began settling in France and intensifying their operations. Then, in 911 Charles the Simple, king of the West Franks, made a deal with Rollo, the Viking leader. The Northmen would be given a large tract of land along the coast, and Rollo would receive baptism and be married to a French princess. His followers accordingly became Christians and took up residence in the promised territory that was called Normandy. Now known as Normans, they still retained their Viking energies, and in the next two centuries they were to invade England and overthrow the Anglo-Saxon monarchy, establish kingdoms in southern Italy and Sicily, and play an important part in the Crusades.

While the Vikings were terrorizing Europe, the first effort to win them was made by the monk Ansgar (801–65). He preached in Denmark and Sweden with little success, but then he became archbishop of Bremen where he had an effective ministry and laid the groundwork for the eventual conversion of Scandinavia. His successors in northern Germany carried on the work of evangelizing the area called Saxony with the aid of missionaries from England, while at the same time regarding themselves as archbishops of the entire region. Still, only in the twelfth century were regular Scandinavian dioceses finally created.

In the last half of the tenth and first half of the eleventh century, three leading kings—Harald Bluetooth of Denmark, Olaf Trygvesson of Norway, and Olaf the Taxgatherer of Sweden—formally made Christianity the official religion of their domains. The reason for renouncing paganism was as much political as religious, as they saw church organization as useful for maintaining an orderly state.

Yet, in Sweden Christianity was slow in taking root, and a struggle between the old and new faiths continued through the eleventh century. One chronicler, Adam of Bremen, left a lurid account of human sacrifices that were a central part of the pagan cult in the shrine at Uppsala: "Dogs and horses may be seen hanging close by human beings. A Christian told me he had seen seventy-two bodies hanging together." Nevertheless the gospel prevailed, and by 1100 the temple had been torn down and a bishopric established there.

Meanwhile, the Norwegian immigrant population in Iceland had been won to Christ after a volcanic eruption had frightened their pagan leaders. The first bishop was seated there in 1056. The conversion of Finland came somewhat later, when the Swedish king took over the territory in the late twelfth century. However, it required another hundred years to win over the entire population to the new faith. Thus, in the Viking states, the final acceptance of Christianity was achieved by the ruling dynasties and within a relatively short time period.

One aspect of the Viking expansion that proved to be much less violent was the movement of the Swedish people known as the Varangians into eastern Europe. Utilizing the river systems, they developed trading links that went all the way to the Black Sea. In the ninth century they established themselves in Novgorod, and soon after one of their leaders, Oleg (879–912), located his capital at Kiev on the Dnieper River. They were also known as the Rus and ruled over the Slavs living in the area.

The growth of commercial and military contacts with Constantinople opened Kievan Rus to increasing Byzantine cultural influence. Some missionary work occurred as early as the 860s, but a definite conversion of the dynasty and the establishment of Orthodox Christianity occurred only a century later. The first member of the ruling family to be converted was Olga in 957. Then in 988 the Kievan ruler Vladimir I, after considering Judaism, Islam, and Western Catholic Christianity, decided to adopt the Eastern Orthodox faith. It was said that his messengers were so overwhelmed with the magnificence of St. Sophia Church in Constantinople that they reported back, "We know not whether we were in heaven or on earth. For on earth there is no such splendor or such beauty, and we are at a loss to describe it."

As part of the agreement with the Emperor Basil II, Vladimir was to receive Basil's daughter Anna in marriage, regardless of the fact that he was known to be a monster of vice, perversion, and cruelty and that he already had several wives and more than 800 concubines. Despite this lack of saintliness, Vladimir was later canonized by the Eastern church and called "equal to the apostles" for his work in converting the Kievan domains. Soon there was a Russian church, organized on the Byzantine model, utilizing Byzantine-style buildings, and acknowledging the Patriarch of Constantinople as its supreme head.

Christianity in Central and Eastern Europe

The area east of Germany and the Adriatic Sea was populated by a rich assortment of peoples, mostly Slavs who had migrated westward and southward and various nomadic groups (Avars, Bulgars, and Magyars) who had moved in from Asia. The Slavs were divided into three linguistic groupings: western (Czechs, Moravians, Slovaks, Poles, Wends); southern (Slovenes, Croats, Serbs, Macedonians); and eastern (Russians, Byelorussians, Ukrainians, Ruthenians). The diffusion of Christianity among these peoples was complicated by rivalry among German, papal, and Byzantine interests.

The most important early missionaries to the Slavs were two brothers, Cyril (or Constantine) and Methodius, whom the Byzantine emperor sent to Moravia in 863. Rather than use Latin as Western missionaries did, they invented a Slavonic alphabet and translated the gospels into it. From the original script, known as Glagolitic, evolved the Cyrillic alphabet. This used Greek characters and became the written language of Serbia, Bulgaria, and Russia. After winning a number of converts, the brothers went on to create a Slavonic liturgy. In 867 they journeyed to Rome and secured the pope's approval for this innovation. In spite of the increasing tensions between Rome and Constantinople they succeeded in remaining loyal to both centers of the church, and the pope even backed Methodius in a petty jurisdictional dispute with the German archbishop of Salzburg who resented the missionary work Methodius was conducting in Slovenia.

Germans themselves carried the gospel to Poland, Bohemia, and Hungary during the tenth and early eleventh centuries. In 968 an archbishopric was created at Magdeburg that had no fixed eastern boundary. The intention was that it would serve as the center for spreading the gospel to the Slavs who lived east of the Elbe River. The most spectacular achievement was in Poland, where the ruler Mieszko (960–92) accepted Christianity. Unwilling either to allow the jurisdiction of the German see of Magdeburg over his church or to come under Byzantine influence, he turned to Rome for help. In 990 he put his lands under the direct protection of the pope, who in turn allowed the creation of a separate Polish bishopric at Gnieszno.

Regensburg in Bavaria was the principal center for missionary work in Bohemia. The first ruler of Bohemia accepted Christianity in 894 and the faith deepened its roots under the legendary godly King Wenceslas (Vaclav) who reigned in the 920s. He had been reared by his devout Christian grandmother Ludmilla, who had struggled against pagan influence. She was strangled by her enemies, thus making her the first Czech martyr. Then Wenceslas was murdered, and he also came to be regarded as a martyr and national symbol. A diocese was established at Prague that was first occupied by Germans, but in 982 Adalbert became the first Czech bishop. For a time both Latin and Slavonic expressions of Christianity coexisted in Bohemia, but when the final break between the Eastern and Western churches came, this was no longer possible. In 1096 the Slavonic liturgy was forbidden there.

About the same time Christianity found its way to Hungary. The Magyars, a Finno-Ugric people from Asia, had moved into the central Danube and for a century raided western Europe. Finally stopped by German forces at Lechfeld in 955, they settled down in the Hungarian plains. German missionaries from Regensburg and Salzburg then worked in the region, and their king, Stephen, decided to become a Christian. In 1000 he accepted a royal crown from the pope and organized a Hungarian church structure that was dependent on Rome.

Although pagan resistance continued, by 1100 nearly all the people in Poland, Bohemia, and Hungary were Catholic Christians. Only the Balts, the non-Slavic peoples located in the north between Poland and Russia, had not been reached with the gospel. The evangelization of these areas—Prussia, Latvia, Estonia, and Lithuania—would take place in the thirteenth and fourteenth centuries.

The South Slavs were converted by cooperative missionary efforts between Rome and Constantinople. Soon, however, the territory

Missions to Scandinavia and Eastern Europe

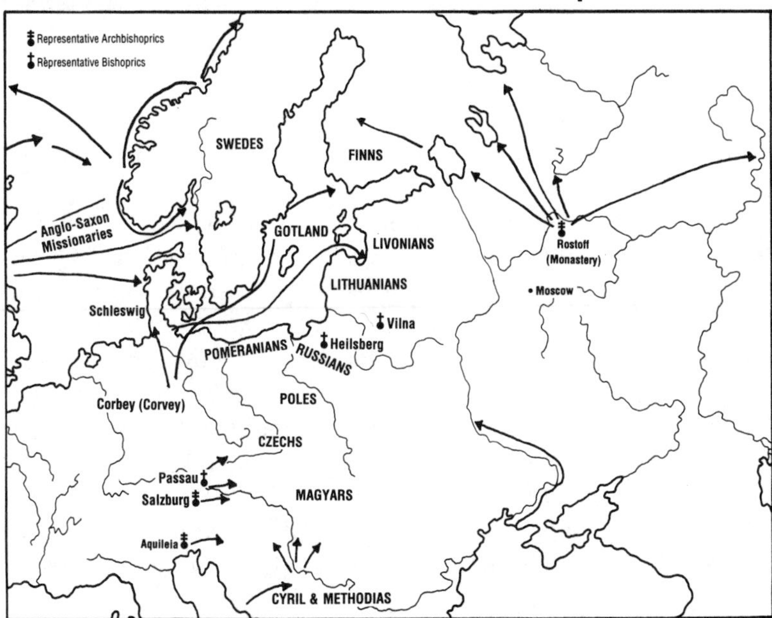

became the scene of bitter rivalry between the popes and patriarchs. The Croats who settled along the Dalmatian coast and the Slovenes who lived farther north accepted Roman Catholicism, but the Serbs and Macedonians in the central Balkans became Greek Orthodox. In Bulgaria, where a Turkic people had migrated from Asia during the 670s and gradually mixed in with the existing Slavic population, even to the point of adopting their language, both the Eastern and Western churches competed in the effort to introduce Christianity. In 864 the Bulgar ruler Boris opted for Orthodoxy and ordered his people baptized. Then, fearful of Byzantine power, he turned toward Rome but soon changed his mind and established Orthodoxy in his domains. The Romanians, who lived north of the Danube and were under Bulgarian influence, also became Orthodox.

The changes of the ninth and tenth centuries in eastern Europe had enduring results. The Poles, Bohemians, Hungarians, and Croats adopted Western or Latin Christianity, while the Serbs, Bulgarians, and Russians accepted Eastern Orthodoxy. The religious loyalties developed in this period were to affect the politics and culture of the region down to the present.

THE RISE OF ISLAM

The most dramatic and far-reaching phenomenon that affected the entire Mediterranean basin from the demise of Rome to the discovery of America was the emergence of Islam and the formation of the Arab empire. This new faith arose out of the life and work of Muhammad (Mohammed). He was born in 570 into the Quraysh tribe, the leading merchant clan in Mecca, a commercial city in the Hejaz area of western Arabia. It was also a religious cult center that, among other things, contained a black stone later alleged as given by the angel Gabriel to Abraham and housed in a cube-shaped structure called the *Kaaba.* As a young man Muhammad managed camel caravans and eventually married his employer, a rich widow. According to Muslim belief, at age forty Muhammad received a vision or revelation, in which Gabriel spoke to him. It is said that although he initially had doubts, he continued to have revelations throughout his later life.

As a result of his experiences, Muhammad began preaching an uncompromising monotheism, a belief in the one indivisible, almighty God (*Allah* is the Arabic word for God). This was the religion of "submission" (*Islam*) to the will of God, and individuals who practiced the faith were called *Muslims,* those who submitted. The creed was a simple one: "There is no God but Allah, and Muhammad is his prophet." This affirmation was the first and most important of the "five pillars," or foundations, of Islam. The others were concerned with religious observance and included the requirement to pray five times each day at specified times, fast during daylight hours in Ramadan (the ninth month in the lunar calendar), give a proportion of one's income to help the poor, and if at all possible make a pilgrimage to Mecca at least once during one's lifetime. Other duties included abstinence from pork and wine, and taking part in the *Jihad,* the "holy struggle" for the faith.

Muhammad's preaching attracted a growing number of followers, which alarmed the leaders of Mecca. They saw his doctrine as a threat to their economic well-being because of the city's position as a cult center where the neighboring polytheistic tribes came to trade and settle their persistent feuds. Hearing of a plot against his life, Muhammad and his followers left Mecca in 622 and settled in Medina, an event known as the *Hijra* ("Flight"). From this is dated the first year of the Muslim calendar. In his new home Muhammad won many converts. He became their civil leader as well because to submit to Allah also meant to obey his prophet. A brilliant military organizer and tactician, he attacked the caravans of Mecca, and in 630 the city capitulated and accepted his religious reforms. By the time of his death in 632 the warring Arabian tribes had accepted Islam and united under his rule.

Although Muhammad left no plans for a succession, his followers chose the capable Abu Bakr (632–34) as *caliph* ("successor"), that is, the civil and religious leader of the Muslim community. Under his direction Arab forces swept into the Middle East and assaulted the moribund Byzantine establishment. He was followed by Umar (634–44) and Uthman (644–56), the first caliph from the great Umayyad family.

In 656 Uthman collected all the sayings of the prophet into a book called the *Qu'ran* ("recitation"). Although there were many other prophets, including Abraham, Moses, and Jesus, who received revelations from Allah, Muhammad is accorded special honor because his was the final and purest statement of the "truth." (Although Muslims regard him as the "messenger" or "prophet" who conveyed Allah's message to humankind, they do not believe he was a god nor do they worship him.) The Qu'ran is divided into 114 chapters, called *Suras,* and includes both prayers and speeches. Since devout Muslims felt it should be studied only in Arabic, this ensured that the Arabic language and culture would predominate. The *Hadith* records the traditions of the prophet, and the *Ijma* consists of the body of law that Muslims should follow. These three religious sources together constitute the *Sunna* or "Path."

Within two decades, the forces of the first three caliphs overran Palestine, Syria, Mesopotamia, Persia, Egypt, and much of North Africa. Then in 656 Uthman was killed and was succeeded by Ali, a cousin and son-in-law of Muhammad, who in turn was assassinated in 661. After this the Umayyads returned to power and created a hereditary dynasty with its capital at Damascus. The majority of Muslims, the Sunnis, followed the Umayyad caliphs, but the adherents of Ali formed dissident groups that persist to the present as the Shi'ite sects.

The Umayyad empire was now an urban kingdom ruled by Arabs, which relied heavily on former Byzantine administrators. They continued the process of expansion, and their empire soon reached from India to Morocco. In 711 the Moors (Islamicized Berbers) crossed the Strait of Gibraltar and conquered Visigothic Spain. They swept north into France, but the Muslim tide finally was halted by

Charles Martel at the battle of Tours in 733. Umayyad forces also threatened Constantinople, but they could not destroy the Byzantine Empire and the two entities settled down into an uneasy coexistence.

During the middle of the eighth century, rebellions broke out against the Umayyads, partly inspired by Shi'ites, and in 750 a new dynasty, the Abbasids, seized control of the caliphate. A few years later they transferred the capital to Baghdad. Islam became more cosmopolitan under their rule, as exemplified by the learning and splendor of the court of Harun al-Rashid (786–809), the most famous of these caliphs. In the tenth century the caliphate's political unity declined as various provinces broke away, but Muslim civilization continued to flourish. Their world was held together by the common religion, Islam, and the common language of government and learning, Arabic, while a network of commercial relations stretched from Spain to India. Thus, Baghdad remained the cultural center of the Muslim world long after its political supremacy had ended.

The importance of Islam for the history of Christianity cannot be overemphasized. As historian Henri Pirenne observed, "without Mohammed Charlemagne would have been inconceivable." The Muslim attacks not only weakened the Byzantine Empire but also opened the way for the creation of the Carolingian Empire in Europe. Their capture of the ancient Christian centers of Jerusalem, Antioch, Alexandria, and Carthage left only Constantinople and Rome to contend for preeminence in the Christian world. It was this situation that enabled the development of a separate medieval Christendom in the West under Charlemagne and his successors.

After disrupting the Roman Empire in the fifth century, the various Germanic tribes eventually converted to Catholic Christianity. In the British Isles the differences between the older Celtic and newer Roman faiths were resolved. Missionaries from this area played a key role in evangelizing Gaul and Germany, bringing these lands under more direct papal control. Fierce Vikings were gradually won to the Christian faith, while the Catholic and Byzantine missionaries reached various Slavic groups in central and eastern Europe, thus creating loyalties that affected political allegiances down to the present. While Christianity was expanding in the North, it was eclipsed in its ancient homeland in the East by the astonishing spread of Islam, which in less than a century reached from the Atlantic Ocean to the Indus River.

6

THE CHURCH UNDER PAPAL MONARCHY

The period from 600 to 1000 has often been called the "The Dark Ages," the time when the Western Roman Empire was replaced by barbarian kingdoms and Europe was battered by attacks from Vikings, Magyars, and Muslims. However, at the turn of the ninth century Charlemagne temporarily unified much of Europe, and the papacy enlisted the aid of the Frankish rulers against the Lombards in Italy. While the Eastern Roman Empire was preoccupied in responding to the Muslim and Bulgar challenges, a new empire was thus formed in the West. Although at first the revived empire amounted to little, eventually it and the papacy became locked in a bitter struggle for the control of Europe.

THE DEVELOPMENT OF THE PAPACY

It was mentioned earlier that, as the political power of Rome declined, the position of the Roman bishop grew in significance. Thus, Siricius (384–99) was the first bishop to use the label *papa* or "pope," and Leo I, "the Great" (440–61), adopted the title *pontifex maximus.* In ancient Rome this designated the priest of Neptune who was in charge of religious affairs. Leo also asserted Rome's primacy over the other churches, declaring that "to deny the pope is to deny Peter; to deny Peter is to deny Christ." Gelasius (492–96), who called himself the "Vicar of Christ," claimed the right to ratify the actions of church councils and to exercise political authority.

The campaigns of Justinian to reconquer lands in Italy resulted in terrible devastation. Rome itself changed hands three times in the battles between the Byzantines and the Ostrogoths. Then the Lombards invaded Italy and settled in the Po River valley in the north. They also established duchies elsewhere in the peninsula, thereby isolating the Byzantine territories around Ravenna from those in the south and, for all practical purposes, cutting Rome off from western Europe.

This was the situation that confronted Gregory I, "the Great" (c. 540–604), who was the founder of the medieval papacy. Reared in a pious and aristocratic Roman family, Gregory studied law and eventually was appointed prefect of Rome. The duties of this position included presiding over the Senate and administering the charities and defense of the city. After his father's death, he resigned from his worldly duties, became a monk, and established seven monasteries on his family's properties. He soon had to give up the contemplative life, as the pope sent him to Constantinople in 579 on a futile quest for Byzantine aid against the Lombards. Seven years later he returned to Rome to help the pope in overseeing the church, and in 590 he was elected pontiff himself.

Gregory's activities set important precedents for later popes and for the medieval church as a whole. Although a humble and godly man, he became heavily involved in secular affairs and assumed the role in Italy previously exercised by the Eastern emperor and his representative in Ravenna. The emperor's inability to deal with the Lombard problem necessitated this. Gregory used the income from the papal lands to deal with the Lombards as well as provide government services for the city of Rome and care for the poor. Because it was the pope rather than the civil authorities who undertook these duties, the papacy ended up ruling central Italy.

Gregory strengthened the position of the papacy through his relations with both the eastern and western parts of the Roman world. By the sixth century these two sections of the empire had drifted apart. In the East there was still an emperor, but he was increasingly concerned with problems in his own realm, while in the West a series of Germanic successor states now exercised political control.

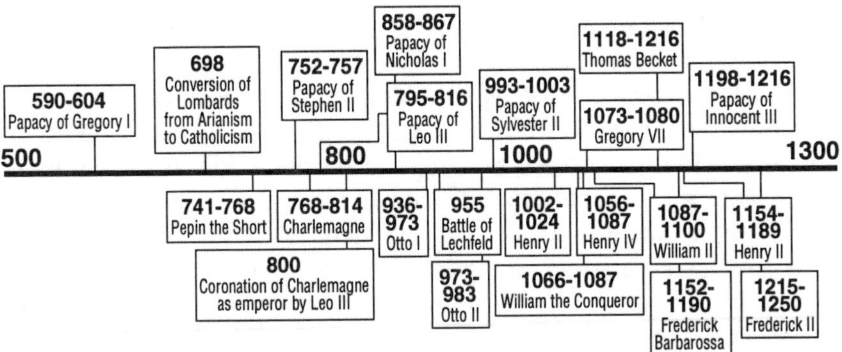

Gregory recognized the rights of the Eastern patriarchs, but at the same time he asserted papal supremacy over the entire church, East and West.

In the West he led the way in missionary activity among the pagans by sending Augustine and his company of monks to preach to the Anglo-Saxons in England. He also established ties with the independent Frankish church and promoted a reform program that attempted to modify its tradition of lay control. In Spain he encouraged the conversion of the Visigoths from Arianism to Catholic orthodoxy and was able to install his friend Leander as bishop of Seville.

Gregory was not only an able administrator, devout monk, and moral leader, but also an influential writer who communicated Christian truth in a concrete way to the unlearned people of early medieval times. His thought, although not original, was expressed in suitable terms for his own and the succeeding generations. This made him an important link between the wisdom and piety of the early church and medieval Christianity. He clarified the doctrine of purgatory and fostered the veneration of relics and the use of images. His ideas were developed in various works, including his letters, dialogues, and an exposition of the book of Job, sermons on Ezekiel and the gospels, and a guide for bishops called the *Pastoral Rule.*

Especially important is *The Four Books of Dialogues on the Life and Miracles of the Saints and on the Immortality of Souls,* which Gregory wrote in 594. They are a series of conversations between the author and a Roman church official. The first three describe the holiness and miraculous aspects of the lives of several sixth-century religious leaders. Gregory states that miracles were not limited to biblical times but were still being performed in response to the prayers and faith of God's people. The last book presents his views on eschatology and is the chief source of the teaching of purgatory for the medieval church. Through his vivid portrayals of heaven and hell, Gregory comforted those who were suffering persecution at the hands of the barbarian forces. The faithful enter heaven immediately after death, but the others who are not prepared to be with God go to purgatory. He then showed how regular participation in the sacrifice of the Mass helps people to pass through purgatory more quickly.

In the exposition of Job, Gregory dealt with this Old Testament book from three aspects: its historical or literal meaning, allegorical significance, and moral implications. The historical treatment would not be considered adequate by modern standards, because he did not know either Hebrew or Greek. Furthermore he showed little acquaintance with Eastern history or culture even though he lived in Constantinople for several years. The allegorical section is of more value, as it contains a system of theology that Gregory read between the lines of the biblical book. The names of persons, places, and things were infused with Christian meanings. For example, Job represents Christ; his wife the sinful human nature; his seven sons the apostles, and hence the clergy; his three daughters the three classes of the faithful laity who are to worship the Trinity; his friends the heretics; and the three thousand camels the heathen and Samaritans. The exposition ends with a summary of Christian ethics.

Gregory's forty sermons on the gospels illustrate the importance of preaching in his time and are made more graphic by the use of vivid illustrations. Many of the exhortations reflected his belief that the end of the world was near. Everywhere he looked he saw signs of the end, such as plagues, barbarian invasions, and the physical decay of the old Roman world. He felt an urgency to warn his listeners of death and to explain to them the danger of hell and the bliss of heaven, thus preparing them for the day of judgment.

His most important work was the *Pastoral Rule,* which was written to guide bishops and served as the standard manual for pastoral theology during the Middle Ages. It describes the sort of person who should be a church leader in terms of his conduct and attitudes toward teaching, and warns of the temptations involved in leadership. Gregory demands celibacy of the clergy and insists that a pastor must be a capable speaker. He urges his readers to teach by example and precept, and insists that a spiritual leader combine compassion with meditation.

Gregory modeled in his own life the counsel that he gave to others. If a beggar died on the streets of Rome, he felt personally responsible, and he gave vast sums to prevent this from occurring.

He did his duty both as a Christian and a Roman gentleman, and he justly deserves his reputation as one of the four great fathers of the Western church, together with Ambrose, Augustine, and Jerome.

The seventh and eighth centuries were a crisis period for the papacy. The followers of Muhammad snatched away from the Byzantine Empire the ancient lands of the eastern Mediterranean and North Africa and pressed in upon Visigothic Spain. At the other end of the European world, the British Isles became a vital center of Christian culture while the new orders of monks spread Christianity north of the Alps. The popes were torn between identifying with the old civilization of the East and the new powers of the North.

Various developments caused relations with the Byzantines to sour. These included a dispute over the use of icons in the church, the emperor's high-handed actions in transferring control over certain dioceses in Illyria and southern Italy from the pope to the patriarch of Constantinople, and the inability of the Byzantines to provide any effective help in dealing with the Lombard problem. This Germanic people, who in 698 had converted from Arianism to Catholicism, rejected papal authority and continued trying to extend its power throughout Italy. The papal response to the Lombard threat was to forge strong links with the Frankish rulers.

THE CAROLINGIANS AND THE PAPACY

Although the Merovingian descendants of Clovis were the nominal rulers of the Franks in the seventh century, the real power was held by the so-called "mayors of the palace" of Austrasia in northeastern France, Pepin I (or Pippin) and his descendants. His son, Charles, who became mayor in 714, halted the Muslim advance into western Europe and as a result of his triumph earned the title *Martel*, or "Hammer." His descendants, who took direct control over the Frankish domains, were known as the Carolingians (from the Latin *Carolus*, or "Charles").

When Charles Martel died in 741, he was succeeded by Pepin III, known as "the Short" (741–68), who was confirmed as the Frankish ruler by Pope Zacharias. After Pepin's coronation in 751 the last Merovingian was sent to a monastery. Upset because the Lombards had seized papal lands, Pope Stephen II made an unprecedented trip across the Alps to meet Pepin in 754. Dressed in sackcloth, he appealed to the Frankish king for aid in recovering these territories. He then anointed Pepin and bestowed upon him the title *patricius Romanorum*

("Patrician of the Romans"). After this, Frankish forces went to Italy and compelled the Lombards to surrender twenty-two cities including the duchy of Ravenna to the papacy. These territories formed the basis of the Papal States, which were to occupy central Italy until the nineteenth century.

When the Byzantine emperor objected, the pope defended the action by referring to a document called the "Donation of Constantine." This alleged that the Emperor Constantine had bequeathed control over the Italian territories to the bishop of Rome, and it also affirmed Rome's primacy over Antioch, Alexandria, Constantinople, Jerusalem, "as well as over all the Churches of God throughout the world." In the fifteenth century this was shown to be a forgery.

CHARLEMAGNE

The greatest of the Carolingian rulers was "Charles the Great," or Charlemagne (768–814), the major figure of the early Middle Ages. When Pepin the Short died in 768, the domains were divided between his two sons, with Charles becoming ruler of northern and southwestern France and Carloman of the southeastern and northeastern areas. However, Carloman died three years later, thus enabling Charles to claim all his father's territory and reunify the Frankish monarchy. Charlemagne was tall (well over six feet); an accomplished horseman, hunter, and swimmer; and above all a brave and tireless warrior. His armies conducted more than fifty campaigns against a variety of enemies on the borders of his realm.

In response to the pope's appeal Charlemagne in 773 defeated the Lombards and became their king. In 778 his forces crossed the Pyrenees into Spain, intending to conquer the Muslim emirate of Saragossa, but they were called back because of trouble in the north with the Saxons. During their retreat they were set upon at Roncevaux by local Basques, who killed one of Charlemagne's officers, Roland. This soon became a legendary event, which was popularized in the great medieval *Chanson de Roland* (*Song of Roland*), with the attackers transformed into Moors (Muslims) to give the incident a heroic Christian aspect.

Although failing in Spain, Charlemagne did conquer Bavaria and Austria. His most difficult task, however, was the subjugation of the fiercely pagan Saxons who lived between the Rhine and Elbe Rivers. In a series of campaigns between 772 and 804 the Saxons were forcibly converted to Christianity, a process criticized by Alcuin, who asked, "How can a man be compelled to believe what he does not believe? You may force a man to the font, but not the Faith."[1] Moreover, these Saxon converts were subjected to harsh legislation that prescribed death for even the slightest infraction of canon law, such as eating meat during Lent. Seeing the resentments these policies were causing, one Saxon leader, Widukind of Westphalia, organized a rebellion that resulted in the death of many of Charlemagne's officers. In retaliation the king ordered the beheading of 4,500 Saxon hostages.

Charlemagne's vast territories were divided into about 300 administrative districts, each under a count. The frontier areas (known as marches) were ruled by margraves. To ensure his power, he sent out pairs of *missi dominici,* which included a layman and a cleric, who traveled through his domains and exercised direct control over the counts. He also ruled by decree, issuing such notable statements of law as, "He who does not nourish the poor is their murderer."

Though Leo III (795–816) had been elected pope, some of the Roman aristocrats still opposed him and accused him of perjury and adultery. In 799 he was violently attacked by a mob, who tried to cut out his eyes and tongue. He managed to escape to the court of Charlemagne, who came to Rome to investigate the charges. Leo defended himself successfully, and his enemies were exiled. Then, on Christmas day in the year 800, as Charlemagne was kneeling in prayer during Mass at St. Peter's, the pope unexpectedly placed an imperial crown on his head and gave homage to him. The people acclaimed him "Charles Augustus crowned of God, great and pacific Emperor of the Romans, long life and victory!" According to Einhard, Charlemagne's friend and biographer, he "declared that he would not have set foot in the church . . . if he could have foreseen the design of the pope."[2]

Charlemagne now was an emperor, and from his palace at Aachen (in French, Aix-la-Chapelle) he reigned over Rome and most of the western part of the old Roman Empire. Although a warrior, he was renowned for his piety as well. He had his architects copy the Byzantine Church of San Vitale in Ravenna and created in Aachen an octagonal chapel that still stands today. There, when he was able to do so, he attended worship services several times a day. The ruler also directed his scholars to prepare sermons, which priests could memorize and deliver in the vernacular. Along with this he promoted liturgical development, especially in the area of music, and he brought in people from the famous School of Singers (founded by

Gregory the Great in Rome) to help in the liturgical reforms. From this followed a process of musical development that over the passage of time resulted in the Gregorian chant, the principal form of church music in the Middle Ages.

Because of his intense desire to elevate the spiritual level of his subjects, Charlemagne promoted reforming churches and monasteries. An important figure in this monastic reform was Benedict of Aniane (750–821). He had been a servant of the king, but after narrowly escaping drowning he decided to become a monk. From his monastery in southern France he sponsored the establishment of a renewed Benedictine rule in the Frankish institutions. His program included the observance of uniform practices by all the houses, regular visitations by royal inspectors, and an increase in the hours of liturgical services.

Another contribution of the emperor was combating the idolatry that persisted among the semi-Christianized Franks. He realized that as long as most of the clergy and laity alike were uneducated, it would be impossible to root out paganism or to realize his vision of a Christian society. He saw "palace schools" as the key to the revival of ancient learning, and he decided to employ Alcuin of York to introduce Latin education into the realm. The result of the emperor's efforts to foster learning was the "Carolingian Renaissance."

Alcuin (c. 735–804) was an English monk who had a great reputation for learning and was a teacher in the prestigious cathedral school of York. Charlemagne commissioned him to carry out an educational reform among the Franks, and from 781 to 790 he lived at the court and devoted his energies to implementing the emperor's scheme. Then he became abbot at the monastery of St. Martin of Tours, where he continued his endeavors. Alcuin restructured the educational system along the lines of the seven liberal arts of the late classical era as spelled out by Cassiodorus. He divided the subjects into two groups, the *trivium* and the *quadrivium.* Included in the former were grammar, dialectics, and rhetoric, and in the latter arithmetic, geometry, astronomy, and music. Latin grammar was the primary subject and embraced not only the structure of the language but also its literature. Dialectics involved the study of systematic logic, while rhetoric focused on written expression. The *quadrivium,* as well as being valuable for church life, provided the intellectual tools to administer the royal estates and other business matters of the king.

Alcuin began with educating members of the royal family, the court, and the clergy. He hoped eventually to have a school in every

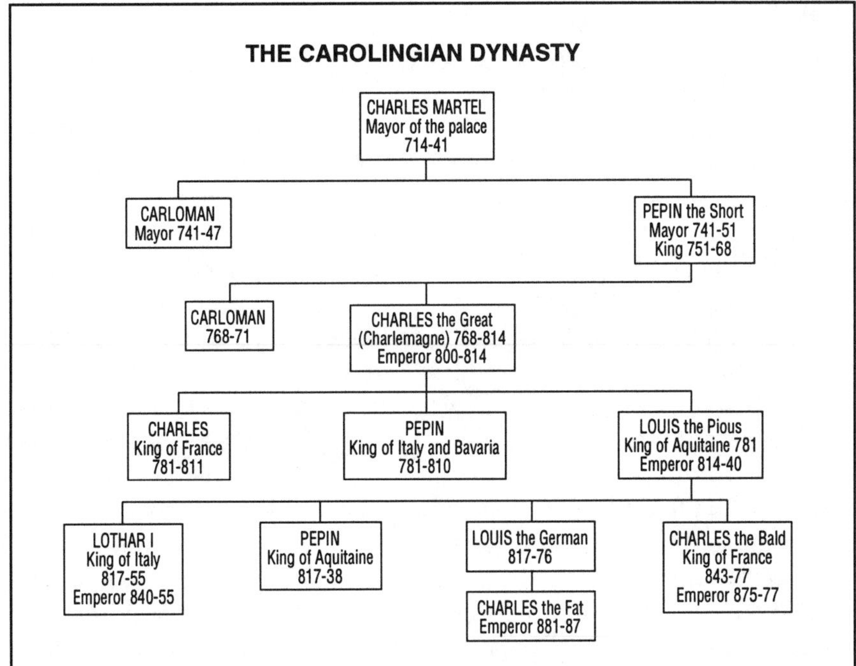

parish that would be open to freemen and serfs alike. He built the court library by collecting the writings of the church Fathers and other ancient authors who reflected Charles's interests in mathematics, history, and astronomy. Alcuin also was interested in establishing the correct texts of these works. He did this by comparing versions, finding the copyists' errors and changes, and developing a perfected version that he placed in the royal library. It would then serve as the text that future laborers in the various monastic *scriptoria* (copying rooms) would use to reproduce the work.

The greatest minds of the day participated in this project, such as Paul the Deacon who is remembered for his *History of the Lombards,* an outstanding work that followed the classical Roman model of historical writing. The court scholars also produced a standard edition of Gregory the Great's works and the Benedictine *Rule.* Their most significant endeavor was refurbishing Jerome's Latin Bible, which in a four-century time span had become corrupted through introduction of words from competing Bible translations and copyists' errors. The corrected version they developed became known as the *Vulgate* (common) text. It was the most widely-used Bible text in the Middle Ages.

Another contribution of Alcuin and his colleagues was the creation of a new style of writing. Most manuscripts from the Merovingian era were essentially illegible even to people at the time. The Carolingian *minuscule* (small or lowercase) script that they developed eliminated the confusing connections between the letters and set a high standard for legibility. The more than 8,000 manuscripts, which were copied in the Carolingian script, form the basis of much of what we know about classical and early Christian texts. The great care given to these manuscripts could be seen in the manner in which they were so beautifully illustrated.

Theological controversies were also a feature of the era. Alcuin sharply attacked the Eastern church for using icons (images of Christ and saints) as objects of worship, although in fact he had misunderstood what was really happening there. Another issue that contributed to worsening relations with the East was the hard-line stance taken by Alcuin and the Carolingian theologians, backed by the emperor himself, on the *filioque* issue, that is, an addition to the Nicene Creed affirming the progression of the Holy Spirit through the Father "and the Son." In Spain a vestige of Visigothic Arianism was seen in the Adoptionist heresy (Christ in his humanity was only the "adopted" Son of God) that was actively promoted by two leading bishops. In 794 Charles called and presided at a council at Frankfurt where Alcuin defended the orthodox doctrine of the eternal sonship of Christ. It condemned the two Spaniards, but four years later Alcuin persuaded one of them, Felix of Urgel, to recant.

Eventually Charlemagne's empire came to include not only France but also Belgium, Holland, Switzerland, northern Spain, and much of Germany and Italy. His achievements were known even in the Muslim world, and Caliph Harun al-Rashid in Baghdad and the emir of Córdoba in Spain sent embassies to him. But since the empire was the creation of the king's own charismatic personality, it lacked the needed military, political, and economic structures to sustain it after his death.

Despite his Christian commitment, Charlemagne had five official wives as well as numerous mistresses and concubines. Such a polygamous situation fostered intrigue; he punished one of his sons with confinement in a monastery for plotting against him. Apparently the polygamous lifestyle troubled the emperor's conscience, as he had hundreds of monks praying for him. When he died in 814, he left all but a fraction of his enormous wealth to endow Masses and the saying of prayers for his eternal salvation.

Before his death Charlemagne chose Louis, his only surviving son, as his successor and instructed him to crown himself emperor.

However, Louis went to Rome in 816 and received the crown from the pope. By this action a foundation was laid for the theory that the pope could choose and depose emperors, an idea that Charlemagne himself would never have tolerated.

Louis the Pious (814–40), although esteemed for his religious devotion, alienated the nobility. His piety made him subservient to the papacy and church officials, but he still supported the reform of monasteries and tried to impose morality upon society. One of his orders declared, "Any man in whose house prostitutes have been found must carry them out on his shoulders to the market place where they will be whipped; if he refuses, he will be whipped with them."[3]

Louis had serious problems with his family and the result was a complicated succession. The years of wrangling led to a permanent division of the empire, and after his death his three sons concluded the Treaty of Verdun (843) that allocated the western area to Charles "the Bald," and the eastern part to Louis "the German." The other son, Lothar (Lothair), inherited the so-called Middle Kingdom, a narrow corridor a hundred miles wide and a thousand miles long, which extended from the Netherlands in the north to Italy in the south. When Lothar and then his son died, Charles and Louis simply divided the Middle Kingdom territories between themselves.

Their incompetent successors were known by such nicknames as "Charles the Fat," "Louis the Stammerer," "Louis the Sluggard," and "Charles the Simple." Furthermore, over the passage of time the western Carolingians lost all effectiveness through the continuing subdivision of their domains and their inability to deal with the Viking threat. After 924 the imperial title was no longer assumed, while the Carolingians competed with another family for its French throne. Then, in 987 the last member of their line died, and the great lords in France replaced him with Hugh Capet, who founded a new dynasty. Meanwhile, Louis the Child, the last Carolingian in the east, died, thus clearing the way for an entirely new political order in Germany.

Germany and the Saxon Dynasty

The eastern realm was divided among five principal duchies: Lorraine, Saxony, Franconia, Bavaria, and Swabia. The dense forests and marshes forestalled any effective unification. Upon the death of Louis the Child in 911, the five dukes ignored the western Carolingians and chose one of their number, Conrad of Franconia, to be the

German king. He was succeeded by the Duke of Saxony, Henry I ("the Fowler"), who established a dynasty that lasted from 919 to 1024.

Henry was an appreciably stronger ruler than his predecessor, and he initiated the practice of expanding German authority eastward into areas inhabited by Slavs, the famous *Drang nach Osten,* the "Push to the East." However, it was his son, Otto I ("the Great"), who developed an effective monarchy in the area and revived the empire of Charlemagne in a German guise. Upon succeeding his father in 936, he set out to bring the five dukes under his control. His method was to give the church large tracts of royal lands and have the bishops and abbots administer these territories, dispense justice, and function as governing princes. The clergy also provided manpower and supplies for the king's armies, and their lands were an important source of income for him. In the "Ottonian system," as it was called, the king appointed his people to vacant ecclesiastical posts, and, since the prelates had to be celibate, they could not make their positions hereditary. However, the system in the long run could not enable a strong monarchy, because the churchmen had no loyalty to the state as such. The only ties were religious and personal, and neither of these could be relied on over a long period.

Despite his regime's inherent internal weaknesses, Otto emerged as the strongest ruler in western Europe. His foreign policy was a model for his successors. First, he worked to keep France weak and divided. Second, he engaged in eastward expansion. His decisive defeat of the Magyars at Lechfeld near Augsburg in 955 discouraged them from making any further raids on Germany. He carried out several expeditions against the Slavs living between the Elbe and Oder Rivers and set up new bishoprics in the region. The bishops fostered missionary work and settled German peasants on their lands. The Germanization program was another example of Otto using the church to carry out his objectives.

The third aspect of his foreign policy was to gain and keep power over Italy. This need for church support explains why Otto tried to conquer Italy. If the German kingdom could exist only with the aid of the church, then he had to control the papacy. Otto's involvement in Italy began in 952, when Adelaide (Adelheid), the widowed Lombard queen, appealed to him for help against her enemy. His military expedition was triumphant. Not only did he rescue and marry the queen, but also he assumed the title of king of Italy. However, problems in Germany kept him from establishing his authority over northern Italy.

After defeating the Magyars, which secured his lines to Italy, he returned there in 961 to dispose of a challenger to his kingship. Then he proceeded to Rome where he was crowned emperor by the pope in the following year. Despite his recognition of papal authority over its central Italian lands, he insisted that future popes must have the emperor's approval before they could be consecrated.

He acted almost immediately to show that imperial control of the papacy was more than a mere form. In 963 he summoned a synod at Rome that deposed the weak and unpopular John XII and replaced him with a more cooperative individual. Otto accused him of a list of sordid crimes and declared that "no pope could take office without first swearing an oath of allegiance to the emperor." This set a precedent and during the next hundred years the popes were often selected by the emperor in spite of repeated protests by the people of Rome.

Otto's assumption of the imperial crown threatened to alienate the Eastern emperors, but gradually they came to accept the existence of two empires, and Otto II (973–83) actually married a Byzantine princess. His reign was less successful than his father's, and he died in Rome after suffering a major defeat in southern Italy at the hands of the Muslims (the so-called Saracens), who had established themselves there in the 830s. Otto left as his heir a three-year-old child (Otto III) who was reared by his mother Theophano almost as a Byzantine prince. In fact, Adelaide and Theophano ruled the kingdom until he took power in 994, an almost unheard of situation at this point in time.

Otto III planned to make Rome his capital. He built a magnificent palace and elevated the greatest scholar of the age, Gerbert of Aurillac (c. 945–1003), to be Pope Sylvester II. Otto had the grandiose dream of a great Christian commonwealth, with church and empire united and ruled from Rome, but the policy could not succeed because he lacked a real basis of power in Italy. His support lay in the Saxon army because the Romans never voluntarily accepted his rule. When he died at the age of twenty-one, he was followed by Henry II (1002–24) from a younger branch of the line. Henry was concerned with maintaining his position in Germany and could not master Italy.

More noteworthy was the cultural revival under Otto III. An important aspect was a rediscovery of the natural sciences, mainly due to the influence of Gerbert who had studied in Spain and was renowned for his knowledge of mathematics and science. Some credit him with the introduction of Arabic numerals to Europe and the invention of the pendulum clock. At Reims, where he had been head teacher at the cathedral school and later archbishop, Gerbert expanded the study of mathematics and reintroduced logic (dialectics). The latter helped students to organize and integrate the knowledge that was now flooding into Europe, and it laid the foundation both for the revival of philosophy in the eleventh century and the university system that soon would flower in medieval Europe.

Norman and Plantagenet England

In contrast to the increasingly confused state of the empire was the more organized monarchy of the Normans in England (1066–1154). In the eleventh century the land was ruled by the Vikings with the exception of Wessex. After the reign of some Danish kings, power was for a brief time again in the hands of an Anglo-Saxon, Edward the Confessor (1042–66). As his mother Emma was a Norman princess, Edward had spent much of his youth in her homeland. Having no heirs, he promised the throne to his cousin William, the duke of Normandy, and this was supported by Pope Alexander II. But after his death the English council of nobles chose Edward's brother-in-law, Harold Godwinson, as successor. To enforce his claim, William invaded England and defeated Harold at the Battle of Hastings on October 14, 1066. William, who became known as "the Conqueror," then was crowned king of England at Westminster Abbey.

The Norman conquest was an enormous shock to the English, especially the upper classes. William viewed the supporters of Harold as rebels and confiscated their lands. Practically all the land in England came into the king's hands, and he allowed those who served him to use it. Thus, private ownership of land almost ceased and the most complete system of feudalism in Europe took its place (see chapter 7). He also built castles to control the population and made a survey of all the properties (the *Domesday Book* of 1086) for taxing purposes. The local people were further antagonized by the Normans' policy of setting aside large tracts of forest land as their private hunting preserves.

Since William of Normandy had received the support of the papal reformers in Rome prior to the invasion, he instituted changes in the churches that in the late Anglo-Saxon period had become as corrupt as those in Merovingian France. He separated the civil from the

Ninth-Century Europe

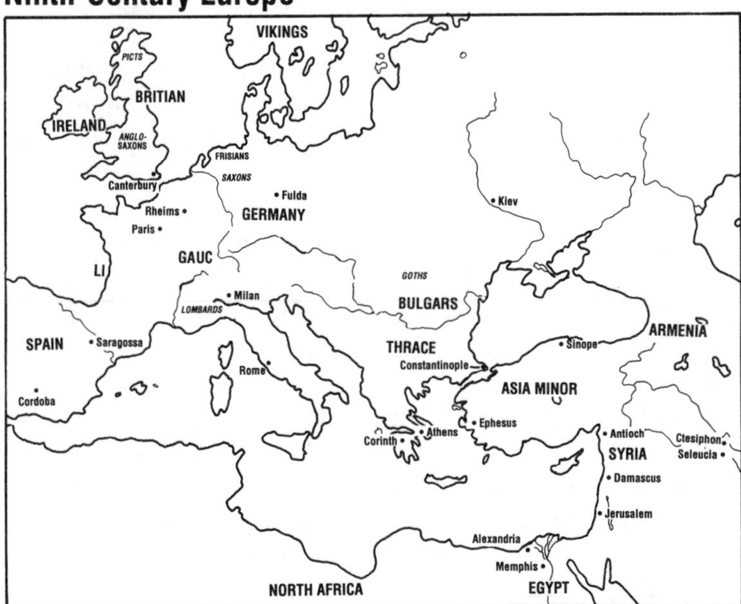

church courts, decreed that no pope could be recognized without royal assent, and declared that no excommunications could take place without royal permission. William also brought in Norman clergy, such as Lanfranc who became the archbishop of Canterbury, and the Normans erected numerous new church buildings throughout the land.

The next ruler, William II (1087–1100), completely ignored the rights of the church. He looked upon clerical property as something to be looted and would not recognize any pope for some years. A serious illness led him to appoint the devout Anselm as archbishop of Canterbury in 1093, but after recovering he returned to his normal irreverent ways and exiled Anselm to France. William was followed by his brother Henry I (1100–35), who negotiated a compromise with the church in 1107. The king gave up the practice of installing bishops, but in return they would render allegiance to him as their feudal overlord for the lands they held. This action would have European-wide significance.

During the period 1135–54 England was racked by civil war, and the church regained considerable independence. With the coronation of Henry II (1154–89) the period of anarchy closed, and the new king set out to reestablish control over his realm. He was the founder of the House of Plantagenet (Angevin) whose kings governed England from 1154 to 1399. Henry proved to be one of the most capable rulers in the country's history. Through inheritance and marriage he controlled a vast region stretching from Ireland to southern France. For the next two centuries the English monarchs ruled half the territory of France as well as their holdings in the British Isles.

Henry wanted to extend his authority over the justice system, make the application of English law more uniform, expand the use of juries, and bring all important lawsuits before his own judges. This led to a bitter dispute between the king and the church, because in medieval England a separate system of ecclesiastical courts existed, which had complete jurisdiction over many types of cases, including clergy accused of criminal offenses. This exemption from the secular law was called "benefit of clergy" and included not only priests and monks, but also students and certain professional people. These privileges were important because the penalties assessed by church courts were usually more lenient than those decreed by the royal judges. One egregious example was a case involving a cleric who had murdered a knight and was cleared of the crime simply by taking an oath in a church court.

One of Henry's chief lieutenants was Thomas Becket (c. 1118–70) who functioned as a judge, diplomat, and financial adviser. He was not only the king's right-hand man, but also his close personal friend. They even drank, hunted, and caroused together. Then in 1162 Henry had Becket named archbishop of Canterbury. By this appointment the king hoped to avoid conflict with ecclesiastical authority and to gain the full support of the church in his work of rebuilding the government.

This proved to be a mistake, since as leader of the English church, Becket switched from being a strong backer of royal authority to a staunch defender of the church's rights. He resigned his secular offices, much to the dismay of the king, and renounced his worldly life. He even wore a hair shirt, visited the sick, and washed the feet of beggars. In other words, he experienced a conversion that made Christianity a vital force in his life instead of a mere form.

In 1164 Henry attempted to gain control over the church courts by issuing the Constitutions of Clarendon, whose most important provision was the elimination of "benefit of clergy." This meant that a cleric accused of a civil crime would have his case heard in a secular court. Henry wanted all Englishmen to be subject to the same law so that justice would be more equally administered. Becket, however, believed that the state was infringing on the power of the church. After months of struggle Becket went into exile in France. This lasted for six years as he resisted all efforts to mediate the dispute and condemned any clergyman who cooperated with Henry.

Finally, Becket returned to England to continue his opposition to the king. He excommunicated those who had cooperated with the royal government in the disputes, and they went to Normandy where Henry happened to be at the time and complained to him about their treatment. The king reacted angrily: "What a pack of fools and cowards I have nourished in my house, that not one of them will avenge me of this turbulent priest." Four knights took Henry at his word, crossed the channel, and without his knowledge or consent, on December 29, 1170, murdered the archbishop as he was officiating at a service in Canterbury cathedral.

The immediate result of Becket's killing was such an outpouring of rage that Henry was forced to perform public penance and to acknowledge church control over those activities Becket had insisted upon. Thus, Becket secured a greater victory by his death than he could have won if he had lived. He was canonized in 1173 and became the most popular saint in English history. People from all parts of the realm flocked to his place of martyrdom, and an enduring work in English literature, *The Canterbury Tales* by Chaucer, describes a group of pilgrims on their way to worship at his shrine.

Henry was married to Eleanor of Aquitaine in 1152, one of the most beautiful and wealthy women in Europe. They had eight children, but she left Henry in 1173 because of his constant infidelities and encouraged her sons to rebel against him. Henry said about them, "From the devil they came, to the devil they will go." He held his own against them for a while but was forced to make an unfavorable peace in 1189 and died brokenhearted.

One son, Richard I (1189–99), spent only five months of his reign in England and did nothing significant there. He was known as "the Lion-Hearted" for his exploits during the Third Crusade. The other son, John (1199–1216), was equally incompetent. In 1207 he opposed Pope Innocent III's candidate for archbishop of Canterbury and was excommunicated. Faced with a possible invasion from France, John abjectly yielded to the pope in 1213. Then to raise funds for a war in France he tried to coerce his barons into providing him with more money and military service. They were already being taxed at a high rate and did not wish to participate in an expedition that they saw as futile. As expected, John's army suffered a crushing defeat, and now all the feudal barons united against him. In 1215 they presented to him a statement of their grievances (the "Magna Carta") and forced him to respect their rights. Although later generations tried to read into it all the liberties that the English gained through centuries of struggle, it was really only a feudal document drawn up by nobles seeking to protect their own financial interests.

During the reign of the next king, Henry III (1216–72), the barons demanded the right to participate in the government, and Simon de Montfort called for the meeting of a parliament in 1265. Two knights from every shire and two representatives from every borough were to participate in a representative assembly, which eventually became the House of Commons. The king's Great Council, which included the leading nobles and higher clergy, developed into the House of Lords.

Henry's son, Edward I (1272–1307), was known as the English Justinian for his extensive legal reforms. He is also remembered for his conquest of Wales and construction of a network of castles such as Harlech and Caernarvon. He had his son installed as the prince of Wales, a custom followed by subsequent English monarchs. Similar attempts to control Scotland were less successful, and the rivalry between the two peoples would continue for several hundred years.

France under the Capetians

The new dynasty established in 987 by Hugh Capet, duke of Orleans, ruled in France until 1328. For much of the first two centuries their realm was centered on Paris, as powerful counts dominated the other parts of France. One important supporter of the French monarchy was the twelfth-century churchman, Abbot Suger of St. Denis in Paris. He was a financial adviser to Louis VI and served as regent while the king took part in the Second Crusade. His abbey, named for the city's patron saint, Dionysius the Areopagite (named in Acts 17:34), was the first structure to be built completely in the new Gothic style (1136).

Philip II Augustus (1180–1223) was the first Capetian who succeeded in gaining control over many of the lands held by the English kings in France and thereby build the power of the monarchy. At the pope's invitation, his son crushed the Albigensian heresy in the south, thus enabling further expansion there.

The greatest king of the era was Louis IX (1226–70), who was noted for his piety and passion for justice. He implemented various legal reforms and generously allowed the English to keep their coastal territories in France. Moreover, Louis built the Sainte Chapelle, one of the most exquisite medieval structures standing today, to house the crown of thorns that he acquired from Constantinople. He also took part in two Crusades. During the first one he was captured in Egypt and had to be ransomed, and in the second he died of dysentery in Tunis. Contemporaries marveled that "the holy king loved the truth so much that he kept his promise even to Saracens." Two decades after his death the good king was declared a saint.

THE PAPACY AND THE EMPIRE

During the period of imperial disintegration a noteworthy leader became pope, Nicholas I (858–67). While Gregory I achieved the supremacy of the papacy in Italy, Nicholas made it a major force in western Europe. He became involved in political affairs in both the Carolingian and Byzantine empires, and to justify this intervention he cited the "False Decretals," a set of documents forged around 850 that greatly enhanced papal power. They were allegedly compiled by Isidore of Seville two hundred years earlier and included the Donation of Constantine and many authoritative letters from early popes.

Most of the other ninth and tenth century pontiffs were worldly figures. Several were assassinated, and abuses like simony (purchase and sale of church offices) and clerical marriage were commonplace. During this period of corruption and degradation, power over the papacy was for a time exercised by the notorious Theodora and her daughter Marozia. Each of them was connected with a half-dozen popes in the capacity of mistress, mother, or murderess. Referred to by some as the "pornocracy," this was the low point in the history of the papacy.

In 1024 a new dynasty, the Salian or Franconian, assumed power in the empire and reasserted royal authority. Henry III, in his capacity as a ruler of Italy, called a church council in 1046 that deposed an immoral pope and elected the first in a line of competent individuals. Unwittingly, the imperial action was helpful to the papacy, since it took control of the institution away from decadent rival factions and placed people of high character in the church leadership. But by this time the popes had lost control even in spiritual matters as royal power extended to the selection of bishops, who were crown appointees and took their secular duties more seriously than their sacred ones.

When Henry IV became emperor in 1056, he found himself facing a papal reform movement. It was led by capable figures like Peter Damien, Humbert of Silva-Candida, and Hildebrand, all of whom had served in the court of Leo IX (1049–54). They encouraged Pope Nicholas II to issue a decree in 1059 affirming that popes should be chosen by the college of cardinals rather than the emperor. Hildebrand, their leader, was elected Pope Gregory VII in 1073, and under him the church-state contest reached its highest intensity. After spending twenty years in the curia, he had developed a most exalted view of the papacy. In 1075 he drew up a set of propositions called the *Dictatus Papae*, among which are:

> That the Roman pontiff alone is rightly called universal.
>
> That he alone has the power to depose and reinstate bishops.
>
> That all princes shall kiss the foot of the pope alone.
>
> That he has the power to depose emperors.
>
> That his decree can be annulled by no one, and that he can annul the decrees of anyone.
>
> That he can be judged by no one.
>
> That the Roman church has never erred and will never err to all eternity, according to the testimony of the holy scriptures.
>
> That he has the power to absolve subjects from their oath of fidelity to wicked rulers.

Pope Gregory issued orders to bishops and rulers throughout western Europe deposing clergy guilty of simony and forbidding married priests from celebrating Mass. To free the church of lay interference in the appointment of bishops, he took actions that led to the "investiture" controversy. This refers to the ceremony in which a vassal swore loyalty to his lord and received from him the insignia of office. Gregory's ban on lay princes investing bishops challenged the practice in Germany whereby the emperor hand-picked the prelates and relied on them for support. What followed was a bitter and complex struggle between the two, in which the emperor tried to depose the pope and Gregory excommunicated Henry, a move that released the ruler's vassals from their oaths of allegiance and left them free to overthrow him. The most dramatic incident came when Henry crossed the Alps in January 1077 and stood in the snow at Canossa for three days begging the pope's pardon. The victory was more symbolic than real, as Henry soon defied him again. He invaded Italy in 1080 and forced Gregory to seek refuge among the Normans in the south (who had just expelled the Saracens and formed their own state in Italy), where he died in 1080.

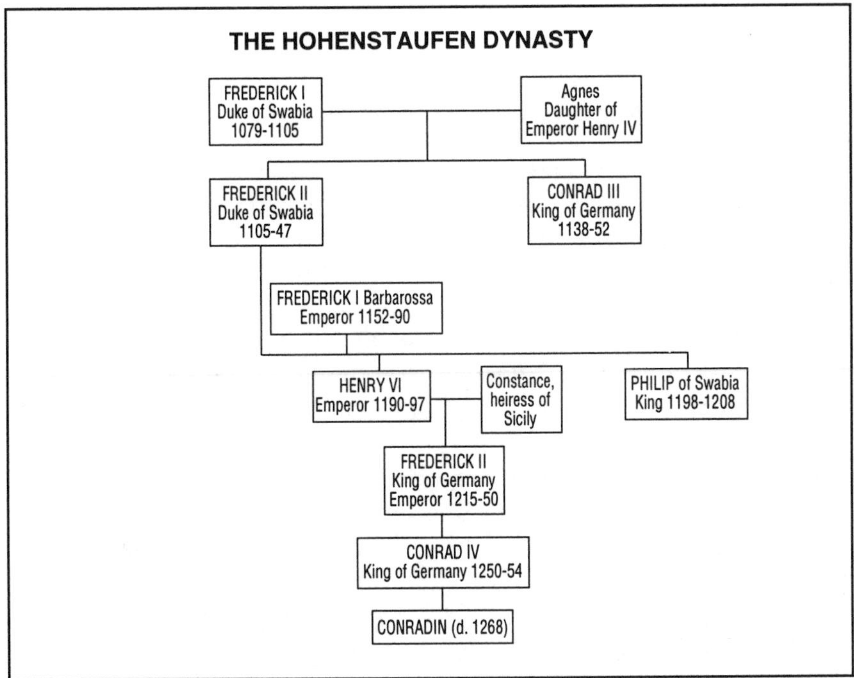

The investiture controversy was eventually settled by a compromise between Henry V and the papacy in the Concordat of Worms (1122). The emperor agreed that bishops should be elected by the church and given their spiritual investment by the archbishop. However, the ruler was to be present at the election and could invest the bishop with the symbols of the secular power of the office.

After this, a new German dynasty emerged, the Hohenstaufens from Swabia. The first member took the throne in 1138, but more important was Frederick I, Barbarossa, or "Red Beard" (1152–90). He renewed the power and unity of the empire in Germany but was less successful in subduing Italy. His plan was to restore the influence over the papacy lost during the investiture controversy. For the first time the term "Holy Roman Empire" appeared in public documents, implying rather pointedly that the emperor's authority came from God alone. Barbarossa wanted the same kind of power over the pope that he had over the prince-bishops in Germany. Moreover, he hoped to become the leader of Christendom and perhaps even recreate the Roman Empire of Constantine. With this goal in mind he embarked on the Third Crusade, but in 1190 he drowned in a river in Asia Minor while on the way to the Holy Land.

INNOCENT III AND THE HOHENSTAUFENS

Papal power reached its height under Innocent III (1198–1216). Like Gregory VII he had an exalted view of the papacy, as indicated in this statement: "The pope holds a position betwen God and man. Though he is less than God, yet he is greater than man. He judges everybody, but is himself judged by none." He also claimed political power: "No king can reign rightly unless he devoutly serves Christ's vicar." Likening the two to the sun and moon, he said, "In the same way the royal power derives its dignity from the pontifical authority."[4]

From a noble family in Rome, Innocent was educated in law and theology. Upon becoming pope he set out to provide moral authority and leadership in both secular and ecclesiastical affairs. He was hard-working, attentive to details, had clear goals, and was totally committed to being the head of Christendom. His endeavors were many. He sponsored the Fourth Crusade, which, much to his chagrin, attacked Constantinople instead of Palestine. He also supported crusades against the Bogomils in the Balkans and Albigensians in France, and approved the new orders of mendicant friars, the Franciscans and Dominicans, which were used to combat these heresies (see chapter 7).

When King John in 1207 refused to accept the papal nominee, Stephen Langton, as archbishop of Canterbury, Innocent placed England under an interdict. This meant a suspension of almost all public services of the church. In 1209 after John confiscated all the English church lands, Innocent excommunicated him. When he continued to resist, the pope declared the throne vacant and invited the French king to invade the country. In 1213 John made his peace with the pope, surrendered England to him as a fief, and received it back as a vassal.

Innocent also forced the French ruler to submit to his will. Philip II had married Ingeborg of Denmark without ever having seen her. Then, when he first set eyes on his new queen, he said that a shiver went down his spine. Feeling such an intense personal distaste for her, he had the French bishops annul the marriage, but Innocent put an interdict on France until Philip restored her. When Emperor Otto IV invaded Sicily, thereby threatening the security of the Papal States, Innocent excommunicated him and in 1212 secured the election of Frederick II of Hohenstaufen, his ward.

The climax of Innocent's career was the Fourth Lateran Council, which he convened in 1215. Among the seventy decrees issued by the illustrious assembly of prelates were: the requirement that Christians should confess their sins and take communion at least once a year at Easter, the acceptance of transubstantiation as dogma, Jews were not to appear in public during Holy Week, and Jews and Muslims were to wear distinctive garb for public identification. The council reflected the unity and universality of Christendom at its peak in the Middle Ages.

Frederick II, however, turned out to be a bitter disappointment to the papacy. He gave virtual independence to the German princes so that he could concentrate on controlling Italy, resulting in a life-and-death struggle with the pope who tried to crush his power. Frederick's own character complicated the problem, for he combined a Western outlook with the style of an oriental sultan. He organized southern Italy in a kingdom that set an example for later Renaissance states. He was a linguist, physician, poet, and patron of learning. He was interested in Arabic culture, had a harem of Muslim women, made a treaty with Muslim rulers while on a crusade, and believed in astrology. For his tolerance and lack of faith, the papacy denounced him as "this scorpion, spewing poison from the sting of its tail."

One pope, Gregory IX, excommunicated Frederick and in 1241 called a synod to depose him, but he intercepted the ships carrying the prelates to Rome and took them captive. The next pope, Innocent IV, refused to rescind the excommunication and charged him with sacrilege and heresy. After Frederick's death in 1250 the papacy set out to exterminate the house of Hohenstaufen and secured the help of the French count, Charles of Anjou. He defeated and executed Conradin, the last of the line, in 1268.

The papal triumph produced instability both in Italy and Germany. The removal of imperial interference in northern Italy permitted the city-states like Milan, Genoa, Venice, and Florence to flourish in the next two centuries. The fluid situation in Germany enabled an insignificant noble from Swabia, Rudolf of Hapsburg, to be elected emperor in 1273. Eventually his family would dominate much of Europe.

The Reconquista in Spain

The Muslims had conquered all but northern Spain within a few years of their invasion. In 756 the sole surviving member of the Umayyad dynasty fled there from Damascus and formed an emirate that soon controlled most of the peninsula. Córdoba, the capital, with its numerous libraries and schools became the cultural center of Europe by the eleventh century. The great mosque that held 5,500 worshipers can still be seen today. Christians (the Mozarabs) and Jews enjoyed considerable freedom in Muslim Spain. In fact, many Christians converted to Islam, but others resisted the new order. A center of inspiration for the latter was the shrine of St. James (Santiago de Compostela) in northwest Spain. It claimed to have the relics of the apostle and attracted innumerable pilgrims during the medieval era.

The great Muslim leader Al-Mansur (981–1002) conducted periodic raids against the Christian north, and his army of Moors even sacked Compostela. But after this success, the emirate of Córdoba rapidly declined and fell in 1031. Muslim Spain then fragmented into several petty states, while the resurgent Christian kingdoms—Castile, Navarre, Leon, and Aragon—began a counteroffensive against the Moors known as the *Reconquista* (Reconquest).

The struggles between the various Christian and Moorish powers continued through the eleventh and twelfth centuries. The decisive victory by the Castilians at Las Navas de Tolosa in 1212 ensured that the final success of the Reconquest would just be a matter of time. Only the stronghold of Granada in the far south remained in Muslim hands. In the reconquered lands Muslims at first were treated in a similar way as Christians had been under Islamic rule. They were free to practice their religion and culture but suffered from civil discrimination, including the payment of special taxes. Many Moors then emigrated to North Africa while others became Christians, especially as a result of Franciscan and Dominican missionary work. In the later Middle Ages pressures on the Moors would become increasingly severe.

During the high Middle Ages (1000–1300) dynastic states had developed in England, France, and Germany. Generally the English and French monarchs cooperated with the popes. As the Gregorian reforms revitalized the papacy and it became a territorial power in central Italy, the popes sought to assert authority over all secular powers. This led to a bitter conflict with the empire's rulers, who wished to control Italy as well as Germany. Finally, the Spanish success in the Reconquista inspired the idea of crusades to free the Holy Land from Muslim domination.

7

THE MEDIEVAL CHURCH IN THE WEST

By the year 1000 a revival of civilization in Europe was under way. Stability returned as the barbarian invasions that had plagued the West since the fourth century came to an end. The growth of towns and trade led to the developments in education, church organization, art, and architecture that resulted in the flowering of medieval cultural life. A period of expansion ensued in a movement often called the "medieval frontier," which led to the Crusades, the settlement of unoccupied forests and marsh lands, and the conversion of the peoples of northern and eastern Europe.

FEUDALISM

By their conversion to Christianity the second wave of invaders, the Magyars and the Vikings, were incorporated into Western society in the same fashion as the earlier migrants. Before this was achieved, however, an intricate and diverse system known as feudalism had developed. Feudalism's institutions enabled local government to function when no organized state existed. Feudalism originated in response to the Viking invasions, against which governments could not offer protection. To be sure, an earlier form existed in late Roman times, when men had to follow the occupation of their fathers, the agricultural classes were dependent upon large landowners who took authority into their own hands, and the church itself was a landholder.

In the mid-ninth century the Carolingians decreed that every man and every parcel of land should have a lord. Warriors or "vassals" acknowledged their dependence in a voluntary, personal relationship whereby the lord gave them land and they in turn agreed to fight for him. Political leadership thus devolved to the area controlled by a castle, with public power (including the administration of justice, police functions, defense, and taxation) enforced by private individuals. The knights, heavily armored cavalrymen, usually dominated those who did not have the wealth or ability to become like them.

Although many exceptions existed, there were some common elements in the lord-vassal relationship. By the ceremonies of homage and fealty, a knight promised to give military service for a stated number of days annually. He also provided the lord with hospitality, advice and counsel on matters affecting his lordship, and, on occasions, money. In turn, the lord assumed an obligation to protect his vassal.

The vassal would serve in the lord's court, and the lord provided justice based upon judgment by peers. The vassal treated his lord with honor, respect, and courtesy, while the lord responded with similar deference. As with any agreement, the mutual obligations of lord and vassal depended on good faith, and, failing that, on force. If the lord did not fulfill his side of the agreement, the vassal could renounce his oath of allegiance. Should the vassal fail in his duties, the lord could reclaim the land that he had let out as a "fief."

Because bishops and other church officials controlled large amounts of land, they were drawn into the feudal order, and conflicts between a churchman's role as servant of God and his position as a secular lord frequently arose. As with lay nobles, the clerical aristocracy had the responsibilities of lordship. They owed homage and fealty to their overlords, participated in government, managed vast estates with dependent serfs, exercised authority over their knights, and amassed wealth. The times demanded that the bishops serve as governors as well as pastors, and it was difficult to harmonize this dual role.

Unfortunately for spiritual values, the public functions required of feudal bishops meant that they had to be loyal to the secular lords

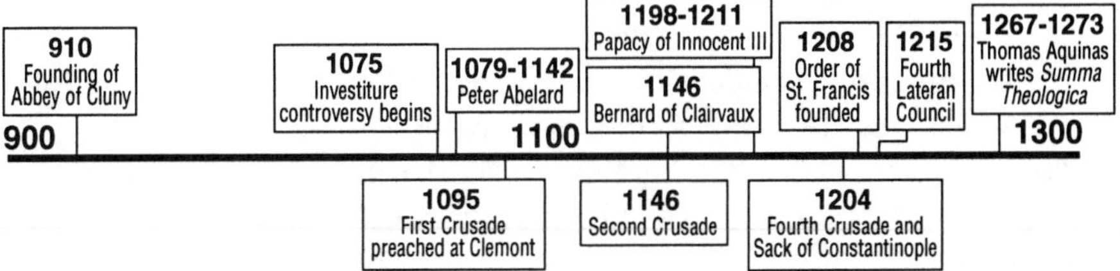

over them. Consequently, these laymen demanded a voice in the election of bishops, and in many areas of Europe they obtained the right to select the servants of God as well as the servants of Caesar. It is no wonder that religious leaders had trouble separating their loyalties or that clerical reformers called for a reordering of priorities. The feudalization of the church was the background for the Gregorian Reform mentioned above, since by this time there was no distinction between church and state, nor agreement as to the powers of the laity.

THE MANORIAL SYSTEM

Historians often divide medieval social structure into those who fought, those who worked, and those who prayed. Although an oversimplification, it is true that some were involved in the feudal system as knights, others worked the fields as serfs, and many served the church in various capacities. Since the knights needed free time to refine their martial skills, they lived on property called manors and received support while they trained. True, there was no typical manor, and the economic and social relationships existed in various combinations on these lands. Ordinarily a village would consist of several manors and thus be subject to several lords.

The lord's rights over his peasants (customarily known as serfs) included the things needed for his support, so he could spend his time in war, governance, and leisure. The various dues and services took the place of taxes, insurance payments, military service, and other obligations expected of people today. The serfs on the manor planted, cultivated, and harvested the lord's land. In addition, he received a share of the crops from common lands, such as hay from the meadows. He also had the right to a specified number of days of work performed by his serfs, to their labor in maintaining roads and bridges, and to tax them if a money economy existed. He could also charge them fees in kind for economic functions over which he held the monopoly, such as the use of the brewery, winepress, flour mill, and baking ovens.

In this hierarchically ordered world the peasant did have rights. Like all manorial obligations, they varied greatly, but generally the serf was subservient only in the relationship with his master. He was equal to others below the knightly caste, had the right to sue and be sued in court, and was not subject to any lord other than his own. Unlike a slave, the serf was bound to the soil, that is, the land he worked could not be taken from him. This gave him the security of steady work and income. In addition to the dues paid in kind, he owed the tithe to his parish church and certain other money payments.

Even in this rough society, custom and tradition gave the peasant relief from his life of constant drudgery. There were a great number of religious holidays on which he did not work, and he enjoyed the festivities and pageantry of tournaments, fairs, and executions. He had a garden plot of his own, was not obliged to render military service unless his own village was attacked, and was fed by the lord on the days he worked the latter's land. The superior had obligations as well, since the lord owed him protection and land, the two things that a peasant most needed. In addition, he provided a church, a priest, seed at planting time, and communal facilities like ovens and mills.

In the eleventh century, thanks to the reestablishment of public order and security and the introduction of new tools and technology, conditions among the peasantry improved. A new type of axe enabled farmers to cut back the forest, and windmills were invented to drain marshes, thus opening new lands for cultivation. The horse collar and moldboard plow broke the tough northern soils, while the development of wind and water driven gristmills and the introduction of the three-field system of crop rotation led to greater production of crops. Thus, the increase in food output enabled modest improvements in living standards for the peasantry.

The Growth of Towns

The middle class, or "bourgeoisie," who engaged in commerce and manufacturing and lived in the towns originated from the peasant class. The revival of long-distance trade in the eleventh century was what fostered the growth of these communities and the economic activities carried on there. This was due to the maritime connections of the Italian city-states with the East and resulting availability of luxury goods, English production of raw wool and the emergence of the Flemish towns as manufacturing centers of fine woolens, and a rising demand for the products of the Baltic area.

Local industry also contributed to the expansion of trade. Goods produced in the small workshops of craftsmen in the towns were intended for export instead of merely being made for domestic consumption. Also, the craftsmen organized into guilds, which were a combination trade association, civic or service club, and fraternity. The craft guilds regulated conditions of manufacture, pricing, criteria of quality, and standards of admission to the craft. In turn, the merchants formed associations to facilitate trade, especially in foreign locations, and to help thwart competition. Just as feudal relationships contained elements of social security, so too did the guilds. They provided a kind of life insurance through the apprentice system, which ensured that a deceased member's surviving sons would learn their father's trade, and it engaged in many kinds of corporate activity for the benefit of all.

A town received its freedom from the feudal lord through a charter, and the usual method of obtaining one was by negotiation, purchase, or as a gift. The surplus food resulting from the agricultural revolution made such population centers possible. The merchants and artisans living there supported themselves by their occupations and bought food from farmers. The townsman differed from his rural neighbor in that he had freedom of movement and, through his guild, a large measure of self-government. Town dwellers also taxed themselves and assisted in the military defense of their community.

Although the medieval environment was primarily rural, the towns and cities were the centers of intellectual innovation. Among the cultural developments associated with them were the university, vernacular literature and drama, and the Gothic cathedral, the most distinctive artistic feature of the Middle Ages. The patronage of wealthy townsmen enabled a genuine cultural renaissance in the period from the mid-eleventh to the late twelfth century.

Medieval Monasticism

Accompanying the economic resurgence in medieval Europe was a spiritual renewal. Its origins lay in the reform movement that began with the founding of the monastery at Cluny in Burgundy in 910. The Cluniac reform included a return to the strict Benedictine rule, cultivation of the spiritual life, and a stress on worship. Attention was also paid to sound economic organization and independence from financial control by laymen. As the Cluniac order established new monasteries, each of them were tied to the "motherhouse" (the headquarters of the order). They thereby evaded local control, and were responsible only to the pope. By the middle of the twelfth century, when its influence reached a high point, within the Cluny orbit were more than three hundred houses and many prominent church figures. The Cluniacs served as an inspiration to other institutions and individuals who were not formally linked to the order. One was the German monk Hildebrand, who as Pope Gregory VII, gave his name to the eleventh-century papal reform.

The spirit of renewal was also evident in the formation of new monastic orders. The success of the reformed papacy together with cultural expansion had led to a crisis in Benedictine monasticism. The rise in power of popes, bishops, and kings undermined the monastic role in culture. Education now was centered in the bishops' schools rather than monasteries. The growth of nonmonastic clergy and stable civil government made the monasteries obsolete as oases of culture. In response to the changed situation, a number of new orders appeared.

The most influential was the Cistercians, founded in 1098 at Citeaux, France, as an offshoot of a Benedictine house. One of its leaders, Stephen Harding, drew up a rule that emphasized manual labor instead of scholarship and private rather than corporate prayer. The Cistercians located their community houses in the most isolated places and accepted no tithes, gifts, or lay patronage. Believing that "to work is to pray," they took upon themselves the tasks of farming, cooking, weaving, carpentry, and other duties of life. Their churches were plain, with no ornaments or treasures, and they owned no personal possessions. They were allowed seven hours of sleep in the winter and six in the summer. After gathering for communal prayer, the brothers spent the rest of the day in manual work, meditation, reading, and worship services. Their diet was spare—vegetables, fish, and cheese—once a day in summer and twice in winter. Even in the coldest regions, a fire was allowed only on Christmas Day.

In spite of this strictness, the Cistercians were a phenomenal success, and by the end of the twelfth century there were hundreds of houses. Its most remarkable leader was Bernard of Clairvaux (1090–1153). He arrived at Citeaux in 1112 and then went to Clairvaux, where he founded the first of more than sixty-five new monasteries and wielded a continentwide influence. He was so persuasive in convincing men to enter the monastery that mothers hid their sons, and wives their husbands, when he came fishing for souls. In his enormously popular and appealing sermons on the *Song of Solomon* and his work *Why and How God Is to Be Loved,* Bernard described the Christian life as an experience of progress in love. Under him, the monks' concerns were widened beyond contemplation to missionary work and pastoral care for their neighbors. Despite his impact, by the end of the twelfth century the Cistercians were becoming wealthy, lax, and ineffective.

The decline of the Cistercians coincided with the passing of the importance of cloistered monasteries. The growth of towns and cities rendered the security of the monastery less necessary and in fact presented a new challenge to the church. Because the traditional expressions of faith were failing to cope with the worldliness of the emerging urban society, many churchmen perceived the need for a new form of spirituality that would enable them to work in the world but at the same time maintain a monastic lifestyle. They decided that the answer was for a group to vow to live together under a strict rule but also go preach and teach among the people. Two orders that operated in this fashion were the Premonstratensians (founded 1120), who had a rule resembling the Cistercian one, and the Augustinians (founded 1256), who used the rule of Augustine.

At the beginning of the thirteenth century appeared the preaching monks or friars ("brothers"). They were "mendicant" orders, that is, they had a highly ascetic lifestyle and depended on charity (begging). The friars preached in the parishes and town squares, taught in the schools, and eventually dominated many of the universities. The two most important orders were the Franciscans and Dominicans.

The Franciscan order was founded by Francis of Assisi (1182–1226), the son of a cloth merchant who gave up his wealth to live a life of prayer and simplicity. Gathering a band of followers, he wandered the hills of Tuscany, worked occasionally, preached, and nursed the sick. He taught that complete poverty relieved the brothers from cares and made them joyous before God. Approved by the pope in 1209, the brothers were known as the Friars Minor, wore dark gray, and went barefoot. As the society grew, living from begging and the work of their own hands became more difficult. Those who insisted on adhering to the original teachings of Francis and maintaining a regimen of poverty were known as the Spiritual Franciscans (or Fraticelli). They were persecuted for refusing to obey a papal decree authorizing the order to own property.

The founder of the Dominican order was Dominic de Guzman (1170–1221), a Spaniard who was sent to southern France to preach against the Albigensians. There he realized the need for an educated clergy who could communicate with the people and win heretics back to the church. His order, recognized in 1216, focused on teaching and preaching. Hence the Dominicans' official title was the Order of Preachers. Wearing a white habit and black cloak, they spread throughout Europe as "the watchdogs of the Lord" (a pun on the Latin name *Dominicanus—domini canis*) to root out heresy and combat ignorance.

The Dominicans were the first order to abandon manual labor and put intellectual effort in the forefront, and their academic emphasis contrasted with Franciscan anti-intellectualism. They established schools and produced such leading theologians as Albert the Great and Thomas Aquinas. However, the two orders soon became more alike, since the Franciscans founded educational institutions to train young friars.

Both groups carried on social, pastoral, educational, and missionary work. They served lepers and the sick, a practice that encouraged the study of medicine. They were also effective preachers, although difficulties with local clergy frequently arose, since parish priests were usually not well trained. Burning with zeal, they made a deep impression on their their hearers. Their sermons were marked by humor and effective stories from everyday life. Their devotional books and religious poetry still convey the message of Christ today.

Like the Dominicans, the Franciscans opened schools at the university centers, and they produced such distinguished scholars as Bonaventure (1221–74), William of Ockham (1280–1349), and Roger Bacon (c. 1214–92). Also noteworthy was their missionary activity. In 1214–15 Francis went to Spain, hoping to convert the Moors, but illness prevented him from continuing on to Africa. In 1219 he made a preaching tour with eleven companions to eastern Europe and Egypt. Both orders encouraged the study of Eastern languages so missionaries could communicate with the Muslims. During the thirteenth century they preached and founded houses in the East and North Africa.

Especially memorable was the work of the Franciscan Raymond Lull (c. 1232–1316). A native of the island of Majorca, he dedicated

The Crusades

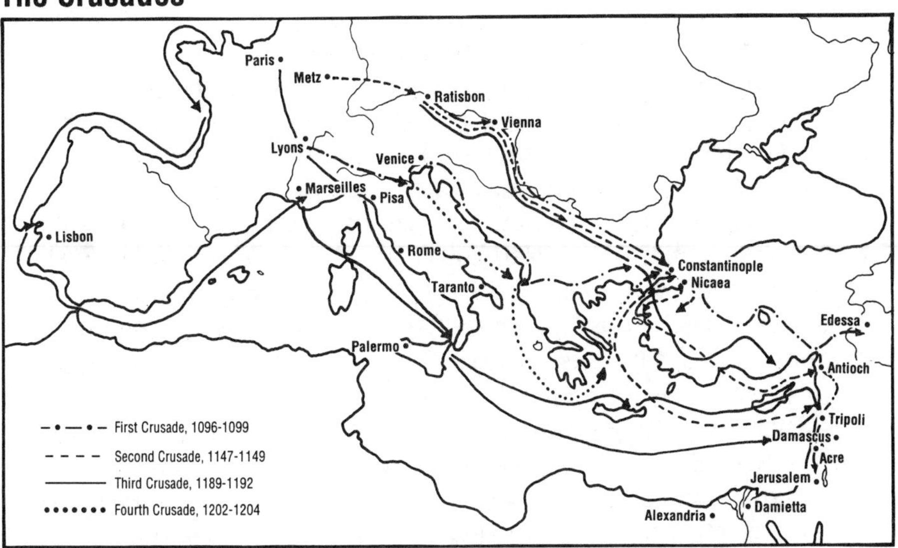

his life to winning Muslims to Christ. Not only did he learn Arabic but he also persuaded the ruler of his homeland to found a monastery where Franciscans could study the language and his methods of approaching Muslims with the Christian message. He made missionary journeys to Tunis and Algiers but was unsuccessful in enlisting support from the kings of Europe for his project. A distinguished theologian in his own right, he worked out a system of unifying all truth, which he believed would lead to a reunion of the Latin and Greek churches and eventually the conversion of all humankind to Christianity.

THE CRUSADES

The preaching of the friars in the East might have resulted in a peaceful penetration of the area by Latin Christianity had it not been for the increasing tensions between Byzantium and the West. At the beginning of the eleventh century the Greek church still was on reasonably good terms with Rome, but then the Crusades caused a complete breakdown in relations. On the surface these were religious wars that aimed at recovering the Holy Land from Muslim control, but in reality the factors leading to them were much more complicated. The Islamic conquest of the Middle East had succeeded in the first place because the Christian populations had offered little or no resistance, and the Monophysite churches even regarded Arab-Muslim rule as preferable to that of Byzantium. Thus there was no popular demand from these Christians to be "liberated."

Moreover, the Carolingians had claimed the right to protect the "Holy Places" in Palestine and the Western pilgrims who traveled there. The Muslim caliphs preferred the interference of the distant Franks to the much more threatening presence of the Byzantines. The increase in the frequency and size of pilgrimages in the tenth and eleventh centuries focused European attention more on the East. Many Crusades were organized by the Cluniac monks who built abbeys and hostels along the way. Often armed escorts accompanied pilgrims, and they traveled in large groups, such as in 1064–66 when 7,000 Germans went to Jerusalem.

There was also a growing awareness of "Christendom" as coextensive with Europe and possessing the right to defend the faith against the "Saracens." This was abetted by the initiation of the effort in the eleventh century to "reconquer" Spain from Muslim rule, the prototype of the later Crusades, and the successful campaign by the Normans to expel the Saracens from Sicily (1072–91). Furthermore, the capture of Jerusalem by the Seljuk Turks, a fiercer Muslim group than the Arabs, and their stunning victory over the Byzantine forces that same year sent shock waves reverberating throughout Christendom.

The Byzantines made several appeals to the West for military aid to repel the Turks, but nothing resulted from these until Pope Urban II delivered his famous speech at Clermont, France, in 1095 that launched the First Crusade. At the council the pontiff declared, "From the confines of Jerusalem and from the city of Constantinople a horrible tale has gone forth. . . . An accursed race, a race utterly alienated from God . . . has invaded the lands of those Christians and depopulated them by the sword, plundering and fire." The Turks were allegedly guilty of such atrocities as desecrating churches, torture and murder, and raping Christian women. He also appealed to French honor: "Recall the greatness of Charlemagne. Start upon the road to the Holy Sepulchre, to tear that land from the wicked race and subject it to yourselves." At the conclusion of his address a shout rose from the crowd, "Deus Vult!" (God wills it). Delighted with this response Urban made "Deus Vult" the battle cry of the Crusades, and suggested that each warrior wear the sign of the cross upon his clothing.

In the months that followed, papal representatives traveled throughout Europe enlisting recruits to go to the Holy Land to fight the Turks, the most notable of whom was Peter the Hermit. The First Crusade (1096–99) was mainly French in character, and its leaders were prominent nobles—such as Raymond of Toulouse, Godfrey of Bouillon (duke of Lorraine), Robert of Normandy, and Stephen of Blois.

As the rag-tag bands of knights and supporters lumbered through central Europe on their way to the Holy Land, they paused to terrorize Jewish communities, whom they accused of persecuting the early Christians and aiding the Islamic conquest, and they extorted money from the Jews to help finance the venture. This marked the first large-scale outbreak of anti-Semitic violence in medieval Europe. Eventually the Crusader forces reached the East, captured Jerusalem in July 1099, and massacred the Muslim population, one of the most disgraceful events in all of Christian history. They created the Latin kingdom of Jerusalem and several other states along the eastern Mediterranean coast, thus maintaining a balance of power between the Byzantines and Muslims. In the process they repeated this pattern of reckless violence against the indigenous populations again and again.

Actually, the hold of the Europeans was fragile and other Crusades soon followed. Italian maritime cities like Venice, Genoa, and Pisa provided a lifeline, in that they conveyed pilgrims to the East and sent supplies and recruits to fight the Muslims, but their commitment to a spiritual venture in Palestine was at best minimal. At this time two new religious orders were formed, the Knights Templar and the Knights Hospitaller (Knights of St. John), which combined monasticism and militarism. Their members were soldier-monks who originally were to aid and protect pilgrims, but soon their duties were expanded to include the defense of the Crusader states. In 1189 German soldiers and merchants in the Holy Land formed a third order, the Teutonic Knights.

Because the Latin Kingdom of Jerusalem was losing ground to a Muslim advance, the pope directed Bernard of Clairvaux to call Christians to a Second Crusade. In 1147 King Louis VII of France and Conrad III, the Holy Roman Emperor, led an expedition that was marked by a series of disasters, most notably an ambush near Damascus, and after two years their forces melted away. A Crusade preached by the man with the greatest reputation for holiness in Europe and led by royalty had failed. The fiasco angered medieval Christians and many came to feel that the "treachery" of the Greeks was the main reason for the failure. Consequently, Bernard suggested that a campaign be mounted against Constantinople, a wish that would be fulfilled in 1204.

Within a few years the Muslims consolidated their power under their most distinguished sultan, Saladin (1138–93). First, he gained control over Egypt by 1174 and then conquered most of Syria. In 1187 he captured Jerusalem, but did not massacre the Christian population, and he reduced the power of the coastal crusader states. When news of this reached the West, the three leading monarchs of the time, Emperor Frederick Barbarossa, Richard I of England, and Philip II of France, undertook an entirely lay effort to free the Holy Land (Third Crusade, 1188–92), but little resulted from it. Barbarossa died on the way and Philip returned home after quarreling with Richard, who did negotiate a treaty with Saladin giving Christian pilgrims access to Jerusalem.

After this Europeans gradually lost interest in the crusading ideal, and Muslim power in the East was completely reestablished. When the few knights who answered Pope Innocent III's call to the Fourth Crusade (1202–4) were unable to pay the passage charges demanded by the Venetians, the two groups struck a bargain and attacked Constantinople instead. Other efforts followed that were pathetic, like the Children's Crusade (1212) and the Fifth Crusade against Egypt (1219). Still others were militarily effective, such as the Sixth Crusade conducted by Frederick II in 1228–29, which briefly regained possession of Jerusalem. Louis IX of France accomplished nothing in his crusading expeditions of 1248–50 and 1270. In 1291 the era came to an end with the fall of Acre, the last crusader state. However, though the Crusades alienated Byzantine Christians, the cultural changes resulting from two centuries of contact with the East had a lasting effect on Western life.

Latin Missionary Expansion

The Crusades were only one way in which Western Europeans responded to the presence of non-Christian neighbors. Another was the continuing eastern movement of the Germans. In the eleventh and twelfth centuries this resulted in the forcible conversion of the Slavic Wends living between the Elbe and Oder rivers and an influx of German farmers into the region. Bishop Otto of Bamberg undertook a successful missionary effort in Pomerania in the 1120s, and with the arrival of German settlers the assimilation of the Slavic Pomeranians was completed. In the thirteenth century the Polish king invited German colonists to occupy areas in Silesia and Poznan (Posen) that had been devastated by Mongol raids.

Along the Baltic coast crusading-style ventures were the order of the day. The Knights of the Sword, formed in 1202, was a German military order that conquered much of Estonia and Latvia within two decades, although they had to compete with Scandinavians for mastery of the region. In 1226 the Polish king invited the Teutonic Knights, who had relocated in Europe and assisted the Hungarian king in converting the Turkic Cumans in Transylvania, to undertake a similar venture among the heathen Prussians. The Knights plunged into the task with vigor, and their crusade as champions of Christianity and Germanism was comparable to the one in Spain. After they absorbed the holdings of the Knights of the Sword in 1237 and finished the conquest of Prussia in 1285, the entire southern coast of the Baltic was open to Christian mission and German trade and colonization.

The Knights intended to continue their drive into Russia, but Catholic expansion was halted by Alexander Nevsky, prince of Novgorod (1219–63). He defeated the Germans at the celebrated "Battle on the Ice" on the frozen surface of Lake Peipus in Estonia in 1242 and then placed himself under the rule of the Mongol khan. This ensured the survival of Eastern Orthodoxy in Russia (see chapter 8), an action for which he was made a saint.

A century later the Teutonic Knights finally wore down the resistance of the Lithuanians, and in 1385 their king, Jagiello, was baptized. However, he at once allied with the Polish ruler to hinder further German advances, and in the following century their combined forces defeated the Teutonic order and restricted its power to Prussia.

Still, Latin Catholics saw the vast Mongol empire as a missionary opportunity. Two Franciscan friars, John of Planocarpini in 1245–47 and William of Rubruquis (or Rubruck) in 1253–55, traveled to the court of the khan and brought back glowing reports. The Nestorians (see chapter 8) had already had enormous success in this area, and the Catholics hoped to duplicate this. In the late thirteenth –early fourteenth centuries Franciscans and Dominicans established a chain of missions across Asia, reaching from the Black Sea-Caucasian region to Persia, India, and even China. Best remembered is John of Monte Corvino, a Franciscan who took charge of the work in Peking in 1294 and was named archbishop by the pope in 1307.

It seemed at first that the Mongol rulers might accept Christianity, but then the western branch adopted Islam, thus cutting off communications with the missions, and the victory of the Ming dynasty in China in 1368 resulted in the expulsion of all foreigners there. By now Europe was distracted by wars, plagues, and political-religious controversies, and missionary enthusiasm waned.

Cathedral Schools and Universities

The stability and optimism of the high Middle Ages (1100–1300) resulted in the growth of learning and of universities. During the earlier period monasteries were largely responsible for education. A learned monk was assigned to teach novices (new monks), and as his fame spread, adults from other houses would come to study with him. Often young men from well-to-do families studied under the monastic tutor and afterwards joined the clergy or took up secular work.

By the twelfth century the cathedral schools had come to the fore. The chancellor, the chief cathedral dignitary after the bishop and dean, taught the liberal arts and theology to the advanced students, while other teachers instructed youths in Latin grammar. Scholars were generally destined for service in the church. A license to teach, awarded by the chancellor, was the predecessor of a university degree.

The theological debates that took place in the schools contributed to the reawakening of intellectual life in Europe. One significant controversy involved Berengar (c. 1000–88), who was at the cathedral school of Tours. The issue was the meaning of the words of consecration in the Mass: "This is my body, this is my blood." Berengar agreed that a real and true change takes place in these elements, but he said the change is spiritual and the bread and wine remain of the same substance. Lanfranc and others insisted that the underlying substance of the bread and wine was changed to Christ's body, blood, soul, and divinity, while the "accidents" (touch, taste, sight, and smell) of the bread and wine remained the same. After a long and bitter controversy Lanfranc's definition of "transubstantiation" became the accepted view.

Another debate was over Christ's work on the cross and how his death could bring about reconciliation between God and man. The dominant teaching had been Origen's (see chapter 2), who believed that through sin humankind had subjected itself to the devil and the mark of this was death. God wished to free men but could not as the

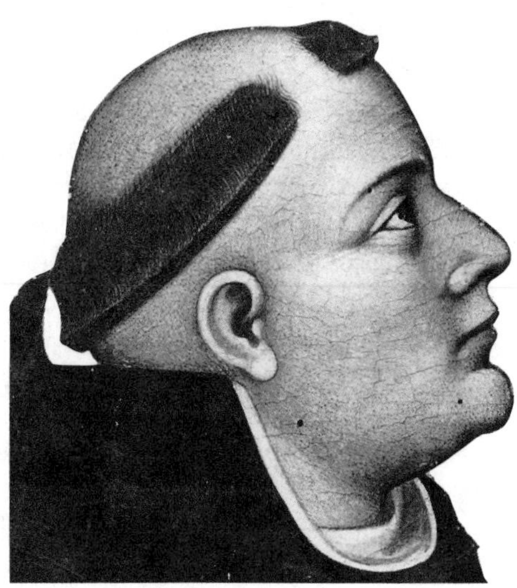

Thomas Aquinas

devil's claim was just. Consequently, to neutralize this claim a ransom was paid in the form of one over whom Satan had no right, that is, a sinless man. Thus, the devil was tricked when Christ was crucified, and now God can justly save whomever He pleases.

Anselm of Canterbury challenged this in *Why God Became Man.* He argued that when a person sins he breaks the right order of the universe and is alienated from God. Being just, God must receive a satisfaction for sin before he can forgive the sinner. Christ, the sinless man, was sent by the mercy of God to offer the satisfaction owed by the human race. This provided a whole new understanding of the incarnation and atonement.

Perhaps the leading teacher in this period was Peter Abelard (1079–1142) in Paris. It was his *methods* more than his *conclusions* that upset many churchmen. As he stated, "The first key to wisdom is this constant and frequent questioning. . . . For by doubting we are led to question, by questioning we arrive at the truth!" Abelard used this approach in the book *Yes and No,* where he demonstrated that tradition and authority alone were not sufficient to answer such questions as "Is God omnipotent?" "Do we sin without willing it?" and "Is faith based upon reason?" He quoted authorities on both sides and left the contradictions unresolved. However, his pupil Peter Lombard (c. 1100–69) used reason to answer many of the same questions in his work *The Sentences,* a popular theological textbook. The technique of setting up contradictory statements concerning a problem and then resolving them by reason would prove to be the key feature of scholasticism.

The cathedral schools were the catalyst for the foundation of universities. A city with a well-known cathedral often became the center for many schools, and scholars would rent rooms and students would pay to listen to lectures. From this situation emerged the university. In fact, the term *universitas* originally described a guild of teachers or scholars who banded together in self-defense against the town in which they were located, or to discipline lazy students or teachers. Professors organized the universities of northern Europe, whereas in Italy it was the students who formed the guilds. The first universities obtained their charter from the pope; later ones applied to the secular rulers for recognition

The earliest universities included Bologna, Paris, Salerno, Oxford, Cambridge, Padua, Salamanca, and Toulouse. They were fairly small by modern standards, the largest having between 3,000 and 4,000 students. Although they taught the seven liberal arts (see chapter 6), logic or philosophy tended to dominate the undergraduate curriculum. The graduate faculties taught medicine, law, and theology.

At Paris, a young man could begin his studies at age twelve, but the privilege of lecturing in theology was not granted until one was thirty-five. The only entrance requirement was a knowledge of Latin. The first four years' work that culminated in the Master of Arts (A.M.) degree consisted of study, a teaching assistantship, and thesis defense. He could then go on to study law, medicine, or theology. If he decided to earn the Doctor of Divinity (D.D.) degree in theology, he would spend six years concentrating on the Bible and Peter Lombard's systematic theology. Three additional years' study of the writings of the church Fathers and the Bible led to the Doctor of Sacred Theology (S.T.D.), which qualified the scholar to teach theology in the same way that the A.M. entitled him to teach the arts.

The most famous college at Paris was the Sorbonne. The English universities, Oxford and Cambridge, were modeled on Paris. The colleges resembled the groups of canons at a cathedral, where the clergy lived together under a rule. Although the professors and students were supposed to be churchmen, their conduct suggested that their minds were often on other matters.

SCHOLASTICISM

The distinctive method of theological and philosophical speculation in the medieval schools was scholasticism. It sought to reconcile Christian revelation with the philosophy of Aristotle, which had been transmitted to western Europe through the Muslims and Jews of Spain and southern Italy. It drew from various sources. One was Platonic "realism," which held there were ideas (universals) in God's mind—perfect forms or essences, such as chair, man, honor, and tree—and the individual things (particulars) that people actually perceive. Another was Abelard's emphasis on the right of the philosopher to use his own reason. Also important was Aristotle's world-system, which became known to medieval scholars around 1200. This relied completely on reason and operated without reference to the Christian God. Such concepts as the prime mover, eternal motion, a denial of creation and providence, uncertainty about immortality and the soul, and a morality based on reason alone were extremely upsetting to people at the time.

The genius of two Dominican theologians, Albertus Magnus (Albert the Great, 1193–1280) and his pupil Thomas Aquinas (1224–74), was to bring these ideas together into a logical system that maintained the distinction between the realms of divine revelation and human reason and that used all human knowledge in the investigation of divine mysteries. Thomas's *Summa Theologiae* was the greatest medieval theological work and its influence is still seen today. In it he argues that God's existence can be known through His effects in the world, things that all can see. But God is known not only through "nature" but also through "grace," by His revelation in Scripture.

Thomas's goal was to harmonize faith and reason. Accepting Aristotle as a guide in reason and Scripture as the rule of faith, he shows that there is a meaningful relationship between the two. Though some doctrines can only be known through revelation, such as the Trinity, original sin, the incarnation, and the resurrection, they are not necessarily contrary to reason. Rather, revelation supplements and perfects but never contradicts the conclusions of reason.

This method is illustrated in a discussion of the providence of God. Aristotle stated that God (or the "Unmoved Mover") neither knows nor cares about the world; yet the Bible affirms frequently that God is intimately concerned with His creation. However, this was not a real contradiction, because God as the maker of the world is its ultimate cause and comprehends the effects of this creation. Since He knows everything in Himself, He knows of the whole creation. Also, because He created time, His knowledge of His work is eternal.

Thomas then explained logically the doctrines of immortality, creation, and judgment. He made a clear distinction between the way knowledge is gained in the present world, and what an individual learns after death. In this world comprehension is gained through experience, either directly or indirectly, but in heaven an individual will learn through "mystic knowledge." The apostles and prophets were privileged individuals, who could experience God in a mystic fashion before their death, but this cognizance was limited to them. By distinguishing in this way between sense experience and heavenly knowledge, Thomas thus could draw a clear difference between science and the Christian hope.

Faith and Worship

The church dominated the intellectual and artistic life of the age because it satisfied the religious needs of Europeans. One source of its strength was flexibility, that is, the capacity to embrace a variety of religious beliefs and practices so long as the essentials the faith were maintained. Further, the regular conduct of divine services, provision of spiritual guidance, and presence of the church's ministers at the times of life's greatest crises and joys gave people the comfort that comes from routine.

Also important were the sacraments, which were believed to confer grace upon those who received them. Peter Lombard set the number at seven in his *Sentences,* and this was ratified at later church councils. Both the Eastern and Western churches accepted the sevenfold enumeration: baptism, confirmation, communion or Eucharist ("Thanksgiving"), penance, extreme unction, holy matrimony, and holy orders.

Baptism removed the stain of original sin, signified adoption as a child of God, and made the recipient a member of the church, the mystical Body of Christ. Confirmation, bestowed by the laying on of hands by a bishop, qualified one to be a full participant in the sacramental and institutional life of the church. The Eucharist, the point in the Mass where the bread and wine were transformed by God through the priest's prayer of consecration into the body and blood of Christ, gave the communicant the benefits of the sacrifice of Calvary in a metaphysical fashion. Included in penance were confession to a priest, acceptance of a penalty, and the absolution of sins sincerely repented. Extreme unction involved the anointing of the sick with holy oil by a priest. It assisted in the cure, or if one was dying, it strengthened his or her soul. In holy matrimony, the marriage of two baptized people, the parties themselves were the ministers and the priest the appointed witness. Marriage was thus placed under the purview of the church. Holy orders, bestowed by bishops in the laying on of hands, made a man a bishop, priest, or deacon, depending upon the situation. Involved here is the concept of apostolic succession, the idea that the ministry was derived from the apostles through an unbroken sequence of ordinations of bishops.

One could argue that the sacramental system was a psychologically sound approach to the Christian life because each of these came at certain passages or crisis times—birth, puberty, marriage, illness, and death. They supported the person by combining a tangible act with some more abstract theological meaning.

The church used many different methods to bring its message to the public. Foremost was the planting of a house of God wherever there were believers or potential converts. Churches, cathedrals, oratories, and shrines were everywhere, and their doors were open to any who wished to enter. The religious work of the church, "the cure of souls" as it was called, was performed by the priests and some in the monastic orders. Missionaries and the friars who preached in the open air brought the word to those who did not attend divine services. Public rituals and processions also attracted the attention of the unconverted.

To reinforce the spoken word, the church utilized music, sculpture, painting, and stained glass. There was also an appeal to the supernatural through relics and miracles. Every major parish had its collection of relics and a patron saint, both of which were believed to have power to heal and bless the worshipers. In short, the church tried all that was humanly possible to attract and hold the populace.

THE VIRGIN MARY

The most popular of the medieval saints was the Virgin Mary. Although her cult originated in the early church, it was encouraged by the use of the term *Theotokos* ("the bearer of God") at the ecumenical church councils (see chapter 3). The concern there was to reinforce a belief in the deity of Christ and the reality of the incarnation against Arian and Monophysite dissenters. At first the cult of the

Virgin was strongest in the East, but by the ninth century it had sunk deep roots in the West as well.

She was believed to be the mediator between God and humans, in that she prayed to her Son to have mercy on sinners. Born without sin (the "Immaculate Conception"), ever virgin and sinless in her life, and taken up into heaven at her death (the "Assumption"), she was the ideal combination of purity and maternal affection. By the thirteenth century she was also known as the Queen of Heaven, and the respect given to her surpassed all previous limits. Although she was venerated with a worship higher than that offered to other saints, it was officially understood that she would not receive the worship reserved for her Son, who was God. Her miracles included helping the poor, healing the sick, and comforting the lonely.

Most church doctrines developed from the work of theologians and the decisions of councils, but the veneration of Mary passed into church teaching from popular religion. To the people she was "Our Lady" or in French, "Notre Dame." There was a tendency to look on Christ as a stern and unapproachable judge, and the increased attention paid to Mary was an example of efforts to adopt a more kindly and gracious view of God. Mary was a loving mother who, because of her own tragic experience, could sympathize with people. This is well expressed in the famous thirteenth-century hymn to Mary, the "Stabat Mater," whose opening stanza reads:

> By the cross her vigil keeping
> Stands the Queen of sorrows weeping,
> While her Son in torment hangs;
> Now she feels—O heart afflicted
> By the sword of old predicted!—
> More than all a mother's pangs.

The extent of the Virgin's popularity in the twelfth and thirteenth centuries could be seen in the many cathedrals and churches dedicated to her, such as Notre Dame de Paris and Notre Dame de Chartres.

HERETICAL GROUPS

After 1200 there was a growing rigidity in faith and order, an erosion of that flexibility that had been a source of the church's

Rheims Cathedral in France

strength. As its structure and doctrines were more precisely articulated, deviation from the official norms was more common and "heresy" became a serious problem. However, there were several ways in which one might deal with religious nonconformity. The friars, with their preaching and exemplary lives, were one response. Another was conversion, the use of teaching to restore the erring to the fold. Most ominous was that followed by Innocent III, who had the views of French heretics condemned at the Fourth Lateran Council (1215) and proclaimed a crusade against them. Thus, an increasingly popular technique was to torture and execute those who obstinately persisted in their heresies.

There were reasons for this strong reaction. Members of heretical groups often engaged in violence against the faithful, especially when they became part of a social protest movement such as the intolerant Albigensians. Also, to people in the medieval world, nothing was more important than the salvation of their eternal souls. Those who endangered souls should be treated as one does an inflamed appendix: remove it before it can cause more trouble.

In the earlier Middle Ages, the teachings of most heresies were so intellectual and abstract as to leave people indifferent or bewildered. But in the late twelfth century, the Gregorian Reform encouraged the dangerous idea of "apostolic poverty" (the clergy should not possess great wealth), thus resulting in an undercurrent of criticism of abuses in the church. Also, because the new movements of dissent were practical, not intellectual, they had mass appeal.

One was the Waldensians, whose founder Peter Waldo, a merchant of Lyon, felt called to a life of apostolic poverty in 1173. The beliefs of his followers included nonrecognition of ecclesiastical authority, vernacular services, a symbolic interpretation of the Eucharist, denial of the validity of infant baptism, rejection of purgatory, an austere lifestyle, and pacifism. Although the papacy considered their ideas as heretical, in fact they were genuinely Christian in an ecumenical sense. Persecution led to the movement's spread across the continent. The French Waldensians found refuge in the Alps of Savoy and Piedmont and survived to the present, while others went to central Europe where they may have influenced both John Hus and the Reformation.

On the other hand, Albigensianism, which emerged in the late twelfth century, really was another religion. Its stronghold was in southern France at the town of Albi in Languedoc. Also known as the Cathari (the "pure ones"), its beliefs were drawn from oriental mystery religions, Manichaeism, and heretical sects in the Eastern church, most notably the Paulicians and Bogomils. The Albigensians held a radical dualism, that is, there was both an evil and a good god who contended in history and in individuals for victory. Life was a struggle between these gods and their principal forces, spirit and matter. Since they preached the gradual purification from all matter, including their own bodies, their lives were ones of extreme asceticism. They also rejected the sacraments, hell, and the resurrection, and saw the clergy and doctrines of the Catholic church as perverted. Although in theory they were pacifists, in practice they were quite violent. After trying in vain to convert them by sending several missions, Innocent III declared the Albigensian Crusade of 1209. Conducted with brutality against violent resistance, the campaign wiped out the Albigenses.

Another instrument to combat heresy was the Roman Inquisition. Founded in 1233 by Pope Gregory IX, this was an ecclesiastical court that operated under Roman law principles of investigation and interrogation. The pope sent inquisitors, mainly Dominican and Franciscan friars, who held tribunals to hunt out heretics. When the inquisitors came to town, dissidents were given a period of time in which they could appear voluntarily and renounce their errors. Those who did so were discharged with a light penalty. Then people were summoned to tell the inquisitors about heretics whom they knew.

While there were some safeguards for the accused, the advantage in the trial lay with the prosecution, particularly after the introduction of torture in 1252. At this stage a confession would deliver the heretic to a heavy penance and punishment. If the accused continued to maintain innocence and not renounce the heresy, he or she was turned over to the secular authorities for condemnation and execution.

The same hardening of attitude was shown toward the Jews, the perennial outsider in Christian society. This was in sharp contrast to treatment they experienced in the early Middle Ages under the Germanic kings, who valued their roles as moneylenders and merchants. During the Carolingian era their economic activities were greatly appreciated, as such services were scarce in an underdeveloped society. In fact, some Jews even owned large estates in the French wine-producing region.

By 1050 the new militancy of Latin Christianity and growth of popular piety led to a marked increase in animosity toward Jews. Economic and political changes prepared the way for this sad condition. Since the feudal relationships that proliferated during this period demanded the taking of a Christian oath, land-owning Jews were forced into the towns where they engaged in handicrafts and trade. Then the growth of guilds, each of which was organized around the veneration of a particular saint, led to their exclusion from the crafts. Soon the the only profession left to them was the exchange and lending of money, thus adding an economic factor to the already existing religious antagonism. Now they were hated for usury (lending money at interest), but, in an age when commercial activities were risky at best and when they had trouble collecting from Gentiles, Jews found it necessary to charge as much as 50 percent interest on loans.

No amount of malicious gossip about Jews seemed too ridiculous for Christians to believe. They supposedly poisoned wells, engaged in cannibalism, sacrificed Christian children (the infamous "blood libel"), and, most absurdly of all, stole the sacramental bread from the altar and stabbed it with a knife in order to make Jesus suffer again.

Finally, the Fourth Lateran Council decreed that Jews had to wear distinctive clothing and be confined to ghettos. Later the kings of England, France, and Spain used the religious argument to expel them and to confiscate their property. Some Jews converted but others moved eastward and settled in Germany and Poland. Actions during this period laid the basis for subsequent expressions of anti-Semitism and deprived medieval society of perhaps its most literate and valuable ethnic group.

THE CHURCH AND ART

The most important area of artistic achievement was the church structures, and the sculpture and painting associated with them. Two architectural styles predominated during this period—the Romanesque and the Gothic. The Romanesque was reflected in a great burst of church building during the eleventh century, which produced an estimated 1,587 new structures in France alone. The roof was a thick half-cylinder of stone called a barrel vault, whose weight forced the builders to construct uniform, heavy walls. The emphasis was on horizontal lines, which gave the worshiper a feeling of repose and solidity. Since windows were few and small, to lighten the interior churches were hung with tapestries or painted bright colors, and statues, chalices, and reliquaries were gilded and jeweled. Freestanding stone sculptures were used to ease the heavy effect of Romanesque construction.

A gradual shift from Romanesque to Gothic style occurred in the later twelfth century. Characterized by delicacy and detail, the support needed for a Gothic structure was placed outside the walls in flying buttresses. The use of pointed arches made possible a very tall structure that emphasized vertical lines directing the worshipers toward heaven. Gothic churches were light in two ways: the design enabled the stonework to lose its massive weightiness, while the stained-glass windows constituted a work of art. Not only were the windows works of art, the pillars, doors, and nearly every other part of the cathedral were sculpted. Gothic churches had structural detail that was comparable to the works of the medieval theologians.

In the thirteenth century rivalry sprang up among the cities as to which could erect the highest cathedral structure. As a result, each was built according to a specific design, although, because a church took generations to complete, the plans would often be altered. Constructing the church was a community project involving professional architects, craftsmen, and laborers.

Medieval art expressed a coherent system of values and a view of the universe based on an understanding of Christianity. Its purpose was to point to the spiritual reality that underlay the material world. Artists used a highly developed system of symbolism and allegory to present their ideas, one where most things had a spiritual as well as a literal meaning. For example, fire represented martyrdom or religious fervor, a lily stood for chastity, an owl (the bird of darkness) often could mean Satan, and a lamb stood for Christ as the sacrifice for sin.

Artistic achievement reached its height in the Gothic cathedral. It combined the medieval version of a place of worship, theater, art gallery, school, and library. The market place was in the area of the cathedral, plays were staged on its steps, strangers slept there, and townsmen would meet in the side-aisles.

Since it was the house of people as well as the house of God, the cathedral was a mirror of the world. All artistic works were naturalistic, detailed representations of beasts, Bible stories, and the allegories of vices and virtues. The structure of society was seen in carvings that portrayed ministers, knights, craftsmen, peasants, and tradesmen in their various activities. Theology was reflected in the structure of the building—the upward reaching toward God, the layout in the shape of a cross, and the altar situated in the east, facing Jerusalem. Every detail of belief, from the triune Godhead to the creation, from the death of Christ to the last judgment, appeared in sculpture, paintings, mosaics, and stained glass. The harmony found in such a structure signified the ideals of medieval art and thought.

At no time in history had Christianity been so pervasive a social influence as it was in medieval Europe. Although the two halves of Christendom were drifting steadily apart, their respective churches dominated political, cultural, and intellectual life. Renewed efforts to expand the frontiers of Western Christendom occurred, but beginning in the early fourteenth century an economic depression affected Europe. This led to a general malaise marked by violence, disease, political instability, and pessimism, and the ensuing century of discontent and bitterness shattered the medieval synthesis of church and society.

8

THE MEDIEVAL CHURCH IN THE EAST

The distance between Orthodox Christianity in the East and the Latin church of the West steadily widened. Not only did its patriarch function under the shadow of the Byzantine emperor, but there were also differences in language, liturgy, doctrine, and church politics. Then the Crusades delivered a death blow to East-West relations, while the increasing Muslim pressures on the empire led to its demise in 1453. At the same time, disagreements over the Chalcedonian definition of Christ caused other Christian groups to become estranged from mainline Orthodoxy. These included Monophysites in Armenia, Egypt, Ethiopia, and Syria, and the Nestorians in Mesopotamia, central Asia, China, and India.

BYZANTINE EMPERORS AND PATRIARCHS

Constantine's transfer of the capital from Rome to Byzantium in 330 had momentous consequences. Not only would the Byzantine Empire last more than a thousand years, but making Constantinople the seat of the empire also meant the elevation of that city's chief bishop. At the time of the Council of Nicaea (325), the city possessed only a small local see, but it grew so rapidly in importance over the next century that in 451 the Council of Chalcedon declared, "The most holy Church of Constantinople, the New Rome, shall have a primacy next after Old Rome." By 600 its bishop was called "Archbishop of the City of Constantine, New Rome, and Ecumenical Patriarch."

The history of the Byzantine Empire is replete with palace intrigues and military revolutions. More than sixty emperors were murdered or forced to abdicate. In contrast to the pope in Rome, who served as the chief spiritual and political authority in the West quite independent of secular rulers, the powerful figure of the emperor always overshadowed the Orthodox patriarch. Although the emperor in his role as the vicegerent (deputy) of Christ was an exalted layman who had the right to preach, he could not legitimately introduce doctrinal changes without the support of the patriarch and a council of bishops. To be sure, the Byzantine emperors were more interested in preserving the unity of their fragmenting empire than in doctrinal purity. But their efforts to maintain links with the West were made increasingly difficult by the Lombard invasion of Italy, Slavic migrations into the Balkans, and the unrelenting attacks of the Bulgars in the north and Muslims in the east.

The emperors attempted to resolve the knotty Monophysite problem through a series of compromises. The most noteworthy was the *Henoticon*, or "Edict of Union," proclaimed by Emperor Zeno with the encouragement of Patriarch Acacius in 482. The *Henoticon* took the stance, one that was popular with the followers of Cyril of Alexandria, that the definition of Christ affirmed at the councils of Nicaea (325), Constantinople (381), and Ephesus (431) was sufficient. Although it condemned the Monophysite leader Eutyches, the document left open an honest difference of opinion on the matter by not affirming the hard-line position taken at the Council of Chalcedon. Zeno hoped by this means to bring about reconciliation between the adherents of the varying views on the two natures of Christ. While many "moderate" Monophysites accepted the decree, the more extreme ones would not yield. At the same time, the pope objected that the *Henoticon* ignored the *Tome* of Leo, and he excommunicated both Acacius and Zeno, resulting in the Acacian Schism between West and the East (484–519).

Theodora, the wife of the great emperor Justinian, sympathized with the Monophysites and even gave refuge in her apartments to their bishops, whom he had deposed. Justinian himself set out to unite the church around the "orthodox" view of the natures of Christ

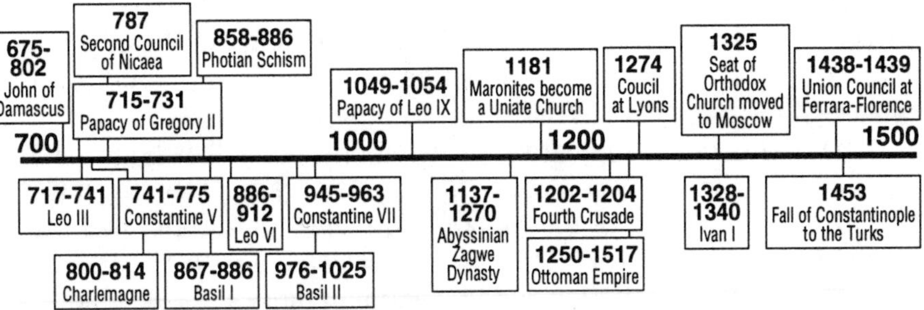

and thereby provide a spiritual basis for his political effort to reunite East and West. But then, in an effort to win over the Monophysites, the emperor issued an edict in 544 condemning the so-called "Three Chapters," the writings of three prominent bishops accused of Nestorian tendencies who had been cleared at Chalcedon a century earlier. He secured the agreement of the four Eastern patriarchs and brought Pope Vigilius to the capital, to pressure him into giving assent as well.

To ratify his condemnation of the Three Chapters, Justinian convened the Fifth Ecumenical Council at Constantinople in 553. Vigilius protested that only a dozen of the 165 bishops at the meeting represented the Western churches and the emperor's efforts at conciliation came to naught. He had alienated the West, infuriated the Nestorians, and even failed to win over the Monophysites. As a result, his hope of establishing religious and cultural unity was frustrated.

An important development took place during the reign of Heraclius (610–41). The Sassanid Persians invaded Syria and advanced into Palestine and Egypt in 619, thereby threatening the empire's grain supply. The Persian king even removed the legendary "True Cross" from the Church of the Holy Sepulchre. When Heraclius approached him for peace terms, the Zoroastrian ruler replied, "I shall not spare you until you have renounced the Crucified One, whom you call God, and bow before the Sun [i.e., Ahuramazda]." Meanwhile, the Avars menaced the north, Slavic raiders reached almost to the walls of Constantinople, and the last Roman forces were expelled from Spain by the Visigoths.

It appeared that Heraclius might have to move the capital to Carthage, when Patriarch Sergius came to the rescue. He offered the treasures of the church to the emperor, thus enabling him to raise an army that defended Constantinople from the barbarian attacks in 625–26. Heraclius then defeated the Persians and recovered the True Cross. By 630 he had restored Syria, Palestine, and Egypt to the empire. This was but a few years before the Islamic onslaught overwhelmed most of these territories.

Thus it became imperative to heal the religious division with the Monophysites in the East. Following Sergius's lead, Heraclius in 633 proposed acceptance of the Monophysite view that Christ had one *energeia* ("operation" or "activity") to correspond with His one nature. Nevertheless, the strongly Chalcedonian monks in Palestine led by Sophronius, patriarch of Jerusalem, opposed this usage and Sergius turned to Rome for support. Pope Honorius, however, said that the proclamation of new doctrines was solely the responsibility of church councils, and Sergius dropped the idea.

However, in his eagerness to win the strong Monophysite party in Egypt without losing the support of the Western church, Heraclius (with the approval of Sergius) proposed another idea that Pope Honorius originally had suggested. To replace the unsuccessful *Henoticon,* he advanced the concept of Monotheletism, which he hoped would replace the Monophysitism rampant in the eastern provinces. Sidestepping the dispute over whether Christ had one or two natures, this doctrine affirmed the oneness of his human and divine *wills* and thus should be acceptable to both the Chalcedonian and Monophysite factions. At first this ingenious statement pleased churchmen on both sides of the divide, but when Heraclius published an edict in 638 containing the dogma of the one will, the Egyptian Monophysites rejected it. A bitter struggle ensued that so alienated the Copts from the Byzantines that it helped set the stage for the Arab conquest of Egypt in 641. They offered no resistance to the Muslim invaders.

Monotheletism was also condemned by the pope in 647, who then excommunicated the patriarch of Constantinople for accepting the doctrine, and East-West tensions simmered over the next few years. When Emperor Constantine IV (668–85) realized that Monotheletism not only failed to reconcile the Monophysites but also alienated the West, he invited the pope to send delegates to Constantinople for the Sixth Ecumenical Council in 681. The assembly decreed that Christ had "two natural wills and two natural operations, without separation, without change, without division, and without confusion." Through this action the great Christological controversies that had torn the church for more than three centuries came to an end.

Besides condemning some popular amusements, the council also proscribed certain Western practices such as fasting on Saturday and clerical celibacy, thus causing another breach with Rome that lasted until 710. It also ruled that Christ should no longer be depicted symbolically (for example, as a lamb) but only as a living human being. This reflected the widening gap between the Eastern and Western churches and set the stage for yet another conflict between them.

THE ICONOCLASTIC CONTROVERSY

By the sixth century both the imperial government and the Orthodox church were encouraging the production of icons (from the Greek *eikôn*)—two-dimensional paintings of Christ, the Virgin, saints and angels. These were believed to have healing and protective powers. The icon of the Virgin was even credited with saving Constantinople from foreign conquest, although the Muslim Arabs did conquer the eastern provinces of the empire with relative ease. But Leo III, who established the Isaurian Dynasty (717–802), was able to repel the Arab assault on the capital in 718.

Leo launched the iconoclastic controversy, the opposition to the use of icons, which raged for more than a century. Because he was from Syria, some feel he may have been influenced by the Muslim accusation that Christians were idolaters, while others credit his hostility to icons to Jewish sources. Be that as it may, Leo concluded that the veneration of icons violated the second commandment and was the reason for Byzantine defeats. Then he interpreted a volcanic eruption on the island of Thera in 726 as evidence of God's wrath and forbade any kneeling before images. Four years later he ordered the removal of all icons from church and public places, thus incurring the wrath of the patriarch, whom he replaced, and the monks. Pope Gregory II, who favored icons as symbols of divine reality, protested the emperor's action, but Leo retaliated by withholding revenues from Byzantine lands in Italy and transferring Illyricum to the patriarch's jurisdiction. This reflected once again the deepening rift between the two churches. Leo was unable to depose the pope as he had the patriarch, and in the following years the papacy moved steadily closer to the French descendants of Charles Martel and away from dependence on the empire.

Leo's son, Constantine V (741–75), brutally enforced the iconoclastic decrees. He excommunicated and tortured the supporters of icons and tore down their monasteries and convents, ordering the residents to marry or be exiled. The emperor further humiliated the iconophiles by parading them in the Hippodrome with famous prostitutes. He replaced icons with the cross, the Bible, and elements of the Eucharist.

On the other hand, the most articulate defender of icons was John of Damascus (c. 675–749). A monk at St. Sabas near Jerusalem, he was such a distinguished theologian that posterity regards him as the last of the Eastern church Fathers. In the *Three Apologetic Discourses* John argued that while "worship" should be reserved for God alone, icons were worthy of "veneration." As he forcefully put it, "When we venerate icons, we do not offer veneration to matter, but by means of the icon, we venerate the person depicted." To deny the validity of icons was to deny the reality of the Incarnation.

The Empress Irene (780–802), an ambitious and dynamic personality who served as regent for her young son and then deposed him, not only was the first woman to exercise imperial rule in her own right, but was also favorably disposed toward icons. She and her appointee, Patriarch Tarasius, called the Second Council of Nicaea in 787 to restore the veneration of icons. Delegates from Rome were present and this came to be known as the Seventh (and last) Ecumenical Council. Its decrees used the argument of John of Damascus to defend icons, but the faulty translation that reached the West led people there to believe that icons had been given the same reverence as the Holy Trinity. Because of this misunderstanding the Council of Frankfurt, which Charlemagne had convened in 794 for other reasons (see chapter 6), rejected the decrees, further exacerbating East-West relations.

A renewed wave of iconoclasm was initiated by Emperor Leo V (813–20) who believed that the Byzantines had lost two battles to the heathen Bulgarians because the Christians worshiped icons. His response was a campaign to destroy all icons. He replaced the existing patriarch with an iconoclast and imprisoned those who venerated them. A subsequent emperor, Theophilus, exiled and even executed icon users.

For support the iconophiles turned to a monk in Constantinople, Theodore of the Studios (759–826), and found in him an eloquent spokesman. He maintained: "For this reason Christ is depicted in images, and the invisible is seen. He who in His own divinity is uncircumscribable accepts the circumscription natural to His body."[1]

Then, the imperial widow, Theodora, who ruled as regent for her young son, Michael III, decided to restore icon veneration. She convened a synod in 843 that condemned iconoclasts, confirmed the decrees of the Seventh Ecumenical Council of 787, and brought the bitter dispute to a conclusion.

THE PHOTIAN SCHISM

Another controversy that plagued the Eastern church began in 858 when Michael III appointed Photius, a layman, to the patriarchal office. He had been a professor of philosophy at the Imperial Academy in Constantinople and was the author of the important *Myriobiblion* (*The Library*), a scholarly commentary on 279 pagan and Christian authors. He is often called the Father of Byzantine Humanism. However, Pope Nicholas I refused to recognize Photius as patriarch and excommunicated him.

Nicholas's opposition to Photius was due not only to his exalted view of papal power, but also to the continuing rivalry with the East over control of the church in the Balkans. In retaliation the patriarch assembled a council at Constantinople four years later, which denounced the Western church for certain customs in ritual and fasting and for the inclusion of the *filioque* clause in the Nicene Creed (see chapter 6). At the same time Photius excommunicated the pope.

It should be noted that the Photian schism occurred at the very time the Eastern and Western churches were competing for the allegiance of the newly converted Bulgarian ruler Boris and that missionaries from both groups were evangelizing the south Slavs. Although the schism was healed soon after the death of Nicholas (867) and dismissal of Photius (886), it was not a cause but a symptom of the widening cleft between the communions. The real issue was papal supremacy, and it was only when this matter came to the fore that the doctrinal differences were rehearsed and debated.

THE GOLDEN AGE OF BYZANTIUM

With the accession of the Macedonian Dynasty in 867, the Eastern empire entered upon its "golden age" and expanded to Syria and Armenia. Founded by Basil I, this dynasty held sway for nearly two centuries. The Macedonian family certainly produced a curious variety of rulers. Basil's son, Leo VI (886–912), was a scholar and writer who specialized in legal studies. When the patriarch refused to sanction his marriage to a fourth wife, he sought and received the pope's blessing. Their son, Constantine VII (945–63), was a noted patron of the arts and learning who composed manuals of statecraft in which he explained the tactics of Byzantine diplomacy and the court ceremonies appropriate for the various times of the Christian year.

Basil II (976–1025) was notorious for the conquest of Bulgaria that earned him the epithet, "The Bulgar Slayer." His conflict with his Balkan neighbor resembled Charlemagne's Saxon wars in length and brutality. He blinded 14,000 prisoners, leaving only one in every hundred with a single eye to lead the rest of them home. The Bulgarian king was said to have died of shock when he beheld his mutilated subjects. It was not, however, until 1037 that the Byzantines finally established firm control over the region. Finally, after a series of weak rulers, in 1056 the Macedonian line died out and a quarter century of anarchy followed.

The Schism of 1054

Near the end of this high-water mark in Byzantine history occurred the famous schism of 1054. There were definite reasons that the growing estrangement between the Eastern and Western churches turned into open conflict. The papal reformers (see chapter 6) were critical of Greek customs and church discipline, which they regarded as immoral since the Eastern priests could marry. Consequently, the Normans, who were currently seizing the last remaining Byzantine territories in southern Italy, compelled Orthodox churches there to adopt the Latin rite and clerical lifestyle. Moreover, the problem had a political dimension, as Emperor Constantine IX had formed an alliance with the German emperor and the pope to check the Norman conquest.

The campaign against the Byzantine churches in Italy provoked the Patriarch Michael Cerularius (1043–59), an ambitious and haughty man, to order all Latin churches in Constantinople to adopt the Greek rite. He also condemned the Westerners for their use of unleavened bread in the communion, which he labeled a Jewish practice. The emperor, who favored reconciliation, invited Pope Leo IX to send a delegation to Constantinople to negotiate the differences, and the legates, led by Cardinal Humbert of Silva-Candida arrived in the capital in 1054. Many of these misunderstandings had arisen because, after the sixth century, few Greeks knew Latin, and fewer Latins knew Greek.

The papal embassy was received with courtesy by the emperor, who sincerely wanted to uphold good relations with the West, but

Carolingian and Byzantine Empires

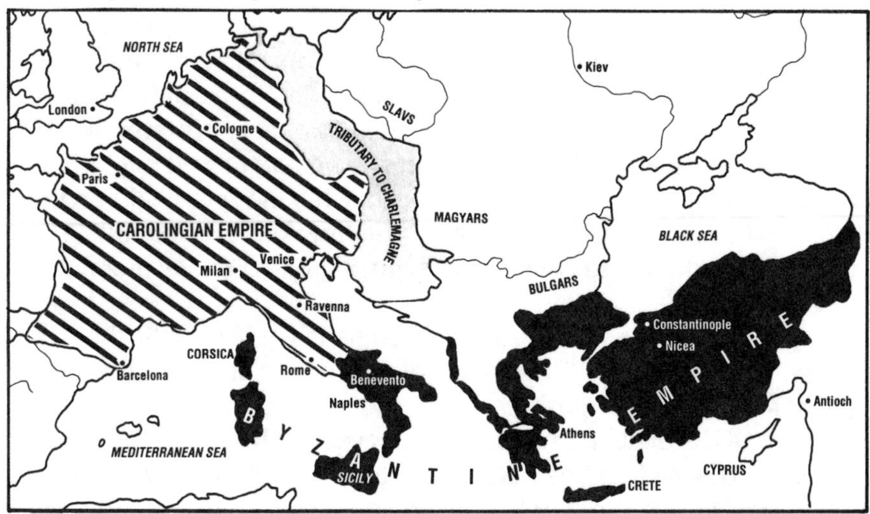

the ecclesiastical representatives from the two sides proved to be intransigent. Humbert, an arrogant man, accused the Easterners of suppressing the *filioque* clause. They responded that the addition of this point to the creed had never been authorized by a general council of the church. At the same time, Cerularius called their credentials into question because he received word that Pope Leo had just died.

On July 16, 1054, an angry Humbert and his colleagues left the city, but not before they had laid a decree of excommunication against the patriarch on the high altar of the Church of St. Sophia. Cerularius responded by convening a synod that excommunicated the papal legates. As historian John J. Norwich assesses the event, "More strength of will on the part of the dying Pope or the pleasure-loving Emperor, less bigotry on the part of the narrow-mined Patriarch or the pig-headed Cardinal, and the situation could have been saved."[2] (The mutual excommunications were only lifted in 1965, after a meeting of reconciliation between Pope Paul VI and the Patriarch Athenagoras.)

Still, relations between East and West continued. The two parts of Christendom were not conscious of an unbridgeable gulf separating them, and people on both sides hoped the misunderstandings could be resolved. However, the Crusades introduced a new spirit of hatred and bitterness that made the schism final.

THE CRUSADES

The Muslims in the East were a continuing threat to the Byzantine Empire, but the tenth century emperors who found themselves surrounded by enemies on all sides succeeded in defeating in turn the Muslims, Bulgarians, and Armenians. Just then, however, a new foe appeared, the Seljuk Turks, a people who had moved out of central Asia into the Middle East, accepted Islam, and pressed in on the empire. In 1071 they defeated the Byzantine forces at the battle of Manzikert and invaded Asia Minor, depriving Byzantium of more than half of its realm.

With the accession of Alexius Comnenus (1081–1118) the Byzantine fortunes revived. An able soldier, politician, and diplomat, Alexius stabilized the position of the empire and prevented its disintegration. (His daughter Anna wrote a revealing history of the times, the *Alexiad,* which critics have hailed as the finest medieval biography.) Alexius found not only a depleted treasury and a government whose authority was seriously undermined but he also faced a ring of enemies in Italy, the Balkans, and Asia Minor. The Turkish occupation of the latter not only broke the eastern front but more importantly it cut off his principal source of military manpower, since most of the Byzantine soldiers came from this region.

When Alexius learned that divisions had opened in the Seljuk ranks, he decided to seize the opportunity to recover his lost domains. But because he lacked sufficient soldiers for a counteroffensive, he appealed to Pope Urban II for Western mercenaries (knights) to assist him. However, the emperor had not anticipated that the help would be sent to liberate Jerusalem from Muslim control. For him the needs closer to home were far more pressing. In other words, a Byzantine ruler like Alexius could not conceive of a crusade in a Western sense. After 400 years of fighting Muslims, he saw absolutely no point in going to Jerusalem if the rear in Asia Minor were unprotected. In fact, he was prepared to come to terms with them, if the empire were threatened by attacks in the Balkans or elsewhere. Further, geography and tradition indicated that war with the adherents of Islam was the specific responsibility of the Eastern Roman Empire, not Christendom in general.

When the Crusaders arrived in Constantinople in the winter of 1096–97, Alexius was alarmed. He had hoped that Urban would help him recruit mercenaries for his own armies; now a horde of 50,000 knights bubbling with religious enthusiasm descended on his capital. He decided to provision them well, surround them with guards so they would not loot the city, obtain an oath of allegiance from their commanders, and move them as soon as possible across the Bosporus into Asia Minor. However, he incurred the displeasure of his newly found allies when he made a peace treaty with the Turks after the fighting had ceased.

This seeming treachery induced the Crusaders to create their own states in the Middle East that would relieve them of dependence on imperial assistance. Their invasion had occurred at an opportune time, as the political realm of Islam was now divided, and major rival states (caliphates) existed in Baghdad, Cairo, and Córdoba. The Crusaders moved south through Syria and Palestine and took Jerusalem in 1099.

Their conquests extended along a strip of eastern Mediterranean coastline and were divided into several kingdoms and counties. For almost 200 years they constituted a foothold of Western Christianity in the East, but in these territories the clash between the Greek Orthodox and Roman Catholics resulted in total alienation. For example, Antioch in Syria, which the Crusaders captured in 1100, had a Greek bishop who was in communion with the patriarch of Constantinople. When Alexius demanded that the city be restored to the Eastern empire, the Crusaders refused. Thus the Orthodox bishop's position became untenable. He left the city and moved to Constantionple. The Westerners chose another bishop who was a Latin, but the Orthodox one refused to resign, leaving two claimants to the ancient Patriarchate of Antioch. Similar situations arose when the Crusaders seized Jerusalem and Constantinople.

The rapport between the Byzantines and the Frankish Crusaders was so bad that Patriarch Michael III (1169–77) declared, "Let the Muslim be my master in outward things rather than the Latin dominate me in matters of the spirit." In 1182 angry Byzantines massacred all the Latins they could find in Constantinople. Then relations between East and West reached their absolute nadir in the Fourth Crusade (1202–4).

The knights from western Europe who set out for the East on the Fourth Crusade contracted with the Venetians to transport them there. To repay them for this service, the Crusaders agreed to sack the Christian town of Zara on the Adriatic coast, a rival of Venice. Then a young Byzantine prince, Alexius Angelus, asked the Crusaders to place him on the throne in Constantinople, and in return he promised to provide them with the needed financial and military support to conduct the Crusade. The Westerners naively believed that in enthroning a rightful ruler they would be performing a work of justice and charity.

Carried on Venetian ships, they proceeded to the East. But when the Crusaders discovered that Alexius was unacceptable to the people of Constantinople, they were in a real bind as to what to do next. Finally they decided simply to conquer the city. On Good Friday 1204 the Crusaders ran amok in Constantinople, and the ensuing looting and pillaging lasted three days. According to Byzantine accounts, they tortured monks, raped old ladies, slaughtered infants, and ransacked churches and libraries. Then they named a Venetian, Thomas Morosini, as the new patriarch of Constantinople and imposed the Latin church in Thrace and most of Greece.

During the period of the Latin patriarchate (1204–61), only three small Byzantine states survived, Epirus in Albania, Trebizond on the north shore of Anatolia, and Nicaea. From the latter came Michael Palaeologus, who expelled the Westerners from Constantinople in 1261, restored the Orthodox church, and established a dynasty that lasted until the fall of Constantinople in 1453.

MONASTICISM AND MYSTICISM

Meanwhile, East and West grew further apart in their theology and understanding of the Christian life. The East emphasized mysticism whereas in the West the tradition of the church Fathers was replaced by the more intellectual approach of scholasticism (see chapter 7). This was clearly reflected in fourteenth-century Hesychasm (taken from the Greek word for "quietness"), a development in which the West had no part whatsoever. To understand this controversy, one must remember that Eastern monasticism stressed total detachment from worldly temptation, unceasing prayer, and a heartfelt Christian experience that led to one becoming "deified" (2 Peter 1:4), that is, the believer would share the divine illumination and become mystically united with God.

The remote monastery at Mt. Athos in northeastern Greece became the center of the Hesychast movement. Its adherents put special emphasis on repetition of the "Jesus Prayer": "Lord Jesus Christ, Son of God, have mercy on me a sinner." It was to be done in a certain physical manner, with the head bowed, chin resting on the chest, eyes fixed on the center of the body, and carefully controlled breathing. They believed that through this "prayer of the heart" one could see God's "divine light" in a spiritual sense, a light identical to that which surrounded Jesus at the Transfiguration.

Critics of the Hesychasts, such as Barlaam the Calabrian (c. 1290–c. 1348), said that the teaching was gross superstition, because one could not know God directly. However, its defenders, particularly Gregory Palamas (c. 1296–1359), a monk at Mt. Athos, claimed that it was the "uncreated energies of the Godhead that they experienced, but not the essence of God as such." Through the energies God becomes visible, approachable, and communicable. After considerable debate, Hesychasm as expressed in the theology of Gregory was endorsed at three councils in Constantinople between 1341 and 1351, and henceforth became an accepted part of the Eastern Orthodox tradition.

ATTEMPTS AT CHURCH UNION

Two important efforts were made to bring about a reunion of the Eastern and Western churches, the first in the thirteenth century and the second in the fifteenth century. The moving spirit behind the first attempt was Michael VIII Palaeologus who ousted the Crusaders from Constantinople. To safeguard his empire from further attacks by Westerners, he needed the support and protection of the papacy, which could be secured through a union of the churches. Thus, the emperor decided to attend a council at Lyons in 1274, accompanied by those Greek bishops who were willing to discuss a settlement. The Orthodox delegates consented to recognize papal claims to supremacy and to accept the Nicene Creed with the inclusion of the *filioque* clause. But when Michael returned to Constantinople, the overwhelming majority of his people and clergy rejected the union as a purely personal agreement between him and the pope. Despite his efforts, the pope excommunicated Michael in 1282 for his lack of success in implementing the terms. The union of Lyons was formally repudiated by Michael's successor, who even denied him a proper Christian burial for his alleged "apostasy."

A second council to heal the East-West rift was convened by the pope in response to an offer from the Byzantines for church union in exchange for help in their struggle with the Turks. It met at Ferrara and Florence in 1438–39 and finally ended up at Rome in 1445. Emperor John VIII, the patriarch of Constantinople, and a large delegation from the Byzantine and other Orthodox churches attended. Even the Russian and Abyssinian churches were represented. Both sides made a genuine attempt to resolve the issues dividing them, and eventually they agreed upon a formula of union. But when it was publicly proclaimed in Constantinople, it was overwhelmingly rejected. As one Byzantine noble exclaimed, "I would rather see the Muslim turban in the midst of the city than the Latin mitre."

The Council of Florence, as it is usually called, also attempted unions with some Monophysite and Nestorian churches, but these amounted to nothing. Much more significantly, however, its decrees formed the basis for the various Eastern Rite Catholic churches ("Uniates") that continued to use Orthodox rituals but gave their allegiance to Rome.

Meanwhile, in the late thirteenth century a new group of Turks who were displaced during the Mongol expansion appeared in Asia Minor. At first they served the Seljuks as mercenaries, but, under their leader Osman (hence the name Ottoman Turks), they asserted their independence and by 1340 controlled northern Asia Minor. Known for their military prowess, they were aided by the weakness of the Byzantine Empire itself, which had never recovered from the effects of the Fourth Crusade. Constant in-fighting among the various segments of the population only added to the empire's difficulties, while the Christian kingdoms of Serbia and Bulgaria absorbed much of its Balkan lands.

The Turks then moved into the Balkans and overran the Christian states. They were poised to capture Constantinople, but then the renowned Turkic conqueror Tamerlane (Timur) swept into Asia Minor and in 1402 routed the Ottoman army at Angora (Ankara), captured the sultan, and temporarily broke their power. Soon the Turkish fortunes revived and in 1453 they made their final assault on the hapless Byzantine capital.

The fall of Constantinople sent many Eastern scholars with their manuscripts to the West, helping to stimulate the Renaissance. At the same time, some Easterners interpreted the event as God's punishment for the concessions made by the emperor and patriarch at Florence. It also encouraged Moscow to declare itself the "Third Rome," thereby asserting its claim to be the legitimate heir of the Roman Empire and defender of the Orthodox faith.

The Ottoman Turks, who allowed the various religious groups self-government as *millets* (autonomous "nations"), ironically gave the Orthodox patriarch greater power than he had under the emperors, since they now regarded him as the official religious and political

The Spread of Eastern Christianity

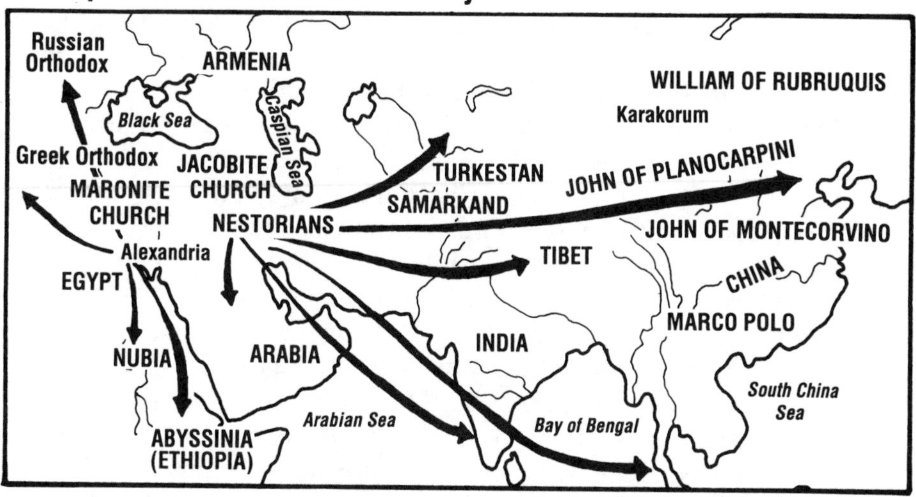

head of all Christian groups in their empire. He was able to centralize the power of his patriarchate over previously "autocephalous" areas and replaced Slavonic bishops with Greek candidates. It would not be until the overthrow of Turkish rule in the nineteenth century that independent churches would again exist in Greece, Bulgaria, and Serbia.

RUSSIAN ORTHODOXY

As mentioned earlier (see chapter 5), the Orthodox faith had spread to Kievan Russia in the tenth century. By the time of Yaroslav the Wise (1019–54), a Russian by the name of Ilarion was appointed as the metropolitan (archbishop) of Kiev instead of a Greek bishop. After 1250 the position alternated between a Greek and a Russian prelate. In 1299 the seat of the Russian Orthodox church was transferred from Kiev to Vladimir, and then in 1325 to Moscow. The fact that the Russian Christians, following the precedent set by Cyril and Methodius, utilized Slavonic instead of Greek, helped to set them apart from the Byzantine church as well as the Roman Catholic West. Indeed, in contrast to the West, which insisted on a uniform Latin liturgy (until 1963), the Orthodox practice of allowing its various branches to use their vernacular (Slavonic, Coptic, Ge'ez, Syriac) had the unintended effect of cutting them off from the Greco-Roman heritage and from each other. Adding to the isolation of the Russians was the Mongol (Tatar) occupation during the years 1237 to 1480.

From the Byzantines the Russians learned to despise the Latin Catholics as heretics, a hatred that was reinforced by the attacks of the Swedes in 1240 and the Teutonic Knights in 1242. The Knights had taken advantage of the Mongol invasion to carry out a Catholic Crusade, but Alexander Nevsky of Novgorod repulsed the Germans and also submitted to the khan. His efforts insured the preservation of the Orthodox faith from the threat of Latinization.

During the Mongol era Russia was divided into several petty states, whose princes were subject to the Tatar khan and paid an annual tribute. The Grand Duchy of Moscow emerged as a leading principality in the fourteenth century, and its ruler Ivan I (1328–40) persuaded the khan to appoint him the tribute collector for all the Russian vassal states. He used this to assert his authority over the others. Grand Duke Dmitri, supported by the monk Sergius of Radonezh (1314–92), who founded the famous monastery of the Holy Trinity near Moscow and is regarded as the greatest Russian saint, rebelled against the Mongols. Although unsuccessful, Dmitri showed that they were not invincible and increased the prestige of Moscow. In 1480 Ivan III finally threw off the Tatar yoke and subjected the other Russian princes to his rule.

Isidore, the last Russian metropolitan of Greek origin, accepted the union with the Roman church at the Council of Florence. But upon Isidore's return to Moscow in 1441, the grand duke denounced the agreement and arrested him as an apostate. In 1448 the Russian bishops elected his successor without approval from Constantinople. From this point on the Russian church was autonomous, and in 1589 the metropolitan of Moscow formally assumed the title of patriarch.

He was able to do this because the Muscovite rulers had established themselves as the successors of the Byzantines. In 1472 Ivan III married the niece of the last emperor, assumed the Byzantine titles of "autocrat" and "tsar" (Caesar), and began using the double-headed eagle of Byzantium as his state emblem. Moscow had now become the "Third Rome" and claimed to be the protector of Eastern Orthodoxy.

OTHER EASTERN CHURCHES

In addition to the Greek and Russian Orthodox churches there was a rich variety of Eastern churches, some of which were in communion with Rome and others that had their own independent patriarchates. The most important of the "Greek rite" churches that became part of Roman Catholic Christianity was the Maronites. The church took its name from St. Maron (d. 410), a Syrian priest with a great reputation for holiness and wisdom who attracted many disciples. Its members were active missionaries, and they founded other monasteries whose heads acted as bishops for their regions. The Muslim takeover of Syria created new problems for the Maronites, and after the destruction of their main monastery they took refuge in the mountains of Lebanon, where in 939 they transferred the patriarchate from Antioch. This patriarch was both the civil and religious head of the community, while local landlords controlled the scattered villages.

For a while they had little contact with the outside world, but the Crusades reopened relations with the West. They were accepted as fellow Christians by most Crusaders, to whom they gave valuable information about the terrain. In 1181 they placed themselves under papal authority. In 1215 the patriarch attended the Fourth Lateran Council, and the pope granted him formal recognition as a bishop.

The Maronites thus became one of the "Uniate" churches, that is, an Eastern church that acknowledged papal authority but retained its own liturgy, traditions, and discipline. Though Arabic-speaking, they used the Syriac liturgy. Today the Maronite "Patriarch of Antioch and the East" leads what is the largest group of Christians in Lebanon. The Maronites serve as the bulwark of Catholicism in the eastern Mediterranean.

There are some other small Uniate groups that maintain ties with Rome. The most important is the Arabic-speaking Melkites (Melchites) in Egypt, Palestine, and Syria. After the fall of Constantinople they first turned to Moscow and then in the seventeenth century submitted to Rome in order to secure Western aid. In 1724 the pope recognized a Catholic Melkite patriarch in Damascus, which is known today as the Antiochian Orthodox Church. A few Coptic Uniates are found in Egypt, while a small "Chaldean" Uniate church of Nestorian origins exists in northern Mesopotamia. An Armenian offshoot in Cilicia (eastern Turkey) from 1294 to 1441 was oriented toward Rome, and one group of Malabar Christians in South India is currently in communion with Rome.

THE MONOPHYSITES

Many of the Eastern bodies were estranged from mainline Orthodoxy because of their adherence to Monophysitism. One is the Armenian church. Representatives of this body, one of the oldest in the East, did not attend the Councils of Ephesus and Chalcedon because the area was under Persian rule at the time, and so the Monophysite Christology continued to prevail there.

Although originally a rather aristocratic faith, Armenian Orthodoxy became genuinely a people's religion after the Arab conquest. The church then repudiated all connections with Byzantine Christianity and developed in its own unique ways. With the coming of the Turks, the Armenians began to suffer persecution. During the Crusades they drew nearer to Rome for reasons of political expediency but rejected the papal effort at reunion at Florence. After the fall of Constantinople, the sultan allowed the Armenian bishop to establish a patriarchate and administer a *millet* that had jurisdiction over the Monophysite communities in Eastern Turkey and the Middle East.

Because of the Armenian people's dispersion and the frequent periods of persecution, the church became closely identified with the nation. Thus the leaders and theologians of the church became noted for their conservatism in doctrine, tradition, and ritual. Any attempt to introduce changes in these was regarded as an act of treachery against the nation itself. Its spiritual head was the *catholicos,* similar to a patriarch, and now the latter is his title. His seat is at the monastery of Etchmiadzin near Erevan in the Republic of Armenia.

The Coptic (Egyptian) church traces its ancestry to St. Mark the Evangelist and is distinctive for its emphasis on monasticism and use of the ancient Coptic language in worship. It was a staunch defender of Monophysitism, as Chalcedon seemed to signify a Greek victory over the indigenous culture of Egypt. A long, bitter struggle ensued for the patriarch's seat between the Orthodox and Monophysites, but the latter won out since this enabled the Copts to assert independence from Byzantium. Arab rule finally ended Byzantine persecution and brought some relaxation of pressures, but the heavy taxation induced many to convert to Islam. Also, harassment still occurred, as when the Caliph al-Hakim (996–1021) destroyed 3,000 churches and massacred thousands.

The Crusades were an unmitigated disaster for the Copts. Since these were "Holy Wars of the Cross," Egyptian Muslims vented their wrath toward all Christians, whether Latin, Greek, or Coptic. The Latin Crusaders also persecuted the Copts as schismatics, people worse than heretics, and even denied them access to the holy places in Jerusalem. Repression reached its height in the Mamluk period (1250–1517) because of periodic mob violence. During the Turkish rule (1517–1798) their conditions improved, and they served as financial officials and tax collectors for the Ottomans. Then, in the nineteenth century the Coptic church finally achieved freedom of worship and could assert its identity, even though it was becoming an ever smaller minority group in an Islamic society. Today its patriarch uses the title of "pope."

Christianity had extensive influence in Nubia, the upper Nile area stretching from Aswan to Khartoum. The Orthodox-Monophysite struggle spilled over into the south, with the latter winning out. This ensured that the church there would be an extension of the Egyptian variety. The Arab efforts to conquer the territory failed, and for the next 500 years the Nubian kingdoms were independent. Ties were maintained with the Coptic church, and one kingdom alone was reported to have 400 churches. Although there were some monasteries, they did not play as important a role as in Egypt. The language of worship remained Greek, but in the later Middle Ages the indigenous Nubian tongue, written in Greek characters, was used for religious texts. In his attack in 1172–73 Saladin destroyed churches and monasteries and captured and enslaved the Nubian bishop and many clerics. The Mamluks in Egypt mounted further assaults on the Christian kingdoms, and by the late sixteenth century all traces of the Coptic faith in Nubia had been wiped out.

The first ruler of the Ethiopian kingdom of Axum to accept Christianity was Ezana (fourth century), as Ge'ez and Greek inscriptions indicate. Frumentius, a Christian from Lebanon who became the royal treasurer, was instrumental in his conversion. Athanasius consecrated Frumentius as abuna (patriarch) over the Axumite or Abyssinian church around 340. The next event of consequence was the introduction of monasticism in 480 by the Nine Saints, learned Syrian Monophysites, who translated the Greek Scriptures into the indigenous Ge'ez. It remains to this day the liturgical language of the Ethiopian church, although Amharic and others have replaced it as the spoken language.

Settlers from southwest Arabia fostered a strong Jewish influence in Ethiopia. Christians there saw themselves as the rightful successors of the Jews, and the emperor took the title "Conquering Lion of the Tribe of Judah" (Rev. 5:5). Many Ethiopian customs have Jewish links, such as wearing an object representing the Ark of the Covenant, circumcision, ritual cleanliness, a double Sabbath (Saturday and Sunday), the prohibition of pork, and liturgical dances.

With the spread of Islam the Muslims controlled the lowlands, and the Amharic Christians retreated to the high plateaus of the interior where they were inaccessible and invincible. Practically all ties with the Copts of Egypt ended except the consecration of the abuna. Under the Zagwe dynasty (1137–1270) there was an ecclesiastical revival. The eleven remarkable rock-hewn churches of Lalibella (c. 1150–1220) are monuments to Ethiopian devotion during this period.

A new dynasty, the "Solomonic," began in 1270 with the support of the influential monk Tekla Haimanot, and the fortunes of Christianity brightened. King Yekuno-Amlak (d. 1285) gave the church one-third of his kingdom's lands in perpetuity, a fact that explains the great wealth of the church. The national epic, the *Kebra Nagast* (*Glory of Kings*), was written in this period. It holds that the Queen of Sheba who visited King Solomon was from Ethiopia, and that she was seduced by the king. The son resulting from this union, Menelik I, later went to Jerusalem and stole the Ark of the Covenant.

In the reign of Zar'a Yakob (1434–68), Ethiopian representatives attended the Council of Ferrara-Florence in order to seek unity of the churches in the face of Islamic expansion. Afterwards other pilgrims came to Rome from Ethiopia, and Westerners became increasingly aware of this distant land. Meanwhile, Byzantine and Coptic apocalyptic writings gave rise to the hope that the emperor of Ethiopia would unite with the West to defeat the Muslims. This helped fuel the legend of the Christian kingdom of Prester John (see chapter 12). The Portuguese who traveled there in 1490 came to find Prester John, and there were further contacts in the next century. For a brief period in the early seventeenth century, Jesuit missionaries even persuaded the emperor, who was threatened by Turkish expansion, to have his church submit to Rome.

Because the Ethiopians were dependent upon the Coptic church in Egypt for their patriarch, an anomalous situation resulted. The head of their church did not know Ge'ez, and a monk actually had to administer it. This custom remained in effect for centuries, and only after the Coptic church agreed to allow an independent "patriarch-catholicos" could a native Ethiopian in 1959 finally assume the post.

St. Basil's Church, Moscow

Another center of Monophysitism was Syria, where the brilliant and energetic Jacob Baradaeus, bishop of Edessa (c. 500–78), secretly consecrated a rival hierarchy of bishops during the persecution by Justinian. Consequently, the church he founded became known as the Jacobite Church. He was encouraged in his work by Empress Theodora who was from Syria and had strong sympathy for Monophysites. Jacob, who was fluent in Greek, Syriac, and Arabic, had no fixed residence and traveled extensively in Armenia, Syria, Anatolia, Mesopotamia, Persia, Arabia, and Egypt. Everywhere he went he defended Monophysite doctrine and ordained new clergy to replace those who had died or were in prison. Constantly pursued by imperial agents, he earned the nickname *Baradaeus* ("The Ragged") from the shabby clothing he wore as a disguise. Probably no church figure in history ordained as many clergymen as Jacob—reportedly 100,000 priests and 27 bishops.

When the Arabs conquered Syria, they did not distinguish between different varieties of Christians but treated them all as one *millet.* The Jacobites thus enjoyed the freedom that they did not under the emperor. Although small in number, they conducted missionary work in Mesopotamia, Persia, and farther east. This required supplementing the patriarch with a person to exercise jurisdiction over these areas. The first and most significant person to carry this new title, "Maphrian (head) of the East," was Marutha, metropolitan of Tekrit (629–49).

The Jacobites left a rich literary tradition. One noted figure was Jacob of Edessa (633–708), a bishop, theologian, philosopher, and historian who supervised a revision of the Syriac Old Testament and authored biblical commentaries and a historical work called the *Hexameron* (after the six days of creation). Even more distinguished was Gregorius Bar Hebraeus (1226–86), a physician of Jewish descent, who wrote major historical and grammatical works in Syriac and Arabic.

In the thirteenth century the Jacobites were devastated by the Mongol invasions, and they suffered even more when Tamerlane swept through their region. Although small in number, Jacobite remnants survive mainly in Kurdistan and Syria, where they are known as the Syrian Orthodox Church. Although Arabic speaking, their liturgy is still in Syriac. It should be mentioned that people belonging to churches customarily labeled as Monophysite reject this designation as pejorative and prefer instead the name Oriental Orthodox.

THE NESTORIAN CHURCH

One of the greatest missionary churches in the history of Christianity was the Nestorian, which took its name from the fifth-century patriarch of Constantinople who allegedly held that Christ existed in two distinct natures, a human and a divine, but not in one "entity." God and man could not come together; the interchange of divine and human attributes in the person of Jesus was impossible. Nestorius's position deviated very subtly from the Orthodox view of Christ, but it still resulted in great opposition to him. After his condemnation at Ephesus in 431, those bishops who did not accept the majority view formed an independent church. It sunk roots in Syria and Persia and came to be known as the "Church of the East."

To understand the Nestorian acceptance in Persia, one must recognize that the Sassanid dynasty, founded in 227, had established Zoroastrianism as the state religion. Because of their continuing conflict with the Roman Empire, the Persians were hostile to Christianity, which they assumed was their enemy's faith. Persecution was intense at times and thousands suffered martyrdom, especially in the fourth century. However, as the regime's attitude toward Christians mellowed, they could function more openly and their bishops could even hold synods. At one of these in 424, the catholicos of Seleucia/Ctesiphon (on the central Tigris river) was elevated to the status of "The Patriarch of the East," thus freeing the Persian church from dependence on Constantinople and Rome alike.

The Nestorians established a theological training center at Edessa in Syria, which Emperor Zeno closed in 489. The teachers and students then moved to the school at Nisibis in Persia that Bar Sauma (d. 493), a prominent preacher and organizer, had founded. This signified that the movement could no longer function in the empire, and Persians welcomed the Nestorians since the Byzantines regarded them with animosity.

Then, in a long, complex process between the fifth and seventh centuries the Nestorians proceeded to work out the distinctives of their faith. The writings of Theodore of Mopseustia (c. 350–428), a bishop in Asia Minor whose works the Orthodox had roundly condemned, became their criteria for correct doctrine. However, the monk Babai the Great (c. 550–c. 630) developed the definitive synthesis of beliefs on the relation between divinity and humanity in Christ. Also characteristic was their monasticism, which besides being known for its austerity, required each abbot to submit to the local bishop who administered all monastic properties. The strict obedience of monks to ecclesiastical authority meant that the Nestorian hierarchy possessed a powerful army of loyal workers who would strengthen the church and fearlessly penetrate the vast reaches of Asia and the western Indian Ocean in their evangelistic endeavors.

The Muslims, who overran Persia in 637–42, tolerated Christians but made them wear distinctive clothing and refrain from proselytizing and drinking wine. They were also prohibited from using church bells and from erecting buildings higher than mosques. When the Abassid caliphate moved its capital to the new city of Baghdad in 762, the Nestorian patriarch also relocated there and became a respected member of the court as the head of the Christian *millet.* One of these patriarchs, Timothy I (779–823), regarded the Muslims as sent by God to punish the sun-worshiping Persians and the heretical Byzantines. Basing his claim on the tradition that the Magi were from the East, he declared, "Thirty years before all others we Easterners confessed Christ's kingdom, and adored his divinity!" The church grew rapidly, and by the thirteenth century the patriarch presided over 250 bishoprics.

When the Mongols conquered Baghdad in 1258, they massacred 800,000 Muslims but spared the Christians, because the favorite wife of their leader was a Christian. The Mongol rulers gave the Nestorians freedom but soon grew weary of the incessant bickering of their bishops and eventually adopted Islam. Then Tamerlane, the terror of Asia and a hard-line Muslim, destroyed the Mongol Khanate in

1393. This was a frightful disaster for the Nestorians, and those who were not killed or did not abandon their faith fled into the mountains of Kurdistan. A small remnant, who are called the Assyrian Christians, has survived to the present.

MISSIONS IN ASIA

Scholars are just now beginning to comprehend what a vast amount of missionary work occurred throughout Asia dating back to the very beginnings of Christianity. The reason for this ignorance was the ethnocentric Western assumption that the Eastern churches were heretical and therefore their endeavors were unworthy of study. Also, attitudes from the era of imperialism about the "Western" character of Christianity, the "younger churches," and "underdevelopment" obscured the recognition that the extension of Christianity had occurred in Asia long before Europeans had set foot there. In fact, studies of Syriac, Arabian, Chinese, Korean, Japanese, Indonesian, Indian, and Persian literary materials, stone inscriptions, and archaeological materials point to an incredible story of Christian expansion in Asia.

The Nestorians had thriving works among the migratory peoples throughout central Asia, including Turkestan and Mongolia. A report to the Nestorian patriarch in the eleventh century noted that a mass movement among Turks and Mongols had added 200,000 souls to the church. The gospel was carried along the fabled "Silk Route" to China in 635, where the T'ang emperor T'ai Tsung granted toleration and a metropolitan bishop was in place by 670. In the thirteenth century a Chinese became the Nestorian patriarch (Yahballaha III) and another (Rabban Sauma) traveled to Europe, visited several rulers, and celebrated a Syriac rite Eucharist before the pope. Documentary and archeological sources reveal that Christians were working in Sri Lanka (Ceylon) in the fifth and Indonesia in the seventh centuries, and in Korea and Japan during the seventh to ninth centuries. By the time of the High Middle Ages in the West, churches existed in the mercantile communities throughout Southeast Asia.

Especially important are the many works in India. Syriac rite Christians, who were well established in southwest India and the Maldive Islands by the fourth century, developed close ties with the Nestorians. The "Malabar Christians" controlled much of the pepper trade, and their "Church of St. Thomas" numbered about 200,000 in 1400. The coming of the Portuguese led to hard times for the indigenous Christians, as the outsiders tried to force Roman Catholicism on them. In the resulting conflicts and divisions some Christians became Jacobites, others Nestorians, and the majority affiliated with Rome, thus leaving a complicated picture of denominationalism in India.

During the Middle Ages the Christians in the East became isolated, fragmented, and marginalized. Eastern Orthodoxy drifted apart from Latin Catholicism but took root among the Bulgars and Slavs, especially in Russia. Byzantine Christianity also separated from its close cousins, the Monophysites and Nestorians. However, at a meeting in 1990 representatives of the Oriental Orthodox (Monophysite) and the Greek Orthodox churches concluded that their differences were based on misunderstandings. Representatives of both sides accepted the first three ecumenical councils, condemned Eutychianism and Nestorianism, and agreed to lift their anathemas against each other.[3] Pulling back from 1500 years of polemics, they came together around Cyril of Alexandria's formula, "the one nature (*physis*) of God's Word Incarnate," thus quietly bypassing Chalcedon.

PART 2

THE REFORMED AND REVIVED CHURCH

(1300 – 1789)

9

THE MEDIEVAL CHURCH DECLINES

By the close of the thirteenth century nearly all the structures were in place that would characterize the Roman Catholic church until the Reformation two hundred years later. However, these institutions were as much of a hindrance as a help to organized Christianity during the fourteenth and fifteenth centuries because they were dependent on a stable and unchanging society. But the period was one of rapid change caused by wars, plagues, and economic crises.

THE AUTUMN OF THE MIDDLE AGES

At the time the popes replaced the emperors as the leaders of Christendom, strong kings were emerging in western Europe. Although they could not compete with the popes for European leadership, they were strong enough to withstand papal interference within their kingdoms. The question was no longer whether the pope or the emperor was supreme but, rather, whether Christendom itself would be more than a vague expression for a collection of separate nations.

The French and English people each developed a sense of national consciousness during the long, weary struggle known as the Hundred Years' War (1337–1453). It originated from Edward III's desire to control France as well as England. His claim to the French throne was based on flimsy legal grounds and French resistance led to war. English knights and longbowmen repeatedly invaded France, and the technological superiority of the longbow was demonstrated in their great victories at Crécy, Poitiers, and Agincourt. By 1419 the English controlled most of northern France, and Henry V was recognized as heir to the throne. But then he died and was succeeded by his nine-month-old son, which gave the French King Charles VII the opportunity to renew the conflict.

He was urged on by Joan of Arc, an illiterate peasant girl and devout mystic who was convinced by visions that it was her duty to defeat the English. In 1429, at the age of seventeen, she was allowed to lead an army that soon regained much of northern France and enabled Charles's coronation in Rheims. However, the English captured Joan, and the ungrateful Charles made no effort to ransom her. She was turned over to the Inquisition, which tried her on trumped up charges of heresy and witchcraft and ordered her burned. The tragic death of the saintly "Maid of Orleans" in May 1431 so outraged the French that their armies resumed the offensive. By 1453 the English had been ousted from all of France except Calais, and the Hundred Years' War was over.

The conflict weakened the feudal nobility in both countries, as many of them died in battle and left no heirs. According to feudal law, their lands reverted to the king who then awarded them to loyal followers and created a new nobility. The new methods of warfare also diminished the value of the cavalry, which was manned by aristocrats.

The French kings who consolidated their power by extending the royal domain gained the support of a public that associated peace, order, and the expulsion of the English with the monarchy. The war taxes were continued in order to finance a permanent army that was used in campaigns against the unemployed mercenaries who roamed the country. People gladly paid for protection from these outlaw bands.

In England, on the other hand, the authority of Parliament increased. Whenever the king needed money for the war, he had to obtain the consent of the people's representatives, and they demanded concessions before they would vote the funds. The English baronial class divided into two factions—the houses of Lancaster and

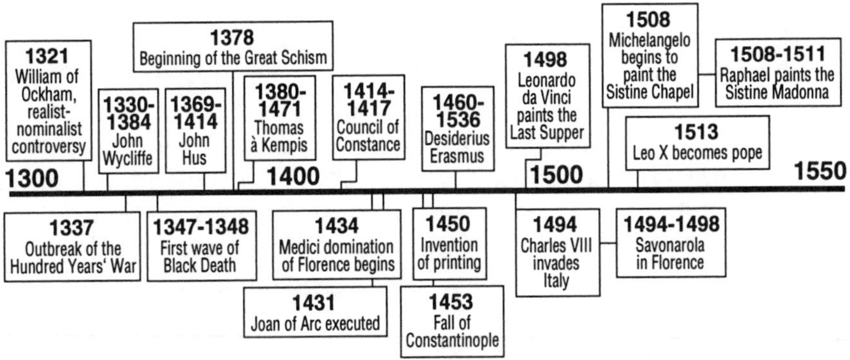

York. The emblem of Lancaster was the red rose and York the white rose. As they struggled for control of Parliament and the monarchy in the Wars of the Roses (1453–85), the feudal nobility virtually exterminated itself. This enabled Henry VII of the Tudor family to take power, and his dynasty, through Henry VIII and Elizabeth I, eventually fashioned England into a strong state.

During this period Germany developed quite differently from France and England. In contrast to the centralization and incipient nationalism in the west, the forces of particularism prevailed in Germany. The medieval conflict between empire and papacy produced a situation where the individual territorial units of Germany and its growing cities maintained a high degree of independence. The princes of these regional units were entitled to take part in the choice of the emperor and were therefore called "electors." In the struggle several emperors concerned themselves more with extending control over Italy than with conditions in Germany, while the popes on occasion backed rival emperors in an effort to find a leader with whom they could get along politically. The critical imperial interregnum of 1254–73 further intensified political fragmentation.

In 1273 the electors chose the Swiss prince Rudolph of Hapsburg because he appeared to be financially and politically weak and no threat to their independence. Rudolf wisely discarded any ambition to rule Italy and turned his attention to building a strong royal domain in southeastern Germany by appropriating the lands of feudal lords who died without heirs. This laid the territorial basis for the Hapsburg dynastic future. Following his death in 1291 the electors selected emperors from various houses. This effectively paralyzed the imperial government and shifted the balance of power to the German princes.

To deal with this chaotic situation, Emperor Charles IV introduced an electoral mechanism through the Golden Bull of 1356. (The title came from the gold seal affixed to the document.) It designated seven individuals who would always choose the emperor: the archbishops of Mainz, Trier, and Cologne; the king of Bohemia; the duke of Saxony, the margrave of Brandenburg; and the Count Palatine of the Rhine. When an emperor died, these seven "electors" would meet promptly and name a successor. They possessed sovereign rights within their domains, and each electoral territory was to be inherited as a unit and not divided among heirs. By omitting any reference to the pope's right to confirm or veto an election or to administer the empire during a vacancy, the Golden Bull effectively eliminated papal involvement in imperial affairs. But by recognizing the sovereignty of the territorial states, no meaningful framework existed to maintain internal security and peace.

At this time Europe also entered a period of economic and social dislocation. In the High Middle Ages, along with the expansion of trade, commerce, and industry occurred an increase in arable lands. German peasants moved eastward into areas thinly settled by Slavic peoples and cleared forests and drained marshes. Much of this was organized, financed, and carried out by religious orders, especially the Benedictines and Cistercians whose rules stipulated that they were to make a living by farming. The revival of commerce gave landlords and peasants alike an incentive to produce more than they needed for themselves. Commutation, the substitution of money payments for manual service by serfs, began to eat away at the manorial system, and by the thirteenth century, many formerly unfree peasants become tenant farmers. As the value of land and the price of agricultural products rose, the small freeholders profited, but landlords who lived on fixed rents and fees experienced a decline in real income.

After the mid–fourteenth century, European agriculture slipped into a serious depression that affected landlords and peasants. Economic expansion stopped as a population decline reduced both the supply of labor and the market for goods produced. When agricultural prices fell, those peasants who paid a fixed rent to the lords could not meet their obligations. Since the old bonds that had held peasants to the soil essentially no longer existed, many simply moved away and their fields went uncultivated. Some went to more prosperous areas and others settled in the towns. As the prices of nonagricultural goods tended to hold firm or increase, the landholding class was caught in a severe cost-price squeeze. Some lords hired laborers to work the land, but with the labor shortage rural wages tended to rise. Attempts to roll wages back through government intervention failed.

A key factor in the population decline was the bubonic plague epidemic—the "Black Death"—a disease carried by lice living on rats, which was brought to Europe from the Orient in 1347. The plague first appeared in Sicily and then swept across central and western Europe following the main trade routes. The victim experienced high fever, aching joints, swelling of the lymph nodes, and a blackening of the skin from subsurface bleeding. After a couple days of excruciating pain he or she usually died. The Black Death wiped out as much as 30 to 40 percent of the population in some areas. After a brief respite, the plague returned again in the 1360s and 1370s, and at regular intervals thereafter.

One result of the plague was the flagellants, a bizarre movement embraced by thousands of people who traveled about whipping themselves in hopes of gaining divine forgiveness and avoiding death. In Germany the fear-crazed populace blamed Jews for the Black Death, and nearly 50 percent of them perished from the murderous attacks of their neighbors as well as from the ravages of the disease.

Because so many peasants died, there were not enough people to work the land, and the survivors demanded higher wages. Thus, the ravages of the plague, the misery caused by the Hundred Years' War, and the attempts to curtail wages provoked many peasant revolts. In France the most serious was the Jacquerie, which broke out in 1358. It took its name from Jacques, a common nickname for the French peasant. In this uprising desperate rural mobs attacked manor houses and committed many atrocities.

England's major peasant revolt began in 1381. Its leader, Wat Tyler, was aided by John Ball, an excommunicated priest who had long been an agitator for the rights of common people. Ball kindled the passions of angry mobs in Kent with talk of equality and an age to come when there would be no rich or poor. They marched on London and many sympathetic citizens welcomed them into the city. As the royal government was currently in disarray because of conflicts in the north, King Richard II negotiated with the insurgents. He issued charters providing for civil emancipation and amnesty for the revolutionaries, but his ministers had no intention of honoring the agreements that he had made. After Wat Tyler was treacherously murdered, the leaderless rebel bands were persuaded to leave London, and their revolt was put down with great brutality. John Ball, the people's prophet, was hanged, disemboweled, and quartered. In Germany peasant revolts broke out a century or so later, and these had a great effect on the Reformation.

The Decay of Scholasticism

The uncertainty and ferment of the period led to the crumbling of the medieval synthesis of theology, philosophy, and the arts. A renewal of the debate between the realists and nominalists at the universities, such as Oxford and Paris, marked the beginning of this process. The achievement of Thomas Aquinas in reconciling Aristotle and the Christian faith was subjected to criticism by scholars such as William of Ockham (d. 1349), who demolished the system of philosophy that had furnished a rational basis for theology.

The medieval platonists, known as "realists," taught that there are certain immutable forms or ideas (universals) that exist in the mind of God and can be perceived by divine illumination, without reference to particular things. Aquinas held that in order to reach these forms one must gain knowledge through the apprehension of objects.

Ockham, however, stated that only individual things actually exist and that universals have no real existence; they are merely names or terms. His philosophy was called "nominalism," from the Latin word *nomen* ("name"). He rejected the proofs for God based upon observed data, but as a devout Franciscan he did not wish to destroy faith in God. Thus, he insisted that he was freeing Christianity from the shackles of reason. One should believe in God, but not because of logical necessity.

Ockham also applied his ideas to the organized church of his day. He sought to show that the emperor should be completely independent of the pope, that the only authority in spiritual matters was the Bible, and that a general council of the church was superior to the papacy. By the time of his death nominalism was firmly established in the Franciscan order, and the conviction was growing among the faithful that a general council was needed to reform the church.

More radical than Ockham's criticisms were those presented in Marsiglio of Padua's *Defensor Pacis* (1324). For him the enemy was not a corrupt clerical hierarchy, as Ockham taught, but rather the influence exercised by the clergy in secular affairs. Marsiglio applied nominalism to the problems of the state and asked, "Where does political authority actually reside?" His answer was in the individual citizen, not in the idea of the state (a universal). As to the question "What is the church?" his reply was that it is composed of individual Christians and is not a supernatural institution with a life of its own.

Thus nominalism was a seedbed for political ideas that would undermine the authority of the papacy.

Decline of the Institutional Church

The church had developed into a monarchy that rivaled those of the newly emerging nation-states. Pope Boniface VIII (1294–1303) ignited a conflict by insisting that temporal rulers owed obedience to the church and forbidding them from taxing the clergy without papal permission. Both the kings of England and France challenged this position. Edward I had Parliament pass a law that forbade the clergy from acknowledging the pope's claim to temporal power, while Philip IV banned the export of all money from France. These actions forced the pope to rescind his orders.

Then a bitter quarrel broke out between Philip and Boniface over the condemnation of a French bishop for treason, and in 1302 the pope threw down the gauntlet in the bull *Unam Sanctam,* perhaps the most extreme argument for papal authority made in the Middle Ages. It proclaimed that "it is altogether necessary to salvation for every human creature to be subject to the Roman pontiff." Philip responded by sending an agent to Italy to arrest Boniface, but the effort failed and the aged pontiff died a few days later. No ruler in Europe had come to his aid and no succeeding pope punished Philip. This showed just how much the power of national monarchies had grown.

In 1305 a Frenchman, Clement V, was chosen pope, and he took up residency in the more comfortable environs of Avignon in southeastern France. Later critics called this "the Babylonian captivity of the church." The popes during this period were French and their policy pro-French. Finally Gregory XI left Avignon in 1377 and returned to Rome. When he died the following year, the Romans were determined at all costs to keep the papacy. Under the threat of mob violence the cardinals chose an Italian, Urban VI, but he so alienated them by his tactlessness and plans to reform the sacred college that they declared his election invalid and replaced him with Clement VI, who went back to Avignon.

Thus began the Great Schism, which divided Christendom for nearly forty years and dealt a severe blow to papal prestige. There were now two popes, each claiming the power of the keys to heaven, and no one could be certain that the sacraments were being administered by a validly ordained priest. The money to maintain two separate papal courts meant increased financial exactions, and European rulers sided with whichever pope whose favor was to their political advantage.

All agreed that the schism must be healed, but only a pope could call the necessary general council. Neither pope was willing to do that. One suggestion to solve the dilemma came from some scholars at the University of Paris. Known as "conciliarists," they insisted that a general council possessed an authority superior to the pope and therefore could act independently. They drew on Marsiglio's work to support the notion that the papacy was a human institution and all important questions of faith should be referred to a council representing the entire Christian community.

Cardinals from both factions tried to break the impasse at a council at Pisa in 1409. Unfortunately, neither pontiff agreed to step down in favor of the individual elected by this council, and now there were three popes. The result of this fiasco was that Emperor Sigismund decided that a general council was necessary, and he forced the Pisan pope, John XXIII, to call it.

The Council of Constance, which sat from 1414 to 1418, had three tasks—heal the schism, suppress heresy, and reform the church. It deposed all three popes and replaced them with Martin V (1417–31), who was now the sole head of the church. It dealt with the problem of heresy by executing the Bohemian advocates of reform, John Hus and Jerome of Prague, but their followers continued the struggle on behalf of their ideals (see below). As for reform, it accomplished nothing at all. It did issue the decree *Sacrosancta,* which declared that a general council was superior to the pope, and *Frequens,* which called for regular meetings of church councils, but subsequent popes ignored these completely. They had no intention of allowing any diminution of their power, and the conciliar movement quietly ended.

The Pressures for Reform

In this era, which historians have labeled the Renaissance (rebirth), the Catholic church faced many problems, but perhaps the most serious of all was the failure of the popes to provide spiritual leadership. For all intents and purposes, they had become Renaissance princes, and they hoped to build a strong state in central Italy so that the Avignon disaster would not recur. It seemed sensible at the time, but in fact it set the stage for the Protestant revolt of the sixteenth century.

THE LATE MEDIEVAL PAPACY

Boniface VIII (1294-1303)
Benedict XI (1303-4)

Beginning of the Avigon Papacy

Clement V (1305-14)
John XXII (1316-34)
Benedict XII (1334-42)
Clement VI (1342-52)
Innocent VI (1352-62)
Urban V (1362-70)
Gregory XI (1370-78)

THE GREAT SCHISM

Roman Popes	Pisan Popes	Avignon Popes
Urban VI (1378-89)		Clement VII (1378-94)
Boniface IX (1389-1404)		
Innocent VII (1404-6)	Alexander V (1409-10)	
Gregory XII (1406-15)	John XXIII (1410-15)	Benedict XIII (1394-1423)

COUNCIL OF CONSTANCE—REUNITES THE CHURCH, 1415-17

The Renaissance Papacy

Martin V (1417-31)
Eugene IV (1431-47)
Nicholas V (1447-55)
Calixtus III (1455-58)
Pius II (1458-64)
Paul II (1464-71)
Sixtus IV (1471-84)
Innocent VIII (1484-92)
Alexander IV (1492-1503)
Julius II (1503-13)
Leo X (1513-21)

Some contemporaries did protest against the direction the church was going. The most significant of these were John Wycliffe, John Hus, and mystics like the Brethren of the Common Life. Wycliffe (1330–84), a late-medieval scholastic, is often called the "Morning Star of the Reformation." Born in Yorkshire, he spent most of his life at Oxford University. In two important books, *On Divine Dominion* and *On Civil Dominion*, he declared that dominion (lordship over all things) belongs solely to God. Although God has granted a measure of lordship to human beings in return for service, a person who sins forfeits the right to this. A cleric whose life manifests a lack of grace should be deprived of his position. Should the church fail in this disciplinary action, then the state must do so. By insisting that all powers, civil and ecclesiastical, are contingent upon their possessor being in a right relationship with God, Wycliffe suggested that even the authority of the pope depended upon his personal character.

In *On the Church* Wycliffe claimed that formal membership in an ecclesiastical body does not guarantee salvation. The church is the spiritual company of believers, with Christ at its head. Salvation is a matter between an individual and Christ, and the pope heads only the visible church at Rome. In his last years, he came to the radical conclusion that the pope was the Antichrist and even taught that transubstantiation was wrong and that the holy communion was simply a celebration of the spiritual presence of the body and blood of Christ.

Wycliffe was an eloquent and persuasive teacher, and he built up a body of "poor preachers," itinerants who spread out across England propagating his doctrines. Moreover, since a knowledge of the Bible was basic to his approach, he encouraged the translation of the Latin Scriptures into English. This Bible version, together with his sermons and tracts, were widely disseminated by the Lollards, as the followers of Wycliffe were called. Parliament outlawed the Lollards in 1401, which drove the movement underground, and some scholars argue that the lingering sympathy with Wycliffe's views explains why the English Reformation began with such ease.[1]

His teachings were particularly influential in Bohemia. Charles IV (1346–73), Holy Roman emperor as well as possibly the greatest Bohemian king, had made Prague a center of international culture by establishing a university in 1348 and had encouraged the growth of Czech national consciousness. When his daughter Anne married Richard II of England in 1382, a large number of Czechs accompanied her. Among them were students who returned to Bohemia with copies of Wycliffe's writings, where they found favorable reception.

The landmark personality here was John Hus (1369–1415). Preacher at the Bethlehem chapel and professor at the university in Prague, he embraced Wycliffe's views and began demanding similar reforms. He also preached against the sale of indulgences, challenged the primacy of the pope, and emphasized the supreme authority of Scripture. When he attacked the papacy and the hated German upper class, he gained a large following. In fact, in 1409 he induced the Bohemian king to change the university's constitution to give the Czech professors a decisive voice in academic matters, and the German teachers and students migrated to Saxony where they organized the University of Leipzig. Now rector of the university, Hus fell afoul of the church when he condemned a papal crusade in Italy and was excommunicated by the archbishop of Prague in 1412. This cost him the king's support, and he spent the next two years outside the capital preaching, writing, and gaining wider audiences.

Wishing to settle the conflict in Bohemia, Emperor Sigismund invited Hus to the Council of Constance in order to defend his views. Although the emperor gave him a safe-conduct letter, the cardinals accused him of heresy and imprisoned him. Rather than jeopardize the success of the council, Sigismund decided to sacrifice Hus, who was then tried, condemned, and burned at the stake on July 6, 1415.

The outraged followers of Hus rebelled against the emperor and plunged Bohemia into a religious war. Under the leadership of their brilliant commander, Jan Zizka, the outnumbered Hussites won one victory after another. However, a split between the radical Taborite wing and the more moderate majority (the Calixtines) blunted the Hussite campaign against the imperial forces. The moderates then defeated the Taborites and made peace with Rome in 1436. They accepted papal supremacy, but in return the laity was allowed to receive both the bread and the cup in the communion and abuses among the Czech clergy were to be eliminated. The Hussite movement kept the idea of church reform alive until it emerged full-blown among the Protestants.

Also important were the movements of popular piety, commonly summed up under the heading of "mysticism." Operating outside the formal structure of the church, the mystics reacted against the rigid institutionalization of Rome, especially the teaching that salvation comes through the sacraments only when they are administered by an ordained priest. Instead, they stressed personal morality and the inner life of the spirit. In place of the sacraments and the priesthood, they emphasized Christ Himself as the mediator between the soul and God. The movement centered in the cities where secular education had created a reading public for their sermons and devotional books.

The leading German mystic was the Dominican Johannes Eckhart von Hochheim (1260–1337), usually known as Meister Eckhart. An ability to express his ideas with a clarity born of personal experience and conviction made him a powerful spiritual force. As his sermons were copied down by nuns who heard him preach in convents and excerpted in devotional books, they reached a wide audience.

Through Gerard Groote (1340–84), mysticism became a vital force in the Netherlands. He urged people to strive for communion with God and achieve personal transformation by imitating the life of Christ. Instead of abstruse theological speculation, he emphasized morality, piety, and good works. After his death the band of disciples who had gathered around him formed an association known as the Brethren of the Common Life. This was an order of laymen who lived under self-imposed regulations but were not bound by monastic vows. They served the poor and founded more than two hundred schools in the Netherlands and Germany. Deventer, their principal academy, had the most advanced instruction north of the Alps, and such leading writers of the age as John Gerson, Desiderius Erasmus, and Thomas á Kempis were students at Brethren schools.

The clearest expression of Brethren mysticism is the devotional book, *The Imitation of Christ,* by Thomas á Kempis (1380–1471). He stressed thorough study of the Bible, prayer, introspection, and sincere effort to lead a holy life. Only the pure in heart can achieve the goal of every mystic, namely, that close communion with God that transcends the bounds of human intellect. Although the Brethren of the Common Life and other mystics throughout Europe did not criticize orthodox doctrine as such, still they were a threat to the established church. Their emphasis on ethics and disdain for speculative theology reduced the importance of official Catholic teaching and led to a laicization of religion.

Unfortunately, fifteenth-century popular piety had a dark side as well, that is, the belief in witches. The easiest way to explain the troubles of the times was to blame a witch. These beings supposedly had special dealings with the devil who empowered them to torment godly people. They were also provided with images and charms that were used to destroy crops and kill livestock. In an age when infant mortality was high, midwives were often accused of being sorceresses. Other witches allegedly could transform themselves into animals or possessed the bodies of men in order to seduce women. Pope Innocent VIII issued a bull in 1484 that defined witchcraft as heresy and instructed the Inquisition to eradicate it. Later, two inquisitors published a manual called *The Hammer of Witches*, which explained how to deal with the phenomenon, and thousands went to their deaths for alleged witchcraft.

BEGINNINGS OF THE RENAISSANCE

During the fourteenth and fifteen centuries Italy was a geographical area lacking in political unity. While France and England were evolving into dynastic states as their monarchs centralized their authority at the expense of the nobility, the territorial city-states of Italy thrived due to their commerce with the eastern Mediterranean. These wealthy areas also profited from the hostility between the German emperor and the pope. With the weakening of the imperial power and the transfer of the papacy to Avignon, the political vacuum in Italy was filled by the city-states, each of which ruled some area around it and quarreled with its neighbors over land and the control of trade routes.

Most had a republican form of government in the Middle Ages. At the beginning of the Renaissance, however, despotic regimes took over. Usually an aggressive leader gained power for a limited time and then sought to establish a hereditary succession. These rulers often tried to expand their territory, which appealed to the pride of the citizenry and also insured the hostility of neighboring states. The result was an ongoing crisis situation that helped keep them in office.

A good example of this pattern of development was Milan, a major city in the fertile valley of the Po River. An expanding economy created a new aristocracy of wealth that challenged the old landed aristocracy and demanded a share in political power. With its growing commercial strength and territorial base, Milan rivaled both Venice and Florence in wealth and prestige. In the twelfth and thirteenth centuries its government was based on a grand council in which all the free citizens were represented and a group of twelve men served as executive officers. In 1277 Otto Visconti overthrew this republican system, and by 1395 the emperor had made his family the hereditary rulers of Milan.

Florence, the leading Italian Renaissance city-state, was a prosperous republic with an unstable political tradition. However, the control of the city did not pass into the hands of military leaders but was held by the cloth merchants who gradually became international bankers. The production and export of woolen cloth was the city's most important economic activity, and it employed about one-third of the population. The great cloth merchants essentially created a constitution that deprived the nobility of meaningful political power. Those of more modest means who belonged to the craft guilds supported the merchants, and in 1434 the Medici family, posing as champions of the common people, gained power in the city.

Under the Medici, particularly Cosimo (1434–64) and Lorenzo the Magnificent (1478–92), Florence pursued a policy of diplomacy and political maneuvering that made it the center of an Italian balance of power system. The Medici, who were munificent patrons of learning and the arts, also saw to it that their prosperous city took the leading role in the culture of the Renaissance.

Lying to the south and stretching like a band across the peninsula were the Papal States. During the popes' residency in Avignon, these territories fragmented as destructive feuds raged between rival cities and warring families. In 1353 Innocent VI sent a representative to reestablish papal authority in central Italy, and his success paved the way for the return of the popes to Rome. Only when they had overcome the conciliar movement, however, could they turn their attention to setting up a strong administration in the Papal States. This was the achievement of a group of individuals called the "Renaissance popes."

Growth of Humanism

Although the artistic and intellectual contributions of northern Europe during the fourteenth and fifteenth centuries were substantial, they paled in significance to that of Renaissance Italy. For many years historians have taken their understanding of this period from a work of the Swiss historian Jacob Burckhardt, *The Civilization of the Renaissance in Italy* (1860). He maintained that the Renaissance was the spontaneous creation of the Italian people during the fifteenth century. It was something new with no roots in the past—an expression of individuality and an outburst of genius that was manifested in brilliant artistic works and immortal literature. However, more recent scholars have shown that Burckhardt's concern with culture and ideas led him to neglect the religious, political, social, and economic factors of history, and his classic historical interpretation requires considerable qualification.

Certainly, the people at the time thought that a rebirth of ancient Greek and Roman civilization had occurred, but modern critics tend to emphasize that it was a transitional period between medieval and modern times. They agree that some ideas of the Renaissance were taken from the past while others stretched into the future and anticipated modern life, but they insist that many things were unique to the period itself. Most do agree that the Renaissance was characterized by restless curiosity, especially about humanity itself, and it was from this emphasis that the most distinctive features of the period emerged. Thus, Burckhardt was correct to say that the Renaissance had burst with creativity and its artists were among the finest that Western civilization has produced.

Dante Alighieri (1265–1321) was perhaps the earliest individual to display the characteristics of Renaissance individuality, but in his complex personality were elements of medievalism as well as of the modern world. Dante apparently came from a respectable Florentine family and was active in local politics. However, when his party lost out, he was banished from Florence and never returned home again. His principal work, *The Divine Comedy,* was completed during the long years of exile and travel.

His poem is an allegory of man's attempt to gain salvation, but

Michelangelo's Moses

unlike medieval works on the subject, it does not focus on personified abstraction. Rather, Dante used actual historical persons to describe, in a figurative manner, what he regarded as the realities of Christian thought—sin and punishment, remorse and repentance, and God's love and mercy. In the poem, he passes successively through Hell, Purgatory, and Paradise with three guides to lead him. In the first two regions the poet Virgil directs his steps; for most of Paradise, it is Beatrice; and, for the final vision of God, Bernard of Clairvaux.

In *The Divine Comedy* Dante showed an astonishing knowledge of science, theology, history, and the classics. He essentially created the modern Italian language through this masterpiece, and it is considered to be the summation of medieval life and thought. However, some elements of the poem did not fall into the medieval outlook. Dante rejected the claim of the church to control every aspect of an individual's life, and he fearlessly consigned several popes to hell for heresy, simony, cowardice, and avarice. His treating of pagan and Christian elements side by side showed a respect for classical culture uncharacteristic of medieval writers. *The Divine Comedy* exercised such a profound effect on the people of fourteenth-century Italy that, within one hundred years of his death, professorships to study the poem had been established at Florence, Venice, Bologna, and Pisa.

The pioneer in the recovery of the classical heritage was Petrarch (1304–74), often called the father of humanism. Born in Arezzo, a small town near Florence, he studied law at the universities of Montpellier and Bologna. After his father's death he gave up legal studies and became a monk so as to be eligible for benefices from wealthy patrons. He lived comfortably and traveled extensively throughout western and central Europe before finally settling in Italy.

Petrarch had been interested in the classics from childhood, and he imparted his passion to many of his acquaintances and through them to an ever-widening group of scholars. He discovered manuscripts of the works of Virgil, Horace, Livy, Ovid, Cicero, Seneca, and Juvenal, among others, and inspired humanists to search for copies of the classics. His epic poem *Africa,* which extolled the conqueror of Hannibal, Scipio Africanus, won him the poet's crown in Rome and started the vogue of glorifying classical times. He also compiled biographical sketches of famous Romans in *Concerning Illustrious Men* in order to show their great accomplishments and superior wisdom and virtue.

What individuals such as Dante and Petrarch did was encourage the growth of humanism. This term was derived from *humanitas,* a Latin word used to describe the civilizing force of art and literature in the widest sense. Medieval scholars had known the classics, but the Renaissance approached these texts in a different manner. No longer did they serve merely as sources for sermon illustrations or tools for logic, but now they were appreciated for their own sake.

Before the study of the classics could begin, however, a more systematic program of manuscript collection was needed. This was the contribution of the rulers of the Italian cities who spent vast sums of money to obtain Latin and Greek works. Many of these had been copied hundreds of years earlier and were damaged by fire, water, or worms. In many cases, medieval copyists had made additions and comments to the text that had to be removed. Finally, dictionaries and encyclopedias were composed to provide those studying the classics with material to aid them in the understanding of various references and allusions.

The revival of classical studies began with Latin literature, since the early humanists could not read Greek, but soon the first professor of Greek appeared on the scene. He was Manuel Chrysoloras who had been sent to Italy in 1396 by the Byzantine government as an ambassador to appeal for military aid against the Turks. The following year he began lecturing in Florence, and then in Milan and Pavia, before returning to Constantinople in 1403.

This contact with Greek scholars stimulated Cosimo de Medici to found the Platonic Academy in Florence. This was a small group who met to discuss Plato's philosophy and their problems of the day in the light of his teachings. In order to facilitate this interaction, Cosimo provided Marsilio Ficino (1433–99) with a villa and an endowment that enabled him to spend the rest of his life translating and interpreting Plato. The Platonic Academy flourished during the later fifteenth century, and among its outstanding scholars was Giovanni Pico Della Mirandola (1463–94), who introduced the study of Hebrew to Christian Europe and attracted students to Florence from as far away as Germany and England. The Medici foundation served as a prototype for similar academies elsewhere in Italy and eventually throughout Europe.

A major humanist contribution was the science of textual criticism. The best example of this new approach was how Lorenzo Valla demonstrated the false origins of the "Donation of Constantine." This document was allegedly the record made by the Emperor Constantine that turned the control over the western part of the empire to the bishop of Rome, and the medieval popes used it as a justification for their "temporal" (landholding) power. Valla utilized philological and historical arguments to show that it could not have been written in the fourth century but was of much later origin. By analyzing the many anachronistic words and customs in the document, he convinced his contemporaries that it was an eighth-century forgery. His method was to be widely used in sixteenth-century Germany when Luther and others embraced the critical approach of the Renaissance.

Renaissance Culture

Not only did the Renaissance recover the great literature of antiquity, but it also produced works of genius in painting, sculpture, and architecture. The new artistic approach began with the work of Giotto (1266–1336).

Italian painting prior to Giotto's innovations was a flat, flowing linear style based on a tradition that had not changed in half a millennium. During these years painting had been a church art designed to teach those who could not read. To achieve this, however, all unnecessary details were removed in order to avoid distracting the viewer's attention from the main theme. Often three or four events were put into the same picture and gestures were exaggerated to make a point. Since painting was an attempt to convey on a two-dimensional medium a three-dimensional world, a person in medieval times regarded the portrayal of a man as "real" in the sense that it reminded him of a man. To present a more accurate illusion of reality artists had to learn how to give a sense of perspective through the use of proportion and of light and shadow.

Giotto, however, broke with the medieval symbolic world and adopted a "naturalist" approach, whereby individuals were painted in lifelike positions and groups, interrelated as humans usually are. Still, because he did not know the laws of perspective, his people look round, solid, and statuelike. This is exemplified in his many pictures of St. Francis such as those in the church at Assisi and the Bardi chapel in Florence.

Renaissance art did not move forward in an unfaltering fashion. When the Black Death swept over Italy, Giotto's emphasis on man was ignored, and art turned back to more traditional modes of expression. By the end of the fourteenth century, however, artists again picked up the thread of realism. What revived the movement Giotto had begun was a competition in 1401 to select an artist to design new bronze doors for the Baptistry of San Giovanni in Florence. Two of the city's most respected sculptors, Filippo Brunelleschi (1377–1446) and Lorenzo Ghiberti (1378–1455), entered the contest. The competition panel was to be a depiction of Abraham's sacrifice of Isaac. Although Brunelleschi's entry showed a greater intensity of religious feeling, the judges chose his rival's because of its superior unity of mood and greater attention to classical body lines. Thus Ghiberti went on to produce the famous "Doors of Paradise," which even to this day astonish the viewer with their indescribable beauty.

The frescoes of Masaccio (1401–28) also revived the realistic approach of Giotto. Brunelleschi had discovered a principle of perspective that the size of objects could be reduced in the background, and Masaccio adopted this in his "Holy Trinity" on the walls of the church of Santa Maria Novella in Florence, a work that was exceptional in its physical realism and portrayal of emotion and character. At the same time, Donatello (1386–1466) broke with traditional patterns of sculpture. A student of Ghiberti, he freed sculpture from its medieval function of embellishing architecture, reduced the amount of detail in his statues, and gave them a solid, heavy, determined air. Much of the inspiration for his work came from the study of human anatomy, a science that was just starting to develop.

Now that the Italians had mastered the art of depicting nature through painting, they began to search for deeper meanings. At first, the Renaissance artists had been members of the craft guilds and did not have much formal education. But as they secured patrons among the upper classes, they began rubbing shoulders with philosophers and humanists and picked up ideas from the intellectual elite. From the Florentine Academy the artists learned that love of the physical world was one of the steps leading to love of God, and they introduced this notion into their work by making the human body look more attractive than it was. The more beautiful nature became, they believed, the closer it would be to God. This led them to study the body more carefully than ever and to place a much greater emphasis on nudes.

The three best-known artists of the high Renaissance, Leonardo da Vinci (1452–1519), Michelangelo (1475–1564), and Raphael (1483–1520), represent this new approach. Although da Vinci was more interested in experimental science, his Last Supper fresco in Milan and portrait of Mona Lisa are masterpieces of Western art.

But with Michelangelo platonism triumphed, as he idealized the human form in statues like the David in Florence and the Pietà in Rome. Born a Florentine and taken into the Medici family circle as a young man, he left home for Rome in 1494 and spent much of the remainder of his life there. One of the greatest artistic geniuses of all time, in addition to sculpture, he painted, designed buildings (the new St. Peter's Basilica), and wrote poetry. His fresco on the ceiling of the Sistine Chapel is probably the most imposing single painting of the Renaissance. It is a magnificent synthesis of pagan form, Christian thought, and Old Testament subject matter that dazzles spectators with its vivid use of color.

Raphael was born in Urbino but settled in Rome in 1508. In his various madonnas he tried to achieve a beauty greater than that found in nature. His art combines the naturalistic goals of earlier fifteenth-century artists with the idealization of the human form found in Michelangelo.

The Renaissance Papacy

Among the most significant patrons of Renaissance art and culture were the popes of the era. From the accession of Nicholas V in 1447 to the sack of Rome in 1527, men who were preoccupied with the more worldly aspects of scholarship and culture and with building a strong state in central Italy occupied the papal throne. Nicholas V (1447–55) not only carried out a building program in Rome but more significantly engaged in book collecting. He employed agents who searched for rare classical manuscripts and humanists who translated and corrected them. Ancient Greek writers, including the Greek fathers, were translated into Latin and thus made available to people in western Europe. His collection of thousands of manuscripts formed the basis for the new Vatican library.

Perhaps the most fascinating of the Renaissance popes was Pius II (1458–64), a skilled humanist whose *Commentaries* give penetrating insights into his life and times. From a poor noble family, he traveled incessantly in the service of the church, and before becoming pope he had distinguished himself as an essayist and Ciceronian orator.

Corruption became rampant in the papacy during the reign of Innocent VIII (1484–92). After spending a profligate youth at the court of Naples, he was ordained a priest. Rising in the church's service, he eventually became pope, but his habits did not change. He fathered sixteen children, whom he openly acknowledged and whose weddings he then celebrated in the Vatican. He constantly engaged in wars and disputes with other Italian states, and financing these campaigns kept the church in debt.

As his death approached, Innocent supposedly begged the cardinals to choose a successor who was better than he. However, they ignored his plea, and with the pontificate of Alexander VI (1492–1503) the papacy reached spiritual rock-bottom. Rodrigo Borgia had advanced rapidly in the church and became a cardinal at twenty-five. A shrewd businessman, he accumulated a fortune that he used to gain the papacy. His personal life was so immoral that by the time of his election he had fathered several children. Although he managed the papal finances prudently, his goal was to establish a principality in central Italy for his family. He turned this project over to his son, Cesare Borgia, who was legendary as an unscrupulous murderer. Alexander assigned control over the papal palace to his daughter Lucretia, who had already been married three times by the age of twenty-two. After Alexander's death, Cesare was forced to leave Italy. Although he supported Portuguese missionary work abroad and negotiated the famous line of demarcation that forestalled war between Spain and Portugal over imperial issues (see chapter 12), he was an utter disgrace to the church.

His successor Julius II (1503–13) tried to repair the damage by curbing the practice of simony and reducing nepotism. However, he led the papal army in person and was a man of such restless and

St. Peter's Basilica, Rome

fierce temper that people spoke of him as "terribilita." Most important, by the time of his pontificate Rome had replaced Florence as the center of Renaissance culture. To emphasize the grandeur of Rome, he demolished the old basilica of St. Peter and directed Bramante to draw up plans for what would be the greatest church in Christendom. As the great building project progressed, Julius commissioned Michelangelo's frescoes in the Sistine Chapel and Raphael's decoration of the papal apartments.

Leo X (1513–21), who followed Julius, was the second son of Lorenzo the Magnificent and had been made an archbishop at the age of eight, a cardinal at thirteen, and pope at thirty-seven. A man of expensive tastes, he was convinced that the head of the church should not live the austere, simple life of Christ and the apostles. At his coronation he entered Rome in gorgeous robes, passing through arches erected in his honor as though it were an ancient triumphal procession. During his pontificate, Leo packed the curia and the administration of the Papal States with members of the Medici family and justified his high living with this memorable phrase: "God has given us the papacy; let us enjoy it." His love of art, music, and the theater made Rome the cultural center of Europe, but to achieve this was extremely costly. Julius II had been a frugal pope, but the money he had accumulated was soon exhausted by Leo, and the papacy found itself deeply in debt.

As has been shown, most Renaissance popes were guilty of nepotism. Relatives who were often incompetent or underage were given positions in the church. At times these were "nephews," or bastard sons such as Cesare Borgia, while several popes themselves began their career in the church because of nepotism. Their exquisite tastes, expensive lifestyles, and political involvements led to many fiscal abuses. Church offices were bought and sold. Julius II and Alexander V were elected by bribing a majority of the college of cardinals. Indulgences were sold with great regularity, and some even tried to forge and sell papal bulls. The Renaissance popes shared the outlook of their fellow nobles who felt that a luxurious existence would gain respect for their office. While this made possible some of the finest art of the Renaissance, it also led to widespread criticism.

Many, especially among the lower classes, disapproved of the lifestyles of the higher clergy. Preachers of repentance who denounced the abuses of both the laity and clergy drew great crowds. Among these fiery evangelists none was better known than Girolamo Savonarola (1452–98). His life and ministry illustrate how the Italian Renaissance was not as secular and worldly as many have claimed. Born into a family of modest means in Ferrara, trained in the humanist tradition, and destined for a career in medicine, at the age of twenty-two he decided to enter the Dominican order.

In 1482 he was sent to Florence, and there he began calling for repentance and conversion in sermons that were filled with apocalyptic prophecies. The times were ripe for such a message since the Medici regime was at war with France, and economic conditions were severely depressed. The Medici had become too powerful, and not only the lower classes but also other merchant families now reacted against their display of wealth and luxury. The Church of San Marco filled with people anxious to hear Savonarola deliver his latest pronouncements against the Medici and other high-living princes and ecclesiastics. Many penitents delivered up such vanities as lewd books, nude pictures, costume jewelry, false hair, and frivolous attire to be burned in huge bonfires.

Savonarola's popularity reached its height when he persuaded King Charles VIII of France, who had invaded Italy, not to sack Florence. The Medici's regime collapsed and was replaced by a new republican government that was heavily influenced by Savonarola's preaching. He predicted that a great disaster would strike Italy, but a golden age would dawn in Florence and spread to all the world. Florentines, including the humanist scholars Ficino and Pico Della Mirandola, enthusiastically supported these prophecies. Pope Alexander VI worried about Florence's newly found friendship with France, because he did not wish to have a French ally flanking the Papal States. Thus, the austere Dominican found himself pitted against the most infamous Renaissance pope. Alexander tried to persuade Savonarola to leave the city, and when this failed, offered him a bribe, namely, a cardinal's appointment. Still unsuccessful, the pope then excommunicated Savonarola in 1497. The friar claimed, however, that the excommunication was invalid and that only God could cut him off from fellowship. He continued to preach and say Mass, but the city government, threatened by the pope with an interdict, asked him to suspend his clerical duties. Savonarola had now lost the support of the wealthy citizens of Florence, and the Franciscans who never cared much for the Dominicans turned against him as well. He was then charged with heresy, tried, and executed.

The Northern Renaissance

The ideas of the Italian Renaissance soon spread into northern Europe, and the chief exponent of the new learning was the "prince of humanists," Desiderius Erasmus (1469–1536). Like many contemporaries, he believed that the study of an accurate text of Christian sources combined with the Greek and Latin classics would bring about a renewal of Christianity. Born at Rotterdam, Erasmus traveled widely and studied incessantly. A student at the Brethren of the Common Life school in Deventer, he was directed toward a religious life, but a brief experience as a monk convinced him that he was not suited for monastic life. Further studies in Paris and Italy oriented him in the direction of humanism. His close acquaintance with John Colet and Thomas More in England strengthened his resolve to seek the reconciliation of faith and reason, devotion and scholarship, Scripture and literature. He thus became the great synthesizer of the northern Renaissance.

Both Erasmus's writings and personal life reflected this harmony of religious and secular thought. In the *Enchiridion* he pleaded with people to be concerned with the meaning of religious devotion and to practice their beliefs instead of merely professing them. He declared, "What point is there in your being showered with holy water if you do not wipe away the inward pollution from your heart." He then went on to say, "You venerate the saints and delight in touching their relics, but you despise the best one they left behind, the example of a holy life."[2] Erasmus promoted biblical scholarship by publishing in 1516 his own translation and the first printed edition of the Greek New Testament. He also edited the works of several early church Fathers.

The religious concerns of Erasmus and other Christian humanists were reflected throughout early sixteenth-century Europe. They published widely, promoted and influenced elementary school education, and even occupied chairs of literature, language, and classical studies in the universities. For example, Johannes Reuchlin, the foremost scholar of the Hebrew Bible, taught at Tübingen University. Juan Luis Vives, the brilliant Spanish humanist, was for a time professor at the University of Louvain and subsequently at Oxford. Other Spanish humanists taught at the new University of Alcala, founded in 1509 by Cardinal Ximénez de Cisneros. Similarly, John Colet founded St. Paul's School in Westminister that was directed toward humanistic learning.

Perhaps the most important contribution of the Renaissance in northern Europe was the discovery of printing with movable type. There had been two earlier classical revivals in Europe, one under Charlemagne in the eighth century and one during the twelfth century led by scholars such as John of Salisbury. Why the Renaissance had a lasting effect while the earlier movements did not was because the classical movement of the fifteenth century was disseminated in print. Printing enabled cheaper books, a wider reading public, and a new outlook.

Paper, ink, and the techniques of printing from carved wooden blocks or metal dies had long been known, but the process was slow and expensive because each letter had to be carved separately. About 1450 Johann Gutenberg of Mainz in Germany began making interchangeable metal letters instead of wooden blocks; since this metal type could be used over and over again, the production of books became relatively inexpensive. With incredible speed this new technique spread across Europe, and by 1500 printing presses were operating in at least one hundred communities. More than thirty thousand different works had been published, totaling altogether between six and nine million volumes. With the coming of the Protestant Reformation the printed word proved to be invaluable in spreading the new religious ideas.

These two centuries were a time of testing for institutions that had held sway for centuries. The concept of Europe as the *Republica Christiana,* with the papacy as its spiritual ruler and the Holy Roman

Empire as its secular ruler, had broken down. Even as it tried to redefine its role, the Roman Catholic church lost spiritual leadership. The new dynastic states were supported by the middle class, who, aided by advances in technology and improved credit procedures, was rapidly becoming the dominant class. In the nonmaterial realm, the era prepared society for the future. While the humanists strove to recover what they believed to be the lost intellectual and moral grandeur of classical antiquity, they bequeathed to posterity new ideas and attitudes. Methods of government that they articulated were the basis for modern theories of constitutionalism. Attempts by painters, sculptors, and architects to reproduce classical masterpieces led to important discoveries in technique and design. In their efforts to understand the work of antiquity, humanists not only developed a modern historical outlook but also sparked a parallel Christian attempt to return to the sources. Thus, the way was now open for the Reformation.

10

THE REFORMATION IMPACTS THE CHURCH

In 1500 it was still possible to speak of Christendom instead of Europe. Rather than being a geographical description, this term was a spiritual concept that involved allegiance to a body of thought. It expressed the unity of Europeans under the Roman Catholic church. All people, except some pockets of minorities—Jews, Muslims, Eastern Orthodox Christians, and extreme sectarians, worshiped according to the same ritual, accepted the church's claim to a monopoly on the way of salvation, and recognized the pope as the supreme authority on faith and morals. But within fifty years, the Protestant Reformation had shattered this religious unity. Northern Germany, Scandinavia, and parts of Switzerland, Holland, Scotland, and England were permanently lost to Rome, while sizable groups in France, Bohemia, Poland, and Hungary accepted the new understanding of salvation taught by the Reformers. Even the Roman Catholic church was deeply affected by the Reformation, and it survived only by becoming a different organization from what it had been in the Middle Ages.

THE LUTHERAN REFORMATION

On October 31, 1517, a German professor of theology named Martin Luther (1483–1546) posted a sheet of paper containing ninety-five propositions, "theses" for debate, on the door of the Castle Church at Wittenberg. This was a normal occurrence in his day because those who wished to initiate a learned debate on a subject used a church door as the equivalent of a bulletin board.

The theses questioned the validity of indulgences, a practice that the medieval church had developed to assist in the salvation of souls. They were based on the belief that Christ, the Virgin Mary, and the saints had accumulated an excess of good deeds (the "treasury of merits") that the church through the pope could draw upon to forgive the amount of temporal punishment (in purgatory) for sin that ordinary persons would have to suffer. At first, these reductions in purgatorial time before entering into heaven were given to individuals who went on a crusade or a pilgrimage or performed some other meritorious act. Gradually the conditions for the granting of such pardons were relaxed, and by the late fifteenth century they could be obtained by giving money to the church. For all practical purposes, dispensing of indulgences had become an industry employing quasi-professional salesmen. The questions that Luther raised about this practice were not intended to cause a division in the church, but that is what happened.

Luther was the son of a copper miner in Saxony. Since his father wanted him to have a legal career, he began studying at the University of Erfurt in 1501 and received an M.A. in 1505. However, in the latter year a terrifying experience during a thunderstorm induced the young Luther to abandon his worldly pursuits and enter the monastery of the Augustinian hermits in Erfurt. In 1507 he was ordained to the priesthood, but his first Mass was such an intensely awesome experience that he felt utterly inadequate.

Luther's introspective and questioning nature was such that his monastic superior, Johann von Staupitz, recommended that he continue his studies at the University of Wittenberg, and in 1512 he earned a doctorate in theology. He was then appointed professor at this university, an institution founded by the electoral Duke of Saxony in 1502. In addition to teaching, Luther served as a pastor at the town church and as administrative overseer of the Augustinian monasteries in electoral Saxony. On one occasion he was sent on monastic

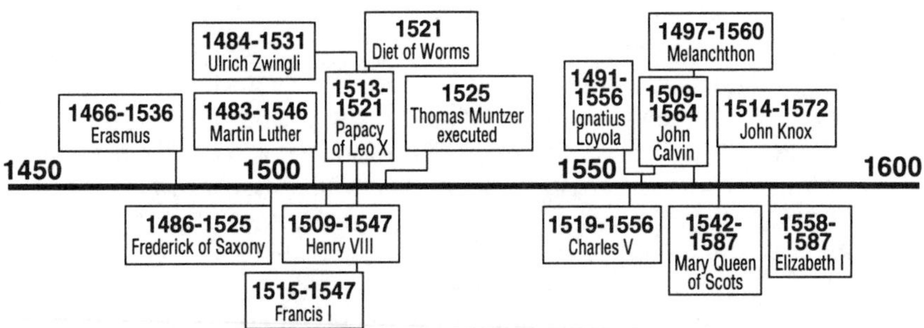

business to Rome, where the worldliness of the city that he believed to be the center of spirituality deeply disillusioned and disgusted him.

The early theological lectures that Luther gave were on the Psalms, Romans, Galatians, and Hebrews. The notes for these indicate that he abandoned the traditional medieval form of textual analysis. Concentrating on questions of sin, grace, and righteousness, he followed the teaching of Augustine of Hippo, thereby rejecting the scholastic approach. What led Luther to rethink theology was the state of despair he found himself in before the presence of God. He wanted the assurance of divine acceptance, but, conscious of the enormity of sin, he saw in God only an unrelenting justice that condemned all human efforts to seek forgiveness. His desire to satisfy the penalty for sin by the various works prescribed by the church and the Augustinian order only increased his sense of frustration.

Finally, the solution to Luther's spiritual crisis came from this sense of total helplessness before God and from the writings of the apostle Paul. His "evangelical discovery" was that a person is not justified by works but rather by faith in the finished work of Christ. An individual can do nothing to deserve the forgiveness of God, but if he believes in Christ, God will bestow salvation and eternal life upon him through the gift of the Holy Spirit. All of this comes through faith—by abandoning oneself to the message of the gospel. Here Luther describes his experience:

> I greatly longed to understand Paul's Epistle to the Romans and nothing stood in the way but that one expression, "the justice of God," because I took it to mean that justice whereby God is just and deals justly in punishing the unjust. My situation was that, although an impeccable monk, I stood before God as a sinner troubled in conscience, and I had no confidence that my merit would assuage him.

> Night and day I pondered until I saw the connection between the justice of God and the statement that "the just shall live by his faith." Then I grasped that the justice of God is that righteousness by which through grace and sheer mercy God justifies us through faith. Thereupon I felt myself to be reborn and to have gone through open doors into paradise. The whole of Scripture took on a new meaning, and whereas before the "justice of God" had filled me with hate, now it became to me inexpressibly sweet in greater love. This passage of Paul became to me a gate to heaven. . . .
>
> If you have a true faith that Christ is your Saviour, then at once you have a gracious God, for faith leads you in and opens up God's heart and will, that you should see pure grace and overflowing love.[1]

Luther's discovery of justification by faith alone and its companion doctrine, the priesthood of all believers, was quite revolutionary. If a person could go directly to God for forgiveness of sins, then the entire church structure, which existed for the primary purpose of mediating between humans and God, was rendered unnecessary. Although he rejected the priesthood and the hierarchy of the church, Luther never changed his conservative belief that society needed a structure to endure. But his attack on the church progressed from one issue to another until very little of the old institution was left immune from his criticisms. For example, he argued that pastors were not priests but individuals whose role was preaching the Word of God. As for the layers of clergy, they were seen as a way for corrupt Italians to steal money from honest Germans.

As it turned out, Luther proved to be an extremely capable individual who communicated his ideas in a most effective manner. During the next thirty years he produced an unbelievable amount of books, pamphlets, sermons, letters, and hymns. It has been calculated that he published something every two weeks, and today his collected works (the authoritative Weimar edition) comprise more than one hundred massive volumes. At times he could be coarse and vicious, but this did not lessen the appeal of his writings. Without Luther the Protestant Reformation would not have succeeded.

It was the ninety-five theses that catapulted the obscure but brilliant scholar-monk into a position of prominence. These propositions were not meant to be inflammatory but were rather cast in the form of a probing inquiry. For instance, he raised these issues:

> This license in the preaching of pardons makes it no easy thing, even for learned men, to protect the reverence due to the Pope against the calumnies, or, at all events, the keen questionings, of the laity.
>
> As, for instance: Why does not the Pope empty purgatory for the sake of most holy charity and of the supreme necessity of souls—this being the most just of all reasons—if he redeems an infinite number of souls for the sake of that most fatal thing, money, to be spent on building a basilica—this being a slight reason?

Despite their conciliatory wording, the theses sparked a controversy because they not only focused on moral and theological issues but also called attention to the economic and political abuses of the church. Luther sent copies of them to several acquaintances and some leading churchmen in Germany, including Albert of Hohenzollen whom he felt was responsible for the abuse of indulgences. What he did not realize was that the indulgence campaign in 1517 was the result of a financial deal between the papacy and the German prince. Albert was a typical aristocrat who advanced his career through the church. He was already archbishop of Magdeburg, but now he wanted to add to his holdings the archbishopric of Mainz because the holder of this position also was one of the seven electors of the Holy Roman Empire. As noted earlier, the empire was not ruled by hereditary right but rather through the choice of an emperor from a field of candidates. Albert's problem was that holding more than one church appointment was the sin of pluralism, and thus special permission from Rome was required. Since a dispensation of such importance required the payment of a large sum of money, Albert and Pope Leo X agreed that the German prince would make a generous contribution for the construction of St. Peter's in Rome. The pope authorized Albert to take the profits from an indulgence sale in Germany to fulfill his contribution.

A Dominican friar, Johann Tetzel, was employed to act as manager for the campaign. Tetzel's flamboyant approach outraged Luther, since he offered people a "plenary" indulgence, that is, total remission of all their time in purgatory and immediate entrance into heaven at their deaths. Particularly galling was the catchy sales jingle, which sounded like the product of a modern-day advertising agent: "As the coin in the chest rings, so the soul from purgatory springs." It was to challenge this abuse that Luther posted the theses for debate. Indulgences were a blatant contradiction of his insight that the just shall live by faith *alone.* The papal representatives, however, felt that the practice of indulgences was too valuable to give up, and they began attacking Luther.

From that moment on the German "reformer" and his conservative opponents were on a collision course. Convinced of the truth of his position, Luther swayed public opinion through printed pamphlets and brochures written in the vernacular and illustrated with dramatic woodcut pictures. In 1518 he was summoned to appear before a general meeting of his order and won many of his fellow Augustinians to his "theology of the cross."

Soon afterwards he was called to Rome to answer the charges lodged against him, but at the request of Frederick of Saxony this demand was not enforced. The elector protected Luther, partly because he was proud of his young professor of theology but even more so because he did not like the practice of indulgences. This resulted from his desire to keep the money at home so he could expand his own collection of relics of the saints and make Wittenberg a major center for pilgrims. This was an anomalous aspect of the man who supported Luther against the traditional church. A papal legate at Augsburg then heard the case, but this accomplished nothing since Luther refused to recant and instead appealed to a general council of the Christian church.

In 1519, during a debate with John Eck at Leipzig, Luther was forced to admit openly that many of the ideas of John Hus were not heretical and that he should not have been condemned. Thus, Luther acknowledged that not only the papacy but also general councils of the church could be mistaken and that the only certain basis of authority was the Scriptures. In 1520 a papal bull condemned forty-one statements from his works as heretical, and Luther replied by burning the document publicly. Another bull excommunicated him and left his punishment up to the secular authorities.

Emperor Charles V allowed Luther to speak for himself at a meeting (or diet) of the German princes and territorial rulers at Worms in 1521. Luther acknowledged at the assembly that some of his books were abusive and others dealt with debatable points, but he refused to disavow his basic evangelical convictions.

> Unless I am convicted by Scripture and plain reason—I do not accept the authority of popes and councils, for they have contradicted each other—my conscience is captive to the Word of God. I cannot and I will not recant anything, for to go against conscience is neither right nor safe. Here I stand, I cannot do otherwise. God help me, amen.[2]

His speech won the day among the German people, but after a period of deliberation the imperial diet declared him and his followers political outcasts and called for the suppression of his teachings. Charles did honor the safe conduct pass that he had given Luther to attend the diet, but Frederick, unwilling to take any chances, had Luther kidnapped as he returned home. For protection he was taken to a secluded castle, the Wartburg, where he spent almost a year in hiding.

The leisure that Luther now enjoyed after such a busy life caused him to become depressed and to question the stand he had taken against the church. A statement of Eck returned to taunt Luther: "How can you assume that you are the only one to understand the sense of Scripture? Have so many centuries gone wrong? What if you are in error and are taking so many others with you to eternal damnation?"[3] Even the devil himself came to mock him, so Luther believed, and he threw his ink well at the specter. Realizing the need for some project to fill the lonely hours, he turned the period of self-doubt into one of great achievement by translating the Bible into German. Luther drew heavily on Erasmus's annotated Greek New Testament and brought the Bible to the reader through his vigorous style and clarity of expression. As he put it, "When I translate Moses . . . I want to make him so German that no one will know he was a Jew." The result was a version as understandable to the humble man in the marketplace as to the learned scholar at the university, and it effectively established German as a literary language.

A new crisis confronted Luther when he returned to Wittenberg. During his absence his followers had radically altered the form of worship, destroyed relics, images, and pictures, and damaged church property—all in the name of the gospel. He responded with a series of sermons in which he insisted that one may continue any religious practice that is not specifically condemned in Scripture. His more zealous disciples reacted negatively to this conservative stance and replied that one may only do what is commanded in the Bible. These arguments led Luther to work more closely with the secular authorities in building a new church to replace Catholicism, which was collapsing in Germany. To provide pastors for the "evangelical" churches (the term used by the Lutherans) he relied upon the University of Wittenberg where he continued serving as a professor. Several individuals helped him in this task, the most outstanding being Philip Melanchthon (1497–1560), a classical scholar who was his most loyal supporter and constant companion. Melanchthon was appointed professor of Greek and Hebrew at Wittenberg when he was only twenty-one years old, and his systematic and analytical mind proved of great use in drafting the early Lutheran doctrinal statements, such as the Augsburg Confession of 1530.

Luther's theological development was essentially complete by 1521; his later work amplified and clarified his original insights. The main points of his theology were summarized in three works written in 1520. The first, *Address to the Christian Nobility of the German Nation,* argued that the civil authorities should reform the church because the hierarchy would never allow changes that might threaten their privileged position. Not only did he support lay leadership in general, but also he made several specific proposals, including affirming the need for clergy to marry, underscoring the necessity for the state to feed the poor, calling for peace with the Hussites, and abolishing the saying of Masses for the dead. In a prophetic comment he urged that heretics should be convinced to change their ideas with books and arguments rather than by persecution, otherwise "the hangmen would be the most learned doctors in the world and there would be no need of study."

The second treatise, *The Babylonian Captivity of the Church,* was an attack on the sacramental system of the Roman church. Luther accepted only two sacraments, baptism and communion, and rejected the other five because their observance was not commanded by Christ in a specific statement in the Bible. In the third book, *Freedom of a Christian Man,* while opposing papal tyranny, Luther cautioned believers not to ignore the ethical aspects of the Christian life. Drawing on Paul's teaching in Galatians, he counseled Christians against the extremes of legalism and hedonism. He explained that the Christian life must be characterized by faith and love. A believer is the lord of all and subject to no one through faith, but he is the servant of all and subject to everyone because of love. Faith binds a Christian to God and love to his fellow human beings. A person must first be born again through Christ before good works can be done, because they proceed from a life of faith. As Matthew 7:18 declared, "A good tree cannot bear bad fruit, and a bad tree cannot bear good fruit."

The year 1525, when Luther became embroiled in two controversies, one with Erasmus and the other with Thomas Müntzer, marked a major turning point in the Reformation. For several years humanists such as Erasmus welcomed Luther's reforming activities, but after 1521 most of them came to feel that he had gone too far and

Four Reformers: Farel, Calvin, Beza, and Knox

had changed from one who wanted to give friendly advice to the church into an enemy of the traditional faith. By 1524 the gulf had so widened that Erasmus rejected the Lutheran view of grace in his *Essay on Free Will.* He said the Scriptures supported the Catholic position that salvation came through faith and works; he cautioned Luther to be less dogmatic and more ready to accept correction. Infuriated, the Reformer responded with the *Bondage of the Will* (1525), which emphasized human depravity and condemned the Dutch humanist. The bitter debate with Erasmus over free will revealed just how much humanist support Luther had lost.

The problem with Müntzer was even more ominous for the future of the Reformation. This controversy grew out of an effort to better the condition of the peasants of Germany who, like their counterparts elsewhere in sixteenth-century Europe, were abused and mercilessly exploited by the landlords. Some of these poor wretches wrote down their frustrations in *The Twelve Articles of the Swabian Peasants.* They demanded the right to choose their own pastors; to be relieved of paying exorbitant taxes, tithes, and rents; and to be able to hunt, fish, and cut wood in the common forests. Encouraged by Luther's defiance of church authorities and statements about the equality of all before God, they mistakenly assumed that he would support their cause.

Led by Thomas Müntzer (1489–1525), Luther's one-time follower who believed that the Second Coming was at hand and that the wicked must be destroyed to prepare the way of the Lord, armed peasants attacked their upper class masters as enemies of God. In defiant, frenzied sermons Müntzer exhorted the peasants, "Strike while the iron is hot" and "Don't let your swords cool off! Don't let them become feeble!" Acting on this advice, they pillaged churches, destroyed castles, and threatened the very fabric of society. As the rebellion spread, tempers flared and many even demanded the common ownership of all property.

Luther's harsh reaction to the revolt was consistent with his previous statements. Although he had accused the lords of corruption and cruelty and had urged them to stop oppressing the peasants, he had never favored social revolution. He did not believe that it was possible to reform both the church and society at the same time. The very thought of social upheaval terrified him. In his anger Luther responded with a most unfortunate pamphlet, *Against the Thieving and Murderous Hordes of Peasants,* in which he denounced them with the most vicious statements. He advised the rulers to "smite, slay, and stab, secretly or openly, remembering that nothing can be more poisonous, hurtful, or devilish than a rebel. It is just as when one must kill a mad dog; if you don't strike him, he will strike you, and the whole land with you."

The lords, who scarcely needed the Reformer's advice, brutally suppressed the revolt at Frankenhausen in 1525. The slaughter on the battlefield and the subsequent reprisals resulted in the death of countless thousands of humble people. Despite the fact that Luther had never wavered from his position of a hierarchical society, the peasants felt that he had betrayed them. After 1525 the evangelical movement depended even more on the rulers, who became of critical importance in carrying out the Reformation in Germany. They even gave the name of "Protestantism" to the new movement when they "protested" against an action taken by the Catholic-dominated Diet of Speyer in 1529, which discriminated against the adherents of the evangelical faith.

The same year that witnessed the break with the humanists and the Peasants' War was also decisive in Luther's personal life. At this time he married Katherine von Bora, a former nun whom he had helped to escape from a convent. Even though Luther entered the union with reluctance, he found great happiness with "Katie." Their relationship set the tone for the Protestant definition of marriage, which he aptly called the "school for character."

The next period of the Reformer's life was taken up by a dispute with Ulrich Zwingli over the meaning of the communion. It culminated at the Colloquy of Marburg in 1529 that was held in an effort to heal the widening rift in the Reformation, especially since the forces of Catholicism were regaining strength. Luther reluctantly participated in the meeting, as he believed that his theological differences with the Swiss Reformer were irreconcilable. The major issue involved the matter of the bodily presence of Christ in the Eucharist. As expected, they reached no agreement and the basic principle of church division, so characteristic of later Protestantism, had reared its ugly head.

During these controversies Luther continued teaching, writing, and exercising leadership of the German Reformation. When negotiations with the Catholics broke down after the Diet of Augsburg in 1530, the Protestant princes formed a defensive alliance, the Schmalkaldic League, which meant armed resistance against the emperor. Despite the adulation of his students, colleagues, and fellow churchmen, his final years were overshadowed by the numerous conflicts among the Lutherans and by the consequences of having advised Philip of Hesse that bigamy was permissible at certain times. The realization that a reliance on Scripture did not preclude sharp differences in interpretation, the continuing struggle with Rome, and the debilitating impact of physical ailments led to the bitter tone of many of his last publications, especially those against the papacy and the Jews. In the worst of these, Luther recommended that all Jews be deported from Europe to Palestine. If that could not be done, they should be forbidden to engage in trade and forced to earn their living by farming. He urged that synagogues should be burned and Jewish books destroyed.

When Luther died in 1546, the Reformation lost its most prestigious leader. Moreover, not only had Lutheranism failed to win over the Roman church, but also the Swiss Reformers, the south German cities, and the Anabaptists had all produced their own versions of reform, while the Lutherans themselves were torn by dissensions. Nonetheless, by mid-century Lutheranism had become the leading faith of Scandinavia. Since these lands were heavily indebted to north Germany for their cultural legacy, it was not surprising that a German religious movement was welcomed there.

Reformed Protestantism

Although Luther provided the spark that lit the fire of the Protestant Reformation, there were other impulses toward religious change at the time. One of these was found in Switzerland, by now a loose collection of cities and small states referred to as "cantons." The early Swiss Protestant, Ulrich Zwingli (1484–1531), studied under some humanists in Vienna before becoming a priest in Zurich. Here he rejected the more aristocratic aspects of humanism and began criticizing abuses in his own church. However, he never entirely abandoned his earlier training, and the changes he brought to the church combined the practical piety of Erasmus with the biblicism of Luther. He was also more eager to turn away from tradition and to act politically and militarily to defend his version of Christianity. Thus, Zwingli combined humanism, theology, and radicalism.

The occasion for his break with Rome came when he began advocating eating meat during Lent. In so doing he raised a number of questions about church rules and practices, and the Zurich city council called for a formal disputation to resolve the controversy. Held in 1523, the debate between Zwingli and the Catholics resulted in a victory for the Reformer. A second disputation that year led to the destruction of images in churches and an end to the saying of Masses. Although he was inspired by Luther, as mentioned above, he parted company with the German leader over the meaning of the Lord's Supper.

Not only was Zwingli influential in Switzerland, but he also commanded a following in southwestern Germany. However, he suddenly passed from the scene in 1531 when he was killed during a battle between the Catholics and Protestants in Switzerland. Although he was succeeded by such capable individuals as Heinrich Bullinger in Zurich, John Oecolampadius and Oswald Myconius in Basel, and Martin Bucer in Strasbourg, the leadership of the Swiss and south German Reformation passed to Geneva and a new figure, John Calvin.

The most powerful force in the second generation of Reformers, Calvin (1509–1564) was not Swiss but French in origin. The son of a notary in Noyon, Picardy, he began the study of law at the insistence of his father. But then the father died and the youth was freed to pursue his first love, namely, humanistic literary studies. He even wrote a commentary on the Stoic philosopher Seneca's *On Clemency*.

The book's argument for the existence of a supernatural and omnipotent providence had deeply impressed the young scholar.

Because he identified with the cause of religious reform, Calvin's career as a Renaissance scholar was cut short. Lutheran ideas had spread among French university students, and in 1533 a major dispute developed between the conservatives and the reformers. After a period of indecision, King Francis I backed the conservatives because he feared that the Protestants were a threat to national security. Since Calvin had joined the new religious movement, he had to leave France and settled in Basel. By this time he had been converted to Christ, but his experience seemed rather prosaic when compared to Luther's. There was no drama or great emotional trauma such as accompanied the German Reformer's change of direction. Calvin simply developed an absolute conviction of God's omnipotence and that he was chosen to advance the kingdom of God on earth. However, one thing was clear. Even after his conversion, the combination of legal and humanistic training that he had received would determine his written expression and the methodology of his biblical scholarship.

Calvin was deeply influenced by Luther and went along with most of his theology. Their differences stemmed from Calvin's greater reliance on the Old Testament and his belief in double predestination. Following Augustine of Hippo, he emphasized God's majesty and humankind's total helplessness before Him. In an attempt to answer the question that every Christian asks who has tried to share the gospel with others, namely, why do some believe and others reject the Word, Calvin taught that God gives the gift of faith to some and denies it to others. According to Ephesians 1:4, these decisions were made before the foundation of the world and cannot be changed. While it is true that Christ died for all, he intercedes with the Father only for the ones who have been elected to salvation. For those who shared such a sense of assurance, predestination produced a sense of missionary purpose and a willingness to stand up against any earthly power that opposed the plans of God's elect. In effect, this belief encouraged the peoples of the Netherlands to rebel against their Spanish ruler and led to significant transformations of religion and government in several other countries.

Calvin set forth his theology in what was to be the classic statement of Protestant thought, the *Institutes of the Christian Religion*, the first edition of which was published in 1536. It revealed that Protestantism had a new leader who possessed an impressive mastery of the Scriptures and church Fathers. Over the years he periodically revised and expanded the work but the basic outline remained unchanged. It provided a solid statement of faith to which his followers could turn in their struggles with the Catholics.

During a brief amnesty, Calvin returned to France but was soon forced to flee once more. Intending to go to Strasbourg where Protestants were welcome, he briefly stopped at Geneva in July 1536. William Farel, a local clergyman, spotted him in a church service and challenged him to stay and assist in the religious reformation of the city. With the exception of a three-year stay in Strasbourg (1538–41), Calvin spent the remainder of his life in Geneva where he carried out a far-reaching program of reform and established a model Protestant community. The Genevan church became a model for Calvinists, whose strongholds were in France, western Germany, the Low Countries, Scotland, England, Poland, and Hungary.

Calvin's variety of Protestantism was known as "Reformed." It differed from the Lutheran system in that the church was an institution alongside the state, not subordinate to it. The church was an independent organization, which maintained its own life and used its position to correct the state when necessary. Calvin rejected the office of bishop (retained in several varieties of Lutheranism) and replaced it with a government consisting of a carefully structured set of assemblies (later called presbyteries or classes) that included both ministers and laypeople. The Reformed churches put great stress upon ecclesiastical discipline because it recognized that the church encompassed all of society, the elect as well as the damned.

As Protestant refugees flocked into Geneva, Calvin began giving lectures to instruct these individuals in the Reformed faith. These informal classes led to the founding of the University of Geneva, which became the intellectual center of Protestantism. Pastors who received training there were sent back to their homelands to preach the gospel. As Calvin put it, "Send me wood and I will send you back arrows." The earliest destination for Calvinist missionaries was France, and by 1555 congregations of Huguenots, as the French Reformed were called, existed throughout the land. That same year they met in Paris to establish a national organization and draft a confession of faith. By 1562 many nobles had become Huguenots, thus giving an aristocratic and subversive element to the faith, as the Wars of Religion soon demonstrated.

In the Netherlands Calvinism was introduced by ministers from

The Reformation

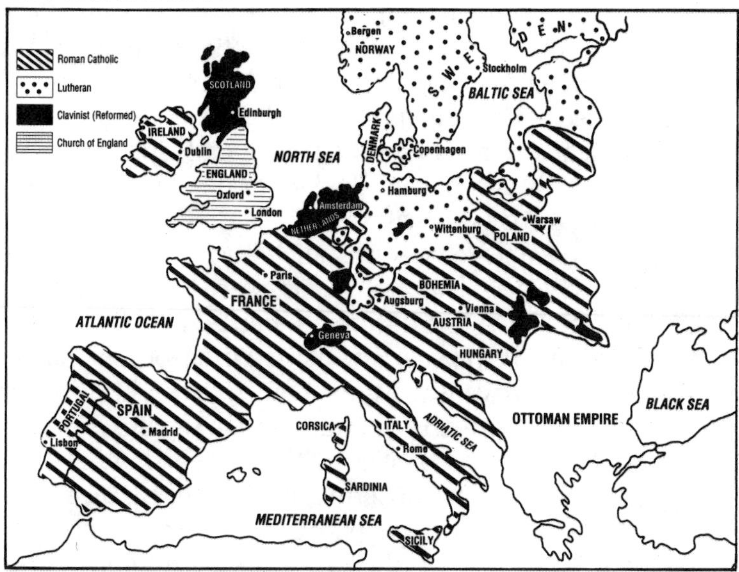

both France and Geneva. The Belgic Confession was adopted in 1566, and the acceptance of the Reformed faith led to a long war of independence against the Spaniards. Scotland was won to Calvinism largely through the efforts of John Knox (c. 1514–72). Trained in Geneva by Calvin himself, the "thundering Scot" led a relentless and ultimately successful crusade against the Catholic nobles and the regime of Mary Queen of Scots. He achieved to a great degree the conversion of the entire kingdom to the Reformed faith. Calvinism also deeply influenced the theology of the Church of England and formed the basis of Puritan thought.

THE ENGLISH REFORMATION

In many respects, the English Reformation was an independent movement resulting from the initiative of the king, although during the 1520s several scholars in Oxford and Cambridge Universities showed great interest in Luther's reform ideas. One of the more important intellectual links between England and the German Lutherans was William Tyndale. His significance was due to the many pamphlets that he wrote and to his brilliant translation of the New Testament. Also, remnants of the Lollards still survived and propagated their anti-papal teaching. Yet, the Reformation in England in its early stages was not anti-Catholic, but it resulted rather from the desire of Henry VIII for a male heir. Despite the break with Rome he remained, at least in his own opinion, a Catholic, but after 1534 there was no place for the pope in his version of the Christian faith.

Henry wanted to divorce his wife, Catherine of Aragon, because after eighteen years of marriage their only child was a daughter, Mary. No woman had sat on the English throne for centuries, and with memories of the brutal civil wars of the previous century in his mind, Henry felt that a male ruler was imperative. In addition to wanting to establish an orderly succession, his affection for Catherine had turned into loathing, as he had become enamored with Anne Boleyn, a young lady-in-waiting. Perhaps to rationalize his actions, he had come to believe that his marriage was wrong. Catherine was his older brother's widow whom he had married for diplomatic reasons. Church law, based on such Scriptures as Leviticus 20:21 prohibited such a union, but the pope had granted special permission for the marriage.

In 1527 Henry petitioned the papacy for an annulment, but because Catherine was the aunt of Charles V, whose troops occupied Rome at the time, no action was taken. A determined and impatient person, Henry decided that he had waited long enough. Believing that England had always been a place where the king had no superior other than God Himself, he saw papal approval for the divorce as unnecessary since the English church could grant it. Thus, in 1533 Thomas Cranmer, archbishop of Canterbury, annulled the marriage and validated the king's earlier secret wedding to Anne Boleyn. The pope responded by excommunicating Henry. Catholics accordingly regarded the daughter of Henry and Anne, Elizabeth, as illegitimate.

In 1534 the adoption of the Act of Supremacy, which made the king, not the pope, "the only supreme head in earth of the Church of England," signaled the decisive break with Rome. Although most English accepted the division without protest, a few such as Sir Thomas More, the brilliant humanist and author of *Utopia,* refused to renounce allegiance to Rome and consequently were beheaded for treason. Many of the subsequent changes in the church met with the approval of the influential classes, especially the dissolution of the monasteries. After a report accused them of corruption, in 1536 and 1537 they were closed and their endowments seized, thus providing the government with extra income and eliminating potential centers of Catholic opposition. Many monastic properties were given or sold at bargain prices to the upper classes, thus making them supporters of the break with Rome.

Although the king now was head of the church of England, its doctrine and practice remained largely unchanged. Despite a few innovations, such as the placing of an English translation of the Bible in every parish church for the use of laymen, Henry reaffirmed Catholic belief and practices in the Act of Six Articles (1539). This law, passed by Parliament at the king's request, upheld transubstantiation, clerical celibacy, private Masses, and confession.

Henry continued his quest for a male heir and finally his third wife gave him a son, Edward VI, who succeeded him in 1547. A sickly boy of ten, Edward's rule was exercised by advisors who were predominately Protestants. The new regime canceled the Act of Six Articles, made English the language of church services, and allowed clergy to marry. To replace the Catholic order of worship, Cranmer produced the *Book of Common Prayer.* It was written in beautiful, stately English, and in a second edition it clearly expressed Protestant doctrine. In Edward's brief reign England moved from Catholicism toward Reformed Protestantism.

However, this trend was reversed after Edward died in 1553 and his successor, Lady Jane Grey, was executed. Mary Tudor came to the throne. As Catherine of Aragon's daughter, her great ambition was to restore England to the Roman church. She pushed laws through Parliament that repealed the religious changes of her father and brother, and in theory England became Catholic once again. Actually, however, the situation had changed so drastically that Mary could not succeed in turning back the clock. One major obstacle was the lack of funds for projects like restoring the monasteries. Even the queen realized that these lands could never be taken away from their influential owners. She also lost the support that Tudor monarchs had enjoyed when she married her cousin Philip II of Spain, whom the English thoroughly disliked.

Another of her mistakes was persecuting Protestants. More than three hundred persons including Archbishop Cranmer were burned at the stake. These executions earned for her the epithet, "Bloody Mary," an indication of the contempt her subjects felt for her. Protestants who fled to the continent, the so-called Marian exiles, such as John Foxe, author of the *Book of Martyrs,* saw to it that people would never forget those who perished for their faith. Mary died in 1558, bitter and discouraged, realizing that her half-sister Elizabeth would follow her to the throne.

Whether Elizabeth wished to be a Protestant or not, circumstances forced her to take the Reformed position. Although Catholics saw her as illegitimate and thus ineligible to be queen of England, she did permit a modest amount of religious diversity for the sake of national unity. When the Marian exiles returned home and helped restore Protestantism, the break with Rome was renewed and the use of Cranmer's prayer book resumed. However, the religious settlement of 1559 was carefully balanced so that those with Catholic leanings would not be unnecessarily alienated. Elizabeth was declared "Supreme Governor of the Church" rather than "Supreme Head" to avoid offending those who felt that a woman should not be head of the church or believed that the pope or Christ was its head. As for the ministry, the traditional Catholic offices of bishops, priests, and deacons were retained. In 1571 Parliament approved an essentially Protestant statement of faith, the Thirty-nine Articles. A masterpiece of studied ambiguity, it was a summary of Anglican beliefs that remains authoritative to this day. In short, the church of the English Reformation was somewhat of an anomaly due to its marriage of Reformed doctrine with an unreformed medieval Catholic structure.

The Radical Reformation

Some enthusiasts in the evangelical movement, people who at first approved of the ideas of Luther and Zwingli, wished to see more radical changes than the major Reformers believed wise or even possible. They were commonly called Anabaptists because of their view on baptism, but the groups actually lacked cohesion and constituted a number of small, divergent sects. Some useful generalizations can, however, be made about them. The Anabaptists taught that the "visible" church must include only those who had experienced regeneration through faith in Jesus Christ and publicly testified to their faith through "believer's baptism." Since one must understand the Christian message in order to believe, baptism was administered only to those old enough to realize what they were doing. Since they had already been baptized as infants, critics labeled them as Anabaptists, people who practiced rebaptism. In their own view, however, infant baptism was invalid.

Anabaptists were also deeply moral and ethical people who, for the most part, insisted on the primacy of Scripture and the separation of church and state. Furthermore, they repudiated armed conflict, capital punishment, and the taking of oaths.

The majority of Christians at this time still regarded the baptism of infants as a most important sacrament and the rite of initiation into a church that encompassed all within the bounds of the state. Moreover, even though some of their leaders were highly educated, most Anabaptists belonged to the lower classes. Consequently, they were looked upon as antisocial radicals, and Lutherans, Reformed, and Catholics alike persecuted them. Despite the cruel punishments to which they were subjected, they continued to profess their faith because they believed that true Christians should expect mistreatment from the worldly authorities.

Anabaptists first appeared among Zwingli's followers in Zurich in 1523. Two of their leaders were Conrad Grebel and Felix Manz whose success in winning converts outraged the city leaders. Manz was executed by drowning (a cynical "rebaptism") and Grebel, along with his followers, was exiled. Those who remained in Switzerland went underground, enabling the movement to survive until the next century, while the refugees spread Anabaptism into south Germany and Moravia. Strasbourg was the center of the movement from 1527 until 1533 when Martin Bucer, the Protestant church leader there, became frightened by the separatist views of the Anabaptists and ordered their expulsion.

One of those who ministered there was Melchior Hoffmann (1500–43), who claimed to be one of the two witnesses of Revelation 11:3 and urged Anabaptists to give up nonviolence and establish Christ's kingdom by force. Although he was jailed, a disciple, Jan Matthys, led a group to Münster in Westphalia where his preaching was so successful that they gained control of the entire town and forced rebaptism upon the residents. Asserting that he was Enoch sent to prepare the way for Christ, Matthys established a communitarian order and introduced a new law code. After his death in combat in 1534, John of Leiden set himself up as King of Zion, introduced polygamy, and killed or expelled those who would not submit to him.

This so upset Lutherans and Catholics alike that they joined forces to besiege the town. Despite a heroic defense, it was captured in 1535 and most of the male Münsterites executed with a cruelty reserved for social revolutionaries. The leaders' corpses were even placed in iron cages and hung in a church tower. Not only did this episode give the movement a bad name, but also it provided an excuse for further persecution.

However, the scattered and despised remnants renounced all forms of violence and lived simple, quiet, and humble lives. Their most important new leader was a former Dutch priest, Menno Simons. Converted in 1536, he rallied the discouraged Anabaptists of the Low Countries and northern Germany. Stressing pacifism and the demonstration of a life of faith through good works, he organized his followers into Christian communities that were separate from the worldly social and political establishments. For him the focus of the Christian life was the church, not the state; believers were to be in the world but not of the world. They became known as Mennonites and thrived in spite of their suffering. At one time they made up one-tenth of the population of the Netherlands. Then they migrated to eastern Europe and later to Russia and the New World.

Another center of Anabaptism was Moravia where Balthasar Hubmaier and Jacob Hutter represented the two wings of the movement. Hubmaier, the leading intellectual among the Anabaptists, had been a student of John Eck and a professor at the University of Ingolstadt before his conversion in 1525. Leaving the priesthood, he eventually settled in Moravia. Here he converted and baptized two leading nobles who in return allowed him to preach in their territories. He won thousands of converts and wrote several pamphlets that skillfully presented the Anabaptist position. Among those who joined him was Hans Hut, an advocate of community of goods and total pacifism. Because Hubmaier's followers would not accept Hut's pacifist views and rejection of contemporary society, the Moravian Anabaptists split. Meanwhile, the Catholic Hapsburgs gained control of Moravia and rooted out what they considered as heresy. With the execution of both Hubmaier and Hut, it seemed that the movement was finished.

However, Jacob Hutter, who provided leadership during the crucial years 1533–36, saved the Moravian settlements from destruction. He organized the brethren into closely knit congregations with common ownership of goods based upon the practice of the apostolic church as recorded in Acts 5. The Hutterites, as they were called, became a viable, socially cohesive, and active community. Although Hutter himself was martyred and the movement went through some trying times, it remains as one of the most successful survivals of Anabaptism. From Moravia the Hutterites wandered into eastern Europe and eventually to North America, always maintaining their communitarian institutions.

Two other noteworthy groups of the radical Reformation were the Spiritualists and the evangelical rationalists. The former rejected external forms of religion and emphasized inner communion with the Holy Spirit. Their leader, the Silesian noble Caspar Schwenkfeld (1490–1561), taught that true believers should withdraw from the

Mainz Cathedral in Germany

church and form prayer groups of the truly regenerate. He urged his followers to become avid Bible students although he did not insist that they be rebaptized. A vestige of the Schwenkfelders survives in Pennsylvania.

The latter group, the evangelical rationalists, rejected the traditional doctrines of the Trinity and the deity of Christ. One noteworthy adherent to this view was Michael Servetus, who was executed for heresy in Geneva. In Poland and eastern Europe rationalist theology was institutionalized through the influence of Faustus Socinus (1539–1604). The Socinians organized their churches along Calvinist lines, but they put less emphasis on church discipline. Jesuit-directed persecution led to their expulsion from Poland in 1658, but a remnant survived in Transylvania under the Turkish rule. Modern Unitarianism is intellectually linked to the Socinians.

The Catholic Reformation

By the 1540s Roman Catholicism seemed to be a dying faith. The Protestants had won most of Germany, and it appeared that the rulers in other parts of Europe might follow Henry VIII's example and establish national churches. But because of the Catholic Reformation (also known as the Counter-Reformation) this did not happen.

Instead, the renewal spearheaded by a regenerated papacy that placed a greater stress on spiritual leadership and several new religious orders enabled the church of Rome to meet the Protestant challenge.

In the revolutionary turmoil caused by Luther it is easy to forget that the Protestant success was never more than partial. Although badly shaken, the papacy was surprisingly resilient. Ironically, the pope emerged from the struggle with greater control over the territory left to him than his predecessors had over the entire Western church. The Reformation split the church but forced Rome to organize for war, and this entailed giving more power to the leader.

Among the religious orders that worked for reform were the Barnabites, Capuchins, Theatines, Carmelites (their leading lights, Teresa of Avila and John of the Cross, were outstanding figures in Catholic mysticism), and above all the Jesuits. Ignatius of Loyola (1491–1556), the founder of the Jesuits (Society of Jesus) who was from the Basque country of northwest Spain, entered the military service of the Spanish king. In 1521, while fighting in a war with France, Loyola was seriously wounded in the leg by a cannon ball. During his time of recuperation he read a devotional book that changed his life and inspired him to become a soldier for Christ. He entered a monastery where he spent nearly a year in ascetic practices, experienced mystical visions, and composed the essence of his great manual of spiritual warfare, *The Spiritual Exercises.* After a pilgrimage to Jerusalem and studies in Spain, in 1528 he entered the University of Paris where he attracted several associates who worked through the *Exercises* and became fired with his ideals. After completing their studies, Loyola and six companions vowed to live a life of poverty, chastity, and service in the Holy Land or, failing that, to go anywhere at the behest of the pope. Since a war in the east prevented them from going to Jerusalem, they applied to Pope Paul III, who in 1540 approved their request to become an order of the church. In 1548 they chose Loyola as the "general" for the Society of Jesus. He provided the group with a "Constitution" that set up a paramilitary structure with obedience, discipline, and efficiency as the key ideas. Unlike other religious orders, the Jesuits took a fourth vow of unconditional obedience to the pope, and they worked in the world rather than withdrawing into a cloister. They placed heavy emphasis on education and missionary work as the means to strengthen and propagate the Catholic faith.

The church also clarified and redefined its teachings. The process was complicated by medieval doctrinal cleavages, especially the nominalist-realist conflict. The nominalists, exemplified by William of Ockham, held ideas much like those of Luther, while the realists, such as Thomas Aquinas, followed a theology that provided logical proofs and was based on Aristotelian thought and method. The doctrinal clarification took place at the Council of Trent, which met periodically between 1545 and 1563. Composed mainly of Italian bishops and abbots who tended to follow the lead of the pope, it was presided over by two papal legates and was thoroughly under the influence of the Jesuits.

The Tridentine (from Trent's Latin name) reforms can be grouped into two categories, disciplinary and dogmatic. The disciplinary matters included luxury, simony, nepotism, and other clerical abuses. Far more significant, however, were the dogmatic reforms. They followed the lines laid out by Thomas Aquinas who in effect was made the official theologian of the church. Each doctrinal canon stated a Protestant point of view and then the Catholic refutation, which often, on the surface at least, was a double compromise. Authority was to be based upon Scripture and tradition with the Latin Vulgate, including the Old Testament apocryphal books, acknowledged as the official Bible of the church. Vernacular translations could only be used with papal approval. Salvation combined the work of God and man, and included both predestination and the exercise of free will. Justification was not only by faith but also by good works. The practice of indulgences would continue but with reforms to prevent abuses. The system of seven sacraments was also retained. Enforcement of the conciliar decrees was left in the hands of the Vatican. This meant that resistance by royal or local authorities would preclude their implementation in some areas.

In order to disseminate what had been decreed at Trent, every bishop was directed to establish a school and a seminary in his diocese. The Jesuits quickly took the initiative in developing this educational system, and they remain the leaders in Catholic learning to this day. An illustration of the new policy was the work done in Switzerland by Charles Borromeo (1538–84), the archbishop of Milan. He sent papal legates into the area who returned with dismal reports about conditions in the Catholic church there. They accused the clergy of being lazy, immoral, and ignorant and claimed the Protestants profited from this sorry state of affairs. Borromeo followed up by founding the Helvetian College at Milan to train priests for service in the Swiss cantons. Then he created colleges in Switzerland proper, one of which still exists at Lucerne. By 1600 the efforts of Borromeo had halted the advance of the Reformation in the alpine nation.

Since the printing press had so effectively spread Protestant thought in Europe, Pope Paul IV decided in 1559 to establish the "Index of Prohibited Books." The Council of Trent ratified this action, and it became the notorious blacklist of works whose philosophies and doctrines were deemed adverse to the teachings of the Roman church. The Index eventually listed everything from the writings of Karl Marx and Martin Luther to novels by Albert Camus, and was only discontinued in 1966. The Vatican also established its own printing press, which later played a major role in spreading the Catholic faith.

In the Middle Ages, the repression of doctrinal deviations was handled by the Holy Office of the Roman Inquisition. In 1480 this was revived in Spain to fight heresy. Ferdinand and Isabella sponsored the institution, which sought to counter Jewish and Moorish influences, making it a key factor in the forced conversions and expulsions of these unfortunate peoples. During the Reformation the Spanish Inquisition targeted the Erasmians and even mystics like Teresa of Avila. In 1542 the Holy Office was revived in the Papal States by Paul III, and among its victims in the following century was Galileo.

The Inquisition was an ecclesiastical court that conducted heresy trials under the leadership of a Grand Inquisitor. In Spain this person was nominated by the king and approved by the pope. He in turn chose a high council of five men who were confirmed by the king. There were also nineteen local courts in each province. The orthodox and scholarly Dominicans conducted the Spanish Inquisition. Evidence was provided by pious laymen, who were given rewards for reporting heresy.

Each person charged was given a month to prepare his defense, and one could be sent to prison only by the unanimous vote of the inquisitors. The trial was conducted secretly, and the defendant did not face the accusers, although there were occasional exceptions. Torture was used to extract confessions. If the accused repented early in the proceedings, he might be released and required to do public penance. If he were found guilty or relapsed into heresy, he would be turned over to the state for punishment, usually by fire. In Spain the public executions occurred at a huge spectacle called the *auto-da-fe* (act of faith), which the king often attended. At times, many accused heretics were burned simultaneously. The Inquisition proved to be an effective bulwark against the voicing of divergent opinions.

The many changes of the sixteenth century made the Roman Catholic church a more disciplined and tightly governed institution. Also, although Protestantism brought hope and a spirit of joy to many, it deprived others of such reassuring instruments of grace as pilgrimages and the performance of little concrete acts that are so much easier than going through the inner conflicts that bring about new life in Christ. The initial reaction of Rome had been simply to condemn Protestant teaching, but once the failure of this became obvious, the old faith renewed itself from within and began a reform of its own. Whether its actions constituted a "counter" or a "Catholic" reformation is a matter of dispute. If the church had been content with a mere rejection of the "heretical" teachings of the Reformers, then only a counter-reformation took place. However, the decisions of the Council of Trent, the renewal of religious life, and the development of a better system of clerical training pointed to a more positive response to Protestantism and a renewal of commitment to the Christian message. In this sense, it was truly a reformation that changed the very fiber of Catholicism and made it into a modern institution. It was now ready to do battle with the Protestant forces in the religious wars.

11

RELIGIOUS CONFLICTS PLAGUE EUROPE

The sixteenth and seventeenth centuries were a period marked by intense ideological turmoil. Whereas power struggles and dynastic rivalries were always a feature of European politics, the addition of religious hatred made conflict more terrible and bitter. In the many wars, Catholics were pitted against Protestants, Protestants against Protestants, and at times Catholics against Catholics. They often became civil wars as Europeans battled each other, believing they were "saints in arms" called to crush those whom they indiscriminately labeled as "anti-Christ." Because of the key role that religious issues played in this extraordinary circle of violence, historians have frequently lumped the clashes together under the not altogether satisfactory rubric "wars of religion."

Responses to the Wars of Religion

Many of the monarchs of Europe grew weary of the incessant fighting and tried a number of methods to stop these struggles. Four possible options were available to them—partition, compromise, suppression, and toleration.

Two illustrations of the first of these tactics were the attempts to end the conflict between the Lutherans and the Catholics in the Holy Roman Empire and the struggle between the Huguenots (Protestants) and the Catholics in France.

War had come to the empire in 1546, and at first Charles V and the imperial Catholic forces seemed to be winning, but then Protestants managed to regroup and neither side could win a decisive victory. The results were the conclusion of the (religious) Peace of Augsburg in 1555, and a year later Charles's retirement and division of his vast realm between his son Philip and brother Ferdinand. The Augsburg agreement provided that the ruler of each territorial state in the empire would determine the faith of his subjects—either Lutheran or Catholic. People who dissented from the prince's determination in their territories were allowed to move to neighboring ones where their faith was recognized. Calvinism, however, was excluded as an option, and ecclesiastical lords (bishops and abbots) who turned to Protestantism could not convert their territories into secular states. State boundaries thus served as the borders between the rival faiths—the principle of partition.

In France a similar form of religious conflict broke out in 1562. Calvin had been sending pastors there for some years, and by 1562 at least 10 percent of the population had adopted the Reformed variety of the Protestant faith. This rapid growth, along with the conversion of many important nobles, frightened the Catholics. When Henry II died in 1559, he left the monarchy in a shambles. Three of his sons successively occupied the throne during the next thirty years and under their rule monarchical prestige eroded still further. At first the queen mother, Catherine de Medici, managed to keep peace between the Catholics and Huguenots, and even arranged a meeting between representatives of the two faiths to work out a compromise (Colloquy of Poissy, 1562). However, the talks came to naught and hostilities ensued.

Religion was only one factor in the struggle. Many nobles and townspeople were also seeking to free themselves from royal control. As in all civil wars, great cruelty marked the fighting. Entire cities were wiped out, assassinations were frequent, and the number of refugees was enormous. Royal power declined as province after province fell under the control of the great nobles.

One of the most tragic events was the massacre of St. Bartholomew's Day, August 24, 1572. The occasion for this was the impending marriage of Henry of Navarre (he also belonged to the Bourbon

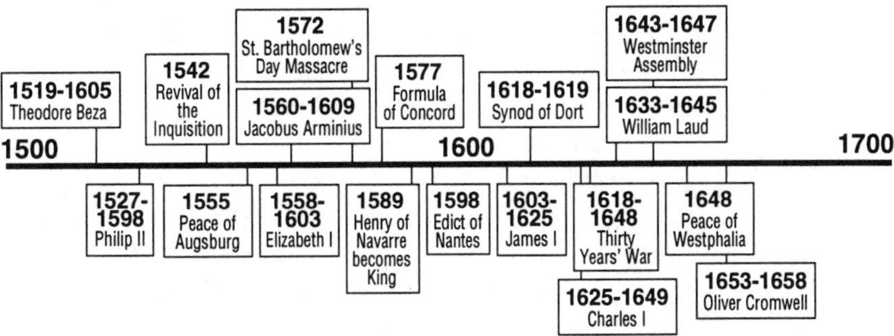

family, a rival of the Valois dynasty), to Margaret of Valois, sister of the current ruler, Charles IX. This relationship opened the possibility that a Protestant might eventually become king of France. Catherine, who was determined that this should not take place, plotted with the Catholic faction to slaughter those Protestants who had gathered in Paris for the celebration. When the nobles were assembled, the Catholics at a prearranged signal (the ringing of church bells) began killing all the Protestants they could find. Parisian mobs quickly entered the fray, and the slaughter even spread to the provinces. Estimates of the dead ran into the tens of thousands, and in the words of a contemporary observer, "The streets were covered with dead bodies, the river stained, the doors and gates of the palace bespottted with blood. Wagon loads of corpses, men, women, girls, even infants, were thrown into the Seine, while streams of blood ran in many quarters of the city."[1]

This touched off a new round of fighting, and conflict raged on and off for the next seventeen years. Henry of Navarre fought with two mutually antagonistic Catholic rivals, King Henry III and Henry, duke of Guise, but then the latter two were assassinated and he was left in 1589 as the prime contender for the throne. Taking the title of Henry IV, the Huguenot champion recognized that the civil wars would soon resume, but he defused this by deciding to shed his Protestantism and become a Catholic. He is reported to have said, "Paris is worth a Mass."

Thus, peace finally came to a war-weary France through the efforts of Henry IV. His conversion to Catholicism secured the allegiance of most French people but alarmed the Protestants, who now saw themselves as isolated and in great danger. To allay their fears and retain their loyalty, he issued the Edict of Nantes in 1598. This granted the Huguenot minority civil rights and allowed them to have their own military units and to fortify two hundred towns in order that they might feel secure. Protestants could worship privately everywhere in France, while certain public worship places for them were officially designated, including some nobles' estates. Here again was the principle of partition.

The second method used to bring peace between rival religious groups was compromise, whereby a state worked out a settlement that would satisfy most of its people and then forced everyone else to submit to it. This happened with the Church of England (Anglican) under Elizabeth I. To be sure, Elizabeth's settlement was partly a product of her own personality. As the daughter of Henry VIII and Anne Boleyn (who was executed for alleged adultery and treason), she grew up in an atmosphere of fear and anxiety. Although many historians believe she would have preferred to be a Catholic, she could not rule England as an adherent of Rome. Elizabeth's strongest supporters were Protestants, but the Catholic church, which regarded her as illegitimate because of her birth from an unrecognized marriage.

Elizabeth sponsored a statement of faith for the Anglican church, the Thirty-nine Articles, which were essentially Protestant. But some points, such as the one on Holy Communion, were left deliberately vague. The liturgy was similar to that of the Roman Catholic church, except that it was in English. The monarch functioned as the "supreme governor" of the church, which was administered by a group of bishops.

Although some clergymen rejected the settlement, most of the people were content with it. Opposition to the Anglican compromise came from devout Catholics led by the Jesuits, while the extreme Protestants (known as the Puritans) were also dissatisfied with the arrangements. As a result, both groups were persecuted for their dissenting beliefs.

A third way of handling religious conflict was suppression. A state chose one side in a dispute and then set out to eliminate the other by murdering or exiling its adherents. This tactic was utilized in many parts of Europe, but especially in Spain where Philip II was by far the greatest practitioner of the method. The most powerful ruler of the last half of the sixteenth century, Philip worked tirelessly to build his dynasty and to strengthen the Roman Catholic church in the face of the Protestant advance.

The symbol of his reign was El Escorial, a massive stone edifice erected on a barren hillside northwest of Madrid that was a combination palace-monastery-mausoleum. It was a most unusual royal residence, because it lacked sufficent space to house the officials of his court yet contained the monks' residence, royal tombs, and a large central church to which his bedroom was adjacent. Philip viewed the Roman Catholic church as essentially an agent of the government and assumed that it should help him politically and financially. Like most rulers of the period, he regarded any religion other than his own as a threat to his power.

Philip used the Inquisition (see chapter 10) to bring pressure to bear on all who deviated from Catholic orthodoxy. Heresy was declared to be a crime against the state, and civil officials carried out the punishments. All those who refused to renounce their faith, whether they were Protestants, Jews, or Muslims, automatically fell into that proscribed category. The Inquisition ruthlessly hunted them down, and they were jailed, tortured, and executed. Jews and Muslims were forced to convert to Christianity, and those who rejected baptism were killed or driven out of Philip's domains. As for the Protestants, they were compelled to return to the Roman church, and their movement in Spain died out completely.

Although the suppression policy was successful in Spain, Philip made an enormous mistake when he used it in his possessions in the Netherlands. To stop the spread of Calvinism there, Philip ordered the strict enforcement of laws against heresy. He went even further to exclude local nobles from his government entirely or relegated them to minor posts and replaced them with aristocrats brought in from Spain. This policy, which some historians have interpreted as racist in nature, seriously undermined his position there with both Catholics and Protestants. Then, in 1567 the latter rioted and smashed religious images, art objects, and stained glass windows in the Catholic churches. Philip responded by promptly sending in an army. His commander, the duke of Alva, unleashed a reign of terror against the inhabitants of the Netherlands, killing many thousands in just six years. As the fighting raged on, the Calvinists moved to more secure positions north of the Rhine, leaving the southern provinces (modern-day Belgium) to the Catholics. In 1579 ten southern provinces formed a league to defend Catholicism, and two years later the seven northern provinces declared their independence from Spain.

The new political entity called itself the United Provinces and chose William of Orange as its leader. Although some French diplomats nicknamed him "the silent," he actually was an extraordinarily articulate and friendly person. His resolute determination, patience, and belief in government by consent of the people upheld the spirit of resistance among the Dutch. Since each of the seven provinces was fairly independent of the others, it required considerable tact and effort on his part to keep them working together. The frustrated Philip offered a large reward to anyone who would kill the Dutch ruler, and in 1584 a young Catholic fanatic assassinated him.

Nevertheless, the revolt continued under the leadership of William's son, and Philip decided to stop the English from helping the Dutch by sending the famous Spanish Armada in 1588. It was also intended to eliminate Elizabeth whom he bitterly hated and to regain England for the Catholic faith, but the venture failed. After Philip's death, a twelve-year truce in the war with the Dutch was called, but then fighting resumed. Finally, their independence was recognized in 1648. The result of the policy of suppression was decades of war, which drained the national treasury and caused the loss of some of Spain's richest provinces.

The last method used to handle religious differences within a state was toleration. In the sixteenth and seventeenth centuries this was not at all viewed with favor as it would be in more recent times. William of Orange was one of the few people in early modern Europe who favored the idea that the state should allow different faiths to coexist in freedom within its boundaries. Through his influence, freedom of conscience became the rule in Holland, and during the seventeenth century the land was a refuge for the persecuted from all over Europe. Toleration, a policy that seems so reasonable today, was thought by most rulers of that time to be a dangerous shortcoming. To tolerate a religious view with which one did not agree was surely proof that one's personal faith was weak.

The bottom line was that despite all attempts by European rulers to resolve the religious conflicts, they continued unabated. Finally, in 1618 the simmering hatreds and resentments broke out in all their irrational fury in the bloodiest of the religious wars of the Reformation era.

THE THIRTY YEARS' WAR

Of all the areas of Europe torn by the conflict between a reformed Catholicism and Protestantism, the one that suffered the most devastation was the Holy Roman Empire. Historians have long wrestled with the question of why Protestantism lost its drive in the place of its birth, whereas Catholicism became increasingly more confident. One factor was the economic decline of Germany resulting from the shift of European trade routes. Another was disappointment over social conditions. Although the Reformation had reaffirmed the importance of sound doctrine, it had less impact on the society as such. Superstition, immorality, and social injustice flourished in the land of the Reformation, and human beings proved to be very resistant to change.

As the Roman Catholic church increasingly reasserted its power in Germany, a strain was placed on the terms of the Peace of Augsburg. As already mentioned, the rulers in each area chose between Roman Catholicism and Lutheranism, and their subjects had to conform to the official religion or leave the territory. Another provision of the Augsburg peace was the "ecclesiastical reservation," which required the spiritual ruler of a church territory to give up his land if he decided to become a Protestant. This was designed to halt the "secularization" of church property and keep the three ecclesiastical votes (Mainz, Cologne, and Trier) for the Holy Roman Emperor in the hands of Catholic electors, thus insuring a permanent majority in the electoral college. But since there was no adequate legal provision to enforce the ecclesiastical reservation, when disputes occurred their outcome depended on the strength of the contending parties.

A prime example of the problem was the conversion of Gebhard Truchsess (1547–1601) who in 1577 had been named archbishop of Cologne. In 1582 he announced that he was going to become a Protestant, marry, and make both Catholicism and Lutheranism legal in his domain. The ecclesiastical reservation was invoked, and an army was sent to oust Gebhard and replace him with the Catholic duke Ernest of Bavaria. Truchsess had been promised Protestant support, but only a small force from the Palatinate came to his aid because the Lutheran princes suspected that he favored Calvinism.

An imperial diet at Regensburg in 1608 tried but failed to relax Protestant-Catholic tensions. The same year the Protestant (also known as the Evangelical) Union was formed. It consisted of most of the German Reformed and Lutheran princes led by Frederick IV, the elector Palatine of the Rhine. In 1609 the rival Catholic League was organized under the leadership of Duke Maximilian of Bavaria. War fever rose, but individuals of good will on both sides tried to reach a settlement without a resort to arms. However, resolving territorial issues between the two confessions became ever more difficult.

Although each side saw conflict as inevitable, the outbreak of the Thirty Years' War surprised both. Before tracing the course of the struggle, some general comments about it would be helpful. For one thing, it was three struggles telescoped into one—Protestants versus Catholics in Germany, a civil war in the Holy Roman Empire between the emperor and the princes, and an international contest between France and the Hapsburgs (Austrian and Spanish) for European hegemony in which other powers were often involved. Historians customarily divide the war into four main phases: Bohemian (1618–25), Danish (1625–29), Swedish (1630–35), and French (1635–48). The seemingly never-ending hostilities and the involvement of hundreds of thousands of soldiers devastated the areas where the fighting took place. It began as a religious conflict, but during the latter two phases it became essentially a political contest in which the Catholic Bourbon house of France, frightened by the growth of Hapsburg power, sent troops and money to support the Protestant cause.

The political or dynastic side of the struggle led to the conclusion of the Peace of Westphalia in 1648, which ended the war in Germany, although hostilities between Spain and France continued for another decade. The settlement was the first modern international peace treaty and was the precursor of many others to follow. It certainly reflected how far secularization had progressed in Europe. At the previous great international gathering more than two centuries earlier, the Council of Constance, the issues of business were matters of belief, authority, and church structure; now they were questions of state, dynastic power, and territorial acquisition.

The Thirty Years' War began in Bohemia. Although a Slavic land, its king was one of the electors of the Holy Roman emperor. The Bohemian nobility selected the king, and during the last century the choice had been a Catholic Hapsburg. But by this time, many Czechs (another name for Bohemians) had become Protestants. In fact, the region had been a trouble spot for the Roman Catholic church ever since the time of the reformer John Hus. The most militant among the Czech Protestants were those who adopted Calvinism. The Reformed church in Germany and its allies in Bohemia were apprehensive about the extension of Hapsburg power and the strengthening of the Catholic church. Their fears seemed confirmed when the Hapsburg emperor Matthias in 1617 secured the election of his cousin Ferdinand as king of Bohemia. Educated by the Jesuits in strict Catholicism, Ferdinand began persecuting Protestants despite promises to the contrary.

The first act of open defiance was the "defenestration of

SOLUTIONS TO THE RELIGIOUS QUESTION

PARTITION	COMPROMISE	SUPPRESSION	TOLERATION
Divide a country into Protestant and Catholic territories, and the ruler of the region determines the faith that will be practiced by the populace	The state works out a compromise that settles the religious differences and everyone is forced to adhere to this	The state chooses one side in the religious question and eliminates all dissenters through execution and exile	The state allows different faiths to coexist in freedom within its boundaries
Peace of Augsburg in Germany, 1555 Wars of Religion in France, 1562-89, results in Henry IV deciding to become a Catholic but giving Huguenots freedom to practice faith in areas where they predominate	Elizabeth I and adoption of the Thirty-nine Articles defining the beliefs of the Anglican Church	Mary Tudor in England Philip II suppresses all dissent in Spain but fails in effort to impose Catholicism on the Dutch	Holland in the late sixteenth and seventeenth centuries Roger Williams in Rhode Island and William Penn in Pennsylvania stipulate that all faiths will have freedom of worship

Prague." On May 23, 1618, two Catholic representatives of the king who had come to put pressure on the Czechs were thrown out of a window in the Prague castle but were not seriously injured. Jubilant Catholics hailed the incident as a miracle; Protestants pointed out that the men had landed on a manure pile. After the incident the Protestant Union sent aid to the Bohemian rebels. In 1619 the representative assembly of the nobility, the estates, convened to depose Ferdinand and elect Frederick V, elector of Palatine, as their new king. He was a handsome, young German Calvinist prince and head of the Protestant Union. He could have been elected Holy Roman emperor, as Protestants now controlled four of the seven votes, but actually he ruled for such a brief time that he is known as "the winter king." When the Hapsburgs attacked Bohemia, Frederick did not receive the aid he expected from the international Calvinist community and the Protestant Union. Ferdinand, who now had become emperor, on the other hand, was backed by Spain, the pope, Bavaria, and the Catholic League. In November 1620, at the Battle of the White Mountain west of Prague, the count of Tilly, commanding the forces of the Catholic League, crushed Frederick's troops, and the winter king had to flee.

Jesuits soon arrived in Bohemia to force Catholicism on the people. Refusing to bow down to the ruthless policy of reconversion,

150,000 people left Bohemia. The lands of the old Protestant nobility were confiscated and given to loyal Catholic supporters of the Hapsburgs. Tilly followed up this victory by conquering the Palatinate and forcing Frederick into exile. The Protestant Union was dissolved and Emperor Ferdinand gave Duke Maximilian of Bavaria the electoral seat from the Palatinate.

The sweeping Catholic victory alarmed the other Protestant princes of Germany, and for help they looked to Christian IV, king of Denmark and Norway, thus inaugurating the second phase of the war. As duke of Holstein, the Danish king was also a prince of the empire. He had built his power and wealth by controlling the entrance to the Baltic Sea. He now decided to intervene on behalf of the German Protestants as a means of gaining more territory for himself. The Dutch and the English gave him the economic aid needed to go to war. Emperor Ferdinand, feeling the need for additional support to meet the Danish challenge, struck a bargain with Albrecht von Wallenstein, a strange, sinister, mercenary soldier of boundless ambition. Wallenstein, who had become rich from lands seized from Bohemian Protestants, agreed to furnish an army of 20,000 men at no cost to the empire as he would provision it by a system of robbery. In a brilliant campaign against the Danes he subjugated most of North Germany and forced King Christian to withdraw from the war in 1629.

The Hapsburg Catholic tide was now at its height, and it looked as though forcible conversion would be the order of the day for most German Protestants. The Protestant losses were great, but none were more symbolic or enduring than that of the Palatine library. The Bavarian troops who conquered the area seized the library of Heidelberg, a great treasure of manuscripts and books, and shipped it to Rome, where it remains to this day. More significant, however, was the Edict of Restitution, which the emperor issued a few weeks before the treaty with the Danish king. It decreed the restoration of all church lands that Protestants had taken since 1552. This included two archbishoprics, twelve bishoprics, and about 120 monasteries and other foundations. Also, only adherents of the Augsburg Confession of 1530 would have free exercise of religion, and all other "sects" were to be suppressed. This not only upset the Protestant princes, who perceived it as a warrant for their destruction, but also Catholic rulers who were apprehensive that Ferdinand would use it as a device to extend Hapsburg control over Germany. In addition, the princes feared Wallenstein, whose extortion and cruelties had aroused considerable animosity, and they demanded that his army be dissolved. In an effort to allay their suspicions, Ferdinand dismissed Wallenstein and ordered his forces disbanded.

If the Edict of Restitution had been fully enforced, Protestantism in Germany might have been wiped out. Although difficulties with the Catholic princes hampered Ferdinand, the death blow to his dreams came when Gustavus Adolphus, king of Sweden, landed in Germany in 1630. A brilliant soldier, statesman, and devout Lutheran, Gustavus was one of the most important rulers of the era. Before invading Germany he had already defeated the Danes, Russians, and Poles. He entered the Thirty Years' War not only to save Protestantism but also to ensure Swedish control of the Baltic Sea region. An indication of the changing character of the war was that part of the financing for the Swedish expedition came from the Catholic king of France, whose adviser was the powerful Cardinal Richelieu (1585–1642).

At first the German Protestant princes were frightened by this foreign incursion, but after Tilly's army sacked the city of Magdeburg they began to support the Swedes. In 1631 Gustavus defeated the imperial forces at Breitenfeld in Saxony. He moved on to capture Prague and won again at Rain on the Danube in 1632, where Tilly was killed. These victories enabled him to restore freedom to Protestants in southern Germany. In desperation, Ferdinand recalled Wallenstein and gave him a *carte blanche* to counter the Swedish advance. At the crucial Battle of Lützen (near Leipzig) in 1632 the Protestants won, but Gustavus was killed in action. The Swedish army remained in Germany and the fighting continued on, but its influence was declining. Wallenstein was now operating freely and even carrying on his own foreign policy. When it appeared that he was trying to take over political power, the emperor dismissed him. Then, in February 1634 under mysterious circumstances Wallenstein was assassinated, although it is uncertain whether Ferdinand actually had ordered this.

A settlement was reached in 1635 that included a compromise over the Edict of Restitution, but the French decided to continue the war. Utilizing mercenaries at first and later mobilizing a French army, Richelieu was determined to reduce Hapsburg power. The war had now lost all religious significance and was a dynastic struggle. Battling Austria, Spain, and Bavaria, France gained the upper hand through its superior resources and leadership. At the same time, Denmark and Sweden fought with one another, while Sweden allied with France. The result was that the Hapsburgs were defeated so decisively that Spain sank to the status of a second-rate power while France assumed the top rank among the European states.

After four years of talks at two cities in Westphalia, Münster and Osnabrück, the conflict was brought to a close in 1648 in a series of treaties known as the Peace of Westphalia. It was a victory for Protestantism and the German princes and a defeat for Catholicism and the Hapsburgs. Among its terms were the reconfirmation of the territorial principle of the Peace of Augsburg and the addition of Calvinism as a prince's religious option. The settlement also allowed Protestants to keep the lands taken from the Roman Catholic church after 1624. It recognized the sovereignty of more than three hundred princedoms, free cities, and bishoprics, and it required that the emperor secure their consent before making laws, raising taxes, recruiting soldiers, or deciding on war or peace. Since these petty units argued continually, agreement on most issues was virtually impossible. The independence granted them made the unification of Germany under a single ruler essentially out of the question. Other significant provisions of the peace included recognition of the Netherlands and Switzerland as independent states, approval of Hapsburg control over Bohemia (including the right to recatholicize the area), restoration of part of the Palatinate to Frederick V's heir, the granting of electoral dignity to the duke of Bavaria (thus making eight electors), and the extension of the territories of the elector of Brandenburg to compensate for land that was ceded to Sweden.

The war left Germany so exhausted that recovery took almost a century. The armies had lived off the land, and the soldiers, mostly mercenaries, taking no pity on the civilians, had sacked cities and pillaged the countryside, and for amusement had raped, burned, and tortured. Disease and famine further helped to reduce drastically the population. A malaise settled over Germany, making it easy for France to keep it divided.

The Peace of Westphalia did settle many of the long-standing religious differences. Catholics and Protestants now realized that they must live together since neither was strong enough to destroy the other. Forced compromise provided opportunity for toleration, although at the time some did not appreciate this and called for renewed war. Angered by concessions made to Protestants relating to secularized church properties, Pope Innocent X objected strenuously to the treaty, while among the Protestants the exiled Bohemian Brethren demanded that their homeland be restored to them. Since neither group gained much of a hearing, it was clear that the religious wars in Europe had ended.

THE ENGLISH REVOLUTION

One of the few major European countries not directly involved in the Thirty Years' War was England. Internal troubles so occupied the attention of the English during the era that continental involvement was not feasible. The seventeenth century began with the death of Elizabeth I and the accession to the throne of a new family, the Stuarts, in the person of James I (James VI of Scotland). He was well-educated, of an intellectual bent, and the author of several books, including *The True Laws of Free Monarchies,* but he was naive about English affairs. The Tudors before him had been despotic, but they cultivated popularity with the people and involved the Parliament in their actions. James tried to follow in their footsteps, but his authoritarianism antagonized the English.

The major problem of his reign was the struggle with Parliament. Although it was not a democratic institution as such, it was a powerful group, representing the nobility and high clergy (House of Lords) and the rich town merchants and leading country families (House of Commons). The conflict that began under James would last through four Stuart reigns and would end with England transformed into a constitutional monarchy, with the House of Commons, rather than the king, as the real ruler of the land.

Underlying the struggle were radically different philosophies of government. The theory of the crown was that of the divine right of kings, namely, that God had placed the sovereign on the throne as his representative and anyone who resisted the king was acting against God. Parliament, on the other hand, supported the historic rights of Englishmen and held that control over one's person and property may not be taken away without the consent of the individual involved. The courts of common law helped Parliament protect the rights of the ordinary person and check the king's power.

The Stuarts and Parliament clashed over religion, economics, and civil rights, but religion seemed to occupy first place in the struggle. The Puritan party, the group within the Church of England that demanded simpler church services and a more pronounced Protestant theology, was a major bloc in the House of Commons. Anticipating a Protestant attitude on the part of the Scottish Calvinist king, the Puritans presented James in April 1603 with the Millenary Petition (from the Latin word for one thousand; its authors claimed that that many signatures were on it). It asked him to terminate practices in the Church of England they regarded as offensive, such as making the sign of the cross in baptism, wearing certain vestments, and using a ring for marriage. The petition also asked that clerical marriage be allowed and ecclesiastical abuses eliminated. In 1604 he met with them at Hampton Court palace, but his only concession was to commission a new translation of the Bible. The Authorized (or King James) Version, which was completed and published in 1611, had a profound effect on shaping the English language and culture.

Another important event of his reign was the Plantation of Ulster in 1611. This marked the beginning of the officially-sponsored settlement of Scottish Presbyterians in Northern Ireland as a means of diluting the strength of Catholicism in the Emerald Isle.

Over the next two decades the Puritans in Parliament fought a running battle with James. They urged him to intervene on the Protestant side in the Thirty Years' War, and they wanted his son Charles to marry a Protestant princess. The king did not follow either of these suggestions.

Although James may have quarreled with the more extreme Protestants, he did not favor Roman Catholics. The Jesuits encouraged his assassination, the most famous attempt of which was the Gunpowder Plot of 1605. The conspirators, led by Guy Fawkes, planned to blow up the king and Parliament, but the plot was exposed. In the reaction that followed, many Catholics were executed and an oath of allegiance was required of those who were not taken into custody. The English were haunted also by the specter of the "black legend," a term Protestants associated with Philip II and his Catholic crusade.

In the reign of Charles I, which began in 1625, religious strife intensified. Whereas James was a Calvinist, Charles was an Arminian (see below). Growing Arminianism among the clergy had contributed to divisions within the church. In 1633 Charles appointed William Laud (1573–1645) as archbishop of Canterbury, with instructions to enforce a uniform liturgy even if it meant driving the Puritans from the church. In doctrinal matters Laud was more tolerant than the Puritans, but he insisted on complete conformity in worship procedures. It was a matter of great importance to him that the communion table be placed at the east end of every church and that all should bow when the name of Jesus was mentioned. Using the Court of High Commission and the Court of Star Chamber (where royal power prevailed), Laud saw to it that severe sentences were

The Religious Wars

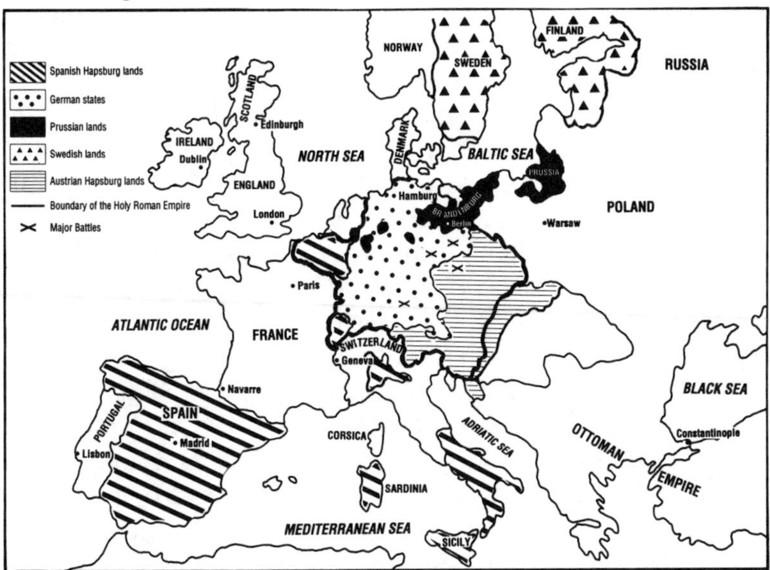

imposed on deviants. His extremism was a major factor behind the Puritan emigration to New England in the 1630s.

Economics also divided the monarchy and Parliament. The House of Commons played a key role in the revenue-collecting system of the English kings, but both James and Charles lacked the patience to work with Parliament and tried to raise money on their own through forced loans, ship money (taxes for coastal defense), forest fines, sale of knighthoods, and granting of monopolies. Popular resentment against these revenue enhancement devices, many of which were based on old laws that had not been enforced for years, increased steadily.

The issues relating to civil rights took several forms, such as free speech in Parliament, resistance to forced loans, and arbitrary imprisonment. Needing to secure his revenue sources, Charles I in 1628 reluctantly agreed to the Petition of Right, which safeguarded Englishmen from arbitrary taxes (those without parliamentary consent) and guaranteed other rights. But Charles soon wrangled with Parliament over financial matters, dismissed the body, and ruled without it for eleven years, in defiance of the Petition of Right.

By 1640 Charles was at war with the Scots, who two years earlier had concluded the National Covenant affirming the Presbyterian faith. As he was in desperate need of money to pay for an army, he finally convened the Parliament, which immediately demanded the resolution of various grievances before it would vote any funds. After three weeks he dismissed the "short Parliament," but following another military disaster in the north he called it back into session. This was known as the "long Parliament," since it technically remained in existence until 1660. It was now the rallying point for opposition to royal absolutism. Puritan forces in the body allied with the Scots in 1643 through the Solemn League and Covenant, whose signatories agreed to make the religious practices of England, Scotland, and Ireland as nearly uniform as possible and to reform religion "according to the Word of God and the examples of the best reformed churches." By this adoption of Presbyterianism England was plunged into civil war.

A little-known Puritan member of Parliament, Oliver Cromwell, created his own regiment, the legendary Ironsides, soldiers who were dedicated Christians as well as fierce fighters. He proved to be a military genius as he led the parliamentary forces (called "Roundheads" because they wore their hair cut short) to victory over the royalists (the "Cavaliers"). After a lengthy period of conflict, fruitless negotiations, and double-dealing, the king was captured and, at the behest of radicals within Parliament, was executed in 1649. England then became a republic (the Commonwealth) led by Cromwell, who ruled with a contingent of Congregationalists (Independents) in the Parliament known as the Rump.

Now that Congregationalists had the upper hand, the alliance with the Scottish Presbyterians was a dead letter. When the Irish and Scots recognized as king the slain monarch's son Charles II, Cromwell's forces in 1649 and 1650 crushed their rebellions. In particular, the brutal massacre at Drogheda was never forgotten by Irish Catholics. Because of ongoing difficulties with Parliament, Cromwell dissolved the body in 1653 and set himself up as "lord protector" under the Instrument of Government, the only written constitution in English history.

The Westminster Assembly, which met during the Civil War period, worked out a church settlement to replace the Anglican Establishment, but the Presbyterianism formulated there was not enforced after Cromwell came to power. The fragmentation of the Puritan position actually led him to become more tolerant of religious differences among Protestants. In fact, he allowed Jews to return to England, but neither they nor Catholics had religious liberty as such. During the 1650s the austerity usually associated with Puritanism held sway in national life. The Christmas festival was abolished, the marriage ceremony was made a civil act, and theaters were shut down.

After Cromwell's death in 1658, unrest mounted so rapidly that Parliament decided in 1660 to invite Charles II to assume the throne. He had spent the last decade in exile in France, where he had come to admire the absolutism and Catholicism of his cousin Louis XIV. Neither of these qualities were to endear him to the English people, but he did agree to rule with Parliament. The "Cavalier Parliament," elected in 1661 and overwhelmingly royalist in composition, set the tone for the "Restoration." It passed a series of measures, the Clarendon Code, which provided a legal basis for persecuting Puritans. Among other things, civil officials were required to take the sacrament according to the Anglican rite and clergymen to accept everything in the Book of Common Prayer. Dissenters from this were called "Nonconformists" and were forbidden to hold religious meetings. More than 2,000 clergymen lost their pulpits and 5,000 persons were jailed because of the laws. The Scottish Covenanters rebelled against the Episcopalian restrictions in 1668 and again in 1679, but they were put down.

In the secret Treaty of Dover of 1670, Charles promised Louis XIV to restore Catholicism to England as soon as possible in return for a French subsidy. But when he tried to fulfill this by issuing a Declaration of Indulgence that allowed freedom of worship in private homes for Catholics and Nonconformist Protestants, Parliament reacted so violently that he abandoned the plan. To reinforce its victory, Parliament in 1673 passed the Test Act, which required all officials to take communion in the Established church. It had the practical effect of excluding Dissenters from public life and was not repealed until 1828. After an anti-Catholic scare in 1678–79 a law was passed excluding Roman Catholics from Parliament. The king's brother, James, duke of York, openly professed Catholicism, and Parliament tried to remove him from the royal succession, but to no avail. Charles remained Anglican but did confess Catholicism on his deathbed.

When James II came to the throne in 1685, he openly tried to restore Catholicism. He appointed Catholics to army commands and to teach at universities. To win support among the Dissenters, he included them in his Declaration of Liberty of Conscience in 1687. But when seven Anglican bishops were charged with treason for not supporting the Declaration, a court acquitted them. Many hoped simply to ride out the reign of the aging monarch (he was fifty-five), but then a son was born to him, which meant a certain Catholic succession. Both the Anglican (Tory) and Puritan (Whig) parties in Parliament united against the king and in 1689 formally offered the crown to William of Orange in Holland (grandson of Charles I) and his wife Mary (daughter of James II). Meanwhile, James had fled to France, and the new monarchs arrived and were seated without opposition. This came to be known as the "Glorious Revolution." Later that year, Parliament passed the Toleration Act and the Bill of Rights, which guaranteed certain civil rights and parliamentary supremacy and allowed freedom of worship to all except Unitarians, Roman Catholics, and Jews. Although a provision in the Toleration Act stated that only Anglicans could serve in the government and the army, exceptions could be made to this restriction. Laws adopted in 1701 provided that no Catholic could ever occupy the throne and the monarch could not leave England without consent of Parliament.

The new English parliamentary regime found justification in the political writings of John Locke. His *Two Treatises of Government* (1690) argued that government is a contract between ruler and the citizens and that revolution is justified if the contract is broken by arbitrarily denying the people their natural rights to life, liberty, and property. He also claimed that the most effective form of government is one based on a representative system. In an irony of history, Locke's apology for the revolution of 1688 was used by the American colonists in 1776 in their revolt against the British. He was also the foremost philosphical spokesman of the time for religious liberty, and in his *Letters Concerning Toleration* (1689–92) he pleaded for freedom for all but atheists and Roman Catholics, whom he felt were a danger to the state.

James attempted a comeback in 1689 by rallying his followers in Ireland and Scotland. Decisively defeated at the Battle of the Boyne in Ireland on July 1, 1690 (subsequently a national holiday for Scotch-Irish Protestants), he returned to France where he died in 1701. His son James and grandson Charles Edward, with French support, tried in vain to bring about a Stuart restoration in Scotland, and the so-called Jacobite movement died out after 1746. To render the tie with the north permanent, the Act of Union was passed in 1707. Scotland would henceforth be represented in the Parliament in London, but its separate laws and legal administration would remain intact, and the Presbyterian church (Church of Scotland) would continue as its establishment.

ARMINIAN CONTROVERSY

Even as soldiers were killing one another in the name of the gospel of Christ, their fellow churchmen fought with words to define the faith more precisely. Doctrinal quarrels were often intertwined with political struggles and led to conflicts between various groups within the churches. One of these, the dispute between the Arminians and the strict Calvinists, centered in the Netherlands. The former took its name from Jacobus Arminius (1560–1609), a theologian who was trained at Leiden and Geneva prior to becoming a pastor at Amsterdam. The Reformed theology of his day had been developed from the view of Calvin by Theodore Beza (1519–1605) and other Reformed scholastics. These men emphasized biblical literalism, strict double predestination, and presbyterian church government. Arminius reacted against this rigid system, and proclaimed that God's offer of grace was universal and that individuals possessed the freedom to respond to God in faith.

In 1603 he was appointed professor of theology at the University of Leiden despite the protest of Francis Gomar (1563–1641), another theologian at the school. The controversy between the two centered on the precise meaning of predestination. Arminius expressed in a forthright manner his opposition to certain aspects of Calvin's theology and suggested that Calvin made God the author of sin and denied genuine freedom to human beings. Gomar, a strict Calvinist, strenuously countered these views, and the bitter debate that followed led to a division in the Reformed church. Arminius wanted the convening of a national synod in order to bring the two sides together. Even political leaders were drawn into the debate, but no agreement had been reached by the time of his death.

The followers of Arminius continued to spread his teachings, and in 1610 they issued a document called the "Remonstrance," which pleaded for toleration and set forth the five major points of Arminianism: (1) the eternal decree of salvation applies to all who believe and persevere in the faith; (2) Christ died for all; (3) the Holy Spirit must help one to do those things that are truly good such as having faith in Christ for salvation; (4) God's saving grace is not irresistible; and (5) one can fall from grace. Many prominent figures in the Netherlands, including theologian Simon Episcopius (1583–1640), statesman Jan van Oldenbarneveldt, and the leading scholar of the day, Hugo Grotius, sided publicly with the Arminian cause.

The Synod of Dort (Dordrecht) was convened in 1618–19 to resolve the controversy. Invitations were sent to all Calvinist churches in Europe, and twenty-seven of the more than one hundred delegates at the meeting came from Germany, Switzerland, England, and Scotland. The Arminians, or Remonstrants as they were frequently called, were condemned in a fivefold set of canons (decrees). This point-by-point refutation of the Remonstrance of 1610 defined the teachings of the orthodox Calvinist faith as total depravity, unconditional election, limited atonement, irresistible grace, and the perseverance of the saints in grace. (Theological students ever since have used the acronym TULIP as a mnemonic device for these five points.) Provincial synods and local presbyteries were ordered to dismiss Remonstrants serving churches under their care. In the years to come, the Reformed church in the Netherlands adhered rigidly to the doctrine defined at Dort, and its theologians interpreted these statements by elaborating their meaning according to Aristotelian categories.

The controversy between the Arminians and the strict Calvinists had a political dimension. The two leading Dutch politicians of the period took different sides in the dispute. Maurice of Nassau backed the Gomarists and Jan van Oldenbarneveldt favored the Remonstrants. It was not only religion that separated the two, as Maurice wished to make his family (the House of Orange) monarchs, while Oldenvarneveldt wanted the merchant aristocracy to control the country. The religious sincerity of Maurice was especially dubious, since he allegedly said that he did not know whether predestination was blue or green, but his strong orthodox stand allied him with the staunchly Calvinistic Dutch. At the time of the Synod, Maurice moved against his enemies. Oldenbarneveldt was arrested, tried for treason, and executed; Episcopius was exiled; and others, such as Grotius, were imprisoned.

The movement seemed to be finished in the Netherlands, but when Maurice died in 1625, the Arminians were allowed to return. Episcopius was the leading light in the refounded Remonstrant church, which still exists. Frederick Henry, who succeeded his brother Maurice as political leader, realized that a rigid orthodoxy was as unsuited to the country as was an absolute monarchy and that forcing the adherents of the various faiths to conform could produce economic ruin. The long-run result of the bitter struggle was an official policy of toleration. Though the Arminian quarrel in the Netherlands was laid to rest, the debate continued in other places. England provided fertile soil for the growth of Arminianism. Many followers of

Oliver Cromwell

Archbishop William Laud accepted the more liberal variety of Calvinism and passed the teaching on to the Latitudinarians (i.e., those tolerant of variations in doctrine) who flourished at the beginning of the eighteenth century. The English Unitarians were also Arminians, as was the great evangelist John Wesley. Through Wesley's Methodism, the doctrine has come down to the present as an important theological stream, and Arminian-Reformed arguments are still of concern to many.

LUTHERAN CONTROVERSIES

The Lutherans were also wracked by controversies during the later Reformation era. As in the earlier stage of the Reformation, theological and political problems were intertwined. The Peace of Augsburg (1555) was concluded with the understanding that a final settlement of the problems would be made at a later time, but this gave the German Protestants too little political and legal security. Thus, when theologians representing the Lutherans and Catholics met at Worms in 1557 to iron out confessional differences, the divisions among the Protestants encouraged the Catholics to postpone a settlement.

The Protestant situation was complicated by the spread of Calvinism in Germany, since several rulers, most notably Frederick III of the Palatinate, had introduced the faith into their principalities. Though he deviated from the Lutheran position, Frederick claimed to follow the Augsburg Confession so that he could be protected by the rights guaranteed to those who adhered to this symbol. Other German Reformed theologians and princes followed his example.

Another division within German Protestantism was that of the Gnesio-Lutherans ("true Lutherans"), a group that followed Matthias Flacius Illyricus (1520–73), a noted scholar and church historian. They rejected the ideas of Melanchthon and his followers who were called "Philippists" after Melanchthon's given name. The Gnesio-Lutherans accused the latter of being too conciliatory toward Roman Catholics, and they set out to develop Lutheran teaching so as to distinguish it from both Catholicism and the views of the Philippists. In the adiaphoristic controversy they accused their opponents of making concessions to Catholicism with regard to such ceremonies as confirmation, extreme unction, veneration of the saints, and the Mass. The "true Lutherans" maintained that nothing is an *adiaphoron* (a matter of indifference) if it touches on any aspect of Christian truth.

Perhaps the most important Lutheran conflicts revolved around the Lord's Supper. Although Lutheran teaching rejected the dogma of transubstantiation, it held firmly to the real presence of the body and blood of Christ in, with, and under the bread and wine. Calvin tried to harmonize Lutheran and Zwinglian views by stating that the believer truly received the body and blood of Christ in the elements of the communion, but in a spiritual manner.

In a controversy over eucharistic views that began in 1552 between the Lutheran Joachim Westphal and Calvin himself, the differences between the Reformed and the Lutheran positions came into sharp focus. Melanchthon and his followers, who refused to become involved in the debate, were accused of sympathizing with the Calvinist position and were denounced as crypto-Calvinists. Thus the presence of Reformed teaching in Germany exacerbated the debates within Lutheranism. Actually, the Lutherans and Calvinists agreed on many matters, but the Reformed generally rejected liturgical worship, stressed greater participation in the solution of social problems, and took differing positions on Christology and the sacraments.

One group of prominent theologians who were centered in the Universities of Leipzig, Rostock, Marburg, and Tübingen, sought to check the fragmentation of Lutheranism by charting out a mediating position between the extremes. Their efforts led to the adoption of the Formula of Concord in 1577, a confessional statement designed to settle the controversies by replacing the separate creeds that had been adopted in the various Lutheran territorial churches. At the root of the problem were the many differing interpretations of the Augsburg Confession. The Formula of Concord with its precise and emphatic language steered a middle course among these in order to spell out what Lutherans really believed. In 1580 the Formula was published together with the three ecumenical creeds (Apostles, Nicene, and Athanasian), the Augsburg Confession (1530) and Apology (1531), Luther's Small and Large Catechisms, the Schmalkaldic Articles (1537), and three earlier drafts of the Formula in the *Book of Concord.* This work, which became binding on two-thirds of German Protestantism, clearly defined the differences between Lutheran and Catholic as well as between Lutheran and Reformed teaching. It was the definitive statement of Lutheran orthodoxy and corresponded to the similar action taken on the Catholic side at the Council of Trent.

Systematization of doctrine within Lutheranism could now proceed, and it was done through elaborate statements based on proof-texts. This method, used in simple form by earlier Lutheran theologians, flowered in the works of the seventeenth-century orthodox scholars. In contrast to the Lutherans, the German Reformed could not work out their own formula of concord and continued to focus on the Heidelberg Catechism of 1563 as their main doctrinal statement. By now the University of Heidelberg had become the intellectual center of a movement that encompassed a number of territories and cities in the Rhineland and western Germany. An important milestone in the spread of the Reformed faith was the conversion of Elector John Sigismund of Brandenburg from Lutheranism to Calvinism in 1613. Partly as an outgrowth of this shift, the country's ties with Saxony and the Hapsburgs came to an end, and that would be a major factor in the rise of Brandenburg-Prussia to great power status after the Thirty Years' War.

From this time, the Protestant rulers of Germany were divided into two groups: the Lutherans (led by the elector of Saxony, who tried to keep the old order intact) and the Reformed (led by the elector Palatine, who wished to take an active part in the struggles of the Calvinists of western Europe). Animosities between these two groups kept the Protestant forces divided and enabled the Catholic Reformation to make impressive gains. At the same time, it meant Germany would play no role in Europe's expansionistic drive overseas, unlike the Catholic lands of Portugal, Spain, and France, and Protestant Holland and Britain. For a time continental Protestantism languished in inward-looking orthodoxy, but eventually the fresh breeze of pietism would bring new life and a broader vision of the church's mission.

12

THE CHURCH EXPANDS BEYOND EUROPE

The revival of long-distance commerce and the accompanying growth of a town-based, capitalist economic system were contributing factors in the earliest expansion of the European church. Combined with the dynamic intellectual and spiritual changes of the Renaissance and Reformation these factors produced a far-reaching curiosity about the lands beyond Europe. New developments in military and especially naval technology enabled Europeans to venture out on the open seas and to engage in successful combat with other peoples in distant places. While many dissipated their energies in the seemingly incessant religious conflicts and jockeying for power, others sought new opportunities for economic gain and spiritual conquest. From the late fifteenth through the early seventeenth centuries Europeans had gained mastery of the oceans and established coastal footholds in various parts of the world.

EUROPEAN OVERSEAS EXPANSION: THE IBERIAN PHASE

The Iberian states, Portugal and Spain, initiated the process, and in some respects this was a continuation of the Crusades. It was a militant, violent confrontation of Western Christians with people holding vastly different views. This expansion of Christianity had a transforming, but not always positive, impact on the faith itself. The responsibility for spreading the faith was carried by specific countries and more or less supervised by their monarchs. The Portuguese conquest of Ceuta in Muslim Morocco in 1415 and the Spanish elimination of Granada in 1492, the last Islamic stronghold in the Iberian peninsula, could be seen as crusading ventures. They became natural impulses for further expansion. Alongside the material motivation for overseas enterprises was a clearly expressed obligation to spread Christianity. Conversion was an aspect of conquest.

The first step in overseas expansion was the Portuguese intrusion in Morocco. This provided them with a listening post in Africa and stimulated the desire to tap into the lucrative gold trade with the peoples south of the Sahara. Informed circles in Europe knew of the fabulous wealth of the Mali kingdom, whose ruler Mansa Musa had depressed the price of gold in the Islamic metropole of Cairo when he visited there on a pilgrimage to Mecca in 1331. Prince Henry, known as "the Navigator" (1394–1460), a younger son of King John I, had participated in the Ceuta campaign and became interested in exploration of the West African coast. His sponsoring of naval expeditions and establishment of a research center at his castle made possible the Portuguese hegemony in the East.

He expressed a desire to engage in trade with the Africans and to carry Christianity to them. However, the prospect of a direct water route to the "Indies" loomed on the horizon, and in 1488 the first Portuguese seamen reached the tip of South Africa. In 1497 Vasco da Gama rounded the Cape of Good Hope and sailed to India, returning home after two years with a cargo of Eastern merchandise. Subsequent expeditions laid claim to Brazil and the East African coast, crushed the Arab naval forces in the Indian Ocean (who had been the middlemen in the East-West trade), and founded a chain of trading posts.

Alfonso de Albuquerque captured Goa in 1510 and made this the seat of Portuguese rule. He instituted control of the sea lanes as his country's power base. With strong points in East Africa, the Persian Gulf, Malacca in Malaya, Indonesia, and various places in India and Ceylon, the Portuguese were masters of the Indian Ocean. Later in 1557, they established the colony of Macao in China. The preservation of this loose, far-flung system was entrusted to the "governor" or "viceroy" at Goa.

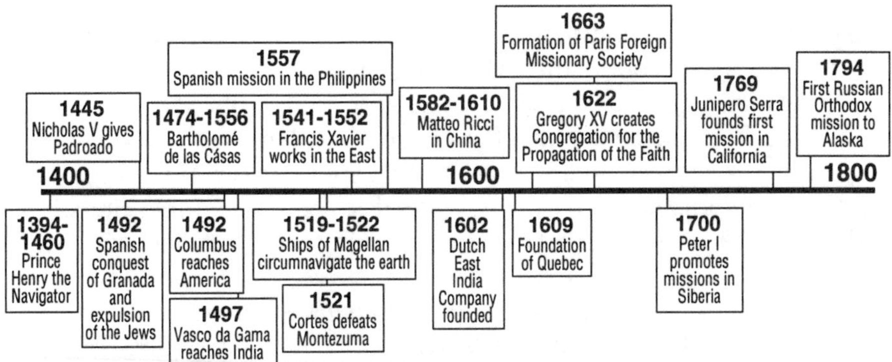

During the union of Spain and Portugal in 1580–1640, the Dutch effectively demolished the Portuguese monopoly on Indian Ocean trade, and several of its bases were lost. However, Brazil, Angola, and Mozambique remained major colonial possessions. For about thirty years the Dutch controlled parts of Angola and Brazil, but they were ousted in 1661. With the discovery of gold in 1693 and diamonds in 1728, the wealth of Brazil formed an important part of the revenue of the crown. Angola and Mozambique served primarily as sources of slaves for Brazil, but some Portuguese did eventually settle there.

Spain entered the picture a few years later. Through a process of study, meditation, intuition, and calculation, the Genoese sailor Christopher Columbus concluded that Asia lay a reasonable distance west of Europe. After eight years of futile efforts in various directions, he finally persuaded Queen Isabella of Castile to provide financial support for a venture. On October 12, 1492, he touched land in the Bahamas and in subsequent journeys established Spanish rule in Hispaniola. Other Spaniards conquered the neighboring islands and explored the coastal regions of the Caribbean.

The Italian Amerigo Vespucci participated in an expedition that explored the northern coast of South America, and, after reading his descriptions of what clearly was not India but a new continent, the famed cartographer Martin Waldseemüller produced a map in 1507 that named the new land after Amerigo. Vasco Nuñez de Balboa crossed the Panamanian isthmus in 1513 and viewed the Pacific Ocean, Hernando Cortés seized the capital of Aztec ruler Montezuma in 1521, Francisco Pizzaro crushed the Inca empire of Peru in 1533–35, and other explorers and conquistadores fanned out through Florida, Mexico, Central America, and South America to establish Spanish rule. With the settlement of Buenos Aires in 1580 the continental stage of Spanish expansion ended, and they concentrated on the occupation of the vast areas staked out earlier. However, pioneers continued to move into new land north of the Rio Grande and south of the Plata rivers.

The Portuguese seaman Ferdinand Magellan, who had entered Spanish service, left in 1519 on the first round-the-world voyage to establish claims in the East. He touched in the Philippine Islands in 1521, where he was killed, but possession was not taken until an expedition in the 1560s.

In Latin America, power in the colonial system was centralized in the king, and the administration was handled by the Council of the Indies in his name. It prescribed the policies, prepared the ordinances, made appointments, supervised the church, and acted as a court of appeal. The subunits in Latin America were two (later four) vice-royalties, which in turn were subdivided into audiencias, captaincies-general, presidencies, and several varieties of local government.

Many Spaniards went out to the colonies, and those who remained permanently came to be known as "creoles." They were lower in the social scale than the "peninsulares" who came directly from Europe and occupied administrative positions. By 1574 the Spanish had founded nearly 200 cities and towns whose white population approached 160,000. The "mestizos," offspring of Spanish men and Indian women, adopted the Spanish language and culture but were looked down upon by the whites. At the bottom of the social scale were native Americans and African slaves.

The economic system was based upon large Spanish land holdings and native peonage, the *encomienda* system of tenant farming, where peasants worked for the landlords in perpetuity. Considerable wealth was also generated through gold and silver mining, commerce, and some small-scale manufacturing. Through its land holdings and economic enterprises, the Roman Catholic church became one of the wealthiest institutions in Spanish America. At the end of the colonial era estimates were that it owned half of all the land there in Mexico.

The Spanish and Portuguese ventures represented the two basic types of "colonialism" practiced by Europeans. A significant number of Spaniards went out from the "mother country," settled in the foreign territories over which a modicum of political control had been established, and introduced their culture. On the other hand, the Portuguese created colonial enclaves that either were tolerated by the local rulers who profited economically from their presence or were maintained by the use of armed force. They were always susceptible to attack by European rivals.

EXPANSION: WESTERN EUROPEAN AND RUSSIAN PHASES

Although the English had dabbled with exploration (voyage of John Cabot, 1497; Martin Frobisher's quest for the Northwest Passage, 1576–78) and in the Elizabethan era preyed upon Spanish shipping (Francis Drake, John Hawkins), they only began colonization in earnest after the turn of the seventeenth century. The North American colonies were private ventures secured by royal charters, but they had to compete with others. The Dutch arrived in New York in 1609 (Henry Hudson's voyage) and established New Netherland in 1626. A Swedish commercial settlement existed on the lower Delaware river from 1638 to 1655.

Further north was the French foothold. Jacques Cartier had visited the lower St. Lawrence region in 1534–35 and claimed it as "New France." Samuel de Champlain founded Quebec in 1609 and worked assiduously in later decades to develop Canada as a colony. Pioneers received little support from the homeland until the reign of Louis XIV, under whose auspices the territory prospered. Fur trading was the major industry on the Great Lakes frontier, and French influence was extended to the Mississippi by the late 1600s. With the influx of more settlers in the following century, New France experienced considerable economic growth.

The real focus of interest, however, was the Caribbean. Spanish exploitation of the native peoples had left the islands depopulated and in ruin. For example, the Taíno people of Hispaniola, which in 1492 ranged in population between 400,000 and two million, had declined to a mere 16,000 by 1518. Then, in the early seventeenth century sugar culture was introduced and produced an economic revolution. The crop was grown on plantations, and a seemingly unlimited labor supply was available in Africa. An extensive slave trading network developed as at least ten million human beings were transported across the Atlantic, and the islands became great sources of wealth. Slaves were also landed in Brazil, where they made a key contribution to economic development and to the unique racial mix that exists there today. Slave labor also was used in British North America and the coastal areas of the Caribbean region. After earlier occupying islands in the Antilles, the English in 1655 seized Jamaica from Spain, and joined Holland, Denmark, and France in the competition for colonial and naval power in the area.

To facilitate the African side of the commerce in slaves and other commodities, various European countries established trading centers along the West African coast. These trading centers, such as the famous fortress of Elmina on the Gold Coast, changed hands repeatedly, while the local African rulers kept the Europeans at bay. Portugal, Spain, England, France, Holland, and even Brandenburg had enterprises there in the seventeenth or early eighteenth century.

The major new factor in European expansion in this period was the Dutch. After their initial success in the struggle for liberation from Spanish rule, they developed the most effective merchant marine in Europe. Their ships penetrated the Indian Ocean late in the sixteenth century, and the Dutch East India Company was formed in 1602. The firm's headquarters were at Batavia (Djakarta) in Java, and it soon supplanted Portugal as the master of the Indian Ocean. Between 1638 and 1658 it held control of Ceylon and in 1652 founded a settlement at the Cape of Good Hope. For two centuries Holland was the only Western country to have contact with Japan. A Dutch West India Company (founded 1621) carried on trade in the Atlantic Ocean for much of the century, maintained the colony in North America, acquired territories in the Caribbean, and temporarily ruled northern Brazil.

However, the English under the leadership of Oliver Cromwell pursued a program of commercial and naval expansion that the Dutch could not match. The Navigation Act (1651) was designed to thwart the Dutch carrying trade, and in 1664 the English ousted them from their North American base and renamed it New York. As Dutch power waned, the stage was set for the titanic struggle between Britain and France that dominated the eighteenth century.

The Russian conquest of the vast forest and tundra region of Siberia was the only real occupation of the Asian continent to occur in this period. The forces of Tsar Ivan IV secured the Volga basin by overcoming the last bastions of the Muslim Tatars (Kazan, 1552; Astrakhan, 1556), and this opened the way for Russian expansion east of the Ural Mountains. In 1581–82 a band of Cossacks under Ermak conquered the Siberian khanate, and they moved rapidly through the river systems establishing fortified towns at strategic points. Fur traders followed the rivers and carried on a brisk commerce.

Within a century the forest region of Siberia was largely under Russian control. However, the Chinese halted the Russian advance in the East, and a border between the powers was drawn in the Amur valley by the Treaty of Nerchinsk of 1685. The presence of strong Islamic states in the grassland and desert regions to the south effectively thwarted Russian expansion in these areas until the later eighteenth and nineteenth centuries. Economic activity in Siberia was dependent on the collection of furs that were Russia's main item of commerce with the West. By the eighteenth century colonists, many of whom were exiles, began to settle on the land and engage in mining or farming. The white population of Siberia grew from 70,000 in 1662 to one million in 1783.

After Nerchinsk, eastward expansion continued, and Kamchatka was annexed in 1699. Vitus Bering was then sent to explore the area further east, and his work laid the foundation for Russian rule in Alaska in the eighteenth century.

CHRISTIANITY IN THE IBERIAN EMPIRES

Based on precedents set by the thirteenth-century pontiffs who claimed that they had sovereignty over the whole earth, including lands that were not yet Christian, Pope Nicholas V endorsed Portuguese expansion into West Africa in a bull in 1454. It authorized King Alfonso I to take control of and exploit other lands in the future and commissioned him to undertake the Christianization of these territories. The Portuguese crown had been given the "missionary patent" (*padroado*), that is, he was to equip, finance, and send out missionaries to Africa and by implication to the Indies as well.

Then Columbus appeared on the scene and outflanked Portugal by traveling in the other direction and claiming the territories he had found for Spain. In order to resolve the problem of which country should take possession of the new lands, Pope Alexander VI (himself a Spaniard) issued a bull in 1493 dividing the world along a line in the Atlantic running from pole to pole west of the Azores, in effect giving Spain the entire western hemisphere. Included in the bull was a missionary patent as well. Ferdinand and Isabella were directed "to send articulate, God-fearing, well-trained, and experienced men who would instruct the inhabitants there in the Catholic faith." The two neighbors confirmed the papal decision in the Treaty of Tordesillas (1494) that moved the line a little farther west, thus unwittingly giving Portugal a claim on Brazil. The Treaty of Saragossa (1529) drew a demarcation line in the East that allowed the Mariana Islands to fall within the Spanish jurisdiction.

Columbus himself was steeped in late-medieval piety. His well-known *Journal of the First Voyage to America* reveals that he engaged in prophetic speculations and saw his mission as to win souls for Christ in the newly discovered lands. He regarded himself as the "Christ-bringer" and selected names hallowed in the church for the territories he discovered. Other Spaniards, however, were less motivated by "God" and more by "gold" and "glory." These conquistadores created sizable empires with considerable potential for abuses. It was up to the church to restrain the baser instincts of the white settlers, and the key to this lay in the patents. The crowns of both countries were empowered to exercise far-reaching controls over the missionary enterprises in their respective empires. They could thus empower the church to work for a more just colonial order.

In Spain the patronage, which was based upon papal bulls of 1501 and 1508, made the crown responsible for the maintenance of the church and conversion of the Indians. In return, the ruler chose missionaries for the colonies in America (and later in the Philippines), and they could not return home without royal permission. The papacy permitted the state to collect the tithes (church taxes) in the colonies and use these to fund the church there. The king had the right of appointment to all ecclesiastical posts—bishops, heads of religious houses, and even parish priests—and no church, convent, or school could be founded without royal authorization. Churchmen abroad could not communicate with Rome except through royal channels. Actions of synods were submitted to the colonial viceroy or other responsible official who had veto power.

Although some secular priests went as missionaries, the primary source of workers was the religious orders, both older ones such as the Benedictines, Dominicans, Franciscans, Augustinians, and various minor orders, and the new ones that were the offspring of the Catholic Reformation, the Capuchins and Society of Jesus (Jesuits). The Jesuit order, with its total commitment both to recovering peoples lost to Protestantism and to carrying the faith beyond the geographical frontiers of Christianity, was the largest supplier of missionaries in the sixteenth and seventeenth centuries. The Portuguese monarch allowed the Jesuits to establish a missionary training school at the University of Coimbra in 1542 that prepared more than 1,600 workers for service in the course of two centuries.

With a few exceptions, such as the "Pious Fund," an endowment provided by private individuals for missions in California, lay Catholics contributed virtually nothing to the financial support of missions. Some of the funding came directly from the state, but by and large the religious orders and congregations carried out work on the basis of their own resources. Moreover, many missions were

Trading Empires of the Sixteenth and Seventeeth Centuries

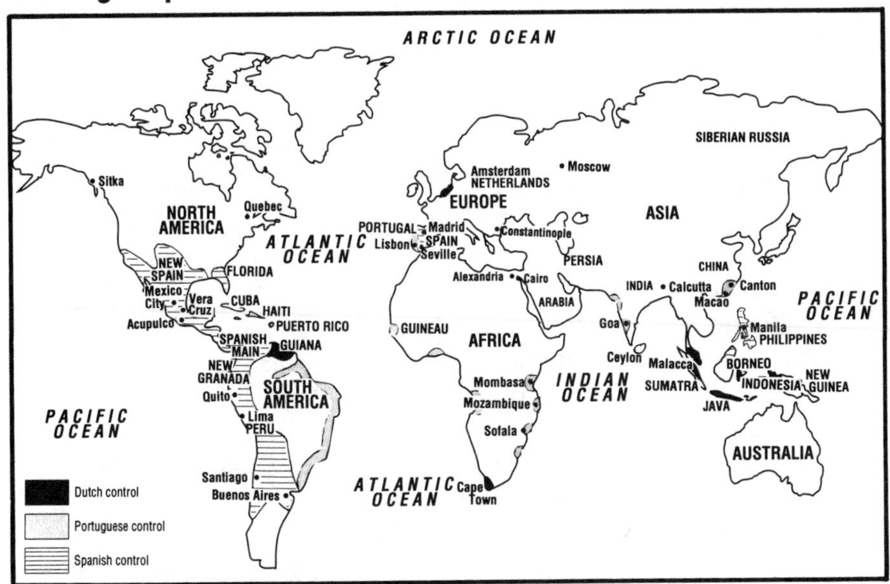

partly or completely self-supporting. The labor of the indigenous Christians in the communities covered the costs of the enterprises, and some missionaries, most notably Jesuits, engaged in commerce directly.

The most noted example of the self-supporting enterprise was the Jesuit mission in Paraguay and the Parana basin. Here the Indians were gathered into villages (*reductions*) where they were provided protection, given Christian instruction, taught various trades, and allowed to develop a consciousness of identity. The church was the center of community life, and the people lavished their devotion on the structure and worship services. They engaged in agriculture, raised cattle, and made handicraft items that were sold to support the village. The clerics formed an Indian self-defense force to resist marauding slave raiders. By 1767, when the Jesuits were expelled, perhaps 106,000 Indians were living in thirty-eight villages under the supervision of eighty-three missionaries. The removal of the fathers left them at the mercy of settlers who destroyed much of what had been achieved.

Since the pope had granted them both civil and ecclesiastical power, the Spanish monarchs theoretically were responsible for safeguarding the Indians from exploitation by the white settlers as well as providing them with spiritual ministries. The reality was often otherwise. The conquistadores had crossed the Atlantic to accumulate wealth for themselves, and they forced the Indians to work in mines and fields. The result was indescribable cruelties and the destruction of the indigenous peoples through disease, overwork, and brutality. As the Indian populations declined, especially in the West Indies, their numbers were supplemented by the importation of slaves from Africa. Although some settlers saw the Indians as subhuman and incapable of being Christians, the papacy in particular was forceful in its demands for missionary work. The result was many forced conversions and baptisms.

Although some popes and kings were concerned about the ongoing mistreatment of the Indians in Spanish America, missionaries were the primary defenders of native rights. By far the best known of these and a role model for missionaries of all persuasions, whether Protestant or Catholic, was Bartholomé de Las Cásas (1474–1566). His father had sailed with Columbus, and in 1502 Bartholomé himself settled in Hispaniola. After managing a plantation for some time, he sought ordination as a priest and went along on the first expedition to conquer Cuba.

He became so troubled about the way the aborigines were being mishandled that he went to Spain to plead their cause. He won the favor of Cardinal Ximenes who appointed him protector-general of the Indians. Las Cásas returned to the New World with a group of monks to seek enforcement of the royal laws on behalf of the Indians. The settlers persuaded his associates that he was some sort of visionary who was ruining the colonies, and they turned against him. He traveled to Spain again to seek help, and his enemies told the king that the colonies would be ruined if slave labor was banned. He countered by proposing that he be allowed to found a colony where the Indians would be decently treated. Arriving back in 1520, he set up his experiment on the coast of South America (modern Venezuela), but it failed.

Three years later he joined the Dominican order. Following the theological path of Thomas Aquinas, the greatest of the Dominicans, who had taught that unbelievers may not be compelled to become Christians because belief is a matter of the will and personal decision, Las Cásas rejected forced conversion and demanded that the Indians be given the possibility to choose Christ freely. In 1535 he established a new mission in Guatemala, publicly supported the cause of mistreated Indians in Mexico and Peru, and preached nonviolence and enforcement of the laws prohibiting enslavement of Indians. At the age of seventy he was appointed bishop of Chiapa in Mexico, and engaged in a bitter struggle with the white laity of his diocese over abuse of the Indians. In 1547 he returned to Spain for the last time to urge the monarch to uphold the rights of the Indians.

He then retired but continued contending for the cause dear to his heart with several significant publications. A much celebrated action was his disputation in Valladolid in 1550–51 with the Spanish theologian Juan Ginés de Sepùlveda, who argued on the basis of just war theory that it was necessary to subdue the Indians by force and then to convert them. Las Cásas's clinching argument was, "Are not all people human?" Although his efforts to halt the enserfment of the Indians through the *encomienda* system were in vain, he did succeed in shaping the humanitarian legislation embodied in the Spanish *Laws of the Indies* (1542). His influence was also seen in the development of Spanish mission strategy with its emphasis on organizing the native peoples into Christian communities, paternalistic settlements that were separate from the corrupting influence of white colonials.[1]

Although untold numbers of missionary monks shared his views, the number of Spanish clergy was not very high. Soon creoles and, in the following century, even a few mestizos and Indians were ordained. As Latin American society stabilized, a sophisticated ecclesiastical structure emerged that mirrored the Spanish political system.

How much the new faith replaced the old belief systems of the Indians is a matter of debate. Many pre-Christian practices and rites continued, especially in Aztec Mexico and Mayan Central America, in such guises as festivals, rituals, and sacred sites. This is exemplified in the veneration of Our Lady of Guadalupe, who appeared to an Indian near Mexico City in 1531. A cult with some traditional rites grew up around the alleged miracle-working power of a painted image of the Virgin that she had given him and that has been housed in various structures on the site, including the massive basilica presently there.

Also, missionary activity spread through the northern frontier areas as evidenced by the Jesuit and Franciscan missions in Texas and New Mexico in the late seventeenth and early eighteenth centuries, and those in California founded by Junipero Serra (1713–84), an ascetic friar who possessed remarkable administrative ability. Through the labors of 146 Franciscan fathers between 1769 and 1845, around 100,000 Indians were baptized, many of whom lived on the twenty-one missions they had founded. This was perhaps the most successful mission-community system in the New World, and they were the most important economic and social institutions in Old California.

In Portuguese Brazil the spread of Christianity resembled that of Spanish America, but there were differences. Since there were no preexisting civilizations, the work was mainly among tribal peoples. Portugal was spread so thin by its vast overseas enterprises that little attention was paid to Christianizing the area. Thus, the propagation of Christianity was much more incomplete than in Spanish America, although the Jesuits did devote attention to missionary work there, and the persistence of the old ways is especially evident in the famous Brazilian Mardi Gras observances. Perhaps the strongest advocate of Indian rights was the Jesuit Antonio Vieira (1608–97), who in 1655 obtained a decree from the king that was designed to protect the native peoples in their settlements. In his sermons he condemned white residents for their mistreatment of Indians and blacks.

In short, the church in Latin America faced the triple challenge of retaining its hold on an increasingly indifferent white settler population, evangelizing the Indians, and ministering to the Africans who had been imported as slave labor. The style of the Christianizing enterprise in general was to induce the Indians to lead a settled life under the tutelage of the missionary fathers, who in turn fought against white colonialist exploitation of the indigenous folk and obtained the enactment of protective measures by the crown. As a result, many in the white lay population bitterly resented the missionaries.

Portuguese Missions in Africa

Among the factors that stimulated the original European interest in Africa was the legend of Prester (Presbyter) John, a Christian ruler who had been cut off from the West. It was believed that if contact could be reestablished, the Christian world could outflank the Muslim empires and go on the offensive. A variety of medieval traditions located him anywhere from India to Western Asia, but by the mid-fourteenth century he was assumed to be some place in Africa, most likely Ethiopia. In 1487 Portuguese King John II sent Bartholomew Diaz south to seek the kingdom of Prester John, but he turned back after passing the Cape of Good Hope. Pero de Covilhã went by the overland route and did reach Ethiopia, where he was well-received. In 1520 a Portuguese embassy from India arrived for a six-year stay, and its chaplain, Francisco Alvarez, published a detailed account of religious life in the Christian kingdom. Several Jesuits served in Ethiopia in subsequent years and tried to bring the Monophysite church into submission to Roman Catholicism.

The Prester John legend had also attracted Prince Henry the Navigator's attention, and his desire to find a Christian ally in Africa as well as to win souls to Christ were among the motives for his coastal expeditions. Since the pope had charged the Portuguese king to foster missions in Africa, priests went along on the ships and filed numerous reports of conversions and baptisms from the Canary Islands to the Guinea coast. In the ensuing 250 years, various orders attempted work in West Africa, but no lasting Christian communities were formed.

More important was the baptism of the Bakongo ruler in 1491, who even changed the name of his capital Mbanza to that of São Salvador. Although he fell away from the faith, his son Alfonso remained a Christian and upon succeding to the throne fostered Christianization of the kingdom. Although noticeable acculturation followed (adoption of Portuguese ways as well as religion), this did not filter down to the masses. He did send some men to Portugal for education (including the priesthood) and dispatched an embassy to the pope in 1513. However, the level of commitment was not very high, and the missionary undertakings over the next two centuries left little trace.

Further south in Angola, Portuguese missionary work resulted in numerous baptisms and the alleged conversion of the entire city of Luanda, where a cathedral was built. With the ordination of a few African priests, the faith persisted here more than in the Congo.

In East Africa virtually no missionary effort was attempted, although Portugal built a huge stronghold in Mombasa called Fort Jesus to protect its commercial interests. The first effort was in Mozambique where in 1560 the Jesuit missionary Gonçalo da Silveira converted the leading members of a coastal community and then penetrated to the interior (modern-day Zimbabwe), where he baptized the most powerful ruler in southern Africa, the Monomotapa. But the king feared that the missionary was a Portuguese agent and had him murdered the following year. Various missions followed in the next century, and a Dominican even baptized one of these kings in 1652, an event that was greeted with jubilation in Lisbon and Rome, but in the long run the work failed to take root in the Zambezi region. No black clergy were ordained in Mozambique for three centuries. On the other hand, some of the European clerics were even involved in the administration of *prazos*, large and profitable agricultural estates operated along feudal lines.

Missions in the East

Missions were an integral part of Portuguese expansion. As Diogo do Couto (1542–1616), the soldier-historian of the empire, put it, "The kings of Portugal always aimed in this conquest of the East at so uniting the two powers, spiritual and temporal, that the one should never be exercised without the other."[2] The patronage assured Portugal that other countries would not seek a share in the imperial booty under the guise of missionary interest. Thus, priests and friars supported by the crown accompanied the ships and were part of every fort-factory (trading station) complex. Under the king's authority was the archbishop of Goa, who was the primate of South and East Asia. The missionary force was originally restricted to Portuguese subjects, but the multinational character of the Jesuit order and the intrusion of Spanish and French clergy soon undermined this.

From a spiritual standpoint, the missions were marginal operations at best until the arrival of Francis Xavier, a landmark figure in the dissemination of Christianity. Born in 1506 to a noble family in Navarre, Spain, as a student at the University of Paris he became a disciple of Loyola and helped organize the Society of Jesus. While in Rome he answered a request of the Portuguese monarch for missionaries for the East and sailed in 1541. A man with boundless energy and commitment, over the next eleven years he traveled incessantly in India and Ceylon, visited Malaya and the East Indies, established a Christian presence in Japan, and was preparing to open a mission in China when he died in 1552.

Xavier prepared the way for the Jesuit missionary effort in Asia. He recruited members for the Society, arranged for them to come from Europe, created a training college at Goa for indigenous Christians, and personally worked at various places in South India where he gained thousands of converts. The first Jesuit contingents arrived in 1545–46, and before long the Society had founded stations in numerous places in the subcontinent. Their attempt to establish a mission at the court of the Mogul emperor in Delhi was noteworthy but its success minimal. Most missionaries ended up ministering among lower caste peoples and the Europeans in India.

More dramatic were the achievements in Japan. In 1547 Xavier found a young Japanese man whom he took to Goa where he was baptized. Two years later Xavier traveled with the youth to his home in Kyushu, the southern Japanese island, where he served as an interpreter.

St. Michael's Russian Orthodox Church in Sitka, Alaska

He remained there two years, made converts, and launched the mission. Other Jesuits followed and the new faith spread rapidly. By 1582 there were 200 churches and 150,000 Christians, which meant that a larger percentage of the population was now Christian than would be true in the twentieth century. Since the mission staff was small, some attempts were made to train a Japanese clergy, and a bishop under the Portuguese patronage arrived in 1596.

Although the pope had reserved Japan for the Jesuits, in the 1590s Dominicans and Franciscans began working the territory as well, and rivalries broke out among the orders. In 1587 the shogun (military ruler of Japan) Hideyoshi issued an edict against Christianity and ordered all missionaries to leave the land, but only a decade later, after the squabbles erupted, did he begin to enforce it by executing two dozen Christians. After a year of persecution the pressures eased, missionary work resumed, and the Christian population soon surpassed the 400,000 mark. The port city of Nagasaki itself had become predominately Christian.

Then in 1614 the Tokugawa shoguns began a vigorous crackdown. They feared that Christianity was the opening wedge for a European takeover of Japan or that the missionaries and Japanese Christians would back some group opposed to the dynasty. Over the next twenty-five years all foreign missionaries were expelled or executed, while indigenous believers were forced to renounce their faith. Those who refused were subjected to brutal horrors—crucifixion, burning by slow fires, or beheading. At least 4,000 people suffered martyrdom.

After a rebellion in 1637–38 in which several thousand Christians were involved, the regime sealed off the country to European commerce. Former Christians were sought out and forced to trample on a cross or representation of Christ to prove they had recanted. Japanese ships were forbidden to go abroad, and persons returning from any such voyage would be killed. The latter fate would befall Europeans as well who landed in Japan. Only the Dutch were allowed to send one trading mission per year to Nagasaki, and they had to conceal all items connected with Christianity while in port.

However, some Christians survived in the remote areas of Kyushu and secretly passed their beliefs on to their children. Baptism was administered, and the Ten Commandments, some prayers, and basic doctrines were transmitted. The existence of this vestigial Christian community, which numbered more than 15,000, was discovered after the reopening of Japan in the later nineteenth century.

In China, as in India and Japan, the Portuguese provided the opening for missions. Although Francis Xavier's effort to initiate a mission was in vain, others followed. The Jesuits started a college in Macao, and in 1576 an episcopal see was established there for which the Portuguese king provided financial support. The union with Spain in 1580 ensured that the Philippines would also be a source of workers.

The Jesuits, however, took the initiative, and 456 workers from this order went to China between 1552 and 1742. The leader of the Asia mission, Alessandro Valignano (1539–1606), had energetically promoted the Japanese work and provided the theoretical underpinnings for what was the most dramatic Christian undertaking of the age. Following the trail blazed by Francis Xavier, he sought to form truly indigenous churches in Japan and China, ones that would be totally separate from the Iberian control inherent in the *padroado* patronage. The Jesuits intended to win these peoples for Christ, not European culture.

As he had done in Japan, Valignano called for adapting the Christian religion to Chinese traditions and customs, as that would enable reaching the higher echelons of society, and in turn the faith would penetrate the entire populace. His protégé was the landmark figure in the Chinese mission, Matteo Ricci (1552–1610), who after studying mathematics, astronomy, and cartography, went to Goa in

1577 and Macao in 1582. The following year he and a co-worker set out to win the respect and friendship of the ruling elite as the first step in introducing Christianity. They located in a provincial capital near Canton, demonstrated to the scholar-bureaucrats their uncanny knowledge of clocks, calendars, and map-making, and through this gained access to higher circles.

Ricci also became familiar with the Chinese classical works and wrote essays in the language on Western science and the Christian faith. He adopted the garb of a Confucian scholar and utilized as names for God terms found in the classics. He regarded the veneration of familial ancestors and of Confucius as a cultural rite without real religious significance and allowed his converts to continue observing these. He endeavored to show that Christianity was not antagonistic either to the family or the state.

In 1601 Ricci reached Peking and won a number of important officials and an imperial prince to Christianity. A decree of 1611 authorized the Jesuits to make a correction of the Chinese calendar, and thereafter they made a variety of scientific contributions. They were in effect placed in charge of the government's astronomical bureau. Since the respect at court was so great for them, they were able to weather the dynastic change from the Ming to the Manchus. Johann Schall von Bell (1591–1661), a German Jesuit, not only directed the bureau and served as the emperor's scientific adviser, but also he built churches and preached throughout the empire. In 1657 he was joined by Ferdinand Verbiest of Belgium (1623–88), who under the brilliant Emperor K'ang Hsi (reigned 1662–1722) made astronomical instruments, designed cannons, and helped arrange the diplomatic settlement of 1685 with the Russians.

As hostility toward Christians declined, the number of ministries expanded and missionaries from various European countries and religious orders entered the country. For example, a Chinese Christian, known by his baptismal name of Gregory Lopez, studied in Manila, became a Dominican, was ordained a priest, and returned to serve his homeland. Then in 1690 he was named bishop of Nanking. Actually, by 1700 the missionary staff was barely more than one hundred and the number of Chinese Christians was 300,000 at the most, so the real impact of the faith on this vast population was minimal.

Farther south in the Philippine Islands, a process of Christianization occurred analogous to that in Latin America. Because of the royal patronage, missionaries from various orders traveled in the Spanish ships and received official support and protection. At the same time their activities were subject to royal control. The early missionaries also sought to protect the indigenous people from the rapacity of white settlers. Most notable was Domingo de Salazar (1512–94), first bishop of Manila and a student of Las Cásas. He condemned practices used to subjugate the local population and fought against the greed and cruel policies of civil officials.

The Spanish missionaries followed methods that had been developed in America, namely, an emphasis on replacement of pagan rites with Christian festivals and the founding of schools, hospitals, and associations for prayer and charity. However, the Portuguese were hostile to the Spanish clerics when they carried on missionary work in China or India, as they felt the patronage gave them exclusive rights to evangelize in these areas. This was the source of numerous tensions in the seventeenth and early eighteenth centuries.

An important indigenous missionary in Asia was Joseph Vaz (1651–1711), an Indian from Goa. Already serving as a priest in his home, he decided to start a work in Ceylon (Sri Lanka) where the Dutch were trying to stamp out the Catholic church. In 1689 he entered the island in disguise and ministered secretly in homes until the Dutch authorities discovered him. Then he escaped to the independent kingdom of Kandy, whose ruler allowed him freedom to evangelize. He brought in other Indian priests from Goa, and soon the work was flourishing. In 1696 he was appointed vicar-general for the island, which meant he was now head of a totally Asian church, a unique event in this period.

Russian Orthodox Expansion

In the sixteenth century the Russian Orthodox church was linked to the expansionist program of the tsars. If newly subjugated peoples were won to the Russian faith, this would aid in their assimilation. Thus, missions received state backing. Instead of individual monks working on their own initiative, the work was done by larger groups under the direction of the ecclesiastical authorities. For example, an archbishopric was created in Kazan in 1555 under Abbot Gurij, who effected the conversion of the Cheremissian Tatars by offering them tax exemptions and freedom from serfdom. This pattern was repeated over the next two centuries with other peoples.

With the opening of Siberia, Orthodox priests and monks, supported by the regime, followed the fur-traders and soldiers. Several local tribes were converted and an archbishopric set up in Tobolsk in 1620. As the seventeenth century progressed, monasteries and mission stations were established in various locations. For example, after the city of Irkutsk was founded in 1652, Orthodox missionaries began working among the Buryat Mongols who lived in the areas around Lake Baikal. However, they only converted about 13 percent of the people. The majority retained their traditional Shamanist and Lamdaistic Buddhist beliefs. The nomadic life of many Siberian tribes made missionary work difficult.

Like his predecessors, Tsar Peter I used missions as a device for assimilating non-Russians and strengthening his authority. His main ally was Filofei Leszcynski, metropolitan of Tobolsk, who founded new works throughout northern Siberia. He had imperial authorization to remit taxes for those who were baptized. New churches were frequently erected on the sites of traditional worship centers.

Most of Kamchatka had been won by they mid-eighteenth century, and the first mission was sent to Alaska in 1794. An Alaska diocese was created with Ivan Venyaminov (1797–1879) as its first resident bishop. In 1848 he built a cathedral at Sitka, which had one of the most thriving Indian missions north of Mexico.

The Mediterranean and Near East

The treatment of the Jews is one of the most discouraging chapters in Christian history. The record of persecution from the Crusades through the expulsions from Western and Central Europe is a dismal one, and the only havens Jews found were in Muslim Spain and in distant Poland, where various rulers in the thirteenth and fourteenth centuries had granted settlement rights. However, in the Reconquista they lost out in Spain, and, following the urging of Torquemada, Ferdinand and Isabella in 1492 ordered the expulsion of all Jews who refused to become Christians. (Portugal did likewise in 1497.) This deprived the country of 170,000 of its most productive subjects at a time when it needed all its resources to sustain its European power and overseas empire. The Iberian, or "Sephardic," Jews were scattered throughout the Mediterranean world, with some going to the Netherlands and America.

Those who had converted under the intense pressure (the so-called Marranos or "new" Christians) were regarded with suspicion and harassed by the Inquisition. From time to time between the sixteenth and eighteenth centuries conscious efforts were made in Italy to convert Jews. In Poland Jesuit missionaries worked among the

Eastern, or "Ashkenazic," Jews to win them to Catholicism, while, after the Russian annexations of Polish territories between 1648 and 1795, the large Jewish population was subjected to increasing discrimination and efforts to convert them to Russian Orthodoxy.

Elsewhere, Christianity was in retreat. The Ottoman Turks chipped away at the moribund Byzantine Empire and in 1453 conquered its last bastion, Constantinople. They continued on the offensive through much of the sixteenth century, captured Belgrade, Rhodes, Cyprus, and most of Hungary, and were barely halted outside Vienna in 1526. Their ships dominated the Mediterranean, and a second assault on Vienna occurred in 1683. The resulting situation for the Greek Orthodox church was grim. Many converted to Islam, and those who remained Christians suffered from discriminatory taxes. To man the janissary (elite Turkish) military forces, Christian youths were taken from their homes and reared as Muslims. Many churches were converted into mosques, most notably the cathedral of Hagia Sophia in Constantinople.

The only significant advance against Islam was in Spain, where the Reconquista was completed in 1492, and the remaining Moors were forced to become Christians. Those who rejected baptism were driven out between 1502 and 1524. The Inquisition was used to ferret out old beliefs and practices among the Moriscos, as the former Muslims were known. Those new Christians who continued to practice their old cultural traditions were finally expelled in 1609.

The Propaganda

The increasing tempo of Catholic missionary work led to the creation of a special agency in the Roman Curia to coordinate this far-flung effort. There was no unity in mission methodology among the various religious orders, and the excessive control that the Spanish and Portuguese crowns exercised through their patronage had a negative impact on the mission outreach. Also, a shortage of workers had developed because the Iberian powers generally excluded all but their own nationals from missionary service in their territories.

Although the idea that Rome should take a firm hand in initiating and directing mission effort had been discussed since the late 1560s, it was in 1622 that Gregory XV created the Congregation for the Propagation of the Faith, commonly known by its Latin short title, the *Propaganda.* At the outset it was composed of thirteen cardinals and other lesser officials. Since its jurisdiction embraced all matters

Bartholomé de Las Cásas

relating to missionary activity, the Propaganda had broad powers. It began by soliciting from all the religious and missionary orders and papal nuncios in foreign lands information about the status and progress of mission work, a summary of the methods used to propagate the faith, and a list of missionaries. The body then sifted, classified, and analyzed the data to determine the principal problems missions faced. After identifying the obstacles and failings, the Propaganda set out to improve methodology, increase the number of workers, and foster the development of an indigenous clergy.

In order to assure a unified effort, the Congregation insisted that authorization for missionary work had to be obtained through it. Missionaries were to report regularly on the status, prospects, and resources of their enterprises. It examined candidates as to their fitness and encouraged the orders to set up schools for those who hoped to serve in the East. In 1627 under the pontificate of Urban VIII, the Propaganda founded a seminary in Rome, the *Collegium Urbanum,* to train men for the priesthood from various nations who would go anywhere in the world at the behest of the pope to propagate or defend the faith. It also created its own press in 1626 to produce Christian literature for the mission enterprise, and by the end of the eighteenth century it published books in forty-four Asian and African languages, making it the foremost printing establishment in Europe.

To counteract the Iberian patronage, the Propaganda inaugurated the practice of having the Holy See appoint "apostolic vicars" for the East. These were bishops who exercised power directly under the pope. Since they were not diocesan bishops in the normal sense, they were less vulnerable to pressure from secular rulers. They were in effect roving missionaries who received their directions through the Propaganda and were expected to work for the preservation of cultural and social autonomy in the non-Western lands where they served. However, the Propaganda was never able to wrest missionary control away from the Spanish and Portuguese crowns in their colonies, but it was responsible for work in northern Europe, North America (until 1908), and most other places in Africa, Asia, and the Pacific islands.

An important personality was the Jesuit Alexander de Rhodes (1591–1660), who had established friendly ties with the royal court in Vietnam and brought a self-sustaining church into existence. He created the written language of Vietnam with his Annamite dictionary, grammar, and catechism. After returning to Rome in 1645, he challenged the Propaganda to appoint apostolic vicars to carry on missionary work in East Asia. He also came in contact with a group of devout priests in Paris called the "good friends," and, with his encouragement two of them, François Pallu (1628–84) and Pierre Lambert de la Motte, were appointed apostolic vicars. In 1664 they began working in Siam and founded a school to train priests.

Growing out of their circle was an important new organization, the Société des Missions Étrangères (Foreign Missionary Society), formed in Paris in 1663. This differed from the religious orders that engaged in missionary work, in that propagating the faith among non-Christians peoples was its sole objective. It carried out Pallu's vision of creating an indigenous *secular* clergy for the young Christian communities in Southeast Asia. The society believed that "regular" priests, members of religious orders directed from Europe, could not provide leadership to root the church in the non-European lands. Even when they did ordain native secular priests for their missions, the orders dominated them and did not allow them to develop normal leadership skills. Thus, the solution was for the parish clergy to be seculars drawn from the indigenous people and under native bishops.

To this end, the society opened a seminary in Paris that trained secular priests to preach the gospel and develop indigenous Christian leaders. A similar institution was created in Quebec in 1668, which maintained ties with the Paris society until the British conquest of French Canada. The group did have some workers in China, but the main focus of its attention was Indochina, where reportedly in the later eighteenth century there were 150,000 Christians. However, both Spain and Portugal criticized the appointment of the two apostolic vicars as a violation of the patronage right granted by Rome. They also feared that this would provide an opening wedge for French imperialism, which of course proved to be true. In 1787, the apostolic vicar of the society, Pigneau de Behaine, secured French naval assistance to restore an ousted monarch of Annam in return for territorial concessions, and that marked the beginning of the long French involvement in this land.

In spite of the Propaganda's efforts to develop more native clergy, the process was about as slow in the territories under its jurisdiction as in the realms where Iberian colonial rule prevailed. European clergy continued to predominate throughout the world.

Rites Controversies

The Congregation for the Propagation of the Faith's work in Asia was greatly endangered by the struggles over rites in India and China, and the papal decisions in these effectively closed the door to future missionary adaptation to the local culture. The first of these, the Malabar rites controversy, arose over the decision of the Jesuit Robert de Nobili (1577–1656) to allow Christians in his Madura mission on the Malabar Coast to retain their existing customs. The missionaries would try to adjust their own way of life and preaching to indigenous practices instead of transforming the people into Europeans. The caste system was retained, and Nobili lived and ate as an Indian and studied the Vedanta and other Indian religious writings in order to reach the Brahmin intelligentsia, some of whom he did convert. He was the first European to gain first-hand knowledge of Sanskrit and the Vedas. He insisted that a difference existed between religious rites and civil customs and justified the latter by removing superstitious elements and redirecting them in a Christian path.

Others were suspicious of his tolerance of existing ways and feared that he was jeopardizing Portuguese mastery over India as well. He was brought before the Inquisition in Goa, which split over the matter, and it was submitted to Rome. In 1623 the pope sided with Nobili, who then resumed his work, and Christianity spread rapidly in the region.

The issue was revived at the end of the century by French enemies of the Jesuit mission in South India, dragging the Propaganda into the affair. After four decades of political wrangling and ecclesiastical backbiting, Pope Benedict XIV ruled in 1744 that all missionaries there must swear a sixteen-point oath that essentially repudiated nearly all adaptations to the Indian culture. Only in 1940 did the Holy See finally nullify the oath.

The Chinese rites struggle was even more serious and far-reaching. Matteo Ricci had allowed Chinese Christians to observe the traditional practices of honoring Confucius and familial ancestors. He saw the retention of these "nonreligious" practices as absolutely necessary if any large-scale conversion of Chinese society were to occur. His Jesuit successors continued the policy, but when the Dominicans and Franciscans began working in China they challenged the Confucian rites as religious superstition and compromise with paganism. Intense wrangling between the parties went on for years, both in China and Europe, and even Emperor K'ang Hsi entered the controversy. Pontifical rulings in 1704, 1715, and 1742 concluded (without coming to terms with their key role in Chinese culture) that the rites were incompatible with the Christian way of life and an oath of submission to the papal decrees was imposed on missionaries. (These were rescinded in 1939.) The upshot of the rejection of the Chinese rites was the expulsion of most missionaries and widespread persecution of Christians.

Though brisk in the sixteenth and early seventeenth centuries, Roman Catholic missionary effort stagnated over the passage of time and by the late eighteenth century had come to a standstill. The dependence on patronage and the link with colonial policy were clearly the fatal flaws in the enterprise. Portuguese missions were particularly weakened by the sixty-year union with Spain that opened the way for the Protestant powers of Europe to prey on their possessions. Also, they encountered more firmly established and resistant indigenous religious cultures in Asia than the Spanish did in the Americas and the Philippines. The decline of Spanish power in the seventeenth and eighteenth centuries left missions more at the mercy of white settlers, while the suppression or expulsion of the Jesuit order by the major Catholic countries and its dissolution by the pope in 1773 deprived the church of its most effective missionary force. Religious skepticism and indifference in the Enlightenment era further undercut missionary enthusiasm. Although European Protestantism was not yet a significant threat to Catholic hegemony overseas, seeds were being sown by the pietist movement that would eventually produce a new worldwide explosion of Protestant missionary endeavor.

13

ORTHODOXY AND ABSOLUTISM SHAPE THE CHURCH

A long period of controversy followed the rediscovery of the gospel by the Reformers, and out of these quarrels came the definition of the Protestant position. The disputants drew heavily upon the philosophy of Aristotle to express their ideas, and this neo-Aristotelianism was a general trend in both Protestant and Catholic circles in post-Reformation Europe. Already popular in such southern European universities as Padua in Italy and Coimbra in Portugal, the movement spread to the Protestant universities in Germany by the end of the century. The Christological issue among the Lutherans, predestinarian disputes among the Reformed, and debates between the two over the Lord's Supper led to the precise definitions of doctrine that was known in the seventeenth century as Protestant orthodoxy.

PROTESTANT ORTHODOXY

Although later generations stereotyped orthodoxy as dead, this was a misconception. Within both post-Reformation communities in Europe appeared a number of major theological thinkers whose works were highly regarded and whose influence among contemporaries was considerable. Johann Gerhard (1582–1637), professor of theology at Jena, was the major Lutheran dogmatician of the age. His *Confessio Catholica* (1634–37) was a forceful defense of the Protestant faith and *Loci Theologici* (1610–22) was an outstanding work in Lutheran dogmatic theology. Abraham Calov (1612–86), professor at Wittenberg, produced dozens of works covering the major topics of theology. Besides conducting an ongoing struggle against efforts to unite the various Reformation and Roman Catholic churches, he authored a significant Bible commentary and the twelve-volume *Systema locorum theologicorum,* a systematic theology that was the leading expression of Lutheran scholasticism. Johann Andreas Quenstedt (1617–88), also a professor at Wittenberg, wrote the *Theologia didactico-polemica*, which was so complete, concise, and systematic that few subsequent Lutheran theological works ever came close to equaling it.

The Reformed churches produced scholars of similar stature. Johann Heinrich Alsted (1588–1638), a scholar in the Rhineland and later in Transylvania, sought to unify all knowledge through an approach that combined Aristotelianism with the scholasticism of the French philosopher Petrus Ramus (d. 1572) and other intellectual currents. In a single work, *Encyclopedia Septem Tomis Distincta,* he brought together the whole range of knowledge—metaphysics, logic, geology, and the other sciences—and these volumes were used throughout the academic world of the century. Gisbert Voetius (1588–1676), a professor at Utrecht, was the leading exponent of scholastic Calvinism. He vigorously defended the independence and purity of the church, argued that truth in religion and philosophy began with Scripture, condemned the toleration of erroneous doctrines, and insisted on a personal life of devotion and strict morality. François Turretin (1623–87), professor at Geneva, published the *Institutio theologiae elencticae,* an important treatment of Scripture based on Calvin and the Canons of Dort that profoundly shaped the nineteenth-century Princeton theology of Charles Hodge.

The goal of Protestant orthodoxy was to unify all theology and to harmonize all knowledge with its understanding of God. The orthodox theologians turned out massive literary works that were tightly outlined through many divisions and subdivisions and that make difficult reading today. Orthodox writers generally presented their views in a standardized format that centered on the doctrine of salvation and progressed through the history of salvation, focusing always

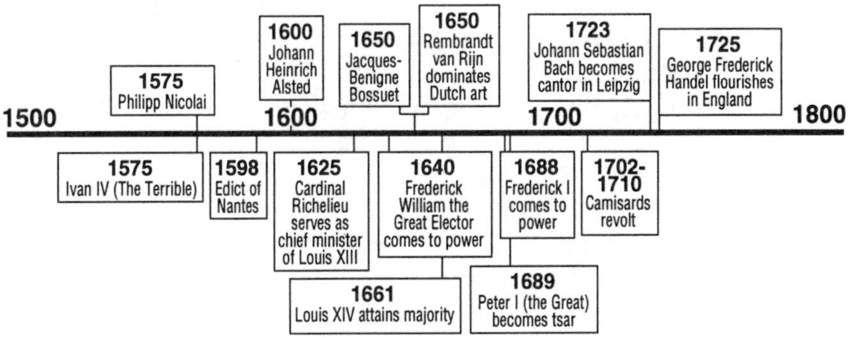

on how one attains it. Such teaching relied heavily on Aristotle and certain medieval logicians for the structure of its arguments, but its basis was always Scripture.

Orthodoxy's primary emphasis was the Bible as the foundation of theology. It is God's Word and therefore trustworthy, and the external statement (the actual words of Scripture) was not distinguishable from the underlying meaning. Orthodoxy believed that God inspired the prophets and apostles to write the message they received from Him. The divine Word thus communicated was preserved in Scripture without error, resulting in a Bible that was the infallible norm for Christians as well as the court of final appeal in all theological disputes. Since Scripture is its own best interpreter, difficult passages could be understood with the aid of clear ones. Stress was placed on the literal interpretation of Holy Writ, that is, taking it in its ordinary and readily apparent sense.

With regard to the Deity, the orthodox were interested in the union of the divine and human natures of Christ in one Person. They debated how the natures affected one another and interacted in Christ. Firm believers in God's creation, they saw humankind as the crown of His work. But Adam sinned and fell, and because of the unity of the race the corruption of sin passed from generation to generation. Humans were under God's wrath and subject to both temporal and eternal punishment unless they had experienced regeneration through Christ.

In their definition of evil and sin, however, the Lutheran and Reformed orthodox parted company. The Calvinist idea that God somehow preordained evil according to His secret will (the basis for the doctrine of double predestination) was rejected by the Lutherans who held that God permits evil and set limits to its exercise but is not responsible for it. Lutherans held to a single predestination: the elect are those God ordained to salvation while the reprobate are those He foresees will lack saving faith at death.[1]

Lutherans maintained that one could pass from spiritual death to life only through the operation of the law and the gospel. The law is God's eternal and unchanging wisdom for righteous living. Summarized in the Ten Commandments, it demands acts of goodness as well as a pure heart. But since humankind cannot obey the law, its role is not to save but to condemn. Forgiveness comes only through Christ's redeeming love and sacrifice and is received in penitent faith. In contrast to medieval Christianity, the orthodox held that repentance involved only contrition and faith. (Confession and absolution were dropped.) Contrition is the proper effect of the law, which threatens, accuses, and condemns; faith is the proper effect of the gospel, which comforts, edifies, and saves. By helping people to grasp the importance of sin and punishment, the law drives them to repentance. The gospel brings forgiveness through Christ and good works play no role in repentance. Since salvation cannot be earned, good works are the fruits of faith. The deeds performed by Christians are a means of glorifying God and helping one's neighbor.

The orthodox of both confessions taught that the sacraments (baptism and the Lord's Supper) were the New Testament counterparts of the Hebrew rites of circumcision and the Passover. Old Testament sacrifices were seen as types of the coming Messiah, and God's promise of forgiveness was applied to the individual through the sacraments. The invisible church was the congregation of all saints and believers, whereas the visible church included everyone who professed faith in the gospel. Those who associated with Christ in only an external way would be separated from the true believers on the Day of Judgment. Then the world would be destroyed by fire, and the faithful would receive eternal life while the wicked would be cast into hell.

Orthodox Spirituality

Although one might gain the impression from the massive tomes of the orthodox theologians that it was a movement of dead intellectualism, in fact their age was distinguished by warm and vibrant faith. Out of the turmoil, suffering, and conflicts of the seventeenth century flowed some of the most intensely spiritual statements of the Christian faith ever seen. Philipp Nicolai (1556–1608) was a pastor in Westphalia who buried 1,300 parishioners during a dreadful plague, yet he wrote two of the most beautiful chorales in Lutheran hymnody: "Wake, Awake for Night Is Flying" and "How Brightly Beams the Morning Star." Johann Heermann (1585–1647) was a pastor in the town of Koeben, Silesia, which was virtually destroyed in a fire, swept by the plague, and sacked by marauding armies in the Thirty Years' War. During the period when he lost all his possessions and fled for his life, he wrote the profound hymn "O Dearest Jesus, What Law Hast Thou Broken?"

By far the greatest hymn writer of the era was Paul Gerhardt (1607–76), whose significance in German hymnody rivals that of Charles Wesley in the English-speaking church. He was first a tutor, then provost at Mittenwalde in Brandenburg, and finally pastor at the prestigious St. Nicholas Church in Berlin. Then he fell out with the Prussian ruler because of his strong Lutheran stance and unwillingness to compromise with Calvinists, and was dismissed from his position. After a time of great hardship, he eventually was appointed archdeacon in Luebben, Saxony, where he remained until the end of his career. His last years were marked by personal tragedy; his wife and four of his five children preceded him in death.

In the furnace of affliction Gerhardt wrote more than 140 hymns. They reflected his own personal experience and the social calamities of the age. He conquered his doubts through a strong faith based upon divine working in nature, the church, and Scripture. He was deeply conscious of sin and even more so of God's grace and forgiving power. His best-known texts included "O Sacred Head Now Wounded," "Jesus, Thy Boundless Love to Me," and "O Lord, How Shall I Meet Thee?"

Calvinist hymnody differed from the Lutheran in that it was directed almost exclusively toward the Old Testament Psalms. Creative writers produced "metrical" versions of the sacred texts, that is, they were recast in meter (poetic verse), set to music, and then sung in unison without instrumental accompaniment except in Holland where an organ continued to be used. The *Geneva Psalter* (1562) was a volume of metrical psalms in French that was translated into German and Dutch, and for a long time it was the only hymn book of the continental Reformed churches. In some English and Scottish churches that could not afford books or where the parishioners were largely illiterate, the psalms were "lined out." A leader would read a line at a time, and the congregation would sing it.

Deep religious feelings were also expressed in the devotional works of the age of orthodoxy. They were popular presentations of the Christian faith intended for use by individuals and groups to aid in prayer and meditation. Many of them were modeled on *The Imitation of Christ,* by Thomas à Kempis. Lutheran writers even produced special prayer books for soldiers, travelers, and expectant mothers.

By far the most influential author of devotional works was the pastor Johann Arndt (1555–1621). His four (later six) *Books on True Christianity* and *Little Garden of Paradise* were widely used, and the former was one of the most significant devotional books in Christian history. He stressed the mystical union of the believer with Christ—that is, it did not suffice simply to demonstrate one's faith through correct belief, one must also engage in moral purification and righteous living. Accordingly, penitence and a close personal relationship with the heavenly Father who redeemed humankind was necessary. Other important seventeenth-century devotional volumes included Lewis Bayly's *The Practice of Pietie,* Johann Gerhard's *Holy Meditations,* Johann Heermann's *Practice of Piety,* and Heinrich Mueller's *Heaven's Kiss of Love.*

The Territorial Church Principle

The establishment of the territorial principle through the Peace of Augsburg (1555), whereby the various princes in the Holy Roman Empire determined the religious confession of their subjects, either Catholic or Lutheran, and its confirmation and extension to Calvinism in the Peace of Westphalia (1648), had a debilitating impact on the vitality of the Protestant church in Germany. The situation was made worse by the adoption of monarchical absolutism by most German princes in the later seventeenth and early eighteenth centuries. This meant not only a mandated uniformity of belief among the people in each principality but also that the head of state exercised the dominant role in the church itself.

The rulers issued edicts dealing with ecclesiastical matters in their territories much like they made secular laws, and they extended their authority over nearly every aspect of church life. Bishops or synods were not allowed to function independently of royal power. Sovereigns usually appointed consistories or ratified the individuals who were chosen, and through these strategies controlled church finances, discipline, and appointment of clergy. The clerical head of the church was a general superintendent, and each diocese (or similar administrative unit) had a director who saw that the ecclesiastical policies and wishes of the ruler were carried out. Disputes within the church were settled by clerical "visitations" that the prince sanctioned and whose reports were forwarded to him.

Princes also interfered in doctrinal areas, even though they often had little theological knowledge, and in effect they functioned as "Protestant popes" for their subjects. Johann Gerhard justified this by arguing that the church was divided into three groups: the civil authority, the clergy, and the rank and file or laity. Each of these estates had a specific divinely ordained role: civil rulers were responsible for the government; the clergy were to advise the rulers, discipline the people, and administer the sacraments; and the laity were to follow the directions of the ruler and clergy.

The real power clearly lay in the hands of the prince. He exercised authority over the other two groups and regarded himself as the divinely appointed guardian of both the spiritual and material welfare of his subjects. Some contemporary writers justified the prince's authority on the basis that the legal rights formerly exercised by the hierarchy of the Catholic church had now devolved on the civil rulers of the German Protestant states, while others went further to suggest that the pope and his representatives had usurped the powers that rulers originally had received directly from God and that enabled them to act on his behalf by establishing civil government.

Pastors in continental Protestant countries were essentially under the control of the civil authorities, and their task was to explain doctrines to the laity. However, the political situation contributed to a reduction in the status and quality of the clergy there. Unlike the Catholic and Anglican churches, few aristocrats entered the clerical professions. Ministers were drawn from the lower classes and were looked down upon by the nobility. In many German universities the theological faculty was the only one open to people of humble origins, and Protestant clergymen accordingly had less polish and ability to adjust to higher society than their Roman Catholic counterparts. But what they lacked in sophistication and cultural understanding was counterbalanced by a stress on book learning that bordered at times on pedantry. The scholastic theology emphasized verbiage and the use of Latin, Greek, and Hebrew phrases in sermons, even though few listeners had any idea what this all meant. Thus, to aid in communication the preachers often used fables, illustrations, strained metaphors, and strange images.

The life of the typical pastor was not an easy one. Although he had studied at a university, he often spent many years working as a tutor or teacher before finally obtaining a pulpit. Even then his position was never secure, as he might fall into disfavor with a prince or local dignitary and be dismissed. Village pastors were often so poor that they had to supplement their income by continuing to teach or by engaging in such activities as farming, beekeeping, or brewing. The favored members of the clergy were the court preachers and theological professors. Lutherans were particularly respectful of theological faculties, and from this eventually emerged the concept of academic freedom that was the distinctive contribution of the German universities to higher education.

In spite of the style of scholarship, strained expression in sermons, and total absence of any prophetic emphasis in their preaching, numerous pastors in the period were deeply spiritual men who were conscientious in the care of souls. Many Lutherans dedicated themselves to instructing the young through the catechism and even heard private confessions from parishioners. In a popular book, Voetius advised Christians on how to lead a godly life. His prescriptions included prayer, fasts, vigils, and devotional exercises in one's struggle against the world, the flesh, and the devil. He gave advice on how to visit those who needed consolation and to die with dignity at the end of one's earthly pilgrimage.

Catholic Renewal

As the age of orthodoxy settled over Europe, the zeal of both Protestant confessions waned and the faith became largely inner-directed. Even the French Calvinists, who through the Edict of Nantes had been granted legal and civil rights and freedom of public worship, lost much of their zeal, and the same was true with Dutch Calvinists who lived in a country that by now had a fairly advanced policy of religious toleration. However, a significant revival of Catholicism paralleled the Protestant decline, and the healthy state of the Roman Catholic church and clergy in France coincided with other areas of national achievement. The seventeenth century was the golden age of French literature, and this encouraged the clergy to artistry in preaching and religious writing.

The political and social atmosphere stimulated by King Louis XIV also was a factor. He expressed his delight in hearing a minister preach who not only was eloquent but also passionately believed what he said. The clergy hoped to make him a better person and through him reach the entire nation, and his own personal interest in

Peter the Great

religion made worship attendance fashionable at court and assisted the church in exercising influence on French life.

The freedoms that the Huguenots enjoyed through much of the century (until Louis began cracking down on them in the late 1670s) spurred the Catholic clergy of France to greater faithfulness. Since they could not depend on persecution to counter Protestantism, they were forced to use preaching and a caring ministry to win people and thereby meet the Huguenot challenge. Especially important was François de Sales (1567–1622), who engaged in missionary work in Savoy, an area of strong Huguenot influence. His diligence in working to win people back to Catholicism led to his eventual appointment as bishop of Geneva. His preaching and writings, especially the *Introduction to the Devout Life* (1609) that sought to show the possibility of leading a life of Christian devotion amid worldly distractions, had a profound influence on Catholic piety. He was the spiritual mentor of a deeply devout widow, Jeanne Françoise de Chantal (1572–1641). In 1610 she formed the Order of the Visitation (also known as the Visitandines or the Salesian Sisters), which devoted itself to education and care of the sick. John Bosco, a nineteenth-century admirer, founded the Society of St. Francis de Sales (Salesian Fathers) in 1859, which eventually became one of the three largest Catholic missionary and teaching orders.

Another devout personality was Vincent de Paul (1580–1660), who early in his priestly career decided to devote his life to the poor. He created two major religious orders, the Lazarists (or Vincentians) in 1625, a missionary and preaching congregation, and the Sisters of Charity in 1633. Members of the latter devoted themselves entirely to the sick and the poor. During the civil strife known as the Fronde he organized extensive relief work among the suffering population. In his preaching he stressed the incarnation and one's total dependence on the merits of Christ.

The most prominent figure in the Catholic renewal in France was Jacques-Bénigne Bossuet (1627–1704). Not only was he the greatest preacher of the seventeenth century, but he also possessed a remarkable knowledge of the Bible, church Fathers, and intellectual trends of the day. He served as bishop of Meaux, tutor to the crown prince, and court preacher, took an active role in controversies with Protestants and deviant wings of Catholicism, and authored several books.

Bossuet is especially remembered for his vigorous defense of the divine right of kings. He maintained that the king (referring of course to Louis XIV) received his mandate to rule from above and would be responsible to God, not to any ecclesiastical representative on earth, for how he carried out this trust. Because the institution of monarchy was of divine origin, all subjects were expected to give their allegiance to the sovereign. If he failed to rule wisely, he would be judged by God. It was not up to the people or the church to make this determination.[2]

Monarchical Absolutism

The character of European Christianity was profoundly shaped by the rulers of the time. Monarchical absolutism arose in early seventeenth-century France, reached its pinnacle during the reign of Louis XIV, which lasted until 1715, and was imitated by most continental sovereigns. The strategy of the early architects of absolutism was to bring an end to the incessant strife that had torn France during the Wars of Religion by upholding the ideal of national unity as superior to religious unity and the monarch as the one person around whom the entire country could rally.

Thus, as mentioned above, the Huguenot Henry IV, who came to the throne in 1589, formally converted to Catholicism because that was the faith of the great majority of his subjects. But then he proceeded to grant political and religious freedom to his former coreligionists in the Edict of Nantes. He was a "politique," that is, he saw the state and its continuing existence as of the highest importance, and the religious issue simply had to take a back seat to the secular political concerns of the state. As a result, the bitter conflict between French Protestants and Catholics receded.

Cardinal Richelieu, whose position in the church was the result of political influence and whose concerns were mainly secular, emerged in the middle 1620s as chief minister to Henry's successor Louis XIII, and he carried the process further. As virtual ruler of France, in the name of the king he curtailed the power of the territorial nobility by prohibiting them from engaging in duels and private warfare and fortifying their places of residence (castles). He also deprived the Huguenots of the right to armed self-defense after brutally suppressing their rebellion at La Rochelle in 1628. To reduce the influence of the nobility Richelieu initiated the practice of appointing provincial officials called *intendants*, who were of the middle class and directly responsible to the royal government.

After Louis and Richelieu's deaths, another political churchman, Cardinal Jules Mazarin, became prime minister. The nobles resorted to arms in the Fronde (1648–53) in order to regain their positions of prominence, and Louis XIV, who became king in 1643 at the age of five and was subjected to a regency during this unpleasant time, determined that he would never tolerate such a situation again.

In 1661 Mazarin died and Louis attained majority. He then went on to identify himself totally with the French state ("I am the state" was his famous motto) and to implement absolute rule. He chose intendants and other officials who were loyal to him, directed most of the operation of the government through councils that reported to him personally, and made all important decisions. He legislated through decrees that were dutifully registered by the major law courts, and he even imprisoned people by royal order without trial.

Louis's talented finance minister, Jean Baptiste Colbert (1619–83), directed commerce, industry, agriculture, and finances. He also administered the colonies through a system of mercantilism, a concept of economic nationalism that involved careful government regulation. Under his capable leadership government revenues tripled but Louis's wars made a balanced budget impossible. The two also encouraged literature, science, and the arts, and founded academies that brought expression in the French language to a peak of perfection. In fact, it began to supplant Latin as the language of educated and cultured people in Europe. Louis's emblem was the sun, the center of the universe, and his subjects referred to him as the "Sun King" while others in Europe called him the "Grand Monarch."

He welcomed Bishop Bossuet's characterization of the king as chosen by God to rule and be responsible to Him only. Since he was God's agent on earth, the people were obliged to submit to him without question. To ensure that the nobility would no longer be a source of resistance, Louis constructed a huge palace and park complex at Versailles, just outside Paris. This was the most magnificent building project of the century, and in the splendid rooms of the structure several thousand nobles lived and were waited on by 4,000 servants. Since he loved ceremony and display, court life revolved around an elaborate social calendar with the sun king at the center of all the activity. The nobles spent their lives in idleness—participating in the royal rituals, receptions, gambling, hunting; attending concerts, plays, and balls; or engaging in licentious living while they gossiped about others. Flattery and hypocrisy were the keys to success at court, and the more sensitive people were demoralized. Versailles marked the virtual ruination of the French aristocracy as a class, and although the nobles did enjoy a resurgence after Louis's death, they were set on a downward path of moral decline that would end with the great revolution a century later.

In his determination to centralize control, Louis decided to abandon the toleration of non-Catholics. With their special rights the Huguenots seemed to be a state within a state, and Catholics were urging upon him a restoration of religious unity in France. Although in post-Reformation church-state relations power had unquestionably shifted to the side of the state, still the idea of an inseparable linkage between the two persisted, and Louis perceived the existence of the Huguenots as a threat both to his rule and to the established Roman Catholic faith. Thus, in 1679 he began chipping away at their privileges. He closed churches and schools, and boarded soldiers in their homes. The latter made life so unpleasant for the Huguenot families that some even converted to Catholicism to escape this.

Finally on October 22, 1685, a royal order revoking the Edict of Nantes was put into effect. It required all Reformed pastors to leave the country and churches to be destroyed. Huguenot schools were no longer permitted, the children were to be sent to Mass regularly, and everyone born into the "false religion" was to be rebaptized. No formal practice of religion outside the Roman Catholic church would be allowed, but individual adults could still enjoy "freedom of conscience." Unlike the clergy, laypersons were forbidden to emigrate because their skills were needed to strengthen the national economy. Those caught trying to flee would have their property confiscated and be sentenced to the galleys.

The result was massive resistance. Many of the Reformed people worshiped silently or held clandestine services in homes or in the woods. Manhunts ferreted out the pastors who had not left, and they were usually hanged. Huguenot children were torn from their homes and placed with Catholic parents. In spite of persecution an underground church flourished. Apocalyptic mystics in southern France known as the Camisards revolted in 1702, and the brutal conflict that resulted lasted until 1710. They were inspired by the writings of the noted Reformed theologian Pierre Jurieu (1637–1713), an advocate of full liberty of conscience and of resorting to arms to combat those who used violence to deny religious freedom. Despite official opposition, Antoine Court (1696–1760) brought together the remnants of the French Reformed in the first provincial synod in 1715. Before long a training school for ministers was founded in Switzerland, and discipline and order returned to the scattered congregations. With the onset of the Enlightenment the pressures rapidly eased, Huguenots regained limited civil rights, and during the French Revolution and Napoleonic era full religious liberty was granted.

However, some 200,000 French Protestants left after the Edict was revoked in 1685, most of whom were skilled craftsmen or experienced soldiers and sailors. The refugees were cordially welcomed into such Protestant lands as Holland, Prussia, England, and the colonies in South Africa and North America, and they contributed immeasurably to the economic life and culture of their new home countries. To be sure, France lost only 1 percent of its population in the illegal emigration, but these were among its most productive citizens, and this did severe damage to the social and economic fabric of the country. The lavish expenditures on Versailles, the mistreatment of the Huguenots, and Louis XIV's insatiable lust for national power that took France into one war after another (including the first real global conflicts) undid much of the work of French absolutism.

German Absolutism

The methods of Louis XIV were imitated in other parts of Europe, especially in the patchwork of states that constituted post-Westphalia Germany. Imitations of Versailles sprang up in such places as Potsdam, Dresden, Munich, Hanover, and Ludwigsburg (near Stuttgart).

The German princelings established civil services, introduced mercantilism and efficient revenue collection systems, created standing armies, kept their thumbs on the churches, and adopted the French court manners, styles, and even language. The main difference here was that the nobility were incorporated into the system and given the preeminent roles in the officer corps and civil service. In return for submitting to the absolute authority of the king or prince and faithfully serving him, they were allowed a free hand on their own landed estates. Thus, the social position of the middle class and peasantry deteriorated in the age of German absolutism.

The most successful application of the absolutistic methods was by the Hohenzollern family in Brandenburg-Prussia. The elector of Brandenburg, Frederick William, in 1640 inherited a set of sandy territories scattered across northern Germany stretching from the Rhine to Poland, some of which had been devastated in the Thirty Years' War. He succeeded in building an army on the basis of the landed gentry (Junker class) that was efficient and completely loyal to him, and he was able to increase the territorial base and economic strength of the state remarkably.

Particularly significant was William's attitude toward religion. Although a Calvinist, he recognized that many of his west German subjects were Catholics and those in Brandenburg and East Prussia were Lutherans. Since he was seeking to tie his domains together by moving officials and soldiers around, he understood that any effort to impose confessional uniformity would undermine his efforts at unity. Frederick William followed the lead of Georg Calixtus (1586–1659), a professor at the University of Helmstedt who had developed a theological system called "Syncretism." That doctrine was designed to bring about a reconciliation between Lutherans, Calvinists, and Catholics on the basis of the Scriptures, Apostles' Creed, and the accepted faith of the first five centuries of the church. Thus, the "Great Elector" adopted a policy of forcing toleration on his subjects, whether or not the clergy liked it. This also explains why it was so easy to integrate thousands of Huguenot refugees in the country after 1685, and they enriched the economy immeasurably.

His son Frederick I (1688–1713) acquired the title of king of Prussia and founded the new university at Halle that was to become a major center of German pietism. His grandson Frederick William I (1713–40) built the army into the fourth largest in Europe, even though Prussia ranked only twelfth in population. He perfected the idea of limiting the officer corps to the landed nobility, developed a

Absolutist States in Europe

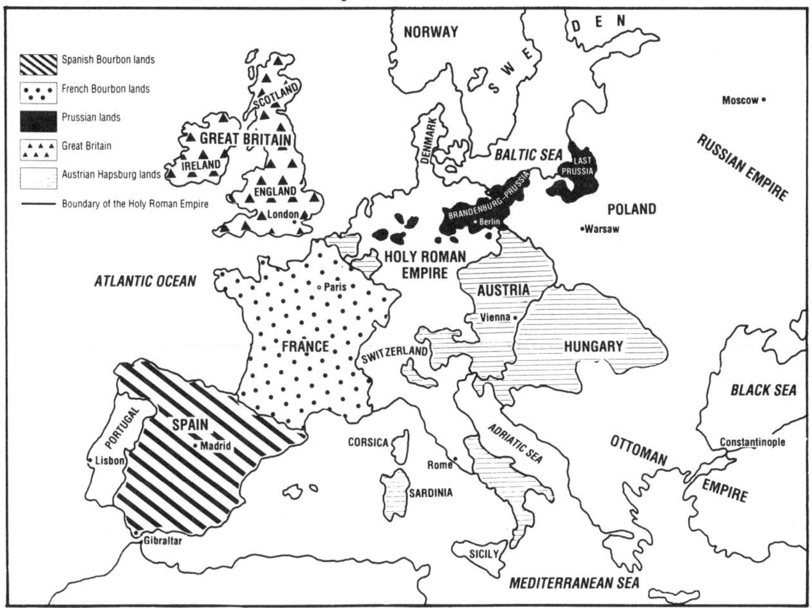

scheme to conscript soldiers from the peasantry, and thus founded Prussian militarism. A deeply pious ruler, he hated laziness and frivolity and even closed theaters because he considered them "temples of Satan." Like his predecessors, however, he had no intention of imposing confessional homogeneity on his domains. For him the churches were not only places where the gospel was preached but also useful public institutions that could inculcate such values as integrity, loyalty, submission, and obedience. Also under his reign the first state-supported program of elementary education was established. In these the "four Rs" were taught—religion, along with reading, writing, and arithmetic.

Actually, Frederick William I was such a harsh disciplinarian and so cruel, miserly, and lacking in spiritual depth that his son Frederick II (1740–86), known as Frederick the Great, when he came to power, rejected his father's faith and maintained only the most tenuous ties with the church. At the same time, he utilized the powerful army bequeathed to him in two major wars that built Prussia into a great power and laid the groundwork for the later development of German nationalism. As for the church, it clearly gained nothing more from monarchical absolutism in Prussia than it did in France; and because religion was used to support the political status quo, its vitality was dissipated. Nowhere was this more evident than in Russia.

Christianity and Absolutism in Russia

As mentioned earlier the prince of Kiev had accepted Eastern Christianity, but during the Mongol period the center of gravity shifted north to Moscow. The Muscovite ruler Ivan III (1440–1505) elevated Russian Orthodoxy, claimed the heritage of the Eastern Roman Empire, brought Byzantine culture to his domains, and asserted that Muscovite Russia was the "Third Rome." His grandson Ivan IV (1538–84) launched a program of eastward expansion that resulted in Russia taking control of the forest regions of Siberia during the next century.

Although known for his extreme cruelty (as Ivan the Terrible, he mercilessly suppressed the nobility and killed his own son in a fit of rage), he did establish some trade ties with the West and sponsored a plan to build churches in all communities so that the people might hear the gospel. Moreover, these were also places where ordinary folk could learn to read and write. The priests gave the worshipers lessons in basic skills and taught the Bible in picture form through icons and frescoes so that even the illiterate gained an understanding of the Scriptures. Thus, the Orthodox faith sank deep roots among the common people. In 1589 he raised the head of the Russian church to the rank of patriarch, thus making him equal to the other four patriarchs of the Eastern church.

There was strong competition between Rome and Moscow for the ecclesiastical allegiance of people in the vast region of Eastern Europe. Although most were Catholic, many in the western Ukraine (also known as Ruthenia) were Orthodox and under the jurisdiction of the metropolitan of Kiev. However, in 1443 the pope arranged with the Polish king who then ruled the area to name a Roman Catholic metropolitan. Within a century most of the churches had reverted to Orthodoxy, but in 1595 Pope Clement VIII and King Sigismund III concluded the Union of Brest-Litovsk, which provided that the Byzantine rite bishops and churches in the western Ukraine would accept papal supremacy but retain their liturgy and discipline. This was called a "Uniate" church, from the Ukrainian word for unity. As the Russian state expanded into these territories in the subsequent centuries, the Ruthenian Uniates were compelled to return to Orthodoxy.

Because Russia remained isolated from the West, it was largely untouched by the developments in the period 1400 to 1700 that had transformed Europe and brought about modern civilization. It had no commercial revolution, no middle class to speak of, no Renaissance or Reformation, and no part in the rise of modern science. The regime was weakened during a period of civil conflict and foreign wars known as the "Time of Troubles" (1598–1613), which ended with the nobles uniting around Michael Romanov to restore order. However, the tradition of strong monarchy remained intact, and this provided the basis for continuing geographical expansion in eastern Europe and Asia and the modernization sponsored by Peter the Great.

A liturgical reform was implemented by Patriarch Nikon (1652–60) to bring it in conformity with Greek and Ukrainian practices, which assisted his ally Tsar Alexis in absorbing the Ukraine. Many were dissatisfied with the changes in the ritual, such as the amount of prostrations during the reading of a prayer or the number of fingers needed to make the sign of the cross. But they were even more unhappy with Nikon's failure to address the problems of spiritual and moral corruption. For these reasons they broke with the official church. They became known as "Old Believers."

The reign of Peter I (1689–1725) marked the turning point in Russian history. A monarch as absolute as any in the West, he undertook a program of forced modernization and westernization that was designed to strengthen the state and make Russia a world power. He was a study in contrasts. On the one hand, he was a crude and savage giant of a man, coarse in manners and speech, with a violent temper, who delighted in obscene, drunken orgies and in torturing his foes. On the other hand, he possessed boundless energy and an insatiable desire to make Russia great. He even traveled abroad in the early years of his reign in order to learn firsthand about European ideas and technology. He hired hundreds of Western craftsmen, technicians, engineers, and teachers to work in Russia.

Then he embarked on refashioning Russian society. He ordered his people to shave off their beards and wear Western-style clothing. He advocated the use of tobacco, hitherto regarded as sinful, and brought women out of their traditional seclusion. He fostered learning by establishing schools and printing presses and requiring educated people for the civil service. The most striking symbol of his westernization program was the founding in 1703 of a new capital city near the entrance to the Baltic Sea that he called St. Petersburg. This "Window to the West" would serve as a counterweight to Moscow, which he saw as too conservative and set in its ways.

To enhance national power he reformed the army and civil service. He introduced a poll tax that provided a sound financial base for the military establishment, implemented a system of conscription to provide a solid body of professional soldiers, and created the first Russian navy. He changed the basis of nobility from mere ancestry to that of state service. Upper class men were encouraged to become officers, and if they rose high enough, they received titles. Even educated people of lesser status could ascend in this system of "service nobility," which lasted in Russia to 1917. Like their counterparts in Prussia, instead of being excluded from the administration of the realm, they were co-opted into the system and made dependent upon the tsar. He also promoted economic development through trade agreements, subsidies for factory construction, and agricultural improvements. The real objective of Peter's reforms was to enable Russia to conduct wars of expansion against neighboring countries, especially Sweden.

The Russian Orthodox church was a particular target of the tsar. Since the church had opposed many of his reforms, Peter decided not to nominate a successor to the patriarch when he died in 1700. Instead, he took control of the office himself and decreed that only a part of church income would return to the church. In 1721 he resolved the patriarchical vacancy by creating a Spiritual College (later called the Most Holy Synod) to govern the church. Composed of twelve clerics nominated by the tsar, its chair or procurator, was a lay civil official who answered directly to the monarch.

Thus, the Russian Orthodox church was transformed into little more than a department of state with the priests as low-paid civil servants. They were even required to report to the police any evidence of treason or anti-government action revealed in the confessional. The higher clerics were under the oppressive thumb of the state. Peter also dissolved a number of monasteries, ordered revisions in the liturgy, and reformed ecclesiastical education. In spite of this virtual nationalization of the church, the level of piety at the grass roots remained high. This would be an essential element in conservative Russian nationalism in the nineteenth century, but the church itself lacked the will or the spiritual strength to check the power of the tsarist autocracy.

Many Russians who opposed westernization and the new practices joined the ranks of the Old Believers, even though this meant persecution that included execution or exile to remote parts of the realm. They continually condemned the official church as apostate and the tsarist order as that of the Antichrist. Many of the dissenters withdrew into tight communities that prospered and contributed to

Russian economic development. Their number amounted to perhaps 20 percent of the population, and the regime was never able to stamp out the movement. There was also a flowering of radical millenarian sects, some of whose members engaged in bizarre behavior.

A treaty signed during the reign of Catherine the Great ending a war against the Turks (1774) acknowledged the Russian monarch's right to intervene in the Ottoman Empire on behalf of the sultan's Orthodox subjects. This would have serious political implications in the nineteenth century. Also she decreed that church and monastic lands should be state property, which cost the church three-quarters of its income. Through this the church became even more an instrument of the state.

Russia's chief rival for mastery of the Baltic was Sweden. There There strict Lutheran orthodoxy had become the religion of the land, which enabled the monarchs to enhance their control. The charismatic Gustavus Adolphus did much to establish the Lutheran identity of Sweden. His daughter Queen Christina (1644–54), one of the most fascinating personalities of the century, tried to check the growth of the nobility and, failing in this, publicly converted to Catholicism and went to Rome. Charles XII (1697–1718), the most famous of the Scandinavian kings, was locked in a struggle with Peter I during his entire reign, and his death marked the end of Swedish greatness.

THE BAROQUE STYLE

The age of orthodoxy and absolutism saw a remarkable flowering of the baroque style, an art expression that rapidly replaced Renaissance classicism and was characterized by flamboyant forms and elaborate ornamentation. The term originally was used disparagingly by critics, but in the meantime the style has come to be recognized and appreciated. The baroque is overwhelming in effect because of its breathtaking extravagance and grandeur. For example, a painting of the era featuring a group of figures is clear and natural, but the individuals cannot be visualized by themselves. The suggested movements of the bodies and the direction of the eyes blend together to provide a dramatic situation and create a whole that is greater than the sum of its parts. In barogue architecture the interior of a building combined painting, sculpture, and structural features to create a grand unity. An early expression of this is to be seen in Il Gesu, a Jesuit church in Rome. There the painting on the ceiling (*The Worship of the Holy Name of Jesus*) is skillfully merged with the altars and the remainder of the structure to give an awesome effect. The theatrical quality of baroque art and architecture lent an impressive larger-than-life quality to its productions.

The center of the new style was Rome. In the seventeenth century the city was virtually redone in the baroque. The new (or remodeled) churches and public buildings were lavishly ornamented and decorated with cherubs and angels, twisted and bent columns, and intricate designs in gold and marble. The most prominent architect of the era was Giovanni Lorenzo Bernini (1598–1680), whose masterpiece was the plaza in front of St. Peter's Basilica. With its two semicircles of colonnades, it overcomes the viewer with the sense of being lost in an immense religious institution.

The Catholic Reformation assisted in spreading the baroque style throughout Europe. In Spain the emphasis on color and ornamentation was particularly evident. The major artist was Jose Churriguera (1650–1723), who decorated the newly completed cathedral in his native town of Salamanca with bright colors and also designed the city square. The Spanish baroque had a great influence on Portugal and in the Iberian possessions in America, especially Mexico, Peru, and Brazil.

Vienna was redesigned after the defeat of the Turks in 1683, and churches, palaces, and monuments were built in the baroque style, while gothic buildings were remodeled to match the new construction. Palaces like the Belvedere and Schönbrünn were striking masterpieces. Other Austrian cities like Salzburg and Innsbruck and the magnificent abbey of Melk are baroque landmarks.

In Germany proper there was a building boom in the new style. The rulers of the various principalities competed in employing architects and constructing impressive palaces, churches, and monasteries, and often they exceeded their financial means. The elector of Saxony, Augustus II (1694–1733) set out to transform his city of Dresden into "Florence on the Elbe," and the keystone in the ambitious project was the elegant Zwinger palace that took ten years to build. The Wittelsbach dukes in Bavaria filled Munich with baroque churches and palaces and converted it into a major cultural center.

The new style affected the French as well, although they tended to incorporate more classicism into their buildings. Further, they paid attention to the practical aspects of life and designed more convenient room arrangements. The influence of the baroque was particularly obvious at Versailles. Not only was the structure impressive in

George Frederic Handel

its own right, but also it was calculated to blend into an environment of gardens, statues, fountains, and a grand canal. The entire setting was a pompous, lavish symbol of the era of absolutism. French architects also produced numerous other palaces and churches, the most noteworthy being the Invalides, Ste. Geneviève (Panthéon), and Fontainebleau.

In the mid-eighteenth century appeared an extreme variation of the baroque called the rococo. Taken from the French word *rocaille,* meaning stone or rock work, it referred to the style of interior decoration of French buildings around 1720–60, but it became an international art style with its greatest flowering in Catholic Bavaria. It was characterized by an elaborate system of ornamentation and decoration that stressed lines rather than space, the exuberant use of color, and different materials such as stone, fresco, gilded woodwork, and even tapestry for a delicate overall effect. Among the major rococo artists was Giovanni Battista Tiepolo (1696–1770), who was noted for his ceiling frescoes that created the illusion of sky, sunlight, and clouds. Another was Dominikus Zimmermann (1685–1766), who specialized in creating a unity of light and color that resulted in a joyously festive mood. The rococo style can be seen today in such splendid structures in southern Germany as the Würzburg Residence, the village church of Wies, and the monastic church of Ottobeuren.

Other art forms reflected the baroque. The seventeenth century was the age of portrait painting and the greatest master was unquestionably Rembrandt van Rijn (1609–69), the Dutch painter who used dark backgrounds and touches of light to study his subjects. Space and light were essential elements in most examples of baroque painting as well. Peter Paul Rubens (1577–1640) and his many pupils created an illusion of endless space so that the viewer would think of infinity. Diego Velasquez (1599–1660), the principal Spanish painter of the era, produced numerous portraits of figures in the royal court. Bernini was the leader in sculpture as well as in architecture, and he is responsible for many of the works that were commissioned for churches, papal tombs, and fountains that embellish the city of Rome today.

The baroque was also an era of great musical achievement. It marked the end of the five-hundred-year dominance of polyphony in music (where one part was no more important than the other) and the emergence of harmonic music. Baroque music consisted of a single element, the melody, supported by harmony. It found expression especially in instrumental music, the opera with its pageantry and exaggerated emotions, and the oratorio, a sacred work that combined the efforts of soloists, a choir, and orchestra. Since it was not a part of the liturgy, the oratorio provided an ideal opportunity for musical experimentation. This variety of composition originated in the mid-sixteenth century with musical performances in the Oratory of Philip Neri in Rome. The Jesuits used the new genre, and it was quickly picked up by Lutherans in Germany who already had chorales, cantatas, and passion music that were not necessarily performed as part of a regular church service.

The organ came into its own in the baroque era. Designers like Gottfried Silbermann (1683–1753) built lavish pipe organs for the new churches as well as installed them in the older gothic structures. The baroque composers wrote music for the organ, and many were accomplished organists in their own right.

There was an abundance of first-rate musical figures in this period. The Venetian Claudio Monteverdi (1567–1643) bridged the Renaissance and baroque, wrote brilliant church music, and is regarded by some as the creator of modern music. His pupil was Heinrich Schütz (1585–1672), court director at Dresden and the most important Lutheran composer before Bach. His choral music is quite significant and widely sung today. Georg Philipp Telemann (1681–1767) and Dietrich Buxtehude (1637–1707) wrote distinguished choral and organ music, and the latter profoundly influenced the young Bach. Henry Purcell (1659–95) was the greatest native English composer between the Elizabethan era and the late nineteenth century. He was organist of Westminster Abbey and produced outstanding instrumental and choral works.

Two individuals, however, stand out from their colleagues because of their superb technical ability and musical genius. George Frederic Handel, or in German Händel (1685–1759), a Saxon who already gained an outstanding reputation in his native Halle, as well as in Hamburg and Hanover, resettled in midcareer in England, where his patrons were the Hanoverian kings, George I and II. He wrote primarily for large public audiences, and even his brilliant religious compositions, such as the oratorios *Messiah* and *Judas Maccabeus*, were intended for public performances in concert halls rather than churches. His themes were drawn from aspects of eighteenth-century English life, such as folk music, country dances, London street cries, the quiet countryside, and even storms at sea. Although foreign-born, Handel is even today England's most beloved composer.

Johann Sebastian Bach (1685–1750) was not only one of the greatest composers of all time but also a devout Christian. He spent almost his entire life in central Germany—in Thuringia and Saxony—and except for a few years when he worked for the prince of Anhalt, he was employed in churches, especially at St. Thomas Lutheran in Leipzig, where he served his last twenty-seven years as cantor (minister of music). Although he wrote several important pieces of secular music, he saw his vocation as service to God and his church. His love for Scripture and the church was translated into a fusion of faith and music, theology and liturgy. For him, to compose music was an act of faith, and to perform it was an act of worship. In his great cantatas, oratorios, passions, organ compositions, and *Mass in B Minor*, he carried out this perception of a divine calling to create music appropriate to God's praise. He set the biblical story to music in such a way as to reveal God's presence to the congregation and to bring about a conversation with the Almighty.

Neither the political nor religious orthodoxy did much to advance the cause of the church in Europe. Yet spiritual and cultural vitality were evident in many places, and the potential existed for more vibrant expression of the Christian faith. This was especially the case in Britain and Germany, where spiritual energies could be channeled into a variety of Protestant movements, and in France, where a Catholic alternative existed.

14
PURITANISM AND PIETISM AROUSE THE CHURCH

For more than a century after Luther had thrown down the gauntlet to the medieval church, Europe was torn by conflicts in which religion played a leading role. Only after the middle of the seventeenth century did the concept of the modern state, with its stress upon territorial sovereignty and the central position of the monarch, begin to predominate. Thereafter the struggles were between states and their rulers, and spiritual concerns took a back seat to raison d'état and balance of power politics. Monarchs sought to control the churches in their domains, and religious unity was seen as an element in the strength of the state. Although these developments were debilitating to the church as a spiritual institution, still pockets of religious vigor existed in the age of orthodoxy and absolutism.

English Puritanism

Calvinist ideas had sunk deep roots in Britain. Scottish Presbyterianism was a vigorous faith, and leaders like Andrew Melville (1545–1622) challenged the Stuart kings to abandon their allegiance to the episcopal system. By the seventeenth century Presbyterianism had become for all practical purposes the national church of Scotland, and it did much to shape the character of this hardy folk in the north. Because they banded together in covenants in 1638 and 1643 to resist the imposition of episcopalian church government and liturgy, they were called "covenanters." Leading divines (theologians) like George Gillespie (1613–49) and Samuel Rutherford (1600–61) rejected the exercise of royal authority in church matters.

There was also a strong Reformed element within the Church of England, and its representatives became increasingly dissatisfied with the compromises of the Elizabethan Settlement. They wished to "purify" the church of "popish" remnants, and their struggle increasingly took on a political character. As mentioned earlier, these "Puritans" were intimately involved in the conflicts between the Stuarts and Parliament that eventually led to civil war and the establishment of a military dictatorship under Cromwell.

In brief, the Puritans wanted to exclude from Anglican worship anything that was not commanded by Scripture. They stressed the importance of conversion, which meant a fundamental transformation of one's entire being and attitudes, and the expectation that the believer would live a godly and disciplined life. Puritans also believed that all work was within the sphere of Christian concern and that pastors and priests were not to be elevated over the ordinary members. Their aim was for the Church of England to have a pastor in every parish who would faithfully proclaim the Word of God, properly administer the sacraments, and discipline immoral church members. The application of Protestant doctrine to the believer's life was the task of the church, and those who did not meet the high standards of belief and obedience to God's law should be excluded from the church. Although many have ridiculed or condemned the disciplined lifestyle that was the hallmark of Puritanism, for individuals in the seventeenth century this was a satisfying experience. It was linked to the joy that they found in worship and the life of service to God.

The Puritans were a profoundly disruptive force in the Church of England, which, under Elizabeth I, had been constituted as a centralized hierarchy under the control of bishops and an inclusive institution. The Puritans advocated instead the idea of a "gathered" church, one comprised only of the faithful who were in covenant with God and each other. Puritanism, which had begun as a reform movement that centered on simplified worship patterns, biblical preaching, and conversion, thus increasingly emphasized "independency" (freedom from episcopal control) and the congregational form of church government.

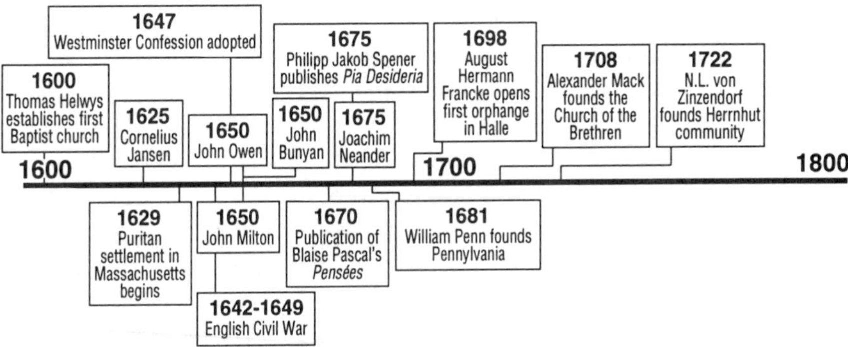

By the late sixteenth century some Puritans were convinced that the only way to complete the Reformation was to separate from the Anglican church.

Robert Browne (1550–1633) was one of the earliest Separatists. In the early 1580s he formed his own congregation and published tracts championing radical reform and gathered, covenanted Congregationalism. Another group of Separatists was led by John Robinson (1572–1625). In the first decade of the new century they met at Scrooby Manor and then moved to Holland to avoid persecution. Many in the group grew dissatisfied with life in a foreign land, and under the leadership of two lay members, William Bradford (1589–1657) and William Brewster (1567–1644), part of them sailed to the New World on the *Mayflower* in 1620, although Robinson remained behind in Leiden. These "Pilgrim Fathers" were the pioneers of Congregationalism in America.

The most enduring of the Puritan Separatist movements from this era were the Baptists. They went beyond the other contemporary reformers to equate infant baptism with spiritual adultery and to insist upon baptism for adult believers. John Smyth (1570–1612) was an Anglican priest who turned to Separatism and in 1607 led a congregation to Holland with a lay associate, Thomas Helwys (1550–1616). Within two years they reorganized along what they considered were New Testament lines, adopted believers' baptism, and issued a ringing declaration of religious liberty that condemned any kind of state regulation of beliefs. In 1611 Helwys took some followers back to London and established the first Baptist church on English soil. Although some have tried to establish a firm link between the Mennonites and the early English Baptists, most historians feel that they arose directly out of English Puritanism and Separatism.

The earliest group was known as General Baptists since they

held to an Arminian view of the atonement. In the late 1630s emerged the Particular Baptists, so called because they accepted the Calvinist teaching of an atonement limited to the elect. Each developed independently of the other. The latter was more willing to accept the Church of England as a true church. By the 1640s the Baptists were regularly practicing baptism by immersion, and by mid-century they had come to use the name "Baptist" to distinguish themselves. During the English Civil War many of them served with distinction in the Parliamentary army. Cromwell favored them when he was in power, but after the Restoration they were classified as Dissenters and lost their privileges. Around 1639 the first Baptist church was established in North America in the colony of Rhode Island.

A flowering of radical Puritan sects occurred during the troubled years of the 1640s. With the abolition of the episcopal system in the Church of England, the Westminster Assembly of Divines was convened in 1643 and continued irregularly in session until 1649 in order to devise an alternative form of the church and to guide Parliament in its religious decisions. The assembly recommended the establishment of Presbyterianism and in 1647 adopted the famous Westminster Confession as a Presbyterian statement of faith, but then a split occurred in the assembly between the Independents (Congregationalists) and Presbyterians. After Cromwell came to power, he followed the advice of the prominent Independent John Owen (1616–83), and a moderately pluralistic situation was allowed, whereby churches could be pastored by Presbyterians, Independents, or Baptists.

The more extreme sects, however, were not tolerated in Cromwell's England. The Levellers, led by John Lilburne (1614–57), an officer in the Parliamentary army, interpreted liberty in Christ as including political democracy. They advocated universal male suffrage, equality before the law, and freedom of religion (hence their name—everyone level in law and religion).

Other sects engaged in millennial speculation and looked for the second coming of Christ. The Puritan revolution and overthrow of the monarchy simply added fuel to the fire of prophetic speculation. The Diggers, following the teachings of Gerrard Winstanley (1609–52), believed that the earth, because it was God's creation, was the property of all people. In 1649 they occupied the commons at St. George's Hill in Surrey, planted crops (hence their name), and formed a commune, but the authorities broke up the venture. They were religious mystics who believed in a universal atonement and were preparing the way for Christ's return. Many Marxists today interpret the Diggers as a forerunner of communism.

The most radical apocalyptic group was the Fifth Monarchy Men. They drew on the prophetic passage in Daniel 2 about the four major empires that would rule the world and concluded from Revelation that the kingdom of God (the "fifth monarchy") would be in the millennium, the one-thousand-year reign of Christ on earth. Although many at the time speculated about the return of Christ, the Fifth Monarchy Men believed it was truly imminent and proclaimed that the saints should not compromise with the old order whatsoever. Instead, they should join together in assemblies under the control of Jesus Christ and create a new form of government for England. Cromwell's establishment of the Protectorate frustrated their hopes of a millennial kingdom.

While the mainstream of Puritanism moved toward systemizing doctrine and church life and a number of prominent theologians and preachers, such as John Owen and Richard Baxter (1615–91), produced substantial volumes on major points of dogma and godly living, some were attracted to the idea of the mystical experience with Christ or the "inner light." One of the more influential figures in mysticism was Jakob Boehme (1575–1624), a German shoemaker, who authored several widely read books on the topic. An individual influenced by Boehmist thinking was a young English Puritan, George Fox (1624–91), who in 1646 after a long, painful struggle came to rely on the "Inner Light of the Living Christ." He became a traveling minister, condemned religious controversy, and preached that truth was to be found in God's voice speaking directly to the soul—hence the label "Friends of Truth" that was quickly attached to his movement.

His followers were content simply to be called "Friends" or "Quakers," allegedly a nickname given by a judge in 1650 after Fox had exhorted the magistrates to "tremble at the word of the Lord." Drawing upon the inner light belief, they taught that the Holy Spirit's power is given to all people and is not limited to the Scriptures. Since each individual received the inner light, all are equal in the church. In their plain "meeting houses" they worshiped without ministers, sacraments, or liturgy, thus pushing the Puritan idea of removing the vestiges of Catholicism to its extreme limit. Clergy and structured services were unnecessary, as the Spirit would inspire those whom He wished to speak during the meeting times. The Quaker message was that people needed only to repent and worship God inwardly, with the heart.

In spite of persecution the group grew rapidly, at first among the poorer classes but soon also among those of wealth (for example, William Penn, son of a prominent admiral and founder of a Quaker colony in America in 1681). Many converts came from the General Baptists. The Quakers were distinguished by their commitment to nonviolence, refusal to take oaths, addressing one another by first names and in familiar address forms, and wearing simple clothes. They also taught the equality of men and women and were among the first to protest against horrible prison conditions and slavery. The most systematic presentation of Quaker theology was the *Apology for the True Christian Divinity,* by Robert Barclay (1648–90).

Both the Baptists and Quakers gave special opportunity for women to minister. In the Netherlands, England, and North America Baptists had women clergy, and in one London congregation as many as one thousand people attended special services where women could preach. Among the "errors, heresies, and blasphemies" condemned in a seventeenth-century anti-Baptist tract was the use of "she-preachers." The Quaker view was that all were illumined by the Holy Spirit and thus welcomed to stand up and speak. Quaker women went on missionary journeys from England to such distant points as North America and Turkey. For example, Elizabeth Hooten, who was past sixty years old, traveled to New England where she was beaten, imprisoned, and exiled to the wilderness.

The difficulties that Puritans experienced under Stuart rule earlier in the century induced many of them to emigrate to America. A group of well-to-do Puritans, who had formed the Massachusetts Bay Company in 1629 as a business venture, decided to move the entire enterprise to North America the following year. By 1643 when the reins of government in England had passed to the Puritan-dominated Long Parliament, more than 20,000 people had made their way to New England. Under such talented leaders as John Winthrop (1588–1649), the company's governor, John Cotton (1584–1652), pastor of the Boston church, and Thomas Hooker (1586–1647) in Connecticut, the Calvinist variety of the Congregational church tradition sank roots in the New World. Members were required to make a public "declaration of their experience of a work of grace," and this assured that the church would be in the hands of genuine believers. Only church members could vote or hold office in the government of the colony. Since a knowledge of reading and writing was essential to understand the Bible and to be mature Christians, every town was required to set up schools to teach the children. In order to insure a dependable supply of trained ministers, Harvard College was founded in 1636. A printing press was brought over and in 1640 the first book was published, a metrical version of the Psalms. The New England Puritans wrestled with knotty theological questions like the nature of man as a moral being, one's preparation for receiving God's grace, qualifications for church membership, and relationships among the various congregations.

Puritans were not just interested in constructing a righteous society, but also contributed to the development of English literature. Two of the most significant figures in the seventeenth century were John Bunyan (1628–88) and John Milton (1608–74). Arrested in the persecution that accompanied the Restoration in 1660, Bunyan languished in prison for several years. There he produced several works, including *The Pilgrim's Progress*, published in 1678, which established him as one of the most influential religious writers of all time. With vivid imagination, he traced the journey of a man named Christian from the City of Destruction to the Heavenly City. Bunyan's allegory was essentially a description of his own spiritual pilgrimage, which likened the spiritual journey that every Christian takes through life to a physical journey beset with dangers and adventures.

Milton's two immortal works, *Paradise Lost* (1667) and *Paradise Regained* (1671) dealt with the fall and redemption of humankind. The former reflected the personal tragedies he had experienced —the death of two wives and two children, his blindness, and the loss of his government post and income after the accession of Charles II to the throne. Another major work was *Areopagitica* (1644), a landmark defense of freedom of the press. He protested the strict official censorship of the time and explained why people should be allowed to publish their opinions freely.

Catholic Spiritual Ferment

The relative vigor in French Catholicism produced significant controversy. A lengthy struggle over the nature of the relationship of the French church with Rome (Gallicanism) was resolved in favor of maintaining firm allegiance to the pope while allowing French bishops a certain measure of autonomy. A more difficult problem was that of Jansenism. A Flemish academic theologian and bishop, Cornelius Otto Jansen (1585–1638) declared that the ceremonies of the church obscured a crucial fact. A person can only be saved through God's love and grace operating on the heart, and this love comes to those whom God chooses. Jansen's rejection of free will and stress on predestination sounded suspiciously like Calvinism, and enemies of the movement accused him and his followers of being "warmed-over Calvinists." The Jansenists responded that they were not Protestants, but at the same time they were deeply concerned about the moral laxity of their fellow Catholics and what they saw as an over-emphasis on the place of free will in Catholic doctrine. In many respects, this was analogous to the challenge that Puritanism was offering to Anglicanism.

Jansenism was introduced into France by Jean Duvergier, abbot of St. Cyran, who won many people to the cause, including several members of the influential Arnauld family. The center of the movement was the Cistercian convent at Port Royal, near Paris. Jansenist piety and doctrine actually did not deviate substantially from accepted Catholic beliefs. They probably would have been tolerated, except that their independent turn of mind and the moral emphasis of their preaching struck a sour note with those in positions of spiritual authority in France. Not only did they call for purity and holy living among the clergy but they also began questioning the secular power of the church. Personally, they led strict, austere lives, stressed popular participation in religious functions, practiced simple forms of worship, and engaged in direct study of the Scriptures and church Fathers. On the other hand, they turned on the Jesuits whom they accused of "laxist" teachings, that is, that they far too easily granted absolution for sins. Such laxness, the Jansenists said, encouraged immorality.

As the movement spread, numerous clerics and pious laypersons settled at Port Royal and dedicated themselves to lives of scholarship and contemplation based upon Jansenist principles. One of these was Blaise Pascal (1623–62), a philosopher and scientist who among other things contributed early theoretical work to the development of the computer. One day, while reading the gospel of John, he had a remarkable religious experience, a vision of Christ. He was so overcome by joy that he yielded himself to this wonderful Being. He then abandoned his career of scientific inquiry, joined the Jansensist community, and devoted his writing talents to the support of their cause.[1]

In 1656 Pascal published the *Provincial Letters,* which not only defended Jansenist piety but more importantly attacked the whole

Francke at Halle, Germany

Jesuit system of casuistry. He claimed that the Jesuits actually undermined the Christian faith by teaching a morality based on what a person does rather than on what he or she ought to do. This morality held that the end justifies the means and that mental reservations may be used to qualify one's word. His brilliant wit and moral fervor struck such a telling blow that the Jesuits thirsted for revenge against a movement that so penetratingly exposed their own weaknesses.

A deeply devout believer in his own right, Pascal had intended to put out a book designed to win others to Christ, but his untimely death prevented him from doing so. However, the notes for this were gathered by his associates and published in 1670 under the title of *Pensées.* This simple but profound work contended both intellectually and emotionally for the existence of God and the reality of faith. Yet, Pascal added, in light of his own personal encounter with Jesus Christ, "the heart has its reasons, which reason does not know." He argued that in the search for truth reason was neutral, and evidence for the existence of God could never replace faith. One comes to know truth not just by reason alone but also through the heart. "We shall never believe with a vigorous and unquestioning faith unless God touches our hearts; and we shall believe as soon as He does so."[2]

In order to convince unbelievers that they should seriously consider Christianity, Pascal propounded his famous "wager," which combined a skeptical attitude with his own mathematical scholarship on the calculation of probabilities. His reasoning went like this: God is a good bet. People should gamble that God exists and act on that assumption. If they are right, they win everything; if they are wrong, they have lost nothing.

The Jansenist controversy quickly attracted the attention of King Louis XIV. He was alarmed by the large number of influential people who identified with it, and he sensed that its emphasis on strict moral behavior was an implicit criticism of his own lifestyle. For a long time he was concerned it might be a threat to his absolute power, while his Jesuit confessors complained about the movement and urged him to ask the pope to denounce it. Finally, in 1709 the king took action. He closed the convent at Port Royal and two years later had the building torn down. In 1713 Pope Clement XI dutifully condemned Jansenism in the bull *Unigenitus*, but it remained a significant force in France for decades, and it was freely tolerated in Flanders.

At the same time, the Roman church had to respond to the challenge of Quietism, a type of mysticism that rejected all the active forms of worship. Quietists saw intellectual activity in the spiritual realm (such as theology) as useless and said God alone must work in the soul while the individual remains totally passive. Their idea of contemplation involved the total abandonment of the self to the will and operation of God in the soul. Thus, good works, prayers of petition, examination of one's conscience, confession, and even meditation on the sacred humanity of Christ and His work on the cross were irrelevant.

Quietism was inspired by Miguel de Molinos (1628–96), a Spanish priest who lived in Italy and whose *A Spiritual Guide* set forth guidelines intended to lead one to an eventual union with God. The Jesuits persuaded the pope to condemn his views, but Quietism spread to France where its followers emphasized passive prayers as the main activity for Christians. The leading light in the movement was Jeanne Marie de la Motte Guyon (1648–1717), a woman from an important family who after being widowed at an early age spent her life in religious endeavor. In her famous work, *Short and Very Easy Method of Prayer* (1685), Mme. Guyon taught the single-minded contemplation of God through which the soul would lose all interest in its own fate. Even the truth of the gospel paled to insignificance before "the torrent of the forces of God" to which an individual must yield. At this point one reached "perfection" and no longer had to perform specific acts, except charity, but simply live in repose with God. One would become indifferent to all things concerning body and soul and repulse all distinct ideas, even those having to do with Christ's attributes.

Her views stirred great controversy, and she was repeatedly arrested and even imprisoned. Bishop Bossuet accused her of being mentally unbalanced and teaching a false mysticism, and he ordered her to stop preaching. However, François Fénelon (1651–1715), archbishop of Cambrai, defended Mme. Guyon, insisting that she had discovered a method of prayer suited to bring the individual close to God. Whether her emotional mysticism paralleled that which was beginning to appear in German Protestantism at this time is highly debatable, but renewal movements clearly were developing in both confessions.

German Pietism

In the era of stifling state-church religion that had settled over seventeenth-century Germany, it became increasingly evident that doctrinal orthodoxy was not enough and that the land desperately needed a revival of the evangelical fervor that had animated the early Protestant Reformation. The movement that arose in the church in response to this situation was labeled by its critics as "pietism." The term was accepted by its adherents and later commentators to identify the new religious outlook. Pietism was a Bible-centered moralism that emphasized personal conviction of sin, repentance, conversion, and a new existence in Christ. The forgiven Christian would manifest Christ in his or her daily life through personal holiness and sensitivity to the needs of others. Worship would be an emotional experience, and little effort would be devoted to harmonizing faith and reason. Religion was highly personal and had to be felt inwardly. Pietism thus was a reaction against intellectualism, religious authorities, and formalistic creeds.

The person most closely identified with German Pietism was Philipp Jakob Spener (1635–1705). Born in Alsace and educated at Strasbourg and other universities, from 1666 to 1685 he held the position of senior minister at Frankfurt am Main and gained a reputation as one of the leading pastors in Germany. In 1686 he was appointed court chaplain to the king of Saxony in Dresden and five years later accepted a call from the Prussian ruler to the prestigious church of St. Nicholas in Berlin, where he remained until his death.

In his early years Spener had been deeply influenced by various modes of Lutheran and Reformed piety, particularly that of Jean de Labadie (1610–74). He spent some time with Labadie in Geneva and later published one of his tracts in Germany. Labadie was a Reformed preacher who blended Jansenism with Calvinist piety to structure a strongly experiential, otherworldly, mystical faith that emphasized separation and small group meetings. Spener also came to see that a conversion experience—a rebirth—was necessary for the Christian life. He preached on this topic many times, and toward the end of his career he published a large collection of sermons on the topic.

Spener argued that the second birth was an act of God and the beginning point of faith in the individual. A process of growth followed the creation of the new inner man that led ultimately to the point where one's entire existence would reflect Jesus Christ. He used the analogy of the draftman's compass to illustrate what takes place. God's action of rebirth constitutes the center, the fixed point, while the other leg—the individual's faith, piety, and moral and social standards—traces out the circle, which is the boundary of his existence. Thus, the born-again person's total being was determined by the center point, Jesus Christ. Victory over temptation, sin, and even Satan himself was now possible. Through the ongoing process of sanctification the believer would become increasingly like Christ.[3]

This led to his ideas on how the church could be improved. This included strengthening the program for religious instruction of children (the catechism), combating ignorance and moral deficiency among the clergy, and encouraging more lay involvement in religious activities. To accomplish the latter, he introduced the practice of holding private meetings of small groups for the purpose of cultivating holiness, the coventicles or *collegia pietatis,* the first of which he implemented in 1670. The gatherings took place in his home, and both men and women attended—although they were seated separately and only the men were allowed to speak. They discussed the previous Sunday's sermon or passages from a devotional book. The meetings were designed to bring the participants nearer to God and to promote a purified life, and they were to be small "churches within the church" that would aid the pastor in his spiritual duties and return the church to the level of the early Christian communities.

Spener spelled out his concepts in more popular form in the small book *Pia Desideria, or Heartfelt Longing for a God-Pleasing Reform of the True Evangelical Church* (1675), originally written as a preface to a new edition of Arndt's *True Christianity*. Spener's work is regarded as the classic statement of Pietism. After commenting on the prevailing moral laxity of both clergy and laity, he affirms the possibility of reform and sets forth six concrete proposals to achieve this:

1. More extensive public and private reading and study of the Bible
2. A renewed emphasis on the priesthood of all believers, which would insure larger participation on the part of the laity
3. The cultivation of the spiritual life through deeds of love to one's neighbor and not just knowledge alone
4. Avoidance of theological disputation
5. A procedure for training future ministers that would couple piety with learning by including devotional literature in the curriculum
6. Encouragement of preaching that would have edification and the development of the inner man as its goal.

On other occasions, Spener wrestled with the problem of life in a sinful world by maintaining that Christians should always relate to the society around them but not absorb its values. Thus he denied many worldly pleasures and insisted upon moderation in such things as the use of alcoholic beverages, but at the same time he urged Christians to serve others in every way they could. Spener had high hopes for society because of his strong belief in the coming kingdom of God. Although he did not set a date for the new age, he looked for the conversion of the Jews, the destruction of the Roman Catholic church, and the glorious spread of Christ's rule over the whole earth. The church should be a pilot project for the future kingdom by fostering revivals and philanthropic enterprises.

The orthodox responded with hostility to the pietist challenge. They charged that Spener's conventicles were divisive elements in the church, the emphasis on spiritual living neglected the importance of correct doctrinal beliefs, the role of the sacraments was minimized, and the door was opened to the reception of special (that is, extrabiblical) revelation. The theological faculty of the University of Wittenberg accused the pietists of being guilty of 284 heresies, and Spener's critics labeled him among other things as a Rosicrucian, chiliast, Quaker, and fanatic. It was obvious that the orthodox establishment saw itself threatened by such appeals for change and for departure from that which was familiar, customary, and comfortable.

The second most important figure in the development of Pietism was August Hermann Francke (1663–1727). Through his practical works he did more than anyone else to spread the pietist vision beyond the confines of Germany. As a student he became deeply interested in biblical studies, and, although only in his twenties, he distinguished himself as a Hebrew scholar. Immediately after coming to know Spener personally, Francke had a profound conversion experience. When he expressed his new understanding of the Bible and theology in his academic lectures at Leipzig University, a revival resulted. These reform views sparked great controversy both at Leipzig and in a brief pastorate at Erfurt. Then, in 1692 Francke became pastor of the struggling congregation in Glaucha, a poverty-stricken suburb of Halle, and was also appointed a teacher of Greek and Hebrew at the newly founded University of Halle. In 1698 he advanced to professor of theology and did much to orient the theological faculty in a pietist direction.

His reputation as spiritual leader grew rapidly. Not only was he a pastor, an academic, and the enthusiastic promoter of pietistic ideas, but he also was concerned about meeting the physical needs of people, a matter that he regarded as inseparable from conversion and revival. The modest beginning of Francke's famous social-service endeavor in Halle was a school he started in 1695 for poor children in his parsonage. So many pupils came that he soon had to find another facility, and then in 1698 he constructed the first of what would be a large complex of buildings just outside the Halle city wall. Largely due to his efforts, the sleepy town on the Saale River became the international center of Pietism. Gifted with limitless energy, boundless enthusiasm, great organizational ability, and a flair for what in a later time would be called public relations, within three decades Francke's institutions had grown into a small city that accommodated 3,000 people.

From his position at the university Francke inspired untold numbers of students to serve God as pastors in Germany and as missionaries in such distant corners of the world as America and India and there raised funds for their support. He maintained extensive ecumenical ties, and through these his reform ideas were carried to many countries. He even fostered research into foreign languages in order to facilitate the study and translation of the Bible and furthered the publication and distribution of the Scriptures from his base at Halle.

A major factor in the growth of Pietism was the wide dissemination of English Puritan devotional and theological literature. Works by the leading Puritans were translated into German, some of which

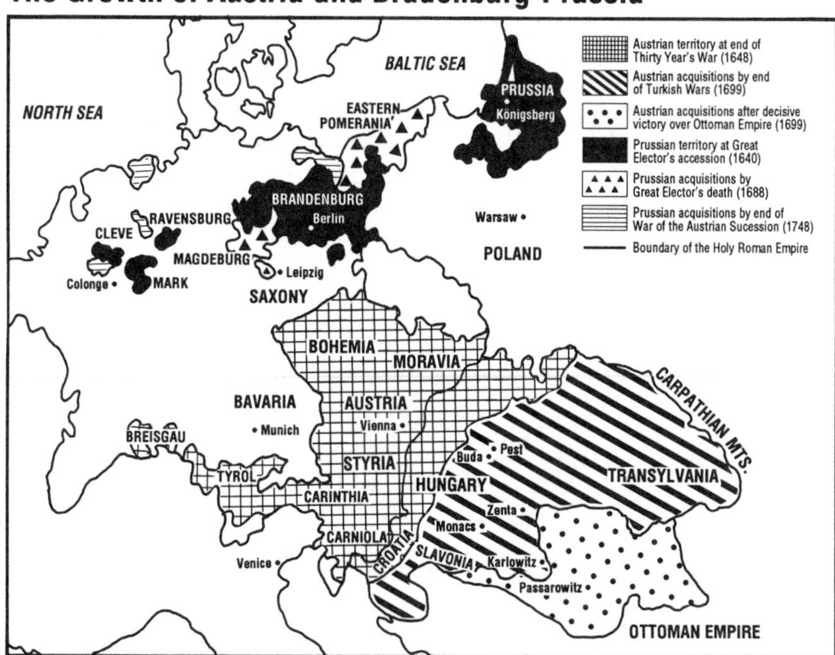

went through many editions, and these books circulated freely among devout Lutheran clergy and laypeople.

As Pietism spread through Germany and Scandinavia, a notable center of the movement developed in Württemberg. The best-known figure in Swabian Pietism was Johann Albrecht Bengel (1687–1752). As a student at Tübingen, he was influenced by pietist teachers and studied the works of Spener and Francke. In 1713 he even spent some time at Halle. Upon his return he accepted an appointment at a theological college at Denkendorf near Esslingen, where he served for twenty-eight years and distinguished himself as a scholar in biblical exegesis and textual criticism. During his last decade he occupied high church positions where he continued to influence pastors in the direction of Pietism.

One of Bengel's most popular works was the *Gnomon Novi Testamenti,* a critical New Testament based on the Textus Receptus. It consists of annotations on each verse and is a model of philological scholarship. It went through numerous editions, was translated into many languages, and even today is still widely used. Bengel also engaged in intensive study of the book of Revelation and set June 18, 1836, as the date for the beginning of the millennium. He was strongly criticized in his day for such speculation, but his eschatological views were in the tradition of Spener. As a pietist, he positively proclaimed a liberating vision of the kingdom of God. He was forthright and clear in rejecting the naive views of progress held by many in the age of rationalism that had set in during his last years.

Pietism also found a favorable reception among the Reformed churches in western Germany, particularly in the Rhineland. Theodor Untereyck (1635–93), who had studied with the leading Dutch theologians of his time and was strongly influenced by Puritan literature, inaugurated the first Reformed conventicles during his pastorate in Mülheim/Ruhr in the 1660s. Then he spent his last twenty-three years at St. Martin's church in Bremen, which he made into a veritable nursery of Reformed Pietism. Among those influenced by Untereyck were the hymn writer Joachim Neander and the important theologian Friedrich Adolf Lampe (1683–1729), who creatively linked the federal theology prominent in Dutch Calvinism with German Reformed Pietism.

Brethren and Moravians

Pietism was a reform movement within the established or territorial churches in Germany, but two important separatist bodies sprang from it, the Church of the Brethren and the Moravian Church, as they are known in North America today. The Brethren began in 1708 at Schwarzenau in Hesse when Alexander Mack (1679–1735) baptized eight people in the local river. Mack had been influenced by radical Pietism, particularly that of Ernst Christoph Hochmann von Hohenau (1670–1721) who had been converted while a student at Halle. He was a strong mystic who saw the church as primarily spiritual in character and minimized the importance of structures. Unlike other Lutheran pietists, Hochmann was a separatist. He wandered around Germany preaching revival and often experienced persecution and imprisonment.

Like his friend, Mack had concluded that the New Testament required separate groups of believers rather than a state church. He settled in one of the few areas of Germany where religious dissenters were allowed to practice their beliefs, the county of Wittgenstein. The local ruler had adopted the policy of toleration, partly because of personal conviction but mainly because he needed settlers. The early Brethren decided to restore what they felt were apostolic practices. These included baptism by trine (or triple) immersion (once face-forward in the water for each Person of the Trinity), the love feast (consisting of a common meal, foot washing, and celebration of the Lord's Supper), anointing of the sick with oil, laying on of hands for

Christian service, congregational church government, and opposition to war, the taking of oaths, and wearing gaudy or "worldly" clothing.

Eventually the long arm of an intolerant Holy Roman Empire reached into the small region and the Brethren were persecuted, even as their itinerant preachers founded other churches in various locations in western Germany and Switzerland. As the situation in Europe worsened, they considered emigration to America. William Penn had encouraged sectarians to come to his colony, and his agents had distributed literature in Germany presenting it as an attractive place to settle. In 1719 the first group of Brethren took up residence in Germantown, just outside Philadelphia, and in 1729 Mack himself led a group across the Atlantic. By 1735 almost all the Brethren had relocated in the new world. Those who remained behind either joined the Mennonites or died out. The immigrants fanned out into the Pennsylvania frontier, and with their distinctive beliefs and lifestyles the Brethren (also known as Dunkards, Dunkers, or Tunkers, from the German word "to immerse") became a permanent part of American religious life.

The Moravians, led by Count Nikolaus Ludwig von Zinzendorf (1700–60), were another sect of radical pietists. He was born into a very pious noble family. Spener was his godfather and the grandmother who raised him could read the Bible in the original languages and engage in the most profound theological discussion. This young aristocrat spent six years at Francke's preparatory school in Halle. He then studied law at Wittenberg University (he had preferred to enter the ministry but his family would not allow it), and after graduation in 1721 he became an official at the court of the king of Saxony. Around that time he received an inheritance that he used to purchase an estate at Berthelsdorf, fifty miles east of Dresden. Frustrated that he could not become a minister, the devout youth felt he might be able to serve God by directing the religious life of the tenants.

A short time later a group of Protestant refugees crossed over the nearby border and at Zinzendorf's invitation settled on his land. They were remnants of the old Moravian, or Hussite, church (known as the *Unitas Fratrem* or *Brüder-Unität*) that had been driven out of their homes by Hapsburg persecution. Under his leadership they founded a village called Herrnhut ("watched over by the Lord"), adopted a modified communitarian lifestyle, and introduced what they regarded as apostolic practices such as the foot-washing rite, the kiss of peace, and casting lots to determine God's will. Their communal religious life included daily worship services, division into "choir" groups (based on age, marital status, and sex), religious education, and an active program of foreign missions. They spent their everyday life in common occupations, and also engaged in instrumental and vocal music. The unmarried were separated by sex, but families lived together and the children were reared in child care centers.

In 1727 Zinzendorf left his government post in order to devote full time to the colony. As his religious thought matured, he gradually moved away from the Halle pietists. He stressed "heart religion"—a deep, mystical experiential faith—as well as Christian community, worldwide evangelism, and the forming of ecumenical relationships. Although he remained a Lutheran, he showed a remarkable tolerance toward other creeds and even devised a plan for the reunion of the Protestant, Roman Catholic, and Eastern Orthodox churches. He was also criticized for holding some mystical beliefs that even the pietists found extreme. In 1737 he received Lutheran ordination, but before long circumstances forced him and his Moravians to form a separate church organization. For eleven years he was even exiled from Herrnhut. He spent his later life in extensive travels and engaged in pastoral and missionary work, preaching, and writing.

Zinzendorf had created a model missionary, service oriented, ecumenical free church that was based on a common experience of salvation, mutual love, and an emphasis on deep, emotional religious expression. The latter was illustrated particularly in his hymns, prayers, poems, and daily "watch words," or *Losungen.* Even today, many people in a variety of Christian communions utilize the annually selected Moravian watch words as a devotional exercise.

Pietism's Social Concern

Perhaps the most vital feature of Pietism was its outward look. Although one turned inward in order to establish a direct relationship with God through faith in Jesus Christ and the Bible was read for personal encouragement, warning, and consolation, at the same time salvation had to be demonstrated by a holy life. The forgiveness of sins and the creation of a new person were bound together. However, holiness did not mean just engaging in "religious" exercises like contemplation, introspection, prayer, seeking visions, or ecstatic utterances, nor was it total separation from the world in order to avoid the stains on one's soul that might be received there. On the contrary, it was expected that Christians would relate to the society around them but not be taken over by the world and its values. They understood fully what Jesus meant when he told his disciples that they were to be in the world but not of the world. The inner strength provided by being in Christ energized individuals as they went out in the world to do God's work there.

Although pietists practiced some forms of asceticism, they did not necessarily feel it made a person more holy. Because the pleasures of the world could get in the way of service to God and fellow human beings, one had to dedicate himself to hard work and self-discipline. One's time was valuable and it should be used in God's service, not frittered away in trifling activities.

Pietism stimulated enthusiasm for education and philanthropy. Spener encouraged the founding of a residential workshop in Frankfurt that would provide shelter and employment for needy people, and a number of German cities established similar institutions. Much more important was the aforementioned endeavor of Francke. His vision of a better world involved not only changes in the church but also a reordering of human structures in the interest of a more just society. His work at Halle was meant to be a model for others.

This could be seen in his educational institutions. He created four types of schools at his foundation. The highest was the *Paedagogium,* a residential school in which the sons of nobles were trained for careers in the army and civil service. The second was the Latin School, an academic preparatory school for the sons of merchant and professional families who were university-bound and would eventually become theologians, lawyers, physicians, and businessmen. The third and largest was the German School, which gave a basic education to the sons *and* daughters of the common people. Finally, there was an elementary school for the very poor children, especially the orphans who lived at the foundation.

Francke employed university students as teachers. They were mainly theology students, which reflected his conviction that they should live as well as study the Christian faith. To improve the quality of teaching, he established a "Seminary of Preceptors" in 1699 as a training institution, and in 1707 it was expanded into a five-year course that included two years of humanities and three years of practice teaching. This was the first organized program of teacher education in Germany. The idea behind this was not only to train good teachers but also theologians who would spread his pedagogical ideas everywhere. This linkage between the university and lower schools was one of Francke's major innovations.

Education also bridged class distinctions. By utilizing students in the schools, capable young men from families of limited means would have the opportunity to obtain a university education. Also, sons from middle class families were allowed to enter the elite *Paedagogium,* while of the ninety-six orphans housed in the foundation in 1706, sixty were enrolled in the Latin school. Francke placed great emphasis on allowing each pupil to develop according to his or her ability. The curricula reflected the pietist desire that education should be relevant to life. Not only did the pupils learn reading and writing, and study the usual academic subjects, but also they took nature walks, went on field trips to art studios and workshops, and were expected to acquire the basics of some trades.

The main goal of pietist education was the development of godly character. The theology students, who themselves were dedicated, gracious, and devout, served as role models for the pupils. It was hoped that the latter would also become individuals who were temperate, responsible, concerned for others, honorable, pious, and kindly. Francke did not depend on the harsh discipline practiced in other schools of his day but saw to it that the children were treated with compassion and consideration. At the same time, he advocated close supervision and control of the pupils and demanded that they learn manners appropriate to their place in society. Thus, a school was not just a place where information was transmitted; it was also an institution to transform character.

At the time of his death in 1727, these remarkable schools employed 183 teachers and approximately 250 student assistants and enrolled nearly 2,300 children. This encouraged other wealthy citizens and princes to become interested in fostering education, the most important of whom was the Prussian king, Frederick William I. His famous decree of 1717 establishing state-supported elementary schools was inspired by the example of Francke in Halle. Seminaries were also created under pietist direction to train teachers for these schools. Thus, it was on the foundation of the pietist-type schools that the later Prussian educational system, the best in Europe, was built.

The Francke foundation was a beehive of other philanthropic activities besides the orphanage and schools. It was a training and sending center for foreign missions (see chapter 16). In 1698 a home for widows was erected where they could live in comfort with medical and spiritual care. When a physician donated his property and services to the foundation in 1702, this enabled the creation of a

THE
LAMENTABLE
COMPLAINTS
OF
NICK FROTH the Tapſter, and
RVLEROST the Cooke.
Concerning the reſtraint lately ſet forth, againſt drinking, potting, and piping on the Sabbath day, and againſt ſelling meate.

Printed in the yeare, 1641.

medical and pharmaceutical dispensary. The establishment had its own hospital, which was the first in Germany where medical students received clinical instruction. In 1699 a retail bookstore was opened that had branches around the country. A library was founded in 1708 that was open to the general public. A press came into being in 1697, and a printing plant was set up four years later that produced Bibles and religious literature.

Of crucial significance in the latter enterprise was Karl Hildebrand, Baron von Canstein (1667–1719). From a prominent Prussian family, he was trained as a lawyer and became a court official in Berlin. There he came under the influence of Spener, who introduced him to Francke's work. A deeply devout layperson, he became totally committed to the foundation and did all he could to promote its work. Besides engaging in fund raising, he donated large sums himself and personally funded 50 percent of the costs of the *Collegium Orientale,* the working group of scholars that Francke had formed to do research in oriental and modern languages in order to expand biblical knowledge. He maintained a branch of the book sales operation in his Berlin house and used his political connections to find positions for pastors, military chaplains, and tutors who had been trained in Halle.

One of Francke's supporters suggested that the foundation press should be used to publish Bibles and that they be distributed from Halle. Inspired by the idea, Canstein assumed leadership of the venture and raised money for it. By 1710 Bibles were rolling off the press, and nearly 2.5 million copies of the Scriptures were produced during the next decades. After his death it was renamed the Canstein Bible Society. Although in the nineteenth century it would be overshadowed by the newer Bible societies, the Canstein Society was the foremost distributor of the Scriptures in Europe in the eighteenth century.

PIETIST LITERATURE

Pietist hymns and devotional literature had much in common with that produced by the Orthodox. Quite influential was the hymnwriter Joachim Neander (1650–80), a teacher and pastor in the Reformed church. In 1674 he began using Spener's idea of small group meetings for worship at the Reformed grammar school in Düsseldorf and was dismissed for doing so. He then became a pastor in Bremen. In his short life he wrote more than sixty hymns, including the beloved "Praise to the Lord, the Almighty." Most significantly, he was the first Reformed musician to break with the Calvinist practice of using only metrical psalms in their worship services. At this time even Lutheran hymns were forbidden in Reformed churches. The Calvinists felt they were human productions and believed that God could only be worshiped properly through divinely inspired hymns, namely, the Psalms.

Gerhard Tersteegen (1697–1769) was another important Reformed pietist. He had been apprenticed to a shopkeeper at Mülheim/Ruhr and was converted in 1716. Though his origins were in the Reformed church, he became increasingly an unattached mystic. For a few years he took up the trade of a solitary ribbonmaker and spent his free time as a spiritual counselor—writing letters, visiting people, and occasionally speaking. Later he became a tutor and a medical social worker, but he never married or entered the ministry. Strongly influenced by Quietism, Tersteegen was one of the most profound of the Protestant mystics, as reflected in his one hundred hymns.

A major Lutheran hymnwriter was Francke's son-in-law, Johann A. Freylinghausen (1670–1739). Although he was a teacher of theology and homiletics and involved in the administration of the foundation, he was also known for the *Geistreiches Gesangbuch*, the most important collection of pietist hymns. The first edition appeared in 1704 with 683 hymns. In the 1741 edition it had expanded to 1,582 hymns, 44 of which he had composed. They were characterized by depth of feeling and a clear understanding of Scripture.

Some of the early pietist hymns were produced by the Württemberg groups, of which Philipp Friedrich Hiller (1699–1769) was the most noted. A student of Bengel and a pastor, he wrote 1,073 hymns of varying quality, which were published in the *Geistliches Liederkästlein* (1762–67). The Moravian leader Zinzendorf also composed more than 2,000 hymns, some of which are found in modern hymn books ("Jesus, Thy Blood and Righteousness").

The Orthodox devotional works found great favor with the pietists. Arndt's *True Christianity* and other writings were quite popular. Sermons by Spener and Francke were published and widely distributed. The devotional collection by Johann Friedrich Starck (1680–1756), a pastor in Frankfurt am Main, *Daily Handbook in Good and Evil* (1727–31), is still used today. In 1730 the first German devotional paper, *Spiritual Tidings,* was published in Berleburg, and between 1726 and 1742 the seven-volume *Berleburg Bible* was produced. This was an original translation accompanied by a radical pietist commentary and exposition of the text. Tersteegen also wrote much devotional material, including the highly mystical *Selected Biographies of the Saints.*

Even as Pietism seemed to be ascendant in the German churches, it was already being undermined by the forces of rationalism gathering under the banner of the Enlightenment. By midcentury it was in retreat, and even such bastions as Halle fell under Enlightenment influence. Yet the historical impact of Pietism was enormous. For one thing, it released the Protestant faith from the bonds of tradition and restored the primacy of personal decision in spiritual matters, thus contributing to the growth of human freedom. Second, in contrast to spiritual mysticism, Pietism forestalled the growth of a vague "Christianity" outside of and opposed to the church. It avoided an anti-institutional religiosity that could have been directed against the church. Third, Pietism renewed and strengthened the ideal of primitive Christianity as exemplary for the present. Finally, with its emphasis upon the spiritual side of life, the uniqueness of personal supremacy of feelings and emotions over the intellect, Pietism helped pave the way for German romanticism and the rise of nationalism. Within two generations the religious sentiments that had been so aroused by Pietism would be transferred to a new, albeit quasi-religious entity, the *Volk* and nation.

15

SCIENCE AND ENLIGHTENMENT CHALLENGE THE CHURCH

The seventeenth and eighteenth centuries witnessed the rise of a new attitude toward nature that led to the development of modern science and dramatic changes in human life. This new outlook caused Western civilization to take on a much more secular character and enabled the West to extend its domination throughout the world by means of superior naval and military technology. It culminated in a radical alteration of thought that became the foundation of modern society. Such an awareness of science and technology did not emerge suddenly, as if out of nowhere, but rather it had deep roots that extended to antiquity and developed through the Middle Ages.

MEDIEVAL SCIENCE

The medieval view of science was a synthesis of ancient Greek ideas and Christian theology. The Scholastics were deeply impressed by the work of Aristotle because it gave an orderly account of nature. Following the great Greek thinker, they believed that every creature, according to its degree of perfection, had an assigned place in the universe. A "great chain of being" descended from God and the angels through the physically perfect stars, planets, sun, and moon to the four elements of this world—earth, water, air, and fire. In this system the earth stood motionless at the center of nine hollow spheres that rotated around it daily. Later called by scholars the "geocentric" explanation of the universe, the medieval understanding was that seven mysterious, crystal-clear "spheres" surrounded the earth, each of which contained a heavenly body, arranged in the following order of distance—the moon, Mercury, Venus, the sun, Mars, Jupiter, and Saturn. An eighth held the fixed stars, and an outer ring called the "first mover" (*primum mobile* in Latin) caused all the spheres to move around the earth in precise, clock-like fashion every twenty-four hours.

Unlike in the modern conception of the universe, distance within this system was not vast and endless. One medieval writer stated that if a person could travel forty miles a day, he could reach the sphere of the fixed stars in 8,000 years. Although God was the source of all power and movement, still, in line with popular astrology, it was believed that the spheres could influence events on earth. For example, Saturn made people sad and brought disaster, Mars produced war, Venus encouraged love, and Jupiter brought prosperity. The sun constantly lit the entire universe and night was the cone-shaped shadow cast by the earth. Because the sun moved while the earth stood still, night was thought to be a long, black finger revolving like the hands of a clock. Space was neither dark nor silent, and when people gazed into the night sky, they looked through darkness but not at it. Most late medieval scholars actually had come to think of the world not as flat but rather as a globe, but they assumed the existence of rather strange creatures in other lands because they had such limited contact outside Europe.

The medieval view differed greatly from twentieth century cosmology, but it did seem to fit observed phenomena. Anyone could plainly see the movement of the heavenly bodies in a circular path around the earth. Also, the world seemed to be standing still in the midst of all this motion. Christians read their theology into science, and the greatest medieval poem, Dante's *The Divine Comedy,* described the universe in geocentric terms, placing heaven above the earth and hell beneath, in the southern hemisphere. At the center of this system was the earth, the home of humanity, the crown of God's creation. Here Christ came to suffer and die for human redemption. Moreover, the hierarchical structure of the universe assured people

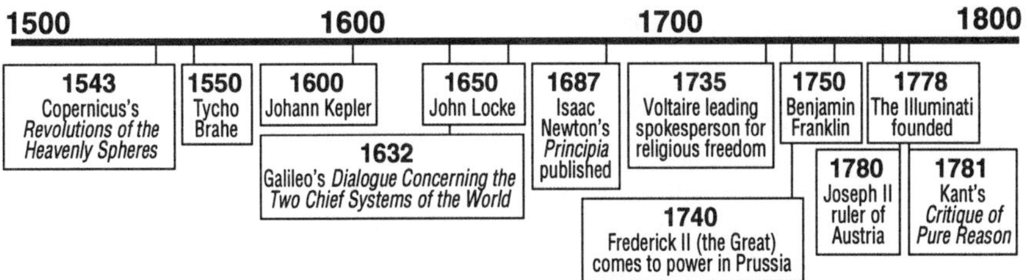

that God was in control. The geocentric theory found support in Joshua's command that the sun should stand still (Joshua 10:12–13), in Ecclesiastes 1:5, and in various statements in the Psalms.

Even in ancient times, however, some astronomers questioned the simplistic geocentric system. In the second century A.D. Claudius Ptolemy explained the variations in planetary motion by suggesting that the earth was not exactly at the center of the universe. He also maintained that the heavenly bodies moved on their spheres in small circles, called epicycles, while the spheres themselves revolved around the earth. Muslim scholars translated Ptolemy's work, and it came to the attention of Christians during the twelfth century. Despite the corrections Ptolemy had made in the Aristotelian geocentric view, the Scholastics found still more errors in the system, and by the sixteenth century it had become apparent that modifications were needed in the tables of planetary movements.

Attempts to describe astronomical phenomena more accurately led to a revision in cosmology and the beginning of what historians call the "scientific revolution." The pioneer of the new outlook, Nicolaus Copernicus, was born in Poland in 1473 and educated in Italy where he studied canon law, medicine, and mathematics. After the completion of his training, he was appointed to the staff of a cathedral in East Prussia where he devoted his time to church administration, a medical practice, and the study of classical writers and astronomy. In 1515 the pope invited scholars to submit proposals for calendar revision, and in the process of working on the project attention was drawn to the flaws in the Aristotelian-Ptolemaic system. This problem fascinated Copernicus, since he knew about the work of Aristarchus of Samos, a Greek astronomer in the third century B.C., who had suggested that the earth rotated on its own axis and along with the other planets revolved around the sun.

The Polish thinker decided to make mathematical calculations based on a heliocentric (sun-centered) hypothesis to find out if they could account for planetary motion more accurately. The model of the universe that he developed retained some medieval notions like epicycles and the perfect circular movement of the heavenly bodies, but it departed enough from traditional Christian views to upset the intellectual community of his day. Martin Luther reflected the outlook of most sixteenth-century scholars when he declared, "This fool wishes to reverse the entire science of astronomy; but sacred Scripture tells us that Joshua commanded the sun to stand still and not the earth."[1] This kind of observation disregarded what some modern biblical interpreters call "the principle of phenomenal (appearance) language."

Scientists also attacked the new theory by pointing out that if the earth revolved on its axis, there would be a constant wind. Copernicus replied that this would not happen because the atmosphere revolved at the same speed and in the same direction as the earth. They argued further that if the earth moved around the sun, then the stars would change position in the sky. Copernicus answered that the distance traveled by the earth was so small compared to the distance to the stars that the actual change in position could not be measured. However, the greatest problem for the heliocentric view was the need for a new explanation of gravity and motion. It took a century of debate and thought before the brilliant English scientist Isaac Newton would supply this through his law of universal gravitation.

Despite Luther's less than enthusiastic endorsement of Copernicus's hypothesis, his *Six Books Concerning the Revolutions of the Heavenly Spheres* ironically was published in Wittenberg in 1543, a few weeks before the author's death. Its impact on the early modern scientific community was dramatic, and the scholarly response fell into three categories.

First were those who upheld the traditional Aristotelian position. They made little use of mathematics and experimentation and continued to rely on logical arguments derived from a few basic premises.

A second group, led by Tycho Brahe and Francis Bacon, advocated the inductive method of reasoning. They believed that scientists should formulate hypotheses based upon observed phenomena and experiments that others could repeat, and eventually such work would lead to the truth.

The third group, which operated from a Platonic understanding of nature and reality, relied upon the deductive approach. They believed that the important details of the universe could be explained by mathematical calculations. Copernicus, Galileo, and Kepler fell into this category.

The Danish astronomer Tycho Brahe (1546–1601) deviated from Copernicus by arguing that the five planets revolved around the sun, which in turn moved around the immobile earth. His much more important associate, Johann Kepler (1571–1630), in an attempt to harmonize the work of Copernicus and Brahe discovered that the planets moved in an elliptical rather than circular manner around the sun. He also accurately calculated the speed of planetary motion. In the process of formulating these ideas he unwittingly helped to lay the groundwork for modern science. However, Kepler would scarcely be considered a scientist in the twentieth-century definition of the term. He was a pantheist who held that the universe was an expression of deity and that God was especially revealed by the sun.

Most significantly, Kepler launched the search for a single law that could be expressed mathematically and would explain the motion of the universe. Before this could be achieved, a greater comprehension of motion was necessary and this was the contribution of Galileo Galilei. Born in Pisa in 1564, he taught mathematics at the universities of Pisa and Padua and then was appointed a resident scholar at the court of the duke of Tuscany. Despite his many observations that served to support the heliocentric rather than the medieval view of the universe, he always remained somewhat leery of nonmathematical proofs for this because he believed that mathematics held the primary key to knowledge.

One of the first scientists to use a telescope, Galileo noticed four moons that revolved around Jupiter, spots on the sun, and the rough surface of the moon. Since Aristotelian cosmology could not account for these irregularities, he concluded that the heavenly bodies were not made of a pure and perfect crystalline substance because the sun had dark spots and the moon and planets seemed to be made of the same materials as the earth. In addition, he was convinced that whatever made things move on earth must also cause the revolutions of the heavenly bodies. Thus, he saw mass and motion as the twin concepts that explained the universe.

Galileo's *Dialogue Concerning the Two Chief Systems of the World: The Ptolemaic and the Copernican* (1632) presented these ideas in the form of a debate about the merits of the new conception of astronomy. Written in Italian, the language of the people, rather than Latin, the book's rejection of the medieval view angered many conservative Catholics. To his critics he said, "The Bible tells us how to go to heaven, not how the heavens go." Despite his friendship with some members of the papal curia, he was brought before the Inquisition and forced to deny his scientific ideas. His books were banned, and he was placed under house arrest near Florence, where he died in 1642.

In contrast to the treatment of Galileo was the freedom and wide acclaim received by Isaac Newton, the scholar who developed the foundation for the modern understanding of the universe. Born in 1642 and educated at Cambridge University, where he became professor of mathematics at the age of twenty-seven, Newton later served as president of the prestigious Royal Society of London for Improving Natural Knowledge for twenty-five years.

Because he was not only a genius but also a very eccentric person, Newton is difficult to assess. Occasionally he would put aside his studies for long periods of time, but when he returned to them he could bury himself in his work. He was known to lose himself in thought to the point that he would wander toward his college dining hall, become distracted, and then return to work unaware that he had not eaten. Often he was pressured to finish tasks by friends or when rivals claimed to have solved scientific problems before him. Once, the astronomer Edmund Halley, his close friend, discovered to his dismay that Newton had worked out some precise calculations for a problem but then mislaid them while others were trying to do what he had forgotten. He also spent time on wild speculations, drawing upon biblical numerology to set the date for the end of the world.

One wonders how he was able to combine imagination and accuracy in the right amount to produce such influential work. Yet this proud, ingenious person devised a model of the physical universe accepted for generations. His worldview remains scientific truth for most people today, and it is regarded as accurate in all realms of nature except at the atomic level and speeds approaching that of light.

In 1665–66 Newton was forced by an outbreak of the plague to leave Cambridge and seek refuge in his country home. There he devised a series of mathematical calculations that brought together the concepts of planetary motion elaborated by Kepler and the concepts about motion on earth discovered by Galileo. He demonstrated that the same force caused planets to stay in their heavenly orbits and objects to fall to earth. This "law of gravity" extended to all parts of the universe. His proof for the view was based on the fact that the moon moves toward the earth at the same rate of speed that an object falls within the earth's atmosphere, sixteen feet per second. Because the requisite figures to support this contention were not available at the time, his findings were not published until 1687 when they appeared in his massive work (in Latin), *Mathematical Principles of Natural Philosophy.* The *Principia,* as the book is usually identified, explained the universal law of gravity and defined centrifugal force, momentum, and inertia in mathematical terms. It also showed that the pull of the moon and the sun caused tides, the earth and other planets were flattened at the poles, and the path of comets could be tracked because they were under the sun's influence.

In addition to being the capstone of the cosmological revolution, Newton's scholarly work established the methodology of modern science. Included in this approach were three basic principles. First was the insistence on *experimentation.* Newton was very suspicious of general ideas and felt that wherever possible they should be tested by experimental observance. Second, he believed in the law of parsimony, or *simplicity.* This states that when there are several valid explanations for a phenomenon, the simplest one is to be preferred. Third, he relied on extensive use of *mathematics.* The universal law of gravity was cast as a mathematical formula: the product of the masses and the square of the distance between them. It was this combination of experimental observation and mathematics that constituted the foundation of modern science, and by the early eighteenth century the Newtonian worldview was accepted by most educated Europeans. Alexander Pope spoke for more than just Englishmen when he wrote:

> Nature and Nature's Laws lay hid in night:
> God said, "Let Newton be!" and all was light.[2]

Reaction Against Science

Despite such lavish praise, the medieval view did not give way graciously before the onslaught of the new science. Those who defended Aristotle reacted in a narrow and belligerent fashion to individuals such as Galileo who tried to present their ideas to a wider audience. The shocking nature of the heliocentric theory to people in the sixteenth and seventeenth centuries could rightfully be compared to the controversies generated by Darwinian evolutionary teaching in more recent times.

In addition to Galileo another martyr for the cause of scientific change was Giordano Bruno. An Italian Dominican who was forced to leave his order in 1576 for alleged heresy, he wandered around Europe lecturing, teaching, and writing. A versatile genius, he mastered philosophy, theology, and natural science. Bruno was influenced by the writings of Hermes Trismegistos, who was believed to have been a mysterious scholar who predated the coming of Christ and inspired Plato. The Hermetic tradition, which encouraged the use of magic and the worship of the sun, led Bruno to reject the Aristotelian view and support the heliocentric theory. But he went beyond the conservative aspects of the Copernican outlook to suggest that the universe was infinite and consisted of innumerable worlds similar to the solar system. He maintained that the Bible should be followed for its moral teachings but not as an astronomical textbook.

In 1591 Bruno was invited to Venice by one of the city's rulers who wished to learn a method of memorization from him. Disappointed by his studies, he denounced Bruno to the Inquisition. In 1600 he was condemned to be burned for his heretical teachings, but before he died Bruno addressed his judges with the poignant lines that have inspired lovers of intellectual freedom ever since: "Perhaps your fear in passing judgment on me is greater than mine in receiving it."

The atmosphere of intolerance and persecution that followed in the wake of the scientific revolution affected not only scholars but also socially different people who were popularly labeled as "witches." The period 1600–1680 marked the high point of the European witch scare, and thousands of these unfortunate men and women fell victim to the anxieties of their neighbors. It was commonly believed that they made secret agreements with the devil and regularly attended "sabbaths." Travel to these meetings was said to be supernatural and involved the use of flying broomsticks or winged goats. The attendees allegedly worshiped the devil, who appeared either as a black-bearded man, a toad, or a goat. After listening to strange music and participating in disgusting acts of homage, the witches then engaged in sexual orgies with Satan and his servants. Often feasts of roasted children, fricassee of bat, or unearthed corpses took place. When they were not at these assemblies, the witches supposedly suckled familiar spirits manifested as bats, toads, or moles. They also caused infertility in newlyweds, diseases, and storms.

THE GEOCENTRIC THEORY

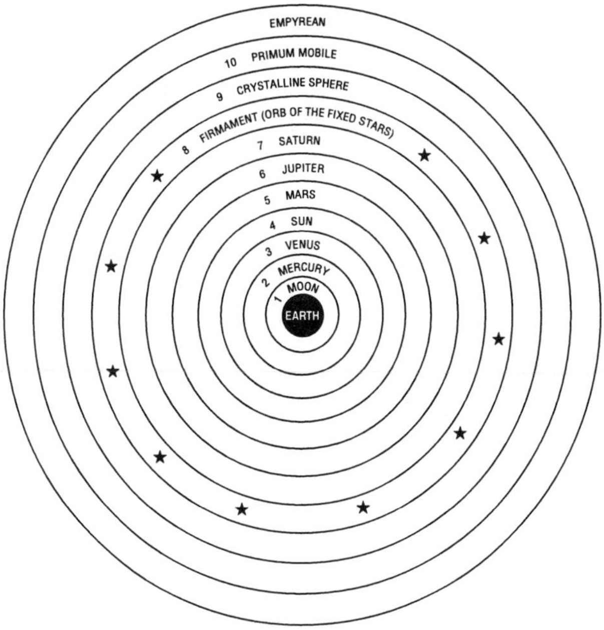

Torture was used to extract from people accused of being witches the evidence for these charges. Although horrible pain would make a person admit almost anything, there were unquestionably some individuals who really did believe they were witches. Most of those who confessed were cruelly executed.

Scholars in the seventeenth-century Age of Orthodoxy routinely included discussions of witchcraft in their works and some even published encyclopedias on the subject. These works maintained that every detail of witchcraft was true and that all objections to the persecution of these emissaries of Satan must be silenced. Most writers believed the number of witches was actually increasing and the reason for this sorry state of affairs was the "leniency" of judges. Although another factor contributing to the renewed emphasis on witchcraft was the struggle in Europe between Catholics and Protestants, still the primary blame for the terrible persecution must be located in the confusion resulting from the transition from the medieval cosmology to the modern scientific outlook.

Between 1630 and 1700 most informed Europeans came to accept the heliocentric viewpoint and the mathematical-mechanical description of the universe as explained by Newton. Thus, an emphasis on uniform law and rationality led inexorably to the decline of belief in witchcraft. Evil beings in league with the devil could not easily exist in a world governed by Newtonian laws. The turn in thinking was illustrated well by the reaction of the judge at one of the last witchcraft trials in England. He dismissed the case with the sarcastic remark that there was no law against traveling between London and Oxford on a broomstick.

THE ENLIGHTENMENT

The new scientific outlook of the seventeenth century was one of certainty about the ability of human reason and experience to solve all problems. Impressed by the achievements of the natural scientists in discovering the laws of the physical universe, the men of the eighteenth-century Enlightenment believed they could find laws that governed society and human behavior. As they attempted to do this, they changed their method from a reliance on mathematics to a more literary approach.

The new movement of social change centered in France among a group of radical writers called *philosophes*, or philosophers. It is preferable to use the French term to refer to these individuals because they did not engage in philosophical speculation as such, but rather they were popularizers and propagandists. They were not so much interested in advancing the frontiers of knowledge as they were reconstructing society according to natural laws and reason. To accomplish this, the philosophes wrote plays, histories, novels, political tracts, works of literary criticism, and scientific studies. Aiming to reach a large audience, they used the vernacular rather than Latin and developed an interesting, clear style of writing. Many of them earned enough from the sale of their books to live comfortably, while others had private means or were supported by wealthy patrons.

Beginning in France, the Enlightenment radiated to other areas of Europe—Germany, Austria, Russia, Britain, Italy, Spain—and even to the American colonies, where individuals under the influence of the philosophes were leading figures in the Revolution. The most famous spokesperson for the new social movement was François-Marie Arouet (1694–1778), who took the name of Voltaire. Born into a middle class family and educated at a Jesuit school, he studied law for a time but abandoned this for a literary career. He established his reputation as a writer of classical tragedies and throughout his life wrote for the theater. Voltaire was one of the first "best-selling" authors. During one seven-year period a million and a half copies of his books were sold. He penned his first work at age seventeen, and by the time of his death his published writings filled more than seventy volumes.

As a young man Voltaire was imprisoned in the infamous Bastille in Paris for insulting a noble and was forced to go into exile in England. He enjoyed the freedom that he experienced there and acquired an enthusiasm for the ideas of Newton and John Locke. He devoted himself to the task of enlightening his native land as well as the entire world through applying their teachings to the old aristocratic societies. Returning to France, he published the *Philosophical Letters on the English* (1734), in which he compared the freedom of speech and religion, equality before the law, and equal taxation —which he believed existed in Britain—with the injustices and inequality in France. The government compelled him to flee from his homeland once more, and this time he settled just across the border in Switzerland. In spite of his friendship with aristocrats, princes, and kings, he never abandoned his belief in social justice for all people, which was based upon the principles of personal liberty, legal equality, and freedom of thought and expression.

Another leading philosophe, Denis Diderot (1713–84), publicized the new scientific approach through a massive work known as the *Encyclopédie.* The series of twenty-eight volumes was composed over a twenty-year time span (1751–72), and seven supplementary volumes were penned a few years later. The contributors included nearly all the leading figures in the French Enlightenment. More than a mere collection of facts, the articles explained that people could improve themselves only if they replaced faith with reason as a guiding principle. As their ideas constituted a threat to existing authority, the earlier volumes were suppressed. However, by the time the last book in the series appeared, the *Encyclopédie* had triumphed over intolerance and could be openly distributed. A unique feature of Diderot's magnum opus was the inclusion of 3,000 pages of illustrations that were especially helpful to physicians, scientists, and skilled craftsmen. The contributors constantly criticized existing institutions and ideas. For example, the article on the goddess Juno ridiculed the cult of the Virgin Mary, the one on salt pointed out the injustice of regressive taxes on the poor, and another on the Swiss city of Geneva condemned the government of France.

Deism

The complicity of the Roman Catholic church in the social injustices of the time led most philosophes to adopt a new religious outlook known as "deism." First expressed by a group of English writers beginning with Lord Herbert of Cherbury in the first half of the seventeenth century, it rejected belief in special revelation. The latter supposedly corrupted the purity of natural religion by introducing conflict and superstition in place of agreement and truth. Lord Herbert contended that the following ideas were common to all religions: (1) the existence of a Supreme Being, (2) the need or obligation to worship that Being, (3) the importance of virtue and piety as part of worship, (4) the necessity of repentance from sins, and (5) divine rewards and punishments in both the present and future life. Those who rely on reason recognize the validity of these points. This was the teaching of the true church that existed before people were misled by the priests and prophets of the various religions. It was the rites and doctrines of institutional religion that were the source of the most savage persecutions in history. Deism also denied any direct intervention of God in the natural order. His function was that of the "first cause," the watchmaker who fashioned the world in the beginning like a clock. He then wound up His creation, and in accordance with His design it now runs smoothly without any need for further involvement.

Lord Herbert's ideas found fertile ground in eighteenth-century Europe because geographical expansion had widened people's knowledge of other faiths. During the Middle Ages Christendom seemed to stand at the center of history, but when seafarers, merchants, and missionaries returned to Europe with stories of millions of people in China, India, and elsewhere who had never heard of Christ, some began to doubt the exclusive claims of Christianity. The worship of "nature's God" and the use of "natural theology" (knowledge of the divine that was not derived from revelation, i.e., Scripture) seemed to offer a solution to the problem.

Natural theology had had a long and respectable history in the church, but something happened to it because of the scientific revolution. It had developed a mechanistic and materialistic view of the universe in which the abstractions of the mathematicians were increasingly believed to be true and the worldview of the Bible less so. When placed against the mechanical regularity of the new science, the miracles reported in the Bible appeared fanciful and irrational. Time and space had exploded to such vast dimensions that the Christian account of history extending from creation to the last judgment and focusing on a tiny entity in the universe seemed petty and irrelevant. Deism offered a way to be religious and at the same time in tune with the new scientific understanding.

During the first half of the eighteenth century in England, deists and orthodox theologians disputed over miracles and the Old Testament prophecies of Christ. Some deists, such as the Third Earl of Shaftesbury, declared that all descriptions of God that depicted His vengeance, jealously, and vindictiveness were blasphemous and that He was a gentle, loving, and benevolent Being who intended for humans to behave in a kind and tolerant fashion. But deists lost in the struggle with the defenders of Christianity who demonstrated a vitality in their faith not found in a natural religion that was liberated from revelation. Deism was shown to be a collection of ideas rather than a living faith. If one pursued the quest for the rational proof of religion, he would end up a skeptic. The validity of the Christian faith rested on an inner experience with God, not on the existence of a vague, impersonal first cause. Thus, in England the choice was between Christianity and skepticism. Those who remained Christian tended to join the Wesleyan or evangelical revival, while the ones inclined toward skepticism turned away from religion altogether and devoted their attention to other activities they regarded more useful.

Although the debate died out in England, it was pursued with vigor on the continent. In France the chief spokesperson for rationalism was Voltaire. He was more capable than the English deists, and French Catholicism had few able defenders. Voltaire felt he had identified its problems as priestly exploitation, superstition, intolerance, and persecution. He advocated tolerance for all religions except the institutional church, which he denounced with such colorful phrases as "crush the infamous thing." He hoped "to see the last king strangled in the bowels of the last priest." Voltaire was a foe of revealed religion, arguing that the Bible was full of absurdities, contradictions, errors, and immoralities, and it depicted a God unworthy of the title of Supreme Being. He also championed natural religion, one in which the moral virtues of love and kindness would resolve the social ills caused by erroneous belief.

Advocates of deism were also to be found in Germany. Hermann Samuel Reimarus (1894–1768), a scholar of the ancient Near East at Hamburg who was one of the "founding fathers" of biblical criticism, contended that the miraculous element was introduced into Scripture because of the fanaticism and deceit of the biblical writers. He explained the origins of Christianity from a naturalistic standpoint. For him the great miracle of revelation was the world, and in nature one could find God, morality, and immortality.

Gotthold Ephraim Lessing (1729–81), the well-known dramatist and the son of a pastor in Saxony, had been trained in Lutheran orthodoxy, but he abandoned this for the Enlightenment. He published one of Reimarus's works and opened the door to critical study of the Bible. Lessing insisted that the life and personality of Jesus might be different from that portrayed in the gospels and the subsequent teaching of the church. He also questioned whether authentic belief could properly be bound up with historical events and denied that revelation could take place in history. If religious truth was genuine, it had to be so universally and was of a different order from that of historical events.

In two important works, *Nathan the Wise* (1779) and *The Education of the Human Race* (1780), Lessing called upon his readers to adopt a "natural" or "positive" religion, one that recognized God, formed noble conceptions of Him, and directed individuals to keep these in mind in all that they did and thought. The "inner truth" of religion could not be derived from a written tradition but might be felt and experienced. However, he said, there was no Lord of history within history who would provide people with final truth. For him the guidelines of the Bible were childish and those of reason were mature.

German rationalism did not go unanswered. The major philosopher of the eighteenth century, Immanuel Kant (1724–1804), a professor at Königsberg in East Prussia who had been trained as a pietist, sought to combine rationalism and orthodox Christianity. In such works as the *Critique of Pure Reason* (1781) he stated that science and reason did not provide proof of the existence of God, the moral law, and immortality. Science described the world but could not provide a guide for ethical living. Such human experiences as the awareness of beauty, conscience, and religious feeling were real even though science could not deal with them. They were instincts implanted by God to teach humans good and evil and to force them to choose between right and wrong. He called this the "categorical imperative." Kant's insistence that science was limited and that moral truth came in a different way than scientific knowledge refuted the naive rationalism of the philosophes.

Europe in 1715

Deism was also popular in the American colonies. Natural religion was introduced in the New World through the writings of English rationalists and became even more in vogue on this side of the Atlantic. Moreover, the books of the French philosophes were widely read. Some scholars argue that the majority of the leaders of the revolution and the new nation were deists. Among the best-known of these were George Washington, Thomas Jefferson, and Benjamin Franklin.

The lifestyle of Washington resembled that of an English country gentleman of his day, since he was a vestryman and a frequent but not regular church attender. However, he never took Communion and his official papers clearly reveal Enlightenment views of religion. He often referred to God as "the great Disposer of Events" or "Father of Lights" but seldom as "the divine Author of our blessed religion." Open-minded, with a firm sense of dignity, a believer in religious liberty, he manifested no interest in Christian theology or belief in the deity of Christ.

Like Washington, Jefferson practiced the easy-going Anglicanism of wealthy Virginians and served his turn on the vestry as those of his social class did. He enjoyed reading deist literature and shared its outlook. Rejecting the writings of Paul, Augustine, Plato, and the Platonists, he spent his life searching for what he considered "the pure teachings of Jesus" that had been obscured by these theologians and mystics. Jefferson eventually went beyond deism to become a Unitarian, following the ideas of Joseph Priestley.

When political foes accused him of unbelief, Jefferson responded that he indeed was a Christian and as proof pointed to his commitment to the pure and noble teachings of Jesus. He proceeded to strip away the work of Paul and other theologians and to isolate from the gospels the words of Jesus Himself. The things Jesus said and did, he maintained, reveal the mark of a superior, sublime mind standing out like "diamonds from a dunghill." What survives of Jesus' teachings is a moral code that places one's duty to others alongside duty to oneself. Jesus made no claim to be God and His mission was to teach brotherhood, hence correcting the distorted view held by the first-century Jews.

His understanding of Jesus was best displayed in the *Jefferson Bible,* which remained buried in his papers and was only published in the twentieth century. This was a scissors-and-paste job done in a notebook where the "genuine" passages from the four gospels were cut out and arranged side-by-side. Sections reporting miracles (including Christ's resurrection) and theological discourses were omitted.

Another important colonial leader, Benjamin Franklin, went even further to exercise a gentle cynicism toward evangelical faith. Like many Bostonians, Franklin abandoned Puritan Calvinism early in his career. As a printer and publisher in Philadelphia, he befriended George Whitefield, but the famous evangelist was never able to win him to evangelical Christianity. Franklin recorded his observations of Quakers, Baptists, Brethren, Jews, and Roman Catholics with the tone of an uninvolved student of comparative religion. For a time he was attracted by Anglicanism, but he seldom attended church. Rejecting any orthodox creed, he adopted a few simple affirmations including belief in a Supreme Being, a future state, and rewards and punishments.

In a manner typical of American deists, Franklin considered the deity of Christ a matter of tolerant indifference. As he stated in a well-known letter to Ezra Stiles,

> It is a question I do not dogmatize upon, having never studied it, and think it needless to busy myself with it now, when I expect soon an opportunity of knowing the Truth with less Trouble. I see no harm, however, in its being believed, if that Belief has the good Consequence, as it probably has, of making his Doctrines more respected

> and better observed; especially as I do not perceive, that the Supreme takes it amiss, by distinguishing the Unbelievers in his Government of the World with any peculiar Marks of his Displeasure.[3]

Here one sees a trace of the Enlightenment view that religion was necessary for the lower classes. Voltaire, for example, remarked that he wanted his servants to be Christians so that they might be influenced by their faith to behave more honestly and diligently.

FREEMASONRY

Another attempt during the Enlightenment to apply reason to religion and society was expressed in the Masonic order. Organized Freemasonry began in 1717 with the establishment of the Grand Lodge in London. For disillusioned Christians Masonry became a new faith based upon a belief in the power of nature, and it provided ceremonies and rituals open to a variety of interpretations. Its essential social nature, reinforced by secrecy, gave an extraordinary sense of community to those who were alienated from the Christian church.

The roots of the Masonic movement go back to the Middle Ages when each craft had a guild or similar organization that provided benefits and mutual support for its members. By the eighteenth century, however, the free market had come to dominate society, and the old economic structures lost out. Gradually most guilds had become purely ceremonial institutions, and their power to control wages, the quality of goods produced, and the labor force disappeared. Only the stonemasons' guilds, which emphasized the unique mathematical and architectural skills of their members, were able to continue in a new and dynamic historical role.

By the late seventeenth century various masonic "lodges," as their guilds were starting to be called, in Scotland and England began admitting gentlemen who were not craftsmen into their order. Many of the new members were wealthy and could contribute capital for the construction projects of those who were already lodge members. The ancient tradition of the mason added to their prestige because they were responsible for building the great churches and cathedrals as well as the palaces of kings and impressive public buildings in the cities. They also drew upon a legendary history that traced their roots back to the building of the Egyptian pyramids and the Temple of Solomon.

The same documents that contained the mythical beginnings of the guild specified moral responsibilities and decreed that masonic teachings be kept secret so that the building techniques of the individual masters could be restricted to guild members. Then, as Neoplatonic and Rosicrucian elements were added to the ideas of the medieval craftsmen, the stonemason's tradition was transformed into a lodge for individuals of any background. These changes caused a reinterpretation of the tools of the mason into a system of symbols for personal morality and transformation. The practitioners of the "royal art," as Masonry was called, worshiped the God of Newtonian science, the grand architect of the universe, as a powerful symbol of order, regularity, and stability.

Much of the appeal of Freemasonry in the eighteenth century lay in its claim to be in contact with a universal wisdom that was revealed in the mathematical and architectural skills displayed in ancient buildings. The prestige attached to the Masonic lodges attracted an impressive group of members that bridged profound social differences. A new form of social relationship emerged that captured the imagination of educated Europeans, both nobles and commoners. Its members sought to apply the Masonic ideas of social mobility, religious toleration, and dedication to science to the larger society.

No better example could be given of the significance of their ideals than in the American colonies. If there is one thread that runs through the movement for independence and the founding of a new republic in America, it is the Masonic order. During the revolution the lodges became rallying points for the colonials in their struggle with their British rulers. Freemasonry had actually come to America shortly after the founding of the Grand Lodge of London. Benjamin Franklin joined one of the first lodges in 1731 and was elected grand master of the Pennsylvania order in 1734. George Washington was initiated into the Fredricksburg (Virginia) Lodge Number Four in 1752. Other American patriots who belonged to the Masonic order included Alexander Hamilton, Patrick Henry, John Paul Jones, and Paul Revere.

The spread of Freemasonry into France and other European lands led to a closer identification of its ideals with the Enlightenment. The rituals and symbolism of the craft tradition were embellished into a system of higher degrees and rites that incorporated the legends of the Knights Templar, Teutonic Knights, and Knights Hospitaller of St. John. The continental Masonic bodies not only stood for deism and equality but also became avidly anticlerical and functioned as cells for political and social reform.

The most radical of these groups were the Illuminati, a Masonic sect founded in Bavaria in 1778 by Adam Weishaupt (1748–1830), who had been trained in a Jesuit school and for a while was a professor of canon law. It sought to spread knowledge and stimulate humanistic ideals and brotherly love among its members, and its goal was the establishment of a classless society and a patriarchal state. The Illuminati repudiated the claims of all existing religious bodies and professed to be those in which the illuminating grace of Christ (Heb. 6:4) alone resided. Because they were organized into an elaborate system requiring absolute obedience to superiors (much like the Jesuits) and advocated a vague form of social revolution, the Illuminati provided a convenient symbol and whipping boy for those who were fearful of conspiratorial movements to overthrow the status quo.

Reforming the Social Order

The attempt of the philosophes to apply Newtonian science to society led them to stress the importance of natural law. They believed firmly that rational laws regulated the universe and human society. Acting on this assumption, they applied the test of reason to social institutions and traditions and expressed an optimistic faith in progress. The most important expression of this optimism was the Marquis de Condorcet (1743–94), whose *Sketch for a Historical Picture of the Progress of the Human Mind* predicted that humankind was destined for unlimited progress in all fields because it had found and applied the method of reason to arrive at truth.

The society to which the philosophes applied the test of reason, France in the "old regime," was obviously in a traditional and irrational situation. Thus, they advocated a variety of programs for revitalizing economic, religious, and political life. In economics the "Physiocrats," whose spokesperson was François Quesnay (1694–1774), advocated replacing the crumbling mercantilistic system with a doctrine of *laissez-faire*, that is, people should be able to do as they wished without government control over their economic activities. The most famous expression of this new doctrine was the *Inquiry into the Nature and Causes of the Wealth of Nations* (1776), by the Scottish economist Adam Smith. He argued that individuals were motivated by self-interest in the economic realm and that if each person were allowed to pursue his own path, this would serve the good of the entire society.

The social implications of the Enlightenment view of religion were enormous. Especially noteworthy was the demand for toleration. The philosophes pointed out that it was unreasonable, foolish, and immoral to force a person to accept ideas that went against his or her conscience. Intolerance was an affront to the Christian teaching of love. Faith was a matter of individual concern, and society should have no control over it. Thus, the Enlightenment marked a quantum leap forward in the struggle for religious liberty.

One form this campaign took was the attack on bigoted religious laws. Voltaire led the way with his involvement in the famous Jean Calas case. The latter was a Protestant in Toulouse who had been charged with murdering his son to keep him from turning to Catholicism and was executed in 1762. This enraged Voltaire who embarked upon a three-year effort to clear the man's name. After looking over the court record, investigating the matter personally, and publishing a number of pamphlets on the case, Voltaire concluded that the dead son was mentally unbalanced and actually had committed suicide. His unrelenting demands for a reconsideration of the matter induced the courts finally to declare Calas innocent and to dismiss the judge responsible for this miscarriage of justice.

The philosophes' attack on religious laws led to an insistence on a more rational and humane approach to other victims of eighteenth-century justice. Slavery, inhuman treatment of the insane, and the torture of prisoners all came under attack. The Italian philosophe Cesare Beccaria in a landmark work, *Crimes and Punishments* (1764), argued for the application of reason to criminal justice. He called for laws to be fair and clearly stated. The aim of punishment was not to be vengeance but the prevention of further crime. The penalty should fit the offense, justice was to be speedy, and torture and capital punishment should be abolished. The state should reward good deeds and educate people about the dangers of a life of crime. Beccaria's work led to penal reform in many areas of Europe, most notably in Catherine the Great's Russia and Revolutionary France.

Enlightenment programs for a better society assumed that changes in government would be necessary. The philosophes regarded people as by nature basically good, rational, and capable of being educated. If natural laws were discovered and explained to people, they would follow them and form societies where human happiness would flourish. Since oppressive institutions were the creations of ruling elites for their own benefit, a transformation of the political system would be for the good of all. Although they thought

Adam Smith

in terms of states, the philosophes' belief in rationality led to a cosmopolitan outlook. With the triumph of natural law, a united and uniform world civilization would emerge in which all nations would cooperate.

Enlightenment political thinkers followed John Locke (1632–1704) in assuming that governments originated in contracts that people formed with rulers to protect individual rights. They held that citizens might revolt against the regime if it failed in its duty. But most philosophes did not support democratic or representative government, and they were comfortable with monarchical systems so long as these operated on a rational basis.

The most sophisticated of the political theorists was Charles de Secondat, Baron de Montesquieu (1689–1755). Unlike the others, he did not support the idea of enlightened despotism, nor did he believe that all people were alike. A French noble, he opposed royal absolutism as much for its inefficiency as for its tyranny, and his *Persian Letters* (1721) satirized the social, political, and religious institutions of the age. He was especially critical of intolerance on the part of the church. In 1726 Montesquieu toured Europe to find out for himself what conditions existed elsewhere, and the trip included a stop in England, where he was deeply impressed by the governmental system. After returning home and reflecting on the British situation for some years, he produced his most famous work, *The Spirit of the Laws* (1748).

Using a comparative technique to discover the fundamental principles of politics, he claimed there were three types of governments—republics, monarchies, and despotisms. The form of a state depended upon its natural environment and history. Republics flourished in small countries, monarchies in moderate-sized areas located in the temperate zone, and despotisms in large empires in the hot or cold climates. He urged France to emulate England and establish a separation of powers that would safeguard liberty. He said that in England the executive, legislative, and judicial branches were separate, and checked and balanced one another. Although Montesquieu actually misunderstood the English system, his thinking influenced those who drafted the American Constitution of 1787 and other constitutional liberals in the nineteenth century.

Rousseau: The Outsider

A radical exception to the general outlook of the philosophes was the work of Jean-Jacques Rousseau (1712–78). In many respects, he was the bridge between the Enlightenment and the revolutionary age that followed. He was also precursor of romanticism, the dominant intellectual movement of the early nineteenth century. Born in Geneva, he ran away from home at age sixteen and always felt alienated from the society around him. His own unhappy life undoubtedly shaped his view of the world.

Rousseau asserted that individuals in a natural state are basically good, since nature is characterized by a warmth of feeling and love for others However, progress and the growth of civilization corrupt people. The good qualities of humankind stem from emotion and the evil habits from reason, and so intuition and emotion are better guides to conduct than philosophy and reason. In *New Heloise* (1761) and *Emile* (1762) he described an educational program that would enable people to preserve their innate feelings for virtue and justice.

In his most important work, *The Social Contract* (1762), Rousseau set forth the idea of a government that would preserve as far as possible the natural equality of people. He stated that citizens in the process of forming a government merge their individual wills into the "general will" and agree to accept the latter's decisions. If individuals try to place what they believe to be their own interests above the general will, inequalities and injustice result. Those who try to do this must be forced to obey the general will. However, he did not explain the mechanisms for carrying out this policy, nor did he seem to realize that compelling one to behave according to the wishes of the general will could lead to the denial of individual freedom and tyranny. His *Social Contract* was so ambiguous that it has been used to justify both democracy and totalitarianism.

Enlightened Despotism

Although the philosophes in general argued for individual freedom and natural rights, they did not necessarily advocate democracy. They were quite willing to settle for kings who would apply Enlightenment principles. In other words, they felt a state could function best if it were under the absolute rule of an "enlightened despot" who, aided by a group of educated persons, would establish freedom of thought and promote education and material progress. A number of eighteenth-century monarchs seemed to fit the role outlined by the philosophes. These included Frederick II of Prussia (1740–86), Catherine II of Russia (1762–96), and Joseph II of Austria (1780–90). Actually, they adopted more benevolent programs not so much because they agreed with the philosophes, but rather because they recognized that their own interests could best be served by the application of reason to their states.

National prosperity would mean an increase in tax revenues, and more efficient administration could strengthen the control of the government. Thus, these monarchs improved agricultural techniques, reformed laws, ended torture, and fostered public health through the construction of hospitals and asylums. They endeavored to raise the educational level of the populace, establish a greater measure of religious tolerance, and in Catholic lands to rein in the power of the papacy.

The scientific revolution and Enlightenment essentially formed modern civilization. Ironically, the renowned American historian Carl Becker pointed out in his classic study of the period, *The Heavenly City of the Eighteenth-Century Philosophers* (1932), that the so-called "age of reason" was really an age of faith. What the philosophes in effect tried to do was replace Christianity with a new belief in science and reason and, through this, lead humanity to a veritable heaven on earth. However, their quest for the utopian kingdom of reason was rudely terminated by the bloody era of revolution and war that followed after 1789. Nevertheless, despite the misuse of their ideals that occurred during that tragic quarter-century, the modern world owes much to the philosophes. Religious tolerance, a decline in superstition, the belief in the dignity and inherent rights of the individual, freedom of thought and expression, a conviction that governments should rule for the benefit of the governed, and an appreciation for technology and science and the many benefits that these could bring—all these constitute the legacy of the age of science and the Enlightenment.

16

THE CHURCH SHOWS RENEWED VIGOR

The new worldview resulting from the scientific discoveries and affirmation of reason was not necessarily a mortal threat to the Christian faith. Although some philosophers turned their backs on Christianity and the spiritual power of churches in many places was sapped by dead orthodoxy, doctrinal indifference, and the heavy hand of authoritarian rulers, numerous signs of vitality existed. Most forms of Calvinism still emphasized sound doctrine, while Pietism brought new life to German Lutheranism. In the early eighteenth century a missionary vision began to emerge in continental and British Protestantism, and along with it came a surging wave of renewal that was known variously as Methodism or the Great Awakening. The Enlightenment had not captured Christianity.

THE STRUGGLE FOR WORLD MASTERY

The final victory of Parliament over the Stuart monarchs in the "Glorious" Revolution of 1688 set the stage for the power struggle between Britain and France that dominated the historical scene during the following century. Beginning in 1667, Louis XIV launched a series of aggressive actions to acquire territory beyond his northern and eastern borders, forcing the Dutch to organize coalitions to stop this expansionism. Thus, William of Orange, the Protestant leader of Holland, who was the grandson of Charles I and husband of James II's daughter, welcomed Parliament's invitation to assume the English throne because this enabled him to bring Britain into his anti-French alliance. During two wide-ranging conflicts in 1688–97 and 1702–13 he challenged French maritime power. In the peace settlement of 1713 the fragile North American colonial empire that had arisen in a piecemeal fashion during the seventeenth century gained a measure of security. Here Britain received Acadia (Nova Scotia), Newfoundland, and the Hudson Bay region along with the lucrative *asiento,* the exclusive right to supply slaves to Spanish America.

The next round of the overseas struggle in the 1740s ended with no territorial gain for England, but the French and British colonial forces soon clashed in the New World. What followed was the French and Indian War (1755–60), the American phase of the Seven Years' War. The spectacular capture of Quebec in 1759 sealed the fate of New France, and through the Treaty of Paris in 1763 Britain took possession of all of Canada. However, King George III issued a proclamation closing the new lands in the interior to white settlement and the subsequent Quebec Act of 1774 seemed to insure the domination of French-speaking Catholics, actions that angered the American colonists.

During the American Revolution the French sought revenge against Britain by siding with and giving military and naval assistance to the colonies, and this tipped the balance in the independence struggle. The final rounds of the struggle for world mastery took place during the French Revolution and Napoleonic era, and in 1815 Britain emerged as master of the overseas world. Meanwhile, many of the Loyalists (Tories) fled northward and established themselves in New Brunswick, Nova Scotia, and beyond the Great Lakes, thus giving these territories a much more English composition. In 1791 Parliament adopted the Canada Act, which divided the former New France into Upper and Lower Canada, each having a limited measure of self-government. The law also stated that one-seventh of all land granted would be reserved for the "support and maintenance of a Protestant clergy," that is, the Church of England, but the rights of the Catholic church in predominately French-speaking areas were reaffirmed. The "clergy reserves" remained a bone of contention for

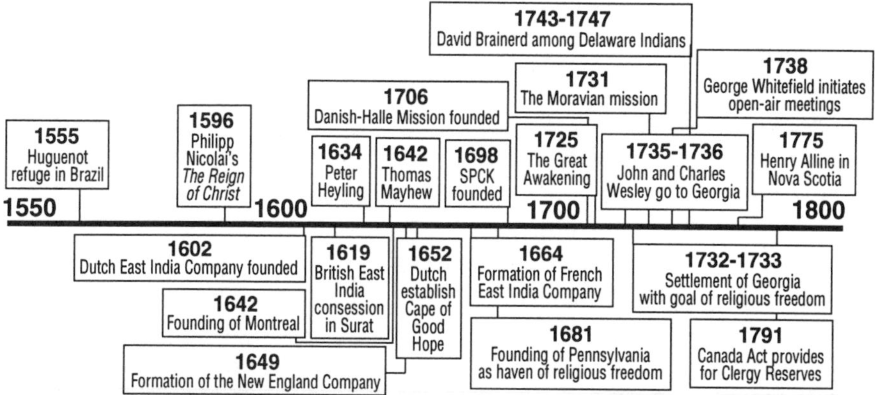

the various Protestant denominations until legislation was adopted in 1840 providing for the division of the money from the land sales among the different groups. The reserves were finally abolished in 1854.

As noted in chapter 12, many of the conflicts between the two maritime powers occurred in the Caribbean region and along the West African coast. But equal to the American struggle in significance was that in India. The Muslim-based Mogul (Mughal) Empire, founded in 1526, was trying to extend control over the entire Indian subcontinent, but it faced opposition from some Hindu princes. After the death of Aurangzeb in 1707, a strong figure whose religious zeal aroused Hindu opposition and undermined political stability, Mogul rule rapidly declined, and no power existed that was capable of resisting European penetration.

During the seventeenth century the Dutch company increasingly directed its attention toward Indonesia, while the British East India Company, chartered in 1600, gradually extended its operations in the subcontinent. In 1619 the Mogul emperor granted the British company trading rights at Surat on the west coast, and eventually it established twenty-seven other posts along the coasts, the most important being Bombay, Madras, and Calcutta. A French East India Company was formed in 1664, which soon obtained concessions at Pondichery and other places, and a small Danish company also operated a trading station on the southeast coast. The great popularity of wares from India and China among the upper and middle classes of Europe meant profits for the companies, but since the trade was largely in one direction there was much dissatisfaction in the commercial companies about the drain of European gold to Asia.

The British called their trading post at Surat a "factory," and the word was subsequently used for all European settlements in India.

Factories were walled compounds containing the residences, offices, and warehouses of the company and its personnel, where the president exercised full political authority. As the East India Company was interested solely in profit, the directors in London discouraged unnecessary risks such as interference in local Indian politics and even missionary work.

This policy changed due to the disorder and instability that set in during the eighteenth century. Then the factories were turned into forts with small garrisons of native troops, which gave protection for company property and nearby residents when warlords appeared or an uprising occurred. Since no strong central government existed and local princes could not provide security, the factory-forts gradually began to exercise political authority over the surrounding territories.

In 1742 Joseph Dupleix became head of the French enterprise. The first European who really understood the political as well as the economic importance of India, he formed alliances with local princes and developed an army of Indian troops (*sepoys*). In 1746 he captured Madras and through personal connections with local princes gained domination over southeast India. But the French efforts were thwarted by superior British sea power and the actions of Robert Clive, a soldier in the British company's service, and Dupleix was recalled in 1754. Three years later, Clive defeated the French-backed ruler of Bengal in the northeast and established a company protectorate over the region. He went on to crush French power in the south, and the Treaty of Paris of 1763 recognized British control in the subcontinent. In 1769 the French East India Company was dissolved.

The British Parliament, concerned that the company had gained too much power and was responsible for the disorders that were now sweeping India, adopted the Regulating Act in 1773, which lessened its political power. The office of governor-general was created that, with an advisory council, would exercise authority over the territory under the company's control. The India Act of 1784 further reined in its powers and made the directors subject to parliamentary supervision.

From their headquarters in Calcutta, Governors Warren Hastings and Charles Cornwallis set out to build an effective administration with a civil service, land taxation system, and an army of Indian troops. The Marquis of Wellesley (1797–1805) established British dominance in the subcontinent through a system of alliances with Indian princes, whereby Britain provided them with protection in return for territorial concessions, control of their foreign affairs, and exclusion of all other Europeans from their state service. Finally, in

1813 Parliament abolished the company's monopoly of trade with India and extended British sovereignty over its territories. Ceylon (Sri Lanka), which was captured from the Dutch in 1796, became a crown possession in 1802.

The establishment of the British and Dutch mercantile empires opened the door for Protestant mission activity. However, the development of a global awareness among the heirs of the Reformation was a slow process. Missionary work was hesitant and sporadic, and enjoyed little official support from the existing churches.

Protestant Missionary Indifference

Luther's recovery of the centrality of the gospel did not result in an outburst of missionary effort, but the universality of the message was clearly evident in his preaching. He believed firmly that the spiritual power of the gospel was such that it would spread without regard to human wisdom and craft. God would do it His way and in His time. Luther directed his message toward pastors and building congregations, in other words, internal development. Protestantism also lacked the institutional structures that medieval Catholicism possessed, which played the key roles in propagating the gospel—ecclesiastical hierarchy and religious orders.

Moreover, the Reformation faith took root in countries that either did not participate in colonial undertakings or were just beginning to do so—Germany, Sweden, Denmark, Holland, and England. The idea of religious freedom was unheard of, and it was unthinkable that Portugal and Spain would tolerate, let alone welcome, Protestant missionaries in their empires. Since the Lutherans did not preach that their congregations had a missionary obligation, their people were not conscious of the political barriers that existed for ministry abroad.

Calvin agreed with Luther that the message would inexorably spread throughout the world because of the sovereignty and power of God. The coming of the kingdom of God would not be the result of human effort. Like the propagation of the gospel, this was something that would happen in God's due time. God calls all people, but whom He had elected we do not know. The Christian's duty is to do everything that will honor God and make His goodness known to all people. Also, the New Testament did not designate any special office in the church that was charged with carrying out missionary work.

The stress on the universal appeal of the gospel revealed an inner orientation toward mission. However, radical movements within the Reformation itself and the mounting pressures of the Catholic counteroffensive restricted the process of congregational strengthening and growth, and the Augsburg religious settlement bound Protestants to rulers who lacked colonial possessions. The only opportunities for spreading the gospel were close by—the Jews and Turks.

There were a few exceptions to this pattern of indifference. In 1555 Durand de Villegaignon established a colony in Brazil with the backing of Admiral Coligny, which was to be a refuge for Huguenots. Calvin sent along a few pastors who attempted some missionary work among the Indians as well as ministered to the Reformed settlers, but because of unscrupulous dealings by the founder and discouragement with the work, the venture collapsed within three years.

Another person of note was Adrian Saravia (1531–1613), a Spanish-Belgian Calvinist who fled to England, held various ecclesiastical posts (including Dean of Westminster) and was a member of the King James Bible translation commission. In a work in 1590 that defended the principle of episcopacy, he identified one of the bishop's principal tasks as that of missionary work among the heathen. The holders of that office were not only to strengthen and edify existing churches but also to aid in the planting of new ones. The work of the apostles must be carried forth in the present age.

As Lutheran orthodoxy began to take hold, an important theoretical work espousing mission entitled *The Reign of Christ* was published in 1596 by Philipp Nicolai (mentioned earlier for his hymnody). He maintained that mission was the function of the church, a vital part of its task of proclaiming the Word of God and caring for souls. His view of mission was both global and ecumenical, in that he saw the Catholic and Orthodox churches as having pursued missionary work for centuries. But he insisted that the Lutheran church should have a central role in the enterprise because it had recovered the full gospel and made the divine Word accessible to all.

Most orthodox dogmatic theologians, to be sure, backed away from making such forthright assessments of mission as Nicolai and Saravia did. However, a century later the noted philosopher Gottfried Leibnitz, who was impressed with the Dutch colonial mission and Jesuit achievements (especially in China), wrote into the purpose statement of the newly founded (1700) Prussian Academy of Science a provision calling for the spread of the Christian faith and values among peoples from other nations and religions.

Relatively speaking, the clearest missionary vision was that of the Anabaptists. This flowed from their understanding of the gospel, the church, and eschatology. Also, the movement was spread by itinerant preachers who used the methods of the early Christians to proclaim the gospel. Their mission field, unfortunately, was restricted to central Europe, and they saw their ministry largely as that of rescuing the "heathen" who had been seduced by their priests into leading ungodly lives. Because of the intense persecutions, the Anabaptists withdrew into their own communities and became known as the "still in the land." Yet, their total dedication and emphasis on preaching the Word of God made them the precursors of the modern missionary movement.

Officially Sponsored Missions

With a few exceptions, missionary work in the seventeenth and early eighteenth centuries was sponsored, or at least sanctioned, by rulers or the managers of chartered companies. (Most colonial trading companies operated under royal charters, which gave them quasi-governmental powers in the areas where their operated.) Among the "lone wolves" was Peter Heyling (1607–52), a young student from Lübeck who was inspired by the writings of Hugo Grotius to become a missionary. He journeyed to Egypt and then to Ethiopia where he made contact with the Coptic church, tutored children from prominent families, and translated the gospel of John. But he was later murdered by Turkish Muslims. Another was Justinian von Welz (1621–68), an Austrian Lutheran whose family was forced to leave their homeland. He experienced a sudden conversion that was inspired by reading the Bible and mystical literature, and in 1664 he published a controversial tract that called for the formation of a voluntary society, the "Jesus Brotherhood," to work for improving the quality of Christianity and converting the heathen. As a layperson he devised a plan for a missionary training school but could not win the approval of church authorities. He then went to Surinam (Dutch Guiana) as a self-supporting missionary and died shortly after arriving.

Worthy of note were the actions of the first Protestant king of Sweden, Gustavus Vasa (1523–60), who initiated missionary work among the Lapps, a non-Christian people in his northern domains. He sent preachers and established schools to win them to Lutheran Christianity. This was essentially a Protestant form of the officially sanctioned missions that already had a thousand-year history.

More significant were the missions conducted under the auspices of the Dutch. Both the Dutch East and West India Companies appointed "chaplains" who were responsible for the spiritual care of their personnel and settlers. In some places the clerics did missionary work on the side. The West India Company provided preachers and schoolmasters for its North American enclave, New Netherland, and engaged in some minimal missionary work among Indians in Brazil during the interlude there.

At its stations on the Guinea coast of West Africa, chaplains were regular fixtures and employees were expected to attend services. There was even a black chaplain at Elmina in the 1740s, a former slave named Jacobus Capitein. His master had taken him to Holland, and after he had received theological education at Leiden he entered the ministry of the Dutch Reformed church. Capitein was the first African to receive ordination in this Protestant body, and he returned to serve in Africa where he died after five years.

In the seventeenth century the Dutch East India Company brought Protestantism to the areas under its control. During the previous eighty-year Portuguese presence in Indonesia, two hundred Catholic missionaries (including Francis Xavier in 1546–47) had worked in the Moluccas. Thus, when the Dutch arrived, they ousted the Catholics, tried to do likewise in Ceylon and some parts of India, and created a Protestant patronate not unlike that of the Spanish and Portuguese crowns. The revised charter of 1623 included the duty to "maintain the common faith," that is, to conform to the Reformed church order of the Netherlands.

Between 1605 and the late 1790s the company sent 254 pastors and 800 nonordained workers who founded churches and schools and published Bibles and religious books both in Dutch and Malay. The company officials determined where workers would be sent and schools opened, assigned them to their posts, and decided what salaries would be paid. Since all the church's work depended on the company, the quality of the Christian enterprise was questionable. The number of pastors actually on the field in any given year never exceeded thirty-four, and many of them could only preach in Dutch.

Although no missionary societies as such were founded, the church in Holland examined those who were to go out and carried on correspondence with them after they reached the East. For a brief time (1622–33) the company financed a "Seminarium Indicum" at Leiden to train men for Christian service. No private fund raising for the support of missions took place. Thousands of baptisms were reported but many of these were coerced, and little work actually was done outside of the Batavia (Djakarta) area in Java.

Example of John Wesley's Shorthand

The Dutch success in Sri Lanka was also modest, since the Catholic presence remained strong. After displacing the Portuguese in midcentury, they tried at first to convert the Catholics but then worked among non-Christians. A few clergy were sent from Holland and some schools and churches founded in the towns. In 1690 two schools were opened to train teachers and catechists, from which some indigenous clergy emerged. Although the number of Protestants may have exceeded 400,000 in the eighteenth century, the faith of the converts was generally superficial.

The major figure in Dutch missions was Justus Heurnius (1587–1652) who in 1616 published *Admonition to Start an Evangelical Witness in the Indies,* a plea for more effective and genuine outreach than that of the Catholics. He went to Batavia in 1624 and served zealously for fourteen years there and in the Moluccas. Besides doing translation work, he proposed providing Indonesians with theological education, but the home churches blocked the idea, fearing this would endanger pure doctrine. The company refused to allow his return after a furlough in 1638.

To be sure, the Dutch theologians did not see missions as exclusively the task of the authorities, but they were unable to arouse much interest in the local congregations. However, their missionary thinking had some impact in Germany and, most important, in Denmark. There the state church decided to found a mission in 1705 in the Danish company's Indian enclave that would have a far-reaching influence.

When the Dutch company established its way station in South Africa in 1652, a catechist was named to conduct prayers, read a Sunday sermon, visit the sick, and teach the Heidelberg Catechism to the small group of settlers. At first, clergy on passing ships administered the sacraments, but in 1665 an ordained person was finally assigned there. The white population at the Cape of Good Hope grew slowly, and refugee Huguenots joined the community after 1685, but the number of churches remained small—seven in 1795. They were under the control of the company and the Amsterdam classis (presbytery) until the British takeover. For a few years some efforts were made to reach indigenous Africans, and the baptism of slaves made it possible for them to become free. Eventually, granting emancipation to baptized slaves was sharply restricted, and in the eighteenth century virtually no concern was shown for the spiritual welfare of either the Hottentots or slaves.

British North America

In the West Indies, Roman Catholicism prevailed in the Spanish islands, and many of the people arriving from Africa were incorporated into the faith. However, in French St. Dominique (Haiti) the West African influence remained quite strong, as exemplified by the voodoo cult, which was a mixture of Catholicism and ecstatic and magical rites. Survivals of African rituals and customs also remained among slave communities in other islands and along the southeastern coast of North America, and these played a significant role in shaping the worship forms of the black church as it emerged in the nineteenth century. As for the islands ruled by Protestant England, the Anglican church ministered to the planters and merchants. The white residents rejected any evangelization of the enslaved African-American population, which they saw as useless and downright dangerous.

On the North American mainland, however, where the number of Europeans was rapidly increasing, most of the Reformation traditions found expression. Although persecution and harassment of minority groups occurred from time to time and in various places, eventually all churches came to coexist in an atmosphere of freedom unknown elsewhere in the world. For example, the Puritan Congregational establishment in New England had to face dissent even within its own ranks. One person, Anne Hutchinson (1591–1643), was expelled from Massachusetts Bay for expressing a variant form of Calvinism and criticizing the leadership elite. Another was Roger Williams (1603–83), a Puritan separatist who incurred the disapproval of the colony's leaders and was forced out. He founded a new settlement in Rhode Island in 1636 and there wrote some tracts defending freedom of conscience, which were the best in the English language and at least a century ahead of their time. Although Williams only briefly identified with the Baptists, both they and the Quakers put down roots in Rhode Island and from this base began spreading their distinctive messages throughout British North America.

In the southern colonies modest Anglican establishments came into being (Virginia's was the most extensive), but other denominations enjoyed freedom. Lord Baltimore's Maryland began in 1634 as a refuge for Catholics, and its celebrated "Act Concerning Religion" (1649) set forth a far-reaching conception of toleration for the time. However, it was annulled during the turmoil of the Cromwell era and eventually the Church of England was established.

Both ethnically and religiously the "middle" colonies were the most diverse territories, and people from a variety of denominations learned to live in harmony. By far the most interesting place was the "Holy Experiment" of William Penn (1644–1718), which really was the antecedent of America's pluralistic society. A remarkable person whose life traversed the distance from the age of Puritanism to the age of Reason, he was the Quaker pacifist son of a famous admiral, a close friend of kings and philosophers, an aristocrat as well as a democratic theorist, and creator of the most successful personally owned colony in the British empire.

Penn was both a practical man of affairs and a man of the spirit. His Pennsylvania was a place where religious freedom, representative government, and cheap land administered under benevolent control provided a haven for oppressed peoples and a model of enlightened rule. Philadelphia became the leading commercial and intellectual center of the American colonies. Not only was Pennsylvania the home of the Quaker movement, but it also was a center for other denominations—Presbyterians, Baptists, Lutherans, German Reformed, and even the Anglicans and Catholics. Eighteenth-century Mennonite and German pietist groups found sanctuary there, while the first independent black denomination in America, the African Methodist Episcopal church, was founded by Richard Allen in Philadelphia.

Although Roger Williams had adopted a highly positive stance toward the Native Americans (Indians) and a clause in the charter of the Massachusetts Bay Company called for winning the country's natives to Christ, the first formal missionary effort was initiated by Thomas Mayhew on Martha's Vineyard Island in 1642. His descendants continued this individualistic work for more than a century. More significant was the systematic program to evangelize the Algonquin-speaking Pequot Indians carried out by John Eliot (1604–90), the pastor of Roxbury Church near Boston. He learned their language and began laboring among them in 1646. Five years later he gathered his converts into the first "praying Indian town." Within two decades about 3,600 Christian Indians lived in some fourteen villages. He also translated the catechism and Scriptures into their tongue, and his crowning achievement was the publication of the Bible in 1663, the first Bible of any kind to be printed in America. Unfortunately, the flourishing enterprise was disrupted during a bloody conflict between the Indians and white settlers in 1675–76, and the towns soon disappeared.

Eliot and his colleagues publicized the work widely, and in 1649 Parliament chartered the Society for the Propagation of the Gospel in New England (renamed the New England Company in 1660). This was the first real Protestant missionary society, and over the next century it provided financial support for his and other Indian ministries in the colonies. The company continued until the Revolution and then shifted its work in the education of Native Americans to Canada.

One of the major contributions in the English missionary advance was made by Thomas Bray (1656–1730), an Anglican rector who with some friends formed voluntary societies to aid in spreading the gospel message. In 1696 the bishop of London appointed him as a special representative to Maryland to help build up the Church of England there. He concluded that good parish libraries were needed for this purpose and in 1698 formed the Society for Promoting Christian Knowledge (SPCK). In the following years it created "charity schools" where poor children could receive an elementary education and religious instruction, established libraries in Britain and the colonies, published religious books and tracts, and corresponded with Protestant churches on the European continent.

After visiting Maryland personally, Bray became convinced that a separate organization was needed to carry on missionary effort per se, and in 1701 he founded the Society for the Propagation of the Gospel in Foreign Parts (SPG). It aggressively endeavored to expand the Church of England's ministry overseas and sent out hundreds of clergy. Its primary activity was in North America and the West Indies, where it focused on reaching colonial settlers who were non-Anglicans, but occasionally some individuals did some work among Indians and black slaves. The group was particularly effective in the southern colonies.

One of the more memorable SPG accomplishments actually occurred outside North America. In 1752 it appointed Thomas Thompson as a chaplain for the main English fort (Cape Coast Castle) on the Gold Coast of West Africa. However, instead of just ministering to the white residents, he began reaching out to the nearby people and even sent some converts to England to be educated. One of these, Philip Quaque, was ordained a priest (the first black to receive Anglican orders), took an English wife, and with SPG support returned to the Gold Coast in 1766, where he served faithfully until his death in 1816.

Thomas Bray also influenced the founding of Georgia. In 1723 he formed a group of "Associates" to administer a fund for supporting libraries and evangelizing blacks and Indians in America. After his death, the Associates used this money to help General James Oglethorpe, a devout soldier and member of Parliament, obtain a royal charter in 1732 for a colony where the poor might be sent as an alternative to debtors' prison. He hoped to make Georgia a humane place free of slavery and rum and one with a strong Anglican presence, although religious freedom would be guaranteed. The social idealism of the venture was illusory, but the colony did become a haven for various groups. One was the Salzburgers, German Lutherans who had been expelled from their homeland by the Catholic archbishop but with SPCK help were resettled in Georgia in the 1730s.

A Scottish branch of the SPCK was created in 1709 that concerned itself with the spiritual welfare of people in the Highlands, but it also subsidized missions to the American Indians. Its most celebrated worker was David Brainerd (1718–47), a Presbyterian from Connecticut who was a protégé of Jonathan Edwards. For four years this young man labored among the Delaware Indians, a number of whom he won to Christ and formed into a church. His journal and diary were masterpieces of inspiration and spiritual edification, and are still popular today.

French North America

French colonization began in the early seventeenth century with settlements at Quebec in the St. Lawrence valley and Port Royal in Acadia (modern-day Nova Scotia and New Brunswick). A ban on the immigration of Huguenots assured that the white residents of New France would all be Roman Catholics. Founder Samuel de Champlain favored missions because he dreamed of a Christian Canada ruled by the French king and peopled by a race of French and Indians who had intermarried. Thus, in 1615 he brought in four Recollects, a reformed branch of the Franciscan order, to aid in Christianizing the population. They were joined in 1625 by five Jesuits, including Jean de Brebeuf (1593–1649).

After a brief interlude of English rule, the Jesuits took charge of the entire mission work. At first they labored among the Huron Indians near Georgian Bay, where they formed communities, intervened in intertribal conflicts, and sought to ameliorate the worst aspects of white rule. By 1648 twenty-two priests were active there. Supporting the enterprise were the Ursuline Sisters, led by Marie de l'Incarnation (1599–1672), who founded the first Indian girls school in Quebec.

However, war broke out between the Hurons and Iroquois, and in 1649 Brebeuf and several other missionaries were brutally murdered by the Iroquois. (Three centuries later he was canonized and named the patron saint of Canada.) Although the Huron mission was terminated, other Jesuits fanned out through the interior, reaching as far as the prairies beyond the Great Lakes and Louisiana in the south. One noteworthy figure was Jacques Marquette (1637–75) who came to New France in 1666 and founded several works. Because of his knowledge of Indian languages he was selected to accompany the Joliet expedition that explored the Mississippi River in 1673. He then started a mission among the Illinois Indians and died soon after of dysentery.

Another significant achievement was the founding of Montreal. The impetus for this came from Jean Jacques Olier (1608–57), a product of the French Catholic renewal movement (see chapter 13). He induced a military figure, Paul de Maisonneuve, to lead a group of committed workers to the upper St. Lawrence, where in 1642 they formed a Christian center to evangelize and care for the native Americans and to look after the spiritual welfare of the white settlers in the

George Whitefield

area. The Society of St. Sulpice, a congregation of secular priests that Olier created, provided clergy for the Montreal outpost, over which eventually the Sulpicians took charge.

The most important figure in the Christian history of French Canada was François Xavier de Laval-Montmorency (1623–1708). From a distinguished old family, he was greatly influenced by the Catholic renewal, had close ties with the group that was to found the Paris Foreign Missionary Society, and was nominated by the Jesuits to lead the church in New France. In 1658 he was appointed as an apostolic vicar and upon arrival in Quebec became a member of the colony's governing council. Laval exercised a firm hand in keeping the church free from lay control, demanded high moral standards from clergy and laity alike, and incurred the hatred of the fur traders for opposing liquor sales to the Indians. Recognizing the need for trained clergy who would be subject to his authority, he opened a seminary in 1663 (now Laval University) that maintained ties with the Paris society. In 1674 he was named bishop of Quebec. He established centralized control over the clergy of Quebec and Acadia, but the Franciscan and Sulpician missionary enterprises still enjoyed some freedom of action.

Laval's creation of a church structure independent of the French crown and staffed with Canadian clergy was the primary factor enabling Roman Catholicism to hold its own after the British takeover in 1763, and thus to maintain that unique position in Canadian life that it has today. At the same time, American Protestants regarded the "popery" of French Canada as the symbol of evil. Therefore, as the British gained control of the maritime colonies and Protestant settlers trickled in, the power of the Catholic church there was reduced. A sad example of the enmity between the two communities was the expulsion of the Acadian French between 1755 and 1763. Many of them were relocated in Louisiana where their heritage is still seen in the "Cajun" (a corruption of Acadian) culture. Actually, although the French established themselves along the Gulf coast in the early eighteenth century, their missionary work in Louisiana never amounted to much.

In fact, a decline in the mission outreach set in due to rivalries among the religious orders, the Jesuit dissolution, and the dampening effect of the Enlightenment on religious zeal. Moreover, missions were drawn into the Anglo-French struggle for supremacy in North America. The French used the Indians as allies, an action that the missionaries encouraged by portraying the Protestant British as a threat to native American souls. Still, mission work resumed in the nineteenth century, and now more than one-half of the Indian population in Canada is Catholic.

GERMAN MISSIONARY ENDEAVOR

German Pietism was a major force in eighteenth-century Protestant missions, and Halle and Herrnhut were centers of the movement. The initial player in this drama was the pietistic King Frederick IV of Denmark and Norway (1671–1730), who wished to do more for the spiritual welfare of the people in his country's trading enclave of Tranquebar, South India. Although assigning chaplains to minister to the Europeans in the factories was a long-established practice, he saw the need to reach non-Christians as well. Finding no suitable candidates among the Danish clergy, the king appealed to Francke, who selected two Halle students for the task, Bartholomäus Ziegenbalg and Heinrich Plütschau.

The youths were promptly ordained in Copenhagen and after a seven-month journey arrived in Tranquebar on July 9, 1706. Both in Denmark and India there was considerable opposition to the venture, but it was so successful that other missionaries schooled at Halle soon followed in their footsteps. In 1714 Frederick set up the Royal

College for Advancing the Cause of the Gospel, which insured official church sanction for Danish missionary ventures. In 1718 he approved the appointment of Hans Egede (1686–1756) as a missionary to Greenland to evangelize the Norwegians there. When he arrived three years later and found none, he turned to the Eskimo population. After years of labor Egede mastered the language, won a few individuals to Christ, and then returned home, where he continued to direct the Greenland work and write about missions.

But it was the Asian venture that really was Frederick's legacy. Although Plütschau soon dropped out, Ziegenbalg served in India until his death in 1719 and established a pattern of action that future Protestant missionaries were to follow. He made schools an integral part of the mission, as he felt new Christians must be taught to read so they could study the Word of God. But if believers were to read the Bible, it had to be in their own language, and so he learned Tamil, completed a New Testament translation in 1714, and was working on the Old Testament when he died. Furthermore, he studied Indian religions and culture in order to be able to preach to the people in a meaningful manner. Ziegenbalg and his co-workers also insisted on personal conversion. They did not deal with large groups and through ruling elites as Catholic missions had done since the early Middle Ages but rather sought to win individuals to Christ. Finally, they formed local congregations and trained indigenous catechists and pastors to lead them, a practice that occasionally disturbed church hierarchies at home. Among the "firsts" of the Tranquebar mission were a girl's school, a printing press, the use of medical personnel, and the ordination of a Tamil pastor (1733).

The "Danish-Halle" work soon became known throughout Protestant Europe. Fifty-six missionaries went out to India and other parts of the world during the course of the century, and many of the letters they sent home were published in a magazine issued from Halle. Francke and his successors also used a large network of correspondents and personal connections to encourage interest elsewhere. Many who heard of the Indian mission even sent gifts to Halle to support it. When Ziegenbalg visited England while on furlough, he was received by King George I as well as the archbishop of Canterbury.

The English connection was important, because the missionary letters were translated and distributed there, and the British East India Company, whose operations were steadily expanding, needed more chaplains for its posts. In 1710 the SPCK agreed to provide funds to support Danish-Halle missionaries who would then work in the company's territories in India. Although German Lutherans, they generally used the Book of Common Prayer and baptized and observed the Lord's Supper in the Anglican fashion. They also worked among the local population as well as in the European community.

One of those, Johann Philipp Fabricius (1711–91), went out to Tranquebar as a Danish-Halle missionary in 1740, soon relocated in Madras, and spent fifty years on the field without a furlough. He produced works in Tamil linguistics and a Bible translation that remained authoritative until the twentieth century. Even more remarkable was Christian Friedrich Schwartz (1726–98), who served in India for forty-eight years. He spent his first years at Tranquebar and then in 1767 was appointed a chaplain at the British post at Trichinopoly. In 1772 the Rajah of Tanjore invited Schwartz to his kingdom, where for a while he was the guardian of the heir to the throne and virtually the prime minister. He also served as a British emissary to the powerful Hyder Ali of Mysore. Although Schwartz was a cultured man who knew several languages and could move freely in high circles, he led a simple, godly life, witnessed constantly to the power of the risen Savior, and trained young Indians for the ministry.

Another Halle figure was John Z. Kiernander (1711–1800), a Swede, who after completing his studies worked as superintendent of the orphanage. Then in 1740 he went to Cuddalore, South India, under the SPCK. Forced to leave during the Anglo-French war in 1758, he relocated in Calcutta and was the first Protestant missionary to serve there. Kiernander preached, opened schools, and eventually built a large church and school that would be a center for the missionaries who came later.

Also trained at Halle was Henry Melchior Muhlenberg (1711–87). In 1742 he went as a missionary to three struggling Lutheran congregations in Pennsylvania, and at once he set out to establish a united, independent, and self-sustaining church. He called for more workers, and by 1748 his energetic leadership resulted in the convening of the first Lutheran synod in America, the Pennsylvania Ministerium. It supervised the growing number of Lutheran churches in the middle colonies and set the standard for synodical organizations in other areas. He has aptly been named "the father of American Lutheranism." His eldest son, Peter, who was born in America, educated at Halle, and pastor of a congregation in Virginia, is remembered for his role in raising a German regiment that fought in the Revolutionary War.

Another area of concern was Jewish evangelism. Johann Heinrich Callenberg (1694–1760), a professor at Halle University, studied Arabic, Persian, and Turkish and prepared Christian literature in these tongues in order to win Muslims. This interest in oriental studies led to a desire to reach Jews as well, and in 1728 he formed the Jewish Institute. It prepared and circulated literature in Hebrew and sent out itinerant missionaries who preached to Jews and cared for converts.

The Moravians (see chapter 14), who were an offshoot of Halle Pietism, undertook the most extensive Protestant missionary operation in the entire century. While visiting Copenhagen in 1731, Zinzendorf met some converts of the Danish-Halle mission, who urged him to send missionaries to their peoples. Upon returning to Herrnhut the count challenged his followers, and J. L. Dober (1706–66) and David Nitschmann (1696–1772) responded. They left the next year for the Danish Virgin Islands where they founded a self-supporting work among the black population and won many to Christ. Other Moravians answered the call to foreign service, and missions were founded in Greenland (1733), Surinam (1735), West and South Africa (1737), Estonia (1738), Labrador (1764), the Nicobar Islands (1769), and among the North American Indians. Dober also ministered to Jews in Amsterdam.

The Moravians established thriving churches in England and Holland, which provided yet more funds and workers for missions. In 1782 it was reported that 175 missionaries were working in 27 places; fifty years later the number had risen to 209 workers and 41 stations. During their first hundred years of missionary endeavor the Moravians sent out 1,199 persons, including 459 women. In the nineteenth century additional fields were opened in Asia, Africa, and Central America.

The main overseas effort was in America. It began with an attempt at settlement in Georgia. In 1733 August Gottlieb Spangenberg (1704–92), who had been working at the Halle orphanage, joined the Herrnhut community and became Zinzendorf's assistant and eventual successor. In 1735 he led a group of ten men to Georgia to form a settlement, and the following year David Nitschmann brought a second party over. Traveling on the ship were John and Charles Wesley, who were profoundly impressed by the piety of these humble Germans. John even lived with them briefly.

The Moravian colony in Georgia was abandoned in 1740 when George Whitefield invited them to Nazareth in eastern Pennsylvania where he intended to set up a school for blacks. But because of differences between the more Calvinistic Whitefield and the Moravians, they decided to acquire a site nearby on the Lehigh River for a new settlement. When Zinzendorf came in 1741, he named it Bethlehem, and the community soon was a little Herrnhut in America. In 1743 the Moravians bought Nazareth, and it became a second communal village. Among others founded in the following years were Lititz (near Lancaster) and Salem in North Carolina. Zinzendorf hoped to unite the scattered German sects in Pennsylvania, but all his attempts at ecumenism failed, and the Moravian church soon took on its own denominational character.

The Indian missions of the American Moravians were a remarkable achievement. They began in 1740 with the Mohican mission of Christian Rauch in New York and Zinzendorf's own travels among the Indians. The best-known missionary was David Zeisberger (1721–1808), who gained the confidence of tribal leaders and founded a number of peaceful Christian communities. But the enterprise suffered continually from white opposition and frontier Indian wars. Particularly disgraceful was the brutal massacre in 1782 of a Christian Indian village in northern Ohio by a colonial militia unit. Zeisberger eventually shepherded his tiny flock of Delawares to Ontario where they could maintain their identity.

THE EIGHTEENTH-CENTURY REVIVAL

It was only a matter of time before Pietism made inroads into Anglicanism, as the Established church suffered from problems similar to those afflicting German Lutheranism. Its teaching buttressed the existing order where each person had a divinely assigned place and social status, and one was to be content with that position. Receiving the sacrament in the Anglican church was the formal test of loyalty to the regime. New waves of thought—rationalism, deism, latitudinarianism (a tolerant outlook that deemphasized correct doctrine), and Unitarianism (rejection of Christ's deity)—along with the corruption and immorality that was rampant in the church contributed further to the spiritual malaise. In other words, "the decay of vital religion," as hymn writer Isaac Watts put it, had left the church an empty shell.

The first challenge to the decadence of the English-speaking church came from the revivals or "awakenings" that swept Britain and the American colonies in the middle third of the eighteenth century.

Count Nikolaus Ludwig von Zinzendorf

These were parallel events, but considerable cross-fertilization among the movements occurred, particularly in the ministry of Whitefield. In Britain the first outbreak of revival happened in Wales under Howel Harris (1714–73), a schoolteacher who was converted in 1735 and began preaching in homes, as he was not ordained. In 1737 he joined forces with Daniel Rowland (1713–90), an Anglican priest who had experienced a spiritual awakening about the same time, and by means of itinerant evangelism they launched what came to be known as Welsh Calvinistic Methodism. Harris settled at Trevecca in 1752 and formed a community that was a center of evangelicalism. Another renewal, albeit not as spectacular as the Welsh one, took place in Scotland in 1741–42.

Clearly the landmark figure in the revitalization movement was John Wesley (1703–91). He and his brother Charles (1707–88) were born into the Anglican rectory at Epworth in Lincolnshire. Their mother, Susanna (1669–1742), exercised a decisive influence on shaping their characters through her own deep personal faith, judicious use of discipline, and practice of introducing the family to Christian devotional literature. John trained for the ministry at Oxford, was ordained, and served as a teacher at Lincoln College. In 1729 he formed the "Holy Club" at Oxford, to which Charles, George Whitefield, and other students belonged. They engaged in prayer, study of the Greek New Testament, and charitable work, and they were nicknamed "Methodists" because they had adopted a disciplined method of spiritual improvement.

In 1735 he and Charles were appointed to the SPG chaplaincy in Georgia and arrived the following year. They traveled on the same ship with a contingent of Moravians, where he was challenged by Spangenberg as to his assurance of salvation. He was supposed to work among the Indians, but after two frustrating years he went back home. Shortly after returning he met Peter Böhler, leader of the London Moravians, who talked to him about the need for a deeper faith. Wesley recorded in his journal that he attended their prayer meeting on Aldersgate Street on May 24, 1738, and while they were reading from the preface to Luther's commentary on Romans, "I felt my heart strangely warmed. I felt I did trust in Christ, Christ alone for salvation." (Just three days earlier Charles, also back in England, had a similar evangelical conversion under Böhler's influence.) The next month John went to Germany and visited Halle and Herrnhut, thus sealing the spiritual bond between Pietism and Methodism.

This paved the way for the Wesley brothers to traverse the land to bring God's message to the people where they were. After twenty years of itinerancy Charles assumed a settled ministry, but as the author of 7,270 compositions he is remembered as perhaps the most gifted and prolific hymn writer in the English language. Among his best known are "Jesus, Lover of My Soul," "Oh, for a Thousand Tongues to Sing," "Love Divine, All Loves Excelling," and "Christ the Lord Is Risen Today."

At Whitefield's suggestion, John began open-air preaching. This gave him more flexibility, as he was unwelcomed in many churches, and he was constantly on the move, speaking wherever he had an audience. In the next half-century he traveled 250,000 miles (mostly on horseback) and preached 40,000 sermons. In his journal Wesley observed,

> I look upon all the world as my parish; thus far I mean, that in whatever part of it I am, I judge it meet, right, and my bounden duty, to declare unto all that are willing to hear, the glad tidings of salvation. This is the work which I know God has called me to; and sure I am that his blessing attends it.

He proclaimed justification by faith, the new birth, and Christian perfection (sanctification). He insisted that a Christian could be holy in this world but not free of all wrongdoing. His preaching in the streets and fields often aroused violent opposition, but he had an absolute fearlessness and complete confidence in God that carried him through the most unnerving situations. The great number of working class people and the "enthusiasm" they demonstrated in his meetings were criticized by some in the upper classes. Others condemned him for preaching outside of churches and for allowing laypeople to preach.

A loyal Anglican, Wesley did not intend to form a new church, but the movement went inexorably in this direction. His goal simply was to declare the gospel to unreached peoples and provide for their spiritual nurture. Following the Moravian model, he created the Methodist "society," which in turn was subdivided into classes and bands. At the meetings the members evaluated each other's spiritual lives and studied the Scriptures. The societies were grouped in circuits (preachers' rounds) and the circuits organized into districts. This structure made up the Methodist "Connexion." The preachers, usually laypersons, met at an annual conference to receive instruction and work assignments.

The real pioneer of itinerant evangelism was Wesley's friend and associate, George Whitefield (1715–70). Converted at Oxford in 1735, after graduation he went to Georgia at the Wesleys' invitation to set up an orphanage. While back in England in 1739 for his ordination, he discovered the value of the open-air meeting, and before long he was preaching to thousands. He played a major role in the Scottish revival and in forming the Welsh Calvinistic Methodist Association. Although the name Methodist first was applied to his followers, theological differences soon arose between him and Wesley. To avoid conflict, he relinquished leadership of the Methodist movement and focused on America where his heart really was and to which he traveled seven times. Whitefield was the best-known preacher in the colonies and the greatest revivalist of the century.

One follower of his was Selina Hastings, countess of Huntingdon (1707–91), who after her conversion became a Moravian and then a Methodist. Like Whitefield she embraced Calvinism, and she opened chapels in various places that combined evangelicalism with a more liturgical worship form. In 1768 she founded a preachers' college at Harris's place in Trevecca to train workers for her group of Calvinist Methodists, which was called the Countess of Huntingdon's Connexion.

Whitefield's preaching tours were an essential element in the "Great Awakening" in America. The colonial revival had its roots in

Calvinist pietist renewal movements in the middle colonies, especially those of the Dutch Reformed preacher Theodorus Frelinghuysen (1691–1747) and Presbyterian Gilbert Tennent (1703–64), but the outstanding personality was undoubtedly Jonathan Edwards (1703–58). A Yale graduate and Congregationalist pastor in Northampton, Massachusetts, his preaching led to a revival in the church in 1734–35. His published accounts of the event were widely circulated in the colonies. Then, in 1740 Whitefield's and Tennent's preaching kindled a revival in Boston that spread as far south as Virginia during the next two years. Because the colonial clergy were deeply divided about the value of the spiritual awakening, laypeople began taking the initiative in religious life, an action that was a major step in the democratization of American Protestantism. At the same time, through his numerous writings Jonathan Edwards precisely and forcefully articulated a Calvinist position that marked him as colonial America's greatest thinker and placed him in the first rank of Reformed theologians.

The Awakening was carried to maritime Canada by Henry Alline (1748–84). In 1775 he had an intense conversion experience, and at once felt a deep conviction that Christ had called him to preach, even though he lacked formal theological education. Thus, during the Revolutionary War years he itinerated throughout Nova Scotia and founded several Baptist and Congregational churches. Because his revival movement did so much to give the Nova Scotian Yankees a new sense of identity, some scholars regard him as Canada's greatest Protestant religious figure.

Protestantism was changing in two ways. One was its growing awareness of peoples outside the familiar European confines who did not know Christ and who needed to be reached with the gospel message. The other was understanding and putting into practice the personal aspect of the Christian faith that was inherent in the conception of the priesthood of all believers. With Catholic power weakening in Europe, Protestantism was situated to forge ahead in the competition for souls. But a crucial question remained unanswered: Would the impending upheaval in Europe facilitate or hinder this process?

PART 3

THE ADVANCING AND GLOBAL CHURCH

(1789 – PRESENT)

17

THE CHURCH IN A REVOLUTIONARY AGE

Between 1760 and 1815 a wave of revolutions swept over the Western world, ranging from protest demonstrations (and resulting governmental concessions) to the great revolution that convulsed France. The result of the political upheavals was the replacement of the traditional hierarchical society with a recognizably modern one. The social ideas of the Enlightenment did much to set the stage for the "age of the Democratic Revolution," as historian R. R. Palmer has characterized the period.

The philosophes based their criticisms of the old order on universal laws that they claimed applied equally to people everywhere. They presented a challenge not only to France and other European states but also to those living in the Americas. These new ways of thinking and looking at the world were subversive of traditional institutions and practices. They especially undermined the Roman Catholic church. Both the Protestant and Catholic churches were forced to face the truth inherent in the Christian message that God had created all humans equal. The evangelicals, however, took this one step further and insisted that all were equally in need of salvation through faith in Christ.

The American Revolution

The first new state founded on the principles of the Enlightenment was in North America. The revolution that led to the creation of the American republic grew out of the conflicts between the English and French during the seventeenth and eighteenth centuries. As mentioned in the previous chapter, these wars were fought not only in Europe but also in the colonial world, resulting in the British triumph in North America and India. However, because British money and soldiers had won the war that ousted France from North America and secured it for the rapidly growing empire, London felt that the colonies should make a greater contribution to their defense costs. The clumsy efforts of the British government to collect taxes for this purpose alienated the colonists and led to the War of Independence.

Religion also contributed to the crisis. During the Great Awakening many colonials had come to expect that they were directly related to God's plan for the end of the age and that the millennial kingdom of Christ was about to dawn. As the revival fires cooled, many clerics mixed the expectation that all nations would be converted to Christ with the commitment to America as the seat of liberty. First, they saw France and then England as the archenemies of civil and religious freedom. This "civil millennialism" defined freedom as the cause of God and civil oppression, rather than formal religion, as the antichrist. The nation itself was seen as the agent of God's activity in history.

The Awakening helped lay the foundation for an American nation on revivalism. Since the Awakening functioned on an intercolonial basis and fostered relations among churches in various geographic regions, it was the first truly "national" event in the colonies. It also made respectable the use in public discourse of such terms as "liberty," "virtue," and "tyranny," and created a model of leadership that called for a direct response from the people. Clergy from various denominations—Baptists, Congregationalists, Presbyterians, Lutherans, Dutch Reformed, even Anglicans—saw themselves as directed by God to awaken and guide the nation into the coming age of millennial fulfillment.

As the crisis deepened, these pastors supported resistance to Britain. Anglican efforts to establish a diocese in the colonies also frightened many colonial ministers, and in a series of joint meetings Congregationalists and Presbyterians declared firmly that they re-

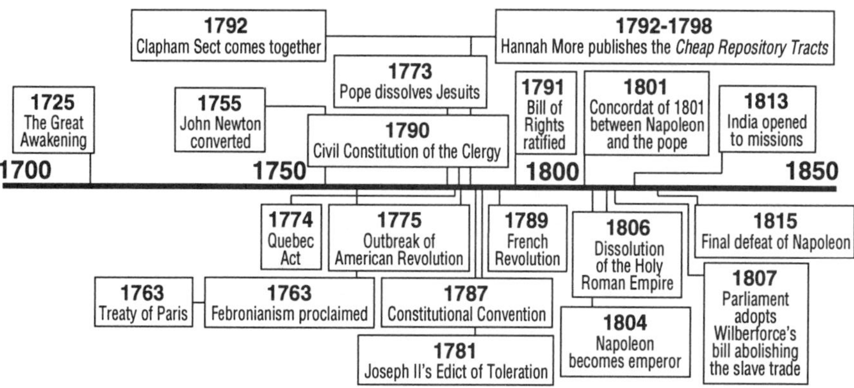

garded episcopacy as the ecclesiastical tool of absolute government. Drawing upon the old Puritan ideal of the covenant, they insisted that government was based on a compact or contract between the ruler and the citizens. Many Anglicans, especially those in the southern colonies, joined in rejecting the imposition of an American bishop from England, and, in fact, two-thirds of the signers of the Declaration of Independence were members of the Church of England.

But other sincere Christians opposed the idea of a war for independence. These included Anglicans in New England and in the middle colonies as well as Methodists. John Wesley himself wrote critically of the Revolution, and many members of his group followed his lead. Wesley was convinced that the revival that had spread through the colonies was being stifled by materialism and this was what really was behind the revolution. Also, he agreed with the teaching that a Christian must not actively resist duly constituted authority. Others opposing the conflict were the peace churches—the Quakers, Church of the Brethren, Moravians, and Mennonites. During the fighting these Christians, who were pacifist by principle, were misunderstood and persecuted by both sides.

Among the more provocative British actions were measures that seemed to favor other parts of the empire (such as duties on molasses and tea) and the imposition of new taxes such as the Stamp Act of 1765. Since most colonial leaders had come to accept the Enlightenment teaching of free trade, the new measures seemed anachronistic as well as threatening to their well-being. The stamp tax, which was to be levied on every printed paper and legal document, was enacted during a time of economic downturn and gave rise to questions on the part of many as to whether Parliament had the right to tax the colonies. Since no American delegates sat in Parliament, colonial leaders argued that this was "taxation without representation." Colonial boycotts and problems in collecting taxes led to the repeal of this and other revenue acts by 1770, but the tea tax that assisted the British East India Company was retained as a token of central authority. When angry colonials dumped a shipload of tea into Boston Harbor in 1773 (the "Boston Tea Party") an infuriated King George III closed the port and revoked the constitution of Massachusetts.

American pastors were already outraged by what they regarded as an unjust British move, but they received an even more severe shock in the Quebec Act of 1774. This measure, which was designed to facilitate the integration of New France into the British Empire, gave broad power to the Roman Catholic church in that area. It officially recognized the church and allowed it to collect its accustomed dues. As the act also extended the boundary of Quebec to include the Ohio country, settlers from New York, Pennsylvania, and Virginia believed they were being blocked from moving into the interior.

In September 1774 the first Continental Congress met in Philadelphia and defied Parliament's right to control the colonies. On April 19, 1775, shortly before a second meeting of the Congress, hostilities between the British troops and a colonial militia occurred at Lexington green and Concord bridge not far from Boston. The colonists felt they were defending their rights as free people, and in their challenge to Parliament and the English king they took the first steps in the direction of both republicanism and human equality. The Enlightenment ideas that had taken root in the New World began to flower.

As violence continued, the Continental Congress formed an army under the command of George Washington, began looking for European allies, and adopted a formal Declaration of Independence on July 4, 1776. Authored by Thomas Jefferson (see chapter 15), its invocation of God reflected Enlightenment deism and essentially put God at the service of the earthly task that the Americans saw before them. Although at first the war went badly, a major victory at Saratoga in the following year encouraged the French to give support to the Americans as a means of reestablishing their prestige in Europe. Meanwhile, representatives of the thirteen former colonies (now called "states") signed the Articles of Confederation that created the United States of America. In 1778 France formed an alliance with the new nation, and their help led to the British defeat and surrender at Yorktown in 1781. In the Treaty of Paris two years later Britain recognized the independence of the colonies.

At once the country faced an economic crisis, as American ships now were excluded from the trade with the British West Indies.

Moreover, social instability due to the lack of authority of the makeshift Articles of Confederation worried the wealthy classes in particular, and they saw the need for a stronger central government. Their concern led to the calling of a convention in Philadelphia in 1787 to revise the Articles. Out of this meeting came an entirely new document, the Constitution, which went into effect in 1789. It created a federal republic, with certain powers reserved to the states and others given to the central government. Under this system the states were clearly more than administrative units of a central bureaucracy. The Constitution also incorporated Montesquieu's concept of the separation of powers into the legislative, executive, and judicial branches. There were checks and balances built into the governmental mechanism to forestall any unit from becoming too powerful and oppressing the others or the people themselves. The judiciary was unique in that it had power to interpret the constitutionality of the actions of the states and the Congress. George Washington, a respected leader whose moral standards were beyond reproach, became the first president of the republic.

The impact of the Enlightenment was especially evident in the Constitution's handling of religion. There was no hint of religious establishment in the document, and one clause in Article VI specifically stated that no religious test would be required for any holder of public office. (This was obviously a reaction to the English Test Act of 1673.) Moreover, because there was uncertainty in some circles about whether individual liberties were sufficiently protected, a set of ten amendments known as the Bill of Rights was passed in 1789 and ratified two years later. The cornerstone was the First Amendment:

> Congress shall make no law respecting an establishment of religion, or prohibiting the free exercise thereof: or abridging the freedom of speech, or of the press, or the right of the people peaceably to assemble, and to petition the Government for a redress of grievances.

Seldom had a state document of such importance so simply and forthrightly posited religious freedom as a human right. Actually, the Constitution reflected the movement for religious liberty that had already arisen in various places, especially Virginia. Just before national independence, James Madison and Thomas Jefferson mounted a campaign, with the support of the Presbyterians and Baptists, to include "the free exercise of religion" in the new state's Declaration of Rights. Then in 1786 they succeeded in obtaining the complete disestablishment of the Anglican church in their state. Madison's *Memorial and Remonstrance* (1785) and Jefferson's *Bill for Establishing Religious Freedom* (written 1779, passed 1786) are two of the most influential documents in the history of religious liberty in America.

Moreover, the Baptists in Massachusetts under the leadership of Isaac Backus played a key role in securing that state's ratification of the Constitution because they approved of its neutral attitude toward religious matters. Even more significantly, Baptist preacher John Leland in Virginia personally impressed upon Madison the need for a constitutional amendment guaranteeing religious liberty, and the strong affirmation found in the First Amendment resulted from this encounter. In 1802 Jefferson, who had now become president, declared that the First Amendment had erected a "wall of separation" between church and state. Denied any support from and relieved of any responsibility for the state, the churches in America existed in a benevolent and free environment that resulted in a flourishing of diverse expressions of faith unlike that ever seen before in a state populated by Christians.

Although the Middle States followed the example of Virginia (Rhode Island and Pennsylvania of course had never had an officially recognized church), the idea of a limited establishment persisted in the South and New England for a few years. But the last vestiges of establishment gave way before the rationalism of the Enlightenment and the revivalist churches that populated the landscape. Thus, from its very beginning the United States's religious life was shaped by free church Protestant denominationalism.

The American success had a profound effect on other peoples. The creation of an independent republic in the New World was widely interpreted in Europe as proof that the ideas of the Enlightenment could be put into practice. It was possible for a people to establish a government based on the rights of the individual.

Catholic Decline

After 1648 the Roman Catholic church as a universal organization slipped into decline. The pope, who had been ignored at the Peace of Westphalia, was seldom consulted on international problems and was not represented at any of the great peace conferences. The various national churches increasingly came to be run by synods of bishops, and the papacy had great difficulty exerting its authority.

A succession of weak popes left the central institution impotent in the face of mounting attacks.

The most significant assertion of the national church idea in the seventeenth century was Gallicanism. At an assembly in Paris in 1682, the French bishops adopted a statement (the Four Gallican Articles) that affirmed that King Louis XIV was not subject in temporal (secular) things to any ecclesiastical power nor could any papal action relieve his subjects from obedience to him. It also held that general councils had authority over the pope, and the crown and bishops could regulate papal interference in France. Although the pope possessed universal spiritual authority, the Gallicans insisted that the state controlled the actual functioning of the church in such matters as the selection of bishops, liturgy, church law, and education.

A further challenge to papal power was a doctrine known as Febronianism. This was set forth in a book published in 1763 by Johann Nikolaus von Hontheim (1701–90), the auxiliary bishop of Trier, under the pseudonym Justus Febronius, which was entitled, *On the State of the Church and the Legitimate Power of the Roman Pontiff.* Although he accepted the primacy of the pope as a recipient of honor and as an executive administrator in Rome, the pontiff was actually a "first among equals." The keys of the kingdom in Matthew 16:19 were given to the whole church, not the papacy alone. The ultimate legislative authority in the church was a general council composed of all the bishops, who held their offices from God, not the pope, and a papal decision could be appealed to the council. Also, when it came to matters of human, not divine law, secular princes were entitled to refuse obedience to the papacy. The author believed that the excessive centralization of ecclesiastical power had caused the Reformation; hence decentralization might facilitate the return of Protestants to the Catholic church.

The pope condemned Hontheim's volume the following year by placing it on the *Index of Prohibited Books,* but four German prince-archbishops affirmed the Febronian principles at a conference in 1786. Accepting only a limited primacy of the pope, they called for episcopal assent to papal decrees and bulls, the cessation of appeals to Rome, and local authority over religious orders. In effect, they intended to form a German national Catholic church, but the lesser bishops were fearful of the power of the larger ones and preferred the distant overlordship of Rome to the more immediate authority of the German princes. The revolt collapsed in 1789 when the archbishops withdrew their statement, but the implications were far-reaching.

The idea of limiting papal authority fell on fertile soil in Vienna where the future "enlightened despot," the young Joseph II, talked about the need for religious freedom in the domains he would eventually inherit. He regarded the entrenched wealth of the Austrian church as an obstacle to economic development and the ecclesiastical control of education as the barrier to the maturing of the Austrian mind. Upon becoming emperor in 1780 he set out to implement a thorough-going reform program that would rationalize the organization of society through statist centralism and authority from above.

In the religious realm, he went considerably beyond French Gallicanism. In 1781 he issued the famous Edict of Toleration, which guaranteed to Protestants and Greek Orthodox the right to have their own church buildings and schools, to own property, and to hold political and military offices. Joseph justified this freedom of worship by saying any church could be made obedient to the state. Later actions allowed somewhat more limited liberties to Jews.

The censorship laws were relaxed, and literary works critical of the church could now be published. Other decrees dissolved monasteries and convents or reduced them in size on the grounds that they were useless or wasteful. Only those that operated schools, hospitals, or other charities were allowed to survive. Thus 700 religious houses were shut down and 38,000 monks turned loose. The properties were confiscated and the revenues from them used to fund a state-controlled reorganization of the parishes, the charitable institutions, and pensions and salary supplements for the clergy. Universal and compulsory public education was also implemented.

Emperor Joseph essentially placed the Catholic church under state control. Bishops were required to take an oath of allegiance to the authorities. Papal decrees had to have government permission in order to be valid in Austria. Clerical education was placed under state supervision, and seminaries were to provide training in science and secular knowledge as well as theology. Orders were issued dealing with minute details of religious practice such as pilgrimages, observance of saints' days, and church furnishings. Pope Pius VI even made a hurried trip to Vienna in 1782, where he pleaded with Joseph to rescind his measures but to no avail. The religious reforms remained intact even after his death in 1790, and for Roman Catholics the term "Josephism" ever since has carried the meaning of the church being under the control of a secular state.

A further sign of the church's weakness was the growing attacks on the Jesuits. Monarchs seeking to gain control of the church within

PROMINENT DENOMINATIONS IN THE THIRTEEN AMERICAN COLONIES

COLONY	FIRST SETTLED	PRINCIPAL DENOMINATIONS	ESTABLISHED CHURCH
Virginia	1607	Anglican • Presbyterian • Baptist	Anglican
Massachusetts	1620	Congregational (Puritan) • Separatist, Baptist	Congregational
New Hampshire	1623	Congregational	Congregational
New York	1626	Dutch Reformed • Anglican • Presbyterian	Anglican (1693)
Maryland	1634	Roman Catholic • Anglican • Presbyterian	Anglican (1691)
Connecticut	1634	Congregational	Congregational
Rhode Island	1636	Congregational • Baptist • Quaker	None
New Jersey	1638	Dutch Reformed • Presbyterian • Quaker	None
Delaware	1638	Lutheran • Anglican	None
North Carlolina	1653	Anglican • Presbyterian • Moravian	Anglican
South Carlolina	1670	Anglican • Huguenot • Presbyterian	Anglican
Pennsylvania	1681	Quaker • Lutheran • Mennonite • Brethren •German Reformed • Schwenckfelder • Presbyterian • Moravian	None
Georgia	1733	Anglican • Moravian	Anglican (1758)
Nova Scotia (Acadia)	1710, 1749	Anglican, but toleration was granted to nearly all faiths	Anglican (1758)

their own domains looked upon the Jesuits, the papacy's chief supporters, as agents of a foreign power. Finally, often after lodging trumped-up charges of intrigues, the rulers of Portugal (1759), France (1764), Spain and Naples (1767), and Parma (1768) ordered the Jesuits expelled from their domains. As demands from around Catholic Europe for the complete suppression of the order mounted, Pope Clement XIV in 1773 reluctantly signed the bull dissolving the Society of Jesus.

A complicated situation existed in the eighteenth-century French church. It was large (130,000 clerics—about one-half of one percent of the total population) and quite wealthy, since it owned 6 percent of the land and derived considerable income from its property. However, an enormous social gulf existed between the simple parish priests and the occupants of posts at the episcopal seats (cathedrals). The local clergy were poor and often minimally educated, but they were hard-working and very much aware of their parishioners' grievances. Nearly all higher churchmen and monks were of aristocratic origins and led gentlemanly lives. Bishops often were men of the Enlightenment whose intellectual horizons were enormous but standards of piety quite limited. For instance, the notorious Talleyrand, who served successive French rulers from the Old Regime to the restoration after 1815, made little pretense of Christian faith, and

King Louis XVI complained that Archbishop Loménie de Brienne of Toulouse did not believe in God.

Religious belief flourished in the villages but waned in the towns and cities, where the upper middle class followed the aristocracy into indifference and unbelief. Yet the church leadership remained woefully out of touch with the changing situation in France. It luxuriated in its wealth, continued to demand censorship of the press, and condemned the relaxation of restrictions on Protestants. The perceptive Alexis de Tocqueville observed that the church was hated, "not because the priests claimed to regulate the affairs of the other world, but because they were landed proprietors, lords of manors, tithe owners, and administrators in this world."[1] They were unaware that a revolution was about to take place that would shatter both the secular and religious props of the existing order, the monarchy and the church.

THE FRENCH REVOLUTION

The ongoing inability of the French government to deal with the problems afflicting the country made a revolution almost inevitable. Although France in general was prosperous, the antiquated social system during the "old regime" left the public finances in a desperate situation. The land owned by the clergy and nobility, the so-called "first" and "second" estates or orders of society, was exempt from taxation, even though it constituted 35 percent of the country's area. This meant the tax burden fell upon the "third" estate, the twenty million peasants and four million artisans and middle class (bourgeoisie) that made up 98 percent of the population. Since most of the taxes were paid by the peasantry, they had good reason to be unhappy. Economic factors were not so important in the alienation of the middle class, as their lot was improving, but they resented the social advantages of the nobility and their exclusion from the better positions in the army, civil service, and church.

From Louis XVI's accession to power in 1774, various finance ministers tried in vain to implement financial and tax reforms, and the government debt mounted steadily. Then the American war placed yet new burdens on the treasury. In 1787 the king called a meeting of high churchmen and nobles (the "Notables") to push through a reform program that would tax all land and involve the cooperation of the taxpayers in provincial assemblies to be elected without regard to social class distinctions. This effort failed, and after months of wrangling, the decision was made to convene the Estates-General of France in May 1789, a body that had last met in 1615. The nobles insisted that such a sweeping tax change could only be made with the consent of the entire nation through its representative assembly. They seriously miscalculated in thinking that they could control the Estates-General, and instead a revolutionary storm was unleashed that swept away the ruling institutions of France.

This body did not represent the "people" but rather the "orders" of French society. However, the third estate, supported by some clergy and a few noblemen, seized the leadership and transformed it into a National Assembly, which would write a constitution and transform the state into one based upon Enlightenment principles. But they had to compete with the Parisian masses, who demanded food and a more just economic system and who were responsible for the great symbolic act of the revolution, the storming of the Bastille, the ancient fortress used as a prison, on July 14, 1789. Then violence spread to the countryside when peasants, inflamed by the Bastille incident, began seizing lands, tearing down fences, and burning manor houses.

The National Assembly responded to the situation by dismantling the remains of the manorial system, abolishing legal class differences, and adopting the Declaration of the Rights of Man and Citizen, a sweeping statement of human rights. Over the next two years it made the nation into a constitutional monarchy and attacked the financial problem by confiscating and selling church property and the estates of nobles. Meanwhile, the king had been rendered powerless.

Many of the nobles who fled the country, the so-called émigrés, turned to foreign powers for help in regaining their lost privileges and property. At the same time, a group in the assembly wanted to export the revolution to other countries. The result was the outbreak of war with Austria and Prussia in April 1792. This gave the radicals (the Jacobins) the leverage they needed to topple the constitutional monarchy, and in September a republic was proclaimed. A National Convention was elected to write a new constitution, and its extremist wing secured the execution of Louis XVI in January 1793.

Meanwhile, the French armies had gone on the offensive and the convention proclaimed that the republic would help people everywhere "recover their liberty." Britain, Spain, and Holland then joined the coalition against France, but a conscript army inspired by love of country and led by able young commanders successfully met the foreign challenge. In addition to supplying the army, the republic's leaders had to deal with internal problems—a revolt among the devout Catholic and royalist peasants in the west, inflation, and food shortages.

To run the government a body called the Committee of Public Safety was created, whose dominant member was a young lawyer, Maximilien Robespierre (1758–94). A disciple of Rousseau, he was the "incorruptible" champion of democracy and a fanatical idealist. Under his rule the committee encouraged people to heroic action, conducted foreign policy, imposed rationing and price controls, and ruthlessly crushed opposition from whatever source it might come. Thus was launched the "Terror," the device that would protect the "Republic of Virtue" from its enemies. However, the great majority of the 40,000 people who died in the Terror were not from the first and second estates, but rather were peasants, workers, and small craftsmen. Only fifteen percent of the victims were noblemen or clergy. Madame Roland, a staunch republican who fell afoul of Robespierre, uttered one of the most stinging indictments of revolutionary idealism as she was placed in the guillotine: "O Liberty, what crimes are committed in your name!"

In his ruthless drive to save the revolution as he conceived it, Robespierre alienated more and more people. Now that the armies were victorious, the need for the Terror had ended, but he turned on even his own supporters. No one seemed free from suspicion, and when he denounced those delegates in the National Convention who opposed him, they feared they would be next and ordered his arrest and execution.

Tensions relaxed quickly, and a reaction set in as people greeted the end of the Republic of Virtue with enthusiasm. Revolutionary ardor cooled, the leaders of the extreme phase were discredited and many punished, thousands of prisoners were freed, émigrés streamed back home, and churches reopened. However, the bourgeoisie made sure they kept control of France through the new constitution adopted in 1795. But mounting economic problems, the on-going war, and enemies on the right and left so threatened the regime that it became dependent on the military, especially the young general Napoleon Bonaparte (1769–1821). Finally, in November 1799 he overthrew the government and established a dictatorship. In 1804 he proclaimed himself emperor. The domestic program he implemented during this period proved to be much more enduring than his imperial ventures, and his legal, financial, educational, and religious reforms laid the basis for a modern state.

Napoleon was the supreme military hero in French history, and his brilliant campaigns from Italy in 1796 to Austria in 1809 dazzled the world. He reorganized Italy into satellite republics and kingdoms and later annexed much of it to his empire, and when the two popes of the time objected to his actions, they were brought to France virtually as prisoners (1799 and 1812). In Germany the annexation of the left bank of the Rhine in 1797 meant the demise of the old ecclesiastical states—the archbishoprics of Cologne, Mainz, and Trier—and set in motion the dissolution of the Holy Roman Empire, which came to a formal end in August 1806. By 1810 Napoleon had reorganized Europe into a vast structure of territories dependent on or allied to France. But then he overextended himself in the futile effort to defeat Britain through economic warfare (the Continental System), a no-win guerrilla war in Spain, and the disastrous Russian campaign of 1812. His empire collapsed like a house of cards in 1813–14, and after a brief comeback in 1815 he was exiled to a lonely island in the South Atlantic.

THE REVOLUTION AND THE CHURCH

In 1789 strong support for reform existed among the lower clergy and even some of the higher as well. Most agreed that monasteries were useless institutions and that church finances needed overhauling. Thus, many clerical deputies voted with the third estate during the early months of the National Assembly. Little opposition was expressed when the assembly in August abolished the tithe (the principal church tax) and manorial rights on church properties and in November confiscated and sold the church lands.

In order to give legal basis to these actions and insure the church's subordination to the state, the assembly on July 12, 1790, adopted the Civil Constitution of the Clergy. This provided for the "rationalization" of the church structure and its personnel. It stipulated state salaries for the clergy, ones that would be more equitable, as those of the bishops were sharply reduced while the parish priests received substantial raises. It also pensioned off a large number of church personnel who seemed to be performing no useful functions, unless they agreed to "purposeful" employment as teachers or parish clergy. The result was the elimination of about 60 percent of the religious establishment in 1789. The Civil Constitution also reduced the number of dioceses and made them coterminous with the new administrative districts of France, the departments. The clergy were to be chosen through lay elections: bishops by the department electors, and priests by district electors, the same people who voted for deputies to the legislative body. The pope was still recognized as the theoretical head of the church, but he no longer could receive tax money from the French clergy or confirm the appointment of bishops. The assembly also demanded that all clergy swear an oath of allegiance to the civil constitution.

In 1791 Pope Pius VI denounced the constitution as schismatic and heretical and suspended all priests and prelates who had taken the oath. The large number of "refractory" or "non-juring" clergy, that is, those who would not swear the oath, led to an open split in the church and the appearance of "anticlericalism" for the first time. This may be defined as opposition to any dogmatic or institutional form of Christianity because the established order in church affairs is viewed as reactionary and a bulwark of political tyranny. It would be a major force in nineteenth-century Europe.

As anticlericalism in the assembly escalated, so the opposition of the non-juring clerics to the "constitutional" church hardened. Soon they were seen as counterrevolutionaries, especially after the war with Austria and Prussia had begun. Many felt Pius VI was the moving spirit behind the clergy coalition, and non-jurors were now suspect as traitors. Around 30,000 to 40,000 non-juring priests emigrated or were exiled, while many others were jailed, and 2,000 to 5,000 were killed. One method of execution was "de-Christianization by immersion," where clerics were tied together in pairs and thrown into the Loire River.

The campaign of de-Christianization reached ludicrous proportions as pagan cults were formed to honor revolutionary martyrs like Jean Paul Marat. Another example was the celebration accepting the new constitution, which took place on the site of the Bastille in August 1793. A member of the Committee of Public Safety stood before a statue of "Nature" and intoned:

> Sovereign of nations, savage or civilized—Oh, Nature!—this great people is worthy of thee. It is free. After traversing so many centuries of errors and servitudes, it had to return to the simplicity of thy ways to rediscover equality and liberty.[2]

Bastille Day itself was commemorated throughout France in a religious fashion. People stood around an open-air altar and took an oath to the nation—*la Patrie.*

Hannah More

In the Republic of Virtue, the "Cult of Reason" supplanted Christianity. Several thousand churches were converted into "Temples of Reason," revolutionary heroes like Voltaire and Rousseau took the place of the Virgin and the saints, and abstractions such as law, truth, liberty, and nature were worshiped. On November 10, 1793, a "Festival of Reason" was held in Notre Dame cathedral in Paris, where the statue of the Virgin was replaced by an actress, to whom hymns were sung. At a service in Beauvais, reason, liberty, and nature were worshiped as three goddesses.

The Christian calendar was discarded in favor of a new one. The year 1 began on the day the republic was founded, September 22, 1792, a week lasted ten days, and Sundays and all church holidays were eliminated. The twelve months were given names representing their seasonal occurrence, and a holiday period at year's end was used to celebrate the revolution. Even the "constitutional" church itself was persecuted, and the priests no longer received salaries or were allowed to teach in the public schools.

Robespierre, a deist as well as a politician, soon saw that the Cult of Reason was alienating too many people and decided to end de-Christianization. Acknowledging that the "Supreme Being" had made France the Republic of Virtue, he gave credit where credit was due. In June 1794 he introduced the "Worship of the Supreme Being," a deistic natural religion that recognized the existence of God and the immortality of the soul. Its rituals essentially were a parody of the Catholic liturgy. This proved no more successful in rallying the masses to the Republic of Virtue, and in fact the peasants in western France (the Vendée), incited by non-juring clergy, were in open revolt against the regime and would remain so for the rest of the decade.

Most historians recognize that the Civil Constitution of the Clergy was the greatest tactical blunder of the French Revolution, and certainly its long-range impact was most unfortunate. Not only did it stir up religious fanaticism and undermine the revolution, but also it guaranteed that the Catholic church in the following century would be hostile to liberalism and democracy everywhere, while at the same time democrats and liberals would become militantly anticlerical. The French church, which had long enjoyed considerable independence, was now thrown into the arms of the pope, and this was a major step in the process of recentralization that would occur in the next decades.

When Napoleon seized power, he recognized that the state needed a religion that would make ordinary people conform to society. Although he claimed to have lost his faith at age eleven and was a pure eighteenth-century rationalist, he concluded that patriotism worked best when it was reinforced by religion and that people needed this authority. As he calmly put it,

> I hold . . . that apart from the precepts and doctrines of the Gospel there is no society that can flourish, nor any real civilization. What is it that makes the poor man take it for granted that ten chimneys smoke in my palace while he dies of cold—that I have ten changes of raiment in my wardrobe while he is naked—that on my table at each meal there is enough to sustain a family for a week? It is religion which says to him that in another life I shall be his equal, indeed that he has a better chance of being happy there than I have.[3]

He also recognized that the refractory clergy were the spiritual force behind the counterrevolution and decided that the way out of the impasse of the last decade was to restore the church. Accordingly, he turned to Pope Pius VII and concluded the Concordat of 1801. The government recognized Catholicism as "the religion of the great majority" of French citizens, allowed the pope a say in the appointment of bishops, and public worship could again take place. The Vatican accepted the loss of church lands (including its own territory of Avignon that the French had seized in 1791) and the end of church taxes. Henceforth the state would pay the clergy's salaries. The pope in effect recognized the French state and civil peace was restored, but Napoleon dispelled any idea of an established church by putting Protestant ministers on the public payroll as well. Pius was invited to attend the imperial coronation in Paris in 1804, but he was not given any role in the ceremony.

Throughout his empire Napoleon implemented the religious reforms of the French Revolution. Everywhere the church lost its position as a public authority alongside the state, its courts and taxing power were curtailed, and much of its lands were confiscated. Protestants, Jews, and unbelievers were accorded the same civil rights as Catholics. On the other hand, the reforms actually strengthened the papacy. The embarrassing institution of the Spanish Inquisition had been abolished, the ecclesiastical princedoms of Germany that asserted their own claims to authority were now gone, and the old monarchies with their strong national churches, like Austria, Spain, Portugal, and France, which formerly exercised so much influence over papal matters had been weakened. With the restoration of the Jesuits in 1814 the way was open for the resurgence of papal authority.

A SPIRITUAL REVOLUTION IN BRITAIN

While revolution was the order of the day on the continent, the British Parliament had achieved the political supremacy that the absolute monarchs had formerly possessed. But it was neither representative nor democratic, since the suffrage was extremely unequal and those seeking election often had to buy votes. Its efforts to bring about a general centralization of the empire failed in America, but Scotland and Ireland were brought fully under its control. The Highland Scots were subdued in the 1740s, whereas the Presbyterian Scots who lived in the north of Ireland and were generally anti-English, were brought into line after the American Revolution. The latter even joined forces with the Catholic majority in trying to free the island from English rule, but their revolt in 1798 was crushed. In 1801 Ireland was formally united with Great Britain into one kingdom.

Improvements in agriculture during the century had contributed to a modest increase in the English standard of living, while the burgeoning industrial economy provided the lower middle class with opportunities for advancement. Pressures for reforming the political system mounted in the years after 1763, and considerable social unrest resulted. Especially outspoken was the eminent political theorist Edmund Burke (1729–97), who pointed to the British failures in America and argued for eliminating the worst abuses in the parliamentary system.

The French Revolution had serious repercussions in Britain, and many wished to see something similar happen in their own country. Tom Paine's tract *Rights of Man* (1791), which appealed to the British to overthrow the monarchy and establish a republic, was quite influential. Joseph Priestley (1733–1804), the noted scientist and leading Unitarian in Britain defended the revolution in a 1791 tract that evoked considerable hostility. However, Edmund Burke's *Reflections on the Revolution in France* (1790) predicted anarchy and dictatorship and urged the English to accept the slow adaptation of their own liberties. He condemned a political philosophy based on abstract principles of right and wrong and insisted that each people must be shaped by its own national history and circumstances, even though the political systems that emerged might differ. By 1792 the unchecked violence in France seemed to vindicate Burke, and to discredit the revolution as the dawn of a new day for political liberty. It also undermined the parliamentary reform movement.

But there was another viable force for change in Britain—evangelical religion. Methodism had spread widely among the lower classes, especially in the new industrial towns in the north. This created tensions with the Church of England establishment and led inexorably to a break. Wesley's use of unordained preachers and itinerant ministers, the creation of separate meeting places and the administration of Holy Communion in these, the formation of a connectional organization apart from the Anglican structure, and the founding of a separate work in America widened the gap. Finally, the formal secession occurred in 1795, four years after the founder's death.

The Methodist revivals had a decisive impact on the established church and, to a lesser extent, the dissenting churches. The term "evangelical" soon came to be applied to the Anglican supporters of the revival, who comprised a "party" within the church. They preferred to work within the parish structures of the church and firmly resisted the employment of unordained preachers. They disapproved of practices commonly associated with Methodism, such as emotional enthusiasm, itinerant preaching, founding of chapels, and perfectionist doctrines. Like George Whitefield, they tended to be

Calvinist in their doctrinal stance. Because they were parish-based and dependent on the support of the local gentry, they tended in their ministries to appeal to the higher socioeconomic levels and to neglect the poorer classes that the Methodists were so effective in reaching. Also, whereas Wesley had a high regard for the New Testament period churches, the evangelicals looked more to the church of the Reformation and the Puritan tradition.

The evangelical revival developed almost simultaneously in a number of places between the 1740s and 1760s as a result of individual conversions. Some found Christ through the reading of devotional works and others through personal contacts. As individual clergymen became converted, they began evangelizing their own parishes and other clergy in the neighborhood and before long small groups formed around them. Among the notable early evangelicals were John Fletcher (1729–85); Augustus Toplady (1740–78), the hymnwriter ("Rock of Ages"); Samuel Walker (1714–61); and Joseph Milner (1744–97), an amateur church historian who was headmaster of a grammar school that William Wilberforce attended. In the London area were such notable figures as William Romaine (1714–95), Henry Venn (1724–97), and, above all, John Newton (1725–1807).

The son of a merchant sea captain, Newton was forced into the Royal Navy as a youth. He deserted his ship in West Africa where he eventually became the servant of a slave trader. For two years he lived a miserable existence but was finally freed and boarded a ship for England. On the voyage home Newton's vessel encountered a violent storm. Faced with the imminent prospect of death, he turned to Christ in faith. He then served for four years as captain of a slave ship, which gave him first-hand knowledge of this odious traffic, but in 1755 his conscience won out and he gave up the sea. After a period of private study, he was ordained an Anglican clergyman and served for fifteen years at Olney in Buckinghamshire where he and the poet William Cowper (1731–1800) produced a famous collection of "Olney" hymns. Among their compositions were Cowper's "God Moves in a Mysterious Way" and "There Is a Fountain Filled with Blood"; and Newton's "Amazing Grace," "How Sweet the Name of Jesus Sounds," and "Glorious Things of Thee Are Spoken." In 1779 he moved to London where he became a leading figure in the campaign against the slave trade and a spiritual counselor to the evangelicals.

Isaac Milner (1750–1820), the brother of Joseph, and Charles Simeon (1759–1836) made Cambridge a center of evangelicalism.

Milner became a fellow of Queen's College in 1776 and its president in 1788, and under him the college became the evangelical stronghold at the university. In 1785 Milner accompanied the young Wilberforce on a trip to Europe and through their conversations the latter was converted. Simeon was appointed vicar of Holy Trinity Church in 1782 and provided spiritual guidance to an entire generation of evangelical preachers. Probably more than any person of the time, he taught evangelicals to hold firmly to the Church of England and to resist latitudinarianism as well as indiscriminate enthusiasm and secessionism.

By far the most important expression of Anglican evangelicalism in the realm of social action was the Clapham Sect. This "brotherhood of Christian politicians," actually a diverse group of laypersons, centered around the parish church of Clapham, a London suburb, whose pastor was John Venn (1759–1813), the son of Henry. They were second-generation evangelicals—wealthy, close to those with political power, well-informed on the matters they dealt with, and adept in the techniques of political persuasion. Following the lead of Wesley as well as the early Anglican evangelicals, they understood the need for organization to make their work effective. Also, they were people of deep conviction who emphasized both conversion and applying their faith to meeting societal needs.

The group became knit together in an astonishing intimacy and solidarity, almost like one large family. They lived and visited in one another's houses, both in Clapham and London proper as well as in the country. They came to be known as "the Saints" because of their religious fervor and desire to establish righteousness in the nation. Various commentators have observed that they planned and worked like a committee that remained in permanent session and that they held "cabinet councils" in their residences to discuss wrongs that needed righting and the strategies they would use to achieve their goals.

The origins of the Clapham Sect may be traced to the relationship established by the Thornton family and William Wilberforce (1759–1833). The wealthy merchant, John Thornton (1720–90), and his son Henry (1760–1815), a prominent banker, were evangelicals. Henry was also a member of Parliament, and in 1792 he not only took up residence in Clapham but also arranged (through Charles Simeon) the appointment of John Venn to the parish church. Thornton's home became the meeting place for the group.

Wilberforce, a cousin of Thornton, was elected to Parliament at age twenty-one and soon became a lively figure in London society.

THE CLAPHAM SECT

The term "Clapham Sect" was coined in the 1840s to designate a close-knit group of Christians, mostly evangelical Anglicans, who resided in the London suburb of Clapham or frequently visited there during the period circa 1792-1815. They were people of high social standing who worked together for social reform and spreading the gospel.

*People who lived in Clapham at least part of this time.

Charles Simeon (1759-1836), vicar of Holy Trinity Church, Cambridge, and mentor to this entire generation of evangelicals
***John Venn** (1759-1813), from 1793 rector of Clapham church and spiritual leader of the group
***Henry Thornton** (1760-1815), prominent banker and member of Parliament who moved to Clapham in1792 and whose home was a meeting place of the group
***William Wilberforce** (1759-1833), member of Parliament, leader of the fight against the slave trade and moral corruption in England, cousin of Thornton
***James Stephen** (1758-1832), lawyer in the West Indies and then in London, also member of Parliament and married to Wilberforce's sister
***Zachary Macaulay** (1768-1838), plantation overseer in West Indies and later headed up the Sierra Leone settlement
***Charles Grant** (1746-1823), official of the East India Company and from 1794 leading director of the East India Council in London, member of Parliament
***John Shore, Lord (Baron) Teignmouth** (1751-1834), governor-general of the East India Company (1793-97)
Thomas Gisborne (1758-1846), clergyman in Yoxall, Staffordshire, advisor to Wilberforce on slavery matters, spent spare time in Clapham
Thomas Babington (1758-1837), member of Parliament from Rothley Temple, Leicestershire, brother-in law of both Gisborne and Macauley
***William Smith** (1756-1835), member of Parliament
***Charles Elliott** (1751-1832), brother-in-law of John Venn
***Edward James Eliot** (1758-1797), brother-in-law of Prime Minister Pitt, was to be governer-general in India but died unexpectedly
Hannah More (1745-1833), writer and educational reformer in Somerset,spent much time in the company of Clapham figures
Granville Sharp (1735-1813), anti slavery figure who secured court decision in 1772 banning slavery in Britian
Thomas Clarkson (1760-1846), prominent figure in abolitionist movement who gathered the data on the slave trade that Wilberforce used
Josiah Pratt (1768-1844), first editor of the *Christian Observer* in 1802; a founder of both the CMS and the British and Foreign Bible Society

CAUSES THEY ESPOUSED

Abolition of the slave trade • Formation of Bible and tract societies to spread the gospel • Foriegn missions and opening India to missionary work • Sunday schools and elementary education • Assistance to the poor and improving lot of the working class • Banning public immorality, brutal sports, and drunkenness • Penal and prison reform • Maintenance of the sabbath

As noted above, he was converted while on a "grand tour" of Europe, and for a time he considered leaving public life and entering the service of the church. However, Prime Minister William Pitt, who wanted to keep him as a functioning ally in Parliament, persuaded him that an active involvement in public affairs was part of one's Christian duty. In 1786 he declared his resolve "to live to God's glory and his fellow creatures' good," and the following year he wrote, "God Almighty has set before me two great objects—the abolition of the slave trade and the reformation of manners."[4]

To achieve the latter Wilberforce used his influence to secure from George III a Royal Proclamation against Vice and Immorality and formed the "Proclamation Society" to put it into effect. This included suppressing "blasphemous" literature, checking the excesses of the liquor traffic, and enforcing Sunday observance. Then he turned his attention to the slave trade, and with the assistance of his allies at Clapham kept hammering away at a reluctant Parliament until finally in 1807 it passed the bill abolishing the trade by British citizens. (In 1833 slavery was abolished in the entire empire.) Others worked to open India to missions, founded missionary, Bible, and tract societies, and gave money to build churches and support clergymen. Among the Clapham figures, besides those mentioned, were the antislavery fighters Granville Sharp and Thomas Clarkson, two top executives in the East India Company, several lawyers and merchants, a number of members of Parliament, and the writer Hannah More.

Regarded by contemporaries as the leading English woman of letters, More (1745–1833) turned from fashionable society and literary fame to a life of charitable endeavors. Newton and Wilberforce encouraged her in her effort to set up schools for poor children and adults at Cheddar in the Mendip Hills, and much of the financing for this came from Clapham figures. She also used her literary gifts to produce the *Cheap Repository Tracts,* 114 of which appeared between 1792 and 1798 and had a circulation of more than two million. They were intended to be wholesome reading material for the working classes that would counteract revolutionary tendencies and radical propaganda.

Some Historical Considerations

In his classic work, *England in 1815* (1913), French historian Elie Halévy set forth the view that Britain was spared the counterpart to the revolution that convulsed France, one that the contradictions in its political and economic system easily could have produced, because of the stabilizing influence of Methodism and evangelical religion. He argued that from 1739 on, economic crises and working class agitation were defused by evangelical preaching and revivalism. Such expressions of religious enthusiasm were the form of popular upheaval least capable of unsettling a social order founded upon inequality and wealth.

Similar arguments had been heard throughout the nineteenth century and Halévy's accomplishment was to popularize them. Some writers, especially socialists and Marxists, have used this to discredit evangelicalism as the opiate of the masses. Others, such as Ford K. Brown in *Fathers of the Victorians* (1961), point to the "social control" practiced by the evangelicals, for example, the program of the Proclamation Society and Wilberforce's conception of "reformation of manners." The paradoxical fact that they were both political conservatives and political innovators has baffled commentators from that time to the present.

The question historians wrestle with is how much evangelicalism was a genuinely disinterested response to the spiritual challenge of the time and how far it was the rationalization of a policy to enhance the power of the ruling classes. To which challenge was Wilberforce most sensitive—the need to rescue souls in peril of eternal damnation or the fear of what might happen if the masses succumbed to Jacobinism? The radical William Cobbett sarcastically defined the issue by saying that the mission of the "Saints" was "to teach the people to starve without making a noise," and to keep "the poor from cutting the throats of the rich." In response, some point out that the evangelicals also summoned the upper classes to a life of responsibility and that they continued the Church of England's traditional teaching on concern for the poor, while adding the element of zeal. On balance, one can say that the achievements of the evangelical reformers were of heroic proportions, and they serve as excellent role models for Christians today. However, their failure to see just how culture-bound their actions were detracts from the overall significance of their work.

On the other hand, Bernard Semmel (*The Methodist Revolution*, 1979) maintains that Methodism (and by implication Anglican evangelicalism) was a "liberal" and "progressive" movement that fostered modernization in Britain. It was the English version of the "Democratic Revolution," and it forestalled a violent counterpart to the French Revolution by preempting the latter's appeal. The Methodist preachers proclaimed a liberating and egalitarian doctrine and gave their adherents a sense of fraternity by integrating them into bands and societies. Wesley's incessant call for self-discipline and political order was articulated simultaneously with the call for a spiritual revolution. By preaching reason, tolerance, and civil and religious liberty, seeing humans as good and capable of perfection in this life, and urging people to assert control over their own lives, the Methodist revolution paved the way for England to become a liberal democracy.

Following in this vein, David Bebbington in *Evangelicalism in Modern Britain* (1989) has pointed to another important dimension of the revival movement, namely, its affinity with the Enlightenment. Contrary to the scores of Christian writers who have uncritically decried the Enlightenment, Bebbington shows that the evangelicals adopted its emphasis on epistemology (the science of knowledge) and affirmed that God had given them self-evident knowledge of Himself, which they should spread to others. They also stressed reason, for as Wesley wrote in 1768, "That to renounce reason is to renounce religion, that religion and reason go hand in hand, and that all irrational religion is false religion."[5] Further, they had a deep appreciation for science and the scientific method, and they stressed "experimental religion."

There were other Enlightenment features reflected in evangelical expression. One was a strong sense of optimism flowing from a belief in divine Providence, the idea that God cared for the world and would enable them to make it a better place. They also felt that God wished all persons to enjoy happiness in this life. The Enlightenment emphasis on moderation could be seen in the actions of Wesley and others who cautioned against the excesses of "enthusiasm." The evangelicals' stress on pragmatism was reflected in such things as open-air preaching, functional church buildings, and lay ministry. Finally, they focused on ethical and moral concerns, and were deeply committed to reform.

The revolutionary era saw both the sweeping away of old structures, both political and religious, and the creation of new ones. Protestantism and Catholicism were greatly affected by the political turmoil. The former was revitalized and the latter purged of old ways. These changes opened the way for renewal after 1815. However, emerging out of the period were new political ideologies that would constitute an even more serious challenge for the church in the decades to follow.

18

THE CHURCH IN AN AGE OF IDEOLOGY

Both the Enlightenment and the French Revolution greatly affected the development of Christianity in the nineteenth century. Rooted in this period were the three major post-Christian ideologies of modern times—nationalism, individualism (liberalism), and Marxist socialism (communism). As traditional religion lost its hold on the "enlightened" intellectual community and eventually on the masses as well, these new beliefs took its place. By the early twentieth century they had assumed the character of religious faith, in that they made ultimate demands on a person and possessed their own sacred symbols, ceremonies, dogmas, inspired writings, saints, and charismatic leaders. Nationalism in particular, and liberal individualism to a lesser extent, became so attached to Christianity that few believers could tell the difference.

International Transitions After 1815

As Napoleon's empire collapsed in early 1814, the victorious powers—Britain, Austria, Prussia, and Russia—concluded a diplomatic alliance against France, restored the Bourbon monarch Louis

XVIII, and sent Napoleon into exile. In the fall they assembled in Vienna and redrew the map of Europe to preserve the balance of power and keep France in check. This included territorial transfers, restoration of deposed rulers, and returning Italy and Germany to their former condition of division, where a variety of states were located on their soil, with Austria exercising strong influence over their political affairs. Napoleon reappeared in France in the spring of 1815, but the coalition dealt him a final blow at the battle of Waterloo. The allies then made a new treaty with Louis XVIII and two agreements for further cooperation—the Holy Alliance and the Quadruple Alliance.

The latter provided a mechanism whereby the allies would meet from time to time to deal with matters affecting the peace of Europe. Four of these "congresses" took place between 1818 and 1822, but then the alliance fell into disuse because of differences among the members about the Greek revolt against Turkish rule and the liberation struggles in Latin America. At the same time, conservative regimes in the major countries sought to suppress all movements toward liberal democracy.

A rising tide of revolution in 1830 swept away some of the reactionary regimes, especially in France. Violence in Britain was forestalled only by parliamentary reforms in 1832 that extended voting power to the growing middle classes and made them allies of the established order. In Russia, however, a liberal movement was put down in 1825, and a Polish uprising six years later was dealt with similarly. Then, in 1848–49 a second wave of democratic revolutions struck that had a much greater impact. The monarchy in France was replaced by a republic, the rulers of Prussia and Austria were forced to grant constitutions, and it appeared that Germany and Italy might even be united. But within two years all the liberal democratic movements had been crushed and a period of sober "realism" followed.

Henceforth, those who wished political change turned away from liberal idealism, peaceful persuasion, and popular protests to the politics of power and the use of "practical" means to achieve their objectives. The stage was set for two decades of violence—the Crimean War (1853–56), a pointless conflict in which Russia suffered a humiliating defeat at the hands of a Western coalition; conflicts in Italy that brought about national unification in 1870; the three wars instigated by Prussia, which created the German Empire in 1871; and the bloody Civil War in the United States (1861–65) that insured the survival of the federal union.

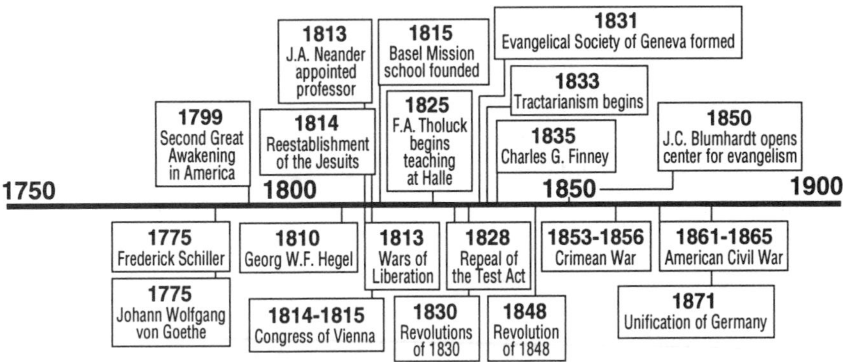

ROMANTICISM AND NATIONALISM

While these political and military events captured public attention, significant intellectual changes were also occurring. One of these was Romanticism, a movement in art, literature, philosophy, and religion. Arising in the 1790s as a reaction to the Enlightenment, it was rooted in the thought of earlier writers such as Rousseau and the Storm and Stress school in Germany, whose main representatives, Johann Wolfgang von Goethe (1749–1832) and Friedrich von Schiller (1759–1805) emphasized the turbulence of the human spirit. Goethe's *Götz von Berlichingen* (1773) and *Sorrows of the Young Werther* (1774) were important preromantic works, while *Faust,* a dramatic two-part poem written in his mature years, was the great masterpiece of German literature. In Britain the leading figures in Romanticism included William Wordsworth, Samuel Coleridge, and Sir Walter Scott.

Romantics rejected classicism and rationalism but stressed emotionalism, sensuality, fantasy, and imagination. Reality was to be found not by rational thought but through one's feelings, the senses, spiritual illumination, and listening to the inner voice. They regarded all experience as subjective and stressed self-consciousness, spontaneity, and originality. A sense of mystery arose out of an inner longing for that which was unknown and unexperienced. Each personality should be allowed to unfold itself freely, according to its own genius and individual characteristics. Beauty, color, adventure, the exotic, and rural life distinguished romantic artistic and literary works, and traditional or prescribed forms were rejected for those that were different, unconventional, and novel. Also there was a deep interest in the past, especially the Middle Ages, as well as in Nordic mythology and folklore. Finally, their art was visionary and even mystical, for as one German poet put it, in the romantic view of life "world becomes dream, dream becomes world."

Romanticism contributed heavily to the rise of modern nationalism. Whereas the Enlightenment philosophes were cosmopolitan in their outlook and emphasized similarities among peoples and nations, the romantics turned inward to their own national origins and traditions. In his four-volume *Ideas on the Philosophy of the History of Mankind* (1784–91), the Protestant pastor and teacher Johann Gottfried Herder (1744–1803) maintained that the educated classes in Germany, who were too dependent upon French thought and manners, should develop their native culture instead. He argued that each *Volk* (people), that is, a body of persons sharing a common language, possessed a unique *Geist* (spirit or genius), and the *Volksgeist* (national character) should be allowed to work itself out in its own way. In order to be authentic, the national culture had to rise from the life of the *Volk*, the common people, and draw its inspiration from them. The *Völker* were a natural feature of the human race, and their diversity was the Almighty's design. Herder's theory of nationalism was purely cultural in nature—there was no political agenda—and this concept of national development was equally applicable to other peoples besides the Germans. Following his lead, various German writers explored their law, folklore, and religion, but after 1800 others began to speak of German cultural superiority. The philosopher J. G. Fichte, in a lecture series in 1807–1808, called for the moral regeneration of the people through education. They should become aware of their unique national character and learn to love their fatherland. An individual could only obtain "freedom" by identifying with the greater personality of the nation, and the Germans had a genius not possessed by other peoples.

The most important philosopher of the time, Georg W. F. Hegel (1770–1831), carried this one step further and emphasized the state. His ideas were contained in a vast, complex system that is difficult to understand, but they exercised an enormous influence. In reaction to Kant, whose critical philosophy left the world of thought in pieces, Hegel saw the universe as one great whole. To him reality was the "Absolute Mind" or the "World Spirit," which revealed itself in nature and history. Each particular person's mind is an aspect of the World Spirit, and intellectual activity is a phase of the Absolute itself.

To explain how this took place, Hegel drew upon a methodology of reasoning known as the dialectic. In this approach, an existing idea, theme, or "thesis" is opposed by or gives rise to its opposite or contradiction, the "antithesis." Out of their conflict emerges an idea or "synthesis" that is both new and superior to its predecessor. This development, which he called the "self-realization of the Absolute Idea," was occurring in nature, science, and the historical process. History changes through the clash of forces in the realm of pure ideas, and the state was one of these ideas. The three main phases of the state's history were the Asiatic, characterized by absolute monarchy; the classical, marked by individual freedom; and last the Germanic, which was a synthesis of freedom in the context of the all-powerful state. At this point of "full consciousness" all people would possess freedom, not just the monarch or the select few.[1]

Hegel's view of the state was not as authoritarian as one might think. Rather he saw it as the highest development of the community, the place where the perfect society would find its existence. It was like Rousseau's general will, the manifestation of the rational spirit of the entire community. Hegel rejected the individualism of the American and French Revolutions, believing that this was contrary to the nature of humanity and reality. In his system the individual only had value and meaning as a part of the greater unified whole. Thus, his preoccupation with the political appealed to the Germans of the time, who were longing for national unity. Although they did not possess unity at that time, still they could feel that it would eventually come through the movement of history.

During the Romantic Age writers from other countries took up Herder's challenge to focus on cultural heritage—their history, language, literature, and art. Among the results were the Greek revival that led to their revolt against Turkish rule, the Magyar resurgence in Hungary that called for greater autonomy within the Austrian Empire, and the Italian nationalist movement against the princes in 1815. Moreover, although the Jacobins in revolutionary France had utilized nationalism to rally public support, during the Napoleonic era it served as a catalyst for resistance to the conqueror. It was a major force in the Spanish insurgency, the Russian effort of 1812, and the German renewal that culminated in the War of Liberation in 1813.

To sum up, nationalism is a sentiment or feeling possessed by a people who come to believe they are different from others, that is, they are a nation, and they desire to affirm this uniqueness. The existence of nationality is not an objective reality that can be determined logically, but rather is irrational, emotional, mystical. The ultimate aim of a nationalist is to create a nation-state, a political order in which those of one's own nationality exercise power.

In the first half of the nineteenth century nationalism was marked by humanity, diversity, and sympathy for others. Following Herder's lead, most early nationalists believed that the fulfillment of national aspirations was essential to the general welfare of humanity. Each one had its contribution to make to world civilization, and society would be richer if the various nationalities were allowed free play. Only after midcentury did the movement begin to turn ugly, and the shift toward exclusivism and national superiority become noticeable.

Still, even in its early stages nationalism showed its face as a rival to the Christian faith. Timothy Dwight (1752–1817), president of Yale College and a landmark figure in American Christianity, bitterly opposed "infidelity," which he saw as the product of the Enlightenment. He called upon Americans to resist the spread of French ideas, since their nation had a special role in the divine plan. God had preserved them during the revolutionary struggle, and they had grown spiritually and physically since then. Many signs now pointed to the advent of a new age, and the kingdom of God was about to come to earth. This would result from revival among Christians and the spread of the American system of religious and political liberty throughout the world, because their nation was God's agent for converting humankind. In countering the French threat to Christianity, Dwight had invested his own land with spiritual significance and identified America with God's purpose.

Romanticism and Religion

Romantics glorified their own powers of self-expression and creativity. They would not give allegiance to any spiritual force superior to their own genius or the objects of their devotion such as nature, liberty, beauty, and love. Some, however, did embrace Christianity. In 1798 the German writer Friedrich von Schlegel had what appeared to be a conversion experience (to Roman Catholicism), and thereafter religious themes filled his works. The poet Novalis in *Christendom or Europe* (1799) portrayed Christianity as the symbol of a universal world faith, the purest example of religion as a historical phenomenon, and the most complete revelation. Both men influenced the young preacher Friedrich Schleiermacher (1768–1834), who was the leading theologian of the nineteenth century and the father of liberal Protestant theology.

Educated in Moravian schools and at Halle, Schleiermacher was shaped by mystical pietism. Appointed as chaplain at a prominent Berlin hospital in 1794, he came into contact with the circle of romantic writers in the city. In fact, Schlegel encouraged Schleiermacher to write *On Religion: Addresses to Its Cultured Despisers* (1799), a defense of the faith to the intellectuals of the day. He argued that rationalism had ignored the true essence of religion, which is feeling. This enables a person to experience God directly. Piety arises from the experience of God (the Infinite) through one's experience of the world (the finite), not by some process of rational reflection. Like the Romantics, he believed that people understood the world in which they lived more through imagination and feeling than through studying it by rational analysis. God is not transcendent but present in the world, and the believer makes contact with Him directly. Instead of being something that grows out of doctrinal expressions or church life, religion is the immediate experience of human existence.

Schleiermacher left the Prussian capital in 1804 to teach at Halle but returned three years later to preach at Trinity Church and then to serve as professor of theology at Berlin University. He held both posts until his death a quarter-century later. He published many works expressing what was a romantic view of theology, the most important being *The Christian Faith* (1821). In this he set forth the idea of the individual believer's absolute "dependence," or "God-consciousness." The failure of dependence is sin, but Christ is the man who was utterly dependent on God in every thought, word, and deed. This means that God existed in Him and therefore He was divine. Hence, Christian doctrines are the expressions of one's religious understanding. The Bible shapes and informs the Christian's God-consciousness but at the same time is a product of this dependence. The fundamental religious awareness led to the development of Christian communities where Jesus' God-consciousness and redemptive work brought believers into a full knowledge of God. For them regeneration occurs by participating in the corporate life of the church rather than simply believing in Christ's death and resurrection. There they experience his God-consciousness.

In these years a number of Romantics turned to the Roman Catholic church, where they found a secure resting place. Noteworthy was the popular writer François René Vicomte de Chateaubriand (1768–1848), who was converted to a living faith. In his famous work *The Genius of Christianity* (1802) he elevated defending the faith from the plane of reason to that of feeling and argued that history revealed Catholicism as a great cultural and moral force.

THE CONSERVATIVES

The "restoration" era that followed Napoleon's downfall was characterized both by a retreat to conservatism and the advance of liberalism. At the Congress of Vienna the old political order was not completely restored; for example, the Holy Roman Empire was not reconstituted, but monarchy was affirmed as the only governmental form that could ensure stability. The best example of this was the Holy Alliance, a proposal of Tsar Alexander I, who at the time was influenced by mysticism and messianism. Many have argued that the inspiration for the Holy Alliance came from Baroness Julie von Krüdener, a writer who had experienced a pietistic conversion and was in his entourage at the time, but most scholars now feel the idea originated with the tsar himself. It was signed by all the European monarchs except the English regent, the pope, and the Turkish sultan, and it proclaimed that international relations would henceforth be based on "the sublime truths which the Holy Religion teaches." The rulers agreed they would abide by the principle that they were brothers, "lend each other aid and assistance" whenever necessary, and recognize no other sovereign than "God our Divine Saviour, Jesus Christ." Although the Holy Alliance had no teeth whatsoever, it essentially maintained the status quo in Eastern Europe until the Crimean War.

The conservative trend was most evident in the Catholic church. As soon as he was freed from French captivity in 1814, Pope Pius VII reestablished the Jesuit order. Then through his secretary of state who represented him at Vienna, Pius regained the papal territories in Italy. He also concluded favorable treaties with several countries and condemned the Carbonari, an Italian nationalist movement. Under him and his successors the "Ultramontane" position triumphed, that is, the full centralization of church authority in the papal curia in Rome, as opposed to national churches or diocesan independence. The popes also fought social liberalism in France and in 1834 drove the popular writer Félicité de Lamennais (originally a traditionalist) out of the church.

Reactionary Catholic "traditionalism" was best represented in the works of Joseph de Maistre (1753–1821) and Louis de Bonald (1754–1840). Émigrés during the French Revolution, they stressed historical development and divine providence over against human autonomy, and called for the restoration of the Bourbon monarchy.

Timothy Dwight

Following the lead of Edmund Burke, they denounced the Enlightenment's emphasis on reason and natural rights. But they went further to attack the entire liberal emphasis on social contract theory and individual liberties. The conservatives also condemned the lack of respect for ecclesiastical authority, and de Maistre in particular affirmed Catholic Christianity as the very foundation of the social order.

In *On the Pope* (1819) de Maistre said all sovereignty is derived from God and vested in the monarch. Because the king's authority is divine in origin, his power may in no way be limited by his subjects. Religion provides the people with a motive for obedience to the ruler and reconciles them to the natural inequalities in society. The church and state must collaborate in promoting human morality and preserving order, and should a conflict between the two arise, the authority of the church automatically takes precedence. He ended by portraying the pope as the supreme political and religious authority in what amounted to a universal theocracy.

German conservatives incorporated an important romantic concept into their thinking, the idea of organicism, and in fact a leading exponent of this was Schleiermacher. The state was not the product of a social contract but rather was an autonomous development and a higher form of life. It grew according to its own laws, and the individual achieved fulfillment and true freedom within the context of the state. Even nationality itself was an organic development. A group of people speaking the same language and having common historical experiences tended to organize themselves politically. Thus, the state was an organism in which the nation had developed in the course of history, and both institutions were divine creations.

According to the organicists, revolution had no place as it would only distort the natural growth of the body politic. The state was rooted in the past, and the ruler, people, and church were all parts of one spiritual organism. State and church, throne and altar, belonged together and should be organized in the same manner, that is, the state monarchical and the church episcopal.[2] One result of this view was King Frederick William III's action in 1817, the tricentennial of the posting of the Ninety-five Theses, uniting the Reformed and Lutheran churches into "one evangelical church"—the so-called Prussian Union. His intention was to achieve a common front against rationalism, which he saw as the enemy of faith, but this provoked reaction from all sides.

The Lutheran conservatives ("confessionalists") mounted a vigorous counterattack. One pastor, Klaus Harms (1778–1855), issued his own ninety-five theses, which condemned rationalism and affirmed basic Lutheran teaching on the forgiveness of sins and the sacraments. As pressures increased to conform, many Prussian Lutherans emigrated to America or Australia, carrying their confessionalism with them. Among the best known of these were C. F. W. Walther (1811–87), the founder of the Lutheran Church—Missouri Synod, and Wilhelm Löhe (1808–72) of Neuendettelsau in Bavaria, a brilliant preacher who remained in Germany but sent out confessionalist missionaries to America. The outstanding scholarly exponent of confessionalism was E. W. Hengstenberg (1802–69), a professor at Berlin. Through his Bible commentaries and the journal he founded in 1827, the *Evangelical Church Newspaper,* Hengstenberg combated rationalism and theological liberalism.

THE LIBERALS

Unlike the Romantics, the liberals drank heavily at the fount of the Enlightenment. They stressed individual freedom—freedom of speech, press, and assembly, and from arbitrary arrest and imprisonment. They regarded a constitutional form of government as the best way to guarantee liberties. In the advanced countries liberals demanded civil rights and more representative governments, while those in other parts of Europe sought written constitutions limiting the power of rulers and made common cause with the aspirations of nationalists. Few liberals, however, would accept popular sovereignty, as they wanted to restrict voting rights to the propertied classes. They regarded mass democracy to be as dangerous as the tyranny of a king. Most agreed with the English utilitarian theorist Jeremy Bentham that the "greatest good for the greatest number" would result if each individual could pursue his or her self-interest with the barest minimum of outside interference.

In other words, they were willing to accept equality before the laws, but they saw nothing wrong with gross inequalities in the distribution of property and wealth. They believed that an individual with initiative, ambition, and enterprise could earn a fortune and that the government should not interfere with private property and its acquisition. In the economic realm this meant a laissez-faire approach, and that put them at odds with both groups that sought to reform the industrial system in the nineteenth century, the Christian humanitarians and the socialists (see chapter 19).

In the theological realm liberalism was reflected first in Schleiermacher's rejection of rational doctrinal belief and stress on subjective feeling that made faith a matter of individual experience. The followers of Hegel, who were inspired by his emphasis on divine immanence (God is *in* the world, not *above* or *outside* it) and on historical development, subjected Christianity to historical analysis. The "Tübingen School" of theologians, led by F. C. Baur (1792–1860) who was appointed to the university in 1826, called attention to what they believed to be distinct strands and theologies within the New Testament and taught a purely historical understanding of the Bible. Baur himself rejected supernaturalism and utilized a dialectical approach to the New Testament. He concluded that it reflected a basic tension between an earlier Petrine or "Jewish" and a later Pauline or "Hellenistic" party in the church. He also held that most of the letters of Paul were not "authentic" because they lacked anti-Judaizing "tendencies." He identified a third grouping, the Catholic or conciliatory books, some of which like Acts were probably written in the second century. He set the precedent for the revisionist biblical criticism that would become the hallmark of liberal theology. Scholars disagree as to whether Baur actually was a Hegelian, but he did utilize historical analysis and viewed church history in dialectical terms.[3]

The decisive break between the old conservative school of biblical interpretation and the new radical antisupernaturalist one came when Baur's student, David Friedrich Strauss (1808–74), published his celebrated *Life of Jesus, Critically Examined* in 1835. He concluded that though a "historical" Jesus lay behind the life recorded in the gospels, His life had been rewritten and embellished by Christian writers to make it fulfill the Old Testament legends and predictions. These pious reflections by Jesus' followers were "myths," that is, truths about him that, although historically inaccurate, were in harmony with their religious feelings and ideas. They were not falsehoods as such, but truths indirectly stated. In a Hegelian sense they expressed the awareness of the writers that Jesus had discovered that God and man are one, and the true God-man is not an individual but humanity as a whole. Jesus must be understood symbolically as the realization of the Absolute Spirit in the human race. Humanity is the union of the finite and infinite, of spirit and nature. Humankind is destined for perfection in its onward and upward march, symbolized in the New Testament in terms of death, resurrection, and ascension.

The French historian of religion, Joseph Ernest Renan (1823–92), carried the discussion even further in his *Life of Jesus* (1863). By using the rapidly developing science of textual criticism, he replaced Strauss's myth theory about Jesus with a rationalist presentation of Him as an enlightened modern man, an itinerant teacher of ethics who was certainly not the Son of God. He was a gentle Galilean who preached a simple morality and dreamed of establishing a utopian fellowship of God's people on earth. But under the influence of John the Baptist, a vain and ambitious Jesus emerged, later transformed into a religious revolutionary. He assumed the role of Messiah, battled with evil as He worked to set up the kingdom of God, and died for His perfect idealism in a struggle against an orthodox and sterile Judaism. As for the resurrection, it was the product of Mary Magdalene's idealized love.

These scholars, who portrayed the essence of religion as purity of heart in communion with a loving God who is everywhere present, ushered in a revolutionary new era of biblical and theological studies. The "life of Jesus" research emphasized getting behind the "Jesus of faith" and "Christ of the creeds" to the "Jesus of history," while the new "higher," or literary, criticism took extreme liberties with Scripture and rejected its supernatural origin. Finally, together with the introduction of Darwinism (see chapter 20) into theological liberalism, higher criticism posed a formidable challenge to orthodoxy, both Protestant and Catholic.

THE CHURCH IN BRITAIN

In many ways the revival of English religion in the nineteenth century corresponded with the growth of the middle classes. Attending services at an Anglican church or Nonconformist chapel was an important part of being respectable. Yet the churches did more than simply reinforce the pursuit of wealth. They taught values like "duty," which cut across self-interest, and an earnestness in making religious faith relevant to everyday concerns animated much of English Protestantism.

Working class church attendance was much lower, but many from this group did take part in Methodist and evangelical Anglican congregations. There were, however, real barriers to church attendance for the poor, as they could not dress properly or afford the pew rents charged in many places. The emphasis on church discipline seemed to fall heavier on the poor, especially their use of alcohol. Also, the growth of organized leisure activities rivaled the church's drawing power.

The one church that clearly possessed the greatest wealth and power was the Anglican. It had the financial means to repair its old buildings and erect new ones, the clerical profession was among the most prestigious in England, and the crown maintained a close attachment. In theory, those who did not receive Holy Communion in the Church of England (Nonconformists and Roman Catholics) were excluded from public life, but various exceptions had been made. The restrictions were finally eliminated when Parliament repealed the Test and Corporation Acts in 1828 and passed the Catholic Emancipation Act in 1829.

Those who were concerned about revitalizing the Anglican church fell into three general categories. The "Low Churchmen" placed primary importance on the inspiration and authority of Scripture, emphasized preaching more than liturgical worship, and were strongly suspicious of Catholic beliefs and practices. The most conservative evangelicals were the "Recordites," who took their name from *The Record,* a church newspaper founded in 1828 that represented their views. The moderate evangelicals continued in the tradition of Charles Simeon and the Clapham Sect, and their journal, the *Christian Observer,* affirmed loyalty to the church. The various factions did work together, and their harmony was reflected in the annual "May Meetings," festivals of evangelical exultation that occurred at Exeter Hall in London.

The "High Churchmen" stressed the continuity with Catholicism, especially apostolic succession and episcopal authority, highly liturgical worship, and the saving power of the sacraments. The Broad Church party tried to steer a middle course and interpreted Anglican doctrines and worship forms in a liberal manner. The most extreme High Churchmen were the "Anglo-Catholics" who emphasized the historical links of the present church with the medieval one.

From their ranks arose "Tractarianism," which began in 1833 with the publication of the *Tracts for the Times*. The authors defended the Church of England as a divine institution, proclaimed the doctrine of apostolic succession, and upheld the Book of Common Prayer as the rule of faith. Many of the tracts were reprints of works by seventeenth-century High Church figures. It was also known as the Oxford Movement, since its leaders, John Keble (1792–1866), E. B. Pusey (1800–82), and John Henry Newman (1801–90) were fellows of Oriel College in the 1820s.

Many in the group edged closer to Rome, especially Newman who was the vicar of the university church in Oxford. While on a trip to Italy in 1833, he wrote a poem that epitomized his spiritual struggle, which was set to music as the hymn "Lead, Kindly Light." Of the twenty-four tracts he authored, the most famous (and last) was *Tract No. 90* in 1841, which attempted to reconcile the Anglican church's Thirty-Nine Articles with Catholic doctrine. It was so roundly condemned that he gave up his pastorate and entered the Catholic church in 1845, thus terminating the Oxford Movement. In 1879 he was made a cardinal. Through his many writings, such as the *Idea of a University* (1852), which set forth his conception of Christian education, and the autobiographical sketch, *Apologia Pro Vita Sua* (1864), Newman had an immense influence within both Anglican and Catholic circles.

The evangelicals breathed new life into English Protestantism. Their concern with winning souls was reflected in the creation of agencies to propagate the Christian faith. Among these were several missionary societies (discussed in chapter 20), the British and Foreign Bible Society (BFBS, 1804), Religious Tract Society (1799), London Society for Promoting Christianity Amongst the Jews (1809), Sunday School Union (1803), and The National Society for the Education of the Poor (1811). Evangelicals were particularly attracted to Bible societies, and many of these sprang up in the British Isles, as well as in the empire and the United States. The BFBS sent agents to the continent who founded Bible societies in various countries, and for a brief time the effort even enjoyed Catholic support in Germany.

John Nelson Darby

However, as the century advanced, more radical evangelicals began to question the value of the Bible, tract, and missionary societies. They saw their "plodding" methods as inadequate and argued instead for supernatural aid through the working of the Holy Spirit. They insisted that Christian workers should depend on God alone to help them carry out their tasks rather than trust in bureaucratic organizations.

The radical strain of evangelicalism was affected by many factors. One was a renewed interest in Calvinism, while another was literary Romanticism, which stressed "natural supernaturalism" (one could discern spiritual significance in the everyday world) along with emotion, experience, and imagination. Also there was a resurgence of premillennialism, the idea that one should not look for the triumph of the church to result in the establishment of Christ's kingdom since His return to earth was imminent. A fourth emphasis was a high view of biblical inspiration and literal interpretation of Scripture.

A noted radical evangelical was Edward Irving (1792–1839), a Church of Scotland minister who pastored a church in London. His eloquence in attacking the moral ills of the age attracted a large following, which included many prominent figures. Soon controversy arose when he preached the imminent return of Christ in glory and encouraged speaking in tongues during public worship. At the same time he held to a High Church view of the sacraments and liturgy.

Finally, in 1833 Irving was dismissed, but by then he and a friend Henry Drummond, a businessman and member of Parliament, had formed the Catholic Apostolic Church. Believing that the Second Coming was near, they set up a structure of twelve latter-day apostles who would sit with the original twelve on the twenty-four thrones mentioned in Revelation 4. Then, by means of a distinctive "sacrament" the church members were "sealed" and became part of the 144,000 of Revelation 7. The group utilized ritual in their services and paid little attention to social issues. Although the movement eventually died out in Britain, it spread to the continent where its German offspring, the New Apostolic Church, remains a vigorous community to this day.

Another important evangelical dissenting group was the "Plymouth," or "Christian," Brethren. It originated in Dublin in the late 1820s and took its name from a large congregation formed in Plymouth in 1831. Seeking to return to the simplicity of the early church, the Brethren met in homes to observe the Lord's Supper, rejected ordained clergy and liturgical worship, and chose elders to rule over the community. Their meetings were marked by a deep devotion to Christ, evangelistic zeal, and strong interest in prophetic matters. Their outstanding teacher, John Nelson Darby (1800–82), was both a student of biblical prophecy and a strong believer in biblical literalism. He formulated the basic tenets of dispensationalism, including the "rapture" of the church prior to the Second Coming. Although a minority view at the time, in the twentieth century it would come to dominate premillennial thought.

When disputes in the later 1840s arose over how much centralized control should be exercised over the assemblies, a split occurred. Those favoring the original principles of the movement became the Open Brethren and mixed freely with other believers. Their best-known figure was George Mueller (1805–98), a German immigrant who pastored a chapel and managed the famous orphanage at Ashley Down in Bristol. It was modeled on the Francke Foundation in Halle with which he was familiar. Mueller pioneered the concept of running the enterprise totally on faith, without fund-raising appeals or support from the church. Darby and his followers formed the Exclusive Brethren whose hallmarks were austere lifestyles and separation from other Christians.

The greatest evangelical churchman in nineteenth-century Scotland was Thomas Chalmers (1780–1847). Ordained in 1803, he experienced a conversion in 1811, which completely transformed his ministerial outlook and emphasis. Four years later he accepted a charge in Glasgow where he developed a parish system that could cope with the problems of an industrial city. It involved appointing elders to oversee the spiritual welfare and deacons to minister to the social and educational needs of the populace.

In 1823 Chalmers accepted a professorship at St. Andrews and then in 1828 at Edinburgh University, where he functioned as the leader and symbol of the evangelical party. Director of the church extension program as well, in six years he oversaw the building of more than 200 new churches. Then trouble arose over the issue of state interference in church affairs, which became a crisis at the general assembly in 1843. When the assembly refused to stand up against the authorities, 200 ministers and elders led by Chalmers walked out of the meeting, an action known as the Disruption. They promptly formed a new body, the Free Church of Scotland, which elected him as moderator. About one-third of the clergy joined the new movement as it set out to duplicate the churches and schools of the Church of Scotland. The schism would not be fully healed until 1929.

The Spread of Revival

The revivals that swept Britain had their counterparts in Europe and America. Germany was particularly ripe for spiritual renewal, as the influence of Pietism had waned under the pressure of rationalism. Once again there was interaction between British and German evangelicalism, similar to the earlier relationship between Pietism and Methodism.

Revival in Germany

Taking the lead in the *Erweckung* (revival) was the German Christianity Society, founded in 1780 by Pastor Johann Urlsperger of Augsburg. His plan was to unite all faithful Christians in an effort to further "true doctrine and true blessedness." Modeled on the English Society of the Propagation of Christian Knowledge (SPCK), it carried out its work through a magazine, personal contacts, and correspondence. Within a few years it had facilitated the formation of missionary, Bible, and tract societies across Europe.

A key figure was its secretary in London and pastor of the German-speaking Savoy Church, Karl F. A. Steinkopf (1773–1859). A native of Württemberg, he spread news about the London Missionary

Society to Germany and was a cofounder of the British and Foreign Bible Society. He helped set up branches of the BFBS in Germany and encouraged his countrymen to give money to the British missions. He also played an influential role in founding German missionary societies.

Revival preachers crisscrossed the land, and some regions like Württemberg in southern Germany and the Wuppertal and Siegerland in western Germany became centers of Protestant piety, a situation that has remained to the present. Some of this enthusiasm even spilled over into the Catholic church, and the best known of the priests involved was Johann Evangelista Gossner (1773–1858). He preached evangelistic sermons in his parish church, held Bible studies and prayer meetings in his home, and even conducted special Bible meetings in Basel for the Christianity Society. The Catholic revival was eventually squelched by the hierarchy, and in 1826 Gossner switched to the Lutheran church. As a Protestant he went on to make significant contributions in the areas of Christian social action and missions.

The influence of some revivalists continued far beyond their time. One was Ludwig Hofacker (1798–1828), essentially a German David Brainerd. A deeply spiritual man afflicted with poor health, his preaching resulted in thousands of people coming to Christ. Although his active ministry scarcely exceeded four years, his posthumously published *Sermons for Every Sunday, Festival, and Holiday* went through innumerable editions and translations and still is one of the most widely distributed works of popular Christian literature in Germany.

Another was Johann Christoph Blumhardt (1805–80), who became pastor at Möttlingen in Württemberg in 1838 and quickly gained distinction as a revivalist and faith healer. After the miraculous cure of an allegedly demon-possessed woman, thousands of people flocked to his parish. Finally, in 1852 he left the pastorate and opened a center for evangelism and international missionary work. Blumhardt deeply longed for the coming of Christ, and he believed that a new Pentecost with a return of the spiritual gifts would prepare the way for the Second Advent. Because of this he is regarded as a precursor of Pentecostalism.

One result of the *Erweckung* was the founding of specialized schools for missionaries and evangelists at Berlin (1800), Basel (1815), and St. Chrischona (1840). The latter was the creation of Christian Friedrich Spittler (1782–1867), secretary of the Christianity

Society in Basel. His plan was to train skilled craftsmen as evangelists and send them out as self-supporting Christian workers. Spittler acquired the vacant church at St. Chrischona near Basel and made this the headquarters of his so-called "Pilgrim Mission." The trainees found their own areas of work and served whatever churches, mission societies, and synods that would accept them.

Also noteworthy were the free church efforts, which resulted from foreign connections. German immigrants who had gone to Britain and America established Methodist congregations in their old homeland during the 1830s and 1840s. The first Baptist work was initiated by Johann Gerhard Oncken (1800–84) who had lived in London and was converted in a Methodist chapel. He worked for various evangelistic groups in North Germany and then in 1834 decided to receive believer's baptism. Through itinerant evangelism Oncken and others founded a number of churches, and the German Baptists later were active in spreading the gospel in other European countries.

The Prussian capital itself became a center of the *Erweckung*, and the University of Berlin provided the two leading academic figures of the movement, Johann August Neander (1789–1850) and Friedrich August Tholuck (1799–1877). Neander was a convert from Judaism, and through zealous Bible study he developed a deep experiential faith. He studied under Schleiermacher and in 1813 became professor of church history at Berlin where he specialized in early Christianity and also published a six-volume general history of the church. An ardent foe of the rationalism of Baur and Strauss, he communicated a warm, living faith to several generations of theological students.

A precocious youth, Tholuck was a student of oriental languages. Through the witness of various people he found Christ as Savior and then switched to theology. After a brief period of teaching at Berlin, he moved to Halle University in 1826 where he served for fifty years. A distinguished and conservative biblical scholar and theologian, he was a sworn enemy of rationalism. But he also carried on an extensive pastoral ministry among the students and sought to develop them into warm, caring Christians. He invited them into his home for Bible studies and discussions about various Christian works, visited and prayed with them in their quarters, and took them along on trips.

Social concern was a hallmark of the *Erweckung*, since at the time many Germans were suffering from economic dislocation. One leader of the movement in Berlin, Baron Ernst von Kottwitz, at his own expense established in 1807 a residence for the unemployed that housed as many as 600 people and provided them with work opportunities as well as shelter. A godly writer in Weimar, Johannes Falk, saw the large number of orphans left in the wake of the Napoleonic Wars and took many of them into his home. He then opened a center where the poor children were given shelter and education and placed in apprenticeships. Also noteworthy was Amalie Sieveking, a member of a prominent Hamburg family who possessed a pietistic faith and ties with British evangelicals. When a cholera epidemic swept the city in 1831, she worked in hospitals to help the disease victims. In the following year, she formed the Women's Association for Care of the Poor and the Sick, a group of Christians who distributed food and visited those in need.

Revival in Scandinavia

The *Erweckung* spread north into Scandinavia. Nikolai Grundtvig (1783–1872), a respected scholar of medieval Nordic literature as well as a pastor in the Danish Lutheran church, underwent an experience of questioning and doubting. He found God in a way similar to that of Luther. His attempts to spark revival in the Danish Church were rebuffed, and he was forced out of the ministry for seven years, a period he spent writing poetry and hymns. Returning to the parish in 1821, he combated rationalism and upheld the Apostles Creed as the church's standard. After several visits to England he promoted more congregational freedom within the state church. Another center of evangelicalism developed on the island of Bornholm in the 1860s. From there lay preachers spread out across Denmark proclaiming justification by grace, reconciliation through Christ's vicarious atonement, and the priesthood of all believers.

In neighboring Sweden numerous preachers of revival were active, most notably Karl Olof Rosenius (1816–68). Although greatly influenced by English Methodism, he remained in the Lutheran church and proclaimed the message of the grace of God in Christ and unmerited forgiveness of sins. Several free churches arose in the wake of his endeavors, most of which came together in the Swedish Mission Covenant of 1878.

Hans Nielsen Hauge (1771–1824) was an outstanding lay evangelist in Norway. Converted at age 25, he began at once to preach the message of salvation and personal holiness. He traveled throughout the country and initiated a popular religious movement within the

Friedrich August Tholuck

state church characterized by self-supporting lay preachers who were linked together in a close network. This emphasis on voluntary activity by laypeople had a powerful effect on the church, although the rationalist clergy bitterly resented Hauge. The Norwegian missionary and evangelistic efforts of the later nineteenth century drew their inspiration from him.

Revival in French-speaking Europe

Although the Huguenot (French Reformed) church had been suppressed by Louis XIV, it made a modest comeback during the eighteenth century (see chapter 13). However, the Lutheran church had been tolerated in Alsace, and here emerged one of the earliest figures in the French Protestant revival, Jean Frédéric Oberlin (1740–1826). A deeply pious pastor, he became renowned for his promotion of education and community self-help enterprises in his parish of Waldersbach. When the French Revolution began he embraced it with enthusiasm, seeing it as the beginning of the kingdom of God on earth, and republican virtues and fraternity as the earthly realization of Christianity. The excesses of the Jacobin regime forced him underground, and he had to hold church services secretly in his home. But he survived the Terror and emerged as a national hero. In him was combined a concern for the welfare of humanity and a deep devotion to Christ. These bore testimony to divine love and power and helped set the scene for the *Réveil* (awakening).

The background of this movement lay in the situation of the Protestant church. It regained its legal rights under a Napoleonic law in 1802, while in Swiss Geneva the French Calvinist church had continued to exist without any interruption. In the French church both an orthodox and a liberal party maintained an uneasy coexistence. By and large, the church, pastors, and people went through the form of religion, but in fact Christianity did not seriously influence their daily lives. However, a religious awakening that swept through the Swiss and French churches dramatically altered this state of affairs.

The primary influence on the revival came from the work of two Scots, the brothers Robert (1764–1842) and James Alexander (1768–1851) Haldane. In 1795 both Robert, who managed the ancestral farms, and James, who was a ship captain for the East India Company, were converted. They gave up their positions and became itinerant preachers, established societies to promote rural evangelism and tract distribution, operated a school to train lay preachers, and adopted Baptist principles of church organization. In 1816–19 Robert went to Geneva and then to various places in France where he held meetings in homes and taught the plenary inspiration and infallibility of the Bible. He also won many converts, who in turn spread the evangelical message among French Protestants.

The three most important people influenced by Haldane's preaching were Jean Henri Merle d'Aubigné (1794–1872), Frédéric Monod (1794–1863), and César Malan (1787–1864). Malan was trained in theology and taught at a Latin school. He had already experienced renewal through the influence of friends, and his faith was confirmed during the Haldane visit. He then became a fearless preacher in Geneva and undertook numerous evangelistic missions throughout western Europe and especially Britain. After he was ousted from the Genevan state church, he joined the Scottish church. Although remaining a convinced predestinarian, he deeply loved souls and proclaimed a fervent message of salvation.

Merle D'Aubígné was a Swiss Protestant who was a student at the University of Geneva when the revival broke out. After serving churches in Hamburg and Brussels, he returned to Geneva in 1831 where he and another figure in the *Réveil,* François Gaussen (1790–1863), founded the Evangelical Society of Geneva to promote the spread of sound doctrine throughout France and French-speaking Switzerland. In 1834 the group established an independent theological school, where both men taught and supported missionaries, pastors, and the distribution of Christian literature. Gaussen's works on the verbal inspiration of Scripture were widely read both in England and France, while Merle d'Aubigné devoted his later years to producing a massive thirteen-volume history of the Reformation.

Frédéric Monod was influenced by Haldane while a student at Geneva and became a bold advocate of Calvinist orthodoxy. For forty-three years he was editor of a journal of contemporary Christianity that helped to clarify orthodox views. Dissatisfied with liberalism in the Reformed church, he formed the Free Evangelical Church in 1849, whose statement of faith opened with a bold formulation of the plenary inspiration and authority of the Bible. His brother Adolphe Monod (1802–56) was converted through contacts with the noted Scottish lay theologian Thomas Erskine. He adhered to the same evangelical principles, including an absolute insistence on biblical inspiration and authority. Adolphe, who did not join the Free Evangelical Church, was the foremost pulpit orator of the French Reformed church.

The cross-fertilization between the *Réveil* and British evangelicalism was remarkable. The French preachers traveled in Britain and their works were translated and widely read there. At the same time, the British and Foreign Bible Society assisted in the founding of the Protestant Bible Society of Paris in 1818, while in 1822 the revived Protestants joined in the growing movement for foreign missions by forming the Paris Missionary Society.

Another significant impact of the awakening was felt in the Netherlands, where in 1828 the young Guillaume Groen van Prinsterer (1801–76), founder of the "Antirevolutinary Party," came to know Christ through the ministry of Merle d'Aubigné. He was a strong critic of that which he labeled as "revolutionary," namely, the enthronement of reason, and he said it must be opposed with the gospel. He argued that individuals must be subject to God through faith, without which there could be no salvation. Further, God's sovereignty must be acknowledged in the political sphere as well as all others. Abraham Kuyper, Holland's most celebrated Christian politician, was Groen's protégé.

Revival in America

Although revival had swept the American colonies in the 1740s, after the Revolution church membership fell to an all-time low—around 5 to 10 percent of the adult population. However, a revival broke out on the frontier in the late 1790s, and it spread rapidly to the eastern cities as well. Known as the Second Great Awakening, this spiritual movement resulted in the evangelical triumph in American religious culture—the "Protestant Century" as historians have labeled the era.

Unlike the "first" awakening, where the older denominations took the lead, here it was the new groups—the Methodists, Baptists, and Disciples of Christ—who dominated and went on to become the largest Protestant denominations. It was more permanent as well, since it left the country more or less evangelical Christian in character for most of the nineteenth century. Also, voluntary societies that fostered foreign missions, evangelism, and a variety of social causes proliferated. Here a key role was played by the Congregationalist preacher Lyman Beecher (1775–1863), who orchestrated many of the enterprises that made up "the evangelical united front."

Another feature was the Arminian emphasis that God gave all people the ability to come to Christ if they would only choose to do so. This theology of action was reflected both in the voluntary organizations and the itinerant evangelists such as Francis Asbury (1745–1816) and Charles G. Finney (1792–1875). Wesley had sent Asbury to the colonies in 1771, and after the Revolution he reorganized the Methodist work there. He utilized a far-flung network of "circuit riders" to reach people on the frontier with the gospel, and his own efforts were prodigious. (He is said to have traveled 300,000 miles, mostly on horseback.) In 1771 he was one of five workers; forty-five years later there were 2,000 ministers and more than 200,000 Methodists in America.

Finney was the best-known mass evangelist in America. He conducted carefully controlled meetings in the country's largest cities as well as on the frontier. He also linked evangelical religion to social reform, especially abolitionism and coeducation for women, while at the same time formalizing the ties between conservative theology and industrial wealth that would later so characterize American Protestantism. Finney served as president of Oberlin College in Ohio from 1851 to 1866. Oberlin was one of the first colleges to admit women and blacks. Through Finney's writings on the moral government of God and the human will he was a significant theologian as well.

Transplanted churches from Europe provided a spiritual sanctuary for immigrants, while African-Americans organized their own churches, which ministered to the needs of a people suffering from the degradation of racism and slavery. The Roman Catholic population was also growing, and some missionary orders used revivalistic techniques to spread their church. Alexis de Tocqueville, who visited the United States in 1831 and saw this outpouring of religious fervor, commented that "there is no country in the world where the Christian religion retains a greater influence over the souls of men than in America."[4]

The new ideologies of the democratic age had a profound impact on the churches, both Protestant and Catholic. Some responded by retreating into the past while others embraced the current intellectual trends uncritically. Evangelical religion made significant advances in Europe and North America, as revival movements energized many churches and the ministry of the gospel went forward with vigor. But problems associated with the Industrial Revolution and the emergence of still more dangerous ideas loomed on the horizon. Christianity in the late nineteenth century would face even greater challenges.

19

THE CHURCH IN AN INDUSTRIAL AGE

The most significant development in modern history occurred not in the political but in the economic realm. The Industrial Revolution profoundly modified human experience. It altered the way men and women worked, transformed the structure of society, enabled ordinary people to attain a higher standard of living, and upset the international balance of power between the Western and non-Western worlds. This made possible the West's most dynamic phase of expansion, a process that had begun with the Crusades and continued with the creation of the seaborne colonial empires. Because of industrialization, hardly any corner of the globe was left untouched by Western economic and political power. Since the largest segment of the Christian church had become part and parcel of Western culture, it too was deeply affected by this process.

THE INDUSTRIAL REVOLUTION

Although scholars debate such issues as the timing and extent of the Industrial Revolution, all agree that the change from hand tools to power-driven machines in doing the work of the world was one of the most fundamental transformations in human history.

British Industrialization

The lead in this was taken by England, where an earlier agricultural revolution had occurred. There the property-owning classes controlled Parliament and obtained legislation enclosing the common lands and open fields, thus placing most of the farmland in the hands of wealthy landlords. Having much larger holdings, they could use more efficient farming techniques to improve the productivity of the land and thereby increase the country's food supply. At the same time, this forced large numbers of small farmers (peasants) to find other sources of employment, which meant that a mobile labor force now existed that would work for wages. The capital generated in the agricultural sector also could be channeled into other ventures, especially manufacturing.

England also had the political and economic infrastructure that made industrialization possible. The stable government allowed the economy to function freely. Since no wars had been fought on English soil since the 1640s, neither civil strife nor invading armies were any real threat to peace and prosperity. The country had a modern and experienced business class and the advantages of a central bank and well-developed credit institutions. England had the largest domestic market in Europe, and most localities were readily accessible by water, either by river and coastal shipping or canals. Through the development of its merchant fleet and colonial empire, England was in a good position to market its chief manufactured product, woolen cloth, and with the development of machinery it could compete with Asia in cotton cloth as well.

The technological breakthroughs that made up the Industrial Revolution first occurred in the cotton textile industry. A series of inventions between 1765 and 1800 enabled an increased output of cotton and the spinning and weaving of cloth. The use of water turbines and steam engines to operate them required factories, so textile workers now labored here instead of in their homes and shops. These changes stimulated the coal and iron industries, and in turn railroads and steamships were built to transport the raw materials to the factories and finished products to markets. By 1850 Britain had become the workshop of the world, producing two-thirds of the world's coal and half of its iron and cotton cloth. London was the

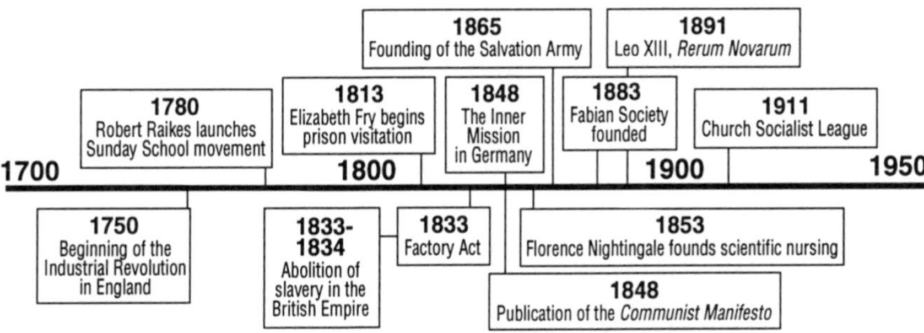

financial center of the globe, and from here capital was exported elsewhere to create new business enterprises.

Industrialization then spread to Belgium and France in the 1820s and 1830s, and to the United States and Germany soon afterward. After 1860 the spectacular rise of the latter two countries began to overshadow Britain, and by the late nineteenth century new industrial centers were developing in Italy, Austria, Sweden, Russia, and even Japan. Capitalists elsewhere simply borrowed the methods developed in Britain and utilized its engineers and capital, but they looked to their own states for assistance to promote industrial growth.

The Impact of Industrialization

The social consequences of these developments were the greatest challenge the nineteenth-century churches faced. The rapid population growth that accompanied industrialization (Britain's increased from ten to thirty million people between 1750 and 1850) shattered the parish system and encouraged the development of itinerant ministries like those of the Methodists. The rural parishes were impoverished by enclosures, while the city churches could not handle the population influx. In the new industrial towns the Dissenting churches seemed more effective in ministering to the new masses than the Established church.

Related to the population increase was the growth of slums. Whole new cities seemed to arise almost out of nowhere, and the unregulated growth placed an impossible burden on urban services —sewage, garbage removal, water supply, public health, police protection, and housing. Building codes seemed almost nonexistent. Structures were erected on the smallest spaces possible and people packed into them. Whole families often lived in single rooms, and in some places family life disintegrated as unnumbered children swarmed in the streets. The heavy smoke and soot of the early coal age darkened the skies and caused respiratory diseases. The stench of the filth and excrement that was underfoot defied belief. Since public transportation was usually unavailable, people had to walk to factories and shops.

The conditions of the factory workers were uncertain at best, and the early years of the Industrial Revolution were the worst, as recent scholarship has shown. Until 1820 food prices rose faster than wages, but then after 1840 real wages started to climb significantly. Also, many family units worked together in the factories and coal mines, and this assisted in maintaining cohesion. On the other hand, the hours of the work week were excessively long, and the discipline of factory life was a new experience for those used to laboring in cottages and small workshops. Because children were usually employed, they had little opportunity to obtain an education. Often their growth was stunted by machine labor, and many suffered debilitating injuries.

As for the factory owners, they swelled the middle class. Some were from already well-established merchant families, but in the early days many were of more modest origins, although that changed by the mid–nineteenth century. There were considerable chances for skilled craftsmen with exceptional ability and initiative. Also people from religious and ethnic groups that had suffered discrimination in the occupations controlled by the aristocracy now had new opportunities. Quakers and Scots played important roles in British industrial development, while Protestants and Jews dominated banking in France.

The new industrialists tended to live modestly and plowed much of their income back into their businesses in order to keep ahead of the competition. They viewed the "poor" as lazy and felt they were doing them a favor by giving them jobs and seeing that they worked diligently and productively. Businessmen did not want government inspectors looking over their shoulders to see that they treated their employees properly. They insisted that if they were left alone to conduct their enterprises as they saw fit, the country would prosper.

The Industrial Revolution's impact on the family was significant. For the middle class the institution of the home and nuclear family replaced the extended family of preindustrial society. The old indifference toward children was replaced by love and concern for them. While the husband worked, his wife stayed home to manage the household and care for the children. Working class families suffered much more stress because of long hours, low wages, often unsafe working conditions, inadequate housing, and the lack of social security in the event of the breadwinner's unemployment, injury, illness, or death.

Along with this a sexual division of labor developed, as only the unmarried women and married women in poor families worked outside the home. Good job opportunities for women were virtually nonexistent, and they were relegated to domestic service, unskilled "sweated" labor, or prostitution. Married women were also subjugated to their husbands and possessed few rights. A wife had no legal identity, could not own property in her name, and was penalized in divorce settlements. Even the wages she earned might belong to her husband.

EVANGELICAL HUMANITARIANISM

Since industrialization was the greatest challenge facing the church in the nineteenth century, the social problems resulting from it could not be ignored. The responses ranged from an acceptance and justification of existing conditions as the will of God to direct assistance for the victims of the industrial order and political involvement to bring about improvement in conditions. The most radical solution was to replace laissez-faire capitalism with some other economic system entirely. Of these options, the one that appealed most to evangelicals was "philanthropy," or voluntary charitable activity.

Various factors made this attractive. It was obedience to Jesus' command to clothe the naked and feed the hungry. It would be the preliminary step to conversion; the poor must be lifted from the depths of misery before they could heed the call to Christ. Others devoted themselves to the performance of "good works" simply because they were deeply moved by human suffering. Thus, the evangelicals' response to social ills was emotional rather than ideological. They saw sin as the root of human misery and the Christian faith as the remedy. Sin was what hindered the spread of the gospel or kept one from living a godly life. As a result the reform efforts tended to be negative in character, that is, they were more "anti" or "against" something than oriented toward achieving some alternative goal or new policy.

Christians felt a responsibility to help those who were suffering and to urge people with wealth and political influence to do likewise. For them, evangelism and missionary work went hand in hand with relief efforts and philanthropy. As mentioned earlier (chapter 17), critics regarded this as "paternalism" and insisted that evangelicals wanted not only to relieve the physical needs of the poor but also to convert and "improve" them as well. However, they were interested in the poor as individuals, each with an immortal soul needing redemption, not just as impersonal victims of a particular socio-economic system. Most Christians did not believe that poverty could be eliminated by reconstructing the social and economic order or that the poor should organize and agitate for change. However, these attitudes gradually altered as the century progressed.

The revived Christians added the element of zeal to the Anglican tradition of concern for the poor, Thus, schemes for doing good flowered in the late eighteenth century. Some examples were orphanages, Strangers' Friend Societies that provided poverty relief, efforts on behalf of prisoners, and basic education. The pathbreaker in prison reform was an earnest evangelical, John Howard (1726–90), who as sheriff of Bedfordshire became aware of the wretched conditions that inmates in the county jail had to endure. He then inspected jails elsewhere in Britain and throughout Europe and found the same pattern of abuse—poor sanitation, rampant disease, and inadequate food and clothing. His famous book *The State of the Prisons,* published in 1777, described the inhumanity of the penal system and called for reforms.

Although Howard did not attempt to secure legal remedies or implement a program for overseeing jails, Elizabeth Gurney Fry (1780–1845), an evangelical minister in the Society of Friends, proved to be more effective. In 1813 she began visiting the women incarcerated in London's notorious Newgate prison, where she read the Bible and prayed with them and supplied them with adequate clothes. Then she began campaigning for better conditions and in 1818 testified before a parliamentary committee on the matter. She even influenced her brother-in-law, T. Fowell Buxton to publish a hard-hitting book on prisons the following year, and their efforts helped bring about penal reform in the 1820s. (Buxton is most remembered for carrying Wilberforce's campaign for abolition of slavery in the British Empire to a successful conclusion in 1833.) Evangelical agitation also brought an end in 1853 to the practice of transporting prisoners to penal colonies.

The Sunday school movement was an important step in public education, and the pioneer was Wesley's disciple Hannah Ball, who opened the first such school in the town of High Wycombe in 1769.

Sunday schools were designed to teach poor children the rudiments of reading, writing, and religion on the one day they had free from work. The promoter of Sunday schools was an evangelical newspaper owner in Gloucester, Robert Raikes (1735–1811), who set up his first school in 1780. The idea caught on so quickly that by the end of the decade 200,000 pupils in Britain were enrolled. The movement spread to the continent and North America, and a national Sunday School Union was formed in Britain in 1803 and in America in 1824. As other educational institutions for the poor proliferated, such as the Ragged Schools, the Sunday schools began to focus exclusively on religious training.

The Clapham Sect (see chapter 17) was the outstanding example of coordinated social effort, and its work reflected the key role voluntary societies played in evangelical philanthropic activities. Starting with the founding of the Bettering Society by Wilberforce and others at Clapham in 1796, charitable organizations formed at an average rate of six a year. By midcentury there were nearly 500 of them, at least three-quarters of which were evangelical in character and control. In 1853 the government created the Charity Commissioners to oversee their efforts.

A divisive issue among evangelicals was factory reform. Most had no use for trade unions, although some early labor leaders were Methodists. On the other hand, the Claphamites were solidly behind restricting child labor and resisted the laissez-faire liberals to obtain the first modest legislation dealing with this. Some had increasing doubts about the factory system and began channeling the energies that had been directed toward abolishing slavery into this new cause. Evangelicals Michael Oastler and George Bull in Yorkshire mounted a Wilberforce-style campaign for strict limitations on child labor in the textile mills, and their ally in Parliament, Michael Sadler, introduced a reform bill in 1832. His investigating committee uncovered shocking abuses, and public interest in a factory bill rose to a fever pitch, but then an electoral defeat removed him from the scene.

His place was taken by Anthony Ashley Cooper, the Seventh Earl of Shaftesbury (1801–85), who would become Britain's greatest Christian social reformer. Of aristocratic lineage, he had been converted as a youth, elected to Parliament as a Tory in 1826, and gained experience in aiding the mentally ill. When George Bull asked Lord Ashley to lead the fight, he responded after a day of prayer and meditation on the Bible: "I believe it is my duty to God and the poor, and I trust He will support me. . . . To me it appeared an affair less of policy than of religion."[1] In spite of the manufacturers' hostility Ashley proceeded to push through the Factory Act of 1833, which restricted the labor of children in the mills and provided for inspectors to enforce it.

Shaftesbury's indefatigable labors on behalf of the poor and oppressed constitute one of the great epics of Christian history. He served in Parliament for nearly six decades and was responsible for legislation promoting public health, restricting female and child labor in the factories and coal mines, outlawing the use of "climbing boys" as chimney sweeps, and improving the housing for urban workers. As chair of the Ragged School Union he promoted education for the poor, and he was involved in dozens of organizations that worked to improve the quality of life for young and old alike. At the same time he was an official in many evangelistic and missionary societies. Above all, he established the doctrine of benevolent state intervention in the organization of industry and commerce to protect the workers' interests.

By the later nineteenth century the number and variety of Christian social service organizations had become staggering. Two of these deserve special comment. One was the Salvation Army, founded in 1865 as the "Christian Mission" by William Booth (1829–1912) and his wife Catherine (1829–90). Both were gifted preachers who were forced out of the Methodist church in 1861 and became freelance evangelists. They settled in London's East End, an area of intense poverty, and began a work where they preached the gospel and a strong holiness message and dealt with social ills at the same time. Their programs included feeding the hungry, shelters for the homeless, labor exchanges for the unemployed, and hostels for women and ex-prisoners. The mission increasingly took on a military structure, and in 1878 it was renamed the Salvation Army. Booth became the "general," the evangelists and workers received ranks, and brass bands were formed. Standard uniforms were adopted in 1880, the same year in which it began the first overseas venture, and corps (local groups) sprang up throughout Britain, the European continent, India, and North America. In 1890 Booth wrote *In Darkest England—and the Way Out,* a best-seller that laid out the facts of poverty and what needed to be done about it. Although the Salvation Army was a highly centralized body, it was the only Christian organization at the time that truly operated on the level of the masses and communicated with them.

Another significant social ministry was that of Thomas John Barnardo (1845–1905), who belonged to a Plymouth Brethren assembly

Anthony Ashley Cooper, Seventh Earl of Shaftesbury

and planned to go as a medical missionary to China. However, one day in 1870 he met a homeless child who inspired him to establish a shelter for destitute boys. A gifted organizer, he founded several orphanages in Britain, and even sent youths to Canada, where employment chances were better. Some have claimed that "Barnardo boys" made up 1 percent of Canada's English population in the early twentieth century.

In Germany the mounting social problems of industrialization also attracted the attention of Christians. An important figure in the Awakening, Theodor Fliedner (1800–64), together with his wife Friederike (1800–42), founded the "deaconess" movement, which opened to women the field of philanthropic work in the Protestant church. Pastor of a village church near Düsseldorf, he had been involved in prison ministry to women. Recognizing the role of women in the apostolic church and their service in ministries to the poor in Holland, he and Friederike in 1836 established a Deaconess Institute to train women as hospital nurses. It was called a "mother house," and the residents learned a variety of skills that they could utilize in church work and charitable service.

The idea caught on quickly and soon other mother houses were founded. In these unmarried women lived in community and took vows of obedience, faithfulness, and devotion to their calling, but these commitments were not as binding as those of a Roman Catholic order. The deaconess movement enabled Christian women to engage in the relief of poverty, sickness, and other human distress. It also provided them with the opportunity to be active in the public life of the church and to apply their faith to practical questions of human need.

The impact of the deaconess movement on the field of nursing was significant. Elizabeth Fry visited the Deaconess Institute in 1840 and founded her Institute of Nursing the following year, and then Florence Nightingale (1820–1910) went there in 1849 and again in 1851, when she spent three months working with the deaconesses. Granddaughter of a Clapham figure, she had a deep personal faith, and Shaftesbury himself encouraged her to take up nursing. Her reorganization of the English military hospitals during the Crimean War (1854–56) marked the beginning of modern scientific nursing. The German emphasis on trained workers and a devotion to duty shaped the whole development of this profession.

The most significant social ministry in nineteenth-century Germany was that of Johann Hinrich Wichern (1808–81). No one since Francke had shown an ability to organize practical religious affairs as he. Wichern linked the Protestant understanding of charity with an effort to rebuild the moral basis of the nation. Like the English reformers he had a vision of the coming kingdom of God where people would experience the triumph of good over evil. This would be assisted by the spread of Christian piety and morals, and religious faith would thrive when the quality of life for the suffering was improved.

Because Wichern's goal was to rebuild human character, not reform social structures, his approach was individualistic. But by including the public life of the person and concern for the moral factors of the social problem, he modified the framework of individualism. Since he rejected social equality and linked his reform program to the Christian-Conservative monarchy of Prussia, Wichern could, like his English counterparts, be regarded as a "Tory reformer."

A native of Hamburg, he was deeply affected by the Awakening as a student in Berlin. Returning to his home town to serve in a parish, he became aware of the social gap between the middle and working classes. He noted the moral and economic deprivation of the working class. In 1833 a patron gave him a building to use as a training school for destitute youths that was known as the *Rauhe Haus* (Rough Place). This humble enterprise quickly developed into a major social service operation, one that would be the most influential in Protestant Germany, essentially because he had a different vision of

Christian work. Whereas Fliedner had focused on local needs with his growing network of institutes and hospitals, Wichern's hope was that he could strengthen religion among all classes of people and thereby rebuild all of Christendom.

Thanks to support he received from the Prussian king during the 1840s he transformed his blossoming social ministry into the "Inner Mission," a term that came to apply to the entire program of charitable work within the Lutheran churches. He saw this as the missionary task of the church within the world, that is, to conquer the remaining anti- and non-Christian elements. He considered these forces as obstructions to the building of Christ's kingdom within the family, church, society, and state. As a result, the Inner Mission was the single most important response of German Protestants to the industrial order. Not only did it cultivate social consciousness among an otherwise indifferent public, but also it worked on a national basis, thus contributing to the growing awareness of the need for both a Germany and a church that was unified.

Among the most beloved Christian social activists, a man known for his simple faith and deep compassion was Friedrich von Bodelschwingh (1831–1910). A prosperous Westphalian farmer who decided to study for the ministry, he was deeply influenced by the Awakening. His first charge was a German congregation in Paris, where he served for six years. Most of his parishioners were factory workers and domestic servants, and through this experience he came to appreciate the problems of the "outsider" in modern society. Returning to his native Westphalia in 1864 to pastor a church in a growing industrial area, he continued to confront the problem of the new economic age. He could not decide whether the "social question" arose from a moral or institutional failure, and even commented once that the working class was pressed between two millstones, "alcohol and capital."

Bodelschwingh had spent years teaching the Bible to young people. Then after experiencing the tragedy of losing four of his own children to disease within a two week period, he renewed his commitment to the suffering and needy. In 1872 he accepted the call to supervise a small home for "epileptic" boys in Bielefeld. These mentally handicapped youths epitomized his eschatological view that one did not build God's kingdom but prepared for Christ's return. Being on the fringes of society, their future lay in God alone. But the hope found in the gospel meant that even the most marginal persons had meaning in God's sight.

Within a few years, the Bethel Institution, as it was called, had grown into an extensive enterprise with farms, sheltered workshops, schools, hospitals, and churches. Bodelschwingh even opened a theological school where students by diligent study of Scripture would gain a firm basis for their faith, and they would put their beliefs into practice in this caring community. By 1914 more than 3,925 people were housed at Bethel and various satellite facilities. It became one of the largest Christian social service institutions in the Protestant world.

The humanitarian impulse penetrated American Christianity as well. By the 1840s revivalism, because it focused on the moral transformation of human character, had spawned a host of social endeavors. The most familiar story is that of the movement to abolish slavery, a major reform effort of Northern evangelicals but not those in the South. Urban social ills were a focus of attention as well, and the work of the Methodist evangelist and cofounder of the holiness movement, Phoebe Palmer (1807–74), was especially noteworthy. After becoming involved in various ministries to the needy in New York, in 1850 she founded the Five Points Mission, a project to house poor families and provide them with schooling and jobs. This was the prototype of Christian institutional work in the slums of the industrial cities.

Philanthropic ventures burgeoned in the United States as they did in Britain and Germany, but only a few examples may be cited. In 1880 the first contingent of Salvation Army workers arrived in New York and soon this endeavor was thriving. In 1896 Ballington and Maud Booth split with the Army because of their unhappiness with its autocratic administration. The new group was called the Volunteers of America, but it retained the Army's quasi-military organization and urban ministry emphasis. In 1872 Jerry McAuley, an Irish immigrant who was converted while in prison, founded Water Street Mission in New York. This was the first "rescue mission" in the United States and the inspiration for hundreds like them in subsequent years. In the 1890s evangelicals created both the Door of Hope and the Florence Crittenton Homes to provide shelter and care for homeless women and unwed mothers.

These and many similar ventures reflected a revivalist and holiness emphasis, and those leading them lived in the cities. In short, the biblical teaching of love as practical assistance to those in need characterized the philanthropic reaction to industrialism.

SOCIALISM

A far different response to the problems of the industrial age was that of socialism. The adherents of this went beyond mere reform to advocate the creation of a wholly new social order. Although there were many varieties of socialism, a common denominator was the call for some form of collective ownership of the productive assets or "the means of production"—land, machines, factories, transportation systems, and banks. Moreover, in contrast to the liberals, socialists rejected laissez-faire capitalism and free-market competition as too wasteful. They preferred instead some kind of cooperative or communal arrangement whereby people would own property in common and share in the proceeds of production. They stressed a fairer distribution of income among the functional members of society rather than simply increasing production.

The early socialists were labeled "utopians" because their ideas were based on extremely idealistic conceptions of human nature. For example, those who followed Robert Owen felt that self-governing communities would do away with the inequalities of life. The disciples of Count Saint-Simon argued that the state should own the means of production but under a hierarchy of talented elites who would reward everyone according to the work they did. Charles Fourier envisioned a society made up of cooperative units of 1,600 people in which everyone did the work that suited their abilities and all shared in the earnings of the venture. Louis Blanc advocated the formation of government-financed "social workshops" that would outperform private enterprises, since the workers would share in their management and profits.

To Karl Marx (1818–83), the most important of all the socialist thinkers, these were the schemes of impractical dreamers. Marx and his colleague Friedrich Engels (1820–95) insisted that rather than create ideal societies, one should work for the destruction of the capitalist system. From its ashes would emerge a new order based upon the just treatment of the workers.

The son of Jewish parents who had converted to Lutheranism, the young Marx himself rejected all religion. After studying philosophy at Berlin, he went into journalism because his radical views kept him from obtaining a university teaching post. However, the Prussian authorities closed his newspaper and forced him into exile. In 1844 he established a lifelong friendship with Engels, also a German, who had gone to England to manage a textile mill that his father owned there and had published a shocking account of the treatment received by the factory workers of the early Industrial Revolution. In early 1848 the two men wrote a political action plan entitled the *Communist Manifesto* for an obscure radical group, the Communist League.

When the revolution broke out in Germany two months later, they returned home, started a newspaper, and tried unsuccessfully to orient events in a socialist direction. When the uprising collapsed in 1849, both went back to England. Engels resumed his business career and helped support Marx, who spent the next thirty years buried in the British Museum library developing the details of his theory. The first volume of *Das Kapital* appeared in 1867, and after Marx's death his disciples compiled two more volumes from his notes. He also wrote several smaller books and many letters to other socialists in an effort to start an international working class movement.

Marx borrowed heavily from earlier thinkers to develop his own system, one that explained why workers lived in poverty and why revolutions and depressions occurred. Rejecting the idealism of earlier socialists as "utopian," he declared his view as "scientific," that is, it was based on the "laws" that governed society and ensured the eventual triumph of the workers. Of these laws, the most basic was "the materialistic view of history," or "historical materialism."

He drew upon two thinkers for this, Feuerbach and Hegel. The philosopher Ludwig Feuerbach (1804–72) wrote in *The Essence of Christianity* (1841) that matter, or nature (the material), was the source of all ideas, the reverse of what Hegel had taught. Further, God was the projection of man, the exalted wish of one's heart, the enlargement of ideas about ourselves. Thus, theology was anthropology, the knowledge of humanity. Marx went one step further to argue that ultimate reality was found not in nature as such but in the structures of economic life. Those who control the means of production (the "ruling class") construct the society in such a way as to benefit themselves. They determine its social relationships, political organs, laws, moral values, and religious beliefs. This inevitably led to the exploitation of others.

However, an economic system naturally expands and production techniques change. This results in the rise of a new class that is quite deeply involved in production, and eventually it challenges the old ruling class. Thus, the basic fact of history is "class struggle." To explain this, Marx drew upon the Hegelian dialectic. The old ruling

Evils of the Industrial Revolution

class is the thesis and the emerging new one the antithesis. Out of their clash (struggle) emerges a new system, one containing the best features of both classes. This process of historical evolution will continue until all classes have "freed" themselves, and the end result will be "communism" or "the classless society." In his time the struggle was between the "bourgeoisie," the industrial capitalist ruling class, and the "proletariat," the wage-earning workers who possessed no assets but their hands and backs.

Most of Marx's literary effort was aimed at exposing the evils of bourgeois society and preparing the way for the proletarian revolution. He argued that capitalist power is based upon profit ("surplus value"), the proceeds that really should have gone to the workers who made the goods, and hence capitalism is "organized theft." Further, the number of capitalists will diminish, because economic power is being concentrated in fewer and fewer hands and the ranks of the proletariat are swelling. The mounting tensions and contradictions within capitalism together with the increasing misery of the laborers will finally lead to a breakdown of the whole system. The workers will then seize power and set up a "revolutionary dictatorship of the proletariat" to carry out the transition to the classless society. Here Marx became a utopian himself, since he believed that in Communism private property would no longer exist, the state ("the executive committee of the ruling class") would be rendered unnecessary, and all would live in a condition of genuine freedom, where each person would contribute according to his ability and be rewarded according to his need.

Although Marx assisted in forming the (First) International Working Men's Association in 1864 and used it as a device to spread his ideas, most of the socialist organizing was done by others. The first German Marxist political party was formed in 1869, and after its union with another socialist group in 1875, the Social Democratic Party of Germany grew rapidly. By the early 1900s it was drawing the largest number of votes of any faction in parliamentary elections. Marxist parties were formed in the other industrialized countries as well, the largest being the Belgian and French ones. Many of the newly formed trade unions were also Marxist in orientation. As the parties and unions increased in strength, differences developed over strategy. The "orthodox" argued that the socialists must work for the revolutionary overthrow of "bourgeois" regimes, while the "revisionists" maintained that since the workers had unions and a political party they could achieve a transfer of power through nonviolent means.

A major influence in producing the latter approach was the "gradualism" espoused by a group of middle class critics of capitalism in Britain known as the Fabian Society. Formed in 1883, its members (including H. G. Wells and George Bernard Shaw) saw socialism as the social and economic counterpart to political democracy, as well as its eventual outcome. Class conflict was not inevitable, and gradual and conciliatory measures would eventually bring about a socialist order. Marxists contemptuously labeled this as "opportunism." The most extreme Marxists turned to syndicalism, an anarchistic movement that called for the violent overthrow of governments and their replacement by workers' unions as the supreme authority.

Relations between the churches and the socialist movements were strained, to say the least. Marx was a "post-Christian humanist" in that he proclaimed human independence from God and religion. For him, religion was the "opiate of the masses," a tool that the ruling class used to maintain its hold. The socialist parties were indifferent to the churches, and working class attendance at worship services sharply declined. The alienation of the laboring masses from the established churches in Europe was already in full swing by the end of the century. At the same time, the hostility of the largely bourgeois churches made reconciliation with the working classes all the more difficult.

CHRISTIAN SOCIALISM

The evangelical humanitarians sought to help the victims of the industrial order, whereas secular socialists viewed the system itself as the primary source of social problems. However, the "Christian socialists" tried to reconcile the divergent approaches. They advocated adjustments in or a revamping of the system itself in order to secure a larger measure of social justice. Most of them proposed a Christian alternative to the existing economic order, and some even worked with socialist or labor parties in the effort to effect change.

Although they differed on points of doctrine and action, Christian socialists were of one mind that the classical liberal approach to economic life was gravely deficient. To be sure, their ideas were drawn from contemporary reformist currents rather than from their own theological study and reflection, but their responses to the social question were moral and religious, not political in nature. For the most part, they were unfamiliar with contemporary socialist theory, while secular socialists were skeptical about their emphasis on spiritual factors and support of voluntary instead of collectivist solutions to social ills. The Christian socialists believed that Christ's kingdom embraced the whole human race and thus humanity could be improved and liberated from the evil conditions of life (e.g., competitive economic practices) produced by sin. Such was not God's intention for His creatures.

Even as the earliest varieties of socialism appeared in France, so did the first expressions of Christian socialism. The Catholic priest and writer Félicité de Lamennais (1782–54) identified poverty as the consequence of human sin. He called for a new order based on the abolition of monopolistic privilege, making credit available to all, and the right of workers to form producer cooperatives ("associations"), but he did not favor the abolition of private property as such. In his short-lived newspaper *L'Avenir* (*The Future*), Lamennais even advocated the separation of church and state and regeneration of the Catholic church. But in 1832 the pope condemned his views, and he resigned from the church and eventually abandoned his faith altogether.

Phillippe Buchez (1796–1865) was a writer who staunchly rejected organized Catholicism yet warmly embraced Christianity and may even have had a conversion experience. He was the chief advocate of independent, voluntary cooperatives. He saw the "right to work," which the associations would make possible, as the fulfillment of the social and political implications of Christ's teachings. Some other French figures espoused vague forms of Christian socialism, but the reactionary church leadership resisted these as well.

In England, however, the idea attracted a greater following. Founder of the self-styled Christian socialist movement was John M. F. Ludlow (1821–1911), a lawyer who was educated in France and learned about socialism there. During the Chartist unrest in 1848 (a moderate movement that through petitions and mass rallies called for a democratic reform of Parliament), he persuaded the liberal Anglican theologian Frederick D. Maurice (1805–72) and the novelist Charles Kingsley (1819–75) that Christians must be concerned about the suffering and injustice experienced by the workers. As Ludlow put it, "the new Socialism must be Christianized." During the next six years they published pamphlets, opened a "Workingmen's College" in London, and formed cooperative workshops for craftsmen. By 1855 the movement had died out because of lack of interest by both church and working class leaders and the distraction of the Crimean War. However, its long-range influence could be seen in the trade union movement, legislation for cooperatives, and working class education efforts.

Christian socialism revived with the founding of the high church Guild of St. Matthew in 1877 by the Rev. Stewart D. Headlam (1847–1924), also a member of the Fabian Society. It was strongly prolabor and looked down on cooperatives, arguing instead that legislation was needed to protect the workers. Headlam declared that Jesus was "the social and political Emancipator, the greatest of all secular workers, the founder of the great socialist society for the promotion of righteousness, the provider of a revolution."[2] However, its main rivals, the Christian Social Union (1889) and the Church Socialist League (1906), attracted more members and offered more radical prescriptions for social ills. They studied working conditions in factories and exposed firms with poor records.

World War I and the Russian Revolution dealt a severe blow to these and the "guild socialist" groups, some of which were associated with the Anglican church. (Guild socialism was a scheme to revive the medieval system of production on the basis of small-scale handicraft guilds.) Because of their middle class character, the societies never reached the urban masses who were becoming increasingly alienated from the churches. Yet, British Protestantism remained favorably inclined toward socialism. A good example was the work of Archbishop William Temple, whose book *Christianity and Social Order* (1942) is still highly respected.

An outstanding illustration of Christian involvement in "party" socialism is J. Keir Hardie (1856–1915). Influenced by the spiritual and ethical values of the Covenanter Presbyterian tradition of his home region in Scotland, he had a deep commitment to social justice. This was strengthened through his conversion at a Moody-Sankey meeting and membership in the Evangelical Union, a Scottish Congregationalist body. He later said that his socialism was derived from the Sermon on the Mount, maintaining that "the only way you can serve God is by serving mankind." He began as a coal miner, became a union agent, and then entered politics. Elected to Parliament in 1892, the following year he helped form the Independent Labour Party. Though it did not take the name "socialist," its program contained a statement endorsing collective ownership of the means of production. It was soon renamed the Labour Party and in 1906 won thirty seats, whereupon Hardie served two years as party chairman.

In Germany the churches saw the industrial order as an enormous challenge. Accordingly, they promoted Sabbath observance, formed city missions to minister to workers and new arrivals from the countryside, and operated train depot missions for travelers. They engaged in many other ventures through the Inner Mission, the principal Protestant response to industrialization. However, they saw the Social Democratic Party as even a greater threat. During the 1880s the German government tried to counter Marxism by a futile effort to ban the party and by offering the workers health, accident, and old age insurance. Thus, socialists came to regard both the church and state as foes.

At first the Social Democrats' stance toward Christianity was a hostile one. Some people argued for atheism or called socialism the new religion for the masses, while others insisted that religion was purely a "private matter." Soon the party moderated this attitude as a strategy to gain more followers. Although the response of most churchmen was purely negative, one Lutheran cleric, Adolf Stoecker (1835–1909), devised a form of Christian socialism as an alternative to Marxism. Through a pastorate in a new industrial town, involvement in the Berlin City Mission, and service as a Prussian court preacher Stoecker came in close contact with the problems of the industrial age. He concluded that God's kingdom could bridge the gap between the old conservative society and the radical new one. The church's emphasis on freedom, brotherhood, and equality before God could reconcile class differences on earth and allow the rich and poor to live at peace with one another.

In 1878 Stoecker founded the Christian Socialist Workers' Party as a rival to the Social Democrats. It called for a variety of reforms to aid the working class and encouraged their loyalty to the church, monarchy, and fatherland. Failing to make any inroads among working class voters, he renamed it the Christian Social Party and turned to the lower middle class. Here he discovered the potent political appeal of anti-Semitism. Through this device Stoecker became a national figure, even gaining election to the parliament, but it discredited him as a Christian socialist and finally led to his dismissal as court preacher in 1890. Although he did engage in other social action ventures in his later years, most people remember him merely as a precursor of Nazism because of his anti-Jewish speeches and activities.

Far different was Christoph Blumhardt (1842–1919), a committed evangelical who was the son of J. C. Blumhardt (see chapter 18). He entered the ministry with his father in 1869 and endorsed the elder's view that Jesus is victor and His kingdom of light will conquer the worldly kingdom of darkness. However, he argued that the institutional church was not witnessing to God's kingdom since it was interested only with details of doctrine, and therefore the proletarians and socialists were the ones who truly had an eschatological hope. Blumhardt became the first Lutheran pastor to join the Social Democratic Party, and in 1899 the local consistory ousted him from his pulpit for publicly supporting a workers' protest movement. In 1900 he was elected to the state legislature of Württemberg as a Social Democrat and served until 1906. Then he dropped out of politics, disillusioned with the Socialist party, which he felt was concerned less with the struggle for justice than with making the most comfortable bargain it could with the unjust world. Still, the stress on God's rule and revelation that pervaded his preaching influenced many twentieth-century theologians, including Karl Barth, Emil Brunner, and Dietrich Bonhoeffer.

His influence was also evident in the work of the "Religious Socialists," a society that was founded in 1906 by Hermann Kutter (1863–1931) and Leonhard Ragaz (1868–1945) in Switzerland. The group identified socialism with the hand of the living God and insisted that the social question would be settled out of the heart of Christianity. Ragaz even joined the Swiss Social Democratic Party, as did Karl Barth. A strong emphasis in the movement was pacifism, which would be a key element in German Christian socialism thereafter. However, in 1919 Barth suggested that religious socialism was a form of political idolatry when it asserted that the service of man,

William Booth, Founder of the Salvation Army

when undertaken in the name of the purest love, becomes the service of God, and he dropped out of the movement. Thanks to Paul Tillich and others, religious socialism flourished in German-speaking Europe, though what the term actually meant to those using it was never very clear. It proved to be an enduring phenomenon, and the Association of Religious Socialists, formed in 1926, still exists.

In the United States hostility to socialism prevailed in both Protestant and Catholic circles, but several influential people did belong to either the Christian Socialist Fellowship (1906) or the Church Socialist League (1911). They were quite different from the British groups, since their members identified with the Socialist Party of America, were conversant with socialist theory, and sought to enlist Christians in the political effort. These persons, many (but by no means all) of whom were liberals, identified the coming kingdom of God with the socialist state. Their success in reaching the mainstream Protestant churches was fairly minimal, and the movement rapidly declined during World War I. However, one lasting result was that a Presbyterian minister, Norman Thomas (1884–1968), would eventually lead the Socialist Party. Also, the work of these Christian socialists did contribute to the spread of that more uniquely American response to industrialization, the social gospel.

THE SOCIAL GOSPEL

This was an indigenous development within American Protestantism that arose in the 1880s, peaked around 1910–15, and declined in the 1920s. Its adherents, who included pastors, educators, journalists, and leaders of social service agencies, grappled with the crisis of industrialism and urbanization and sought solutions to the problems in the Scriptures and Christian theology. Because of the imprecise and polemical use that backers and critics alike made of the term "social gospel," it was defined in a variety of ways, ranging from meaningful societal involvement by Christians to a good-works morality that stripped the gospel message of all spiritual content. Liberal Shailer Mathews called it "the application of the teaching of Jesus and the total message of the Christian salvation to society, the economic life, and social institutions . . . as well as to individuals."[3] On the other hand, conservative opponent W. B. Riley claimed that social gospel preachers "repudiated the shed blood while they pleaded for service of man to man, finer education, fewer tenement houses, flowers in the front yard."[4]

The social gospel was primarily an urban and middle class phenomenon, and it reflected the Protestants' belief in the ultimate goodness of America and ongoing effort to Christianize the nation. Its focus was directed at the poor in the cities, and little attention was paid to the plight of the farmers or African-Americans. Due to the emphasis on saloons and similar vices and on immigration reform, some scholars argue that it was really rooted in small-town values. Moreover, the social gospel relied heavily on public and political means to promote the welfare of society, and in some ways it was the spiritual arm of the reform-oriented Progressive movement in American politics. Finally, the advance of social concerns to center stage in American Protestantism was a direct outgrowth of evangelical activism.

As mentioned earlier, evangelicals with their strong moral impulse that complemented their zeal for souls, were in the forefront of urban social action. For example, following Dwight L. Moody's revival in Boston in 1877, Baptist A. J. Gordon opened the Industrial Temporary Home to provide food, lodging, and jobs for those to whom he was preaching. A. B. Simpson founded the Christian and Missionary Alliance in the 1880s to bring the gospel to the urban poor. The *Christian Herald* magazine, under the leadership of businessman Louis Klopsch, was by the turn of the century the nation's leading sponsor of urban relief efforts. The Salvation Army's work in the American slums grew rapidly. However, where the evangelicals parted company with the social gospel was over its emphasis on pragmatic action. For them, theological beliefs and affirmation of faith in Christ were paramount, and the indifference of many social gospelers to doctrinal concerns seemed to undermine the relevance of the message of eternal salvation.

The foremost preacher of the social gospel was Congregationalist minister Washington Gladden (1836–1916). In his famous address "Is It Peace or War?" (1886), he defended the right of labor to organize. In numerous lectures and writings he called for practical reform measures such as factory regulation, inheritance taxes, and the breakup of monopolies. A noted popularizer of the social gospel was the clergyman Charles M. Sheldon (1857–1946), who wrote *In His Steps, or What Would Jesus Do?* (1896). It portrayed the social regeneration of a community whose leaders modeled their lives on Christ, and it allegedly sold twenty-three million copies. Josiah Strong (1847–1916), whose book *Our Country* (1885) was perhaps the most influential call for urban reform, declared that since the conquest of the West had been achieved, the city was the new frontier. He spent his last thirty years in New York working to bring the principles of social Christianity to bear on urban problems.

The major theologian of the social gospel was Walter Rauschenbusch (1861–1918), a German-American Baptist who in 1887 became pastor of an immigrant congregation in a New York slum and eleven years later a professor at Rochester Seminary. As he gained firsthand knowledge of exploitation and suffering and the indifference of those in places of power to the situation, he became a critic of the established order. He searched the Scriptures for an alternative that would harmonize his deep commitment to personal regeneration with an equally firm realization of the need for social action. In such works as *Christianity and the Social Gospel* (1907), and *A Theology of the Social Gospel* (1917), he emphasized the centrality of sin in producing the social crisis and the building of the kingdom of God as the answer.

The Catholic Response

Catholics lagged behind in their response to industrialism because of papal conservatism, but in Germany efforts were made to confront the problem. In the late 1840s Adolf Kolping (1813–65), a priest in Cologne, formed journeymen's associations to foster religious and moral values and immunize skilled workers to social-revolutionary appeals. (The organization, named after him, with its educational program, clubs, and hostels still exists.) Twenty years later clergy in the Rhineland launched a "Christian Social" movement to counter Social Democratic agitation. The main figure in this was Wilhelm von Kettler, archbishop of Mainz (1811–77), who dialogued with socialist leaders and linked the movement to the German Catholic Center Party.

An important change in course from the papal policy of absolute opposition to working class concerns occurred in 1891 with Leo XIII's encyclical *Rerum Novarum.* Essentially a conservative document that condemned the Marxist idea of a classless society and affirmed private property and the wage contract between workers and employers, it did criticize capitalism for its unbridled greed of competition and the concentration of economic power in the hands of a powerful few. The pope also urged employers to pay a just wage and endorsed modest state intervention on behalf of the weak and poor. He suggested that Catholics form their own trade unions, although for the purpose of moral and religious perfection, not the exercise of political clout. Leo XIII was certainly not the "red pope" as some critics of *Rerum Novarum* labeled him, and Catholic social thought continued to be more conservative than that of Protestants. However, it encouraged some, especially in America, to seek closer ties with organized labor and social reform.

The Industrial Revolution transformed the role of Christianity in Western culture. Its middle class character together with Marxist hostility contributed to a widening gulf between the churches and the working classes. Still, innumerable Christians, many of whose efforts went unheralded and unnoticed, endeavored to bridge the gap and reach those in deepest need with spiritual and physical help, and the same concern for others was seen in the foreign missionary enterprise. A wave of evangelical growth occurred in the later nineteenth century, but the clouds of new, even more menacing ideologies were gathering.

20

THE WORLDWIDE EXPANSION OF THE CHURCH

Although missionary work has been an important element in Christian history, it was usually a concern of the minority. Most European Christians were involved with their own day-to-day existence and gave little thought to people in other parts of the world who had never heard the gospel. Some theologians even regarded missions as unnecessary, arguing that God, in His own way, would enable those who were predestined to salvation to find Christ or that the "Great Commission" (Matt. 28:18–20) was addressed only to the apostles. At the same time, most European seafarers, merchants, and colonizers looked upon the indigenous populations of Asia, Africa, and America as inferiors, if not subhumans, and felt that evangelism among these people would interfere with their pursuit of wealth and power. However, the evangelical revival and Industrial Revolution placed the relationship of Western Christians to the larger world on a totally new footing.

European Imperialism and Missions

The nineteenth century was the great age of European imperialism. It enabled the Industrial Revolution to operate on a global scale and Europe to exercise economic—and, to a large extent, political—hegemony over the world. Prior to this time, Europeans controlled the sea lanes, but on land their power was more or less limited to the coastal regions of Asia, Africa, and the Americas. Such substantial states as Songhay and the Asante in Africa, the Ottoman Empire in Western Asia, the Mogul Empire in India, Manchu (Ch'ing) China, and Tokugawa Japan were effective counterparts to the West. However, the Industrial Revolution altered the global balance of power. It provided Westerners with the technology—steamships, railroads, agricultural equipment, and weapons—to establish their control over, and even to settle lands that belonged to, others. Also, with the introduction of mass education and literacy and the formation of relatively democratic governments, political leaders could enlist popular support for overseas ventures.

Even as Spain, Portugal, and Holland faded into the background as imperial giants, Britain and France came to the fore. Although the British had lost in the American Revolution, they held firmly to their position of power in Canada, the Caribbean, and especially India, which was the jewel of their overseas realm. Then followed the formation of a vast, worldwide empire. The explorer of the South Pacific, Captain James Cook, had revealed the extent of the islands, and his discoveries paved the way for the initial settlement of Australia in 1788 and New Zealand a few years later. In 1800 Britain acquired its first holding in Malaya, and in 1819 Sir Stamford Raffles founded the colony of Singapore, which became a center of British influence in East Asia.

After the abolition of the slave trade in 1807 and the subsequent decline of the West Indian sugar industry, the country's commercial interests shifted their attention increasingly to Asia. The British gradually extended their power throughout the Indian subcontinent, and following the Great Rebellion in 1857, Parliament dissolved the East India Company and assumed direct control there. In 1878 Queen Victoria was proclaimed Empress of India, symbolizing its significance in the British imperial structure as the center of a web of trading activity that spread from China to Africa. Britain also played the key role in forcing the opening of China to Western commerce in the notorious Opium Wars and supported the similar action by the Americans in Japan.

The defense of the "lifeline" to India was a major determinant of British imperial policy. For example, South Africa, which they had

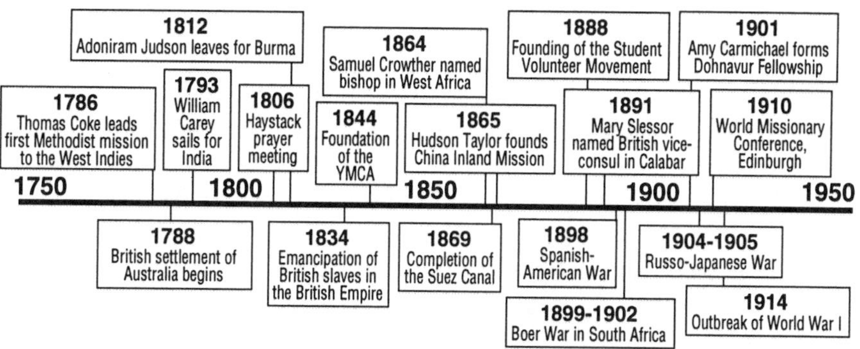

seized from the Dutch in 1795 and again in 1806, now took on strategic importance. Tensions with the Dutch-speaking Boer, or "Afrikaner," population grew steadily, even though they fled from the Cape in the 1830s to escape British domination. But at the beginning of the twentieth century their republics were forcibly incorporated into the new Union of South Africa. With the completion of the Suez Canal in 1869, Egypt took on special meaning as well, and this resulted in the imposition of the protectorate there in 1882. At the same time, British commercial enterprises flourished in East and West Africa.

An important factor in Britain's West African policy was the antislavery movement. Some evangelicals founded Sierra Leone in 1787 as a haven for freed slaves, and Clapham Sect figures soon were involved in the venture. Following the passage of the abolition bill, a British naval squadron operated from Freetown, its capital city, to intercept slave ships, and the rescued Africans were resettled there. Because many of them were won to Christianity and given a modest education, Sierra Leone became the leading edge of British advance in West Africa.

Because legislation—outlawing the slave trade and even emancipation in 1834—did not halt slaving, the evangelical abolitionist T. Fowell Buxton decided that the solution to Africa's problems lay in the development of its own resources. He organized the ill-fated Niger Expedition of 1841 that sought to conclude antislavery treaties with African chiefs, set up farms, and establish commercial operations. This was the first effort at offering the famous "three C's"—Christianity, commerce, and civilization—as an alternative to an economy based on slavery. Convinced that "legitimate" trade would counter slavery, some mission societies in West Africa formed self-supporting communities that produced commodities for sale in Europe. In the last half of the century the same approach was used to attack the slave traffic in East Africa, which was in the hands of Arabs and Swahili peoples. The foremost exponent of this was the renowned David Livingstone, who believed that an economic substitute —commerce and agriculture—would diminish the attractiveness of the slave trade.

Meanwhile, France began rebuilding its overseas holdings with the seizure of Algiers in 1830 and Tunisia in 1881, expansion into the interior of West Africa from its coastal foothold in Senegal in the 1850s, annexation of islands in the Pacific and Indian Oceans, and establishment of its first protectorate in Indochina in 1862. During the course of the century the Russians pressed into Central Asia and took land from China. Their encroachment on India almost led to war with Britain, but the antagonists eventually settled their differences.

In the 1880s the "scramble" for Africa began. The European powers subdivided large parts of the continent among themselves. Germany now entered the colonial struggle by claiming lands in West, East, and Southwest Africa. Belgium fell heir to the Congo (modern-day Zaire), which had been a personal business venture of its king. Italy took lands on the eastern coast and, later, Libya in the north, but its attempt to conquer Ethiopia was thwarted in 1896. In a contest over the upper Nile valley, Britain and France almost came to blows in 1898, and serious tensions between Germany and France occurred over the latter's seizure of Morocco. Meanwhile, Cecil Rhodes's empire building in southern Africa led not only to British domination of the region but also the tragic Boer War.

In Asia, Japan abolished the shogunate in 1868, and the new emperor oversaw an extensive program of political and economic reform. The forces of modernized Japan defeated China in 1895, touching off a scramble for territorial and economic concessions reminiscent of what had happened in Africa. In 1898 the United States defeated Spain and entered the ranks of the imperial powers by taking the Philippines. In a major war in 1905 the Japanese thwarted Russian expansion in East Asia, opened the way for the annexation of Korea five years later, and sent a signal to nationalist leaders throughout Asia that the Europeans were not invincible. The era of Western world domination was drawing to a close.

It was in this context that the global Protestant missionary effort occurred. Workers penetrated the domains of the British East India Company, first as chaplains and then as regular missionaries. A boatload left for Tahiti in 1796, and many more followed it to the Pacific islands. Robert Morrison began his labors in Canton (China) in 1807, where he translated the Bible and laid the groundwork for an enormous expansion of Christian work after the Opium Wars. The first missionaries entered the newly opened Japan in 1859 and Korea in 1884. British and German missionaries were active in Indonesia, and they also founded thriving works in West, East, and South Africa.

Many other efforts are worthy of mention. The Baptist George Grenfell led a major venture in the Congo region. There was a modest enterprise in the Caribbean and extensive endeavors among the American and Canadian Indians, of which Dr. Wilfrid T. Grenfell's work in Labrador was the most famous. Attempts were made in the Near and Middle East and in North Africa to reach Muslims. An intensification of effort accompanied the scrambles for Africa and China, and by the turn of the century the number of workers and amount of funds expended for missions had reached new heights. Many in the missionary community were hopeful that the impending triumph of Christianity and Western civilization meant that the kingdom of Christ was at hand. However, they failed to realize just how shaky the position of the West was.

CHRISTIANITY AND IMPERIALISM

Some interpretive matters need to be mentioned at this point. The Marxist contention that imperialism was (and still is) the by-product of capitalism is accepted without question in many places today, especially in the developing world. This "popular orthodoxy" holds that all varieties of Western imperialist expansion were the result of the capitalistic quest for profits overseas. That involved both the "export of capital" and dependence on the home governments to protect their investments from capitalists in rival countries and from resistance by the indigenous victims of their economic policies.

Thus, imperialism serves as an emotional slogan for leaders of liberation movements, although in reality the historical basis for this view is flimsy at best. The most recent scholarship on imperialism shows that Western bankers in search of profits paid only modest attention to the non-Western areas. Instead, the great bulk of their investments were placed in already developed areas, not newly acquired colonial dependencies. This was clearly the case with Great Britain, the United States, France, and Germany. Some countries that did have or were seeking possessions were quite short of capital, including Russia, Italy, Japan, and Portugal. Further, capital that was invested in new colonial territories did not produce a higher return than domestic investments. Thus, it would be more fruitful to look for the origins of imperialism in other places, such as the quest for national prestige, than in the conspiratorial designs of capitalist interests.

This issue is quite important for historians of Christianity, as such a materialistic explanation of imperialism rules out philanthropic sentiment or spiritual motivation. It means that when Christian missionaries cooperated with imperialism, whether wisely or unwisely, they automatically promoted the exploitative designs of Western capitalism. Missionaries were, at best, the dupes of and, at worst, in collusion with the agents of capitalist imperialism. Further, this interpretation precludes any assessment of positive benefits that might have resulted from the imperial relationship, and from a theological perspective it leaves no room for the workings of divine providence.

A more serious problem for Christians, however, is the relation of imperialism to Western conceptions of cultural superiority. Social Darwinist views (see chapter 21) about the "fitness" of white people to rule the "weaker" races and to bring civilization and enlightened existence to those living in darkness—the "wild tongues that have not Thee in awe" and "lesser breeds without the law," as Rudyard Kipling put it in his poetic hymn "Recessional" (1897)—flew in the face of Christian belief about the universal sinfulness of humanity and the equality of all people before God. As for the racialist version of Social Darwinism—the strongest nation always conquered the weaker ones and the dominant white race seized colonies to prove it was strong and virile—this not only was repugnant to Christianity but also paved the way for the most virulent form of racism—German Nazism.

However, faith in modern civilization was much more seductive, and, in fact, for many it had become a sort of substitute religion, with imperialism as its creed. The French spoke of their sacred "civilizing mission," the Germans of spreading *Kultur,* the Americans of the "blessings of Anglo-Saxon protection," and the British of the "White Man's burden." The latter was taken from Kipling's poem of 1899, which urged Europeans to engage in unselfish service in distant lands to advance the work of humanity. The problem lay in the obvious self-interest and gross condescension that accompanied this noble vision.

As British historian Brian Stanley observes, most Protestant missionaries in the nineteenth century, especially those from Great Britain, believed that missions would transform heathen barbarism into Christian civilization. This was based on four assumptions. First, the cultures that they were penetrating were not religiously neutral but under the control of Satan in all their aspects, including politics, economics, public morals, and the arts. Second, they saw their own nation as a model of Christian culture and society. The Bible and the Reformation had made their country great. Third was the implicit faith in human moral progress that the Enlightenment had contributed to Christian thought. Centuries of Christian influence in their countries had held in check the human sinfulness that had free rein in heathen lands. Finally, the successful efforts in "civilizing" the heathen, as seen in Sierra Leone and some Pacific islands, seemed to validate the contention that this was possible. Only in the twentieth century would people come to recognize that a civilization modeled on post-Enlightenment, Victorian middle class society was not necessarily Christian at all.[1]

Mission Societies and Renewal of the Vision

As was shown in chapter 16, considerable Protestant missionary vitality existed in the 1700s. But the geographical expansion of the faith during the following century was truly extraordinary, given the fact that prior to 1875 the number of workers was relatively small. Many writers see the modern missionary movement as beginning in 1792, the year when William Carey (1761–1834), originally a shoemaker and then a Baptist preacher, published *An Enquiry into the Obligations of Christians to Use Means for the Conversion of the Heathens* and delivered the sermon at a Baptist ministers' meeting with the famous lines "Expect great things from God; attempt great things for God." This inspired the founding of the Baptist Missionary Society (BMS). However, these events actually marked the culmination of a process in the evangelical awakening.

One element in it was the emphasis on the responsibility to preach the gospel to all people. Another was the prophetic or millennial strain that came from Jonathan Edwards, who believed that the last days were at hand and that the spread of the gospel throughout the world, together with the earnest prayers of the church, would usher in the kingdom of Christ. Edwards's influence was reflected both in the Prayer Call of 1784, issued by a group of Baptists and modeled on a similar appeal by him, and the work of Baptist theologian Andrew Fuller (1754–1815), whose *The Gospel Worthy of All Acceptation* (1785) used Edwards's argument that divine sovereignty operated in the propagation of the gospel by human effort. Also, Wesley's associate Thomas Coke (1747–1814) published a plan for a missionary society in 1783 and took the first Methodist mission to the West Indies in 1786. Moreover, in the 1790s the mission-oriented evangelicals were encouraged by the French Revolution, which seemed about to destroy their ancient foe, the Roman Catholic church.

In 1793 Carey, with his family, sailed for India, never to return to England, even for a furlough. Essentially they were illegal immigrants since the British East India Company was hostile to missionaries. It feared that the preaching of Christianity might cause disturbances and undermine its shaky control. However, Carey found a job as manager of an indigo plantation and spent his spare time preaching and doing Bible translation. In 1799 the BMS sent out two more missionaries, Joshua Marshman (1768–1837), a teacher, and William Ward (1764–1823), a printer. Barred from Calcutta, they settled in the nearby Danish territory of Serampore and persuaded Carey to join them.

Later known as the "Serampore Trio," they formed one of the most remarkable partnerships in Christian history. They lived in community, formed a church, set up a printing press, engaged in itinerant evangelism, and translated the Bible into various Eastern languages, including Bengali, Sanskrit, and even Chinese. They also founded a college to train Indians to spread the gospel. Carey himself mastered the world of Hindu thought and essentially created the field of Bengali prose literature. He published a 1,000-page Sanskrit grammar, translated Hindu works into English, taught Indian languages at Fort William College in Calcutta, and even conducted horticultural research.

The creation of the BMS marked the entrance of the Anglo-Saxons into full-scale mission work. It was also a true voluntary society, in contrast to the two earlier Anglican church bodies, the SPG and SPCK (see chapter 16), which had parliamentary funding and royal backing and focused on reaching people in British possessions. To be sure, the SPCK did support the German workers in India, some of whom had been part of the Danish-Halle mission, and others who were chaplains under the East India Company. In 1795 the London Missionary Society (LMS) was formed as an interdenominational society, but within a few years it had become the organ of the Congregationalists. In 1813 the Methodists consolidated some local works into a national missionary society.

In 1799 the evangelical Anglicans, who wished to maintain their churchly identity, created the Society for Missions to Africa and the East, which in 1812 was renamed the Church Missionary Society (CMS). Unlike the Nonconformist bodies, the CMS required that its

Samuel Crowther

workers be ordained. After the high church Anglican SPG took over the SPCK work in India in the 1820s, the SPG's character changed from that of a supplier of colonial clergy to a more general voluntary missionary society. The enthusiasm of the Anglo-Catholics was reflected in the Universities Mission to Central Africa, formed after David Livingstone delivered a famous speech at Oxford and Cambridge in 1857 that challenged his audiences "to carry out the work I have begun."

For a long time the Church of Scotland was torn by dissension over whether to engage in foreign missions and only formed its own board in 1824. Its most renowned worker was Alexander Duff (1806–78), who carried on educational work in India. However, various local Scottish groups promoted missions and some Scots served with the LMS in Africa: for example, John Philip and Robert Moffat, and David Livingstone, the latter's son-in-law. In 1875–76 both the Free Church and the mainline Church of Scotland established neighboring works in Nyasaland (East Africa)—the Livingstonia and Blantyre Missions.

In Britain's colonies the Church of England undertook the effort to meet the spiritual needs first of their European residents and later the native populations as well. Although the American Revolution was past, still three bishops were ordained there between 1784 and 1787 for what was now an independent Protestant Episcopal church.

However, north of the border the Loyalist Charles Inglis (1734–1816) was consecrated bishop of Nova Scotia in 1786, the first colonial bishop in the Church of England. In 1814, after Parliament opened the East India Company's territories to missions, Thomas F. Middleton (1769–1822) was made bishop of Calcutta, and he set out to bring the CMS missionaries, many of whom were still German Lutherans, under the control of the Established church. In the following decades dioceses were set up in Bombay, Madras, and other urban centers. Australia had been under the oversight of Calcutta, but in 1836 William G. Broughton (1788–1853) was appointed bishop of Australia. Over the succeeding years he built up an extensive church structure in the thinly populated dependency. George A. Selwyn (1879–78), who was consecrated bishop of New Zealand in 1841, ministered both to the British settlers and indigenous Maori communities. The first bishop in South Africa, Robert Gray (1809–72) of Cape Town, was seated in 1848, and other bishoprics were created in Africa as missionary work progressed.

In the United States the impetus for creating foreign mission societies was the Second Great Awakening. Students played a major role in this, most notably Samuel J. Mills (1783–1818), who turned to Christ during a revival in his home county and decided to attend Williams College in Massachusetts to prepare for foreign service. Here he found some kindred spirits, and they formed a small group called the Society of the Brethren. One afternoon in 1806 they were caught in a thunderstorm and sought refuge under a haystack near the college. They used the occasion for a prayer meeting and pledged to become missionaries. Mills and others in the circle went on to Andover Theological Seminary where they continued to proclaim their vision. Here they met Adoniram Judson (1788–1850), a young man who was recently converted and had also dedicated himself to foreign service. He would be remembered as the greatest nineteenth-century American missionary.

In 1810 the youths persuaded leaders of the Congregational church to establish the American Board of Commissioners for Foreign Missions (ABCFM). Two years later it sent out the first workers to India, including Judson and his new bride. While studying the New Testament on the voyage, he decided that infant baptism and sprinkling were improper, and upon arrival in Calcutta he had one of the Baptists there immerse him. An associate, Luther Rice (1783–1836), also opted for believer's baptism. They resigned from the Congregationalist society and sought support from American Baptists, who in turn asked the English BMS to take Judson into their work in India. It recommended instead that the Americans form their own board, and accordingly in 1814 the General Missionary Convention of the Baptist Denomination in the United States of America for Foreign Missions came into existence. Forbidden by the company to work in India, Judson went to Burma where he had a long and fruitful ministry. Rice returned home and promoted missions and denominational growth.

Although the ABCFM was best known for its work in the Hawaiian Islands, its ministry among the American Indians, especially the Cherokees in Georgia (the tribes forcibly removed to Oklahoma), and the Nez Perce in the Northwest, was also quite important. Both it and the Baptist society soon became regular denominational boards, an organizational pattern that predominated in the U.S. The Methodists in 1819 and the Episcopalians in 1835 created boards, and nearly all other Protestant denominations followed suit in the ensuing years.

As in England, the missionary societies on the European continent were outgrowths of the evangelical revival. In 1797 Johannes T. Vanderkemp (1747–1811) formed the Netherlands Missionary Society before he left for service in South Africa with the LMS, and for some time it functioned as the Dutch auxiliary of the latter. Similar missionary organizations were formed by awakened Christians in France, Denmark, Sweden, and Norway, but the most important ventures were in Germany.

In 1800 Pastor Johannes Jänicke (1748–1827), who was a figure in the Berlin *Erweckung,* opened a missionary training school in his church, many of whose graduates later served under British boards. In 1815 a mission school and society was founded in Basel, Switzerland. Although it drew the bulk of its support from neopietists in southwestern Germany, its ties with the English were particularly close. By 1833 thirty Basel-trained workers were serving under the CMS, and it subsidized the education of missionaries in Basel until 1858. In the period several other societies were founded in Germany, including the Berlin (1824), Barmen or Rhine (1828), Bremen (1836), Gossner (1836), Leipzig (1816), and Hermannsburg (1849) missions.

The example for these had been provided by the British, and, as in England, the leaders were often people of fairly high social position whereas the missionaries themselves were mainly lower–middle class types, such as clerks and artisans. But in Germany it was a novelty that lay people—simple church folk—banded together without direction from higher authorities to carry out what they saw as the work of God. Actually, the localized, territorial church structure in Germany was conducive to this sort of religious individualism. The societies, which were seen as the free outgrowth of the spirit of missions in the church as a whole, enlisted support throughout the country. Since they were highly ecumenical ventures, Lutheran confessionalists were uneasy about cooperating with either British Anglicans or German Reformed in them. Accordingly their own agencies were more separatist in character.

Societies and boards were necessary because it was extremely difficult to be self-supporting on the mission field. The freelancer, such as Charles Rhenius, who broke with the CMS in South India in the 1830s over the issue of ordination, or the ambitious German Karl Gutzlaff (1803–51), who ran a one-man show in China in the 1830s and 1840s, was clearly the exception. However, the most remarkable missionary in China, J. Hudson Taylor (1832–1905), developed a different approach to the support question, namely the "faith" mission. His China Inland Mission (CIM, founded 1865) had the backing of no church or denomination, and his workers did not receive a fixed salary but instead trusted God to supply their needs. Friends of the enterprise were urged to pray for missionaries and the money needed for their passage and support, but no direct appeals for money were to be made. The society, which would not go into debt, accepted funds from devout Christians around the world. Taylor also required his people to conform as closely as they could to the living conditions of the Chinese, even to the point of wearing their dress. The CIM's aim was to preach the gospel to as many people as possible in the shortest amount of time, and Taylor left to others the organizing of converts into churches. The faith mission model was replicated by various societies before the end of the century: The Evangelical Alliance Mission (1890), Sudan Interior Mission (1893), African Inland Mission (1895), and Liebenzell Mission (1899).

The Indigenous Principle

An important question in mission theory was the development of an independent "native," or indigenous, church. Although it was clearly a concern early in the century, the main discussions occurred between 1840 and 1870, and the principles were enunciated by Henry Venn (1796–1873), secretary of the CMS (1841–72), and Rufus Anderson (1796–1880), foreign secretary of the ABCFM (1832–66). The slogan, "self-governing, self-supporting, and self-propagating," summed up their position. This meant decentralization in mission work and the encouragement of local initiative. Funding for the ministry should come from local sources and not from Europe. National pastors should be ordained and given responsibility for directing their churches, which in turn would grow on their own and win people in the community. This would free up the missionaries from pastoral and administrative duties so that they could get on with the job of evangelism.

A good illustration of the potentialities and limitations of this doctrine was Samuel Ajayi Crowther, the best-known African Christian of the nineteenth century. A Yoruba from modern-day western Nigeria, as a teenager he was captured and sold to Portuguese slavers in 1822. But the British naval squadron stopped the ship and released him in Sierra Leone. There he found Christ, was baptized by a CMS missionary and given the new name of Samuel Crowther, and received an education. He worked as a teacher and evangelist, engaged in linguistic studies, and eventually prepared a first-rate Yoruba translation of the Bible. He also was sent to London for further education and ordained in 1843. On his return, he worked closely with a new CMS mission in the Yoruba country.

In line with Venn's theory, more Africans were ordained and finally in 1864 Crowther was consecrated as bishop of these domains. Venn felt that the missionary role was temporary and once an indigenous church was established, the Europeans would move on. However, the resistance by the expatriate missionaries, who saw this as the impractical, doctrinaire view of a home-based administrator, was too strong. By the 1880s the missionary vision had spread among the educated classes, and the CMS now had an abundance of keen, young European workers who wanted to extend the mission, secure as many converts as possible, and order the church in their own way. Having no interest in a self-governing African church, they ignored Crowther. In 1891 he died a broken man and was replaced by a European bishop.

But the idea of an indigenous church was not dead. It was reiterated by the American Presbyterian missionary to China John L. Nevius (1829–93), who wrote the influential book *Planting and Development of Missionary Churches* (1886). After being invited by missionaries in Korea to review their field in 1890, they adopted his approach and phenomenal growth in their Presbyterian church occurred. The "Nevius method" was fourfold: (1) each Christian should be self-supporting through his or her own labor and be a witness for Christ by word and deed; (2) church methods and organization should be developed only to the extent that the indigenous Christians could take responsibility for them; (3) the church should select for full-time work those who seemed best qualified and whom it was able to support; and (4) churches were to be built in the native style and by the Christians from their own resources.

His "three-self" approach (self-governing, self-supporting, self-propagating) was reiterated by the Anglican missionary to China Roland Allen (1868-1947). This strategy would prove to be decisive in church growth and is the foundation for the enormous expansion of the church in the non-Western world that has taken place in the twentieth century.

Missions and Social Progress

Although the great majority of missionaries saw their primary task as winning the lost to Christ, the movement as a whole had an enormous impact on improving the quality of life in the non-Western world. The introduction of modern medicine, public health, and sanitation was one very real benefit. For example, the early missionary to Japan James C. Hepburn (1815-1911) operated a dispensary in the 1860s and 1870s that treated six to ten thousand patients annually, and he trained medical students there as well.

Another benefit was education, as missionaries universally set up schools and trained people to read and write. This was designed to prepare the way for a self-governing church, since an educated, indigenous leadership was the prerequisite for granting autonomy. But one who had been trained to read the Bible could also read newspapers and political tracts, and, in fact, many of the future revolutionary nationalists were educated in mission schools.

The potential of educational ministry was particularly seen in Japan. Dr. Hepburn and other pioneers tutored students and opened schools, and some of the women began girls' schools as well, which marked the beginning of women's education in Japan. Guido Fridolin Verbeck (1830–98), an American Dutch Reformed missionary, arrived in 1859 and started a school in Nagasaki. Several of his pupils would be leaders of the new Japan. In 1870 the government invited him to Tokyo to establish a school for Western languages and sciences, and this became Tokyo Imperial University with him as its first president. Another result of education was the formation of dedicated groups of students, the Christian "bands," such as the Kumamoto Band formed in 1876. Its most famous member was Niishima Jo,

IMPORTANT PROTESTANT FOREIGN MISSION SOCIETIES
(PRIOR TO WORLD WAR I)

- 1649 Society for the Propagation of the Gospel in New England (New England Company)
- 1698 Society for Promoting Christian Knowledge
- 1701 Society for the Propagation of the Gospel in Foreign Parts
- 1732 The Moravians at Herrnhut begin overseas mission work
- 1792 Baptist Missionary Society
- 1795 London Missionary Society
- 1797 Netherlands Missionary Society
- 1799 Church Missionary Society
- 1810 American Board of Commissioners for Foreign Missions
- 1813 Wesleyan Methodist Missionary Society
- 1814 General Missionary Convention of the Baptist Denomination in the USA for Foreign Missions (American Baptist Foreign Mission Society)
- 1815 Basel Mission
- 1819 Missionary Society of the Methodist Episcopal Church (USA)
- 1821 Danish Missionary Society
- 1822 Paris Evangelical Missionary Society
- 1824 Church of Scotland Foreign Missions Committee
- 1824 Berlin Missionary Society
- 1828 Rhenish (or Barmen) Missionary Society
- 1829 Christian Missions in Many Lands (Plymouth or Christian Brethren)
- 1835 Swedish Missionary Society
- 1835 Protestant Episcopal Church in the USA Missionary Society
- 1836 North German (or Bremen) Missionary Society
- 1836 Gossner Missionary Society (Berlin)
- 1836 Leipzig Missionary Society (Confessional Lutheran)
- 1837 Board of Foreign Missions of the Presbyterian Church in the USA
- 1840 St. Chrischona Pilgrim Mission (Switzerland)
- 1841 Neuendettelsau Missionary Society (Confessional Lutheran)
- 1842 Norwegian Missionary Society
- 1843 Free Church of Scotland Mission (formed after the Disruption)
- 1844 South American Missionary Society
- 1845 Foreign Mission Board of the Southern Baptist Convention
- 1849 Hermannsburg Missionary Society (Confessional Lutheran)
- 1849 American Christian Missionary Society (Disciples of Christ)
- 1857 Universities Mission to Central Africa
- 1859 Finnish Missionary Society
- 1865 China Inland Mission (Overseas Missionary Fellowship)
- 1872 Regions Beyond Missionary Union
- 1872 Mennonite Church, General Conference, Foreign Mission Board
- 1881 North Africa Mission
- 1884 German East Asia Mission
- 1889 South African General Mission (Africa Evangelical Fellowship)
- 1890 The Evangelical Alliance Mission
- 1892 Lutheran Free Church (or Bleckmar) Mission
- 1892 Gospel Missionary Union
- 1893 Sudan Interior Mission
- 1895 African Inland Mission
- 1897 Christian and MIssionary Alliance
- 1899 Liebenzell Mission (Germany)
- 1901 Oriental Missionary Society
- 1904 Sudan United Mission
- 1908 Christoffel Mission to the Blind (Christian Blind Mission)
- 1910 World Gospel Mission
- 1914 Assemblies of God Foreign Missions Department
- 1914 Worldwide Evangelization Crusade

known in the West as Joseph Hardy Neesima (1843–90). Converted while studying in America, he returned with a vision to found a Christian college.

Higher education was a major emphasis, and numerous colleges and universities were established. Noteworthy ones in India included Serampore College (1819), Wilson College in Bombay (1832), Madras Christian College (1837), and the United Theological College at Bangalore (1901). In China there were thirty-three Christian institutions in 1914, the best known of which were Peking, Yenching, and St. John's universities. In Japan the famous Doshisha University was organized in 1874. In the Near East the American University of Beirut and Robert College in Constantinople were founded in the 1860s. The CMS's Fourah Bay College in Sierra Leone (1827) and the Presbyterian Lovedale Institute in the Cape Colony (1841) were pioneer African institutions.

Bible translation was a central concern of the evangelistic endeavor. However, as African historian Lamin Sanneh points out, putting the Bible into the world's vernacular languages acknowledged that in God's eyes there was a plurality of cultures and all were equal before him. Just as neither the Jewish nor Greek culture was superior, so it was with Western culture. The revitalization of the language of a people, especially one that had been unwritten, was an unanticipated by-product of Bible translation. It helped to preserve that people's culture rather than destroy it. He concludes that missionary adoption of the vernacular was tantamount to adopting indigenous cultural criteria for the Christian message. In other words, this is a "piece of radical indigenization far greater than the standard portrayal of mission as Western cultural imperialism."[2]

Missionaries also fought against barbaric and dehumanizing practices. The early workers in India pressured the company and then Parliament to halt the widespread practice of *sati,* the burning alive of a widow on her husband's funeral pyre. They also campaigned against the pilgrim tax that helped to support the great religious festivals. Terrible abuses, such as mutilations and human sacrifices, occurred at these festivals. Another matter that drew the missionaries' fire was the Indian caste system. Although some tolerated it, most were adamantly opposed. As the Bishop of Calcutta said in 1835, it was "eating as doth a cancer into the vitals of our infant churches," and "the distinctions of caste must be abandoned, decidedly, immmediately, and finally."[3] Mission schools helped combat the evil by giving lower caste people a sense of self-worth and teaching that the system was wrong.

A particular concern of the workers in China was the brutal custom of footbinding. As many as 90 percent of the women at the time were forced to endure this painful process that gave them tiny feet. Missionaries fought the practice by establishing girls' schools where it was not allowed and forming "anti-footbinding societies," which set out to influence public opinion against it. By the turn of the century the movement had made considerable progress, thanks to the persistent effort by both expatriate missionaries and Chinese women themselves.

Another women's issue was the cruel practice of female circumcision among the Kikuyu people in British East Africa (Kenya). Mission efforts in the late 1920s to ban the procedure caused deep resentment among the Kikuyu men, and a political crisis resulted. This open confrontation between Christianity and traditional values led eventually to the Mau Mau resistance movement in Kenya during the 1950s.

Slavery was the most compelling issue for the missionaries in Africa. As mentioned earlier, it lay behind the effort to foster so-called legitimate commerce. A good example of this was the work of the Basel Mission in the Gold Coast (modern Ghana). In the 1850s it formed a trading company to market products from workshops and farms that the mission had established to employ Africans. The venture especially prospered from cocoa production, still a staple of the Ghanaian economy.

The most memorable advocate of the policy of indigenous commerce was David Livingstone (1813–73). He arrived in South Africa in 1841 and soon engaged in evangelism in remote areas. This led to his famous journeys into unknown regions, where he looked for people uncontaminated by contacts with whites. Soon he became more of an explorer than evangelist, but he still believed that Africa could be opened to "civilizing influences," that is, missions and healthy commerce. What he regarded as unhealthy were slave trading and oppressive, greedy white settlers like the Boers. He died without seeing the fulfillment of his dream of a chain of mission stations and trading centers in Central Africa.

Although missionaries often knuckled under to imperial power interests and white settler groups, there were some who bucked the tide. One was John Philip (1775–1851), who was sent by the LMS to reorganize its work in South Africa. Arriving in Cape Town in 1819, he was shocked by the white mistreatment of the native population. He believed that blacks and whites were equals and mounted a campaign to persuade the British authorities to grant civil rights to all persons of color. He turned his society's stations into "cities of refuge" for blacks, where they could be safe from intimidation by white residents over labor contract disputes. Philip also tried to have white traders and farmers excluded from border areas, and he obtained legislation abolishing forced labor and affirming legal equality of both races. For his efforts he was bitterly condemned by whites in the colony.

An inspiring story is that of the English Baptist missionary William Knibb (1803–45). He went to Jamaica in 1825 and quickly recognized the plight of the plantation slaves. As he came to see that evangelization and emancipation were inseparable, his preaching against the planter regime grew increasingly militant. His custom of treating the blacks as human beings also upset the planters. When a slave insurrection erupted in 1831–32, Knibb was accused of being an instigator and a white mob burned down his chapel. Since his life was now in danger, he went home and plunged into the campaign for the abolition of slavery in the British Empire. He published documents and lectured about conditions on the island and testified before a parliamentary committee about servitude in the Caribbean colonies. He returned to Jamaica after the emancipation bill passed and immediately took up the struggle against the "apprentice system," a halfway stage between slavery and freedom. For Knibb, the all-important question was justice for his "brothers and sisters," as he called the Jamaicans.

WOMEN AND MISSIONS

The area of church ministry most open to women was foreign missions. Here women could preach, evangelize, plant churches, educate national leaders, and carry on humanitarian work. Although they lacked clerical ordination, they functioned on their own, far from the reach of critics back home. Also, since most of them engaged in "women's work" on the mission field or preached to male audiences of "natives," the male-dominated church simply looked the other way. Not only did missions constitute a meaningful profession for thousands of women, but also millions of others were drawn into the endeavor in some way or other, since almost every denomination had a female missionary society or a women's support group. Historian Patricia Hill remarks that the mission enterprise was "substantially larger than any of the other mass women's movements of the nineteenth century" and greater in size than both the widely heralded Student Volunteer Movement and the Laymen's Missionary Movement.[4]

The wives of missionaries were one element in this. Although some were ignored by their spouses (Mary Moffat Livingstone was a good example of this), many of them were as equally effective in ministry as their men. For instance, Ann Hasseltine Judson, first wife of Adoniram, gained lasting fame from her inspirational writing and assistance to her husband while he was in a Burmese prison. J. Hudson Taylor's first wife, Maria, helped him found the China Inland Mission, and his second, Jennie, was an equal partner with him in the ministry.

The number of female workers swelled. Most societies regarded the wife also as a missionary, and numerous single women went to the field under the regular denominational boards or one of the many women's agencies, such as the Female Education Society (Britain), Church of England Zenana Missionary Society, Woman's Union Missionary Society (United States), or German deaconess orders. In fact, by the 1890s so many single women volunteered for service that the men began to perceive them as a threat.

Often overlooked by historians, some of these women were extraordinary individuals. One was Charlotte ("Lottie") Diggs Moon (1840–1912), a Southern Baptist teacher from Virginia, who went to

China in 1873 and initiated a remarkable teaching and preaching ministry. A fireball of activity, it was said that she did the work of three missionaries. She established an outpost of the gospel in North China where others had tried but failed. Lottie Moon also kept up a barrage of correspondence with the home base that pleaded for missionary recruits and financial support for them. In 1888 this resulted in the launching of the annual Christmas offering for foreign missions in the Southern Baptist churches (named for her after her death), which over time has raised more than $1 billion.

A remarkable personality in the area of medical missions was Dr. Ida Sophia Scudder (1870–1960). Born in India into an old American missionary family, she had at first decided not to follow in her father and grandfather's footsteps. A crisis experience in 1893 caused her to change her mind, and she studied medicine and returned to India as a physician. She opened a women's hospital at Vellore in 1900 and later added to it a nursing school and, in 1918, a medical college for women. Through her great ability as a fund raiser she built a medical training complex that involved the cooperation of fifty missions from ten countries. It came to be known as the finest medical center in India.

Another exceptional figure who worked in India was Amy Carmichael (1867–1951). Born in Northern Ireland, she was deeply influenced by the Keswick Movement (see chapter 21). After a brief stint in Japan she went to South India in 1895, never to return home again. She served in Dohnavur with the Church of England Zenana Missionary Society, which tried to minister to the high caste women who were isolated from the general society. (A *zenana* was the section in a large house where women and girls lived.) A decisive moment in her life was in 1901 when she took into her home a runaway girl who had been destined to become a temple prostitute. Soon other abandoned children and temple escapees came to her, and she began an active program of rescuing abused youths. She called her enterprise the Dohnavur Fellowship, and by 1912 she had 130 children under her care. It functioned as a communal society where all the workers wore Indian dress, cared for and educated the children, and strove to develop Christian character in them. Then she formed a Protestant religious order for single women called the Sisters of the Common Life. Although an invalid after 1931, she became famous through her devotional books, which were marked by an intense spirituality.

The most amazing woman of all was Mary Slessor (1848–1915). From a poor, working-class Scottish family, she was reared in the slums of Dundee. Although she had a limited education and worked in a textile mill to help support her mother and other family members, David Livingstone's death inspired her to volunteer for service in the Presbyterian Calabar mission in West Africa (modern Nigeria). She arrived there in 1876, taught in a school, and learned the language quickly. In 1880 she took charge of the mission at Old Town, where she lived in a mud hut, ate the local food, supervised schools, gave out medicine, resolved disputes, fought against witchcraft and drunkenness, and cared for orphans, many of whom were twins that had been abandoned. Slessor then began a pioneer work among the Okoyong tribe, and she was so skillful in working with people in judicial matters that the British authorities in 1891 named her a vice-consul, the first woman in the empire ever to hold this title. A decade later she moved further inland to work among the Ibos. She so identified with the Africans that in her later years she was known throughout the region as the "Mother of All the Peoples."

African-American Missions in Africa

It is not very well known that African-Americans engaged in missionary activity, and much research remains to be done before the whole story can be told. The earliest such missionary was Daniel Coker (1780–1835), one of the founders of the African Methodist Episcopal Church in 1816. In 1820 he led a small group of free blacks who were emigrating to Sierra Leone and remained there to pastor a Methodist church in Freetown that ministered to slaves set free by the British.

The black Baptists formed a missionary society in 1815, and it directed one of its co-founders, Lott Cary (c. 1780–1828), a freed slave and self-educated preacher in Virginia, to accompany the settlers going to the future Liberia in 1821–22. He established a church and school and tried to reach the indigenous people as well as the emigrants from America. To be sure, Cary's involvement in the ill-conceived effort to "repatriate" blacks to Africa may have damaged his historical reputation, but he contributed significantly to the dominant position Baptists now have in Liberia. African-American Baptists later named a mission board after him.

Another noteworthy effort was initiated by Baptists from Jamaica. In 1838–39 they began raising money for a mission to West Africa, and two volunteers set out on their own but disappeared without a trace. William Knibb pressed their case with the Baptists in London, and in 1840 he convinced them to support the project. An

Mary Slessor

advance party of British Baptists checked out the situation in Cameroon and the nearby Spanish island of Fernando Po and found the missionary prospects to be favorable. The response in Jamaica was enthusiastic, and two men from there, Joseph Merrick and Alexander Fuller, sailed to Fernando Po in 1843. Arriving five months later were two British Baptists and thirty-nine Jamaicans, some who were teachers and evangelists and others settlers. Although it was very poor, the Jamaican church contributed a large sum of money to support the African venture, thereby reflecting a remarkable partnership in mission with its British counterpart.

Though they initiated a promising ministry, within two years the Spanish pressured the missionaries to leave and most of the Jamaicans returned to the West Indies. However, Merrick and his wife relocated on the mainland, where he reduced a local language to writing, began Bible translation, opened a school, and held services. He died in 1849, but a British member of the Fernando Po mission, Alfred Saker, was able to put the Baptist work in Cameroon on a permanent footing.

African-American Methodists and Baptists began missions in South Africa in the 1890s. The Methodists also had works in Sierra Leone, Liberia, and the Gold Coast. These ties with American blacks were important in the emergence of "Ethiopianism," an independent church movement in South Africa in the pre–World War I years.

Roman Catholic Advance

In its non-European heartland, Latin America, Roman Catholicism fell on hard times. With the end of Spanish patronage the liberal revolutionary regimes after 1815 exercised their own forms of control over the church, and Catholicism lost much of its legal and political power and influence. Those governments struggling against the church often found the Protestants to be allies, and this aided a modest advance of the latter, especially toward the end of the century. Although for a while relations with the papacy were fairly good, religion at the popular level was in rapid decline, and after 1850 the liberals increasingly demanded (and in several countries obtained) separation of church and state. The most radical break was in Mexico where even the church's properties were confiscated and religious orders suppressed.

In the latter part of the century a missionary renaissance took root in Latin America. A variety of religious orders worked among the people to win them to (or back to) Catholicism, and the bishops began developing strategies to preserve the faith in the face of anti-Christian movements and growing Protestant competition, including Methodists, Southern Baptists, and various faith missions, who were especially active.

Elsewhere in the world, many older Catholic orders carried on missionary work, but their efforts were not as spectacular as those of the Protestants. Also, nearly one hundred new orders and religious communities were founded that engaged in some kind of missions. They were not as free acting as the Protestant societies, since the Propaganda in Rome exercised some supervision. But the following may serve as examples.

In 1868 a French order called the White Fathers was founded by Cardinal Charles M. Lavigerie (1825–92), Archbishop of Algiers and head of the Catholic church in North Africa. They were secular priests who wore a distinctive white garb and took a vow for lifelong service in African missions. At first they worked among the Muslims, but then in 1877 they were sent to Uganda, where a fierce rivalry ensued between them, CMS workers, and Muslims for religious control of the Bugandan kingdom. Fighting the slave trade was also a major concern of the order, which had stations throughout Central and East Africa.

The Society of the Divine Word was formed by German Catholics in 1875, largely in response to the rapidly growing Protestant effort. Its first mission field was in the Shantung region in China, and the German government used the murder of two of the society's priests by Chinese terrorists in November 1897 as a pretext for seizing a port city there for a naval base. The group established works in Latin America, Africa, and the South Pacific as well. Another important society was an American congregation of diocesan priests known as the Maryknoll Missioners. Formed in 1911, their major fields were in East Asia, but later they opened missions in Latin America and Africa.

MISSIONS AND ECUMENISM

The twentieth-century ecumenical movement originated in and was the fulfillment of the missionary advance. On the foreign fields Christians from many denominations and countries engaged in the common effort of preaching the gospel, and in the non-Christian environments they discovered that the differences among them were really not all that significant when compared to the task before them. Limited funds and the magnitude of spiritual need forced the mission agencies to learn how to cooperate with one another, and the lessons learned there were carried back to the home base in Europe and North America.

One element in the new ecumenical vision was missionary scholarship. Alexander Duff in Calcutta, who was a strong advocate of learning as a means to spread the gospel, promoted the scientific study of missions. In 1867 he was appointed to the first university chair of missions at the Free Church of Scotland's New College in Edinburgh. Another pioneer in mission studies was Gustav Warneck (1834–1910), who held an honorary chair of missions at the University of Halle, edited the first scholarly journal devoted to the study of missions, and published major theoretical works on the history, philosophy, and theology of missions. Julius Richter (1862–1940) authored thirty books and two hundred articles on missions and was named to a new chair of missiology at the University of Berlin in 1913. All three men were strong advocates of ecumenism. *The Muslim World*, founded in 1911, is still the leading journal of Christian-Muslim relations. A more popular magazine that reported on missions from a global perspective was the *Missionary Review of the World*, edited by the prominent American evangelical A. T. Pierson (1837–1911).

Cooperative ventures began on the mission fields in the form of regional consultations and general conferences. Also important were the conferences of the Evangelical Alliance, an international body formed in 1846 to promote unity among churches, which emphasized the full authority of Scripture, Christ's incarnation and atonement, salvation by faith, and the work of the Holy Spirit. At a Union Missionary Convention in New York and an Evangelical Alliance meeting in London, both in 1854, Duff made stirring presentations for missions. A variety of conferences were held in Germany and Britain during the next three decades, culminating in large gatherings in London (1888) and New York (1900) that called for greater unity. Also, cooperative organizations were formed in the major sending countries, such as the Standing Committee of German Protestant Missions (1885), Foreign Missions Conference of North America (1911), and Conference of Missionary Societies of Great Britain and Ireland (1913).

An even more crucial factor was the student movements. The Young Men's Christian Association, founded in England in 1844 by George Williams (1821–1905), a businessman and lay evangelist, spread to the United States in 1851. Soon college chapters of the YMCA were formed (by 1884 there were 181), and these emphasized Bible study, worship, and personal evangelism. Other student groups were in the seminaries and British universities, including one at Cambridge where seven leading athletes vowed in 1882 to become missionaries. The "Cambridge Seven" had a powerful impact on missionary recruitment. At a student gathering at D. L. Moody's home in Mount Hermon, Massachusetts, in 1886, a revival broke out, and one hundred young people pledged to become missionaries.

One of these was a Cornell University student, John R. Mott (1865–1955), who went into college YMCA work. In 1888 he founded the Student Volunteer Movement for Foreign Missions whose watchword was "The Evangelization of the World in This Generation." Mott remained a lay Christian worker his entire life, and like his mentor, Moody, he never received a theological education or was ordained. He was a gifted writer and speaker, creative and energetic organizer, and incessant traveler who circled the globe promoting student work and Christian cooperation. Besides leading the SVM, the student YMCA, and the World's Student Christian Federation, which he formed in 1895, he was the prime mover behind the World Missionary Conference at Edinburgh in 1910.

This was the first truly ecumenical gathering. It was organized by an international committee, and the 1,200 delegates represented 159 mission societies and boards. Seventeen were Asian churchmen. The chief topic of the plenary discussions and commission meetings was missions. A Continuation Committee was named to follow up on the topics investigated and prepare the way for a permanent international missionary council. Mott chaired this body, with Eugene Stock of the CMS and Julius Richter from Berlin as vice-chairman. Its secretary was J. H. Oldham (1874–1969), a dynamic young man who would become one of the leaders of the ecumenical movement. He also edited the *International Review of Mission,* founded in 1912, which was the organ of the new ecumenism. However, the hopes for Protestant unity based on missionary cooperation were rudely shattered by the outbreak of war in 1914.

The extraordinary progress of foreign missions lulled many into thinking that the kingdom of Christ was at hand. The advance of middle class values that they identified with Christian civilization concealed the fact that other ideologies were competing for the allegiance of people both in the Western and non-Western worlds. Already a restive nationalism was afoot in Asia, whereas in the industrial cities of Europe and North America large segments of the population had little or nothing to do with the church. The onslaught of alien ideas and finally the deluge of war would forever shatter the evangelical consensus. Ecumenism would have to be founded on premises other than the propagation of the evangelical gospel.

21

THE CHURCH IN THE TWILIGHT OF THE WEST

Whereas Catholicism was held back by papal conservatism, evangelical Protestantism seemed to be growing. Missionary extension was one aspect of this process. Mass evangelism was another, as many thousands found Christ in the large urban meetings of the era, and the holiness and Pentecostal movements added a powerful spiritual dimension to evangelicalism. However, new ideas that were at odds with the Christian tradition threatened the Protestant and Catholic churches and cast a dark cloud over the optimism so prevalent at the beginning of the twentieth century. Liberals tried to adjust to the changes and conservatives resisted them, but neither could turn back the forces that were causing Western civilization to unravel.

THE POLITICS OF POWER IN A LIBERAL AGE

The Western nations experienced many changes in the late nineteenth century, not all of which were negative. Democratic government advanced throughout northern, western, and central Europe. Political reforms in Britain had extended the vote to almost all men, and in 1911 the House of Lords was stripped of its veto power. In the United States the union had been preserved and slavery eliminated. The creation of the Dominion of Canada in 1867 marked the first example of the granting of political liberty within one of the European colonial empires without resort to violent revolution. Similar dominion status was granted to Australia, New Zealand, and the Union of South Africa after the turn of the century. Even the monarchical empires—Germany, Austria-Hungary, and Russia—had liberalized their regimes. Both Germany and Austria had parliamentary governments, though considerable power still resided in the monarchs. Russia abolished serfdom in 1861.

The two problems that grew more menacing as the years passed were nationalism and militarism. British rule in Ireland was a constant source of dissension in the United Kingdom, while Germany's annexation of the French provinces of Alsace and Lorraine in 1871 permanently poisoned relations between the two neighbors. The multinational empires of central and eastern Europe contained many peoples who desired their own nation-states, such as the Poles, Czechs, Romanians, and Bulgarians. Italy and Serbia wished to include in their boundaries people of their nationality ruled by Austria-Hungary. Ottoman Turkey was a composite of nationalities, several of whom wanted their own states or desired to join with ethnic brethren outside the empire.

To check the possibility of war between Germany and France and to keep the "great powers" from becoming involved in a fratricidal war in the Balkans, German chancellor Otto von Bismarck devised an elaborate system of alliances. Whether this peacekeeping device ever could have worked is a debated issue, but after his dismissal by the young Kaiser (Emperor) William II in 1890, only an alliance with Austria-Hungary was allowed to remain. Imperialism, however, gave nationalism a new face. Britain was concerned about imperialistic rivals and Germany's growing economic power, while the kaiser was demanding "a place in the sun" for his country. The vagueness of Germany's overseas ambitions worried the other countries. Reactionary tsarist Russia did the unthinkable and concluded an alliance with republican France, while Britain settled the colonial differences with its rivals France and Russia. By 1908 Germany felt surrounded and had only one ally, the deteriorating Dual Monarchy of Austria-Hungary, whose Balkan involvements would lead to war.

Militarism accentuated the problem because the great powers had large standing armies and military lobbies that were pressuring

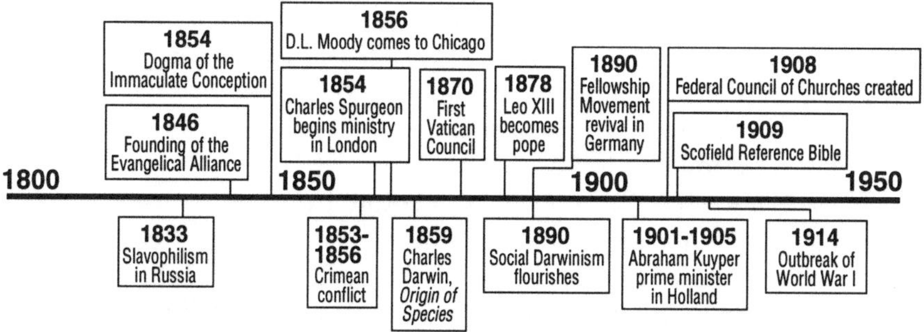

the governments for still greater expenditures. The German decision to build a large navy as a symbol of its national greatness threatened the British, who regarded their naval force as vital to national survival. That drove them into the waiting arms of France. Military leaders with their mobilization and battle plans exercised an inordinate influence on political decision making. This factor, together with the changed alliance system, ensured the virtual impossibility of containing a local war between two great powers. Thus, when a Serbian terrorist assassinated the crown prince of Austria-Hungary on June 28, 1914, the major countries of Europe were one by one drawn into a war that would totally alter the course of civilization. But in the peaceful and prosperous years of the late-Victorian era, few could foresee the cataclysm that lay beyond the horizon.

Roman Catholic Conservatism

With the accession of Pius IX (1792–1878) to the papal throne in 1846, it appeared at first that some liberalization might occur, but the Revolution of 1848 frightened him back into the path of reaction that had gripped the papacy (see chapter 18). He had fled from Rome when radicals set up a republic there, and he returned in 1850 under the protection of French arms. Pius's goal was to strengthen his spiritual authority in every way possible, and he began in 1854 by proclaiming the dogma of the Virgin Mary's immaculate conception. Then in 1864 he issued an encyclical (papal letter to all bishops) listing eighty propositions or "errors" that Catholics must reject. Most of these had been condemned before, but putting them in one package was seen as a formal rejection of the modern world. Included in the Syllabus of Errors were pantheism, naturalism, rationalism, indifferentism, socialism, communism, Freemasonry, Bible societies, public education, freedom of speech, any limitation of the pope's civil power, and many others. Most offensive was Section 80, which condemned the assertion that "the Roman pontiff can and should reconcile and align himself with progress, liberalism, and modern civilization." This encyclical outraged Protestants and liberal Catholics, but they could do nothing about it.

In 1869–70 Pius IX convened a council (Vatican I) to deal with various matters in the church, and he made it the occasion for an even greater assertion of papal primacy. The Ultramontanes, the hard-line papal supporters, greatly outnumbered the liberals at the council, and they secured the passage of a decree affirming papal infallibility. It declared that the pope is infallible "when he speaks *ex cathedra*," that is, in his role as pastor and teacher, and "by virtue of his supreme Apostolic authority he defines a doctrine regarding faith or morals to be held by the Universal Church." On the surface this was a stunning claim, but in fact it was quite circumscribed and the prerogative would seldom be used. Yet the papacy had gained a position of power within Roman Christianity that it did not have even in the thirteenth century, and the great majority of Catholic Christians seemed willing to grant the Holy See this authority. In the age of democracy Rome had erected a fortress for itself against modernity. The unconditional acceptance of papal jurisdiction had prevailed over national and liberal tendencies.

The statement was accepted by all but a handful of dissidents in Germany and Austria. A distinguished church historian, Johann von Döllinger of Munich, led the opposition to the decree and was excommunicated, but he did not join the group that separated in 1871. The latter claimed that the Vatican decrees and other recent pronouncements had created a new church, but they wanted to perpetuate "true" Catholicism. They called themselves "Old Catholics," adopted an episcopal form of government, and acknowledged as binding most of the doctrines spelled out prior to 1054. The Old Catholics, who were never more than a small minority, eventually (1932) established communion with the Church of England. They in effect became German Episcopalians.

While the Vatican Council was in session, war broke out between France and Prussia, and the French garrison was withdrawn from Rome. This was the moment for which the young Italian state was waiting. Its forces promptly moved in and annexed the city, bringing an end to the temporal power of the papacy. In the long run, this action enormously benefited the church. Now that the pope no longer was a secular prince, his spiritual hold on Catholics throughout the world was enhanced.

However, Pius IX was incensed that the Italians had seized his lands, and he withdrew into the Vatican Palace. From this point he posed as the "prisoner of the Vatican," and the "Roman question" embittered relations between the papacy and Italy for the next half-century. The state made a generous offer in the Law of Guarantees (1871), which, although it deprived the pope of his sovereign power, still accorded him all the honors and rights of a sovereign and exempted him from Italian law. He was allowed to retain possession of the Vatican and two other properties, the Holy See would continue to have a diplomatic corps and its traditional police units, ecclesiastics could come and go at will and conduct church business unhampered, and the state granted him an annual allowance equal to the income he would have received from his former possessions.

Pius and his successors refused to accept this because it did not acknowledge the pope's right to be an independent territorial prince. Compromise was impossible since the Italians were not prepared to give back any part of the Papal States. The situation was made worse when right-wing monarchists in France supported the pope's position, something that Italy saw as interference in its affairs. When Leo XIII in 1898 ordered Italian Catholics to abstain from political life while he remained in his "intolerable position," this only stirred more anticlericalism. Only after World War I would the matter be resolved.

In Germany a bitter church-state conflict took place during the 1870s. Known as the *Kulturkampf* (cultural struggle), it was inaccurately portrayed by some liberals as a conflict between modern civilization and an ancient, out-moded religion. Actually it was politically based. For various reasons German chancellor Bismarck feared that the Catholic minority in the Protestant-dominated German Empire was a threat to its security. They had a strong political party, the Center, which was hostile to his regime. The assertion of papal infallibility seemed to be a claim of superiority over the state. The strident demands by some Catholics for intervention to restore the pope's temporal power disturbed friendly relations with Italy. And the danger existed that German Catholics might unite with their counterparts in France and Austria in a war to undo German unification.

Bismarck's program of repression included expulsion of the Jesuits (the traditional instrument of papal authority), abolition of the Catholic bureau in the Ministry of Public Worship, institution of civil marriage, and placing education completely under state control.

Also, he appointed a liberal, Adalbert Falk, as Minister of Public Worship in Prussia and ordered him to defend the rights of the state against the church. Falk was responsible for the adoption of the notorious "May Laws" (1873), which claimed the absolute supremacy of the state. They limited the powers of bishops in disciplinary matters, set up a supreme church court appointed by the emperor, put the training of priests under strict state supervision, and gave the regime veto power in clerical appointments. When Pius IX condemned the measures, Bismarck severed diplomatic relations with the Vatican, cut off all financial support to the German church, and compelled religious orders to leave the country.

Catholic resistance to the state's actions was unyielding, and many bishops and priests were jailed or ousted from their posts. In the parliament the Center Party vehemently criticized the moves. Even some Protestants were sympathetic, as they thought things had gone too far and feared they might be the next victims of high-handed state action. Bismarck, who had not expected to see his measures evoke such a hostile response, was politically embarrassed and began looking for a way out. Finally, with the accession of the more conciliatory Leo XIII to the papal throne, a changed political climate in Europe (the republicans had won out in France and Austria was allied to Germany), and the onset of the anti-Socialist campaign, the policy was reversed and the laws quietly removed from the books. Bismarck's attempt to browbeat the Catholic church and its political party had failed miserably. Since then, the term *Kulturkampf* has become part of the modern political vocabulary and is often used to designate a church-state conflict.

In France, most leading Roman Catholics were opposed to the Third Republic that had been founded in 1870, and they advocated restoration of the monarchy. The government responded with anticlerical laws to keep the church in check. Among these were registration of religious associations, elimination of army chaplaincies, legalization of divorce, and compulsory primary education that included a ban on religious teaching in the public schools. However, in 1890 Leo XIII decided to conciliate the regime by ordering French Catholics to abandon their support for a restoration of the monarchy.

Church-state relations then improved, but soon they suffered irreparable damage in the Dreyfus affair. This involved the court martial and conviction of a Jewish army officer accused of selling secrets to the Germans. When it was shown in 1896 that the charges were false, the country was torn between the defenders and critics of the army. The military refused to admit its mistake or to deal with the anti-Semitism that lay at the heart of the problem. While the republicans lined up behind Captain Dreyfus and demanded justice, the army, royalists, and Catholic clergy supported the original action.

Eventually he was exonerated, but in the meantime the republicans turned on the monarchists and their clerical allies and in 1905 passed a law separating church and state. This guaranteed complete liberty of conscience, stipulated that the state was to have nothing to do with the appointment of clerics or the payment of their salaries (this applied to Protestants and Jews as well), and provided for the formation of private corporations that would take over the property of the church.

The significance of this action can hardly be overstated. Not only did it cancel the Napoleonic agreement with the church (see chapter 17), but more importantly it meant the end of the special relationship between the popes and the French rulers that had originated in 756 when Pepin the Short authorized Stephen II to take control of lands in Italy, thus laying the basis for the papacy's temporal power. An era lasting twelve centuries had come to a close. Moreover, the events of the period help to explain why France, in spite of its strong Catholic heritage, is today one of the most secular countries in Europe.

THE RESURGENCE OF ORTHODOXY

With the rapid decline of the Ottoman Empire the authority of the Ecumenical Patriarch in Constantinople lessened. During the course of the century the Serbian, Greek, Romanian, and Bulgarian churches all became autonomous, and the role of the patriarch was reduced to deciding questions of dogma and consecrating holy oil for all the churches. Meanwhile, the Russian Orthodox church remained closely tied to the state (see chapter 13), and during the reign of Tsar Nicholas I (1825–52) the doctrine of "official nationality" was developed. Proclaimed by his minister of education in 1833, it contained three principles—Orthodoxy, autocracy, and nationality. Autocracy meant the maintenance of the absolute power of the sovereign, which was the indispensable foundation of the state. Orthodoxy indicated that the church's official role was to be the ultimate source of ethics and ideals that gave meaning to life and society in Russia. Nationality referred to the unique nature of the Russian people, which made them a mighty and dedicated supporter of the dynasty and government. To enable the church to do a more effective job of inculcating the people with loyalty to the tsar, more seminaries were founded and the state paid the salaries of the clergy.

For Nicholas I, Orthodoxy was also involved in foreign policy. He asserted the right to "protect" the Orthodox Christians living in the Ottoman Empire, and this led to a diplomatic crisis in the early 1850s. A dispute erupted between Orthodox and Roman Catholic monks over custody of the holy places in Palestine, and the ambitious Napoleon III claimed that France was the protector of Catholics there. Nicholas sent an ultimatum to the Turkish sultan insisting that he settle the Holy Land controversy in favor of the Orthodox and recognize a Russian protectorate over Orthodox churches in the empire. France and Britain urged the sultan to resist the demand, and this helped trigger the Crimean War in 1854.

In the 1830s and 1840s a group of romantic intellectuals emerged who were known as the Slavophiles. They had a major impact on Russian religious thought. They rejected the West and emphasized the superior nature and historic mission of Russia and its Orthodox church. They argued that the Slavs were divinely commissioned to preserve the Christian faith in its purity and that their church and state were the guardians of true Christianity and the ideal society. According to the Slavophiles, the character of the Slav, and especially the Russian peasant, was marked by love, freedom, and cooperation, while the West was decadent. Christianity there had been corrupted by rationalism, papal tyranny, and Protestant individualism. Some maintained that Russia should liberate all Slavs from foreign rule and bring all Christians into the Orthodox fold. It was a renewed affirmation of Holy Russia as the Third Rome.

The leading Slavophile religious philosophers were the laymen Alexis S. Khomiakov (1804–60) and Vladimir S. Soloviev (1853–1900). Khomiakov argued that the Orthodox church was an organic whole, with Christ as the head and the Holy Spirit as the soul, and its essence was unity and freedom. Religious authority rested in the entire body of the church rather than in the Bible or the papacy. Soloviev set forth the concept of "Godmanhood," by which he meant the union of humanity and divinity through the identification of man with Christ, the incarnate Word. He advocated the reunion of the Eastern and Western churches and the establishment of a universal theocracy.[1]

An important late nineteenth-century Russian figure was Constantine Pobiedonostsev, a lawyer who served as procurator of the

Nicholas I, Tsar of Russia

Holy Synod from 1880 to 1905 and was the architect of tsarist reactionary policy. He emphasized the weakness and viciousness of humankind and the fallibility of human reason, hated the industrial revolution and the growth of cities, and saw the purpose of the state as maintaining law, order, stability, and unity. In Russia this could best be accomplished through the autocracy and the Orthodox church. He distrusted the West and wanted to keep Russia as much as possible from becoming contaminated by ideas from that direction. He was opposed to parliaments, trial by jury, newspapers, and secular schools, and he rigidly censored the press. In order to assimilate the diverse peoples of the empire to Russian culture (Russification), he encouraged Orthodox missions among them.

One of Pobiedonostsev's principal targets was the large Jewish population in western Russia and Poland. He declared that one-third of them would convert to Orthodoxy, one-third would emigrate, and one-third would be exterminated. Many pogroms (the Russian word for organized violence against Jews) occurred during these years, and a massive migration of Russian Jews to western Europe and America took place. His anti-Semitism was a frightening foretaste of what would happen in Nazi Germany. In short, he put Orthodoxy solidly on the side of reaction and helped to discredit it in the eyes of thinking people.[2]

The Orthodox church had no more regard for evangelical groups than it did for radical sects like the Molokans and Doukhobors. (In fact, the latter emigrated en masse to Canada in 1898 to escape persecution.) The first Protestants in Russia were immigrants, but eventually the evangelical faith took root among native Russians. Catherine the Great had invited Mennonite and Hutterite colonists from Germany to settle in the Ukraine, while other Germans from a Lutheran pietist background came to southern Russia in the early nineteenth century. Some of these engaged in evangelism, but under Nicholas I such activities were curbed. Even the Russian Bible Society was closed down, but clandestine distribution of the Scriptures continued. In the 1840s Baptists from Germany began work in the Baltic area, and after Nicholas's death they spread across Russia.

Closely related to the Baptists were the pietistic Stundists, whose name came from their practice of regular hours of Bible study. The movement arose in the 1860s. At first they operated within the Orthodox church. But eventually they were forced out. F. W. Baedeker (1823–1906), a German evangelist who had a high social standing and close ties with Brethren circles in England, began working in Russia in 1875 and had some success in reaching upper-class people. One of his converts, an army colonel, organized the first meeting of the Russian Baptist Union in his home in 1884. Because of his connections Baedeker was able to make frequent preaching tours and even visit prisons where he distributed Bibles. The Baptists and Stundists later united to form the core of the "Evangelical Christian-Baptists" in Russia.

Evangelical Advance

Whereas the established churches of Protestant Europe were losing momentum in the late nineteenth century, the American denominations, which were well organized and sociologically homogeneous units, reached a much larger portion of the populace. Not only did denominationalism flower in America but also religious innovation. Adventism, with its emphasis upon the apocalyptic coming of the kingdom of God, developed in the 1840s and was institutionalized in the Seventh-day Adventist Church, which grew into a worldwide denomination through its emphasis on lay dedication and health care. A much more radical adventism was propagated by the Jehovah's Witnesses, founded by Charles T. Russell in the 1870s. What would become the largest of the new faiths was the Church of Jesus

Christ of Latter-Day Saints (the Mormons). It arose in the 1830s, and, after the murder of its founder Joseph Smith in 1844, it divided into two separate churches. The larger branch with its base in Utah became an international denomination, thanks to the intensity of its missionary effort. Another group, small but genteel, was Christian Science, founded in the 1870s. Historian Sydney E. Ahlstrom aptly remarks that these four, plus Pentecostalism, are five religious movements that properly bear the stamp "made in America."[3]

However, more significant than any of these innovations was the American shaping of evangelical Protestantism. This prepared it to survive ideological assaults and function as a truly global faith at the end of the twentieth century. One product of the American environment was mass evangelism. This approach was popularized in the early decades of the century by Charles Finney and became a mainstay of Protestantism in the United States after the Civil War.

Its towering figure was Dwight L. Moody (1837–99). Converted as a teenager in his native Massachusetts, he went to Chicago in 1856 to work as a shoe salesman. At the same time, he became deeply involved in YMCA work, preached, started Sunday schools, and distributed Christian literature. After five years he had become a successful businessman, but he left this career to enter full-time ministry. Though only a layman with no theological training, his reputation as a preacher grew rapidly. Then he met a song leader named Ira Sankey (1840–1908), and in 1873–75 they went together on an extended preaching mission to Great Britain. This proved to be the turning point in his life. The meetings were so successful that he was now in demand all over America. During the next few years the pair held evangelistic services in most of the country's large cities and returned twice to Britain.

Critical to Moody's success was organization. He refused to come to a city until all the ministers in the evangelical churches invited him. A local committee was set up to care for all the arrangements, such as securing a hall, advertising, and fund raising. A volunteer choir was assembled and drilled in selections from Sankey's hymnbook. Ushers were chosen and trained along with "inquiry room workers," ministers and laymen who counseled those who came forward to receive Christ. During the campaign Moody also held workshops for Christian workers who would play an important role in the "follow up" of the converts.

His manner as a preacher was a model of decorum. He dressed like an ordinary businessman, the meetings were carefully planned and run according to a schedule, and he spoke calmly and plainly. His messages were simple and to the point, and he focused on God, sin, and one's need for a Savior. Moody did not expound theology, deal with doctrinal issues, or promote social action, but simply called men and women to Christ. He viewed himself as first and foremost a winner of souls, and his emotionally powerful sermons were designed to achieve this objective. As for the converts, his advice to them was to join a local church right away and get to work for God.

Moody maintained such a grueling schedule of travel, prayer meetings, lectures, instructional sessions with workers, and interviews that his heart finally gave out at age sixty-two. But his legacy lived on in his training school for lay workers in Chicago (now Moody Bible Institute), secondary schools in Massachusetts, and the people touched by his ministry, such as John R. Mott. All the other great preachers between 1870 and 1920 (the "golden age" of itinerant mass evangelism)—Samuel P. "Sam" Jones, J. Wilbur Chapman, R. A. Torrey, Rodney "Gipsy" Smith, William A. "Billy" Sunday, and innumerable other lesser-known figures in the United States, Britain, and Germany—followed the methodological trail first blazed by Finney and converted into a spiritual highway by Moody.

A second American contribution was the "holiness" emphasis. Its origins lay in John Wesley's teaching on perfectionism and the writings on sanctification of such pre–Civil War figures as Charles Finney, Asa Mahan, and Phoebe Palmer. Holiness emerged full-blown in the "camp meetings" that began in the late 1860s, and a variety of groups and publications promoted it in Methodist circles. However, its advocates within the mainline Methodist churches (both North and South) felt increasingly alienated because of indifference to their concerns, and finally they separated and formed their own holiness denominations. The largest were the Church of God, founded by Daniel S. Warner in 1881, and the Church of the Nazarene, started by Phineas F. Breese in 1895.

The hallmark of American holiness teaching was "entire sanctification," a stage of spiritual development beyond conversion. This "second blessing" of the Holy Spirit gave one the ability to resist temptation to commit sin and live a life totally dedicated to God.

The holiness perspective was carried to Britain by William E. Boardman (1810–86), author of the book *The Higher Christian Life*, R. Pearsall Smith (1827–99), and his wife Hannah Whitall Smith (1832–1911). She wrote the popular book *The Christian's Secret of a Happy Life.* The couple propagated holiness doctrines in England while he was there on business, and during Moody's 1873 campaign they joined with Boardman to deliver the message to British ministers. This was followed by a series of conferences at Oxford in 1874 that spelled out holiness and then an invitation in 1875 from an Anglican minister to hold open-air meetings in his Lake Country town, Keswick. This became an annual affair, and the conventions were imitated around the world. The name "Keswick" was affixed to the teaching, but in Europe it is also called the "Oxford Movement."

In the quest for personal holiness, Keswick adherents rejected the perfectionist aspect of sanctification and emphasized instead what they called the "fullness of the Spirit." One had to seek this experience, which was an act of faith in Christ distinct from regeneration in order to achieve victory over sin. The empowering received from the Holy Spirit also enabled one to be an effective servant for Christ. Associated with Keswick were such phrases as the "higher life," "victorious living," "abiding in Christ," "resting in the Lord," "full surrender," "consecration," and "the Spirit-filled life."

Keswick had a deep impact on modern evangelicalism. Moody brought the ideas back to the summer conferences he sponsored at his Massachusetts home, and they rapidly spread through evangelical Bible schools and missionary societies. Keswick terms even found their way into the popular gospel songs. The leading mass evangelists followed Moody's lead and spoke about the filling of the Holy Spirit, while Bible teachers like F. B. Meyer, Andrew Murray, W. H. Griffith-Thomas, and W. Graham Scroggie became household names for British and American evangelicals alike. Keswick had a key impact on the coming of the spectacular Welsh revival in 1905, and its influence was also evident in the Fellowship Movement, a holiness revival that swept Germany between 1880 and 1910. The preachers of this revival were relatively unknown outside of Germany, but the Gnadau Association, which formed around a Keswick-style Bible conference, has preserved the organizational form of the Fellowship Movement.

An outgrowth of the emphasis on holiness was Pentecostalism. It went beyond the second blessing to stress a "baptism in the Holy Spirit" that was accompanied by the "gifts of the Spirit" or "charismata." This was not a one-time event but something that should continue to be manifested in the life of the believer and in the church thereafter. Among the gifts were glossolalia (speaking in tongues), interpretation of the tongues, prophecy, divine healing, and a trance-like experience called being "slain in the spirit."

The movement's beginnings date from 1901 when a woman spoke in tongues at a Bible school in Topeka, Kansas, run by a former Methodist preacher, Charles F. Parham (1873–1929). He later formulated the doctrine that "tongues" is the necessary first sign that one has experienced the Pentecostal blessing. Then William J. Seymour (1870–1922), an African-American holiness preacher, embraced the Pentecostal teaching after coming in contact with Parham. In 1906 he became leader of a holiness mission on Azusa Street in Los Angeles, and one day he began speaking in tongues. Large crowds flocked to the rundown building to share in the experience, and his meetings, which ran for three years, effectively launched American Pentecostalism. From these humble origins a worldwide movement emerged, complete with denominational splits and theological debates over fine points of doctrine.

A European Pentecostalism developed independently through Thomas B. Barratt (1862–1940), a Methodist from Norway who received the Holy Spirit baptism in 1906. It quickly spread to Germany, but the Fellowship Movement split over the matter. In the Berlin Declaration of 1909 the holiness leaders condemned the "tongues movement," and the German Pentecostals went their separate way. The considerable cross-fertilization that occurred between European and American Pentecostals helped to spur the movement's growth.

A fourth American contribution to evangelicalism was the campaign against alcoholic beverages. The antebellum temperance movement, which proved to be the most widespread reform endeavor of the period, was revived after the Civil War through the efforts of evangelicals such as Frances Willard (1839–98) and her Women's Christian Temperance Union and such powerful political organizations as the Anti-Saloon League.

To be sure, temperance groups existed in Britain and Europe, but they were small and mainly sought to curb drunkenness. The Americans, however, went further to forbid any use of alcohol in their own ranks and to pressure the government for a complete ban on the manufacture and sale of all alcoholic drinks. By 1914 laws to that effect were in place in most of the states, and in 1920 National Prohibition was enacted. The evangelicals overwhelmingly supported this action, but Christians in the immigrant churches and Lutherans and Catholics in particular were much less enthused. Many even strongly opposed the measure. Mounting public dissension over National Prohibition finally resulted in its repeal in 1933, but most American evangelicals still practice total abstinence.

Dwight L. Moody

One of the more influential evangelical preachers of the era was Charles Haddon Spurgeon (1834–92). Converted in a Methodist chapel, he became a Baptist and began preaching at seventeen. Three years later he was called to a congregation in London, where he would serve for the remaining thirty-eight years of his life. The church grew so rapidly during his first five years that he had to build a new structure in 1859 called the Metropolitan Tabernacle to house a congregation that now numbered six thousand. He also founded a college to train pastors, an orphanage, and various other social service agencies. An evangelical Calvinist, he was well known for his sermons, which received worldwide distribution and are still read today.

The major effort at ecumenism was the Evangelical Alliance. After considerable discussion by Protestant leaders on both sides of the Atlantic, a meeting was convened in London in 1846 to create a united front to defend biblical Christianity. The intention was to form a group that would promote communication and fellowship among evangelicals throughout the world and assist in spreading the gospel, but the American delegation backed away from involvement when some raised the slavery issue. The conferees finally decided that instead of having one overarching organization, each country would form its own national Alliance. Still, since it was the strongest, the British body kept the lines open to the others, and periodic conventions were held in major cities to bring people together. The various Alliances focused on defending the religious liberty of evangelical Protestants, both in Roman Catholic and non-Christian countries, supporting evangelistic endeavors (for example, Moody and Sankey in Britain, a Bible school in Berlin, and Baedeker's journeys in Russia), encouraging missionary work, and sponsoring a Universal Week of Prayer.

The British and German groups were the most effective in carrying out the goals of the organization. Today the German Alliance functions as a cooperative body for the free churches, while the British Alliance has engaged in many evangelistic, missionary, and relief operations. The creation of the World Evangelical Fellowship in 1951 helped to breathe new life into the concept. Meanwhile, the United States formed a national Alliance in 1867, and among its leaders were the church historian Philip Schaff and social gospel figure Josiah Strong. Its success in promoting ecumenical cooperation was not very spectacular, and by 1900 it was in a state of deep decline. The Federal Council of Churches of Christ, formed in 1908, supplanted it.

The public influence of evangelical Protestants was remarkable. Wealthy businessmen patronized evangelists, and political officials often testified to their faith. British prime minister William E. Gladstone was regarded as an outstanding Christian, while one American president, James A. Garfield, had a been a lay preacher in his youth and openly confessed that he had been "born again." Another president, William A. McKinley, was a devout Methodist layman, and Woodrow Wilson, an active Presbyterian, frequently manifested his Christian values in his presidential actions. William Jennings Bryan, three times a presidential candidate and Wilson's secretary of state, was a highly respected evangelical. In the Netherlands Abraham Kuyper (1837–1920), a Reformed minister and theologian, fought against the liberalism of his day by developing a Neo-Calvinistic "world and life view." This involved forming separate political, economic, and educational institutions so that, through these, the Reformed could confront every aspect of society and culture with a distinctly Christian perspective. In the political realm he became leader of the Anti-Revolutionary Party and served as his country's prime minister from 1901 to 1905.

New Ideas Challenge the Church

The secular ideologies of liberalism, nationalism, and socialism could be seen either as supplements or alternatives to Christianity, but others emerged as the century passed that were frontal challenges to the faith. Among these were Darwinian evolution, Nietzschean nihilism, cultural relativism, and higher criticism. The problems facing the churches because of these developments were enormous as waves of doubt and discontent swept through society. The whole fabric of Christianity was being called into question.

The publication in 1859 of *On the Origin of Species by Means of Natural Selection*, by Charles Darwin (1809–82), did not attract much attention at first, but soon shock waves reverberated through the Christian community. His theory of organic evolution caused consternation analogous to that of Aristotelianism in the thirteenth and the Copernican theory in the sixteenth century.

Actually, the idea that living beings changed and developed was not new. Darwin had arrived at that conclusion fifteen years earlier after studying the works of other natural scientists like Jean Lamarck and Charles Lyell and going on a research expedition to the South Pacific. He even rushed his book into print to beat out a rival who was about to say the same thing. Moreover, evolutionary philosophies, the belief that the way to understand something is to study its development, were already quite common. Both Hegel and Marx utilized this approach, as did the romantic historians of national states. The Enlightenment idea of progress was also an evolutionary concept. Darwin's unique contribution was that he gave evolution the seal of science.

He argued that every species produces more offspring than the environment can support, and they compete with each other for food, shelter, and the chance to reproduce. In the "struggle for existence" some individuals have unexplained variations, like stronger muscles or sharper claws, which enable them to win out, reproduce, and pass on these superior qualities to their offspring. Over time, this process of the "survival of the fittest" leads to change in the species. Thus, all species of living organisms have developed by successive small changes from others that preceded them. The decision as to which off-spring will possess the variations is made by nature, or "natural selection"—that is, a kind of chance. In a later work he applied the theory to human development and said that men were descended from animals.

Many churchmen were alarmed by Darwin's view, as it denied the special creation of humankind and the role of divine Providence in the workings of nature. Others who adjusted their understanding of the natural world to include the Darwinian hypothesis, included such prominent evangelicals as Asa Gray, James Frederick Wright, and James Orr. What they rejected were explanations of the evolutionary process that omitted the role of God in directing it.

Although the "warfare" between science and religion was not so severe as some popular writers at the time claimed, hostility grew rapidly after the turn of the century. Conservatives saw evolution as contradictory to Scripture, and social activists were fearful of its dehumanizing potential. Since the Darwinists could not show conclusively that a true species ever had developed out of another one, debate among scientists as to the accuracy of the hypothesis continued for decades.

What facilitated the triumph of the evolutionary approach was its appeal to the wealthy business classes and its acceptance in two important fields of study—anthropology and biblical criticism. The well-to-do found that it justified their lifestyle, and they became "Social Darwinists." The most famous exponent of this view, that is, the application of organic evolution to society, was Herbert Spencer (1820–1903). He argued that human existence evolves from the simple to the complex and any attempt to interfere with this process would only hinder progress. Evolution as a universal law operated even in such realms as sociology, economics, and politics. Competition among people, business firms, and nations resulted in the survival of the fittest, and governments must not interfere to help the weak or poor.

Some Christians, for example, William Jennings Bryan (1860–1925), recognized that Social Darwinism reduced humans to the purely material level. They no longer had value as creations of God but only as objects of use to society, who could be dispensed with when no longer needed. This feeling lay behind Bryan's unrelenting opposition to the teaching of evolution for which he was so vilified by liberals in the 1920s.

However, most Social Darwinists saw things differently. They agreed with the idea that society was not marked by cooperation and compassion but vicious competition. The successful businessman was the most "fit" regardless of how he gained success. And since survival was the only thing that mattered, no higher standards existed to judge one's actions. The upper classes deserved to be rich because they were "more fit" than the lazy, shiftless poor. In the same manner, "nature" decreed that large businesses would absorb smaller ones, and certain "superior" or "master" races should rule over "inferior" ones—whites over blacks, Germans over Slavs, non-Jews over

Jews. Using the biological theory of evolution one could justify the rule of the strong over the weak in all aspects of life. It is no wonder that the greatest Social Darwinist of all turned out to be one of the most demonic figures in history—Adolf Hitler. He made competition between nations and races the cornerstone of his political program.

Like many of his generation, Hitler was profoundly influenced by the German philosopher Friedrich Nietzsche (1844–1900), who carried Social Darwinism to its logical end. He said that natural selection should be allowed to operate freely in society. The constant weeding out of the unfit would one day produce a race of "supermen." These noble beings with strength of character would rule the masses, and those who perished in the struggle were moral weaklings. Announcing that God was dead, Nietzsche insisted that humankind must go it alone and make its own rules for living. However, the weak try to hinder the strong by inventing religions, such as Christianity, which glorify "slave virtues," like humility, patience, hope, love, acceptance, concern for the weak, and self-denial. To compensate for their weakness, Christians believe in a God who rewards and punishes rather than seeking to improve themselves. Nietzsche declared that mediocrity must give way to talent, and pity to competition. Thus, not only does he share in the blame for the extreme individualism of the modern world, but also his nihilistic teaching contributed to the feeling so prevalent in the twentieth century that life is empty and devoid of meaning.

Anthropology did much to advance the acceptance of Darwinism. Some anthropologists focused on the evolution of races and determined that the whites had developed the farthest, and in that group the Nordics, Teutons, or Anglo-Saxons were the most competent. Others insisted that no one culture or society was "better" than any other and that all institutions were merely a matter of customs, not morals. There was no objective standard to judge social institutions; everything was a matter of social custom and point of view. This relativism was soon to infuse every realm of social science, especially psychology. As for religion, James Frazer in *The Golden Bough* concluded that the rites, practices, and ideas of Christianity were not unique but could be found in primitive societies as well. Moreover, he saw little difference between magic and religion.

One further area where evolutionary ideas had an impact was in biblical criticism. "Lower," or textual, criticism had to do with determining the most accurate text of the document, and during the course of the century scholars found many ancient manuscripts that enabled them to produce a more accurate text of the New Testament. "Higher," or literary, criticism involved questions of literary form, authorship, dating, and purpose of the text and enabled the reader to determine its correct meaning. From the 1830s scholars in Germany (see chapter 18) had engaged in New Testament literary criticism that rejected any supernatural element in the text. Later writers, like J. R. Seeley, Adolf Harnack, and Albert Schweitzer, continued this trend in their "life of Jesus" studies.

The same methodology was applied to the Old Testament by Julius Wellhausen (1844–1918), who contended that the Hexateuch (the first six books of the Bible) evolved from a variety of ancient Israelite cults that were finally centralized in a single temple. Following the lines of the new anthropology, he said that the evolution in religious beliefs progressed from the simple tribalism of the nomadic period to the great writing prophets of the kingdom era and deuteronomic legislation of the seventh century B.C. and culminated in the priestly religion of the postexilic community. These books were not divinely revealed oracles written down by Moses and Joshua, as the church had always believed, but instead were a compilation of "documents" from different periods in Israelite history. Meanwhile, other critics "discovered" that Isaiah was written in two different time periods and Daniel in the second century B.C.[4]

The question of higher criticism caused deep anguish within the Protestant churches, especially those in America. Conservatives labeled its evolutionary approach to the history of Israel and the early church and rejection of the Bible's supernatural character as "destructive" criticism. It undermined the Bible's truthfulness and authority. Higher criticism was a concern in Catholic circles as well, and both branches of Christianity now faced the problem of "modernism."

Catholic and Protestant Responses to Modernism

A conservative papacy was in no mood to accommodate new ideas, as was clear in the aforementioned actions of Pius IX and Leo XIII, and the same was true in Leo's handling of the "Americanist controversy." Isaac Hecker (1819–88), a convert to Catholicism and founder of the Paulist Fathers, had promoted a democratic faith. When his biography was published in Europe, many Catholics there expressed concern that the church had compromised its beliefs by adapting to the American environment. At the same time, James Cardinal

William Jennings Bryan

Gibbons, Archbishop of Baltimore (1834–1921), was working diligently to bring the church into the mainstream of American life, and he promoted the idea that the church could flourish in a society without state support. In 1895 and 1899 Leo XIII addressed encyclicals to the American church criticizing it for "giving indulgence to modern popular theories," but Gibbons assured him that no heresies were being tolerated here.

The reaction to "modernism" was even more forceful. In France the historian Louis Duchesne (1843–1922) exposed weaknesses in church doctrine and tradition in his many books on early Christianity. Biblical scholar Alfred Loisy (1857–1940) taught an extreme theory about the composition of the gospels and declared that the teachings of Christianity were not those of Christ but the early church. In England the Jesuit George Tyrrell (1861–1909) criticized scholasticism and Catholic orthodoxy. First, Pope Leo responded to higher criticism in 1893 by affirming the plenary inspiration and inerrancy of Scripture. Then, Pius X put an end to the whole matter with his decree *Lamentabili* in 1907, which condemned sixty-five errors of the "modernist heresy." He followed this up with an encyclical requiring all bishops, priests, and teachers to take an antimodernist oath. Duchesne recanted, Loisy and Tyrrell were excommunicated, but no split in the church occurred.

The problem of theological liberalism (modernism) was far worse in the Protestant churches. It had originated in this community, and no effective authority structures existed to deal with it as in the Catholic church. The doctrines were well defined by 1900, although few liberals adhered to all of these points:

1. Religious ideas must be adapted to modern culture and modes of thinking.
2. All religious beliefs based on authority alone must be rejected. Reason and experience are equally valid tests of belief and the "essence of Christianity" replaces the authority of Scripture, creeds, and the church.
3. God is present and dwelling in the world and its structures (divine immanence), not above it as a transcendent being.
4. A universal religious sentiment lies behind the institutions and creeds of particular religions, so that ultimately there is no real difference among them.
5. Sin or evil is imperfection, ignorance, maladjustment, and immaturity, not the fundamental flaw in the universe.
6. Jesus signified God's presence in the world through His heroic deeds and death, but He did not perform miracles, nor was He resurrected, except that like all mortals, His spirit and personality lives on.
7. One looks toward the realization of the kingdom of God, which will be an ethical state of human perfection.[5]

Liberal theology was an extraordinarily complex, confusing, and inconsistent body of beliefs. It drew upon many sources: modern science; higher criticism; the social gospel; American Unitarianism; Schleiermacher's concept of God-consciousness; Horace Bushnell's redefinition of traditional doctrines in language that emphasized intuition, human potential, and social progress; the action-oriented experiential theology of Albrecht Ritschl; and Adolf Harnack's theory that one must separate the permanently valid kernel of the gospel from the changing form of life and thought in which it was given.

Modernism made its greatest gains in the centers of higher learning and only later did the ideas filter down to the local church level. The German and British universities accommodated rather quickly, and in America the first centers of modernist thought were Union Theological Seminary in New York and the University of Chicago, represented respectively by the key figures A. C. McGiffert (1861–1933) and Shailer Mathews (1863–1941). In Britain the broad church party in Anglicanism was particularly drawn toward liberalism.

Conservatives reacted strongly to the advance of modernism. Their strategy centered on affirming the integrity of the Bible as verbally inspired and uniquely trustworthy and authoritative. The leading exponent of this was Benjamin B. Warfield (1851–1921) of Princeton Seminary, the great defender of biblical inerrancy. He defined this as meaning that all of Scripture's statements are truthful if interpreted according to the sense in which their authors had intended them.

Another element of the conservative counterattack was a strong emphasis on eschatology, particularly the premillennial return of Christ. Although evangelicals were not united on the question, many were drawn to dispensationalism, which had been brought to North America by J. N. Darby. Through the Niagara and other prophecy conferences of the late nineteenth and early twentieth centuries, and the best-seller by William E. Blackstone (1841–1935) *Jesus Is Coming* (1908), these views were popularized. They seemed to offer a viable alternative to the liberal stress on the advance of God's kingdom and the evangelical realization that American culture was rapidly slipping away from historic Protestant control. By far, the most influential statement of dispensational teaching was the *Scofield Reference Bible*, an annotated version of the Scriptures published by Oxford University Press in 1909. Formerly a lawyer, C. I. Scofield (1843–1921) became a Congregationalist minister after his conversion and spent years in Bible conference work and study before undertaking this project.

An important stage in the organized evangelical resistance was the publication of a twelve-volume paperback series of books between 1910 and 1915 entitled *The Fundamentals.* Two wealthy California oilmen, Lyman and Milton Stewart, financed the project and provided three million copies free to Christian workers around the world. The ninety articles were by respected Bible teachers and scholars on both sides of the Atlantic. They demonstrated that basic evangelical doctrines such as biblical inspiration, miracles, and the resurrection were compatible with modern science and rationality, and that the testimony of personal experience could confirm Christian belief.

Since about 1895 evangelicals had been attempting to define the basic elements (or fundamentals) of the faith that had to be protected from the eroding effects of modern thought. An important illustration of this was the action of the northern Presbyterian church in 1910, which spelled out the five key biblical doctrines to which ministerial candidates were expected to adhere: the inspiration and inerrancy of Scripture; the virgin birth; substitutionary atonement; the bodily resurrection of Christ; and His performance of miracles during His earthly ministry. Others added the deity of Christ and the Second Coming to their list of essentials.

In Britain evangelicals expressed similar concerns about modernism, but their responses were not as well organized or forcefully articulated as those of their North American counterparts. Also, even though conservatives stressed these fundamental beliefs in their struggle with the modernists for the soul of Anglo-American Protestantism, the term "fundamentalism" was not coined until 1920 by a Baptist journalist. By then, however, the contest had taken on a much different character.

Christianity was now in a state of disarray. Even though many Protestants continued to view the world in optimistic terms, the evangelicals were becoming increasingly aware that all was not right. Modernism seemed on the march, particularly in their institutions of higher learning and their social service enterprises. Many had given up on "Christianizing" the world and were looking for the Blessed Hope of the Second Coming. But then, as the flames of war engulfed Europe in 1914, all the illusions of liberal optimism were shattered. The world would never be the same again.

22

THE CHURCH IN A WAR-TORN WORLD

As the world entered the twentieth century, liberal humanists, advocates of social Christianity, and even many evangelicals were certain that the kingdom of God, or at least a better world, was at hand. Perhaps nothing reflected this optimism better than the massive three-volume work by the American Presbyterian missionary to Syria, James S. Dennis, *Christian Missions and Social Progress* (1897–1906). But others questioned whether valid proof for such progress really existed and suggested that the evils of industrialization and urbanization far outweighed the benefits. Certainly the new belief systems of the era were not optimistic or complimentary about human nature. The Marxists saw humans in terms of property relations, the Social Darwinists the survival of the fittest, the Freudians an unknown libido, and positivists scientific rationalism. Then, two world wars, followed by nearly half a century of fearing a third one, buried the optimistic hope of human perfectibility. This situation would profoundly shape Christianity in the twentieth century.

World War I and the Churches

Although Europe seemed to be on a course for war, still the movement for international conciliation had made considerable gains. Peace societies existed in several countries, and a number of international congresses sought to give direction to the cause. Their belief was that from the international community would emerge the institutions that could settle disputes between nations. Formed at this time were the Permanent Court of International Justice (the World Court) at The Hague and the Carnegie Endowment for International Peace.

Working from his Christian perspective, American Secretary of State William Jennings Bryan negotiated conciliation or "cooling-off" treaties to deter countries from rushing hastily into war, and during 1913–14 thirty of these were signed. In 1915 he told a friend that this was one of the God-directed moments in his life. Also, in 1908 churchmen in Germany and Great Britain began visiting each other's countries to foster mutual understanding, and they established contacts with fellow Christians in the United States who shared their concerns. These endeavors so impressed industrialist Andrew Carnegie that he donated a large sum to create the Church Peace Union (CPU; now the Carnegie Council on Ethics and International Affairs). Its goal was promoting interfaith cooperation among Protestants, Catholics, and Jews in advancing peace ideals. In August 1914 representatives from the CPU and the Europeans formed the World Alliance for Promoting International Friendship Through the Churches. Although the CPU was funding the World Alliance, the war limited its work to education and to keeping lines of communication open between Christians on both sides. In 1919 it emerged as a major force in promoting international understanding.

In spite of the well-meaning actions by peace advocates, tensions continued to rise. Only a spark was needed to set off the powder keg of Europe, and it came with the assassination of the Austro-Hungarian crown prince on June 28, 1914. After the diplomats vainly struggled to avert the outbreak of conflict, the armies marched joyously off to war. They naively assumed that they would be back home by Christmas, having solved all the pressing problems their countries faced. What in fact followed was a stalemate, and for the next three years all efforts to break through the enemy lines failed. The so-called civilized peoples of the West engaged in an unprecedented carnage that

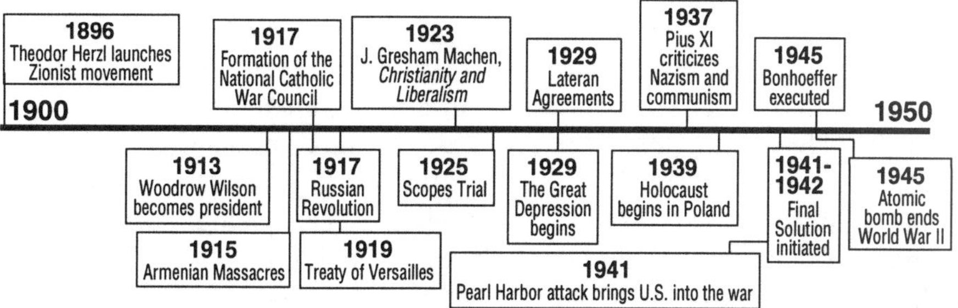

cost more than twelve million lives and wiped out a large portion of the male population between the ages of eighteen and thirty-two. The unleashing of the pent-up emotions of war shattered the optimism of the peace advocates.

This was a "total war" in the sense that it was fought on land, sea, and air, with the industrial complex regimented to guarantee a steady flow of weapons. Governments directed the economies of their countries, strictly controlling industrial output, food production, and the allocation of raw materials and labor. Through a naval and submarine blockade each side tried to destroy the other's economy.

Civilian activities were restricted as well. Civil rights were curtailed to silence criticism of the war effort or combat domestic subversion, however illusory that might be. For instance, Eugene Debs, leader of the American Socialist party, was sentenced to a long prison term for calling it a "capitalist war." Censorship was used to prevent spreading of news helpful to the other side and to strengthen morale. War propaganda portrayed the enemy in the worst possible way and instilled in the people a sense of solidarity and the conviction that they were engaged in a righteous crusade.

Although the Edinburgh Continuation Committee and the peace movement had made progress in the direction of ecumenical cooperation, the dreams of Christian solidarity were dissipated as the winds of war swept over Europe. The mission enterprise was dealt a crushing blow as the funding for overseas ventures was sharply reduced and missionary travel curtailed. The Allies also ignored the "supranationality of missions" principle widely discussed prior to 1914 when they conquered Germany's African and Pacific possessions. They confiscated mission properties and interned or repatriated missionaries of German nationality who were working there. The Allies continued this process in their own territories in India, Africa, and the South Pacific.

These actions ensured that the churches would be drawn into the struggle from the very beginning. Leaders of the German theological and missionary community, including Adolf von Harnack, issued a sharply worded statement in August 1914 that condemned the Allies for blaming Germany for the war and seizing their mission properties. They defended their country's actions as self-defense. The following month British church figures and theologians headed by the archbishop of Canterbury responded with an equally strong defense of their country, and charges and countercharges continued to flow. Pastors on both sides preached the most vitriolic sermons proclaiming the righteousness of their cause and accusing the enemy of the vilest motives and deeds. Although John R. Mott and J. H. Oldham tried desperately to maintain some semblance of ecumenical solidarity, the movement for church cooperation based on the common involvement in missions fragmented. Finally, in 1917 the Germans completely repudiated Mott. On a more positive note, Christian groups on both sides, like the YMCA, worked untiringly to relieve suffering in the war-torn areas and to aid war prisoners and wounded soldiers.

Among the atrocities of the war was one that deeply stirred feelings in the West—the Turkish massacre of the Christian Armenians. An earlier massacre in 1895–97 had attracted international criticism, but it was not as extensive as the one in 1915. The existing conflict between two nationalisms, Turkish and Armenian, was made more serious because Russia and Turkey were on opposite sides of the war, and the Armenian population was evenly divided between the two countries. The Turkish forces turned on their Armenians, and about one million died as a result of murders, mob violence, and deportation death marches. To be sure, the Allies verbally condemned the genocide, but they did nothing to stop it. The matter is significant because it was the systematic extermination of an ancient Christian people, and it provided Hitler with a model he could follow in dealing with Europe's Jews. The Armenian Massacres were the precursor to the Holocaust.

By slanting news reports and exploiting German blunders, such as the sinking of the *Lusitania* and execution of the nurse Edith Cavell, Allied propagandists won the sympathy of influential people in the United States, especially those in church circles. By constantly portraying the conflict in moralistic and ideological terms as a holy war against tyranny, despotism, and militarism, a negotiated peace based on the reestablishment of the balance of power was rendered completely out of the question. Although President Wilson professed neutrality, he edged increasingly closer to the Allies and finally took his country into the war in April 1917. With the involvement of Wilson the idealist and the overthrow of the Russian autocracy the previous month, the argument that the war was a struggle between democracy and authoritarianism took on new life. The Central Powers must be defeated so a new world order could be created.

Most American Christians were enthusiastic in their support of the war endeavor, although the historic peace churches (Mennonites, Quakers, and Church of the Brethren) held to their pacifist principles. Many of their members either were assigned to noncombatant service or refused altogether to wear the uniform. Mennonites who took the latter course were severely persecuted by the civil and military authorities. Some Protestant preachers went to extremes in their war rhetoric, such as evangelist Billy Sunday, who declared, "If you turn hell upside down, you will find 'Made in Germany' stamped on the bottom," or the prominent liberal Presbyterian minister and educator Henry Van Dyke (1852–1933), who advocated that everyone who lifted his voice against the American war effort "should be hung without delay." One found just as boundless enthusiasm for their sides in the sermons of German and British ministers.

Much more important than the nationalism proclaimed from American pulpits was the war's impact on the denominations themselves. The recently formed Federal Council of Churches, which by 1917 represented two-thirds of the nation's Protestants, emerged as the most influential religious force in America. This was due to the FCC's General War-Time Commission of the Churches, which coordinated efforts in social work and dealt with the government. By focusing on practical matters the churches overcame divisions and broke new ground in the quest for unity.

As for the Catholics, their war experience enabled them to become a full partner in the American religious community. Prior to this time the American church lacked a national, cohesive organization. It did not even have the status of an independent unit of the Roman church until 1908. Before that it was a mission under the primary jurisdiction of the Congregation for the Propagation of the Faith in Rome (see chapter 12). Only after 1908 was it equal to the older European branches of the Catholic faith. Through the expert leadership of Cardinal Gibbons, who established a close relationship with President Wilson, and the wartime ministry of the National Catholic War Council, the church developed a united national ministry. In 1919 the agency was given permanent standing as the National Catholic Welfare Conference, and it served as a clearinghouse for Catholic leaders and looked after the church's interests in the political realm. In 1966 two new bodies took over its functions—the National Conference of Catholic Bishops to exercise the joint pastoral ministry, and the U.S. Catholic Conference to handle the public policy matters.

With his idealistic view of the war as a contest of good against evil and democracy against Prussian tyranny and militarism and with his vision of a postwar world where all nations would live in harmony and resolve their differences through an international organ, the League of Nations, Wilson was truly a revolutionary. V. I. Lenin (1870–1924) and his Bolshevik party added a second revolutionary element to the picture when they overthrew the government of the Russian Republic in November 1917 and established a dictatorship. His revision of the moribund Marxist belief system gave it renewed vitality, and Marxism-Leninism became a formidable ideological challenge to democracy, as will be shown below. Aware of how fragile his hold on power was, Lenin immediately concluded a separate peace with Germany. He saw this as the only way to preserve the revolution in Russia.

The Germans were now ready to deliver the knock-out blow on the western front, but the industrial and human resources of the United States precluded a victory. The Allies launched an offensive on every front, the Central Powers collapsed, revolution swept their countries, and the war ended with the armistice on November 11, 1918.

The Flawed Peace Settlement

The dominant mood at the Paris peace conference that followed was one of nineteenth-century nationalism. The Europeans planned to punish Germany and keep it from rising again, while many of the nationality groups wanted to carve up the old empires into new nation-states. The advocates of power politics pushed aside those churchmen and statesmen like Wilson who advocated the new diplomacy of resolving disputes by international law and a supranational organization. The fear of Bolshevism spreading into their countries further stiffened the resolve of leaders not to accept a peace of conciliation. With conservative tides running in the Allied countries, the leaders in Paris were keenly aware of nationalistic and antirevolutionary tendencies back home.

The Treaty of Versailles, signed with their principal foe on June

28, 1919, had the character of a dictated peace, for the Germans were not allowed to participate in the negotiating sessions. Germany was forced to cede territory to its neighbors, submit to severe arms restrictions and an occupation of the Rhineland, and make reparation payments. To ensure fulfillment of the latter, Germany had to accept responsibility for having caused the loss and damages the Allies suffered because of the war "imposed upon them by the aggression of Germany and her allies." This was the so-called "war guilt clause" that the Germans so bitterly resented.

The peace settlement also built a dam in eastern Europe to contain Bolshevism by permitting the creation of several new countries from the territory of the old empires. As the Bolshevik threat eased, these states were torn by class and nationality conflicts and most adopted authoritarian regimes. The colonial possessions of Germany and most non-Turkish regions of the Ottoman Empire were taken and distributed among the victorious powers as "mandates" under the oversight of the League of Nations. This was the world-embracing organization that Wilson had proposed for keeping the peace, and its covenant was included in all the treaties with the Central Powers. The American president regarded this as the most pressing task of the Paris conference, and he made damaging concessions in order to secure its creation. He believed that the League provided the peace settlement with a moral foundation and the machinery to correct errors in the treaties.[1]

An important achievement of the Christian community in the peace settlement was preserving the mission properties. The treaty drafters had included a section authorizing the Allies to confiscate all assets in their lands belonging to German citizens to satisfy debts owed to individuals and the various governments. This would have meant the complete destruction of German missions, but J. H. Oldham and others in the ecumenical group persuaded the drafters to include an exception clause in the document. Article 438 provided that mission holdings would be placed in the hands of "trustees" of the same denomination as that of the society involved. After passions had cooled, the Western trustees quietly returned the properties to their German owners.

The Uneasy Years Between the Wars

The great "civil war of the West" had fatally undermined Europe's world position. The new industrial giants, the United States and Japan, had found places in the imperial sun, the former in Latin America and the latter in East Asia, and both were jockeying for power in the Pacific. Great Britain was under increasing pressure to relax its control over Ireland, Egypt, the Middle East, and India. In fact, M. K. Gandhi's movement in India, with its emphasis on nonviolent resistance, boycotts, and civil disobedience, was greatly admired by Christian peace activists in the West. The Statute of Westminster (1931) accorded Britain's white dominions (Canada, Australia, New Zealand, South Africa, and Ireland) legal equality with the mother country in the British Commonwealth of Nations. Meanwhile, France's effort to promote cultural assimilation in North Africa and Indochina was foundering on the rocks of colonial nationalism. Rising tides of nationalism in China, Japan, and Indonesia were challenges to the Christian communities there.

The casualties suffered in the Western countries were enormous, and in fact almost an entire generation of leaders perished on the battlefields. Their economies were in shambles, and the prospect of German reparations to rebuild them were uncertain. Yet times had changed. The older democratic regimes broadened the base of political participation to include women, while the new ones formed since the war coped with the perplexities of unemployment, inflation, economic reconstruction, and political extremists on the right and left. Such left-wing bodies as the British Labour and German Social Democratic parties now participated in government coalitions, and in most lands a pragmatic democratic socialism replaced the laissez-faire emphasis of earlier times. Even Franklin Roosevelt's "New Deal," though its primary aim was to save the capitalist system, involved considerable state intervention in the economy. Socialism fitted in well with the postwar advance of secularism, but since most socialists had become middle class in their outlook, radical leftists flirted with Communism.

For all the high aspirations of its founders, the League of Nations did not, in the long run, prevent aggression and preserve peace. Wilson failed to obtain Senate ratification of the Treaty of Versailles, and the United States never joined. Since Germany and Soviet Russia were excluded at its founding, the Bolsheviks regarded the League of Nations as a capitalist device to encircle Russia and overthrow Communism, while the Germans viewed it as an instrument to enforce the Versailles treaty and keep their country down. When the two outcast powers did join the League (Germany, 1926; Soviet Union, 1934), they did so only to strengthen their political positions, not because

President Woodrow Wilson

they believed in the new international system. Since most countries conducted disarmament negotiations outside the League and concluded alliances with each other directly, it achieved little besides promoting cooperation in the technical and economic spheres and guaranteeing religious and missionary freedom in the former German and Turkish lands under its mandatory supervision.

Although prosperity returned to Europe by 1924, the recovery was a hollow one. Soviet Russia was still in an economic shambles, and pockets of poverty existed elsewhere. Then, when the downturn began in 1929, nothing seemed able to stop the slide into the abyss of the Great Depression. Desperate for anything that might help, people abandoned the democratic middle and turned to the political extremes.

Anti-Semitism and Zionism

The growth of European racism is a complex topic, but clearly the manufacture of stereotypes like the "noble Aryan" and the systematizing of racial types by physical features were aimed at one group—the Jews. Much of this was rooted in romantic concepts of *Volk* and blood and in Social Darwinistic ideas of racial evolution. Also, the medieval legend of the "Wandering Jew," a man named

Ahasuerus who hurried Christ along the way to His crucifixion and refused Him comfort or shelter and in turn was cursed to a never-ending existence of wandering, was quite popular in this period. It reinforced the view of the Jew as the eternal foreigner, a shiftless, rootless nomad who engaged in commerce—unlike the good Aryan farmer who had roots. Another myth was that of the sinister Jewish world conspiracy, a topic of nineteenth-century fiction that was incorporated into the greatest anti-Semitic book of all times, *The Protocols of the Learned Elders of Zion.* Produced in Russia about 1905, it reached the West in translation in 1918 and has been regarded as gospel truth by Jew-haters ever since.

In contrast was the Enlightenment ideal of Jewish assimilation. This held that Jews could become a part of the larger civilization and that they should have the same rights as all other people. Emancipation—the granting of civil rights to Jews—was achieved in most countries during the course of the nineteenth century. But in the later decades anti-Jewish sentiment once again reared its ugly head, above all in Russia but also in Austria-Hungary and Germany. Theodor Herzl (1860–1904), an Austrian journalist who covered the Dreyfus trial and saw the rampant anti-Semitism in that most liberal of all countries, France, concluded that assimilation was not the solution. He published a book in which he argued that Jews must have their own homeland—a Jewish state.

Herzl was the founder of modern Zionism, the movement to secure a national home for Jews. For him it was a rational response to anti-Semitism, not something based on a deep sense of Jewish national identity. He was unable to negotiate an agreement with the sultan for a Jewish enclave in Ottoman Palestine, but increasing numbers of Jews were going there anyway, a move that alarmed the indigenous Arabs. With Arab nationalism rising throughout the Middle East by 1914, the potential for trouble was already there. However, because Turkey had sided with the Central Powers, sentiment for Zionism grew in the West. Chaim Weizmann (1874–1952), an ardent supporter of the movement in Britain who had connections in high places, persuaded Foreign Secretary Arthur Balfour to support Zionism as a war measure.

In the famous Balfour Declaration of November 2, 1917, he said that the British government "views with favor the establishment in Palestine of a national home for the Jewish people." This was intended to firm up support among American and Russian Jews for the war effort and head off a possible German endorsement of Zionism, and in fact the next month British troops entered Jerusalem. In the peace treaty Britain received a League of Nations mandate over the area, while France assumed a mandate in Lebanon and Syria. Jewish settlers began flocking into mandatory Palestine, bought land, built cities, founded schools and hospitals, and in 1929 created an organ of self-government, the Jewish Agency for Palestine. During the ensuing years the tempo of violence between Jewish and Arab guerrilla groups escalated, and the British were caught in the middle. After Hitler came to power in Germany, Jewish immigration soared and with it Arab resentment as well. Their numbers had risen from 58,000 in 1919 to 450,000 in 1939. For Britain the Palestine problem seemed insoluble.

The Cultural Crisis and Christian Thought

The revolution in ideas that had begun before the First World War spread through the entire population in the 1920s. Western society began to question and even abandon cherished values and beliefs that had guided it since the Enlightenment. Numerous writers rejected the general faith in progress and human rationality and suggested that immediate experience and intuition were as important as rational and scientific thinking. Various prophets of doom spoke of the decline of Western civilization and pointed to history's most destructive war as proof that human beings were a pack of violent, irrational animals.

Doubt, disorder, uncertainty, alienation, and pessimism marked this crisis of the mind. The new physics portrayed a universe lacking any absolute, objective reality. Everything was relative and depended on the observer's frame of reference. Freudian psychology explained human behavior in terms of the irrational unconscious, which was driven by sexual, aggressive, and pleasure-seeking desires that were in constant conflict with the rational and moral parts of the mind. Logical positivism held that the only valid concepts were those that could be tested by scientific experiments or demonstrated by the logic of mathematics. Therefore, one could not speak about such concepts as God, freedom, and morality because they were meaningless.

These developments profoundly affected theology. Since the Middle Ages faith and reason were linked, and the reliability of Christianity was only questioned from the outside, such as by Enlightenment deism, which was really a rival religion. However, in the nineteenth century the concept of divine revelation was doubted, not just by unbelievers but by theologians within the church itself. This was a momentous matter. If God revealed Himself in Christ and redeemed humanity from sin, there must be submission to this authoritative revelation. But now to what must one submit and how much must one believe? These questions divided modern Christians more than did the old denominational separations.

The liberal response was to affirm the new situation, whereas the conservatives rejected it. On the American scene this set the stage for a bruising culture war in the 1920s known as the fundamentalist-modernist controversy. The conservatives challenged the tenets of modernism with prophetic courage and showed that such things as the theory of evolution and the documentary hypothesis of Scripture were incompatible with biblical Christianity. However, in the initial stage of the movement, as exemplified in *The Fundamentals,* the conservatives were moderate in their criticism of the liberals and even cooperated with them in denominational and interdenominational ventures.

But Wilson's holy war against German "barbarism" and for "the survival of civilization and morality" turned the theological contest into a cultural struggle. The conservatives discovered a plausible explanation for the "collapse" of German civilization in modernist theology and Darwinian evolution. Now they saw that the "unbelief" that had destroyed Germany's soul was undermining America's religious and educational institutions. Thus, the stridency and militancy of the World War was transferred to the religious arena. Another factor that stimulated fundamentalist activism was biblical prophecy. The British liberation of Jerusalem from the Turks had cleared the way for the return of the Jews, and for many this meant that the Second Coming was at hand. Then the heavenly army of King Jesus would crush the earthly forces of evil.

In 1919 W. B. Riley (1861–1947), a prominent Northern Baptist preacher in Minneapolis, organized a meeting of conservatives in Philadelphia to launch the World's Christian Fundamentals Association. Its creed was biblical inerrancy and the premillennial, imminent return of Christ. The movement spread rapidly and challenged the modernists on two fronts: the churches and the culture at large. The major denominations and their missionary agencies combated liberalism by pressuring officials to commit themselves to traditional doctrines. Modernists like Shailer Mathews and Harry Emerson Fosdick (1878–1969), who called themselves "evangelical liberals," appealed for tolerance, and insisted they were really preserving the main lines of Christian orthodoxy in an expression more suitable for the times.

It was largely a northern problem, since conservatives controlled the southern denominations. The most dramatic struggles occurred in the Disciples of Christ, Northern Baptist Convention, and Presbyterian Church in the U.S.A. A central figure in the latter group was the brilliant New Testament scholar at Princeton Seminary, J. Gresham Machen (1881–1937), whose book *Christianity and Liberalism* (1923) argued cogently that the two were distinct religions.

In the cultural realm, the movement focused on saving American civilization from the baleful influence of Darwinism, which was charged with causing the revolution in morals and threatening democracy. The fundamentalists secured laws in some states banning the teaching of evolution in the public schools, but the Tennessee law was challenged in the Scopes Trial of 1925. The media made this trial into a circus. The fundamentalists were ridiculed, and the movement rapidly lost its steam. Machen left Princeton in 1929 and started the new Westminster Theological Seminary, and conservatives split from the major denominations to start new bodies, such as the Orthodox Presbyterian Church (1936), the General Association of Regular Baptists (1932), the Southern Methodist Church (1939), Independent Fundamental Churches of America (1930), and the North American Christian Convention (1927).

Because they focused on the single matter of negating modernism, the fundamentalists failed to develop an affirmative worldview and thus were a defeated party in denominational politics. Still, fundamentalism underwent an institutional transformation into a popular religion through the creation of a complex network of Bible institutes, summer Bible conferences, religious broadcasting efforts, and missionary societies. This enabled conservatives to reemerge in the 1940s with renewed vigor.

At the same time, another movement called Neo-orthodoxy supplied more unique answers to the modern dilemma. An important source of this new outlook was Søren Kierkegaard (1813–55), a Danish philosopher whose works were unknown outside his homeland until the twentieth century. He came from a pious family, studied for the ministry but never took a church, and lived a lonely, gloomy existence. He came to see the importance of personal faith based upon a broken heart, rebelled against the popular rationalist explanations of faith, and insisted that truth was perceived through struggle, engagement, and decision.

Kierkegaard declared that "existence is prior to essence," that is, the individual person is more important than any abstraction. He had a deep consciousness of sin and found that the gulf between the remote, majestic God and humankind could be bridged only through faith in Christ. Each person stands alone before God and must find the way to Him through anxiety and despair. One must have an authentic, first-hand faith, not something that came second-hand from the worldly and lukewarm established church of his day. He was the first exponent of existentialism, the philosophy that rejected both romanticism and reason and emphasized one's whole existence (or being) and experience as the basis for living.

It was after World War I that the melancholy Dane influenced theology. The suffering of that conflict discredited faith in science and human perfectability, and many wondered how God would permit such a tragedy. Swiss pastor Karl Barth (1886–1968), who would become the greatest theologian of the twentieth century, published a commentary on Romans (1919) that drew upon the Bible and Kierkegaard and showed the inadequacy of liberalism and the need for genuine faith in God. Rejecting the liberal emphasis on the immanence of God in nature, Barth insisted on His transcendence. Theology was not religious experience or human philosophy but a dependence on God's revealed word. History was not the gradual, progressive development of the good life but "dialectical" or "cataclysmic" in character. He characterized human existence as a tension between God's judgment and grace. The only hope lay in the "crisis of faith," when one repents before God and lives in a state of humility, forgiveness, and obedience. This prepares an individual for participation in the church and the kingdom of God, for which no substitute can be found in any merely human institution.

Although these ideas were similar to those of the Protestant Reformers, Neo-orthodoxy retained some things from nineteenth-century liberalism, including the scientific explanation of nature and human life, the historical nature of religious statements and activities, and the need for relevance on the part of the Christian message. Moreover, because it was not an organized school or movement, it is difficult to find any theologian associated with it who would agree to all these statements. They range from the "orthodox" Barth and Emil Brunner (1889–1956) to Reinhold Niebuhr (1892–1971) and the "liberal" Paul Tillich (1886–1965). In reality it was a synthesis of the old and the new that did much to reestablish the message of the Bible, the unique mission of the church, the importance of theology, and the relevance of the Christian gospel to both personal and social life.

After 1918 religion became more significant and meaningful to

Jews in the Warsaw ghetto

thinking people than it had been before. Not only did the French philosophers Gabriel Marcel (1889–1973) and Jacques Maritain (1882–1973) turn to Catholicism and draw sustenance from their faith, but also the English writers T. S. Eliot (1888–1965) and C. S. Lewis (1898–1963) were deeply committed to Christian values. Through his literary and apologetic works Lewis exercised an enormous influence on Anglo-American evangelicalism, where he is held in high esteem today.

Dictatorships Challenge the Church

The greatest challenge to Christianity in the interwar period was the brutal dictatorships that arose in Italy, Germany, and Russia. They are often labeled as "totalitarian," although most historians are reluctant to use the term because it eludes meaningful definition and is mainly used in a propagandistic context.

Fascism and the Catholic Church

The first was that of Benito Mussolini (1883–1945) in Italy. A former journalist, war veteran, and gifted orator, he founded the Fascist party in 1919, which exploited nationalist discontents and the fear of Bolshevism. He bluffed his way into power in the so-called March on Rome in 1922 and in the following years fastened an iron grip over the country through the use of police supervision, terror, censorship, and propaganda.

In the religious realm Mussolini's main achievement was the reconciliation between the Roman Catholic church and Italian state. Pope Pius XI, elected in 1922 and a bitter foe of Communism as well as traditional liberalism, was willing to wink at the more unsavory aspects of the Fascist regime in order to resolve the Roman Question. Although Mussolini himself was anticlerical, he saw the political advantages of a settlement, and the result was the Lateran Agreements of 1929. The papacy gave up its territorial claims in Italy, acknowledged the Italian ruling dynasty, and agreed to keep out of politics. For its part, Italy recognized the Vatican City as an independent sovereign state, compensated the Holy See for the loss of Rome in 1870, established Catholicism as the "sole religion of the state," extended canon law rules to marriage matters, allowed religious instruction in the schools, and accorded legal standing to Catholic religious orders and associations.

Although Pius praised the dictator as a "man sent by providence," relations between them soon cooled. In 1931 the pope criticized some features of Mussolini's regime, particularly his crackdown on Catholic Action, a large lay organization that engaged in educational and social activities. The *Duce* eventually relented and permitted the association's existence but under tight restrictions. Italian churchmen gave their blessings to overseas ventures like the conquest of Ethiopia and intervention in the Spanish Civil War, and the only criticisms of Fascist actions were in specific matters of church-state competition rather than on broad philosophical or theological grounds. There were also ties between Catholicism and other fascist-type movements in Austria, Spain, Portugal, and Hungary.

The Nazi System and Christian Response

National Socialism (Nazism) in Germany fed upon disillusionment with the war, resentment over the peace, and economic problems. An Austrian-born war veteran and political agitator, Adolf Hitler (1889–1945), built the National Socialist party into a powerful organization after the onset of the depression. Short-sighted conservatives who saw him as an antidote to Communism helped him to become chancellor on January 30, 1933. With his hands on the levers of power, Hitler placed his people in key positions and used force to intimidate foes. Within two years the state was under his absolute control.

Hitler's basic organizational idea was the unity of the German people with the leader (*Führer*) and introduction of the leadership principle into the political, economic, and social structures of the country. By integrating all the competing classes and interest groups into the nation, the Nazis hoped to form an ideal supercommunity, but they could not win the full allegiance of the army and churchmen. Ideologically, the Nazis rejected the Enlightenment, urban life, democracy, and other features of modern existence, and glorified the *Volk*, blood, and soil, holding that Germans possessed various traits bound up with their homeland and environment that set them apart. In a Social Darwinistic struggle between groups and nations, the stronger Germans would displace and destroy the weaker races. One of these was the Russians. Hitler said the Germans needed "living space," which they would obtain by conquest in Russia. Then German farmers would be settled there, away from the corrupting influence of the cities, and provide the raw materials, foodstuffs, and manpower for the "Thousand Year Reich."

In Hitler's racial theory the Jews were the source of all evil, the "culture-destroying race" that gave the world both capitalism and Marxism. Even the Christian faith was a Jewish plot: "The heaviest blow that ever struck humanity was the coming of Christianity. Bolshevism is Christianity's illegitimate child. Both are inventions of the Jew."[2] He saw the "culture-creating" Aryan race as locked in a life-and-death struggle for survival, with the eradication of the Jewish race as an act of social purification that would restore the uncorrupt past. These were the ideological underpinnings of the Holocaust.

The Nazis deprived the half-million German Jews of citizenship rights, and through boycotts, expulsion from their jobs, and constant harassment encouraged them to emigrate. In November 1938 they were victims of a terrible pogrom known as the "Night of the Broken Glass." After the German armies overran eastern Europe, whose Jewish population was far larger, anti-Semitism became much more violent. In Russia Nazi death squads murdered hundreds of thousands of Jews on the spot, while in Poland they were herded into wretched urban slums called "ghettos."

The notorious concentration camps, originally built to break the spirits of the Nazi regime's opponents, had even more ominous overtones for Jews. In 1940–41 six camps were created in Poland, the best known of which were Auschwitz and Treblinka, where the Nazis put into operation the "final solution," the extermination of the entire Jewish population of Europe. Men, women, and children were transported to these "death factories," and in a cold-blooded, calculated manner were beaten, starved, shot, worked to death, used in medical experiments, and gassed. The best estimates place the number of Jewish deaths in the Holocaust at six million, and to this day theologians and philosophers probe the meaning of this incomprehensible tragedy.

The plight of Christians under the Nazi regime was also precarious. Born and raised a Catholic, Hitler abandoned whatever Christian principles he may have had, but he never formally severed his ties with the church or was excommunicated. National Socialism itself was a new faith that appealed to Germans longing for national regeneration. Hitler's attitude toward the churches was political; he envied the power Catholicism had over its adherents but despised Protestantism for its lack of unity and authority. However, during his rise to power he courted members of both churches.

Most Protestants were cool to the postwar republic, whose constitution separated church and state and appeared to be dominated by socialists and Catholics, even though the church continued to have its privileged status. Most churchmen sympathized with the antirepublican right wing and were attracted to Hitler's "national movement" as conditions deteriorated after 1929. They overlooked the anti-Semitic and pagan side of Nazism and praised Hitler's anti-Communism and call for "positive Christianity." A pro-Nazi party even arose in the church called the "German Christians."

Hitler's "seizure of power" was greeted with enthusiasm. Some expected to see the "Marxist" republic replaced with a Christian ruler. His "pro-moral, pro-family" program was also appealing in that he emphasized the importance of childbearing and women's place in the home and pledged to eliminate pornography, prostitution, and homosexuality. But his own policy was purely pragmatic, since he realized the strength the churches had and did not want another *Kulturkampf.* He quickly won over the Catholics, and the Center Party voted for the measure allowing him to rule by decree. After their party and trade unions were dissolved, Hitler signed a treaty with the Vatican guaranteeing German Catholics freedom to practice their religion and the independence of the church. This effectively undermined resistance in Catholic circles.

The Nazis had more problems with the Protestants. The German Christians endeavored to unify all the regional churches into a national one under a Nazi "Reich Bishop" named Ludwig Müller (1883–1945). They also wanted the church to introduce the *Führer* principle and adopt the "Aryan Paragraph," which provided for the dismissal of church personnel who were of Jewish ancestry. But Hitler rejected their idea of a National Socialist state church because he felt the church's sole function was to cater to benighted people who still had religious needs. Any church, even a Nazified one, could be a limit on his power, and before long the German Christians were totally ignored.

The Aryan Paragraph outraged many in the church, and in September 1933 Pastor Martin Niemöller (1892–1984) formed the Pastor's Emergency League to combat German Christian ideas. This marked the beginning of the "Church Struggle." His group repudiated the Reich Bishop and set up an alternative church government structure known as the Confessing Church. Its theological basis was spelled out in the Barmen Declaration of May 1934. Largely written by Karl Barth, it called the German church back to the central truths of Christianity and rejected the totalistic claims of the state in matters of faith.

The Declaration was not intended as a political protest, and the Confessing Church did not plan to spearhead resistance to Nazism. These moves were aimed at defending the orthodox faith against innovations and the heretical distortions of the German Christians. However, the Confessing Church was repudiated or at least ignored by most Protestant leaders and harassed by the Gestapo. Its very presence was an embarrassment to the Nazis, and its witness to Christ's lordship implicitly challenged Hitler's claim to ultimate power. A few church figures, most notably Dietrich Bonhoeffer (1906–45), became involved in the anti-Hitler resistance, but the conservatism and nationalism of most Protestants deterred them from standing up against the evil system. Still, the Confessing Church had challenged the traditional alliance of church and state, and this marked the most radical break in German church history since the Reformation itself.

The Catholics too were drawn into the Church Struggle when the Nazis destroyed the network of Catholic organizations and clamped down on their press and schools. Churchmen were alarmed over the spread of the "new heathenism," and in 1937 Pope Pius XI issued the encyclical *With Deep Sorrow*, which was smuggled into Germany and read from the pulpits on Palm Sunday. It called on Catholics to reject the idolatrous cult of race and state and to maintain their loyalty to Christ and His church. The infuriated Hitler avoided a break with Rome by responding to it with silence. The Nazis kept pressure on the clergy to thwart resistance but did not move against dignitaries such as the Bishop of Münster, who criticized the euthanasia program in 1941.

Christianity under Soviet Communism

The third great dictatorship was established in Russia by Lenin. He had developed a doctrine of the party and the nature of revolution that would ensure the victory of the proletariat, even in a backward country like Russia. Under a tightly organized party the workers and peasants could together overthrow the tsarist regime and set up a revolutionary dictatorship to direct the country's economic development and create a classless society. In 1917 his Bolsheviks identified with the popularly elected councils (*soviets*) and seized power from the tottering republic that had replaced the tsar. As he began putting his theories into practice, his enemies struck back, leading to a bitter civil war and intervention by the Western Allies. The Bolsheviks tried in vain to stir up revolution in the capitalist countries, but when they recognized that the European states drew strength from their empires, the Communists backed colonial liberation as well.

Soon after Lenin's death in 1924, the ambitious Joseph Stalin (1879–1953) came to power. As a boy he had attended the Orthodox seminary in Tiflis, but he abandoned religion for Marxist materialism. Stalin realized the futility of spreading revolution beyond Russia and set out to transform it into an industrialized state on the basis of its own resources so that it could compete with the Western capitalist nations. What followed was the creation of a dictatorship even more brutal than Hitler's, involving the forced collectivization of farms, police terror, slave labor camps, purges of rivals, and Russification of the subject peoples of the old tsarist empire, renamed in 1922 as the Soviet Union. He brought into Communism the "cult of the personality."

Since hostility to all religion was a central theme of Marxism-Leninism, the Russian Communists actively struggled against the church. Not only did they see Christianity as a reactionary social force that impeded progress toward the classless society, but they also considered it an alternative worldview that threatened the power and prestige of the Communist party. For their part, Christians could not accept the secular view that nature was moving humanity toward a final, perfect end or the Marxist-Leninist emphasis on violent class struggle.

In the dying days of the tsarist regime many churchmen believed that the conditions of workers and peasants must be improved, but few were willing to accept socialism. Thus, they welcomed the March Revo-

THE DISHONOURS OF WAR
MARS: "I USED TO BE THE GOD OF BATTLE—NOT BUTCHERY."

lution of 1917 that created the republic. In August 1917 an All-Russian Council (*Sobor*) of the church was convened. It went against public opinion by reintroducing the patriarchal system of church government that had been abolished in 1700 and naming the metropolitan of Moscow, Tikhon (1866–1925), to the post.

When the Bolsheviks took over in November, they confiscated church lands, canceled state subsidies for the church, decreed civil marriage, and nationalized schools. Patriarch Tikhon responded by excommunicating the government leaders, and in open demonstrations church officials called for restoration of the monarchy. Lenin's government retaliated by ordering an immediate separation of church and state and recognizing the equality before the law of all religious groups. Every vestige of religion was banished from the public schools, and all church property was nationalized. Revenue-producing property was kept by the state while buildings used for worship were leased to the congregations free of charge. Tikhon bitterly condemned the seizure of church treasures for famine relief purposes, but he later recanted of his "anti-Soviet actions" and declared loyalty to the regime. A schism occurred when a group of parish priests formed the "Living Church," which endorsed the reforms. However, the *Sobor* in 1923 accepted the Soviet stance, cut all counter-revolutionary ties, and assured the government of its allegiance.

Although the various constitutions guaranteed "freedom of religion and anti-religious propaganda," the 1929 Law on Religious Association strictly limited the activities of churches. They could not engage in social, charitable, or educational work, give material aid to their members, or hold any meetings other than worship services. Also, every congregation had to be registered, extraordinary meetings and religious conferences required special permission, and officials could close a church if they decided the building was needed for some public purpose.

The next decade was one of intense persecution, as thousands of clergymen were jailed or murdered and the survivors treated as second-class citizens and harassed by the secret police. As a result, the Russian Orthodox church was on the verge of disintegration, while the Stalinist terror almost wiped out the Lutheran and ravaged the Evangelical Christian-Baptist denominations. Large numbers of Mennonites emigrated to the Americas in the 1920s, and those who remained behind were persecuted, as were all other religious groups—Roman Catholics, Uniate Catholics, Old Believers, and even Jews and Muslims. The Vatican strongly condemned the persecutions, and in 1937 Pius XI declared that "communism is intrinsically wrong and no one who would save Christian civilization may collaborate with it in any undertaking whatsoever." However, after Russia entered World War II, Stalin allowed the church much more freedom, as he realized it could contribute to public morale and serve to promote Soviet foreign policy.

World War II and the Churches

The expansionist actions of the German and Italian dictators and the militarist clique in Japan led to World War II. In 1941 Russia was attacked by Germany and the United States by Japan, thus setting the stage for the greatest conflict in history. During the 1930s Christians were divided in their attitudes toward the dictatorships. Some were so staunchly anti-Communist that they backed fascist-type movements, and Hitler even found favor with a few Christians. One actually commended him in 1936 for building "a front line of defense against the Anti-Christ of Communism." Liberal Christians tended to favor the left, and some were active socialists, such as Reinhold Niebuhr and Norman Thomas, but few joined the Communist party or condoned events in the Soviet Union.

The American peace movement provided support for isolationist policies, but some liberals came to see a vast difference between 1914 and the current situation and began arguing for American participation in the widening struggle. Outraged by what they regarded as short-sighted pacifism, Niebuhr and others founded the journal *Christianity and Crisis* in February 1941, which challenged church people to reject neutrality and accept intervention as a necessary alternative.

Once war came, churchmen in the various countries pledged loyalty to their regimes, but in comparison to 1914 the commitment was more tentative. In the West, churches supplied servicemen with pastoral care through the military chaplains, the rights of religious conscientious objectors were usually respected, and a few clergy actually opposed the war or at least criticized the obliteration bombing of Germany and Japan. German Protestant and Catholic leaders also urged their people to back the war effort, while the Russian churches enthusiastically supported the "Great Patriotic War." In Japan the small Christian community had been forced to unite into one church, the *Kyodan,* and it urged believers to "promote the great endeavor." Some evangelicals who criticized the patriotic Shinto festivals were persecuted.

In Germany, the conciliatory attitude of church leaders did not prevent the persecution of Christians. Hitler's closest advisers were working toward a "final settlement" in church-state relations as well, and in the "new order" Christianity would be left to suffer what Hitler called a "natural death." In the occupied areas priests and pastors, along with devout laypeople, were treated as common criminals, and thousands were executed or sent to concentration camps. However, some Christians were motivated by their conscience to reject the Nazi regime and even to kill Hitler if necessary to stop the insane violence he had unleashed upon the world. A few were involved in the conspiracy to remove the Führer, and, in fact, the person who planted the bomb on July 20, 1944, was Count Klaus von Stauffenberg, a strong Catholic. Sadly, the explosion only wounded Hitler, and the Nazi retaliation against the resistance was swift. Among the thousands of martyrs were the devout Lutheran layman Count Helmuth von Moltke, the Jesuit Alfred Delp, and Dietrich Bonhoeffer. Martin Niemöller spent more than seven years in concentration camps as Hitler's "personal prisoner."

By and large, however, the Protestant churches lacked the moral courage to resist Hitler, and this was acknowledged in the "Stuttgart Declaration of Guilt" written by Niemöller in October 1945. This was due to their exclusive concern with individualistic personal faith, their traditional submission to the state, and a conservative outlook that permitted them to accept the Nazis' claim to be the only alternative to Communism. Especially controversial was the silence of Pius XII, who ascended the papal throne in 1939 and personally detested both Nazism and Communism. Critics claim that his failure to condemn Nazi aggression or the slaughter of millions of Jews was because he wanted to see Communism destroyed. Defenders argue that he had to be neutral and that German Catholics supported Hitler so strongly that they would not respond to any effort to counteract Nazi Jewish policies.

The Protestant ecumenical movement was also in an awkward position, because it did not want to jeopardize the fate of believers in the Soviet Union, Axis countries, or Japanese-occupied lands by condemning specific sins by national leaders in these places. The International Missionary Council did help the "orphaned missions" of Germany and other European countries in Africa and Asia to continue functioning, thereby demonstrating that a Christian world fellowship was possible. Other ecumenical groups focused on international relief efforts, caring for war prisoners and refugees, and maintaining contacts between churches on both sides.

The war clearly had a devastating impact on Christianity, both physically and morally. Thousands of churches were destroyed, clergy killed, and believers persecuted or uprooted from their homes. The level of violence escalated because of so many new weapons, incendiary bombing, and ultimately the atomic bomb, all of which resulted in the deaths of millions. The deliberate direction of war against civilians, the indifference of so-called Christian political leaders in the West to the sufferings of the Jews, and the alliance of the Western democracies with the tyrannical Soviet Union were all moral issues of great concern to Christians. This led many to question whether a "just war" could any longer be possible, and to suggest that the Christian endorsement of war only led to its intensification.

World War II ended with large parts of Europe and Asia in ruins. But the peace that returned was an uneasy one because a "cold war" between the two allies, the United States and the Soviet Union, soon dominated the international stage. Still, Western power had ended, and the process of colonial liberation meant a new world was coming into being. In these areas Christianity made enormous strides, and within a few decades the numerical center of gravity shifted away from Europe and North America to Asia, Africa, and Latin America. This presented new challenges to the Christian faith in the last half of the twentieth century.

23

THE CHURCH AS A GLOBAL INSTITUTION

The impact of the Cold War on the churches was mixed. In the Soviet bloc countries Christians suffered discrimination, the regimes subjected the churches to constant pressure, and Christianity was driven underground or reduced to political impotence. In the Western lands evangelicalism flourished, but the established churches experienced a continuing fall in attendance. In both areas the public influence of the churches declined, but at least political leaders in the West continued to identify with a church or denomination, whether or not they were actually practicing members. Evangelicals in the United States did much to spread the faith through their expanding missionary force and mass evangelistic efforts. Consequently, the churches in the non-Western world grew by leaps and bounds. But they faced a formidable rival in the resurgent non-Christian religions.

THE COLD WAR RUNS ITS COURSE

World War II did not end with a general peace treaty. The Allied leaders worked out the outlines of the postwar world at various conferences, but deep divisions arose between Stalin and his Western counterparts—Churchill in Britain and Roosevelt in the United States. The latter two looked forward to a new era where every nation would be self-governing, would have equal rights, and would work together for economic security, improved living standards, and the elimination of force and aggression in international affairs.

As the war drew to a close in 1945, the United Nations was formed. The dream of one world where all peoples lived in peace seemed about to be fulfilled. However, this would not be the case. The Soviets, who had experienced attack from the west twice in this century, were adamant about the need for security from any future German aggression. Thus, the Red Army remained in eastern Europe, where they set about installing Communist "peoples' democracies" in these countries. East-West tensions rose as the Soviets paralyzed the UN with vetoes and tried to squeeze the Western powers out of Berlin. The victors did manage to arrange the occupations of Germany and Japan and to conclude peace treaties with Italy and Japan, but a final settlement over Germany proved impossible. Though the Cold War began as a great power rivalry, it rapidly took on an ideological character, as the Soviets preached the doctrines of Communism and called for liberating people oppressed by "imperialists." By 1949 economic recovery and the de facto division of Germany resulted in stability through an uneasy balance of power in Europe, but the struggle spread to Asia where, after a bitter civil war, the Chinese Communists took control of their vast nation.

As leader of the Western democracies, the United States took the initiative to "contain" Communist power by supplying arms and economic assistance to threatened countries. Although containment of Soviet expansion remained the cornerstone of American foreign policy until the demise of the Soviet Union in 1991, many sought to broaden it to include opposition to Communism as a social doctrine, especially after China was "lost." Communism anywhere, whether at home, in Europe, or in the non-Western world, was seen as a threat to American national security. The "witch hunts" of Senator Joseph McCarthy and other investigators were aimed at domestic subversion, whereas foreign aid and military alliances resisted Communist exploitation of weaknesses abroad. This led to direct military involvement in Korea and later in Vietnam.

In the mid-fifties, after Stalin's death and Eisenhower's accession to the presidency, Cold War tensions eased somewhat. The development of the H-bomb and long-range ballistic missiles made war

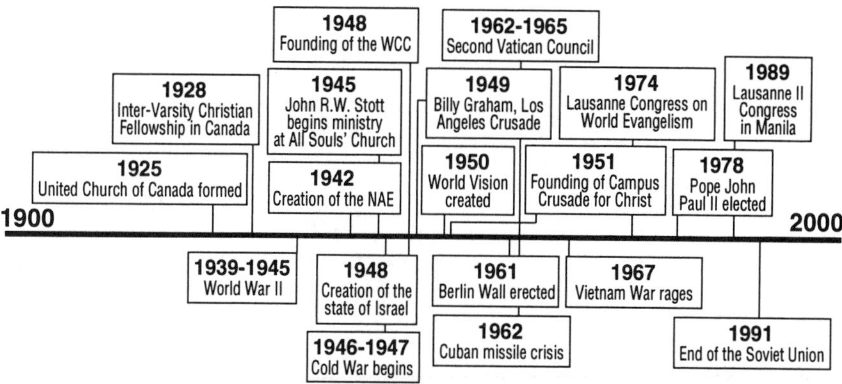

between the two superpowers unthinkable. Both Korea and Vietnam were divided between Communist and non-Communist regimes, and the United States did not interfere when the Soviets cracked down on Poland and Hungary in 1956. Then, when Nikita Khrushchev gained control of the Soviet government, he decided to test Western resolve at the two flash points of Berlin and Cuba. America did not try to stop the building of the Berlin Wall in 1961, but it responded forcefully to the Cuban missile crisis of 1962, and for a few days the two nations poised on the brink of World War III.

This marked the turning point in the Cold War. In the following years more effort was devoted to negotiating differences, while the polarized blocs disintegrated with the defections of China and France, and the United States got bogged down in a bloody and inconclusive war of containment in Vietnam. Meanwhile, the Soviets followed a policy of repression at home and in the Communist bloc, and their entry into Afghanistan in 1979 to prop up a faltering Marxist regime proved to be a disaster. They also sought parity in naval power and strategic weapons with America, and the escalating arms race led both nations to the point of bankruptcy.

In 1985 Mikhail Gorbachev introduced a reform program that opened up Soviet society, but by then it was too late to save the system. As a tidal wave of popular revolutions swept over eastern Europe, the Soviet bloc disintegrated. Finally the Soviet Union itself dissolved into a welter of quarreling national entities. The United States was left as the only international superpower, but its economy was mired in a recession and social tensions were dividing the country.

Colonial Revolutions and the Third World

The collapse of the whole colonial system followed on the heels of World War II. In the forties and fifties all of South and Southeast Asia gained independence, and in the Middle East the old League of Nations mandates were ended. Between 1951 and 1968 all the Muslim states of North Africa and most of the colonies south of the Sahara were liberated. In 1974–75 the Portuguese empire was dismantled. In 1980 Zimbabwe, and in 1990 Namibia, gained independence. The only remaining bastion of white power was in South Africa, which withdrew from the British Commonwealth in 1961 because of criticism of its apartheid policy. A similar process of decolonization occurred in the Caribbean and South Pacific islands.

The most complex problem was in Palestine where the British turned the matter over to the UN, which recommended a partition into Jewish and Arab states. When the Arabs rejected this, the radical Zionists proclaimed the creation of Israel on May 14, 1948. Enraged, the Arab League members immediately attacked the fledgling nation, but they could not suppress the Jewish state. Israel ended up with more territory than had been proposed by the UN commission. Nevertheless, it lived under a constant state of siege and engaged in further conflicts in 1956 and 1967 to improve its defensive position. In the Yom Kippur War of 1973 Israel suffered a temporary setback, and its image of strength was tarnished. But no resolution of the Arab-Israeli dispute seemed possible. In fact, the chances for a peaceful resolution of the problem were diminished by the demands of radical Jewish traditionalists for the removal of all Arabs from Israel and a concomitant hardening of Palestinian resistance in the "Intifada."

The Christian response to the problem was complicated by various factors. Almost all Arab Christians, whether Roman Catholics, Orthodox, or Protestants, firmly backed the Palestinians. Like Arab Muslims, they considered Israel an outpost of Western colonialism, and at the same time they identified with the many Christians who were Palestinians. Western Christians, especially liberals, were tormented by a deep sense of guilt for the Holocaust, yet they wanted to see justice for those who had been driven from their homes. They were afraid to criticize Israeli policy lest they be labeled as anti-Semitic. Nevertheless many condemned the treatment of the Arabs. Conservative Protestants, especially premillennialists, on the other hand, were among Israel's most vocal supporters. Even though all missionary work there was forbidden, still many saw events in Palestine as fulfilling biblical prophecy.

The term "Third World" began to be applied in the 1950s to the less economically advanced or "developing" nations of Africa, Asia, and Latin America. It distinguished them from the two "industrial" worlds—the Western bloc (including Japan) and the Communist bloc led by the Soviet Union. They also saw themselves as "neutral" or "nonaligned," though in fact many of them (like Cuba) were aligned more closely to the Communist bloc. A more accurate term was the "Two-thirds World," and after the fall of Soviet Communism, this phrase was increasingly heard. The UN served as the major forum for these nations to express their views. They called for a New International Economic Order—a reshaping of the global economy that would give them greater access to the investment funds and technology of the West. Since the former colonial world was located in the southern portions of the two hemispheres, the confrontation took on a "north-south" character. The churches responded in various ways to the changing configuration of the world, and in spite of secularizing trends and the resurgence of rival religions they remained as major players on the world stage.

THE COLD WAR AND THE CHURCHES

In Germany the church was part of the Cold War. Konrad Adenauer, the first chancellor of West Germany, was a hard-nosed anti-Communist Catholic, and his Christian Democratic Union party brought together Catholics and conservative Protestants. The churches were not at first divided by the imposed political border running through Germany, and their organizational structure helped to perpetuate the idea of unity. The *Kirchentag* (Church Assembly), the first of which met in 1949, was an innovation in the Protestant church, and the huge crowds that attended revealed the important role they could play in bringing the laity back into church life. Also important in developing Christian awareness among the laypeople were the evangelical academies founded after the war.

Once the political division of Germany became permanent, the Communist regime forced the churches to redraw their boundaries to coincide with the political ones. In East Germany an almost total secularization of public life occurred, but the institutional church was not destroyed. In 1978, after decades of harassment, church leaders reached an understanding with the state whereby it would act as the "church in socialism." On the other hand, the church in West Germany was allowed to function freely. It could assess a "tax" on its members, provide religious education in the schools, and participate actively in public affairs. However, the level of involvement in church life in both German states sharply declined over the years.

In the Communist bloc countries Christians were under intense pressure, although the nature of this varied from country to country and from time to time. On the one hand, the influence of the Catholic church in Poland was considerable; on the other hand, Albania officially banned all religion. Conditions in the other Eastern bloc nations ranged between these two extremes. Irreligion was consciously fostered through the teaching of Marxist materialism in the schools, atheist organizations, and the substitution of secular rites for religious ones, such as the East German "youth dedication." The Stalinist state in Soviet Russia crushed the Uniates, the Greek rite Roman Catholics in the Ukraine, and forced them to become Russian Orthodox. As the level of persecution in Russia rose, the Baptists in 1959 split over whether they should continue submitting to the state regulation of church activities. Josef Cardinal Mindszenty (1892–1975) denounced the Hungarian Communist regime and was sentenced to prison after a mock trial in 1949. Released during the 1956 uprising in Budapest, he sought refuge in the American embassy and remained there for years as an anti-Communist symbol until the pope secured his release.

In every Eastern European country the state exercised influence over the appointment of church officials and assigned to some government bureau the task of overseeing church affairs. There were fewer clergy, and their average ages were higher; fewer people attended services (except in Poland), and far more old churches were closed than new ones built. But this occurred in western Europe as well. The difference was that the West grew more secular even though the state itself was not antireligious.

Another interesting development in the East was the founding of the Christian Peace Conference (CPC) in 1958. Its leader, Josef L. Hromádka (1889–1969), a highly respected theologian at Prague, made the CPC into a major bridge between the two blocs. It promoted conciliation between East and West, Christian-Marxist dialogue, nuclear disarmament, and Third World justice issues. But the Soviet invasion of Czechoslovakia in 1968 essentially discredited the CPC in the eyes of most Westerners.

The major impact of the Cold War on Western churches was to foster anti-Communism. This was especially true in the United States, where liberalism, socialism, and other left-wing orientations were quickly labeled as Communist. Some fundamentalists accused liberal churchmen of being "Reds" or "fellow-travelers." In one incident in 1953 an investigator for the McCarthy committee claimed that the largest single group supporting the Communist apparatus was Protestant clergy. Presidents Truman and Eisenhower repeatedly linked faith in God with the American way of life and contrasted this to Communist atheism. In fact, the addition of "under God" to the Pledge of Allegiance in 1954 and the adoption of "In God We Trust" as the national motto in 1956 were direct results of the Cold War emphasis on God and country.

The Communist regimes of eastern Europe, in spite of their efforts, could not eradicate Christianity. At the popular level, religious feelings ran deep, as evidenced by the enthusiastic reception Billy Graham received in his ventures into the Soviet bloc beginning in 1977. The collapse of Communism began in Poland, where the Catholic church had stood firmly for its rights through the years. The Polish church gained further encouragement from the election of the first Polish pope in 1978. A government based on a highly Catholic working class party (Solidarity) came to power in 1989 and began dismantling the Marxist system. The churches played a major role in the other revolutions as well, such as the prayer services and candlelight marches in East Germany, the crucial support of Cardinal Tomasek to the uprising in Czechsolovaka, and the courageous Reformed pastor Laszlo Tökes who initiated the Romanian resistance to the brutal Ceauşescu government. The unpopular religious laws were dismantled in every country, including Russia. People were allowed to worship freely, and the churches regained control of their confiscated properties.

To be sure, some have argued that the revolutions did not need the churches. Because the Communist governments could no longer supply the economic needs of the citizenry or depend on the backing of Soviet tanks, the people could have risen up on their own. But this view ignores the existing historical conditions. Christianity was the only "opposition," so to speak, that had been allowed in the Soviet bloc, and the Christians, with their alternate worldview to that of the Marxists, had a basis for ethical action. Also, since these governments had repudiated religion, they could not look to the church to gain legitimacy like dictators elsewhere always did. Finally, the churches were part of the national fabric, as they had shared in the historical evolution of the nation. The Communists argued that human unity was in the class, but unity actually was to be found in the family and nation. When it was put to the ultimate test, the Marxist ideology failed.

THE ECUMENICAL MOVEMENT

Even before World War I Protestants in Europe and North America were thinking about Christian cooperation on the international and national level, and the groping attempts at united effort culminated in the post–World War II "ecumenical movement," a generic term referring to a wide range of efforts toward the reintegration of Christendom. Among the early examples of cooperative endeavor were Bible societies, the YMCA, student Christian groups, and Christian Endeavor.

After 1900 national and regional councils of churches began to organize. The first were the Protestant Federation of France, formed in 1905, and the Federal Council of the Churches of Christ in America, founded in 1908 and restructured as the National Council of Churches in 1950. National Christian Councils were created in India, China, and Japan in 1922, and in Korea in 1924. The Evangelical Church in Germany (1922) and British Council of Churches (1942) were important national organizations in Europe. By 1948 there were thirty national councils worldwide, and by 1990 the number had reached ninety.

After World War II several regional councils came into being. The first of these, the East Asia Conference of Churches (later renamed the Christian Conference of Asia) was formed in 1959, D. T. Niles (1908–70) of Sri Lanka becoming its first general secretary. A Methodist evangelist, he was a brilliant organizer and tireless worker in ecumenical causes. Other regional groups included the Conference of European Churches (1959), All Africa Conference of Churches (1961), Pacific Conference of Churches (1966), Caribbean Conference of Churches (1973), Middle East Council of Churches (1974), and the Latin American Council of Churches (1982). All of these endeavored to help the divided churches understand one another and work together, but they did not expect the members to accept a common doctrinal position or surrender any of their autonomy.

Another form of ecumenical cooperation was within specific denominational groups. The earliest was the Lambeth Conferences,

CHRISTIANITY AS A GLOBAL FAITH (1993 DATA)

World Population (total)	5,575,954,000
World Population by Religion	
Christians (all kinds)	1,899,751,000
Non-Christians	
Muslims	1,014,372,000
Nonreligious	912,874,000
Hindus	751,360.000
Buddhists	334,002,000
Atheists	241,852,000
New Religionists	123,765,000
Tribal Religionists	99,736,000
Sikhs	19,853,000
Jews	18,153,000
Minor Religions and Unclassified	190,234,000
Total	3,706,202,000
Total Christians as a percentage of world population	**34%**
Membership by Ecclesiastical Bloc	
Anglicans (Episcopalians)	55,974,000
Roman Catholics (Including Uniates)	1,020,804,000
Protestants	342,696,000
Marginal Protestants	20,020,000
Orthodox (All Kinds)	185,568,000
Non white Indigenous Christians	161,873,000
Secret Believers and Unclassified	112,816,000
Percentage of Christians by Geographical Area	
Africa	16.6%
East Asia	6.2%
Europe	24.1%
North Asia/Former USSR	6.7%
Latin America	25.3%
Northern America	11.6%
South/Southeast Asia	8.4%
Oceania	1.1%

Source: David B. Barrett, "Annual Statistical Table on Global Mission: 1993," *International Bulletin of Missionary Research* 17 (January 1993), 23.

consultative meetings of bishops in the Anglican family of churches, which began in 1867 and were held at ten-year intervals thereafter. The World Alliance of Reformed Churches (1970) resulted from a merger between the agency created by British and North American Presbyterian churches in 1875 and the International Congregational Council. The Baptist World Alliance was formed in 1905 and focused on fellowship and programs in which Baptists could support one another. The Lutheran World Federation was founded in 1947 on the base of an earlier body and is especially well known for its relief activities. The World Methodist Council was created in 1951 as the successor to an ecumenical conference that had been meeting every decade since 1881. Several other denominations also have international organs. Most of them entered into a consultative relationship through the World Council of Churches (WCC) and are known as "Christian World Communions."

The most thoroughgoing efforts at unity was the creation of united churches from different confessional traditions. Most of these emerged after lengthy periods of negotiation and planning. But one exception, the United Church of Christ in Japan (*Kyodan*), was the result of a government mandate in 1941. The first major twentieth-century venture was the United Church of Canada (1925), in which Congregationalists, Presbyterians, and Methodists joined together. The same three groups inaugurated the Uniting Church of Australia in 1977. Quite important were the Church of South India (1947) and the Church of North India (1970), which incorporated Anglicans, Methodists, Congregationalists, and Presbyterians. The major figure in launching the movement that brought about these unions was V. S. Azariah (1874–1945), the first Indian bishop in the Anglican church and a landmark figure in Indian church history. Since 1962 the Consultation on Church Union has been exploring possible routes to a unified church in the United States.

The most important ecumenical venture has been the World Council of Churches. Its roots lay in three earlier bodies. First, the International Missionary Council, formed in 1921, institutionalized the vision of the Edinburgh conference and held major conventions in Jerusalem (1928) and Madras (1938) to coordinate and foster missionary work. Second, the World Conference on Faith and Order met in Lausanne in 1927 and promoted theological dialogue on issues dividing the churches, such as baptism, the Eucharist, the ordained ministry, creeds and confessions, the authority of Scripture, forms of worship, and ecclesiology. Third, the Universal Christian Conference on Life and Work was inspired by the Lutheran archbishop of Uppsala, Nathan Söderblom (1866–1931). In 1925 he convened a meeting on social issues in Stockholm that sought to apply the Christian way of life to contemporary problems. A second Life and Work conference at Oxford in 1937 adopted a theological statement dealing with the Christian task in the modern world. Faith and Order met in Edinburgh that same year and clarified various points on the question of Christian unity.

Most important, the latter two decided to work together to create a representative assembly of the churches. In 1938 a provisional committee was chosen to form the World Council of Churches, with Anglican archbishop William Temple as chair and Willem A. Visser 't Hooft (1900–85) of the Netherlands as general secretary. A founding assembly was planned for 1941, but the war intervened and Visser t' Hooft directed the ecumenical enterprise from Geneva. Once peace had returned, planning resumed and the inaugural meeting took place in Amsterdam in 1948. Subsequent assemblies were held at seven to eight year intervals. Although the International Missionary Council remained as a separate organization, it finally united with the WCC in 1961.

During the war, the infant ecumenical organization was drawn into the anti-Hitler movement. Dietrich Bonhoeffer was working as a courier for the conspirators who were planning to overthrow the *Führer*, and he met with various ecumenical leaders and kept them informed of developments in Germany. However, the British government ignored the pleas for assistance conveyed through the contacts. Bonhoeffer's involvement in this eventually cost him his life.

It was decided that the WCC would be "a fellowship of churches which accept our Lord Jesus Christ as God and Saviour." It would not be a "superchurch" but an instrument whereby the churches could bear witness together to their allegiance in Christ, search for the unity that He wills for His church (John 17:11), and cooperate in matters requiring common action. To achieve these goals the WCC developed a complex structure. It also grew rapidly, from 147 member churches in 1948 to 311 churches in 100 countries in 1991. It was not just a Protestant institution, because the Greek, Russian, and Oriental Orthodox churches also joined, as well as some independent African churches. Although their concept of the church precluded the possibility of formal membership, Roman Catholics did participate in WCC programs.

The enthusiasm for ecumenism in general and the World Council in particular was quite high in many circles, but the movement has been criticized as well. From a theological standpoint some pointed out the flawed, limited, and inconsistent visions of what ecumenism was, and cynics suggested that the movement for unity was a political expediency in the face of dwindling congregations and funds. Unity was exalted at the expense of truth, more emphasis was placed on social action than doctrinal questions, minimizing the importance of proclaiming the gospel and dulling Christian witness through interfaith dialogues. Others criticized the WCC's "liberal" theology, excessive number of bureaucrats who were single- issue "prophets" lacking experience in pastoral work, vague and inconsistent political stances, and waste of time and money on international conferences.

THE EVANGELICAL RESURGENCE

The feeling grew among American fundamentalists that they must cooperate with one another, but they saw the Federal Council as hopelessly modernistic. The first step was taken by Carl McIntire, who was born in 1906, studied with J. Gresham Machen, and followed his mentor and others when they left Princeton Seminary. When they defied the Presbyterian Church in the U.S.A. by forming an independent mission board, they were expelled from the ministry. Then McIntire broke with his colleagues over premillennialism and lifestyle questions and created a new denomination and seminary. In 1941 he organized the American Council of Christian Churches (ACCC), whose theological basis was fundamentalism and exclusivist separatism. No denomination or individual church could join the ACCC unless it formally renounced modernism and severed all ties with the Federal Council.

Another approach to transdenominational evangelical cooperation was that of J. Elwin Wright (1896–1966). In 1929 he formed the New England Fellowship whose cooperative program included radio ministry, Christian education, bookstores, and Bible conferences. He saw the need for a similar fellowship on the national level, and at his urging representatives of nearly forty denominations assembled in St. Louis in 1942 to form the National Association of Evangelicals (NAE). They adopted a conservative statement of faith but rejected McIntire's appeal to join with his militantly separatist ACCC. They opted instead for a fellowship for united action in such fields as evangelism, radio broadcasting, foreign missions, and church-state relations. The NAE took a separatist stance in that denominations affiliated with the Federal (and, later, National) Council would be ineligible for membership, but individual persons and congregations were not held to this requirement. Also, Pentecostal and Holiness bodies might join.

The differences between the two were clear, and the McIntire and ACCC camps bitterly attacked the NAE for its "compromising" and "inclusivist" position. Due to its own negativism and antiliberalism, the NAE could not attract many who might be defined as evangelicals, such as those in the mainline churches and the black denominations. In fact, the largest conservative denominations—the Southern Baptist Convention, Lutheran Church–Missouri Synod, and Churches of Christ—did not join. However, such spinoffs as the Evangelical Foreign Missions Association, National Religious Broadcasters, World Relief Commission, and Evangelical Press Association helped fulfill the cooperative vision.

Far more significant was the emergence of a new generation of fundamentalist intellectuals. Many of them, having received graduate training at major universities, began to be heard in theological and academic circles. Fuller Theological Seminary, founded in 1947, was a center of the new scholarship, and the rapid growth of other colleges and seminaries reflected a thirst for learning among evangelicals. New scholarly societies were formed that represented this outlook, including the American Scientific Affiliation in 1941 and the Evangelical Theological Society in 1949.

In 1947 the thirty-four-year-old journalist and theologian Carl F. H. Henry published *The Uneasy Conscience of Modern Fundamentalism*, which challenged the conservative church to meet the problems confronting the modern mind and society. Henry and others argued that fundamentalism, although it had upheld the integrity of orthodox Christianity in the face of the modernist challenge, now had lost its prophetic character and was a threat to the historic faith. They faulted it for oversimplifying complex theological matters, separating one's faith from everyday life, anti-intellectualism, and having a pugnacious and negative character. They claimed that, in the popular mind, fundamentalism had become loaded with bad connotations, and the positive contributions it made in a critical period of church history had been forgotten.

The "new evangelicalism," a term coined by one of its founders, Harold J. Ockenga (1905–85), represented a vital force in American Protestantism. Within a decade it had maneuvered itself into a position of leadership. This was symbolized in 1956 by the founding of the journal *Christianity Today*, with Henry as editor. The view of unity that the new evangelicals expressed was that of cooperative effort by like-minded people in such areas as evangelism, education, and social action rather than denominational mergers or comprehensive ecumenism. Its strategy was that of "infiltration," not separation, and it would minister to and influence all churches by applying Christian truth to every phase of life.

The key personality who communicated the vision of a broader evangelicalism was William F. "Billy" Graham. Born in 1918, he was converted at an evangelistic meeting and trained at Wheaton College. In 1943 he began his ministry with Youth For Christ, one of the major outreach organizations of the new evangelicalism, and identified with the NAE and its position as a middle way between fundamentalist negativism and modernist heresy. Mass evangelism was clearly his calling, and he became a national figure after a crusade in Los Angeles in 1949 and gained international renown with his London campaign in 1954. By the middle 1950s he was without peer in the field. In his early years he manifested the traits of American fundamentalism—a conservative theology linked with a conservative political and social philosophy that stressed the work ethic, patriotism, the central role of religion in public life, traditional sexual mores and family relations, a strong national defense, and rejection of the foreign ideology of Communism.

However, Graham had a remarkable flexibility and was able to change as the times changed. Although at heart a humble country boy, he could relate to the highest figures in government and business. His contacts with them and wide travels broadened his understanding of the world. His emphasis on "cooperative evangelism," that is, local-level ecumenical support for his various crusades while keeping the machinery firmly in the hands of his organization and evangelicals, contributed immensely to their success. But it gained him the undying enmity of the separatist fundamentalists. He also matured in his understanding of social issues, first abandoning the racial segregation he had learned as a Southerner and then moderating his anti-Communism after visits to eastern Europe. He also came to see the need for nuclear disarmament and to shed his earlier superpatriotism. Most remarkably, he was able to bridge the chasm that separated evangelicals from other expressions of the Christian faith, even to the point of appearing at National and World Council functions and establishing a cordial relationship with Pope John Paul II.

Graham also promoted ecumenism among evangelicals. Not only did he bring them together in his local crusades but also was the prime mover behind the launching of *Christianity Today.* His organization sponsored congresses on evangelism, beginning with a meeting in Berlin in 1966, all of which included a wide range of participants. He facilitated the Lausanne Congress on World Evangelization in 1974 and its follow-up meeting at Manila in 1989. He also held training conferences for itinerant evangelists in Amsterdam in 1983 and 1986. These gatherings, emphasizing the importance of cooperative effort on a global scale to reach men and women for Christ, included not only biblical teaching but also social concern in their scope of vision.

North American evangelicalism spawned countless evangelistic, missionary, educational, and social service institutions that function on an interdenominational, and often international, basis. For example, World Vision, founded in 1950 by Robert "Bob" Pierce (1914–78) to assist Korean orphans, is now among the largest Christian humanitarian organizations in the world. InterVarsity Christian Fellowship, which originated in England and was transplanted to Canada in 1928 and to the United States in 1940, has been a major force in fostering evangelism and interest in foreign missions among students. A closely associated organization, the International Fellowship of Evangelical Students, formed in 1947, assists and encourages indigenous student work in 130 countries. An equally significant student

Harold J. Ockenga

ministry, Campus Crusade for Christ International, founded in 1951, also operates on a global scale. The Lausanne Committee for World Evangelization seeks through conferences, publications, and networking to be a catalyst and facilitator for world evangelism.

Evangelical growth was not simply a North American phenomenon. In Britain, during the interwar years, the division between conservatives and liberals was not so acrimonious as in America. Conservatives were involved in the institutional framework of the churches, where their voices were heard. Some moderate conservatives, such as Baptist W. Graham Scroggie (1877–1958) and Congregationalist G. Campbell Morgan (1863–1945), had visited America and came back deploring the damage that fundamentalism had done to the gospel. Since the cleavage between British liberals and conservatives was not absolute and the evangelicals were broadening in their own understanding of theological issues, British evangelicalism was quite diverse in character.

Like its North American counterparts, the Inter-Varsity Fellowship (now Universities and Colleges Christian Fellowship), formed in the 1920s, stimulated the advance of conservative evangelicalism after World War II. Among its enterprises were the creation of Christian professional societies, establishing Tyndale House at Cambridge in 1945 as a center for biblical studies, founding London Bible College in 1954 to train people for Christian work, and publishing scholarly Christian literature.

Within the Church of England itself, the leader in the movement to bring evangelical Christianity back into the mainstream of its life and thinking was John R. W. Stott. Born in 1921 and educated at Cambridge, he served at All Souls' Church in London, where he had a remarkable ministry from 1945 to 1975. Through his lecturing and writing he became known throughout the world as a first-rate evangelist, apologist, and Bible teacher. He was the organizer of the first National Evangelical Anglican Congress at Keele in 1967, an event that had a decisive effect on the renewal of evangelicalism within the church.

Other notable figures in British evangelicalism included the eminent Anglican churchman and scholar of Islamic law Sir Norman Anderson, New Testament scholar F. F. Bruce, Old Testament scholar D. J. Wiseman, and expository preacher D. Martyn Lloyd-Jones. Also, The Evangelical Alliance Relief (TEAR) Fund, founded in 1968, has become a major social service agency, while the Shaftesbury Project fostered thought and action in the social realm.

In Germany the number of evangelicals was small compared to the United States and Great Britain, but the free churches and Evangelical Alliance promoted evangelistic outreach, and in the postwar years efforts by these and many other groups flourished. Billy Graham went to Germany on numerous occasions, and his meetings drew large crowds. Itinerant preacher Anton Schulte, Ulrich Parzany of the German YMCA, Bishop Rolf Scheffbuch of the Württemberg Protestant Church, and Dr. Theo Lehmann, the leading youth evangelist in former East Germany, are respected figures in German evangelicalism. Trans-World Radio began working in Germany in 1961 and has become a major Christian organization. Also, German evangelicals sponsor a biennial national convention that is designed to be a counterbalance to the *Kirchentag* (Church Assembly) of the mainline churches.

New Currents in Christian Missions

In the interwar years enthusiasm for missions was slipping. Too many still thought in terms of "Christendom," that is, the idea of creating a global Christian civilization with the church serving as the religious center around which nations and peoples would unite. Yet, the tide of rising expectations within the non-Western world flowed in a far different direction. They wished to enhance their own cultural traditions within a framework of democracy, and an expansionist Christendom could only be maintained by coercion. Liberal critics denied that Christianity could validly assert that it was true and all other religions false and suggested that this was a form of cultural imperialism. Missionaries from the mainline churches had great difficulty in adjusting to this new situation, whereas fundamentalists continued to interpret the missionary call as the simple and unambiguous action of saving souls, ignoring sociopolitical matters. Their missions flourished, but the mainline works lost momentum and by the 1930s were experiencing a sharp decline in volunteers and funding. Even the once vibrant Student Volunteer Movement (SVM) had become moribund.

Some influential voices in the church questioned whether missions even had a future, as evidenced by the report of a commission headed by Harvard philosopher of religion William Ernest Hocking (1873–1966) that was published in 1932. Entitled *Re-Thinking Missions: A Laymen's Inquiry after One Hundred Years,* it argued that missions should emphasize social effort apart from evangelism, that missionaries should seek to link their faith with common features they could find in non-Christian religions, and that there ought to be greater unity in missionary activity both between missions and with members of other religions. The goal should not be to create institutional churches on the foreign field but to permeate the fabric of society with creative ideals and eventually to form an international fellowship in which each religion would find its appropriate place.

Fundamentalists simply saw this as further proof that modernism was destroying missions, although most missionaries actually were quite conservative. Many prominent figures fell into that category: Yale professor and Baptist Kenneth Scott Latourette (1884–1968), the premier historian of missions; Robert E. Speer (1867–1947), who served for forty-six years as secretary of the Presbyterian Board of Foreign Missions; Samuel Zwemer (1867–1952), the great worker among the Arab Muslims; and E. Stanley Jones (1884–1973), the renowned Methodist missionary to India; and others. Moreover, as Joel Carpenter demonstrates, 40 percent of the workers in 1935–36 came from boards of conservative denominations and faith missions, and by 1952 the number exceeded 50 percent.[1] Also, the creation of the Student Foreign Missions Fellowship in 1936 and its linkage with InterVarsity Christian Fellowship a decade later ensured that the lost vision of the SVM was given new life on campuses.

Quite significant was the shift in the missionary force from Britain and Europe to North America. Whereas the total number of workers doubled in the course of the twentieth century, the American contingent increased sixfold. In the early 1900s one-third of the Protestant missionaries in the world came from North America, but by 1969 it had risen to 70 percent. The ecumenically oriented mission bodies declined while the evangelical ones grew by leaps and bounds, and the two functioned in almost separate worlds. The number of new mission societies and support agencies also rose dramatically.

There were several reasons for the rapid growth of American mission work. One was the strong theological emphasis in evangelical churches and schools on spreading the gospel. Another was the impact of World War II itself. The rhetoric of conflict and conquest pervaded missionary sermons, while many who had served overseas in the armed forces caught the vision of returning to labor among the peoples there. General Douglas MacArthur's call for missionaries to be sent to Japan also animated the evangelical churches. The introduction of scientific methodology into mission practice through such disciplines as cultural anthropology, linguistics, statistics, and communications spurred the linkage of scholarly research and practical work. Such technology as aviation and radio was harnessed in the enterprise, and specialists in these areas joined the medical and educational workers in the support staff. Finally, great importance was placed on contextualization of the gospel message, church growth, and advancing the kingdom of God.

These ideas underscored the growing influence of the Third World churches, who saw social, political, and economic issues as vital to the process of world evangelization. They stressed a "holistic" approach to mission, in which a deep spirituality would be combined with a concern for each individual's total welfare. Also important was the development of Third World mission-sending agencies, such as those in Korea and Brazil. The numbers of missionaries from non-Western countries climbed steadily in the eighties and nineties. The role of Pentecostal missions, which placed strong emphasis on the role of the Holy Spirit in evangelism, is another important factor in Third World Christianity. Theologians from there, such as the evangelical Orlando Costas (1942–87), frequently faulted Westerners for being captive to an individualism and rationalism that prevented the Word of God from working with full power, and they condemned the "practical unbelief" of professing Christians who oppressed their neighbors.

PENTECOSTALISM AND THE CHARISMATIC MOVEMENT

Before World War II Pentecostalism tended to be associated with the lower socioeconomic classes and was on the margin of evangelical Christianity. However, through the work of evangelist Oral Roberts, whose rise to fame paralleled that of his contemporary Billy Graham, and California dairy farmer Demos Shakarian, who founded the Full Gospel Business Men's Fellowship International in 1951, Pentecostalism moved closer to the mainstream. Then, South African-born David J. du Plessis (1905–87), affectionately known as "Mr. Pentecost," made it into an international movement. He was a pastor and general secretary in the largest Pentecostal church in his country, and in 1947 he began working with the Pentecostal World Conference, located in Switzerland. He later moved to the United States, joined the Assemblies of God, and became involved in the ecumenical movement. To the dismay of many, he was a regular participant in the World Council of Churches assemblies and initiated Pentecostal-Roman Catholic dialogues.

In the 1950s several individuals in evangelical and mainline churches experienced the baptism of the Holy Spirit, and by the early sixties the so-called "charismatic renewal" was growing rapidly. In 1962 du Plessis organized the first meeting of charismatics from non-Pentecostal traditions. In 1967 the renewal spread to the Roman Catholic church, where the Belgian prelate Joseph Cardinal Suenens became its patron. During the seventies and eighties it spread through the American churches; all the larger denominations had charismatic renewal groups and conferences, but considerable tension and fragmenting occurred within the movement. Several leading charismatics had television ministries, including Rex Humbard, Marion "Pat" Robertson, Paul Crouch, Jimmy Swaggart, Jim Bakker, and James Robison.

The movement spread to Britain, where Anglican cleric Michael Harper, an associate of John Stott, received the baptism of the Holy Spirit and in 1964 established the Fountain Trust as a service agency for the charismatic renewal. It also took root in Protestant and Catholic circles throughout Europe. There was an important diffusion of Pentecostalism in Asia, the best-known example being David (Paul) Yonggi Cho, an Assemblies of God pastor in Seoul, Korea, who started a tent church in 1958 and built it into the world's largest congregation, the Yoido Full Gospel Church, with a membership of more than half a million.

In Latin America, Pentecostalism became a major religious force, but it did not retain the ecumenical character it had in North America and Europe. Although the renewal was widespread in the Latin American Catholic church with possibly two million charismatics by the late eighties, the hierarchy itself was extremely hostile to the Protestant Pentecostals. They were regarded as proselytizing interlopers who lured away the faithful, while the evangelicals saw the Catholics as pagans lost in a morass of superstition. By 1987 it was estimated that between 80 and 85 percent of the Protestants were Pentecostals or charismatics. Most of them belonged to indigenous independent churches where they contributed a vital element to Latin American Christianity.

CHANGES IN THE ROMAN CATHOLIC CHURCH

The conservative course of the papacy continued into the 1950s, as exemplified by Pius XII's unilateral action in 1950 decreeing as church dogma the bodily assumption of the Virgin Mary into heaven. However, a major shift occurred with the election of Angelo Roncalli (1881–1963) as Pope John XXIII in 1958. He chose this name to repudiate the John XXIII, who was the Pisan pope at the time of the Great Schism (see chapter 9). He was only expected to be a "caretaker" pope, but he surprised the world by announcing that he would convene an ecumenical council (Vatican II) and by creating the Secretariat for Promoting Christian Unity to foster dialogue with other churches. When Vatican II opened in 1962, John said he wanted to "update" the church because the most effective way to combat error would be to demonstrate the validity of its teaching rather than to condemn falsehoods. Its purpose would be to promote concord and the brotherly unity of all. Although he died after the first session, Paul VI (1963–78) saw the council through to its completion in 1965.

The various decisions of Vatican II radically transformed the Catholic church. The liturgy was to be in the language of the people, not in Latin. The church would be more "collegial" in character, that is, the hierarchy was to be part of the people of God and not separate from them, and the bishops would work together with the pope to guide the church. From a pastoral standpoint the church was in the world, and its mission was to serve the whole human family so that a more humane world might emerge. Greater stress was put upon the revelation in Scripture and the importance of easy access to the Bible by the faithful. Also, because God spoke through other religions, the

Desmond Tutu

church should be in dialogue with them. Since the Jews have a special relationship to the church and may not be blamed for the death of Jesus, anti-Semitism was condemned. Religious freedom for all was affirmed, and no one was to be forced to embrace the faith. Admitting that both sides were responsible for the divisions among Christians, cooperation and dialogue with the "separated churches and communities" on matters of common concern were encouraged.

After Vatican II an encouraging new climate of relationship between Protestants and Catholics existed, including shared worship and ecumenical cooperation. Catholics were now represented on the WCC's Faith and Order Commission, they participated in local councils of churches, and dialogues with other Christian groups from Pentecostals to Anglicans were regular activities. In December 1965 Paul VI and Patriarch Athenagoras of Constantinople revoked the excommunications of 1054 and declared them "erased from the memory" of the church. This was followed by ongoing Orthodox-Roman Catholic dialogues.

Some Catholics were bewildered by the changes and sought solace in breakaway traditionalist congregations, while others who wanted to go further formed underground or "house" churches. That a strong element of conservatism remained was evidenced by Pope Paul's affirmation of the church's traditional stand against all forms of artificial birth control in 1968 and Rome's action in 1979 relieving the enormously popular theologian Hans Küng of professorial responsibilities in the Catholic faculty at Tübingen for being too radical in his views.

Cardinal Karol Wojtyla, enthroned as Pope John Paul II in 1978, also took a conservative stance on such divisive issues as clerical celibacy, ordination of women, and birth control. However, his strong affirmations of political and religious freedom and the visit to his native Poland in 1987 helped to set in motion the revolutions in the Communist world. As the most-traveled pope in history, he has been a firm proponent of ecumenism and highly popular in the Third World.

Christianity and Racial and Ethnic Conflict

A serious problem facing the twentieth-century church was ethnic and racial conflict, as these examples illustrate. Even though the overtones were religious, the Protestant-Catholic struggle in Northern Ireland was really a class and ethnic struggle. Orthodox Greeks and Muslim Turks clashed in Cyprus, where Archbishop Makarios (1913–77) was chosen president in 1960. The Turkish minority, fearful of being overrun by the Greeks, received help from Turkey in 1974, and the island nation was effectively partitioned into two ethnic communities. The struggle between Jews and Arabs in Palestine also had a religious dimension, and there was ongoing strife between Muslim traditionalists and Copts in Egypt and between Muslims and Christians in Nigeria and the Sudan.

The most serious problem was that of apartheid in South Africa. This legal policy of racial separation allegedly ensured pluralism through "separate development" or "cooperative coexistence" and guaranteed peace, freedom, and prosperity for all. In fact, it was a device to uphold white political and economic power at the expense of the nonwhite majority. To be sure, racial segregation dated back to the early days of South Africa, but it became much more intense after the founding of the union in 1910. The apartheid policy grew out of the struggle between the English and Afrikaner (Dutch-speaking) populations, and the Afrikaner Nationalist party gained power in 1948 on a platform of implementing white supremacy. During the fifties the most restrictive laws were passed, including racial classification, requirement of identity cards, prohibition of interracial marriages and sexual relations, segregation of residential areas and public amenities, and creation of "homelands," where black Africans could exercise political rights and have "sovereign independence." Suffrage and the best jobs were reserved for the whites. The army and police acted arbitrarily and brutally to enforce the laws.

The policy turned South Africa into an international outcast while opposition grew at home. But the security police dealt ruthlessly with both moderate critics and illegal resistance groups. The various Dutch Reformed churches were essentially proapartheid, but during the eighties more and more of them turned against it. The World Council of Churches initiated its Program to Combat Racism (PCR) in 1969 to focus world attention on the situation and raise funds to support the resistance. The PCR was heavily criticized in the West for fostering violence. Anglican bishop Desmond Tutu defended it by asking why Bonhoeffer was regarded as a saint in Europe for trying to kill Hitler and rid Germany of the Nazi system, whereas black South Africans who took up arms to defeat the apartheid system were considered terrorists. The WCC also lobbied for disinvestment in South Africa and UN sanctions against the regime.

South African Christians themselves were in the forefront of the struggle: Bishop Tutu, author Alan Paton, Beyers Naudé of the Christian Institute, Reformed minister Allan Boesak, Michael Cassidy of African Enterprise, Pentecostal minister Frank Chikane, Methodist Charles Villa-Vicenio, and church historian John de Gruchy. Christian leaders adopted several statements boldly criticizing the system, of which the Rustenburg Declaration (1990) was especially noteworthy since it was signed by representatives of all churches in South Africa except two hard-line Dutch Reformed groups. It stated that apartheid was sin and heresy and called for concrete forms of restitution. At long last, the South African regime began to dismantle the apartheid system.

Discrimination against blacks was also a serious problem in the United States, and their struggle for justice was long and hard. The civil rights movement was born and nourished in the bosom of the black church. Many of its leaders were children of ministers or at least had been reared as church members, and much of the organizing and direction had come from people in the churches. The central figure, Martin Luther King, Jr. (1929–68), was a Baptist minister. He gave theological direction to the freedom movement and insisted that nonviolence and Christian love always be at the heart of the struggle. From his spiritual background he developed a view of black suffering, the meaning of historical travail, and a faith in God's ultimate victory. Although his message met considerable resistance, especially in the white Christian community, and he became a martyr for the cause of freedom, eventually his vision triumphed.

Ecumenical and mainline denominational leaders were solidly for King and the civil rights movement, but evangelicals tended to lag behind. However, lending support to the cause was Billy Graham, who began holding desegregated crusades in the South in 1953, appointed an African-American (Howard O. Jones) to his associate evangelists staff in 1957. He also spent time in Alabama promoting reconciliation during the heat of the civil rights struggle there in 1965, and refused to speak in South Africa until integrated seating was allowed. During the sixties such African-American voices as William Pannell, John Perkins, and E. V. Hill were increasingly being heard in evangelical circles.

The Old Wine in New Wineskins

The Christian faith was frequently being packaged in new ways. In Africa a rich variety of "Independent" or "African Instituted" churches arose in the early decades of the century, beginning with the "Ethiopian," "Zionist," and "prophet healing" churches in South Africa. Others included the Harriste churches in the Ivory Coast, the Christ Army Church in the Niger delta, the Aladura (praying) churches among the Yoruba of Nigeria, the Kimbanguist church in Zaire, and the Church of Christ in Africa, situated among the Luo in Kenya. They adapted African cultural traits and forms to Christianity, put heavy emphasis on the Holy Spirit and His work, were strongly biblicist in character, and had a deep sense of community. They are growing so rapidly that many predict Africa will soon be the most Christian of the continents.

In the sixties grassroots "base communities" arose among Roman Catholics in Latin America, and the idea spread widely to other parts of Africa and Asia. In these groups, which exist on the margins of the institutional church, poor people study the Bible in the light of their own experience of oppression and re-create the experience of the early church as a participatory community. The region has also been the seedbed of "liberation theology," a complex, multifaceted approach to questions of political and economic liberation. Although its best-known exponents, such as Gustavo Gutiérrez, José Miranda, Juan Luis Segundo, and Leonardo Boff, are Catholics and sometimes draw on Marxist social theory, many Latin American Protestants, such as José Miguel Bonino and the members of the evangelical Latin American Theological Fraternity, are sympathetic to its emphases. It stresses "praxis," that is, the belief that theology is worked out in the experience of the poor and that the Bible should be applied to the situations in which people find themselves.

New theologies and approaches to the faith abounded in the last half of the twentieth century. There were geographical theologies —African, Asian, Korean "minjung" (of the people), Japanese "pain of God," Pacific island "coconut," and Latin American liberation— and many varieties of feminist, black, and political theologies. Also present were transient varieties like the "death of God" and theology of hope. Whereas growth slowed in North America and declined in Europe, churches were mushrooming in Latin America, sub-Saharan Africa, China, Korea, and other places in Asia and the Pacific. However, other forces were at work that would challenge the church as the century drew to a close.

EPILOGUE
ONGOING CHALLENGES TO THE CHURCH'S ADVANCE

As this account of two thousand years of Christian history draws to a close, the church of Jesus Christ is still standing as firmly as ever. It has indeed endured the test of time. As for the future, Christians are convinced that God will continue to work in the historical process. Although they cannot use the tools of modern science to demonstrate objectively and conclusively the operation of the supernatural, nevertheless they perceive God's actions through the eyes of faith. Therefore, they affirm confidently that His church will press forward in carrying out the task He has assigned to it, which is to make His name known to all people. As the church enters the twenty-first century, it faces many challenges, but at the same time these are opportunities for it to bear witness to the one who has called it out of the nations and purchased it with His blood.

THE CHALLENGE OF SECULARIZATION

The most immediate challenge to the church is one with which it has been contending for a long time, namely, the process of secularization. The term *secular* comes from the Latin word *saeculum* (age—that is, the world as considered in the aspects of time) and was used to translate the Greek *aion,* which had the same meaning. In the New Testament, *aion* referred to the "age" that was created by God (Heb. 1:2), in which we live and do good to our neighbors (1 Tim. 6:17), to whose values and standards we are not to be conformed (Rom. 12:2), which will end in the judgment of God (Matthew 24), and will be followed by the age to come where the faithful enjoy eternal life (Luke 18:30). It was the historical time in which people lived in expectation of the promised coming of the Redeemer. However, the word took on a different meaning in the middle ages, where the "secular" came to be identified as the "temporal," the present age, and was contrasted with the "eternal," the realm of the spiritual, sacred, and divine.

In modern times secularization has come to mean more than just a process of living and functioning in the present world. It is now a worldview, which one may call "secularism." This is a philosophy that stresses the material over the spiritual, respect for all truth regardless of its source so long as it leads to human betterment, concern solely for matters in this world and not in another world that may come, and a rational morality that is independent of any reference to God or a realm of spiritual reality. From the standpoint of the secularist, conventional religion is marginal to the operation of the social order, and society is governed by impersonal systems of control, such as bureaucracy, science, technology, and pragmatism (whatever works). Groups that place importance on the supernatural are no longer permitted to play a role in decision making.

Though secularism seems to be the reigning worldview of modern times, its emptiness was demonstrated by the dismal cities of the Industrial Revolution, the tyranny of Hitler, Stalin, and Mao Tse-tung, and the creation of weapons of mass destruction that could eliminate all life on earth. Even in the "enlightened" West, where science has produced the highest living standards in history and the disengagement of the church from the state has allowed both to function more authentically, it has failed to provide meaningful answers to basic human problems. Political corruption, the multiplying threats to the environment, and the menace of new and deadly diseases such as AIDS have helped to shatter the illusion of optimism that gripped the West at the outset of the twentieth century.

Even for many Christians the pace of life in the secular age leaves much to be desired. This is indicated by their intake of tranquilizers, sleeping pills, and other chemicals, and by the statistics on mental health, stress-related diseases, and suicides. They are not immune to the troubles that plague others in the world.

Another variety of secularism is the almost religious devotion to things or processes that on the surface have nothing to do with religion as one customarily understands it. Among the new secular gods of the age are the obsession with sexuality, reliance on the nation-state, belief in technological processes, fixation on entertainment and sports, and desire for material possessions. Although there is nothing intrinsically wrong with these items, still any one of them may demand the kind of total commitment that should be reserved for God alone.

The resurgence of traditional religions in all parts of the world is one evidence of the emptiness of secularism, and this underscores for Christians that they must not ignore the problem at hand and leave to others the task of challenging the world-system. They must not be conformed to the spirit of the times or allow the church to be manipulated by political leaders or others seeking worldly gain.

The response of believers to secularism must be that of bringing their faith to bear on all issues of the day. No realm of life exists that is exempt from God's scrutiny. On the other hand, they should not seek to return to an imaginary golden age of Christian culture or withdraw into some sort of Christian ghetto. They must confront secularism by living in the world and demonstrating how one may have an integrated life whose separate parts are held together by the concept of a Creator God who cares about His universe and has made redemption possible through Christ's death.

WEALTH AND POVERTY

A second challenge facing the church is the extreme divergence between the rich and poor of today's world, a contrast that is often described in terms of the North-South divide. Experts in demographics estimate that by the year 2000 the world's population will be 6.3 billion and by 2025 may reach 8.5 billion. Moreover, 95 percent of the global population growth over this period will be in the developing countries of Latin America, Africa, and Asia. By 2025 Mexico will have replaced Japan as one of the ten most populous countries on the earth and Nigeria's population will exceed that of the United States.

Despite the real progress made in economic growth, public health, and literacy in the Third World, at least 800 million live in "absolute poverty." This is defined as a condition of life where malnutrition, illiteracy, disease, squalid housing, high infant mortality, and low life expectancy are beneath any reasonable definition of human decency. The stark reality is that the North (including eastern Europe and excluding China) has a quarter of the world's population and 80 percent of its income, while in the South (including China) three-quarters of the world's people live on one-fifth of its income. Also, approximately 90 percent of the global manufacturing industry is in the North. Whereas the quality of life in the North rises steadily, in the South every two seconds a child dies of hunger and disease.

Still, the contrast between wealth and poverty does not correspond exactly with the North-South division. Many of the OPEC countries are rich, whereas poverty is found in North America and Europe. In the United States, 14 percent of the people and one-fifth of all children are beneath the poverty line. In Britain more than 10 percent live below the legal definition of poverty and another 10 to 15 percent close to this point. The reality is that a great disparity between wealth and poverty is found not only between nations but also within them.

On the other hand, one-fifth of the world's population lives in relative affluence and consumes approximately four-fifths of the world's production. Moreover, according to a World Bank report in the year 1988 the "total disbursements" from the wealthy nations to the Third World amounted to $92 billion, a figure less than 10 percent of the worldwide expenditures on armaments, but this was more than offset by the "total debt service" of $142 billion. The result was a negative transfer of some $50 billion from the Third World to the developed countries. This disparity between wealth and poverty is a social injustice so grievous that Christians dare not ignore it.

One must not blame God for the situation in which the poor exist. He provided enough resources in the earth's land and sea to meet the needs of all. Nor is it the fault of the poor themselves, since for the most part they were born into poverty, but some of their government leaders may be blamed for corruption and incompetence. Also, it is not necessarily the fault of those in the West. However, Christians become personally guilty when they do nothing about the situation.

In the story of the Rich Man and Lazarus (Luke 16:19–31) there is no indication that the wealthy person was responsible for the poor man's sad plight. Where the guilt lay was in his blind ignorance of the beggar at his gate. He did not use his affluence to relieve the man's need, and he allowed a situation of gross poverty to dehumanize Lazarus. The Rich Man was consigned to hell not because he exploited the beggar but because he ignored him. Christians today are tempted to use the complexities of economics as an excuse to do nothing. God's people need to dedicate themselves not only to evangelism but also to relieving human needs, both at home and to the ends of the earth.

That explains why Christians in the Two-Thirds World place issues of poverty and economic development at the top of their theological agendas. Some Christians in the North have difficulty in understanding why "liberation" is so central to the thinking of their counterparts in Latin America, Africa, and Asia, but they have never faced the stark, dehumanizing reality of grinding poverty. It should come as no surprise that evangelicals in the South, with their strong commitment to the integrity and authority of Scripture, are in the forefront of the endeavor to secure a greater measure of justice for their fellow people. They simply believe what the Bible says.

Never was this dedication to action more eloquently affirmed than in the Manila Manifesto, adopted at the Lausanne II International Congress on World Evangelization in July 1989. With 3,000 delegates from 170 countries, this meeting in the Philippines was the most representative body of evangelicals ever to assemble in one place. The following words were contained in the section entitled "The Gospel and Social Responsibility":

> As we proclaim the love of God we must be involved in loving service, and as we preach the kingdom of God we must be committed to its demands of justice and peace. . . .
>
> Jesus not only proclaimed the kingdom of God, he also demonstrated its arrival by works of mercy and power. We are called today to a similar integration of words and deeds. In a spirit of humility we are to preach and teach, minister to the sick, feed the hungry, care for prisoners, help the disadvantaged and handicapped, and deliver the oppressed. . . .
>
> In our concern for the poor, we are distressed by the burden of debt in the Two-Thirds World. We are also outraged by the inhuman conditions in which millions live, who bear God's image as we do.
>
> Our continuing commitment to social action is not a confusion of the kingdom of God with a Christianized society. It is, rather, a recognition that the biblical gospel has inescapable social implications. True mission . . . necessitates entering humbly into other people's worlds, identifying with their social reality, their sorrow and suffering, and their struggles for justice against oppressive power. This cannot be done without personal sacrifices.[1]

THE ONGOING THREAT OF WAR

The relaxation of international tensions following the demise of the Soviet Union led many people into complacency about the continuing threat of war. Even as the menace of international Communism faded and with it the fear of a nuclear holocaust, its place was taken by a fragmenting nationalism. A variety of mini-nationalisms pointed to the great paradox of the times, namely, bitter divisions in an otherwise increasingly unifying world. Since the end of World War II more than one hundred new states have declared their independence and started on the road to nationhood. Usually unstable and economically weak, these states face severe problems. The appearance of so many new, small countries has even stimulated nationalism among minority groups in the larger, older states. However, the fact that such movements often lead to violence and bloodshed is of no concern to the leaders of these new nations. As one of them put it, "We prefer self-government with danger to servitude in tranquillity."

Most of these states have been accepted as members of the United Nations, thus setting a precedent for other dissident groups that they too should be heard, even those living in situations that have not traditionally been seen as "colonial." Until recently, all existing countries had regarded their dealings with "minority" groups within their boundaries as basically an internal matter, but the nature of international politics is such that this is no longer the case. Leaders of supposedly "oppressed" nationalities seek to gain sympathy for their plight from the world community, and some even resort to terrorism to make their point clear.

The existence of so many new nation-states is a serious matter because they are in such a precarious condition. Given their small land areas and limited resources, the hopes to which independence gave rise cannot be fulfilled by peaceful development. Consequently they may resort to arms to gain what they want. These wars may be fought with conventional weapons, but there is always the temptation to turn to atomic, biological, and chemical (ABC) warfare. The use of chemical weapons by the Iraqis in the 1980s illustrates this point.

What makes this such a frightening threat is the proliferation of atomic weapons. In the 1980s only five countries had them—the United States, the Soviet Union, Britain, France, and China. By the early 1990s it was known that *seventeen* more countries had the capability to produce them. Many believe that in the first decade of the twenty-first century the "nuclear club" may have more than one hundred members. With that many countries possessing nuclear arms, the possibility that they would be used in a war is extremely high.

This gives great urgency to Christian efforts on behalf of peace. As Jesus said, "Blessed are the peacemakers, for they will be called the sons of God" (Matt. 5:9). This and other statements of Christ ought to rule out the use of force in nationality conflicts, but, due to the complexity of these situations, some Christians may still find it expedient to acquiesce in the resort to arms. Certainly there can be no place for nuclear weapons in such struggles, but conventional arms, including the high-tech varieties, are available in staggering amounts.

An objective observer from another planet would conclude that earth is indeed a strange place. There is such a surplus of lethal weapons and yet a scarcity of food for the hungry and shelter for the homeless. Thus, the task confronting the church is an urgent one. It must teach people to beat their swords into plowshares and build a peace in the world based upon a true knowledge of God, just relationships among nations, and a concern for the weakest and most vulnerable in society.

Racism and Ethnicity

Closely related to the problems of war and poverty are racism and ethnicity. A widely accepted definition among the international Christian community holds that racism is

> ethnocentric pride in one's own racial group and preference for the distinctive characteristics of that group; belief that these characteristics are fundamentally biological in nature; [and] strong negative feelings toward other groups who do not share these characteristics, coupled with the thrust to discriminate against and exclude the outgroup from full participation in the life of their community.[2]

Ethnicity has to do with cultural or group identity. Members of an ethnic group (also frequently labeled a "nationality") share a common language and social and cultural institutions, and perceive that these set them apart from other people. Ethnicity is what set the Hebrews apart from other peoples, and the concept of *nation* is recognized in the New Testament (Acts 2:5; Rev. 21:24). Christians themselves, however, constitute "a holy nation" (1 Peter 2:9), and in the apostolic age individual congregations were structured geographically and not ethnically (e.g., the church in Corinth).

Racism and ethnicity are global matters, not something limited to the West. Before European expansion (c. 1500) the various races of the human family lived in relative isolation, but this was gradually modified by mass migrations, both free and forced, and presently there are varying degrees of racial mixture in the world. The change in the racial map of the world did not necessarily make conflict inevitable. What actually promoted it was the nature of European expansion. Possessing technological and military superiority, the Europeans conquered vast colonial possessions in Africa, Asia, and the Americas and transported millions of African slaves to the New World. In the process the Europeans developed a myth of racial superiority to justify their conduct. In the contemporary world, racial and ethnic tensions have steadily been increasing.

Christians are especially equipped to deal with this situation, as the apostle Paul showed in his memorable address to the Athenians (Acts 17:22–31). Athens was among the most racially, ethnically, and culturally diverse cities in the Roman Empire, and he addressed the question of their differences in the sight of God. His sermon emphasized four points.

First, he affirmed the unity of humanity because God is the Creator, sustainer, and Father of all humankind. Consequently, racism is not only foolish but evil, as it violates the creative purposes of God. Second, Paul acknowledged the diversity of ethnic cultures. Despite the fact that God made all nations from one man, "he determined the times set for them and the exact places where they should live" (v. 26). Scripture acknowledges that cultures enrich the total picture of human life, so Christians may affirm both the unity of humankind and the diversity of ethnic existence. Third, although Paul accepted the richness of the various cultures, he did not carry this over into the realm of religion. He did not accept the idolatry on which they were based because God does not tolerate any rivals to his Son Jesus Christ, the only Savior and Judge of humankind. Finally, the apostle declared the importance of the church, which would be a new and reconciled community to which all may belong (v. 34). As Paul declared in Galatians 3:28 and Colossians 3:11, in Christ "there is neither Jew nor Greek, slave nor free." They are one in Him.

John R. W. Stott eloquently sums up the thrust of Paul's address to the Athenians:

> Because of the unity of humankind we demand equal rights and equal respect for racial minorities. Because of the diversity of ethnic groups we renounce cultural imperialism and seek to preserve all those riches of inter-racial culture which are compatible with Christ's lordship.

> Because of the finality of Christ, we affirm that religious freedom includes the right to propagate the gospel. Because of the glory of the church, we must seek to rid ourselves of any lingering racism and strive to make it a model of harmony between races, in which the multiracial dream comes true.[3]

The Environmental Challenge

Perhaps the most serious challenge facing the church of the twenty-first century will be that of preserving the earth. The extent of environmental destruction is alarming, as indicated by such recent disasters as the leak of poisonous gas from a chemical plant at Bhopal, India, in 1984 that killed more than 2,000 people and injured in excess of 200,000 more, the Chernobyl nuclear power plant accident in the Ukraine in 1986 whose lethal effects will not be fully known for decades, the Exxon Valdez oil spill in Alaska in 1989, and the even larger oil spill in 1992 off the Shetland Islands. Such alarming events as the destruction of the Amazon rain forest, the steady elimination of the forests in northern India, the southward advance of the Sahara desert, the acid rain crisis in Europe and North America, depletion of the ozone layer, and the elimination of innumerable species of animals and plants have made the public aware of the need for environmental responsibility.

Unfortunately, secular ecologists accuse the church of being a principal source of the problem because of the statement in Genesis 1:26, 28 that humankind should "subdue" and have "dominion" over the earth and all the life that is in it. Some even say that Christians bear a huge burden of guilt for the exploitation of the environment, and they call for a pantheistic religion joining humans and nature together.

Christians must respond to these charges by showing that Genesis 1 and 2 balance each other. God delegated the dominion to humans, but they were responsible to Him and were to cooperate with the forces of nature. The principle that God owns and supervises the earth is affirmed repeatedly in Scripture: "The earth is the Lord's" (Ps. 24:1), "every animal of the forest is mine, and the cattle on a thousand hills" (Ps. 50:10), and He feeds the birds, makes the lilies grow, and clothes the grass of the fields (Matt. 6:26, 28, 30). This requires conservation of the earth's resources, including the wise use and recycling of manufactured products. The church must promote awareness of environmental responsibility if it is to maintain credibility in today's world.

WOMEN IN MINISTRY?

Few matters in the last decades of the twentieth century have been more divisive, both in Protestant and Catholic circles, than the issue of whether women may be admitted to the ordained clergy. On one side are those who believe that the mission of Christ's church is damaged when half of its members are denied the chance to use their God-given gifts. On the other are those who are equally convinced that the male ministry was instituted by Jesus Himself when He called twelve men as His apostles. Both the traditionalists and the egalitarians appeal to Holy Scripture and to the historical development of the church to support their positions on the role of women in ministry. Each accuses the other of bringing his or her own preconceived views to the Bible and selecting those passages that reinforce the given stance on the matter.

In the nineteenth century, several Protestant groups permitted the participation of women in the public ministry. Among the better-known examples were the American Methodist Phoebe Palmer, Catherine Booth of the Salvation Army, and Hannah Whitall Smith, who helped begin the Keswick movement. In the United States most of the holiness and Pentecostal bodies utilized women ministers and evangelists from their earliest day, but only toward the middle of the twentieth century did the mainline denominations begin in earnest to ordain women clergy. However, at the parish level there was considerable resistance until recently. Now Protestant seminary enrollments are nearly one-third female.

The Swedish Lutherans began ordaining women in 1958, and the Germans followed a few years later. The first German woman bishop was elevated in 1992. The Reformed Church and the Church of Scotland accepted women ministers in the 1960s, and the Baptists and Methodists in Britain and Germany more recently. American evangelicals by and large have resisted the trend, but some evangelicals have argued for women's ordination.

The most serious tensions have been in the Anglican and Roman Catholic churches. In the 1970s both the Canadian Anglican and American Episcopalian churches began the ordination of women, and in 1991 the New Zealand church named a woman as bishop. But the Anglican churches in Britain and Australia were torn by deep dissension. Their decisions in 1992 to allow women priests threatened to split the church in both countries and seriously endangered the efforts of Anglican ecumenists to establish closer ties with Rome. Pope John Paul II adopted a consistently uncompromising stance on female ordination, even though a strong feminist movement within the Catholic church was pressing for this. The Eastern Orthodox churches were even firmer in their rejection of women priests.

It seems clear that this issue will continue to trouble the various Christian communions of the world for years, and even decades, to come. Many devout Christians, multitudes of women among them, cling fervently to the old ways when all that is hallowed seems to be eroding. That is why conservative churches that defiantly oppose women's ordination are still thriving. In order to succeed in the long run, the new Christian feminism will have to demonstrate that gender equality enhances the church's spiritual and moral strength.

THE RESURGENCE OF NON-CHRISTIAN RELIGIONS

One of the consequences of the end of the imperial era has been the resurgence of the non-Christian religions. The twentieth century opened with the triumphalist dream of Christianity conquering the world and is ending with non-Christian faiths on the offensive in many places. From a Christian perspective, even more ominous is the form this counterattack is taking, which is a militant traditionalism. In fact, a major research project initiated in the early nineties at the University of Chicago has attempted to assess the dimensions and long-term impact of this traditionalist resurgence in the various religions of the world, and its findings have been frightening.

Hinduism, the oldest and most complex challenge to Christianity, claims 751 million adherents, mainly in India, or 13 percent of the world's population. Buddhism, its outgrowth, swept through Asia in the third century B.C., then stagnated. But with the post–World War II collapse of colonialism it has experienced a revival. Buddhists number about 334 million, or 6 percent of the world's people, and it predominates throughout East Asia, except in China. Islam is the faith most like Christianity in that it claims to be a universal and, at the same time, the only true religion. With its fervent missionary zeal, Islam is the world's fastest growing religion and claims one billion adherents from Morocco to the Philippines, or 18 percent of the world's population. An additional 12 percent of the world identifies with a variety of other belief systems, including Shinto, Jainism, Sikhism, Judaism, and African tribal religions.

This revival of other faiths has taken place both in missionary endeavors and through political establishment of a state religion, such as in Pakistan, Iran, and Malaysia. Adherents to these faiths maintain that theirs are more relevant to the needs of the people. Such religions present themselves as a way of life that is synonymous with culture. Christianity, on the other hand, is seen as alien and culturally distant. Reaching the followers of the non-Christian faiths is a monumental task facing the church.

In the areas where Communism once held sway is an enormous spiritual vacuum where both Christianity and its competitors are seeking to fill the void. However, the secularized West is rapidly becoming a mission field in its own right. Hybrid Eastern religions compete with numerous other "new religions" for the allegiance of people who have no other god but materialism, and this too is a missionary challenge to the church.

TOWARD THE FUTURE

The preceding list of problems is by no means exhaustive. Others that could be mentioned include the computer age, totalistic claims of some state leaders, the impact of communications technology, alienation in the modern world, family issues (such as divorce, spouse and child abuse, neglect of the elderly, sexual freedom, abortion, homosexuality, and euthanasia), drug and alcohol misuse, illiteracy and ignorance, human rights, employment and work, and industrial relations. Just to think about the multiplicity of challenges confronting the church could lead one to despair. However, the Christian must never waver in his or her belief that God's sovereign power is at work in the world.

Should developments continue as they are now, it is quite possible that sometime in the future the church may be forced to return to an existence somewhat like that which prevailed before the time of the Emperor Constantine. Instead of pretending to be coextensive with the world, it will have to function as the church of a minority and accept a position of conscious antagonism to the world. Whatever the future may hold, Jesus' parting words to His disciples are reassuring:

> I have told you these things, so that in me you may have peace. In this world you will have trouble. But take heart! I have overcome the world. (John 16:33)

NOTES

Chapter 2

1. Tacitus, *Annals* 15.44.
2. Eusebius, *Ecclesiastical History* 8.2.4–5.
3. Origen, *Homilies on Leviticus* 9.1.3.
4. Hippolytus, *Refutation of All Heresies* 9.12.21–22.
5. Minucius Felix, *Octavius* 8.4
6. Ibid., 9.4
7. Ibid., 31.7–8.
8. Tertullian, *Apology* 37.4.
9. Lactantius, *On the Death of the Persecutors* 44.5.

Chapter 3

1. Clement, *Stromateis* 6.8.
2. Tertullian, *On the Flesh of Christ* 5.4.

Chapter 4

1. On Christian legends about Julian, see Robert Browing, *The Emperor Julian* (Berkeley, Calif.: Univ. of California, 1976), 225–58.
2. Hippolytus, *The Apostolic Tradition* 2.20.7–21.1.

Chapter 5

1. Bede, *A History of the English Church* 2.13.
2. Cited from a contemporary source by J. Brondsted, *The Vikings* (London: Penguin, 1965), 58.

Chapter 6

1. Alcuin, letter to Meginfried (796).
2. Einhard, *Life of Charlemagne* 28.
3. Capitulary (820) of Louis the Pious from *Capitularia Requm Francorum* 1, 298.
4. Innocent III, letter to Acerbus (1198).

Chapter 8

1. Theodore the Studite, *First Refutation of the Iconoclasts* 2.
2. John J. Norwich, *Byzantium: the Apogee* (New York: Knopf, 1992), 321.
3. T. Fitzgerald, "Toward the Reestablishment of Full Communion: The Orthodox-Orthodox Oriental Dialogue," *Greek Orthodox Theological Review* 36 (1991), 169–82; cf. also "Joint-Commision of the Theological Dialogue between the Orthodox Church and the Oriental Orthodox Churches," idem., 183–88.

Chapter 9

1. A. G. Dickens, *The English Reformation* (University Park, Pa.: Pennsylvania State Univ., 1991), 46–60.
2. Matthew Spinka, *Advocates of Reform from Wyclif to Erasmus*. Library of Christian Classics (Philadephia: Westminster, 1953), 15:337.

Chapter 10

1. Roland H. Bainton, *Here I Stand: A Life of Martin Luther* (Nashville: Abingdon-Cokesbury, 1950), 65.
2. Ibid., 185.
3. Ibid.

Chapter 11

1. Clyde L. Manschreck, *A History of Christianity in the World* (Englewood Cliffs, N.J.: Prentice-Hall, 1985), 206.

Chapter 12

1. Lewis Hanke, ed., *Tears of the Indians by Bartholomé de las Casas* (Williamstown, Mass.: John Lilburne, 1970), xiii.
2. Charles R. Boxer, *The Portuguese Seaborne Empire, 1415–1825* (New York: Knopf, 1975), 228.

Chapter 13

1. Paul Althaus, *The Theology of Martin Luther* (Philadelphia: Fortress, 1966), 274–86.
2. Paul Hazard, *The European Mind: The Critical Years (1680–1715)* (New Haven, Conn.: Yale Univ., 1953), 198–216.

Chapter 14

1. Robert J. Nelson, *Pascal: Adversary and Advocate* (Cambridge, Mass.: Harvard Univ., 1981), 115–209. See also Alexander Sedgwick, *Jansenism in Seventeenth-Century France* (Charlottesville, Va: Univ. of Virginia, 1977).
2. Blaise Pascal, *Pensées*, Fragments 432, 380.
3. F. Ernest Stoeffler, *The Rise of Evangelical Pietism* (Leiden, the Netherlands: Brill, 1971), 228–48.

Chapter 15

1. John Dillenberger, *Protestant Thought and Natural Science* (London: Collins, 1961), 37; *Luther's Works*, ed. Theodore G. Tappert (Philadelphia: Fortress, 1967), 54:359.
2. R. R. Palmer, *A History of the Modern World*, 7th ed. (New York: McGraw-Hill, 1992), 299.
3. *The Complete Works of Benjamin Franklin*, ed. John Bigelow (New York: Putnam's, 1888), 10:194–95.

Chapter 17

1. Alexis de Tocqueville, *The Old Regime and the French Revolution* (Garden City, N.Y.: Doubleday, 1955), 6.
2. Paul Johnson, *A History of Christianity* (New York: Atheneum, 1970), 360.
3. Alec R. Vidler, *The Church in an Age of Revolution* (New York: Penguin, 1961), 19.
4. R. I. Wilberforce and Samuel Wilberforce, *The Life of William Wilberforce* (1838), 1:149, quoted in John Pollock, *Wilberforce* (New York: St. Martin's, 1977), 69.
5. David W. Bebbington, *Evangelicalism in Modern Britain* (London: Unwin Hyman, 1989), 52.

Chapter 18

1. T. A. Burkill, *The Evolution of Christian Thought* (Ithaca, N.Y.: Cornell Univ., 1971), 382–98.
2. Fritz Fischer, "Der deutsche Protestantismus und die Politik im 19. Jahrhundert," *Historische Zeitschrift* 171 (1951), 480–83.
3. "Tübingen School," in *Evangelical Dictionary of Theology*, ed. Walter A. Elwell (Grand Rapids: Baker, 1984), 1114–15.
4. Alexis de Tocqueville, *Democracy in America* (New York: Schocken, 1961), 1:359–60.

Chapter 19

1. Edwin Hodder, *The Life and Works of the Seventh Earl of Shaftesbury* (London: Cassell, 1887), 1:146.
2. John C. Cort, *Christian Socialism* (Maryknoll, N.Y.: Orbis, 1988), 156.
3. Shailer Matthews, "The Social Gospel," in *A Dictionary of Religion and Ethics* (New York: Macmillan, 1921), 416–17.
4. W. B. Riley, *The Menace of Modernism* (New York: Christian Alliance, 1917), 337.

Chapter 20

1. Brian Stanley, *The Bible and the Flag: Protestant Missions and British Imperialism in the Nineteenth and Twentieth Centuries* (Leicester, England: Apollos, 1990), 160–62.

2. Lamin Sanneh, *Translating the Message: The Missionary Impact on Culture* (New York: Orbis, 1989), 3.
3. Stephen Neill, *A History of Christian Missions* (New York: Penguin, 1964), 278.
4. Patricia R. Hill, *The World Their Household: The American Woman's Foreign Mission Movement and Cultural Transformation, 1870–1920* (Ann Arbor, Mich.: Univ. of Michigan, 1985), 3.

Chapter 21

1. Dmitrij Tschizewskij, *Russian Intellectual History* (Ann Arbor, Mich.: Univ. of Michigan, 1978), 194–97.
2. Ibid., 221–26.
3. Sydney E. Ahlstrom, *A Religious History of the American People* (New Haven, Conn.: Yale Univ., 1972), 1021.
4. "Julius Wellhausen," in *The Oxford Dictionary of the Christian Church*, ed. F. L. Cross (New York: Oxford Univ., 1958), 1444.
5. "Theological Liberalism," in *Evangelical Dictionary of Theology*, ed. Walter A. Elwell (Grand Rapids: Baker, 1984), 631–32; William R. Hutchison, *The Modernist Impulse in American Protestantism* (New York: Oxford Univ., 1976), 2–6.

Chapter 22

1. See the discussion in Richard V. Pierard and Robert D. Linder, *Civil Religion and the Presidency* (Grand Rapids: Zondervan, 1988), 153–58.
2. *Hitler's Secret Conversations 1941–1944* (New York: New American Library, 1961), 34, 330.

Chapter 23

1. Joel A. Carpenter and Wilbert R. Shenk, eds., *Earthen Vessels: American Evangelicals and Foreign Missions, 1880–1980* (Grand Rapids: Eerdmans, 1990), 335–42.

Epilogue

1. J. D. Douglas, ed., *Proclaim Christ Until He Comes* (Minneapolis: World Wide, 1989), 20–21.
2. This was adopted at the 1968 assembly of the World Council of Churches. See *Dictionary of the Ecumenical Movement*, ed. Geoffrey Wainwright, et al. (Grand Rapids: Eerdmans, 1991), 841.
3. John Stott, *Decisive Issues Facing Christians Today* (Tarrytown, N.Y.: Revell, 1990), 225–26.

BIBLIOGRAPHY

ENCYCLOPEDIAS AND REFERENCE WORKS

Anderson, Gerald, et al., eds. *Concise Dictionary of the Christian World Mission*. Nashville: Abingdon, 1971.

Atiya, Aziz S., ed. *The Coptic Encyclopedia*. 8 vols. New York: Macmillan, 1991.

Barrett, David B., ed. *World Christian Encyclopedia: A Comparative Survey of Churches and Religions in the Modern World, A.D. 1900 to 2000*. New York: Oxford Univ., 1982.

Bodensieck, Julius, ed. *The Encyclopedia of the Lutheran Church*. 3 vols. Minneapolis: Augsburg, 1965.

Bowden, Henry W., ed. *Dictionary of American Religious Biography*. Westport, Conn.: Greenwood, 1977.

Brauer, Jerald C., ed. *The Westminster Dictionary of Church History*. Philadelphia: Westminster, 1971.

Burgess, Stanley M., and Gary M. McGee, eds. *Dictionary of Pentecostal and Charismatic Movements*. Grand Rapids: Zondervan, 1988.

Chadwick, Henry, and G. R. Evans. *Atlas of the Christian Church*. New York: Facts on File, 1987.

Cross, F. L., and Elizabeth A. Livingstone, eds. *The Oxford Dictionary of the Christian Church*. New York: Oxford Univ., 1978.

Curtis, Kenneth A., ed. *Dates with Destiny: The 100 Most Important Dates in Church History*. Tarrytown, N.Y.: Revell, 1991.

Douglas, J. D., ed. *The New International Dictionary of the Christian Church*. Grand Rapids: Zondervan, 1978.

———. *New 20th-Century Encyclopedia of Religious Knowledge*. Grand Rapids: Baker, 1991.

———, ed. *Who's Who in Church History*. Wheaton, Ill.: Tyndale, 1992.

Dowley, Tim, ed. *The History of Christianity: A Lion Handbook*. Oxford, England: Lion Publishing, 1990.

Durnbaugh, Donald F., ed. *The Brethren Encyclopedia*. 3 vols. Philadelphia: The Brethren Encyclopedia, 1983,

Eliade, Mircea, ed. *The Encyclopedia of Religions*. 16 vols. New York: Macmillan, 1986.

Elwell, Walter A., ed. *Evangelical Dictionary of Theology*. Grand Rapids: Baker, 1984.

Encyclopedia of Southern Baptists. 4 vols. Nashville: Broadman, 1958–82.

Ferguson, Everett, ed. *Encyclopedia of Early Christianity*. New York: Garland, 1990.

Ferguson, Sinclair B., and David F. Wright, eds. *New Dictionary of Theology*. Leicester, England: Inter-Varsity, 1988.

Harmon, Nolan B., ed. *Encyclopedia of World Methodism*. 2 vols. Nashville: United Methodist, 1974.

Hill, Samuel S., ed. *Encyclopedia of Religion in the South*. Macon, Ga.: Mercer Univ., 1984.

Keeley, Robin, ed. *Christianity in Today's World*. Grand Rapids: Eerdmans, 1985.

Langer, William L. *An Encyclopedia of World History*. Boston: Houghton Mifflin, 1972.

Lewis, Donald M., ed. *The Blackwell Dictionary of Evangelical Biography 1730–1860.* Oxford, England: Basil Blackwell, 1994.

Littell, Franklin H., ed. *The Macmillan Atlas History of Christianity*. New York: Macmillan, 1976.

Lyon, H. R., ed. *The Middle Ages: A Concise Encyclopedia*. London: Thames & Hudson, 1989.

McKim, Donald K., ed. *Encyclopedia of the Reformed Faith*. Louisville: Westminster/John Knox, 1992.

Melton, J. Gordon, ed. *The Encyclopedia of American Religions*. Detroit: Gale Research, 1989.

The Mennonite Encyclopedia. 4 vols. Scottdale, Pa.: Mennonite, 1955–59.

Moyer, Elgin, and Earle E. Cairns, eds. *The Wycliffe Biographical Dictionary of the Church*. Chicago: Moody, 1982.

New Catholic Encyclopedia. 18 vols. New York: McGraw-Hill, 1967, 1989.

Piepkorn, Arthur C. *Profiles in Belief: The Religious Bodies of the United States and Canada*. 4 vols. New York: Harper & Row, 1977–79.

Reid, Daniel C., ed. *Dictionary of Christianity in America*. Downers Grove, Ill.: InterVarsity, 1990.

Steeves, Paul D., ed. *Modern Encyclopedia of Religions in Russia and the Soviet Union*. 4 vols. (30 projected). Gulf Breeze, Fla.: Academic International, 1989– .

Strayer, Joseph R., ed. *Dictionary of the Middle Ages*. 13 vols. New York: Scribner's, 1982.

Wainwright, Geoffrey, et al., eds. *Dictionary of the Ecumenical Movement*. Grand Rapids: Eerdmans, 1991.

Walton, Robert C., comp. *Chronological and Background Charts of Church History*. Grand Rapids: Zondervan, 1986.

Woodbridge, John D., ed. *Great Leaders of the Christian Church*. Chicago: Moody, 1988.

__________. *More Than Conquerors: Portraits of Believers from All Walks of Life*. Chicago: Moody, 1992.

GENERAL WORKS AND SERIES

Aland, Kurt. *A History of Christianity.* 2 vols. Philadelphia: Fortress, 1985–86,

Austin, Bill R. *Austin's Topical History of Christianity.* Wheaton, Ill.: Tyndale, 1983.

Bainton, Roland H. *Christendom: A Short History of Christianity and Its Impact on Western Civilization*. 2 vols. New York: Harper & Row, 1970,

__________. *Christian Attitudes toward War and Peace: A Historical Survey and Critical Reevaluation.* Nashville: Abingdon, 1979.

__________. *The Church of Our Fathers.* New York: Macmillan, 1978.

Baker, Robert A. *A Summary of Christian History*. Nashville: Broadman, 1991.

Bebbington, David. *Patterns in History: A Christian Perspective on Historical Thought.* Grand Rapids: Baker, 1990.

Bouyer, Louis, et. al. *A History of Christian Spirituality.* 3 vols. New York: Winston, 1963–69.

Brown, Colin. *Christianity and Western Thought: A History of Philosophers, Ideas and Movements.* Downers Grove, Ill.: InterVarsity, 1990.

Brown, Harold O. J. *Heresies: The Image of Christ in the Mirror of Heresy and Orthodoxy from the Apostles to the Present.* Garden City, N.Y.: Doubleday, 1984.

Bruce, F. F., ed. *The Advance of Christianity Through the Centuries*. London: Paternoster; and Grand Rapids: Eerdmans.

1. Bruce, F. F. *The Spreading Flame: The Rise and Progress of Christianity from Its First Beginnings to the Conversion of the English*. 1958.
2. Wood, A. Skevington. *The Inextinguishable Blaze: Spiritual Renewal and Advance in the 18th Century*. 1960.
3. Walker, G. M. S. *The Growing Storm: Sketches of Church History from A.D. 600 to A.D. 1350*. 1961.
4. Douglas, J. D. *Light in the North: The Story of the Scottish Covenanters*. 1964.
5. Orr, J. Edwin. *The Light of the Nations: 19th Century Revivals*. 1965.
6. Parker, G. H. W. *The Morning Star: Two Centuries of Violence, from Wycliffe to Luther*. 1965.
7. Atkinson, James. *The Great Light: Luther and the Reformation*. 1968.

Butterfield, Herbert. *Christianity and History.* London: G. Bell, 1949.

Cairns, Earle E. *Christianity Through the Centuries.* Grand Rapids: Zondervan, 1981.

Cambridge History of the Bible. 3 vols. Cambridge, England: Cambridge Univ., 1963–70.

Chadwick, Owen, gen. ed. *The Penguin* [formerly Pelican] *History of the Church*. London and New York: Allen Lane/The Penguin.

1. Vidler, Alec R. *The Church in an Age of Revolution*. 1961.
2. Cragg, Gerald R. *The Church and the Age of Reason, 1648–1789*. 1962.
3. Chadwick, Owen. *The Reformation*. 1964.
4. Neill, Stephen. *A History of Christian Missions*. 1964.
5. Chadwick, Henry. *The Early Church*. 1967.
6. Southern R. W. *Western Society and the Church in the Middle Ages*. 1970.
7. Chadwick, Owen. *The Christian Church in the Cold War*. 1992.

Clebsch, William A. *Christianity in European History*. New York: Oxford Univ., 1979.

Clouse, Robert G., and Richard V. Pierard. *Streams of Civilization: Modern World to the Nuclear Age.* Milford, Mich.: Mott Media, 1980.

Coomby, Jean. *How to Read Church History.* 2 vols. New York: Crossroad, 1985–89.

Cowart, John W. *People Whose Faith Got Them into Trouble: Stories of Costly Discipleship.* Downers Grove, Ill.: InterVarsity, 1990.

Daniélou, Jean, and Henri-Iréné Marrou. *The Christian Centuries: A New History of the Catholic Church.* Mahwah, N.J.: Paulist, 1964.

Dawson, Christopher. *The Dynamics of World History.* New York: Sheed & Ward, 1956.

Dekar, Paul, and Joseph D. Ban, eds. *In the Great Tradition.* Valley Forge, Pa.: Judson, 1982.

Drummond, Richard H. *A History of Christianity in Japan.* Grand Rapids: Eerdmans, 1971.

Dussel, Enrique. *A History of the Church in Latin America: Colonialism to Liberation.* Grand Rapids: Eerdmans, 1981.

Dwyer, John C. *Church History: Twenty Centuries of Catholic Christianity.* Mahwah, N.J.: Paulist, 1985.

The Evangelicals: The Story of a Great Christian Movement. Grand Rapids: Baker, 1989.

Frankforter, A. Daniel. *A History of the Christian Movement: The Development of Christian Institutions.* Chicago: Nelson Hall, 1978.

Frend, W. H. C. *The Rise of Christianity.* Philadelphia: Fortress, 1984.

Gonzalez, Justo L. *A History of Christian Thought.* 3 vols. Nashville: Abingdon, 1988.

__________. *The Story of Christianity.* San Francisco: Harper & Row, 1984.

Harnack, Adolf von. *History of Dogma.* 7 vols. Gloucester, Mass.: Peter Smith, 1976.

Hastings, Adrian. *A History of African Christianity.* Cambridge, England: Cambridge Univ., 1979.

Heritage of Freedom. Oxford, England: Lion, 1984.

Jedin, Hubert, and John P. Dolan, eds. *History of the Church.* 10 vols. New York: Crossroad, 1980–81.

Johnson, Paul. *A History of Christianity.* New York: Atheneum, 1976.

Kane, J. Herbert. *A Global View of Christian Missions from Pentecost to the Present.* Grand Rapids: Baker, 1971.

Latourette, Kenneth Scott. *Christianity in a Revolutionary Age: A History of Christianity in the 19th and 20th Centuries.* 5 vols. Grand Rapids: Zondervan, 1969.

__________. *A History of Christianity.* 2 vols. New York: Harper & Row, 1975.

__________. *A History of the Expansion of Christianity.* 7 vols. Grand Rapids: Zondervan, 1970.

Leonard, Bill J. *The Word of God Across the Ages.* Nashville: Broadman, 1980.

Manschreck, Clyde L. *A History of Christianity in the World.* Englewood Cliffs, N.J.: Prentice-Hall, 1985.

Marsden, George, and Frank Roberts. *A Christian View of History.* Grand Rapids: Eerdmans, 1975.

Marty, Martin E. *Short History of Christianity.* Minneapolis: Augsburg, 1980.

McBeth, H. Leon. *The Baptist Heritage: Four Centuries of Baptist Witness.* Nashville: Broadman, 1987

McGinn, Bernard, and John Meyendorff, eds. *Christian Spirituality from the Apostolic Fathers to the Twelfth Century.* New York: Crossroad, 1985.

McIntire, C. T., ed. *God, History, and Historians: Modern Christian Views of History.* New York: Oxford Univ., 1977.

McManners, John, ed. *Oxford Illustrated History of Christianity.* New York: Oxford Univ., 1990.

Meyendorff, John. *The Orthodox Church: Its Past and Its Role in the World Today.* Crestwood, N.Y.: St. Vladimir's Seminary, 1962.

Meyer, Carl S. *The Church—From Pentecost to the Present.* Chicago: Moody, 1969.

Mirgeler, Arthur. *Mutations of Western Christianity.* South Bend, Ind.: Univ. of Notre Dame, 1968.

Moffett, Samuel Hugh. *A History of Christianity in Asia.* 2 vols. San Francisco: HarperCollins, 1992–.

Montgomery, John W. *History and Christianity.* Minneapolis: Bethany House, 1986.

Neill, Stephen. *A History of Christianity in India.* Cambridge, England: Cambridge Univ., 1985, 2 vols.

Newsom, Carroll V. *The Roots of Christianity.* Englewood Cliffs, N.J.: Prentice-Hall, 1979.

Nichols, James Hastings. *History of Christianity, 1650–1950: Secularization of the West.* New York: Ronald, 1956.

Niebuhr, H. Richard, and Daniel D. Williams, eds. *The Ministry in Historical Perspective.* New York: Harper & Row, 1956.

Niebuhr, Reinhold. *Faith and History: A Comparison of Medieval and Modern Views of History.* New York: Scribner's, 1949.

Pelikan, Jaroslav. *The Christian Tradition: A History of the Development of Doctrine.* 5 vols. Chicago: Univ. of Chicago.

1. *The Emergence of the Catholic Tradition (100–600)*. 1971.

2. *The Spirit of Eastern Christendom (600–1700)*. 1974.

3. *The Growth of Medieval Theology (600–1300)*. 1978.

4. *Reformation of Church and Dogma (1300–1700)*. 1983.

5. *Christian Doctrine and Modern Cultures (since 1700)*. 1989.

Roberts, Frank C. *To All Generations: A Study of Christian History.* Grand Rapids: CRC Publications, 1980.

Schaff, Philip. *History of the Christian Church.* 8 vols. New York: Scribner's, 1909–15. Reprint. Grand Rapids: Eerdmans, 1960.

Shelley, Bruce L. *Church History in Plain Language.* Waco, Tex.: Word, 1982.

Suelflow, Roy. *Christian Churches in Recent Times: Christianity in the 19th and 20th Centuries.* St. Louis: Concordia, 1980.

Tewinkel, Joseph M. *Built on the Cornerstone.* Harrisburg, Pa.: Christian Pubns., 1980.

Treadgold, Donald. *A History of Christianity.* Belmont, Mass.: Nordland, 1979.

Tucker, Ruth A. *From Jerusalem to Irian Jaya: A Biographical History of Christian Missions.* Grand Rapids, Zondervan, 1983.

__________, and Walter Liefeld. *Daughters of the Church: Women and Ministry from New Testament Times to the Present.* Grand Rapids: Zondervan, 1987.

Underhill, Evelyn. *The Mystics of the Church.* Ridgefield, Conn.: Morehouse, 1988.

Van Leeuwen, Arend T. *Christianity in World History: The Meeting of the Faiths of East and West.* New York: Scribner's, 1964.

Vos, Howard F. *Beginnings in Church History.* Chicago: Moody, 1977.

Walker, Williston. *A History of the Christian Church.* New York: Scribner's, 1985.

Walsh, Michael. *An Illustrated History of the Popes: St. Peter to John Paul II.* New York: St. Martin's, 1980.

Warner, Marina. *Alone of All Her Sex: The Myth and the Cult of the Virgin Mary.* New York: Random House, 1983.

Wells, Ronald A. *History Through the Eyes of Faith.* San Francisco: Harper & Row, 1989.

SOURCE COLLECTIONS

Bettenson, Henry, ed. *Documents of the Christian Church.* New York: Oxford Univ., 1970.

Classics of Western Spirituality. 60 vols. (others planned). Mahwah, N.J.: Paulist, 1974–.

The Fathers of the Church. Washington, D. C.: Catholic Univ. of America, 1947– . Projected to reach 100 volumes.

Gorman, G. E., and Lyn Gorman. *Theological and Religious Reference Materials: Systematic Theology and Church History.* Westport, Conn.: Greenwood, 1985.

Leith, John H., ed. *Creeds of the Churches: A Reader in Christian Doctrine from the Bible to the Present.* Atlanta: John Knox, 1982.

The Library of Christian Classics. 16 vols. Philadelphia: Westminster, 1950– .

Manschreck, Clyde D., ed. *Readings in the History of Christianity*, vol. 2. Grand Rapids: Baker, 1981.

Petry, Ray C., ed. *Readings in the History of Christianity,* vol. 1. Grand Rapids: Baker, 1981.

Schaff, Philip. *The Creeds of Christendom.* 3 vols. Grand Rapids: Baker, 1975.

Stevenson, James, ed. *A New Eusebius.* London: SPCK, 1987.

__________. *Creeds, Councils, and Controversies.* London: SPCK, 1966.

GENERAL WORKS IN AMERICAN CHRISTIANITY

Ahlstrom, Sydney E. *A Religious History of the American People.* New Haven, Conn.: Yale Univ., 1972.

Askew, Thomas A., and Peter W. Spellman. *The Churches and the American Experience: Ideals and Institutions.* Grand Rapids: Baker, 1984.

Dolan, Jay P. *The American Catholic Experience.* Garden City, N.Y.: Doubleday, 1985.

Ellingsen, Mark. *The Evangelical Movement: Growth, Impact, Controversy, Dialog.* Minneapolis: Augsburg, 1988.

Gaustad, Edwin S., ed. *A Documentary History of Religion in America.* 2 vols. Grand Rapids: Eerdmans, 1982–83.

____________. *Historical Atlas of Religion in America.* New York: Harper & Row, 1976.

____________. *A Religious History of America.* New York: Harper & Row, 1966.

Grant, John Webster. *The Church in the Canadian Era.* Burlington, Ontario: Welch, 1988.

Handy, Robert T. *A Christian America: Protestant Hopes and Historical Realities.* New York: Oxford Univ., 1984.

____________. *A History of the Churches in the United States and Canada.* New York: Oxford Univ., 1977.

Hudson, Winthrop S. *Religion in America.* New York: Macmillan, 1987.

Lincoln, C. Eric, and Lawrence H. Mamiya. *The Black Church in the African-American Experience*. Durham, N.C.: Duke Univ., 1990.

Lundin, Roger, and Mark A. Noll, eds. *Voices from the Hearts: Four Centuries of American Piety.* Grand Rapids: Eerdmans, 1987.

Marsden, George M. *Religion and American Culture.* San Diego: Harcourt, Brace, Jovanovich, 1990.

Marty, Martin E. *Pilgrims in Their Own Land: Five Hundred Years of Religion in America.* Boston: Little, Brown, 1984.

____________. *Righteous Empire: Protestantism in the United States.* New York: Scribner's, 1986.

Mead, Sidney E. *The Lively Experiment: The Shaping of Christianity in America.* New York: Harper & Row, 1963.

Mulder, John M., and John F. Wilson. *Religion in American History: Interpretive Essays.* Englewood Cliffs, N.J.: Prentice-Hall, 1978.

Noll, Mark A. *A History of Christianity in the United States and Canada.* Grand Rapids: Eerdmans, 1992.

____________, ed. *Religion and American Politics from the Colonial Period to the 1980s.* New York: Oxford Univ., 1990.

Pierard, Richard V., and Robert D. Linder. *Civil Religion and the Presidency.* Grand Rapids: Zondervan, 1988.

Rawlyk, George A., ed. *The Canadian Protestant Experience, 1760–1990.* Burlington, Ontario: Welch, 1990.

Reuther, Rosemary Radford, and Rosemary Skinner Keller, eds. *Women and Religion in America.* 3 vols. San Francisco: Harper & Row, 1981–86.

Sweet, Leonard I., ed. *The Evangelical Tradition in America.* Macon, Ga.: Mercer Univ., 1984.

Wells, David F., et al., eds. *Eerdmans' Handbook to Christianity in America.* Grand Rapids: Eerdmans, 1983.

____________., and John D. Woodbridge, eds. *The Evangelicals: What They Believe, Who They Are, Where They Are Changing.* Grand Rapids, Baker, 1977.

Woodbridge, John D., Mark A. Noll, and Nathan O. Hatch. *The Gospel in America: Themes in the Story of America's Evangelicals.* Grand Rapids: Zondervan, 1979.

Wells, Ronald A., ed. *The Wars of America: Christian Views.* Macon, Ga.: Mercer Univ., 1991.

Wilson, John F., and Donald L. Drakeman, eds. *Church and State in American History.* Boston: Beacon, 1987.

BIBLIOGRAPHY FOR SPECIFIC CHAPTERS

Chapter 1: The Founding of the Church

Balsdon, John P. V. D. *Rome: The Story of an Empire.* New York: McGraw Hill, 1970.

Bammel, Ernst, and.C. F. D. Moule, eds. *Jesus and the Politics of His Day.* Cambridge, England: Cambridge Univ., 1985.

Bruce, F. F. *Jesus and Christian Origins Outside the New Testament.* Grand Rapids: Eerdmans, 1977.

___________. *New Testament History.* Garden City, N.Y.: Doubleday, 1972.

___________. *Paul: Apostle of the Heart See Free.* Grand Rapids: Eerdmans, 1977.

Conzelmann, Hans. *Gentiles—Jews—Christians: Polemics and Apolegetics in the Graeco-Roman Era.* Minneapolis: Fortress, 1992.

Ferguson, Everett. *Backgrounds of Early Christianity.* Grand Rapids: Eerdmans, 1987.

Ferguson, John. *The Religions of the Roman Empire.* Ithaca, N.Y.: Cornell Univ., 1970.

France, R. T. *The Evidence for Jesus.* Downers Grove, Ill.: InterVarsity, 1986.

Gasque, W. Ward. *A History of the Interpretation of the Acts of the Apostles.* Peabody, Mass.: Hendrickson, 1989.

Godwin, Joscelyn. *Mystery Religions in the Ancient World.* San Francisco: Harper & Row, 1981.

Grant, F. C. *Roman Hellenism and the New Testament.* New York: Scribner's, 1962.

Guttmann, Julius, ed. *Ancient Synagogues: The State of Research.* Chico, Calif.: Scholars Press, 1981.

Jeremias, Joachim. *Jerusalem in the Time of Jesus.* Philadelphia: Fortress, 1969.

Macmullen, Ramsay. *Paganism in the Roman Empire.* New Haven, Conn.: Yale Univ., 1981.

Meeks, Wayne A. *The Fist Urban Civilization: The Social World of the Apostle Paul.* New Haven, Conn.: Yale Univ., 1983.

Meyers, E. M., and J. F. Strange. *Archaeology, the Rabbis, and Early Christianity.* Nashville: Abingdon, 1981.

Nash, Ronald H. *Christianity and the Hellenistic World.* Grand Rapids: Zondervan, 1984.

Rhoads, David M. *Israel in Revolution 6–74 C.E.* Philadelphia: Fortress, 1976.

Sherwin-White, Adrian N. *Roman Society and Roman Law in the New Testament.* Oxford, England: Clarendon, 1963.

Taylor, Lily R. *The Divinity of the Roman Emperor.* New York: Garland, 1979.

Tcherikover, Avigdor. *Hellenistic Civilization and the Jews.* New York: Atheneum, 1970.

Theissen, Gerd. *Social Reality and the Early Christians: Theology, Ethics, and the World of the New Testament.* Minneapolis: Fortress, 1992.

Vermes, Geza. *The Dead Sea Scrolls: Qumran in Perspective.* Philadelphia: Fortress, 1981.

___________. *Jesus the Jew.* Philadelphia: Fortress, 1981.

Yamauchi, Edwin. *Harper's World of the First Christians.* San Francisco: Harper & Row, 1981.

__________. *New Testament Cities in Western Asia Minor.* Grand Rapids: Baker, 1980.

__________. *The Stones and the Scriptures.* Grand Rapids: Baker, 1987.

Chapter 2: The Church in the Roman State

Bauer, Walter. *Orthodoxy and Heresy in Earliest Christianity.* Philadelphia: Fortress, 1971.

Benko, Stephen. *Pagan Rome and the Early Christians.* Bloomington, Ind.: Indiana Univ., 1984.

__________, and John J. O'Rourke, eds. *The Catacombs and the Colosseum.* Valley Forge, Pa.: Judson, 1971.

Brown, Peter. *The World of Late Antiquity from Marcus Aurelius to Mohammed.* London: Thames & Hudson, 1971.

Cadoux, C. John. *The Early Christian Attitude to War: A Contribution to the History of Christian Ethics.* New York: Harper & Row, 1982.

Dodds, Eric R. *Pagan and Christian in an Age of Anxiety.* New York: Norton, 1970.

Dörries, Hermann. *Constantine the Great.* New York: Harper & Row, 1972.

Ferguson, Everett. *Backgrounds of Early Christianity.* Grand Rapids: Eerdmans, 1987.

Fox, Robin Lane. *Pagans and Christians.* New York: Knopf, 1987.

Frend, W. H. C. *Martyrdom and Persecution in the Early Church.* Oxford, England: Basil Blackwell, 1965.

Grant, Robert M. *Augustus to Constantine: The Thrust of the Christian Movement into the Roman World.* New York: Harper & Row, 1970.

__________. *Greek Apologists of the Second Century.* London: SCM, 1988.

__________. *Jesus after the Gospels.* Philadelphia: Westminster, 1990.

Harnack, Adolf von. *The Expansion of the Church in the First Three Centuries.* 2 vols. New York: Ayer, 1972 reprint.

Hinson, E. Glenn. *The Evangelization of the Roman Empire: Identity and Adaptability.* Macon, Ga.: Mercer Univ., 1981.

Jeffers, James S. *Conflict at Rome: Social Order and Hierarchy in Early Christianity.* Minneapolis: Fortress, 1992.

Macmullen, Ramsay. *Christianizing the Roman Empire A.D. 100–400.* New Haven, Conn.: Yale Univ., 1984.

Mattingly, Harold. *Christianity in the Roman Empire.* New York: Norton, 1967.

Momigliano, Arnaldo. *The Conflict Between Paganism and Christianity in the Fourth Century.* Oxford, England: Clarendon, 1963.

__________. *On Pagans, Jews, and Christians.* Middletown, Conn.: Wesleyan Univ., 1987.

Pagels, Elaine H. *The Gnostic Gospels.* New York: Random House, 1979.

Rudolph, Kurt. *Gnosis: The Nature and History of Gnosticism.* San Francisco: Harper & Row, 1983.

Schowalter, Daniel N. *The Emperor and the Gods: Images from the Time of Trajan.* Minneapolis: Fortress, 1992.

Simon, Marcel. *Verus Israel: A Study of the Relations Between Christians and Jews in the Roman Empire (135–425).* Oxford, England: Oxford Univ., 1986.

Snyder, Graydon F. *Ante Pacem: Archaeological Evidence of Church Life before Constantine.* Macon, Ga.: Mercer Univ., 1985.

Stevenson, James. *The Catacombs: Life and Death in Early Christianity.* Nashville: Nelson, 1978.

Walsh, Michael. *The Triuimph of the Meek: Why Early Christians Succeeded.* San Francisco: Harper & Row, 1986.

Wilken, Robert L. *The Christians as the Romans Saw Them.* New Haven, Conn.: Yale Univ., 1984.

Yamauchi, Edwin. *Pre-Christian Gnosticism.* Grand Rapids: Baker, 1983.

Chapter 3: Doctrinal Development in the Church

Barnes, Timothy D. *Tertullian: A Historical and Literary Study.* Oxford, England: Clarendon, 1985.

Battenhouse, Roy W. *A Companion to the Study of Augustine.* Grand Rapids: Baker, 1979.

Bray, Gerald. *Holiness and the Will: Prespectives on the Theology of Tertullian.* Atlanta: John Knox, 1980.

Brown, Peter. *Augustine of Hippo.* Berkeley: Univ. of California, 1967.

____________. *The Body and Society.* New York: Columbia Univ., 1988.

Bruce, F. F. *The Canon of Scripture.* Downers Grove, Ill.: InterVarsity, 1988.

Campenhausen, Hans von. *The Fathers of the Latin Church.* London: A.& C. Black, 1964.

Chadwick, Owen. *Early Christian Thought and the Classical Tradition.* New York: Oxford Univ., 1966.

Clark, Elizabeth A. *Jerome, Chrysostom, and Friends.* New York: Edwin Mellen, 1979.

Cochrane, Charles N. *Christianity and Classical Culture.* New York: Oxford Univ., 1940.

Crouzel, Henri. *Origen.* San Francisco: Harper & Row, 1989.

Daniélou, Jean. *Gospel Message and Hellenistic Culture.* Philadelphia: Westminster, 1973.

____________. *A History of Christian Doctrine before Nicea.* 3 vols. Philadelphia: Westminster, 1973–77.

Forell, George W. F. *History of Christian Ethics.* Minneapolis: Augsburg, 1979.

Frend, W. H. C. *The Donatist Church.* Oxford, England: Clarendon, 1971.

____________. *The Rise of the Monophysite Movement.* Cambridge, England: Cambridge Univ., 1979.

Grant, Robert M. *The Early Christian Doctrine of God.* Charlottesville, Va.: Univ. of Virginia, 1966.

____________. *Eusebius as Church Historian.* New York: Oxford Univ., 1980.

Grillmeier, Alois. *Christ in Christian Tradition.* Atlanta: John Knox, 1975.

Jaeger, Werner W. *Early Christianity and Greek Paideia.* Cambridge, Mass.: Harvard Univ., 1962.

Kelly, J. N. D. *Early Christian Creeds.* London: Longman, 1972.

____________. *Early Christian Doctrines.* New York: Harper & Row, 1976.

____________. *Jerome: His Life, Writings and Controversies.* New York: Harper & Row, 1975.

Laeuchli, Samuel. *Power and Sexuality: The Emergence of Canon Law at the Synod of Elvira.* Philadelphia: Temple Univ., 1972.

Metzger, Bruce M. *The Canon of the New Testament.* Oxford, England: Clarendon, 1987.

Pagels, Elaine. *Adam, Eve, and the Serpent.* New York: Random House, 1988.

Pelikan, Jaroslav. *The Excellent Empire: The Fall of Rome and the Triumph of the Church.* San Francisco: Harper & Row, 1987.

Russell, Jeffrey B. *Satan: The Early Christian Tradition.* Ithaca, N.Y.: Cornell Univ., 1981.

Trigg, Joseph W. *Origen: The Bible and Philosophy in the Third-Century Church.* Atlanta: John Knox, 1983.

Chapter 4: The Church after Constantine

Barker, John W. *Justinian and the Later Roman Empire.* Madison, Wis.: Univ. of Wisconsin, 1966.

Barnes, Timothy D. *Constantine and Eusebius.* Cambridge, Mass.: Harvard Univ., 1981.

Bowersock, Glen W. *Julian the Apostate.* Cambridge, Mass.: Harvard Univ., 1978.

Brown, Peter. *The Cult of the Saints.* Chicago: Univ. of Chicago, 1981.

__________. *Society and the Holy in Late Antiquity.* London: Faber, 1982.

__________. *The World of Late Antiquity, AD 150–750.* New York: Harcourt, Brace, Jovanovich, 1971.

Browning, Robert. *The Emperor Julian.* Berkeley: Univ. of California, 1976.

Chitty, Derwas J. *The Desert a City.* Oxford, England: Blackwell, 1966.

Clark, Elizabeth A. *The Origenist Controversy: The Cultural Construction of an Early Christian Debate.* Princeton, N.J.: Princeton Univ., 1992.

Greenslade, Stanley L. *Church and State from Constantine to Theodosius.* London: SCM, 1954.

Herrin, Judith. *The Formation of Christendom.* Princeton, N.J.: Princeton Univ., 1987.

Johanny, Raymond, et. al. *The Eucharist of the Early Christians.* New York: Pueblo, 1978.

Jones, Aarnold H. M. *Constantine and the Conversion of Europe.* Toronto: Univ. of Toronto, 1979.

Jungmann, Josef A. *The Early Liturgy to the Time of Gregory the Great.* South Bend, Ind.: Univ. of Notre Dame, 1959.

Kavanaugh, Aidan. *Confirmation: Origins and Reform.* New York: Pueblo, 1988.

King, Noel Q. *The Emperor Theodosius and the Establishment of Christianity.* Philadelphia: Westminster, 1960.

Knowles, David. *Christian Monasticism.* New York: McGraw-Hill, 1969.

Krautheimer, Richard. *Early Christian and Byzantine Architecture.* Baltimore: Penguin, 1975.

__________. *Rome, Profile of a City, 312–1308.* Princeton N.J.: Princeton Univ., 1980.

Laistner, Max L. W. *Christianity and Pagan Culture in the Later Roman Empire.* Ithaca, N.Y.: Cornell Univ., 1967.

Matthews, John F. *Western Aristocracies and the Imperial Court, A.D. 364–425.* Oxford, England: Clarendon, 1975.

Pearson, Birger A., and James E. Goehring, eds. *The Roots of Egyptian Christianity.* Philadelphia: Fortress, 1986.

Rousseau, Philip. *Ascetics, Authority, and the Church in the Age of Jerome and Cassian.* Oxford, England: Oxford Univ., 1978.

__________. *Pachomius: The Making of a Community in Fourth-Century Egypt.* Berkeley: Univ. of California, 1985.

Talley, Thomas J. *The Origins of the Liturgical Year.* New York: Pueblo, 1986.

Telfer, William. *The Office of a Bishop.* London: Darton, Longman & Todd, 1962.

Temkin, Owsei. *Hippocrates in a World of Pagans and Christians.* Baltimore: Johns Hopkins Univ., 1991.

Workman, Herbert B. *The Evolution of the Monastic Ideal.* Boston: Beacon, 1962.

Chapter 5: European Expansion of the Church

Beck, Hans J. *The Pastoral Care of Souls in South-East France during the Sixth Century.* Rome: Universitatis Gregorianae, 1950.

Brondsted, Johannes. *The Vikings.* New York: Penguin, 1965.

Casey, P. J., ed. *The End of Roman Britain.* Oxford, England: B.A.R., 1979.

Chadwick, Nora K. *The Age of the Saints in the Early Celtic Church.* Oxford, England: Oxford Univ., 1961.

__________, et. al., eds. *Studies in the Early British Church.* Cambridge, England: Cambridge Univ., 1958.

Clarke, H. B., and Mary Brennan, eds. *Columbanus and Merovingian Monasticism.* Oxford, England: B.A.R., 1981.

Collins, Roger. *Early Medieval Spain: Unity in Diversity, 400–1000.* New York: St. Martin's 1983.

Deanesly, Margaret. *Augustine of Canterbury.* Stanford, Calif.: Stanford Univ., 1964.

__________. *The Pre-Conquest Church in England.* New York: Oxford Univ., 1961.

Donner, Fred. *The Early Islamic Conquests.* Princeton, N.J.: Princeton Univ., 1988.

Farrugia, Edward G., et. al., eds. *Christianity among the Slavs: The Heritage of Saints Cyril and Methodius.* Rome: Pont. Institutum Studiorum Orientalium, 1988.

Fry, C. George, and James R. King, eds. *Islam: Survey of the Muslim Faith.* Grand Rapids: Baker, 1980.

Gabrielli, Francesco. *Muhammmad and the Conquests of Islam.* New York: McGraw-Hill, 1968.

Hillgarth, J. N., ed. *Christianity and Paganism, 350–750: The Conversion of Western Europe.* Philadelphia: Univ. of Pennsylvania, 1986.

Hughes, Kathleen. *The Church in Early Irish Society.* Ithaca, N.Y.: Cornell Univ., 1966.

James, Edward. *The Franks.* Oxford, England: Basil Blackwell, 1991.

Kantor, Marvin. *The Origins of Christianity in Bohemia.* Evanston, Ill.: Northwestern Univ., 1990.

Lewis, Bernard. *The Arabs in History.* New York: Harper, 1960.

Macartney, Carlile A. *The Magyars in the Ninth Century.* Cambridge, England: Cambridge Univ., 1930.

Mackey, James P., ed. *An Introduction to Celtic Christianity.* Edinburgh, Scotland: T. & T. Clark, 1989.

MacManus, Francis. *Saint Columban.* Dublin, Ireland: Clonmore & Reynolds, 1963.

McNeill, John T. *The Celtic Churches: A History, A.D. 200 to 1200.* Chicago: Univ. of Chicago, 1974.

Musset, Lucien. *The Germanic Invasions.* State College, Pa.: Pennsylvania State Univ., 1975.

Newby, Gordon D. *The Making of the Last Prophet: A Reconstruction of the Earliest Biography of Muhammad.* Columbia, S.C.: Univ. of South Carolina, 1989.

Reuter, Timothy, ed. *The Greatest Englishman: Essays on St. Boniface and the Church at Crediton.* Greenwood, S.C.: Attic, 1980.

Robinson, Neal. *Christ in Islam and Christianity.* Albany, N.Y.: State Univ. of New York, 1991.

Simpson, William D. *The Historical Saint Columba.* Edinburgh, Scotland: Oliver & Boyd, 1963.

Thomas, Charles. *Christianity in Roman Britain to A.D. 500.* Berkeley: Univ. of California, 1981.

Wallace-Hadrill, John M. *The Frankish Church.* Oxford, England: Clarendon, 1983.

Watt, William M. *The Influence of Islam on Medieval Europe.* Edinburgh, Scotland: Edinburgh Univ., 1972.

Chapter 6: The Church under Papal Monarchy

Abulafia, David. *Frederick II: A Medieval Emperor.* London: Allen Lane/ Penguin, 1988.

Barraclough, Geoffrey. *The Crucible of Europe: The Ninth and Tenth Centuries in European History.* Berkeley: Univ. of California, 1976.

____________. *The Medieval Papacy.* New York: Norton, 1979.

Barstow, Anne L. *Married Priests and the Reforming Papacy: The Eleventh Century Debates.* New York: Edwin Mellen, 1982.

Blumenthal, Uta. *The Investiture Controversy.* Philadelphia: Univ. of Pennsylvania, 1988.

Boussard, Jacques. *The Civilization of Charlemagne.* New York: McGraw-Hill, 1968.

Bullough, Donald A. *The Age of Charlemagne.* New York: Putnam, 1965.

Cantor, Norman F. *Church, Kingship, and Lay Investiture in England, 1089–1135.* New York: Octagon, 1969.

Evans, G. R. *The Thought of Gregory the Great.* Cambridge, England: Cambridge Univ., 1986.

Jackson, Gabriel. *The Making of Medieval Spain.* New York: Harcourt, Brace, Jovanovich, 1972.

Kantorowicz, Ernst. *The King's Two Bodies.* Princeton, N.J.: Princeton Univ., 1957.

Kelly, J. N. D. *The Oxford Dictionary of Popes.* Oxford, England: Oxford Univ., 1988.

Langmuir, Gavin I. *Toward a Definition of Antisemitism.* Berkeley: Univ. of California, 1991.

Lynch, Joseph. *Simoniacal Entry into Religious Life from 1000 to 1260.* Columbus: Ohio State Univ., 1976.

Morris, Colin. *The Papal Monarchy: The Western Church from 1050 to 1250.* Oxford, England: Clarendon, 1988.

Nelson, Janet L. *Politics and Ritual in Early Medieval Europe.* Ronceverte, W.V.: Hambledon, 1986.

Noble, Thomas F. X. *The Republic of St. Peter: The Birth of the Papal State, 680–825.* Philadelphia: Univ. of Pennsylvania, 1984.

Pennington, Kenneth. *Pope and Bishops: The Papal Monarchy in the Twelfth and Thirteenth Centuries.* Philadelphia: Univ. of Pennsylvania, 1984.

Richards, Jeffrey. *Popes and the Papacy in the Early Middle Ages, 476–752.* Boston: Routledge & Kegan Paul, 1979.

Rich, Pierre. *Daily Life in the World of Charlemagne.* Philadelphia: Univ. of Pennsylvania, 1988.

Robinson, Ian S. *Authority and Resistance in the Investiture Contest: The Polemical Literature of the Late Eleventh Century.* New York: Holmes & Meier, 1978.

Runciman, Steven. *The Sicilian Vespers.* Cambridge, England: Cambridge Univ., 1958.

Straw, Carole. *Gregory the Great: Perfection in Imperfection.* Berkeley: Univ. of California, 1988.

Tellenbach, Gerd. *Church, State, and Christian Society at the Time of the Investiture Contest.* Oxford, England: Blackwell, 1940.

Tierney, Brian. *The Crisis of Church and State, 1050–1300.* Englewood Cliffs, N.J.: Prentice-Hall, 1964.

Trachtenberg, Joshua. *The Devil and the Jew: The Medieval Conception of the Jew and Its Relation to Modern Antisemitism.* New York: Harper, 1966.

Ullmann, Walter. *Growth of Papal Government in the Middle Ages.* London: Methuen, 1962.

Van Cleve, Thomas. *The Emperor Frederick II.* Oxford, England: Clarendon, 1972.

Vodola, Elisabeth. *Excommunication in the Middle Ages.* Berkeley: Univ. of California, 1986.

Chapter 7: The Medieval Church in the West

Cohn, Norman R. C. *Pursuit of the Millennium: Millenarians and Mystical Anarchists of the Middle Ages.* New York: Oxford Univ., 1970.

Deanesly, Margaret. *A History of the Medieval Church, 590–1500.* London: Methuen, 1969.

Elkins, Sharon K. *Holy Women of Twelfth-Century England.* Chapel Hill, N.C.: Univ. of North Carolina, 1988.

Evans, G. Rosemary. *Anselm and a New Generation.* Oxford, England: Oxford Univ., 1980.

__________. *The Mind of St. Bernard of Clairvaux.* Oxford, England: Oxford Univ., 1983.

Knowles, David. *The Evolution of Medieval Thought.* New York: Random House, 1964.

__________. *The Religious Orders in England.* 3 vols. Cambridge, England: Cambridge Univ., 1948–59.

Lambert, Malcolm. *Medieval Heresy: Popular Movements from Bogomil to Hus.* New York: Holmes & Meier, 1977.

Leff, Gordon. *Medieval Thought from Saint Augustine to Ockham.* New York: Humanities, 1978.

Lewis, Archibald R. *Nomads and Crusaders, A.D. 1000–1368.* Bloomington, Ind.: Indiana Univ., 1988.

Lewis, C. S. *The Discarded Image.* Cambridge, England: Cambridge Univ., 1964.

Mayer, Hans Eberhard. *The Crusade.* New York: Oxford Univ., 1988.

McGinn, Bernard. *Visions of the End: Apocalyptic Traditions in the Middle Ages.* New York: Columbia Univ., 1979.

Mollat, Michel. *The Poor in the Middle Ages.* Chicago: Univ. of Chicago, 1986.

Moore, R. I. *The Formation of a Persecuting Society: Power and Deviance in Western Europe, 950–1250.* Oxford, England: Basil Blackwell, 1987.

Mortimer, Robert C. *Western Canon Law.* Berkeley: Univ. of California, 1953.

Oakley, Francis. *The Western Church in the Later Middle Ages.* Ithaca, N.Y.: Cornell Univ., 1985.

Powell, James M. *Anatomy of a Crusade, 1213–1221.* Philadelphia: Univ. of Pennsylvania, 1986.

Queller, Donald E. *The Fourth Crusade.* Philadelphia: Univ. of Pennsylvania, 1977.

Rashdall, J. Hastings. *The Universities of Europe in the Middle Ages.* 3 vols. Oxford, England: Oxford Univ., 1936.

Runciman, Steven. *The Medieval Manichee: A Study of the Christian Dualist Heresy.* Cambridge, England: Cambridge Univ., 1947.

Russell, Jeffrey B. *Dissent and Reform in the Early Middle Ages.* New York: AMS, 1982.

__________. *A History of Medieval Christianity: Prophecy and Order.* New York: Crowell, 1968.

__________. *Lucifer: The Devil in the Middle Ages.* Ithaca, N.Y.: Cornell Univ. 1984.

__________. *Witchcraft in the Middle Ages.* Ithaca, N.Y.: Cornell Univ., 1984.

Setton, Kenneth M., ed. *A History of the Crusades.* 6 vols. Madison, Wis.: Univ. of Wisconsin. 1969–89.

Smalley, Beryl. *Study of the Bible in the Middle Ages.* South Bend, Ind.: Univ. of Notre Dame, 1964.

Southern, Richard W. *The Making of the Middle Ages.* New Haven, Conn: Yale Univ., 1953.

Weinberg, Juius R. *A Short History of Medieval Philosophy.* Princeton, N.J.: Princeton Univ., 1964.

Weinstein, Donald, and Rudolph Bell. *Saints and Society: The Two Worlds of Western Christendom, 1000 to 1700.* Chicago: Univ. of Chicago, 1986.

Chapter 8: The Medieval Church in the East

Atiya, Aziz S. *History of Eastern Christianity.* South Bend, Ind.: Univ. of Notre Dame, 1968.

Barnard, Leslie W. *The Graeco-Roman and Oriental Background of the Iconoclastic Controversy.* Leiden, The Netherlands: E. J. Brill, 1974.

Benz, Ernst. *The Eastern Orthodox Church.* Garden City, N.Y.: Doubleday, 1963.

Brown, Leslie W. *The Indian Christians of St. Thomas.* Cambridge, England: Cambridge Univ., 1982.

Charanis, Peter. *The Armenians in the Byzantine Empire.* Lisbon, Portugal: Livraria Bertrand, 1963.

Constantelos, Demetrius J. *Understanding the Greek Orthodox Church.* New York: Seabury, 1982.

Dawson, Christopher. *The Mongol Mission.* New York: Sheed & Ward, 1955.

Dvornik, Francis. *Byzantium and the Roman Primacy.* New York: Fordham Univ., 1979.

———. *The Slavs in European History and Civilization.* New Brunswick, N.J.: Rutgers Univ., 1979.

Fedotov, George P. *The Russian Religious Mind.* Cambridge, England: Cambridge Univ., 1966.

Galavaris, George. *The Icon in the Life of the Church: Doctrine, Liturgy, Devotion.* Leiden, The Netherlands: E. J. Brill, 1982.

Geanakoplos, Deno J. *Interaction of the "Sibling" Byzantine and Western Cultures in the Middle Ages and Italian Renaissance (330–1600).* New Haven, Conn.: Yale Univ., 1976.

Gerostergios, Asterios. *Justinian the Great: Emperor and Saint.* Belmont, Mass.: Institute for Byzantine and Modern Greek Studies, 1982.

Hussey, Joan M. *The Byzantine World.* New York: Harper & Row, 1961.

———. *The Orthodox Church in the Byzantine Empire.* Oxford, England: Clarendon, 1986.

Kidd, B.J. *The Churches of Eastern Christendom.* London: Faith, 1928.

Magoulias, Harry J. *Byzantine Christianity: Emperor, Church, and the West.* Detroit: Wayne State Univ., 1982.

McCullough, W. Stewart. *A Short History of Syriac Christianity to the Rise of Islam.* Chico, Calif.: Scholars Press, 1982.

Mews, Stuart, ed. *Religion and National Identity.* Oxford, England: Basil Blackwell, 1982.

Meyendorff, John. *Byzantium and the Rise of Russia.* Cambridge, England: Cambridge Univ., 1981.

Nicol, Donald M. *Church and Society in the Last Centuries of Byzantium.* Cambridge, England: Cambridge Univ., 1979.

Ouspensky, Leonid, and Vladimir Lossky. *The Meaning of Icons.* Crestwood, N.Y.: St. Vladimir's, 1982.

Pearson, Birger A., and James E. Goerhing, *The Roots of Egyptian Christianity.* Philadelphia: Fortress, 1986.

Runciman, Steven. *The Byzantine Theocracy.* Cambridge, England: Cambridge Univ., 1977.

__________. *The Eastern Schism.* Oxford, England: Clarendon, 1955.

Strunk, W. Oliver. *Essays on Music in the Byzantine World.* New York: Norton, 1977.

Ullendorff, Edward. *The Ethiopians: An Introduction to Country and People*. Oxford, England: Oxford Univ., 1965.

Vernadsky, George. *Kievan Russia.* New Haven, Conn.: Yale Univ., 1973.

Ware, Timothy. *The Orthodox Church.* Baltimore: Penguin, 1963.

Waterfield, Robin E. *Christians in Persia*. New York: Barnes & Noble, 1973.

Whitting, Philip, ed. *Byzantium, An Introduction.* New York: St. Martin's, 1981.

Young, William. *Patriarch, Shah and Caliph*. Rawalpindi, Pakistan: Christian Study Centre, 1974.

Zernov, Nicolas. *Eastern Christendom.* New York: Putnam, 1961.

Chapter 9: The Medieval Church Declines

Aston, Margaret. *Lollards and Reformers: Images and Literacy in Late Medieval Religion.* London: Hambledon, 1984.

Bainton, Roland H. *Erasmus of Christendom.* New York: Scribner's, 1969.

Breen, Quirinus. *Christianity and Humanism.* Grand Rapids: Eerdmans, 1968.

Farthing, John L. *Thomas Aquinas and Gabriel Biel: Interpretations of St. Thomas Aquinas in German Nominalism on the Eve of the Reformation.* Durham, N.C.: Duke Univ., 1988.

Gilmore, Myron P. *The World of Humanism, 1453–1517.* Westport, Conn.: Greenwood, 1983.

Hay, Denys. *The Church in Italy in the Fifteenth Century.* Cambridge, England: Cambridge Univ.,1977.

Huizinga, Johan. *The Waning of the Middle Ages: A Study of the Forms of Life, Thought, and Art in France and the Netherlands in the XIVth and XVth Centuries*. New York: St. Martin's, 1985.

Kaminsky, Howard. *A History of the Hussite Revolution.* Berkeley: Univ. of California, 1967.

Kenny, Anthony. *Wyclif.* New York: Oxford Univ., 1985.

Knowles, David. *The English Mystical Tradition.* New York: Harper, 1961.

Kristeller, Paul O. *Renaissance Thought: The Classic, Scholastic, and Humanistic Strains.* New York: Harper, 1961.

Marius, Richard. *Thomas More: A Biography.* New York: Knopf, 1984.

McFarlane, Kenneth B. *John Wycliffe and the Beginnings of English Nonconformity.* London: English Universities, 1952.

McGrath, Alister E. *The Intellectual Origins of the European Reformation.* Oxford, England: Basil Blackwell, 1987.

Mollat, Guillaume. *The Popes at Avignon, 1305–1368.* New York: T. Nelson, 1963.

Mullett, Michael A. *Popular Culture and Popular Protest in Late Medieval and Early Modern Europe*. New York: Croom Helm, 1987.

Nauert, Charles G. *Agrippa and the Crisis of Renaissance Thought.* Urbana, Ill.: Univ. of Illinois, 1965.

Oberman, Heiko. *Forerunners of the Reformation: The Shape of Late Medieval Thought.* Philadelphia: Fortress, 1981.

__________. *The Harvest of Medieval Theology: Gabriel Biel and Late Medieval Nominalism.* Grand Rapids: Eerdmans, 1967.

Overfield, James H. *Humanism and Scholasticism in Late Medieval Germany.* Princeton, N.J.: Princeton Univ., 1984.

Ozment, Steven E. *The Age of Reform 1250–1550: An Intellectual and Religious History of Late Medieval and Early Reformation Europe.* New Haven, Conn.: Yale Univ., 1980.

Pius II. *Memoirs of a Renaissance Pope.* New York: Putnam, 1959.

Sabean, David W. *Power in the Blood: Popular Culture and Village Discourse in Early Modern Germany.* New York: Cambridge Univ., 1984.

Scribner, Robert W. *Popular Culture and Popular Movements in Reformation Germany.* Ronceverte, W.V.: Hambledon, 1987.

Spinka, Matthew. *John Hus: A Biography.* Princeton, N.J.: Princeton Univ., 1968.

__________. *John Hus' Concept of the Church.* Princeton, N.J.: Princeton Univ., 1966.

Spitz, Lewis W. *The Religious Renaissance of the German Humanists.* Cambridge, Mass.: Harvard Univ., 1963.

Vineis, Raymundus de. *The Life of Catherine of Siena.* Wilmington, Del.: Glazier, 1980.

Wilson, Katharina M., ed. *Women Writers of the Renaissance and Reformation.* Athens, Ga.: Univ. of Georgia, 1987.

Zeman, Jarold K. *The Anabaptists and the Czech Brethern in Moravia 1526–1628.* The Hague: Mouton, 1969.

Chapter 10: The Reformation Impacts the Church

Atkinson, James. *Martin Luther: Prophet to the Church Catholic.* Grand Rapids: Eerdmans, 1983.

Aveling, John C. H. *The Jesuits.* New York: Stein & Day, 1981.

Bainton, Roland H. *Here I Stand: A Life of Martin Luther.* Nashville: Abingdon, 1950.

__________. *Women of the Reformation.* 3 vols. Minneapolis: Augsburg, 1971–77.

Baker, J. Wayne. *Heinrich Bullinger and the Covenant: The Other Reformed Tradition.* Athens, Ohio: Ohio Univ., 1980.

Bouwsma, William J. *John Calvin: A Sixteenth Century Portrait.* New York: Oxford Univ., 1988.

Cameron, Euan. *The European Reformation.* New York: Oxford Univ., 1991.

Cowan, Ian B. *The Scottish Reformation: Church and Society in Sixteenth-Century Scotland.* New York: St. Martin's, 1982.

Eire, Carlos M. N. *War Against the Idols: The Reformation of Worship from Erasmus to Calvin.* New York: Cambridge Univ., 1986.

Elton, G. R. *Reform and Reformation: England 1509–1558.* Cambridge, Mass.: Harvard Univ., 1979.

Estep, William R. *The Anabaptist Story.* Grand Rapids: Eerdmans, 1975.

__________. *Renaissance and Reformation.* Grand Rapids: Eerdmans, 1986.

Friesen, Abraham. *Thomas Muentzer, a Destroyer of the Godless: The Making of a Sixteenth-Century Religious Revolutionary.* Berkeley: Univ. of California, 1990.

George, Timothy. *Theology of the Reformers.* Nashville: Broadman, 1988.

Harbison, E. Harris. *The Christian Scholar in the Age of Reformation.* New York: Scribner's, 1956.

Irwin, Joyce L., ed. *Womanhood in Radical Protestantism, 1525–1675.* New York: Edwin Mellen, 1979.

Ives, Eric W. *Anne Boleyn.* Oxford, England : Basil Blackwell, 1986.

Jordan, W. K. *Edward VI.* 2 vols. Cambridge, Mass.: Harvard Univ., 1968–70.

Kittelson, James M. *Luther the Reformer: The Story of the Man and His Career.* Minneapolis: Augsburg, 1986.

Knowles, David. *Bare Ruined Choirs: The Dissolution of the English Monasteries.* New York: Cambridge Univ., 1976.

Kyle, Richard G. *The Mind of John Knox.* Lawrence, Kans.: Coronado, 1984.

Lortz, Joseph. *The Reformation in Germany.* New York: Herder, 1968.

Marshall, Sherrin, ed. *Women in Reformation and Counter-Reformation Europe.* Bloomington, Ind.: Indiana Univ., 1989.

Mattingly, Garrett. *Catherine of Aragon.* Boston: Little, Brown, 1941.

McGoldrick, James E. *Luther's English Connection: The Reformation Thought of Robert Barnes and William Tyndale.* Milwaukee: Northwestern, 1979.

McGrath, Alister E. *A Life of John Calvin: A Study in the Shaping of Western Culture.* Oxford, England: Basil Blackwell, 1990.

__________. *Reformation Thought: An Introduction.* Oxford, England: Basil Blackwell, 1988.

Oberman, Heiko A. *Luther: Man Between God and the Devil.* New Haven, Conn.: Yale Univ., 1989.

__________. *The Roots of Anti-Semitism in the Age of Renaissance and Reformation.* Philadelphia: Fortress, 1984.

Olin, John C. *Catholic Reform: From Cardinal Ximenes to the Council of Trent.* New York: Fordham Univ., 1990.

Potter, G. R. *Zwingli.* Cambridge, England: Cambridge Univ., 1976.

Smith, Lacey Baldwin. *Henry VIII: The Mask of Royalty.* Boston: Houghton Mifflin, 1971.

Spitz, Lewis W. *The Protestant Reformation, 1517–1559.* New York: Harper & Row, 1985.

Strauss, Gerald. *Luther's House of Learning: Indoctrination of the Young in the German Reformation.* Baltimore: Johns Hopkins Univ., 1978.

Tavard, George H. *Holy Writ or Holy Church: The Crisis of the Protestant Reformation.* London: Burns & Oates, 1959.

Walton, Robert C. *Zwingli's Theocracy.* Toronto: Univ. of Toronto, 1967.

Weaver, J. Denny. *Becoming Anabaptist: The Origin and Significance of Sixteenth-Century Anabaptism.* Scottdale, Pa.: Herald, 1982.

Williams, George H. *The Radical Reformation.* Kirksville, Mo.: Sixteenth Century Journal, 1992.

Chapter 11: Religious Conflicts Plague Europe

Bangs, Carl. *Arminius: A Study in the Dutch Reformation.* Grand Rapids: Zondervan, 1985.

Bireley, Robert. *The Counter-Reformation Prince: Anti-Machiavellianism or Catholic Statecraft in Early Modern Europe.* Chapel Hill, N.C.: Univ. of North Carolina, 1990.

Buisseret, David. *Henry IV.* London: G. Allen & Unwin, 1984.

Collinson, Patrick. *The Religion of Protestants: The Church in English Society, 1559–1625.* New York: Oxford Univ., 1984.

__________. *The Birthpangs of Protestant England: Religious and Cultural Change in the Sixteenth and Seventeenth Centuries.* New York: St. Martin's, 1988.

Eisenstein, Elizabeth L. *The Printing Press as an Agent of Change.* 2 vols. New York: Cambridge Univ., 1979.

Elliott, John H. *The Count-Duke of Olivares: The Statesman in the Age of Decline.* New Haven, Conn.: Yale Univ., 1986.

____________. *Imperial Spain, 1469–1716.* New York: St. Martin's, 1964.

Geyl, Pieter. *The Revolt of the Netherlands, 1555–1609.* New York: Barnes & Noble, 1966.

Gray, Janet G. *The French Huguenots: Anatomy of Courage.* Grand Rapids: Baker, 1981.

Hibbert, Christopher. *The Virgin Queen: Elizabeth I, Genius of the Golden Age.* Reading, Mass.: Addison-Wesley, 1991.

Jones, Norman L. *Faith by Statute: Parliament and the Settlement of Religion, 1559.* Atlantic Highlands, N.J.: Humanities, 1982.

Kamen, Henry. *Inquisition and Society in Spain in the Sixteenth and Seventeenth Centuries.* Bloomington, Ind.: Indiana Univ., 1985.

Kingdon, Robert M. *Geneva and the Consolidation of the French Protestant Movement.* Madison, Wis.: Univ. of Wisconsin, 1967.

____________. *Myths About the St. Bartholomew's Day Massacres, 1572–1576.* Cambridge, Mass.: Harvard Univ., 1988.

Kolb, Robert A. *Andreae and the Formula of Concord.* St. Louis: Concordia, 1977.

____________. *For All the Saints: Changing Perceptions of Martyrdom and Sainthood in the Lutheran Revolution.* Macon, Ga.: Mercer Univ., 1987.

Linder, Robert D. *The Political Ideas of Pierre Viret.* Geneva, Switzerland: Droz, 1964.

Mattingly, Garrett. *The Armada.* Boston: Houghton Mifflin, 1962.

McNeill, John T. *The History and Character of Calvinism.* Oxford, England: Oxford Univ., 1967.

Nugent, Donald. *Ecumenism in the Age of the Reformation: The Colloquy of Poissy.* Cambridge, Mass.: Harvard Univ., 1974.

O'Connell, Marvin R. *The Counter Reformation: 1559–1610.* New York: Harper, 1974.

Parker, Geoffrey. *The Dutch Revolt.* Ithaca, N.Y.: Cornell Univ., 1977.

____________. *Philip II.* Boston: Little, Brown, 1978.

____________. *The Thirty Years War.* Boston: Little, Brown, 1984.

Paul, Robert. *The Lord Protector.* Grand Rapids: Eerdmans, 1964.

Prestwich, Menna, ed. *International Calvinism, 1541–1715.* New York: Oxford Univ., 1985.

Reid, W. Stanford, ed. *John Calvin: His Influence in the Western World.* Grand Rapids: Zondervan, 1982.

Roberts, Michael. *Gustavus Adolphus: A History of Sweden, 1611–1632.* 3 vols. London: Longmans, 1953–58.

Rothrock, George A. *The Huguenots: A Biography of a Minority.* Chicago: Univ. of Chicago, 1979.

Russell, Conrad. *The Causes of the English Civil War.* New York: Oxford Univ., 1990

Solt, Leo F. *Church and State in Early Modern England, 1509–1640.* New York: Oxford Univ., 1990.

Tyacke, Nicholas. *Anti-Calvinists: The Rise of English Arminianism, c. 1590–1640.* New York: Oxford Univ., 1987.

Visser, Derk. *Zacharius Ursinus: The Reluctant Reformer—His Life and Times.* New York: United Church, 1983.

Walzer, Michael. *The Revolution of the Saints: A Study in the Origins of Radical Politics.* Cambridge, Mass.: Harvard Univ., 1982.

Weir, David A. *The Origins of the Federal Theology in Sixteenth-Century Reformation Thought.* New York: Oxford Univ., 1990.

Chapter 12: The Church Expands Beyond Europe

Boxer, Charles R. *The Christian Century in Japan, 1549–1650.* Berkeley: Univ. of California, 1967.

__________. *The Church Militant and Iberian Expansion, 1440–1770.* Baltimore: Johns Hopkins Univ., 1978.

__________. *The Dutch Seaborne Empire, 1600–1800.* New York: Knopf, 1965.

__________. *The Portuguese Seaborne Empire, 1415–1825.* New York: Knopf, 1975.

Carr, Francis. *Ivan the Terrible.* Totowa, N.J.: Barnes & Noble, 1981.

Coles, Paul. *The Ottoman Impact on Europe, 1350–1699.* New York: Harcourt, Brace & World, 1968.

Cronin, Vincent. *A Pearl in India: The Life of Roberto de Nobili.* New York: Dutton, 1959.

Elison, George. *Deus Destroyed: The Image of Christianity in Early Modern Japan.* Cambridge, Mass.: Harvard Univ., 1988.

Elliott, J. H. *Spain and Its World, 1500–1700.* New Haven, Conn.: Yale Univ., 1989.

Friedman, Ellen G. *Spanish Captives in North Africa in the Early Modern Age.* Madison, Wis.: Univ. of Wisconsin, 1983.

Gray, Richard. *Black Christians and White Missionaries.* New Haven, Conn.: Yale Univ., 1991.

Goodpasture, H. McKennie. *Cross and Sword: An Eyewitness History of Christianity in Latin America.* Maryknoll, N.Y.: Orbis, 1989.

Hanke, Lewis. *Aristotle and the American Indians: A Study in Race Prejudice in the Modern World.* Bloomington, Ind. : Indiana Univ., 1970.

__________. *Bartolome de Las Casas: An Interpretation of His Life and Writings.* The Hague: M. Nijhoff, 1951.

__________. *The Spanish Struggle for Justice in the Conquest of America.* Philadelphia: Univ. of Pennsylvania, 1949.

Kennedy, John H. *Jesuit and Savage in New France.* New Haven, Conn.: Yale Univ., 1950.

Konrad, Herman W. *A Jesuit Hacienda in Colonial Mexico: Santa Lucia, 1576–1767.* Stanford, Calif.: Stanford Univ., 1980.

McAlister, Lyle N. *Spain and Portugal in the New World, 1492–1700.* Minneapolis: Univ. of Minnesota, 1984.

MacLachlan, Colin M. *Spain's Empire in the New World.* Berkeley: Univ. of California, 1988.

Pullapilly, Cyriac K., and Edwin J. Van Kley. *Asia and the West: Encounters and Exchanges From the Age of Explorations.* South Bend, Ind.: Cross Roads, 1986.

Rhodes of Viet Nam. *Travels and Missions of Father Alexander de Rhodes in China and Other Kingdoms of the Orient.* Westminster, Md.: Newman, 1966.

Ricard, Robert. *The Spiritual Conquest of Mexico: An Essay on the Apostolate and the Evangelizing Methods of the Mendicant Orders in New Spain, 1523–1572.* Berkeley: Univ. of California, 1982.

Ronan, Charles E., and Bonnie B. C. Oh, eds. *East Meets West: The Jesuits in China, 1582–1773.* Chicago: Loyola Univ., 1988.

Schurhammer, Georg. *Francis Xavier: His Life, His Times.* 4 vols. Rome: Jesuit Historical Institute, 1973–82.

Schwaller, John F. *The Church and Clergy in Sixteenth-Century Mexico.* Albuquerque: Univ. of New Mexico, 1987.

__________. *Origins of Church Wealth in Mexico: Ecclesiastical Revenues and Church Finances, 1523–1600.* Albuquerque: Univ. of New Mexico, 1985.

Song, Raphael H. S. *The Sacred Congregation for the Propagation of the Faith.* Washington, D.C.: Catholic Univ. of America, 1961.

Spence, Jonathan D. *The Memory Palace of Matteo Ricci.* New York: Viking, 1984.

Van Oss, Adriaan C. *Catholic Colonialism, A Parish History of Guatemala, 1524–1821.* Cambridge, England: Cambridge Univ., 1986.

Vigil, Ralph H. *Alonso de Zorita: Royal Judge and Christian Humanist, 1512–1585.* Norman, Okla.: Univ. of Oklahoma, 1987.

Wright, Anthony D. *The Counter-Reformation: Catholic Europe and the Non-Christian World.* New York: St. Martin's, 1982.

Chapter 13: Orthodoxy and Absolutism Shape the Church

Armstrong, Brian G. *Calvinism and the Amyraut Heresy: Protestant Scholasticism and Humanism in Seventeenth-Century France.* Madison, Wis.: Univ. of Wisconsin, 1969.

Bak, Janos M., and Gerhardt Benecke, eds. *Religion and Rural Revolt.* Dover, N.H.: Manchester Univ., 1984.

Barnes, Robin Bruce. *Prophecy and Gnosis: Apocalypticism in the Wake of the Lutheran Reformation.* Stanford, Calif.: Stanford Univ., 1988.

Bergin, Joseph. *The Rise of Richelieu.* New Haven, Conn.: Yale Univ., 1985.

Bonney, Richard. *Society and Government in France Under Richelieu and Mazarin, 1624–61.* New York: St. Martin's, 1988.

Clouse, Robert G. *The Church in the Age of Orthodoxy and the Enlightenment: Consolidation and Challenge 1600–1700.* St. Louis: Concordia, 1980.

Dukes, Paul. *The Making of Russian Absolutism, 1613–1801.* London: Longman, 1982.

Elert, Werner. *The Structure of Lutheranism: The Theology and Philosophy of Life of Lutheranism, 16th and 17th Centuries.* St. Louis: Concordia, 1974.

Evans, Robert J. W. *The Making of the Habsburg Monarchy, 1550–1770: An Interpretation.* Oxford, England: Clarendon, 1979.

Friedrich, Carl J. *The Age of the Baroque, 1610–1660.* New York: Harper & Row, 1962.

Fulbrook, Mary. *Piety and Politics: Religion and the Rise of Absolutism in England, Württemberg and Prussia.* Cambridge, England: Cambridge Univ., 1983.

Hazard, Paul. *The European Mind: The Critical Years (1680–1715).* New Haven, Conn.: Yale Univ., 1953.

Hazelton, Roger. *Blaise Pascal: The Genius of His Thought.* Philadelphia: Westminster, 1974.

Henshall, Nicholas. *The Myth of Absolutism: Change and Continuity in Early Modern European Monarchy.* London: Longman, 1992.

Knecht, Robert J. *Richelieu.* London: Longman, 1991.

Knox, Ronald A. *Enthusiasm: A Chapter in the History of Religion With Special Reference to the Seventeenth and Eighteenth Centuries.* New York: Oxford Univ., 1950.

Leites, Edmond, ed. *Conscience and Casuistry in Early Modern Europe.* New York: Cambridge Univ., 1988.

Lindberg, Carter. *The Third Reformation? Charismatic Movements and the Lutheran Tradition.* Macon, Ga.: Mercer Univ., 1983.

Lupinin, Nickolas. *Religious Revolt in the XVIIth Century: The Schism of the Russian Church.* Princeton, N.J.: Kingston, 1984.

Nelson, Robert J. *Pascal, Adversary and Advocate.* Cambridge, Mass.: Harvard Univ., 1981.

Parker, Geoffrey, and Lesley M. Smith, eds. *The General Crisis of the Seventeenth Century.* London: Routledge and Kegan Paul, 1978.

Perry, Elizabeth I. *From Theology to History: French Religious Controversy and the Revocation of the Edict of Nantes.* The Hague: M. Nijhoff, 1973.

Preus, Robert D. *The Theology of Post-Reformation Lutheranism.* 2 vols. St. Louis: Concordia, 1970–71.

Reynolds, Ernest E. *Bossuet.* Garden City, N.Y.: Doubleday, 1963.

Riašanovsky, Nicholas. *The Image of Peter the Great in Russian History and Thought.* New York: Oxford Univ., 1985.

Scharlemann, R. P. *Thomas Aquinas and John Gerhard.* New Haven, Conn.: Yale Univ., 1964.

Sedgwick, Alexander. *Jansenism in Seventeenth-Century France: Voices From the Wilderness.* Charlottesville, Va.: Univ. of Virginia, 1977.

Tapie, Victor L. *The Age of Grandeur: Baroque Art and Architecture.* New York: Praeger, 1966.

Vierhaus, Rudolf. *Germany in the Age of Absolutism.* Cambridge, England: Cambridge Univ., 1988.

Wolf, John. *Louis XIV.* New York: Norton, 1968.

Chapter 14: Puritanism and Pietism Arouse the Church

Barbour, Hugh. *The Quakers in Puritan England.* New Haven, Conn.: Yale Univ., 1964.

Beeke, Joel R. *Assurance of Faith: Calvin, English Puritanism, and the Dutch Second Reformation.* New York: Peter Lang, 1991.

Braithwaite, W. C. *The Beginnings of Quakerism.* Cambridge, England: Cambridge Univ., 1961.

Breward, Ian, ed. *The Work of William Perkins.* Abingdon, England: Sutton Courtenay, 1970.

Brown, Dale. *Understanding Pietism.* Grand Rapids: Eerdmans, 1978.

Collinson, Patrick. *The Religion of Protestants: The Church in English Society.* Oxford, England: Clarendon, 1982.

Doran, Susan, and Christopher Durston. *Prince, Pastors, and People: The Church and Religion in England 1529–1689*. New York: Routledge, 1991.

Durnbaugh, Donald F. *The Believers' Church.* Scottdale, Pa.: Herald, 1985.

Garrett, Clarke. *Spirit Possession and Popular Religion: From the Camisards to the Shakers.* Baltimore: Johns Hopkins Univ., 1987.

George, Timothy. *John Robinson and the English Separatist Tradition.* Macon, Ga.: Mercer Univ., 1982.

Gwyn, Douglas. *Apocalypse of the Word: The Life and Message of George Fox (1624–1691).* Richmond, Ind.: Friends United, 1986.

Hambrick-Stowe, Charles E. *The Practice of Piety: Puritan Devotional Disciplines in Seventeenth-Century New England.* Chapel Hill, N.C.: Univ. of North Carolina, 1982.

Lake, Peter. *Anglicans and Puritans: Presbyterianism and English Conformist Thought from Whitgift to Hooker.* London: Unwin Hyman, 1988.

———. *Moderate Puritans and the Elizabethan Church.* New York: Cambridge Univ., 1982.

Lovelace, Richard F. *The American Pietism of Cotton Mather: Origins of American Evangelicalism.* Grand Rapids: Eerdmans, 1979.

Miller, Perry. *The New England Mind: From Colony to Province.* Cambridge, Mass.: Harvard Univ., 1953.

Morgan, John. *Godly Learning: Puritan Attitudes Towards Learning and Education.* New York: Cambridge Univ., 1966.

Muller, Richard A. *Christ and the Decree: Christology and Predestination in Reformed Theology from Calvin to Perkins.* Grand Rapids: Baker, 1988.

Olsen, V. Norskov. *John Foxe and the Elizabethan Church.* Berkeley: Univ. of California, 1973

Petersen, Rodney L. *Preaching in the Last Days.* New York: Oxford Univ., 1993.

Ryken, Leland. *Worldly Saints: The Puritans As They Really Were.* Grand Rapids: Zondervan, 1986.

Sommerville, C. John. *The Secularization of Early Modern England: From Religious Culture to Religious Faith.* New York: Oxford Univ., 1992.

Sprunger, Keith L. *The Learned Doctor William Ames: Dutch Backgrounds of English and American Puritanism.* Urbana, Ill.: Univ. of Illinois, 1972.

Stein, K. James. *Philipp Jakob Spener: Pietist Patriarch.* Chicago: Covenant, 1986.

Stoeffler, F. Ernest. *German Pietism During the Eighteenth Century.* Leiden, The Netherlands: E. J. Brill, 1973.

____________. *The Rise of Evangelical Pietism.* Leiden, The Netherlands: E. J. Brill, 1965.

Toon, Peter, ed. *The Correspondence of John Owen (1616–1683): With an Account of His Life and Work.* Cambridge, England: James Clarke, 1970.

Trevor-Roper, Hugh. *Catholics, Anglicans, and Puritans: Seventeenth Century Essays.* Chicago: Univ. of Chicago, 1988.

Wakefield, Gordon. *Bunyan the Christian.* San Francisco: Harper, 1992.

Weinlick, John R. *Count Zinzendorf.* Nashville: Abingdon, 1956.

Chapter 15: Science and Enlightenment Challenge the Church

Aaron, Richard I. *John Locke.* Oxford, England: Clarendon, 1971.

Alexander, John T. *Catherine the Great: Life and Legend.* New York: Oxford Univ., 1989.

Anderson, Matthew S. *Historians and Eighteenth-Century Europe, 1715–1789.* New York: Oxford Univ., 1979.

Baumer, Franklin L. *Religion and the Rise of Skepticism.* New York: Harcourt, Brace & World, 1969.

Brantley, Richard E. *Locke, Wesley, and the Method of English Romanticism.* Gainesville, Fla.: Univ. of Florida, 1984.

Butterfield, Herbert. *The Origins of Modern Science.* New York: Macmillan, 1951.

Cragg, Gerald R. *From Puritanism to the Age of Reason: A Study of Changes in Religious Thought Within the Church of England 1660 to 1700.* Cambridge, England: Cambridge Univ., 1966.

____________. *Reason and Authority in the Eighteenth Century.* Cambridge, England: Cambridge Univ., 1964.

Easlea, Brian. *Witch Hunting, Magic and the New Philosophy: An Introduction to Debates of the Scientific Revolution, 1450–1750.* Atlantic Highlands, N.J.: Humanities, 1980.

Gagliardo, John G. *Germany Under the Old Regime.* London: Longman, 1991.

Gay, Peter. *The Enlightenment: An Interpretation.* 2 vols. New York: Norton, 1977.

Jacob, Margaret C. *The Cultural Meaning of the Scientific Revolution.* Philadephia: Temple Univ., 1988.

____________. *Living the Enlightenment: Freemasonry and Politics in Eighteenth-Century Europe.* New York: Oxford Univ., 1991.

———. *The Radical Enlightenment: Pantheists, Freemasons, and Republicans.* Boston: Allen Unwin, 1981.

Larner, Christina. *Witchcraft and Religion: The Politics of Popular Belief.* New York: Oxford Univ., 1984.

Manuel, Frank E. *The Religion of Isaac Newton.* Oxford, England: Clarendon, 1974.

Martin, Ruth. *Witchcraft and the Inquisition in Venice, 1550–1650.* Oxford, England: Basil Blackwell, 1989.

May, Henry F. *The Divided Heart: Essays on Protestantism and the Enlightenment in America.* New York: Oxford Univ., 1991.

———. *The Enlightenment in America.* New York: Oxford Univ., 1976.

Midelfort, H. C. Erik. *Witch Hunting in Southwest Germany, 1562–1684: The Social and Intellectual Foundations.* Stanford, Calif.: Stanford Univ., 1972.

Reardon, Bernard M. G. *Kant as Philosophical Theologian.* Totowa, N.J.: Barnes & Noble, 1988.

Rockwood, Raymond O., ed. *Carl Becker's Heavenly City Revisited.* Ithaca, N.Y.: Cornell Univ., 1958.

Rupp, Gordon. *Religion in England, 1688–1781.* Oxford, England: Clarendon, 1987.

Scott, H. M. *Enlightened Absolutism: Reform and Reformers in Later Eighteenth Century Europe.* Ann Arbor, Mich.: Univ. of Michigan, 1980.

Sher, Richard B., and Jeffrey R. Smitten, eds. *Scotland and America in the Age of the Enlightenment.* Princeton, N.J.: Princeton Univ., 1990.

Smith, A. G. R. *Science and Society in the Sixteenth and Seventeenth Centuries.* New York: Harcourt, Brace, Jovanovich, 1972.

Stevenson, David. *The Origins of Freemasonry: Scotland's Century, 1590–1710.* New York: Cambridge Univ., 1988.

Stromberg, Roland. *Religious Liberalism in Eighteenth-Century England.* London: Oxford Univ., 1954.

Thomas, Keith. *Religion and the Decline of Magic.* New York: Scribner's, 1971.

Wade, Ira O. *The Structure and Form of the French Enlightenment.* 2 vols. Princeton, N.J.: Princeton Univ., 1977.

Westfall, Richard S. *Never at Rest: A Biography of Isaac Newton.* New York: Cambridge Univ., 1980.

Chapter 16: The Church Shows Renewed Vigor

Andrews, Kenneth R. *Trade, Plunder and Settlement: Maritime Enterprise and the Genesis of the British Empire, 1480–1630.* New York: Cambridge Univ., 1984.

Armstrong, Anthony. *The Church of England, the Methodists and Society, 1700–1850.* London: Univ. of London, 1973

Bowden, Henry Warner. *American Indians and Christian Missions: Studies in Cultural Conflict.* Chicago: Univ. of Chicago, 1981.

Campbell, Ted A. *The Religion of the Heart: A Study of European Religious Life in the Seventeenth and Eighteenth Centuries.* Columbia, S.C.: Univ. of South Carolina, 1991.

Crawford, Michael J. *Seasons of Grace: Colonial New England's Revival Tradition in Its British Contest.* New York: Oxford Univ., 1991.

Dallimore, Arnold. *George Whitefield: The Life and Times of the Great Evangelist of the Eighteenth-Century Revival.* 2 vols. Edinburgh, Scotland: Banner of Truth, 1970–80.

Danker, William J. *Profit for the Lord: Economic Activities in Moravian Missions and the Basel Mission Trading Company.* Grand Rapids: Eerdmans, 1971.

Fiering, Norman. *Jonathan Edwards' Moral Thought and Its British Context.* Chapel Hill, N.C.: Univ. of North Carolina, 1981.

Gaustad, Edwin S. *The Great Awakening in New England.* New York: Harper, 1957.

__________. *Liberty of Conscience: Roger Williams in America.* Grand Rapids: Eerdmans, 1991.

Hamilton, John, and Kenneth G. Taylor. *History of the Moravian Church: The Renewed Unitas Fratrum, 1722–1957.* Bethlehem, Pa.: Moravian Church in America, 1967.

Harmon, Rebecca Lamar. *Susanna, Mother of the Wesleys.* Nashville: Abingdon, 1968.

Hatch, Nathan O., and Harry S. Stout, eds. *Jonathan Edwards and the American Experience.* New York: Oxford Univ., 1988.

Hempton, David. *Methodism and Politics in British Society, 1750–1850.* Stanford, Calif.: Stanford Univ., 1984.

Miller, Perry. *Jonathan Edwards.* New York: Meridian, 1959.

Rack, Henry D. *Reasonable Enthusiast: John Wesley and the Rise of Methodism.* London: Epworth, 1989.

Rawlyk, George A. *Ravished by the Spirit: Religious Revivals, Baptists, and Henry Alline.* Montreal: McGill-Queens, 1984.

Schmidt, Martin. *John Wesley: A Theological Biography.* 2 vols. Nashville: Abingdon, 1962–73.

Snyder, Howard A. *The Radical Wesley and Patterns for Church Renewal.* Downers Grove, Ill.: InterVarsity, 1980.

Stoeffler, F. Ernest, ed. *Continental Pietism and Early American Christianity.* Grand Rapids: Eerdmans, 1976.

Stout, Harry S. *The Divine Dramatist: George Whitefield and the Rise of Modern Evangelicalism.* Grand Rapids: Eerdmans, 1991.

Tanis, James. *Dutch Calvinistic Pietism in the Middle Colonies: A Study in the Life and Theology of Theodorus Jacobus Frelinghuysen.* The Hague: M. Nijhoff, 1967.

Tracy, Patricia. *Jonathan Edwards, Pastor: Religion and Society in Eighteenth Century Northampton.* New York: Hill & Wang, 1980.

Trigger, Bruce G. *Natives and Newcomers: Canada's "Heroic Age" Reconsidered.* Montreal: McGill-Queen's Univ., 1985.

Tuttle, Robert G. *John Wesley: His Life and Theology.* Grand Rapids: Zondervan, 1978.

__________. *Mysticism in the Wesleyan Tradition.* Grand Rapids: Zondervan, 1989.

Tyson, John R., ed. *Charles Wesley: A Reader.* New York: Oxford Univ., 1989.

__________. *Charles Wesley on Sanctification: A Biographical and Theological Study.* Grand Rapids: Zondervan, 1986.

Ward, William R. *The Protestant Evangelical Awakening.* Cambridge, England: Cambridge Univ., 1992.

Winslow, Ola Elizabeth. *John Eliot: Apostle to the Indians.* Boston: Houghton Mifflin, 1968.

Chapter 17: The Church in a Revolutionary Age

Alley, Robert S., ed. *James Madison on Religious Liberty.* Buffalo: Prometheus, 1985.

Anstey, Roger. *The Atlantic Slave Trade and British Abolition, 1760–1810.* Atlantic Highlands, N.J.: Humanities, 1975.

Bailyn, Bernard. *The Ideological Origins of the American Revolution.* Cambridge, Mass.: Harvard Univ., 1967.

Bebbington, David W. *Evangelicalism in Modern Britain: A History from the 1730s to the 1980s.* London: Unwin Hyman, 1989.

Berens, John F. *Providence and Patriotism in Early America, 1640–1815.* Charlottesville, Va.: Univ. of Virginia, 1978.

Brown, Ford K. *Fathers of the Victorians.* Cambridge, England: Cambridge Univ., 1961.

Butler, Marilyn, ed. *Burke, Paine, Godwin, and the Revolutionary Controversy.* Cambridge, England: Cambridge Univ., 1984.

Calhoon, Robert M. *The Loyalists in Revolutionary America, 1760–1789.* New York: Harcourt, Brace, Jovanovich, 1973.

Chadwick, Owen. *The Popes and European Revolution.* Oxford, England: Clarendon, 1981.

Christie, Ian R. *Stress and Stability in Late Eighteenth Century Britain: Reflections on the British Avoidance of Revolution.* Oxford, England: Clarendon, 1984.

Davis, David Brion. *The Problem of Slavery in the Age of Revolution, 1770–1823.* Ithaca, N.Y.: Cornell Univ., 1975.

Dickinson, H. T., ed. *Britain and the French Revolution.* New York: St. Martin's, 1989.

Hales, Edward E. Y. *Revolution and Papacy, 1764–1846.* Garden City, N.Y.: Hanover House, 1960.

Hatch, Nathan O. *The Sacred Cause of Liberty: Republican Thought and the Millennium in Revolutionary New England.* New Haven, Conn.: Yale Univ., 1977.

Heimert, Alan. *Religion and the American Mind: From the Great Awakening to the Revolution.* Cambridge, Mass.: Harvard Univ., 1966.

Howse, Ernest M. *Saints in Politics: The 'Clapham Sect' and the Growth of Freedom.* London: Allen & Unwin, 1971.

Kennedy, Emmet. *A Cultural History of the French Revolution.* New Haven, Conn.: Yale Univ., 1989.

Levy, Leonard W. *The Establishment Clause: Religion and the First Amendment.* New York: Macmillan, 1986.

McLoughlin, William G. *New England Dissent 1630–1833: The Baptists and the Separation of Church and State.* 2 vols. Cambridge, Mass.: Harvard Univ., 1971.

McManners, John. *French Ecclesiastical Society under the Ancient Regime: A Study of Angers in the Eighteenth Century.* Manchester, England: Manchester Univ., 1968.

Miller, William Lee. *The First Liberty: Religion and the American Republic.* New York: Knopf, 1986.

Noll, Mark A. *Christians in the American Revolution.* Grand Rapids: Eerdmans, 1977.

Palmer, Robert R. *The Age of the Democratic Revolution: A Political History of Europe and America, 1760–1800.* 2 vols. Princeton, N.J.: Princeton Univ., 1959–64.

———. *Catholics and Unbelievers in Eighteenth-Century France.* Princeton, N.J.: Princeton Univ., 1939.

Pollock, John. *Wilberforce.* New York: St. Martin's, 1977.

Roberts, James. *The Counter-Revolution in France, 1787–1830.* New York: St. Martin's, 1990.

Semmel, Bernard. *The Methodist Revolution.* New York: Basic, 1973.

Tackett, Timothy. *Religion, Revolution, and Regional Culture in Eighteenth-Century France: The Ecclesiastical Oath of 1791.* Princeton, N.J.: Princeton Univ., 1986.

Van Kley, Dale K. *The Damiens Affair and the Unraveling of the Ancien Regime.* Princeton, N.J.: Princeton Univ., 1984.

———. *The Jansenists and the Expulsion of the Jesuits from France, 1757–1765.* New Haven, Conn.: Yale Univ., 1975.

Chapter 18: The Church in an Age of Ideology

Battiscombe, Georgina. *John Keble*. New York: Knopf, 1964.

Bebbington, David W. *The Nonconformist Conscience: Chapel and Politics, 1870–1914*. London: G. Allen & Unwin, 1982.

___________. *William Ewart Gladstone: Faith and Politics in Victorian Culture*. Grand Rapids: Eerdmans, 1993.

Bowen, Desmond. *The Idea of the Victorian Church: A Study of the Church of England 1833–1889*. Montreal: McGill Univ., 1968.

Bradley, Ian C. *The Call to Seriousness: The Evangelical Impact on the Victorians*. New York: Macmillan, 1976.

Brown, Richard. *Church and State in Modern Britain, 1700–1850*. New York: Routledge, 1991.

Brunschwig, Henri. *Enlightenment and Romanticism in Eighteenth Century Prussia*. Chicago: Univ. of Chicago, 1974

Butler, Perry. *Gladstone, Church, and Tractarianism: A Study of His Religious Ideas and Attitudes, 1809–1859*. Oxford, England: Clarendon, 1982.

Carwardine, Richard. *Transatlantic Revivalism: Popular Evangelicalism in Britain and America, 1790–1865*. Westport, Conn.: Greenwood, 1978.

Chadwick, Owen. *Newman*. Oxford, England: Oxford Univ., 1983.

___________. *The Spirit of the Oxford Movement: Tractarian Essays*. Cambridge, England: Cambridge Univ., 1990.

___________. *The Victorian Church*. 2 vols. New York: Oxford Univ., 1966.

Conser, Walter H., Jr. *Church and Confession: Conservative Theologians in Germany, England, and America, 1815–1866*. Macon, Ga.: Mercer Univ., 1984.

Dawson, Jerry F. *Friedrich Schleiermacher: The Evolution of a Nationalist*. Austin, Tex.: Univ. of Texas, 1966.

Hardman, Keith J. *Charles Grandison Finney, 1792–1875: Revivalist and Reformer*. Syracuse: Syracuse Univ., 1987.

Hylson-Smith, Kenneth. *Evangelicals in the Church of England*. Edinburgh, Scotland: T. & T. Clark, 1988.

Jay, Elisabeth. *The Evangelical and Oxford Movements*. Cambridge, England: Cambridge Univ., 1983.

Kurtz, John W. *John Frederic Oberlin*. Boulder, Colo.: Westview, 1976.

Lebrun, Richard A. *Maistre Studies*. Lanham, Md.: Univ. Press of America, 1988.

Maier, Hans. *Revolution and Church: The Early History of Christian Democracy 1789–1901*. South Bend, Ind.: Univ. of Notre Dame, 1969.

Manwaring, Randle. *From Controversy to Co-Existence: Evangelicals in the Church of England*. New York: Cambridge Univ., 1985.

O'Dwyer, Margaret M. *The Papacy in the Age of Napoleon and the Restoration: Pius VII, 1800–1823*. Lanham, Md.: Univ. Press of America, 1985.

Osen, James L. *Prophet and Peacemaker: The Life of Adolphe Monod*. Washington: Univ. Press of America, 1984.

Pickering, W. S. F. *Anglo-Catholicism: A Study in Religious Ambiguity*. New York: Routledge, 1989.

Reardon, Bernard M. G. *From Coleridge to Gore: A Century of Religious Thought in Britain*. London: Longman, 1971.

___________. *Religion in the Age of Romanticism: Studies in Early Nineteenth Century Thought*. New York: Cambridge Univ., 1985.

Redeker, Martin, ed. *Schleiermacher: Life and Thought.* Philadelphia: Fortress, 1973.

Robbins, Keith, ed. *Protestant Evangelicalism: Britain, Ireland, Germany, and America, c. 1750–c. 1950*. Oxford, England: Basil Blackwell, 1990.

Rosell, Garth M., and Richard A. G. Dupuis, eds. *The Memoirs of Charles G. Finney: The Complete Restored Text.* Grand Rapids: Zondervan, 1989.

Rosman, Doreen M. *Evangelicals and Culture*. London: Croom Helm, 1984.

Scharpff, Paulus. *History of Evangelism.* Grand Rapids: Eerdmans, 1966.

Smith, Timothy L. *Revivalism and Social Reform: American Protestantism on the Eve of the Civil War.* Baltimore: Johns Hopkins Univ., 1980.

Wolffe, John. *The Protestant Crusade in Great Britain, 1829–1860.* New York: Oxford Univ., 1991.

Chapter 19: The Church in the Industrial Age

Battiscombe, Georgina. *Shaftesbury: The Great Reformer 1801–1885.* Boston: Houghton Mifflin, 1975.

Bready, J. Wesley. *England Before and after Wesley: The Evangelical Revival and Social Reform.* New York: Russell & Russell, 1971.

__________. *This Freedom—Whence?* Winona Lake, Ind.: Light & Life, 1950

Cairns, Earle E. *The Christian in Society*. Chicago: Moody, 1973.

Collier, Richard. *The General Next to God: The Story of William Booth and the Salvation Army.* New York: Dutton, 1965.

Cort, John C. *Christian Socialism.* Maryknoll, N.Y.: Orbis, 1988.

Curtis, Susan. *A Consuming Faith: The Social Gospel and Modern American Culture.* Baltimore: Johns Hopkins Univ., 1991.

Dorn, Jacob H. *Washington Gladden: Prophet of the Social Gospel.* Columbus: Ohio State Univ., 1968.

Fishburn, Janet F. *The Fatherhood of God and the Victorian Family: The Social Gospel in America.* Philadelphia: Fortress, 1981.

Gorrell, Donald K. *The Age of Social Responsibility: The Social Gospel in the Progressive Era, 1900–1920*. Macon, Ga.: Mercer Univ., 1988.

Groh, John. *Nineteenth Century German Protestantism: The Church as Social Model.* Washington, D.C.: Univ. Press of America, 1982.

Handy, Robert T., ed. *The Social Gospel in America, 1870–1920.* New York: Oxford Univ., 1966.

Heasman, Kathleen. *Evangelicals in Action: An Appraisal of their Social Work.* London: Geoffrey Bles, 1962.

Hilton, Boyd. *The Age of Atonement: The Influence of Evangelicalism on Social and Economic Thought, 1795–1865.* Oxford, England: Clarendon, 1988.

Ketteler, Wilhelm E. *The Social Teachings of Wilhelm Emmanuel von Ketteler.* Washington, D.C.: Univ. Press of America, 1981.

Lewis, Donald M. *Lighten Their Darkness; The Evangelical Mission to Working-Class London, 1828–1860.* Westport, Conn.: Greenwood, 1986.

Lyon, David. *Karl Marx.* Oxford, England: Lion, 1988.

Magnuson, Norris. *Salvation in the Slums: Evangelical Social Work, 1865–1920.* Grand Rapids: Baker, 1990.

McLean, Iain. *Keir Hardie.* New York: St. Martin's, 1975.

Minus, Paul M. *Walter Rauschenbusch: American Reformer.* New York: Macmillan, 1988.

Misner, Paul. *Social Catholicism in Europe: From the Onset of Industrialization to the First World War.* New York: Crossroad, 1991.

Morris, Calvin S. *Reverdy C. Ransom: Black Advocate of the Social Gospel.* Lanham, Md.: Univ. Press of America, 1990.

Nygaard, Norman E. *Trumpet of Salvation: The Story of William and Catherine Booth.* Grand Rapids: Zondervan, 1961.

Pulker, Edward. *We Stand on Their Shoulders: The Growth of Social Concern in Canadian Anglicanism.* Toronto: Anglican Book Centre, 1986.

Reckitt, Maurice B. *Maurice to Temple: A Century of the Social Movement in the Church of England.* London: Faber & Faber, 1947.

Shanahan, William O. *German Protestants Face the Social Question: Conservative Phase, 1815–1871.* South Bend, Ind.: Univ. of Notre Dame, 1954.

Sperber, Jonathan. *Popular Catholicism in Nineteenth-Century Germany.* Princeton, N.J.: Princeton Univ., 1984.

Stearns, Peter. *Priest and Revolutionary: Lamennais and the Dilemma of French Catholicism.* New York: Harper & Row, 1967.

Ward, William R. *Theology, Sociology and Politics: The German Protestant Social Conscience 1890–1933.* Berne: Peter Lang, 1979.

White, Ronald C., Jr. *Liberty and Justice for All: Racial Reform and the Social Gospel (1877–1925).* San Francisco: Harper & Row, 1990.

__________, and C. Howard Hopkins. *The Social Gospel: Religion and Reform in Changing America.* Philadelphia: Temple Univ., 1976.

Chapter 20: The Worldwide Expansion of the Church

Ajayi, J. F. *Christian Missions in Nigeria, 1841–1891: The Making of a New Elite.* Evanston, Ill.: Northwestern Univ., 1965.

Bayly, Susan. *Saints, Goddesses, and Kings: Muslims and Christians in South Indian Society, 1700–1900.* Cambridge, England: Cambridge Univ., 1990.

Broomhall, A. J. *Hudson Taylor and China's Open Century.* 4 vols. Littleton, Colo.: OMF Books, 1981–88.

Brumberg, Joan Jacobs. *Mission for Life: The Story of the Family of Adoniram Judson.* New York: Free Press, 1980.

Christensen, Thorsten, and William R. Hutchison. *Missionary Ideologies in the Imperialist Era, 1880–1920.* Aarhus, Denmark: Aros, 1983.

Covell, Ralph. *W. A. P. Martin: Pioneer of Progress in China.* Grand Rapids: Eerdmans, 1978.

Davidson, Allan K., and Peter J. Lineham. *Transplanted Christianity: Documents Illustrating Aspects of New Zealand Church History.* Auckland, N.Z.: College Communications, 1987.

Fairbank, John K., ed. *The Missionary Enterprise in China and America.* Cambridge, Mass.: Harvard Univ., 1974.

Groves, Charles P. *The Planting of Christianity in Africa.* 4 vols. London: Lutterworth, 1948–58.

Gunson, Niel. *Messengers of Grace: Evangelical Missionaries in the South Seas, 1797–1860.* New York: Oxford Univ., 1978.

Hopkins, C. Howard. *John R. Mott, 1865–1955.* Grand Rapids: Eerdmans, 1979.

Hunter, Jane. *The Gospel of Gentility: American Women Missionaries in Turn-of-the-Century China.* New Haven, Conn.: Yale Univ., 1984.

Hutchison, William R. *Errand to the World: American Protestant Thought and Foreign Missions.* Chicago: Univ. of Chicago, 1987.

Jacobs, Sylvia M. *Black Americans and the Missionary Movement in Africa.* Westport, Conn.: Greenwood, 1982.

Latourette, Kenneth Scott. *A History of Christian Missions in China.* New York: Russell & Russell, 1967.

McCracken, John. *Politics and Christianity in Malawi, 1875–1940: The Impact of the Livingstonia Mission in the Northern Province.* Cambridge, England: Cambridge Univ., 1977.

Neill, Stephen C. *Colonialism and Christian Missions.* New York: McGraw-Hill, 1966.

Oliver, Roland A. *The Missionary Factor in East Africa.* London: Longmans, 1965.

Piggin, F. Stuart. *Making Evangelical Missionaries 1789–1858: The Social Background, Motives and Training of the British Protestant Missionaries to India.* Abingdon, England: Sutton Courtenay, 1984.

__________, and John Roxborogh. *The St. Andrews Seven: The Finest Flowering of Missionary Zeal in Scottish History.* Edinburgh, Scotland: Banner of Truth, 1985.

Ransford, Oliver. *David Livingstone, the Dark Interior.* New York: St. Martin's, 1978.

Sanneh, Lamin. *Translating the Message: The Missionary Impact on Culture.* Maryknoll, N.Y.: Orbis, 1991.

__________. *West African Christianity: The Religious Impact.* Maryknoll, N.Y.: Orbis, 1983.

Shenk, Wilbert R. *Henry Venn: Missionary Statesman.* Maryknoll, N.Y.: Orbis, 1983.

Stanley, Brian. *The Bible and the Flag: Protestant Missions and British Imperialism in the Nineteenth and Twentieth Centuries.* Leicester, England: Apollos, 1990.

Strayer, Robert W. *The Making of Mission Communities in East Africa: Anglicans and Africans in Colonial Kenya, 1875–1935.* Albany, N.Y.: State Univ. of New York, 1978.

Turner, Mary. *Slaves and Missionaries: The Disintegration of Jamaican Slave Society, 1787–1834.* Urbana, Ill.: Univ. of Illinois, 1982.

Whyte, Bob. *Unfinished Encounter: China and Christianity.* Ridgefield, Conn.: Morehouse, 1990.

Williams, C. Peter. *The Ideal of the Self-Governing Church: A Study in Victorian Missionary Strategy.* Leiden, The Netherlands: E. J. Brill, 1990.

Wills, David W., and Richard Newman, eds. *Black Apostles at Home and Abroad: Afro-Americans and the Christian Mission From the Revolution to Reconstruction.* Boston: G. K. Hall, 1982.

Wright, Marcia. *German Missions in Tanganyika, 1891–1941: Lutherans and Moravians in the Southern Highlands.* Oxford, England: Clarendon, 1971.

Chapter 21: The Church in the Twilight of the West

Bannister, Robert C. *Social Darwinism: Science and Myth in Anglo-American Social Thought.* Philadelphia: Temple Univ., 1979.

Bass, Clarence B. *Backgrounds to Dispensationalism: Its Historical Genesis and Ecclesiastical Implications.* Grand Rapids: Eerdmans, 1960.

Billington, James H. *The Icon and the Axe: An Interpretive History of Russian Culture.* New York: Random House, 1966.

Blocker, Jack S. *American Temperance Movements: Cycles of Reform.* Boston: Twayne, 1989.

Bowker, John. *The Religious Imagination and the Sense of God.* Oxford, England: Clarendon, 1978.

Dayton, Donald W. *Theological Roots of Pentecostalism.* Metuchen, N.J.: Scarecrow, 1987.

Dieter, Melvin E. *The Holiness Revival of the Nineteenth Century.* Metuchen, N.J.: Scarecrow, 1980.

Dorsett, Lyle. *Billy Sunday and the Redemption of Urban America.* Grand Rapids: Eerdmans, 1991.

Frank, Douglas W. *Less Than Conquerors: How Evangelicals Entered the Twentieth Century.* Grand Rapids: Eerdmans, 1986.

Gauvreau, Michael. *The Evangelical Century: College and Creed in English Canada from the Great Revival to the Great Depression.* Montreal: McGill-Queen's Univ., 1991.

Hutchison, William R. *The Modernist Impulse in American Protestantism.* New York: Oxford Univ., 1976.

Jordan, Philip D. *The Evangelical Alliance for the United States of America, 1847–1900.* Lewiston, N.Y.: Edwin Mellen, 1983.

Kurtz, Lester R. *The Politics of Heresy: The Modernist Crisis in Roman Catholicism.* Berkeley: Univ. of California, 1986.

Larkin, Maurice. *Church and State After the Dreyfus Affair: The Separation Issue in France.* New York: Barnes & Noble, 1974.

Livingstone, David N. *Darwin's Forgotten Defenders: The Encounter Between Evangelical Theology and Evolutionary Thought.* Grand Rapids: Eerdmans, 1987.

McManners, John. *Church and State in France, 1870–1914.* New York: Harper & Row, 1972.

Moore, James R. *The Post-Darwinian Controversies: A Study of the Protestant Struggle to Come to Terms with Darwin in Great Britain and America.* Cambridge, England: Cambridge Univ., 1979.

Pollock, John C. *The Keswick Story: The Authorized History of the Keswick Convention.* Chicago: Moody, 1964.

Ranchetti, Michele. *The Catholic Modernists: A Study of the Religious Reform Movement, 1864–1907.* Oxford, England: Oxford Univ., 1969.

Riasanovsky, Nicholas V. *Nicholas I and Official Nationality in Russia, 1825–1855.* Berkeley: Univ. of California, 1959.

Rumscheidt, Martin, ed. *Adolf von Harnack: Liberal Theology at Its Height.* Minneapolis: Fortress, 1991.

Russell, Colin A. *Cross-Currents: Interactions between Science and Faith.* Grand Rapids: Eerdmans, 1985

Russett, Cynthia E. *Darwin in America: The Intellectual Response 1865–1912.* San Francisco: Freeman, 1976.

Sandeen, Ernest R. *The Roots of Fundamentalism: British and American Millenarianism, 1800–1930.* Chicago: Univ. of Chicago, 1970.

Sizer, Sandra S. *Gospel Hymns and Social Religion: The Rhetoric of Nineteenth-Century Revivalism.* Philadelphia: Temple Univ., 1978.

Smith, Gary Scott. *The Seeds of Secularization: Calvinism, Culture, and Pluralism in America 1870–1915.* Grand Rapids: Eerdmans, 1985.

Vanden Berg, Frank. *Abraham Kuyper: A Biography.* St. Catherines, Ontario.: Paideia, 1978.

Wallace, Lillian P. *The Papacy and European Diplomacy, 1869–1878.* Chapel Hill, N.C.: Univ. of North Carolina, 1948.

Weber, Timothy P. *Living in the Shadow of the Second Coming: American Premillennialism, 1875–1982.* Chicago: Univ. of Chicago, 1987.

White, Charles Edward. *The Beauty of Holiness: Phoebe Palmer as Theologian, Revivalist, Feminist, and Humanitarian.* Grand Rapids: Zondervan, 1986.

Chapter 22: The Church in a War-Torn World

Barnett, Victoria. *For the Soul of the People: Protestant Protest Against Hitler.* New York: Oxford Univ., 1992.

Bentley, James. *Martin Niemöller.* New York: Free Press, 1984.

Bethge, Eberhard. *Dietrich Bonhoeffer.* New York: Harper & Row, 1970.

Binchy, Daniel A. *Church and State in Fascist Italy.* London: Oxford Univ., 1970.

Borg, Daniel R. *The Old-Prussian Church and the Weimar Republic: A Study in Political Adjustment, 1917–1927.* Hanover, N.H.: University Press of New England, 1984.

Bromiley, Geoffrey W. *An Introduction to the Theology of Karl Barth.* Grand Rapids: Eerdmans, 1979.

Carter, Paul A. *The Decline and Revival of the Social Gospel: Social and Political Liberalism in American Protestant Churches, 1920–1940.* Hamden, Conn.: Archon, 1971.

Chadwick, Owen. *Britain and the Vatican during the Second World War.* Cambridge, England: Cambridge Univ., 1986.

Coletta, Paolo E. *William Jennings Bryan.* 3 vols. Lincoln: Univ. of Nebraska, 1964–69.

Conway, John S. *The Nazi Persecution of the Churches, 1933–45.* New York: Basic, 1968.

Diephouse, David J. *Pastors and Pluralism in Württemberg, 1918–1933.* Princeton, N.J.: Princeton Univ., 1987.

Ericksen, Robert P. *Theologians under Hitler: Gerhard Kittel, Paul Althaus and Emanuel Hirsch.* New Haven, Conn.: Yale Univ., 1985.

Fox, Richard W. *Reinhold Niebuhr: A Biography.* New York: Pantheon, 1985.

Helmreich, Ernst C. *The German Churches under Hitler.* Detroit: Wayne State Univ., 1979.

Hoover, Arlie J. *God, Germany, and Britain in the Great War: A Study in Clerical Nationalism.* New York: Praeger, 1989.

Kelly, Geffrey B., and F. Burton Nelson, eds. *A Testament to Freedom: The Essential Writings of Dietrich Bonhoeffer.* San Francisco: HarperCollins, 1990.

Laqueur, Walter. *A History of Zionism.* New York: Schocken, 1976.

Longfield, Bradley J. *The Presbyterian Controversy: Fundamentalists, Modernists, and Moderates.* New York: Oxford Univ., 1991.

Marrus, Michael R. *The Holocaust in History.* New York: Meridian, 1987.

Marsden, George M. *Fundamentalism and American Culture: The Shaping of Twentieth-Century Evangelicalism.* New York: Oxford Univ., 1980.

Miller, Robert M. *Harry Emerson Fosdick.* New York: Oxford Univ., 1985.

Pauck, Wilhelm and Marion. *Paul Tillich: His Life and Thought.* New York: Harper & Row, 1976.

Piper, John F., Jr. *The American Churches in World War I.* Athens, Ohio: Ohio Univ., 1985.

Pospielovsky, Dmitry. *The Russian Church under the Soviet Regime, 1917–1982.* Crestwood, N.Y.: St. Vladimir's, 1984.

Rausch, David A. *A Legacy of Hatred.* Chicago: Moody, 1984.

Rudnick, Milton L. *Fundamentalism and the Missouri Synod: A Historical Study of Their Interaction and Mutual Influence.* St. Louis: Concordia, 1966.

Scholder, Klaus. *The Churches and the Third Reich.* 2 vols. Philadelphia: Fortress, 1988.

Stonehouse, Ned B. *J. Gresham Machen: A Biographical Memoir.* Grand Rapids: Eerdmans, 1954.

Trollinger, William V. *God's Empire: William Bell Riley and Midwestern Fundamentalism.* Madison, Wis.: Univ. of Wisconsin, 1990.

Wind, Renate. *Dietrich Bonhoeffer: A Spoke in the Wheel.* Grand Rapids: Eerdmans, 1992.

Wistrich, Robert S. *Antisemitism: The Longest Hatred.* New York: Pantheon, 1991.

Chapter 23: The Church as a Global Institution

Anderson, Gerald H. *Asian Voices in Christian Theology.* Maryknoll, N.Y.: Orbis, 1976.

Barrett, David B. *Schism and Renewal in Africa: An Analysis of Six Thousand Contemporary Religious Movements.* London: Oxford Univ., 1968.

Branch, Taylor. *Parting the Waters: America in the King Years, 1954–1963.* New York: Simon & Schuster, 1988.

Carpenter, Joel A., and Wilbert R. Shenk, eds. *Earthen Vessels: American Evangelicals and Foreign Missions, 1880–1980.* Grand Rapids: Eerdmans, 1990.

Cavert, Samuel. *The American Churches in the Ecumenical Movement, 1900–1968.* New York: Association Press, 1968.

Detzler, Wayne A. *The Changing Church in Europe.* Grand Rapids: Zondervan, 1979.

Dyrness, William A. *Learning About Theology from the Third World.* Grand Rapids: Zondervan, 1990.

Ellis, Jane. *The Russian Orthodox Church: A Contemporary History.* Bloomington, Ind.: Indiana Univ., 1986.

Falk, Peter. *The Growth of the Church in Africa.* Grand Rapids: Zondervan, 1979.

Findlay, James M. *Church People in the Struggle: The National Council of Churches and the Black Freedom Movement, 1950–1970.* New York: Oxford Univ., 1993.

Flannery, Austin P., ed. *Vatican Council II: The Conciliar and Post- Conciliar Documents.* Grand Rapids: Eerdmans, 1975.

Goeckel, Robert E. *The Lutheran Church and the East German State: Political Conflict and Change under Ulbricht and Honecker.* Ithaca, N.Y.: Cornell Univ., 1990.

Hastings, Adrian. *A History of English Christianity, 1920–1990.* London: SCM, 1991.

__________. *Modern Catholicism: Vatican II and After.* London: Oxford Univ., 1991.

Henry, Carl F. H. *Confessions of a Theologian.* Waco, Tex.: Word, 1986.

Hogg, W. Richey. *Ecumenical Foundations: A History of the International Missionary Council and Its Nineteenth-Century Background.* New York: Harper, 1952.

Kirk, Andrew. *Liberation Theology.* Atlanta: John Knox, 1979.

Lowman, Pete. *The Day of His Power: A History of the International Fellowship of Evangelical Students.* Leicester, England: Inter-Varsity, 1983.

Lynch, Edward A. *Religion and Politics in Latin America: Liberation Theology and Christian Democracy.* New York: Praeger, 1991.

Marsden, George M. *Reforming Fundamentalism: Fuller Seminary and the New Evangelicalism.* Grand Rapids: Eerdmans, 1987.

Martin, William. *A Prophet with Honor: The Billy Graham Story.* New York: William Morrow, 1991.

Moodie, T. Dunbar. *The Rise of Afrikanerdom: Power, Apartheid, and the Afrikaner Civil Religion.* Berkeley: Univ. of California, 1975.

Nunẽz, Emilio A. *Liberation Theology.* Chicago: Moody, 1985.

Oates, Stephen B. *Let the Trumpet Sound: The Life of Martin Luther King, Jr.* New York: Harper & Row, 1982.

Pospielovsky, Dimitry. *A History of Soviet Atheism in Theory, Practice, and the Believer.* 3 vols. New York: St. Martin's, 1987–88.

Prozesky, Martin, ed. *Christianity Amidst Apartheid: Selected Perspectives on the Church in South Africa.* New York: St. Martin's, 1990.

Reid, David. *New Wine: The Cultural Shaping of Japanese Christianity.* Berkeley: Asian Humanities, 1991.

Rouse, Ruth, and Stephen C. Neill, eds. *A History of the Ecumenical Movement, 1517–1948.* 2 vols. Philadelphia: Westminster, 1970.

Sell, Alan P. F. *A Reformed, Evangelical, Catholic Theology: The Contribution of the World Alliance of Reformed Churches, 1875–1982.* Grand Rapids: Eerdmans, 1991.

Smith, Christian S. *The Emergence of Liberation Theology, Radical Religion and Social Movement Theory.* Chicago: Univ. of Chicago, 1991.

Steeves, Paul D. *Keeping the Faith: Religion and Ideology in the Soviet Union.* New York: Holmes & Meier, 1989.

Swidler, Leonard. *Küng in Conflict.* Garden City, N.Y.: Doubleday, 1984.

Tiénou, Tite. *The Theological Task of the Church in Africa.* Achimota, Ghana: Africa Christian Press, 1982.

Tutu, Desmond. *Crying in the Wilderness: The Struggle for Jusice in South Africa.* Grand Rapids: Eerdmans, 1990.

Villafane, Eldin. *The Liberating Spirit: Towards an Hispanic-American Pentecostal Social Ethics.* Lanham, Md.: Univ. Press of America, 1992.

Villa-Vicencio, Charles. *Trapped in Apartheid: A Socio-Theological History of the English-Speaking Churches.* Maryknoll, N.Y.: Orbis, 1986.

Watt, David H. *A Transforming Faith: Explorations of Twentieth-Century American Evangelicalism.* New Brunswick, N.J.: Rutgers Univ., 1991.

Wilmore, Gayraud S., and James H. Cone, eds. *Black Theology: A Documentary History, 1966–1979.* Maryknoll, N.Y.: Orbis, 1979.

Epilogue: Ongoing Challenges to the Church's Advance

Azevedo, Marcello C. *Basic Ecclesial Communities in Brazil—The Challenge of a New Way of Being the Church.* Washington, D.C.: Georgetown Univ., 1987.

Clouse, Bonnidell, and Robert G. Clouse, eds. *Women in Ministry: Four Views.* Downers Grove, Ill.: InterVarsity, 1989.

Clouse, Robert G., ed. *War: Four Christian Views.* Downers Grove, Ill.: InterVarsity, 1991.

———, ed. *Wealth and Poverty: Four Christian Views of Economics.* Downers Grove, Ill.: InterVarsity, 1984.

Dayton, Donald W., and Robert K. Johnston, eds. *The Variety of American Evangelicalism.* Downers Grove, Ill.: InterVarsity, 1991.

Douglas, J. D., ed. *Proclaim Christ Until He Comes: Calling the Whole Church to Take the Whole Gospel to the Whole World.* Minneapolis: World Wide, 1989.

Eden, Martyn, and David F. Wells, eds. *The Gospel in the Modern World: A Tribute to John Stott.* Downers Grove, Ill.: InterVarsity, 1991.

Gilliland, Dean S. *African Religion Meets Islam: Religious Change in Northern Nigeria.* Lanham, Md.: Univ. Press of America, 1986.

Martin, David. *A General Theory of Secularization.* New York: Harper & Row, 1978.

May, Melanie A. *Bonds of Unity: Women, Theology, and the Worldwide Church.* Atlanta: Scholars Press, 1989.

Mball, Zulile. *The Churches and Racism: A Black South African Perspective.* London: SCM, 1987.

Neill, Stephen C. *Christian Faith and Other Faiths.* Downers Grove, Ill.: InterVarsity, 1984.

Newbigin, Lesslie. *Foolishness to the Greeks: The Gospel and Western Culture.* Grand Rapids: Eerdmans, 1986.

Padilla, C. René. *Mission Between the Times.* Grand Rapids: Eerdmans, 1985.

Preston, Ronald H. *The Future of Christian Ethics.* London: SCM, 1987.

Samuel, Vinay, and Chris Sugden. *The Church in Response to Human Need.* Grand Rapids: Eerdmans, 1987.

Saunders, George R. *Culture and Christianity: The Dialectics of Transformation.* Westport, Conn.: Greenwood, 1988.

Sider, Ronald J. *Rich Christians in an Age of Hunger.* Waco, Tex.: Word, 1990

Stott, John R. W. *The Contemporary Christian.* Downers Grove, Ill.: InterVarsity, 1992.

___________. *Decisive Issues Facing Christians Today.* Tarrytown, N.Y.: Revell, 1990.

Thorogood, Bernard. *The Flag and the Cross: National Limits and the Church Universal.* London: SCM, 1990.

Walls, Andrew F., and Wilbert R. Shenk, eds. *Exploring New Religious Movements.* Elkhart, Ind.: Mission Focus, 1990.

Wuthnow, Robert. *The Struggle for America's Soul: Evangelicals, Liberals, and Secularism.* Grand Rapids: Eerdmans, 1989.

INDEX OF PERSONS

INDEX OF SUBJECTS

INDEX OF PLACES